PENGUIN REFE

R

A NEW DICTION ... MUSIC

Arthur Jacobs conducted a mixed-voice choir while still an undergraduate at Oxford. Later he joined the Royal Choral Society for the experience of singing under Sir Malcolm Sargent. From 1947 until 1952 he was music critic for the *Daily Express*, and has since worked for many British and overseas newspapers and musical journals. He is at present deputy editor of *Opera*, a record critic for the *Sunday Times* and *Audio Record Review*, and has taken part in many television and radio programmes. He is the author of *Gilbert and Sullivan* (1952), and the editor of *Choral Music* (a Pelican). He lectures on musical history at the Royal Academy of Music, and was George A. Miller Centennial Lecturer at the University of Illinois in 1967.

A champion of opera in English, he himself wrote the very successful English translation used in the Sadler's Wells production of Rossini's *Cinderella*, and has since translated other operas from French, German, Italian, and Russian. Among these are Tchaikovsky's *The Queen of Spades*, Richard Strauss's *The Silent Woman*, Schoenberg's *Erwartung* (all given at Covent Garden), and Alban Berg's *Lulu*. He was the librettist of Nicholas Maw's opera *One Man Show* (London, 1964).

Born in Manchester in 1922, Arthur Jacobs lives in London, loves theatre-going, and hates gardening. His travels as a music critic have taken him from Salzburg to San Francisco, and from Moscow to Auckland, N.Z. (where he was married).

A NEW DICTIONARY OF MUSIC

ARTHUR JACOBS

NEW EDITION

PENGUIN BOOKS

Penguin Books Ltd, Harmondsworth, Middlesex, England
Penguin Books Inc., 7110 Ambassador Road, Baltimore, Maryland 21207, U.S.A.
Penguin Books Australia Ltd, Ringwood, Victoria, Australia

—

First published 1958
Reprinted with revisions 1960, 1961, 1963
Second edition 1967
Reprinted with revisions 1968

—

—

Made and printed in Great Britain
by C. Nicholls & Company Ltd
Set in Monotype Times

INTRODUCTION TO THE SECOND EDITION

This dictionary has been compiled for the inquiring music-lover, whether as listener or as performer. The present revised edition includes many new entries, and hundreds of changes covering recent developments in careers and music-making, but only one or two entries in the previous edition have been dropped.

Its single alphabetical list gives entries for composers, living and dead; for musical works (titles of operas, symphonic poems, etc.); for English and foreign musical terms; for performers and conductors; and for the names of certain well-known musical institutions (for instance Glyndebourne, Scala). Critics and other writers are not generally entered, unless of course they qualify in another capacity: but an exception is made for those whose catalogues of composers' works have become established in common reference. No musical dictionary could shut out Köchel, for example, from whose name the initial K. has become familiar in the numbering of Mozart's works.

The names of composers and musical works have been chosen as being those most likely to be encountered – now or soon. (Several composers listed are still in their early twenties.) Certain additional names are listed chiefly for their possible connexions with other, better-known names. Thus it is useful to distinguish that obscure composer, Domenico Gabrieli, from the other two (and more important) composers of that surname. Similarly, any English-speaking reader whose eye has once been caught by the name of Tchaikovsky's opera, 'Iolanta', will wish to know whether this is not a well-known Gilbert and Sullivan character in Russian guise.

Where an opera is given an entry, a brief explanation of the title follows. Similarly with other works bearing literary or otherwise allusive titles. Not that such a short Dictionary as this can list all such works: in particular, songs and short piano pieces are not generally given their own entries unless the name emphatically needs explanation – Chopin's so-called 'Revolutionary Study', for instance.

Among performers and conductors, a fairly drastic restriction had obviously to be imposed. Only the following are therefore included: (1) those who, although dead, continue prominent through recorded performances (e.g. Gigli); (2) the highest-ranking international artists of today, plus a very few apparently on the verge of attaining that rank; (3) a few who, though not necessarily at the very head of their profession, are known as executants closely associated with composers in bringing out new works, or as conductors in charge of important orchestras.

Readers may incidentally be cautioned against concluding that, because one composer is given twice as many lines as another, he is necessarily twice as important. Certain composers take apparently disproportionate space because their biographies or the nature of their works call for an unusual amount of explanation.

II

Titles of works are, wherever possible, given in English. The enormity of this step may require justification. Although the Germans think of Mozart as having written 'Figaros Hochzeit' and not 'Le Nozze di Figaro', and although the French quite freely translate Wagner's 'Der fliegende Holländer' into 'Le Vaisseau fantôme', a strange and superstitious regard for foreign titles has remained in 'accepted' English usage.

This regard would be more convincing if it were not so frequently applied to foreign titles which are not, in fact, the originals. The Russian opera by Rimsky-Korsakov which has been mounted at Covent Garden as 'Le Coq d'Or' acquired that French title only because Paris happened to be the first west-European city in which it was presented. The string quartet by Smetana which the BBC has on occasion announced as 'Aus meinem Leben' was so named not by its Czech composer but by its German publisher. If our foreign-language sticklers were really sticklers, they would insist on calling these two works 'Zolotoy Petushok' and 'Z mého života'; the rest of us may remain content with 'The Golden Cockerel' and 'From My Life'.

It will not do, even, to translate into English those titles originally in Russian, Czech, Danish, and so forth, and to leave French, German, Italian, and Spanish titles in their original form. A music-lover's horizons will be broadened, like anyone else's, if he knows foreign languages; but there is no case for penalizing him if he happens to know one and not another, or none at all. Still less ought it to be suggested that there are some, but only some, languages that a music-lover somehow 'ought' to know. It may be argued that, in rendering 'L'Enfant et les sortilèges' as 'The Child and the Spells', we are not quite savouring the exact associations of *sortilèges*. Quite so, but we are nearer than Ravel's own publishers, who (presumably with the consent of Colette as librettist) gave, as an alternative title in English, 'The Bewitched Child'. The purpose of this Dictionary is not to provide an exercise in literary discrimination, but – among other things – to give the English-speaking listener a serviceable and revealing identification of musical works.

The happy post-war growth of operatic performances in English, in both Britain and the United States, gives further reason for the use of English titles. An exception is made for certain works of which the foreign title has established itself in what may fairly be called common usage (as distinct from the usage of specialized musical circles). It is too late, for instance, to anglicize 'Il Trovatore' as 'The Troubadour'. Naturally enough, most English versions used in these pages will already be familiar. The BBC sensibly allows Berlioz his 'Roman Carnival'; the New York Philharmonic Orchestra's programmes speak of Debussy's 'The Afternoon of a Faun'. This Dictionary welcomes both. Foreign titles are, however, given in parentheses after the English title; and, where the foreign title is itself reasonably well known, it is also listed in its due alphabetical place with a cross-reference to the main (English) entry.

Where a foreign title refers to a historical or literary figure known in English by another form of name, the English form is preferred: thus 'Joan of Arc' (not Jeanne d'Arc or Giovanna d'Arco) and 'Cinderella' (not Cenerentola or Cendrillon or Zolushka). But an exception is made when the form of name used in musical contexts may be said to have established its identity apart from its literary precursors in English. Thus 'Tristan and Isolde' is listed, not 'Tristram and Iseult'; thus, too, 'Don Giovanni' just scrapes through (though it is a pity not to have, as in French and German usage, the self-evident identification with Don Juan); and the Italians may be conceded the Italian spelling of the Italian name Otello.

American terms, where different from English, have their own entries in these pages – for instance 'half-note' and 'concertmaster'. But English usage is followed ('minim', 'leader') where the things represented are referred to in the course of other entries. An apparent exception, where it might seem that American usage has been followed, is in the case of 'flutist'. But this word is also good English, as any non-musical dictionary will testify, and its superiority to 'flautist' is evident on grounds both of analogy and clarity; similarly with 'English horn'. The time is ripe for an attempt to establish a shared Anglo-American musical terminology: if American writers would abandon their use of the word 'tone' to mean 'note' (as well as to mean so much else), then England might well be glad to cast off the irrationalities of her crotchets and quavers in favour of the self-explanatory quarter-notes and eighth-notes.

In spelling Russian names I have followed the latest (fifth) edition of *Grove's Dictionary of Music and Musicians*. The advantage of uniformity between reference books seems easily to outweigh the unfamiliarity of one or two such forms as 'Rakhmaninov': and the reader looking up 'Rachmaninov' will in any case find a cross-reference. In conformity with this system I have transliterated the Russian 'ya' sound as 'ia' in such names as 'Aliabiev' and 'Liapunov'; but it would be equally logical to substitute 'ya' in all such cases, as indeed other modern systems of transliteration do. In divergence from Grove I have, however, permitted myself the retention of the form 'Koussevitzky' – not only established by the Russian-born conductor during his long American residence, but perpetuated after his death by the Koussevitzky Music Foundation.

III

Even more than other writers, a dictionary-compiler stands on his predecessors' shoulders if he stands up at all. My obvious debt to those modern princes of musical lexicography – the late Eric Blom and the late Percy A. Scholes in England, Nicolas Slonimsky in the United States – is gratefully acknowledged. Mr Slonimsky's generous personal help has included the provision of many newly authenticated dates.

Many friends and professional acquaintances have cheerfully, and sometimes unknowingly, allowed their brains to be picked on this book's behalf. Mr David Cox and Professor Denis Stevens, in particular, read the whole text of the first edition and suggested many an improvement. Among others who generously supplied specialized information were Mr Raymond Bryant, Mr Allan Fry, Dr R. H. Kay, and Mr Harold Rosenthal; the late Mr M. Montagu-Nathan was a kind consultant on the transliteration of Russian names. Past and present members of the BBC's Music staff including Mr C. B. Rees, Mr Barrie Hall, and Mr Deryck Cooke have placed helpful material at my disposal; and I am indebted also to the staff of the Central Music Library (London) and to the diplomatic and cultural representatives in London of various overseas governments. My wife not only assisted in the physical preparation of the typescript but gave a critical layman's (and an expert journalist's) scrutiny to every entry.

Needless to say, final responsibility for the text, and for such shortcomings as survive, remains my own.

A.J.

The second edition has been further revised in this 1968 reprint, particularly in the noting of recent deaths (up to mid-1968) and some important recent works.

A.J.

HOW TO USE THIS BOOK

Most of the abbreviations, symbols, and conventions are self-explanatory, or familiar from general reference books.

Names of languages are given in abbreviation – Cz. for Czech, Dan. for Danish, Du. for Dutch, Eng. for English, Fr. for French, Gael. for Gaelic, Ger. for German, Gk for Greek, Heb. for Hebrew, Hung. for Hungarian, Ir. for Irish, It. for Italian, Lat. for Latin, Norw. for Norwegian, Rus. for Russian, Sp. for Spanish, Swe. for Swedish.

Where SMALL CAPITALS are used in the course of an entry (that is, apart from the opening words of the entry itself) a cross-reference is indicated: i.e. 'Look up this term for further information'.

Alphabetical order follows Telephone Directory practice, all entries beginning with a particular word being grouped together. Thus (to take a hypothetical list):

IN NOMINE
IN THE SOUTH
IN THE STEPPES OF CENTRAL ASIA
INDIAN QUEEN, THE
INGHELBRECHT, DÉSIRÉ ÉMILE
INSTRUMENTATION
INVERSION

and not:

INDIAN QUEEN, THE
INGHELBRECHT, DÉSIRÉ ÉMILE
IN NOMINE
INSTRUMENTATION
IN THE SOUTH
IN THE STEPPES OF CENTRAL ASIA
INVERSION

'A', 'The' and their foreign-language equivalents at the beginning of entries are disregarded for alphabetical purposes. Abbreviations and letter-symbols are placed at the beginning of the sections devoted to their initial letters.

Where possible, full names of persons – and not only their commonly used professional names – are given. But where a part or parts of the holder's full name is not in general use, then such parts are enclosed in parentheses. Such names in parentheses are disregarded for the purpose of alphabetical listing: thus 'Haydn, (Franz) Joseph' would be entered after and not before a hypothetical 'Haydn, Georg'.

Where a date is marked *c.* (*circa*, i.e. approximately), this refers only to the figure immediately following. Thus '*c.* 1555–1602' means 'born about 1555, died definitely in 1602'.

A

A, note of the scale (commonly used for tuning instruments). So A FLAT (A♭), DOUBLE-FLAT (A♭♭), NATURAL (A♮), SHARP (A♯), DOUBLE-SHARP (A𝄪); *A major, A minor,* etc. – see MAJOR. So also *in A,* either (1) in the key of A (major, understood), or (2) indication of a TRANSPOSING INSTRUMENT on which the note written C sounds as A (and correspondingly with other notes): e.g. *clarinet in A,* or, colloquially, *A clarinet.*

A, term used in analysis to symbolize the first section of a piece. So e.g. ABA represents a piece containing one section followed by a different section followed by a repeat of the first.

A, À (It., Fr.), to, at, with, etc. So *a* 2, *a* 3, etc., indication either that a piece is written in so many PARTS, or that a single line of music is to be played by so many instruments in unison; so also *a* CAPPELLA, *a* PIACERE, *a* TEMPO, etc. (in all such cases see under next word).

A.R.A.M., A.R.C.M., A.R.C.O., A.R.M.C.M., Associate of the Royal Academy of Music, Royal College of Music, Royal College of Organists, Royal Manchester College of Music.

ARR. (abbr.), arranged (by).

A.S.C.A.P., American Society of Composers, Authors, and Publishers (usually pronounced as a word and written ASCAP).

AUG., abbreviation of AUGMENTED.

AB (Ger.), off, away. So *Dämpfer ab,* take mute(s) off.

ABA (and similar combinations of letters in musical analysis), see A (2nd entry).

ABE, KOEMI (b. 1911), Japanese composer (cello concerto, piano concerto, seven string quartets, etc.), also conductor in Tokio, and cellist.

'ABEGG' VARIATIONS, Schumann's opus 1, for piano (1830), dedicated by him to a 'Countess Abegg' and consisting of variations on a theme made up of the notes A–B♭–E–G–G (German B = English B♭). Meta von Abegg was a friend of his, but the rank of Countess was imaginary.

ABEL, CARL FRIEDRICH (1723–87), German player of the viola da gamba (also of harpsichord) and composer of chamber music, symphonies, etc. Trained in boyhood under J. S. Bach; settled in London (where he died) and gave concerts there with J. C. Bach.

ABSIL, JEAN (b. 1893), Belgian composer of operas, five symphonies, five piano concertos, four string quartets and two saxophone quartets, cantata 'The Zodiac', etc. Some of his music uses irregular metres.

ABSOLUTE MUSIC, music without direct reference to anything outside itself, i.e. not having words and not being ILLUSTRATIVE MUSIC depicting story, scene, etc.

ABSOLUTE PITCH, see PITCH.

ABSTRACT MUSIC, same as ABSOLUTE MUSIC.

ABT, FRANZ (1819–85), German composer, especially of songs and part-songs in the German style of his period; also conductor in Germany and Switzerland.

ABU HASSAN, one-act comic opera by Weber, produced in Munich, 1811. Libretto by F. C. Hiemer, after an *Arabian Nights* adventure of escaping debtors.

ACADEMIC FESTIVAL OVERTURE (Ger., *Akademische Fest-Ouvertüre*), concert-overture by Brahms, first performed 1881, composed in acknowledgement of a doctorate from Breslau University, 1879. Made up of favourite German student songs. (Another overture so entitled has been written by Broman.)

ACCELERANDO (It.), quickening the pace.

ACCIACCATURA (It., a crushing), an 'extra' note struck just before (or simultaneously with) the main note, but immediately released. Notated with the stem of the note crossed through, as 𝆔

ACCIDENTAL, a sharp, flat, double-sharp, double-flat, or natural sign occurring temporarily in the course of a piece, and not forming part of the key-signature. It conventionally refers only to the bar in which it occurs – not to any succeeding bars, unless repeated there.

ACCOMPANY, to perform with another performer, but in a subordinate capacity; so *accompanist*, *accompaniment* – a piano being usually understood as the instrument unless another is specified. When the performers are thought of as equal partners, e.g. in a violin and piano sonata, then *accompany* and its derivatives are to be avoided.

ACCORDION, instrument having metal reeds which are made to vibrate by the access of air from bellows, actuated by player's hands pushing and pulling; portable, box-shaped. The notes are selected through the action of the player's fingers on studs, or (*piano-accordion*) on studs for the left hand and a piano-like keyboard for the right. Much used in informal music-making, very rarely elsewhere – but see HARRIS (Roy) and GERHARD.

ACCURSED HUNTSMAN, THE (Fr., *Le Chasseur maudit*), symphonic poem by Franck, 1882. On a German poem by G. A. Bürger; the curse is for Sabbath-breaking.

ACHRON, see AKHRON.

ACHTEL (Ger., eighth part), quaver – U.S., eighth-note.

ACIS AND GALATEA, dramatic cantata by Handel with text by John Gay, variously described as a 'mask' (i.e. MASQUE), 'serenata', and 'pastoral'; first performed privately near London, 1721. It had then no connexion with Handel's earlier Italian cantata on the same story (of two pastoral lovers and a villainous giant); but when reviving the English work in 1732 Handel incorporated part of the Italian one.

ACOUSTIC BASS, an organ pedal stop which makes use of an acoustic phenomenon, the RESULTANT TONE, to produce notes an octave lower than the pipes seemingly permit. When the note ordinarily representing 16-FOOT C is depressed, this stop brings into action that note together with the G above it; this then appears to sound the C an octave below, i.e. 32-ft C. Similarly for other notes. This stop is thus said to simulate 32-ft tone.

ACOUSTICS, (1) the science of sound; (2) the sound-properties of a building, etc.

ACT TUNE, piece played between the scenes of an English seventeenth-century theatrical work; cp. ENTR'ACTE, INTERMEZZO.

AD LIB. (Lat., *ad libitum*), at discretion, to be performed as the performer wishes – especially meaning that strict time need not be observed, or that the inclusion of a particular voice or instrument in the ensemble is optional.

ADAGIETTO (It., a little adagio), not quite so slow as ADAGIO.

ADAGIO (It.), slow, a slow movement – slower than ANDANTE, faster than LARGO. *Adagio for Strings*, title of an orchestral work (in elegiac vein) by Barber, first performed 1938 – originally the slow movement of a string quartet.

ADAM, ADOLPHE (CHARLES) (1803–56), French composer of operas including 'If I were King', ballets including 'GISELLE', choral and church music, etc. Also critic.

ADAMS, STEPHEN, pen-name of Michael Maybrick (1844–1913) English composer of 'The Holy City', alleged to have sold at one period 50,000 copies yearly, and other successful 'ballads' of the sentimental English type.

ADDED SIXTH, the major 6th added to the major or minor triad – e. g. or  , A being the added note, the result being called an *added-sixth chord*. Used e.g. by Mahler and Delius and (*ad nauseam*) by jazz and its derivatives, usually for sentimental effect.

ADDINSELL, RICHARD (b. 1904), English composer of music particularly for films and plays – including 'Warsaw Concerto' (fragment for piano and orchestra) in film *Dangerous Moonlight* (1941).

ADDISON, JOHN (b. 1920), English composer, pupil of Jacob. Works include trumpet concerto; overture 'Heroum Filii' (Lat., Sons of Heroes); trio for flute, oboe, and piano; ballet 'Carte Blanche'; much theatre and film music. See POLLY.

'ADÉLAÏDE' CONCERTO, a violin concerto alleged to have been written by Mozart, aged 10, and dedicated to a French princess, Adélaïde. Its authenticity has not been proved.

ADIEUX, LES (in full *Les adieux, l'absence, et le retour*), title given by

Beethoven to his piano sonata in E♭, op. 81a (1809); the 'farewell, absence, and return' are depicted successively in three movements.

ADLER, LARRY (really Lawrence Cecil . . .; b. 1914), American player of the harmonica (mouth-organ) – an instrument he has elevated to concert rank, works having been specially written for him by Milhaud, Vaughan Williams, M. Arnold, etc.

ADRIENNE LECOUVREUR (It., Adriana . . .), opera by Cilèa, produced in Milan, 1902. Libretto by A. Colautti, about an (historical) actress of the Comédie Française, 1730.

AEOLIAN HARP, primitive instrument with strings of different thicknesses but all tuned to the same note, across which the wind is allowed to blow: various HARMONICS result. Named from Aeolus, legendary keeper of the winds.

AEOLIAN MODE, the MODE which may be represented by the white keys of the piano from A to A.

AFFETTUOSO (It.), with feeling.

AFFRETTANDO (It.), becoming faster or more agitated.

AFTERNOON OF A FAUN, THE (Fr., *L'Après-midi d'un faune*), orchestral piece by Debussy, 1892–4, composed as a musical illustration of Mallarmé's poem. Strictly called 'Prelude to "The Afternoon of a Faun"'; Debussy originally intended two other pieces to follow it.

AGE OF ANXIETY, THE, title (from W. H. Auden's poem) of Bernstein's symphony no. 2, for piano and orchestra, first performed 1949 and used for ballet in 1950.

AGITATO (It.), agitated, restless.

AGNEW, ROY (EWING) (1893–1944), Australian pianist and composer of 'Capricornia' (alluding to the Tropic of Capricorn and thus to Australia) and other piano works, etc.

AGON, ballet with music by Stravinsky, produced in New York, 1957: title is the Gr. for 'contest'.

AGRÉMENT (Fr.), equals ORNAMENT.

AGRICOLA, ALEXANDER (?–1506), Flemish composer of church and secular music, pupil of Okeghem; died while working in Spain.

AI (It.), at the, to the (pl.).

AIDA, opera by Verdi, produced in Cairo, 1871. Libretto by A. Ghislanzoni, set in ancient Egypt and named after the Ethiopian princess who is its heroine. (The spelling 'Aïda', with diaeresis, is incorrect in Italian.)

AIR, a simple tune for voice or instrument. (The old English spelling AYRE, and the Italian equivalent ARIA, have acquired more specialized meanings.) The *Air on the G string* is a name given to an arrangement by Wilhelmj (1871) of the 2nd movement of Bach's Suite no. 3 in D for orchestra; in this arrangement, for violin and piano, the piece is transposed from D to C and the violinist plays on his lowest (G) string.

'AIRBORNE' SYMPHONY, work of oratorio type by Blitzstein (first performed 1946) on a text by the composer about the evolution of flying. Uses speaker, singers, and orchestra.

AKHRON, JOSEPH (also spelt *Achron*; 1886–1943), Lithuanian-born violinist (pupil of Auer in Russia) and composer who settled in U.S.A., 1925. Works include three violin concertos and several works with Jewish associations.

AL (It.), to the. (For phrases beginning thus, see under the word following.)

ALABIEV, see ALIABIEV.

ALBANESE, LICIA (b. 1913), Italian-born operatic soprano, American since 1945. Appeared in London, 1937.

ALBÉNIZ, ISAAC (1860–1909), Spanish composer of music in Spanish 'national' style. Child prodigy as composer and pianist; pupil of Liszt in Weimar; spent much of later life in London and Paris. Works include operas (two in English), songs, many piano pieces including cycle 'IBERIA', and a celebrated Tango.

ALBERT, EUGÈNE (FRANCIS CHARLES) D' (1864–1932), Scottish-born composer-pianist, French-English by descent and German by adoption (therefore known also as Eugen d'Albert). Pupil of Liszt; teacher in Berlin; died in Riga. Composed 'Lowland' (Ger., *Tiefland*) and 20 other operas, etc.

ALBERT HERRING, comic opera by Britten, produced at Glyndebourne, 1947; libretto by E. Crozier, after a story by Maupassant about a male 'May Queen'.

ALBERTI BASS, the spreading-out of a left-hand keyboard chord in a rhythmical pattern – e.g.  (from  .) Named after Domenico Alberti (1710–40), Italian composer, who used it extensively.

ALBINONI, TOMASO (1671–1750), Italian violinist and composer of works of CONCERTO GROSSO type; also of more than fifty operas, etc. Bach studied, and adapted from, his music.

ALBORADA (Sp.), morning song (cp. AUBADE); *Alborada del gracioso* ('... of the jester'), piano piece by Ravel in the set 'Mirrors' (1905).

ALBRECHTSBERGER, JOHANN GEORG (1736–1809), Austrian composer and theorist under whom Beethoven studied counterpoint.

ALCESTE, ALCESTIS, see ALKESTIS.

ALCUNA LICENZA, see LICENZA.

ALDRICH, HENRY (1647–1710), English composer of church music, the round 'Great Tom is Cast', etc.; also theologian and architect.

ALEATORIC, malformed word (presumably from Ger. *Aleatorik*, noun not adjective) ignorantly used in place of the standard English term: see next entry.

ALEATORY, dependent on chance or on the throw of the dice (Lat., *alea*). This is rather loosely applied to a tendency (since the 1950s) of some composers to leave elements in their compositions in an indeterminate state. But it might be more strictly confined to compositions in which random chance genuinely plays a part in performance (see CAGE), not to those in which a decision of the performer replaces a decision of the composer. See INDETERMINACY.

ALEXANDER NEVSKY, cantata (drawn from film score) by Prokofiev, first performed 1939, celebrating the victories of the 13th-century Russian prince.

ALEXÁNDER'S FEAST, cantata by Handel, first performed 1736: words mainly from Dryden's poem, referring to Alexander the Great and celebrating the power of music.

ALEXANDROV, ALEXANDER VASSILYEVICH (1884–1945), Russian composer of popular songs, and of the tune adopted as the Russian national anthem from 1944. Also conductor, especially of Russian army ensembles.

ALFANO, FRANCO (1876–1954), Italian composer of operas including 'Cyrano de Bergerac' (after Rostand); also symphonies, string quartets, etc. Completed Puccini's 'TURANDOT' from sketches left by the composer.

ALFONSO AND ESTRELLA, Schubert's only all-sung opera, produced posthumously in Weimar, 1854. Libretto by F. von Schober, about two lovers who are children of a deposed king and a usurping one respectively.

ALFRED, masque by T. A. Arne, produced at Cliveden, Bucks, 1740. Words by J. Thomson and D. Mallet, celebrating King Alfred. It contains 'Rule, Britannia!' (of which the version usually sung today is corrupt).

ALFVÉN, HUGO (1872–1960), Swedish composer of five symphonies and three orchestral Swedish Rhapsodies (no. 1, 'Midsummer Vigil' is the one sometimes called simply 'Swedish Rhapsody'); also of cantatas, a violin sonata, etc. Formerly musical director of Uppsala University.

ALIABIEV, ALEXANDER ALEXANDROVICH (1787–1851), Russian composer of song 'The Nightingale' (formerly often interpolated into the Lesson Scene of Rossini's 'Barber of Seville'); also of operas, etc. (The name is wrongly transliterated as 'Alabiev' in most English references.)

ALKAN, pen-name of Charles Henri Valentin Morhange (1813–88), French pianist and composer of works mainly for the normal piano and the PEDAL-PIANO; his music has some 'advanced' chromatic harmonies.

ALKESTIS, operas by many composers, after Euripides' tragedy. E.g. as 'Alceste', (1) by Lully (libretto, P. Quinault) produced in Paris, 1674; (2) by Gluck (libretto in Italian by R. Calzabigi), Vienna, 1767; as 'Alkestis' (3) by Boughton (libretto from Gilbert Murray's translation of Euripides), Glastonbury, 1922; (4) by Wellesz (libretto, H. von Hofmannsthal), Mannheim, 1924.

ALLA (It.), to the, at the; in the manner of (like Fr. '*à la*').

ALLARGANDO (It.), broadening, becoming slower.

ALLEGRETTO (It., a little allegro), not quite so lively as ALLEGRO.

ALLEGRI, GREGORIO (1582–1652), Italian composer, and singer in the Papal chapel. His Miserere was written down by Mozart, aged 14, allegedly after one hearing.

ALLEGRO (It.), lively, i.e. rather fast (but not as fast as PRESTO).

ALLEMANDE, dance-movement often opening the classical SUITE, in moderate 4-4 time; it was divided into two sections, and usually began with a short note just before the bar-line. The term is French for 'German', but this is not the same as a GERMAN DANCE.

ALLENDE, (PEDRO) HUMBERTO (full surname Allende y Saron; b. 1885), Chilean composer (also violinist, teacher, and folk-music researcher). Works include twelve 'Tonadas' of popular Chilean character, for piano (some also orchestrated); 'The Voice of the Street' for orchestra; songs.

ALMAIN, ALMAND, ALMOND, old English equivalents of ALLEMANDE.

ALPAERTS, FLOR (1876–1954), Belgian composer of symphonic poems (one on the 'TILL EULENSPIEGEL' story), songs with piano and with orchestra, opera 'Shylock' (after *The Merchant of Venice*), etc.; wrote in IMPRESSIONIST style. Also conductor and (1933–41) director of the Antwerp Conservatory.

ALPHORN, wind instrument having a straight wooden tube sometimes as much as 12 ft long. It sounds one HARMONIC SERIES only (like a bugle) with very powerful tone, and is used in Switzerland for attracting cattle (and tourists). The German name is *Alpenhorn*.

ALPINE SYMPHONY, AN (Ger., *Eine Alpensinfonie*), the last of R. Strauss's descriptive orchestral works, first performed 1915.

ALT, term signifying 'high' in special vocal sense – *in alt*, in the octave written immediately above the treble clef, beginning with G; *in altissimo*, in the octave above that.

ALTISSIMO, see preceding entry.

ALTO, (It., high), (1) an unusually high type of adult male voice, employing falsetto – see also COUNTER-TENOR; (2) the lower type of female voice – so designated in choirs, elsewhere usually CONTRALTO (see also next entry); also, sometimes, the corresponding child's voice; (3), in a 'family' of instruments, having range approximately that of an alto voice – e.g. *alto* FLUTE, *alto* SAXOPHONE; (4, *alto clef*) type of clef, written ; it is the normal clef for viola but is otherwise little used; (5, Fr.) viola.

ALTO RHAPSODY, usual English designation for Brahms's Rhapsody for contralto solo, male chorus, and orchestra, first performed 1870; it has a philosophical text by Goethe.

ALWYN, WILLIAM (b. 1905), English composer in broadly 'traditionalist' style, pupil of McEwen. Formerly flutist. Works include four symphonies, concerto 'Lyra Angelica' for harp and strings (referring to an English religious poem of 1610), symphonic poem 'The Magic Island' (after Shakespeare's *The Tempest*); Divertimento for solo flute; much film music.

AMAHL AND THE NIGHT VISITORS, opera for television by Menotti, produced in New York, 1951; later on stage. Libretto by composer, on the legend of the Magi.

AMATI, family of violin-makers of Cremona, functioning from mid-16th to early 18th century.

AMBROSIAN CHANT, type of PLAINSONG introduced by Bishop (St) Ambrose of Milan (340–97), differing from GREGORIAN chant.

AMELIA GOES TO THE BALL, Menotti's first opera, produced in Philadelphia, 1937. Libretto by composer, originally in Italian (*Amelia al ballo*) mocking woman's outlook on social priorities.

AMERICAN FESTIVAL OVERTURE, by W. Schuman, 1939 – based initially on the three-note call of a children's gang in New York.

AMERICAN IN PARIS, AN, descriptive piece for orchestra (including four taxi-horns) by Gershwin, first performed 1928.

AMERICAN ORGAN, type of REED-ORGAN in which air is sucked in through bellows. (U.S. term, cabinet-organ.)

'AMERICAN' QUARTET, name for Dvořák's string quartet in F, op. 96 (1893), composed in U.S.A. and partly prompted by Negro melodies; hence also called 'Negro' Quartet and (in former usage) 'Nigger' Quartet.

'AMID NATURE' (Cz., *V přírodě*), overture by Dvořák, 1891; see also CARNIVAL.

AMOR BRUJO, see LOVE, THE SORCERER.

AMORE, D'; AMOUR, D' (It., Fr.), term applied to some old instruments indicating an ingratiating tone (literally, 'of love'); see main name of instrument, e.g. VIOLA D'AMORE.

AMORE DEI TRE RÉ, L', see LOVE OF THE THREE KINGS.

AMOROSO (It., lovingly), tenderly.

ANCIENT CYMBAL, see CYMBAL.

ANCLIFFE, CHARLES (1880–1952), Irish-born composer of light music including waltz 'Nights of Gladness'.

ANCORA (It., cp. Fr. ENCORE), still, yet; *ancora più mosso*, still more quickly.

ANDA, GEZA (b. 1921), Hungarian pianist, pupil of Dohnányi; resident in Switzerland since 1942.

ANDANTE (It., going) at a walking pace, at moderate speed (between ALLEGRETTO and ADAGIO).

ANDANTINO (It., a little ANDANTE), term apparently indicating either a little slower than andante, or (now more usually) not quite so slow as andante.

ANDERSON, MARIAN (b. 1903), American contralto; overcame various disabilities imposed on her as a Negro; in 1955, became the first Negro to sing in the Metropolitan Opera, New York. Internationally known, e.g. in Sibelius's songs and Negro spirituals.

ANDRÉ CHÉNIER (It., *Andrea* . . .), opera by Giordano, produced at Milan, 1896. Libretto by L. Illica about the historical French Revolutionary poet.

ANDREAE, VOLKMAR (1879–1962), Swiss composer (operas, oboe concertino, etc.), conductor, and director of the Zürich Conservatory.

ANDRIESSEN, HENDRIK (b. 1892), Dutch composer of much Roman Catholic church music, including Masses making use of Gregorian chant; also of opera, three symphonies, etc. Author of a book on Franck and director of The Hague Conservatory. Father of JURIAAN ANDRIESSEN.

ANDRIESSEN, JURIAAN (b. 1925), Dutch composer, pupil of his father (preceding), also pianist and conductor. Works include Sinfonietta Concertante for four trumpets and orchestra; 'Homage to Milhaud' for eleven instruments or quintet; incidental music for stage and radio.

ANERIO, FELICE (1560–1614), Italian composer, mainly of church music; Palestrina's successor as composer to the Papal chapel.

ANFOSSI, PASQUALE (1729–97), Italian composer, especially of operas – including 'La Finta Giardiniera' (The Mock Girl-Gardener) to a libretto later used by Mozart; also church musician in Rome.

ANGEL OF FIRE, THE, see FIERY ANGEL.

ANGLICAN CHANT, type of harmonized melody used for psalm-singing in the Church of England. The melody is four-square in itself, but made metrically irregular by having to accommodate a varying number of syllables.

ANIMATO (It.), animated, lively.

ANSERMET, ERNEST (b. 1883), Swiss conductor – worked with Diaghilev, then (1918) founder-conductor of the Geneva orchestra (Orchestre de la Suisse Romande); gave many first performances of important modern works, especially of Stravinsky. Also writer on music.

ANSWER, a musical phrase appearing to respond to another – particularly in a FUGUE, where the first entry of the main theme is called the subject and the second (at the interval of a fifth upwards from the subject) is called the answer, and so alternately. If the answer exactly reproduces the subject) apart from the displacement of a fifth) it is called a *real answer* and the fugue a *real fugue*; if the internal intervals of the subject are (as usually) slightly modified in the answer, so as to keep the music within the key, then the answer is a *tonal answer* and the fugue a *tonal fugue*.

ANTAR, symphonic suite by Rimsky-Korsakov, first performed 1869 (then called a 'symphony', a description later abandoned by the composer); Antar is the hero of a Syrian tale of chivalry.

ANTHEIL, GEORGE (1900–59), American composer and pianist. Wrote 'Ballet Mécanique' (for aeroplane propellers, bells, motor-horns, etc.), 1927, but later adopted less strikingly unorthodox media and has composed six symphonies, opera 'Volpone' (after Jonson), many film scores, etc. He also wrote an autobiography; crime stories; a syndicated 'advice to the lovelorn' column, etc.

ANTHEM, short solemn vocal composition (hence *national anthem*, authorized for expression of patriotic sentiment); specifically, a short choral work, to a text not necessarily forming part of the liturgy, included in Church of England services – sometimes with organ accompaniment, and either with or without solo parts. Cp. MOTET.

ANTICIPATION, the sounding of a note before the chord of which it forms part, so that at first it is heard as a discord with the preceding chord.

ANTIGONE, operas by various composers, after Sophocles, including one by Honegger, produced in Brussels, 1927 (libretto by Cocteau); another by Orff (with unorthodox, mainly percussive orchestra), directly setting Hölderlin's German version of Sophocles, Salzburg, 1949.

ANTILL, JOHN (b. 1904), Australian composer of ballet 'Corroboree' (evoking Australian aboriginal atmosphere), operas 'Endymion' (on Keats's poem) and 'The Music Critic', etc.; on staff of Australian Broadcasting Commission.

ANTIPHON (from Gk. for 'sounding across') part of Roman Catholic and Greek Orthodox church services sung as responses between single and many voices or between two groups of singers; hence *antiphonal*, adjective used of musical effects drawn from the use of groups of performers stationed apart.

ANTIQUE CYMBAL, see CYMBAL.

ANVIL, orchestra bar-and-striker instrument imitating real anvil; first used by Auber, 1825. Wagner's 'The Rhinegold' demands eighteen.

AP IVOR, DENIS (b. 1916), Irish-born composer of Welsh parentage; qualified doctor of medicine. Works include 'A Mirror for Witches' and other ballets, symphony, piano concerto, cantata 'The Hollow Men' (T. S. Eliot).

APOLLO MUSAGETES (Gk., Apollo, Leader of the Muses), ballet with music by Stravinsky, produced at Washington, 1928. The French version of the title, *Apollon Musagète*, has no claim to usage in English.

APOSTEL, HANS ERICH (b. 1901), German-born Austrian composer, pupil of Schoenberg and Berg. Works include string quartet (with variations on a theme from 'WOZZECK' for Berg's birthday), Requiem, piano solos.

APOSTLES, THE, oratorio by Elgar (text from the Bible), first performed 1903. The first part of Elgar's intended trilogy of oratorios; no. 2 is 'The Kingdom', no. 3 was never completed.

APPALACHIA, 'variations on an old slave song' for orchestra with final chorus by Delius, first performed (in Germany) 1904. (Title from the American Indian name for N. America.)

APPALACHIAN SPRING, ballet with music by Copland, produced 1944. (Title chosen by Martha Graham, for whose company the work was composed: the setting is a 'primitive' American rural community.)

APPOGGIATURA (It., a leaning), (1) musical ornament (chiefly 18th century, now obsolete) consisting of unharmonized auxiliary note falling (or, less frequently, rising) to an adjacent note which is harmonized or implied to be so. Appoggiatura can be either *written*, using an auxiliary note in smaller type – e.g.,  played  or *unwritten*, i.e. to be inserted by performer according to conventions of the period – e.g., a recitative in Handel or Mozart ending  was intended to be sung as ; (2, derived from above) term used in modern harmonic analysis for accented non-harmonized note like the D in the above example (whether or not notated in the above obsolete way) adjacent to following harmonized note less accented than itself.

APPRENTI SORCIER, L', see THE SORCERER'S APPRENTICE.

AQUARELLE, term used for each of two pieces for strings arranged by E. Fenby from Delius's two wordless choruses, 'To be sung of a summer night on the water' (1917). (The term really indicates a type of water-colour painting.)

ARABESQUE (Fr., Eng.; also *Arabesk*, Ger.), title borrowed from visual art and sometimes given to short piece with decorative qualities.

ARBÓS, FERNANDEZ (1863–1939), Spanish violinist, conductor, and arranger – e.g., orchestrated part of IBERIA by Albéniz.

ARCADELT, JACOB (*c.* 1514–*c.* 1575), Flemish composer of masses, motets, madrigals, etc. (one of the earliest practitioners of the madrigal), working in Rome as Papal musician.

'ARCHDUKE' TRIO, nickname of Beethoven's piano trio in B♭ (1811), op. 97, dedicated to Archduke Rudolph of Austria.

ARCHLUTE, type of large lute.

ARCO (It.), bow (of a stringed instrument); (instruction to) play with the bow (cancelling the instruction PIZZICATO).

ARCUEIL, see SATIE.

ARDITI, LUIGI (1822–1903), Italian composer of waltz-song 'Il Bacio' (The Kiss), etc., and conductor; settled in England, 1885, and died there.

ARENSKY, ANTON STEPANOVICH (1861–1906), Russian composer, pupil of Rimsky-Korsakov but not sharing his teacher's pronounced 'nationalism' in music; works include four operas, two symphonies, and (now chiefly heard) piano pieces, chamber music, and songs.

ARIA (It.), air, song, especially one of some complexity in opera or oratorio; '*da capo*' *aria* (as used, e.g., by Handel), one in which the first section is finally repeated after a contrasting section.

ARIADNE AND BLUEBEARD (Fr., *Ariane et Barbe-bleue*), opera by Dukas, produced in Paris, 1907. An almost literal setting of Maeterlinck's play.

ARIADNE ON NAXOS (Ger., *Ariadne auf Naxos*), opera by Richard Strauss with libretto by H. von Hofmannsthal – original version, 1912, designed to be performed after Molière's play *Le Bourgeois Gentilhomme* (with Strauss's incidental music); longer self-contained version, 1916. (Naxos is the island on which Ariadne, at first desolate, later finds consolation from Bacchus.)

ARIETTA (It.), a little or a light ARIA.

ARIOSO (It.), aria-like, i.e. 'normally' sung (as distinct from RECITATIVE) though not necessarily constructed according to the formal balance normally accorded to an ARIA.

ARLECCHINO (It., Harlequin), opera by Busoni, produced in Zürich, 1917. Libretto (by composer) is, despite its title, in German – but set in 18th-century Italy, where Harlequin's mocking defiance of conventional social attitudes brings him success.

ARLÉSIENNE, L', see THE GIRL FROM ARLES.

ARMIDA (or, Fr., *Armide*), operas by several composers based on Tasso's poem of the Crusades, 'Jerusalem Delivered': e.g. (1) by Lully, produced in Paris, 1686 (libretto by P. Quinault); (2) by Gluck, Paris, 1772 (libretto by P. Quinault); (3) by Haydn, Eszterháza, 1784 (libretto, in Italian, by J. Durandi); (4) by Rossini, Naples, 1817 (libretto by G. Schmidt); (5) by Dvořák, Prague, 1904 (libretto by J. Vrchlitzky). See also RINALDO – he and Armida being Tasso's principal male and female characters.

ARMSTRONG, (DANIEL) LOUIS (b. 1900), American trumpeter (earlier, cornetist) famous in jazz and the commercial exploitation of it; led his own band from 1925.

ARMSTRONG, THOMAS (HENRY WAIT) (b. 1898), English organist, composer (choral works, etc.), conductor and teacher; formerly at Oxford University, from 1955 to 1968 principal of the R.A.M. Knighted 1958.

ARNE, MICHAEL (b. 1740 or 1741; d. 1786), English singer and, from childhood, a composer. Works include song 'The lass with the delicate air', and much music for the stage. Illegitimate son of Thomas Arne.

ARNE, THOMAS AUGUSTINE (1710–78), English composer mainly of operas (one in Italian), other stage works, and songs; also of oratorio 'JUDITH'. Wrote masques 'ALFRED' (in which 'Rule, Britannia!' occurs) and 'COMUS'. See also 'LOVE IN A VILLAGE'. Attached as composer at various times to Vauxhall Gardens (London), Drury Lane Theatre, etc. D. Mus., Oxford, 1759 and generally known as Dr Arne. Michael Arne was his illegitimate son.

ARNELL, RICHARD (ANTHONY SAYER) (b. 1917), English composer, also conductor and pianist. Pupil of J. Ireland; lived in U.S.A., 1939–47. Has evolved style with both NEO-CLASSICAL and ROMANTIC traits. Very prolific: works include opera 'Moonflowers', ballet 'Harlequin in April'; five symphonies, and 'Sinfonia quasi variazioni', and a 'Symphonic portrait, Lord Byron'; piano concerto, violin concerto; chamber music, songs, various instrumental solos.

ARNOLD, MALCOLM (b. 1921), English composer, pupil of Jacob; formerly principal trumpet, London Philharmonic Orchestra. Works, cultivating vivid orchestration and straightforward (often humorous) style, include five symphonies and a TOY SYMPHONY, various concertos (one for harmonica, one for piano duet and orchestra) overtures 'BECKUS THE DANDIPRATT' and 'TAM O'SHANTER', various instrumental sonatas, many film scores, ballets 'HOMAGE TO THE QUEEN' and 'Rinaldo and Armida'.

ARNOLD, SAMUEL (1740–1802), English composer of many operas and plays with music; also of church music, harpsichord pieces, etc. Was also organist, and the editor of some works by Handel.

ARPA (It.), harp.

ARPEGGIO (It., from preceding), chord (on piano, etc.) which is performed 'spread out' – i.e. the notes sounded not simultaneously but in succession (nearly always starting at the bottom) as normally on the harp.

ARRANGE, to set out for one performing medium a composition written for another. (Normally this indicates stricter fidelity to the composer's notes, and less artistic licence, than does the term TRANSCRIBE.)

ARRAU, CLAUDIO (b. 1903), Chilean pianist who gave first recital at age 5 and studied in Berlin under Krause (pupil of Liszt); appeared in U.S.A., 1924, and then began world tours. Travels on Chilean 'official' passport and has a street in Santiago named after him.

ARRIAGA, JUAN CRISOSTOMO ANTONIO (full surname Arriaga y Balzola; 1806–26), Spanish composer who studied in Paris and, before early death, wrote symphony and three string quartets notable for classically-proportioned eloquence.

ARS ANTIQUA (Lat., old art), term for the style of Western European medieval music (based on PLAINSONG and ORGANUM) practised e.g. by Pérotin and preceding the ARS NOVA.

ARS NOVA (Lat., new art), term for the musical style current in 14th-century France and Italy, free from the restrictions of ARS ANTIQUA, introducing duple (instead of only triple) time and having more independence of part-writing; practised e.g. by LANDINI, MACHAUT.

ART OF FUGUE, THE (Ger., *Die Kunst der Fuge*), work by Bach, a series of fugues and canons all on the same theme – showing prodigious resource in contrapuntal technique. No instrument is indicated, but the work was demonstrably intended for keyboard (probably harpsichord, possibly organ) – though versions with other instrumentation have been made by several 20th-century musicians. Begun 1748; the final fugue was left incomplete on Bach's death in 1750 (see TOVEY).

ASAFIEV, BORIS (1884–1949), Russian composer ('The Fountain of Bakhchisarai' and other ballets; also operas, four symphonies, etc.); and, under the name Igor Glebov, music critic and writer.

ASCAP, (word formed from the initials of) American Society of Composers, Authors, and Publishers, formed 1914.

ASHKENAZY, VLADIMIR (b. 1937), Russian pianist, joint winner of the International Tchaikovsky Contest at Moscow, 1962 (see OGDON); resident in Britain since 1963, touring extensively.

ASSAI (It.), very; *allegro assai*, very quick.

ASSASSINIO NELLA CATTEDRALE, see MURDER IN THE CATHEDRAL.

ATONAL, not in any key; hence *atonality, atonalism.* (The term *Pantonal*, indicating the synthesis of all keys rather than the absence of any, was preferred by Schoenberg but has never won general acceptance.) As a systematization of atonal music there developed TWELVE-NOTE music.

ATTACCA (It.), attack (verb), i.e. go on to the next section without a break; so also *attacca subito* (immediately).

ATTERBERG, KURT (b. 1887), Swedish composer, conductor, and critic; won international competition for a Schubert commemoration symphony, 1928, afterwards admitting to elements of pastiche in the work. Has also written other symphonies, five operas, etc., sometimes making direct use of Swedish folk-music.

ATTWOOD, THOMAS (1765–1838), English organist (at St Paul's Cathedral, London, from 1796), and composer of church and other music, including notable songs. Pupil of Mozart in Vienna.

AU, AUX (Fr.), at the, to the, etc.

AUBADE (Fr.), morning song (cp. SERENADE); *Aubade héroïque*, work for small orchestra by Lambert, 1942, alluding to the dawn invasion of The Hague by German parachutists. See also ALBORADA.

AUBER, DANIEL FRANÇOIS ESPRIT (1782–1871), French composer of more than 40 operas including 'The Dumb Girl of Portici' (*La Muette de Portici* – see MASANIELLO), 'MANON LESCAUT', and 'FRA DIAVOLO'; also of violin concerto, etc. Director of the Paris Conservatory.

AUBERT, LOUIS (FRANÇOIS MARIE) (b. 1877), French composer of symphonic poem 'Habanera', opera, ballets, songs, etc.

AUBIN, TONY (LOUIS ALEXANDRE) (b. 1907), French composer of cantatas, piano works, songs, etc.; pupil of Dukas.

AUDRAN, EDMOND (1842–1901), French composer chiefly of operettas including 'The Mascot' (*La Mascotte*).

AUER, LEOPOLD (1845–1930), Hungarian-born violinist, famous teacher in St Petersburg – e.g. of Elman and Heifetz – and also in Germany and U.S.A.

AUFFÜHRUNGSPRAXIS (Ger.), the practical aspects of performance – term particularly referring to the necessity, in preparing a performance of old music, of looking beyond the written page into what the composer expected from his interpreter. (Choice of instruments, modifications of note-values, appropriate expression, etc., was often less explicitly detailed in former periods than now.)

AUFSTIEG UND FALL DER STADT MAHAGONNY, see RISE AND FALL OF THE CITY OF MAHAGONNY.

AUGMENT (1) to supplement the numbers of a performing group; so 'augmented choir', etc.; (2) to 'increase' certain intervals – see AUGMENTED; (3) to subject a melody to AUGMENTATION.

AUGMENTATION, the treatment of a melody in such a way as to lengthen (usually doubling) the time-values of its notes. The device is used, e.g. in some fugues.

AUGMENTED, term applied to a type of interval regarded as an 'increased' version of a certain other interval. So *augmented 1st* (e.g. C up to C♯); *augmented 2nd* (C up to D♯); *augmented 4th* (C up to F♯); *augmented 5th* (C up to G♯); *augmented 6th* (C up to A♯ – see FRENCH, GERMAN, ITALIAN SIXTHS); *augmented 8th* or *augmented octave* (C up to next C♯ but one). Note that the *augmented 5th* carries the harmonic implication of the major 3rd too; e.g. the *augmented fifth chord* on C is C–E–G♯, which chord is referred to in dance-bands, etc., as *C augmented* (abbr. *C aug*.).

AULOS, ancient Greek oboe-like wind instrument, having double reed.

AURIC, GEORGES (b. 1899), French composer, youngest member of the 'SIX'. has written much for ballet (e.g. 'Phèdre', after Racine's play) and for films; also piano concerto, piano sonata, etc. Administrator of the two Paris opera-houses from 1962.

AURORA'S WEDDING, see SLEEPING BEAUTY.

AUSTIN, FREDERIC (1872–1952), English baritone and composer; arranged the music of 'THE BEGGAR'S OPERA' for its exceptionally successful London revival, 1920. Made a similar arrangement of 'POLLY'.

AUTHENTIC MODES, see MODE.

AUXILIARY NOTE, in harmony, a note which forms a discord with the chord with which it is heard, but is 'justified' because it lies adjacent (higher or lower) to a note of the chord which is heard immediately before and after – e.g. the D in the following example. 

AVE MARIA (Lat., Hail, Mary), Roman Catholic prayer of partly biblical source. It has been variously set to music. The setting usually described as 'Bach-Gounod' consists of the first prelude of Bach's 'WELL-TEMPERED CLAVIER' plus a melody which Gounod wrote over this (with the title 'Meditation'); to this melody the words of the 'Ave Maria' were fitted by someone else.

AVISON, CHARLES (1709–90), English composer and organist who worked in Newcastle-on-Tyne, and probably studied with Geminiani in London. Works include concertos for string orchestra; also edited Marcello's psalm-settings with English texts. See also GIARDINI.

AVODATH HAKODESH, see SACRED SERVICE.

AVSHALOMOV, JACOB (b. 1919), American composer – born in China of a Russian father. Works include Sinfonietta, Slow Dance for orchestra, choral work 'Inscriptions at the City of Brass'. Also conductor.

AXMAN, EMIL (1887–1949), Czech composer of symphonies, choral works, etc.; pupil of Novák.

AYRE, old spelling of *air*, retained in modern English for a type of English song practised (e.g. by J. Dowland) about 1600 – having its main melodic interest in the top vocal line, with accompaniment for lute (or for other voices) and with the tune repeated for each stanza.

B

B, note of the scale. So B FLAT (B♭), DOUBLE-FLAT (B♭♭), NATURAL (B♮), SHARP (B♯), DOUBLE-SHARP (B𝄪); *B major*, *B minor*, etc. – see MAJOR. So also *in B♭*, either (1) in the key of B♭ (major, understood); or (2) indication of a TRANSPOSING INSTRUMENT on which the note C sounds as B♭ (and correspondingly with other notes): e.g. *clarinet in B♭*, or, colloquially, *B♭ clarinet*. Note that the note represented in English by B is represented in German by H, the Germans using B to mean what is in English B♭. Hence clarinets in German scores may be marked 'in B', etc.

B–A–C–H, in German nomenclature, the notes B♭–A–C–B♮; J. S. Bach himself conceived the idea of using these notes as a theme of the unfinished final fugue of 'THE ART OF FUGUE', and the same combination has been used by many subsequent composers (e.g., Schumann, Liszt, Busoni), generally in tribute to Bach.

BAR., abbr. of BARITONE (voice).

BA♭ BASS, name used in brass and military bands for the lower of the band's two types of TUBA; it is a TRANSPOSING INSTRUMENT in B♭ – the double 'B' indicating a pitch an octave lower than, e.g., the euphonium, also in B♭.

BBC, British Broadcasting Corporation; *BBC Symphony Orchestra*, its chief orchestra, maintained in London – founded 1930, first conducted by Boult. Later conductors included Sargent, Schwarz, and Dorati and (1967) Colin Davis.

B.MUS., abbr. of Bachelor of Music.

BR., abbr. of Ger. *Bratsche*(*n*), i.e. viola(s).

BTB., Ger. abbr. of bass tuba, i.e. the normal orchestral tuba in F.

BWV, see SCHMIEDER.

BAAL SHEM suite for violin and piano by Bloch, subtitled 'Three Pictures of Chassidic Life': named after Baal Shem Tov (Master of the Good Name), 17-century founder of the Jewish pietist sect of Chassidism.

BABA YAGA, 'fairy tale for orchestra' by Liadov, 1904, describing the flight of the witch named in the title.

BABBITT, MILTON (b. 1916), American composer, pupil of Sessions; works, employing SERIAL technique, include string quartet, piano pieces, songs, 'Vision and Prayer' (words by Dylan Thomas) for soprano and 'electronic music'.

BABIN, VICTOR (b. 1908), Russian-born American pianist (pupil of Schnabel) forming two-piano team with his wife, Vitya Vronsky; also composer of two 2-piano concertos, song-cycles, etc.; pupil of Schreker. Director of Cleveland Conservatory, 1961.

BABY GRAND, a grand piano of the smallest size.

BACCHETTA (It., pl. *-ette*, stick), drumstick.

BACCHUS AND ARIADNE (Fr. *Bacchus et Ariane*), ballet with music by Roussel, produced in Paris, 1931. (On the same legend as R. Strauss's 'ARIADNE ON NAXOS'.) Two orchestral suites are drawn from it.

ACEWICZ, GRAZYNA (b. 1913), Polish (woman) composer of three symphonies, cello concerto, four violin concertos, four string quartets, etc.; also violinist.

BACH, German family of musicians, some of whom are listed below; *Bach* without prefaced name or initials indicates Johann Sebastian Bach. For *Bach bow*, see BOW; for *Bach trumpet*, see TRUMPET. See also B–A–C–H (above).

BACH, ANNA MAGDALENA (1701–60), second wife of J. S. Bach who compiled two books of music (by himself and others) for her musical instruction, 1722 and 1725.

BACH, CARL PHILIPP EMANUEL (1714–88), German composer, fifth child of J. S. Bach, pupil of his father. Domestic musician to Frederick the Great of Prussia, until assuming a church post at Hamburg in 1767. Noted keyboard-player, adapting his music progressively to suit trend from harpsichord to piano; wrote treatise on keyboard-playing. Works, showing departure from J. S. Bach's style towards that of Haydn and Mozart, include keyboard concertos and sonatas, symphonies, chamber music; also oratorio and church music.

BACH, JOHANN CHRISTIAN (1735–82), German composer, eighteenth child of J. S. Bach; studied under his father and under his brother C. P. E. Bach. Went in 1756 to Italy, in 1762 to London where he remained, eventually dying there. He was known as 'the English Bach'; influenced Mozart on his visit (aged 8) to London. Works include Italian operas, English songs, about forty piano concertos and other orchestral works, church music in Latin and English.

BACH, JOHANN CHRISTOPH (1642–1705), German composer, cousin of J. S. Bach's father. Wrote oratorios, symphonies, string quartets, etc.; also choral music including motet 'Ich lasse dich nicht' ('I leave thee not', but in English usually known as 'I wrestle and pray'), formerly ascribed in error to J. S. Bach.

BACH, JOHANN SEBASTIAN (1685–1750), German composer; of high repute in his time as organist, but achieved major standing as composer only with posthumous (19th-century) revival. Born at Eisenach; studied under his brother Johann Christoph (not the preceding) and, as boy chorister at Lüneburg, was apparently influenced by Georg Böhm. 'Held organist's or other posts at Weimar, 1703; Arnstadt, later in 1703; Muhlhausen, 1707; Weimar, 1708; Cothen, 1717; then in 1723 to Leipzig as Cantor (director of music) at St Thomas's church, in which post he died shortly after becoming blind.' Twice married, father of twenty children. Works, mostly written as official duty or with some other definite performance in view, include nearly 300 church cantatas (Lutheran), with orchestral accompaniment; ST JOHN and ST MATTHEW PASSIONS, both using his harmonizations of Lutheran chorales; CHRISTMAS and EASTER ORATORIOS; Mass in B minor; 'COFFEE CANTATA', 'PHOEBUS AND PAN' and some other secular vocal works; preludes, fugues, and other works for organ; 'CHROMATIC FANTASIA AND FUGUE', 'GOLDBERG VARIATIONS', 'ITALIAN CONCERTO', 'THE WELL-TEMPERED CLAVIER' and other works for harpsichord and for clavichord; concertos for one, two, three, and (arranged from Vivaldi) four harpsichords, also for one and two violins; SIX BRANDENBURG CONCERTOS (orchestral); 'THE MUSICAL OFFERING' and 'THE ART OF FUGUE', both demonstrating prodigious contrapuntal skill. For the numbering of his works, see SCHMIEDER. See also CHACONNE.

BACH, WILHELM FRIEDEMANN (1710–84), German composer, eldest son and second child of J. S. Bach who wrote some music specially for his instruction. Became church organist, died in poverty; wrote church cantatas, nine symphonies, organ and harpsichord music, etc.

BACHAUER, GINA (b. 1913), Greek-born pianist (of Greek, Italian, Russian, and Austrian descent); first appeared in Britain 1946, later in U.S.A.

BACHIANAS BRASILEIRAS, title given by Villa-Lobos to a set of works (for various instrumental groups with or without voice) intended to synthesize the spirit of J. S. Bach's music and that of the traditional music of Villa-Lobos's native Brazil.

BÄCK, SVEN-ERIK (b. 1919), Swedish composer, pupil of Petrassi in Rome; works, latterly inclining to TWELVE-NOTE technique, include symphony for strings, 'Sinfonia Sacra' for choir and orchestra, sonata for solo flute.

BACKHAUS, WILHELM (b. 1884), German pianist (pupil of d'Albert) who made first concert tour at 16 years of age and later attained world fame.

BACON, ERNST (b. 1898), American composer of opera 'The Tree on the Plains', two symphonies, etc.; also conductor, pianist, critic.

BADINERIE (Fr., a teasing), title of certain quick 2/4 movements in the 18th century, e.g. in Bach's Suite in B minor for flute and strings.

BADINGS, HENK (b. 1907), Dutch composer, born in Java; largely self-taught at first, then pupil of Pijper. Works, showing some affinity with Hindemith's style, include five symphonies, four violin concertos, sonata for carillon, orchestral arrangements of old Dutch songs.

BADURA-SKODA, PAUL (b. 1924), Austrian pianist; has toured widely in Europe and has also visited Australia. Also writer on music.

BAGATELLE (Fr., trifle), short, rather light piece, often for piano – Beethoven wrote twenty-six.

BAGPIPE(s), reed-pipe instrument for which wind is stored in a bag, either (e.g. Scottish Highland pipes) mouth-filled, or (e.g. Northumbrian pipes and Irish 'Uillean' or 'Union' pipes) filled by bellows under player's arm; the former type is the louder. Similar types are found in other countries; most have one or more drone pipes (giving unaltered bass-notes) as well as a pipe for the melody (chanter). The Scottish Highland pipe, though its scale does not correspond exactly to the normal one of the concert-hall, is used with orchestra in Ian Whyte's ballet 'Donald of the Burthens', 1951. See also MUSETTE.

BAGUETTE (Fr.), drumstick.

BAILLIE, ISOBEL (originally Bella; b. 1895), Scottish-born soprano, brought up in Manchester, trained in Milan; first London appearance 1923. Prominent in oratorio and recital. C.B.E., 1951.

BAILLOT, PIERRE (MARIE FRANÇOIS DE SALES) (1771–1842), French violinist, composer of violin music and writer of an instructional textbook on his instrument.

BAINES, ANTHONY (CUTHBERT) (b. 1919), English bassoonist, conductor, and authority on old instruments. Made an arrangement of Handel's WATER MUSIC. Brother of Francis Baines.

BAINES, FRANCIS (ATHELSTANE) (b. 1917), English double-bass player and composer of a symphony for chamber orchestra, trumpet concerto, etc. Brother of Anthony Baines.

BAINTON, EDGAR LESLIE (1889–1956), English composer and piano-teacher who settled in Australia; director of New South Wales State Conservatorium (Sydney) 1933–47. Works include opera, three symphonies, choral setting of Rosetti's 'The Blessed Damozel', piano pieces.

BAIRD, TADEUSZ (b. 1928), Polish composer of 'Erotics' (six songs for soprano and orchestra), 'Variations without a theme' and other orchestral works, piano concerto, theatre and film music, etc.

BAIRSTOW, EDWARD CUTHBERT (1874–1946), English organist (at

York Minster from 1913), composer chiefly of church music, conductor, and professor at Durham University; knighted 1932.

BALAKIREV, MILY ALEXEYEVICH (1837–1910), Russian composer, leader of the 'nationalist' group of composers called THE MIGHTY HANDFUL; also conductor and musical organizer. After nervous breakdown, retired from music 1871–76, becoming railway official; 1883, director of music to the Russian court. Works include two symphonies, symphonic poem 'Tamara'; much piano music including 'ISLAMEY' and a sonata; songs and folksong arrangements.

BALALAIKA, type of Russian plucked instrument usually with three strings and triangular body; made in various sizes, and used singly and in bands for folk music, etc. Cp. DOMRA.

BALFE, MICHAEL WILLIAM (1808–70), Irish composer, also baritone singer; came to London as a boy and later studied in Italy. Composed operas in French, Italian, and English, these last including 'THE BOHEMIAN GIRL' (internationally successful, combining a cosmopolitan operatic style with provision for the Victorian English taste for 'ballads'), 'The Maid of Artois' (see 'MANON'), 'The Rose of Castile'; also songs, cantatas, etc.

BALLABILE (It.), to be danced; in a dancing manner. Cp. CANTABILE.

BALLAD (derived as 'ball', i.e. from dancing), (1) old song (often a FOLK-SONG) telling a story, the music being repeated for each verse; hence – (2) a self-contained song of a narrative nature, e.g. Goethe's 'The Erl King' as set by Schubert or Loewe; (3) song of narrative, explanatory type characteristically found in French opera and also e.g. in Wagner's 'The Flying Dutchman' ('Senta's Ballad'); so Stravinsky calls his narrative cantata on Abraham and Isaac a 'sacred ballad'; (4) sentimental English song of 19th century 'drawing-room' type (also found in English operas of the period); so *ballad concert*, mainly devoted to such songs; (5) see BALLADE. See also BALLAD OPERA.

BALLAD OPERA, opera having spoken dialogue and using popular tunes of the day adapted to new words, the prototype being 'THE BEGGAR'S OPERA', 1728. (The term is also used in various looser senses; Vaughan Williams's 'HUGH THE DROVER', described as 'a romantic ballad opera' has no spoken dialogue, and is not made up of traditional tunes, but is written in an idiom deliberately evoking such tunes.) Cp. BALLAD (1).

BALLADE, (1) instrumental piece suggesting narrative, e.g. four for piano by Chopin, said to be inspired by (but certainly not being literal interpretations of) Polish poems by Mickiewicz. (The word is the French version of BALLAD; its use in English may be justified by the convenience of differentiating the instrumental from the vocal term.) (2) a form of medieval poetry and music; certain polyphonic works e.g. by Machaut are so entitled.

BALLET, (1) form of dancing of Italian origin, becoming established at the French court in the 16th century, and evolving into a recognized art-form with its own traditional technique and conventions; it normally uses orchestral music (specially composed or otherwise) and appropriately full resources of stage decoration. The term is now used in Britain for almost any piece of stage dancing having an artistic purpose and substantial length; but in the U.S.A. it is commonly withheld from works not based on the 'classical' technique of dancing – e.g. the so-called 'modern dance'. (For the somewhat academic distinction between *ballet* and 'divertissement', see DIVERTISSEMENT.) Hence *opéra-ballet* and *ballet-pantomime*, 18th-century French terms differentiating ballet with and without sung words; the term *opera-ballet* is also applied to certain modern ballets with singing, e.g. Prokofiev's 'CINDERELLA'. (But note that the simple classification *ballet* does not exclude the use of voices – as in Ravel's 'DAPHNIS AND CHLOE' – and that Falla's 'LOVE, THE SORCERER' is styled ballet-pantomime, although it has vocal solos.) (2) an alternative spelling of BALLETT, and so pronounced.

BALLETT, type of concerted English vocal composition prominent about 1600 and similar to the madrigal – sometimes, indeed, itself classed as a kind of madrigal; it has a dance-like lilt (as the name suggests) and a fa-la refrain.

BALLO (It.), a dance; *Overture Di Ballo*, linguistically odd title of a concert-overture by Sullivan, 1870, using dance-rhythms.

BALLO IN MASCHERA, UN, see A MASKED BALL.

BAMBOO PIPE, simple wind-instrument of RECORDER type, used mainly educationally, players often making their own instruments; sometimes just called *pipe*, as in Vaughan Williams's 'Suite for Pipes' (four of different sizes), published 1947.

BAND, a numerous body of players, especially of wind or percussion instruments – BRASS, MILITARY, DANCE, PERCUSSION *bands*, etc. The use of the term for a full or string orchestra is almost obsolete, and the supposed prestige of the term 'orchestra' is now borrowed even by dance bands.

BANDURRÍA (Sp.), Spanish plucked instrument, usually with six pairs of strings, each pair tuned to a unison.

BANFIELD, RAFFAELLO DE (b. 1922), Italian composer; works include opera 'Lord Byron's Love Letter' (libretto by Tennessee Williams), ballet 'The Duel'.

BANISTER, JOHN (1630–79), English violinist, composer, and the man who organized the first concerts in London to be open to the public on payment of an admission fee, 1672.

BANJO, fretted instrument of five or more strings, plucked with fingers or plectrum; taken over from U.S. Negro slaves by black-faced minstrel shows, and also used in early jazz – not much else in public, except to provide local 'atmosphere', e.g. in the orchestration of Gershwin's 'PORGY AND BESS' and Delius's 'KOANGA'.

BANKS, DON (really Donald Oscar; b. 1923), Australian composer, resident in England since 1950; pupil of Seiber in London and of

Dallapiccola in Florence. Works, in TWELVE-NOTE technique, include 'Four pieces for orchestra'; horn concerto; setting of Psalm 70 for soprano and chamber orchestra; Divertimento for flute and string trio; violin sonata.

BANTOCK, GRANVILLE (1868–1946), English composer of 'Fifine at the Fair' and other symphonic poems; also of 'Hebridean Symphony' (and other Scottish-inclined works), song-cycles, unaccompanied choral works including a setting of Swinburne's 'Atlanta in Calydon', etc. Professor at Birmingham University, 1908; knighted 1930.

BAR, (1) a metrical division of music, marked on paper as the distance between two vertical lines; so 'two beats in the bar', etc.; (2) such a vertical line itself. (In general the first of these uses is English, the second American – Eng. *bar* equals U.S. *measure*; U.S. *bar* equals Eng. *bar-line*. But two vertical lines close together, indicating the end of a piece or section, are called even in English *double bar*, not *double bar-line*.)

BARBER, SAMUEL (b. 1910), American composer, formerly also singer (e.g. in his own setting, for voice and string quartet, of Matthew Arnold's 'Dover Beach'). Studied in Italy and U.S.A. Works, favouring a traditional-European rather than an overtly American idiom, include operas 'VANESSA', 'A Hand of Bridge', 'Antony and Cleopatra', two symphonies, two Essays for orchestra, ADAGIO for Strings, overture to Sheridan's *The School for Scandal*, cello concerto, 'Capricorn Concerto' (flute, oboe, trumpet, and strings), piano sonata, ballet 'Medea' (also known as 'Cave of the Heart'), cantata 'Prayers of Kierkegaard'.

BARBER OF BAGHDAD, THE (Ger., *Der Barbier von Bagdad*), comic opera by Cornelius, produced in Weimar, 1858. Libretto by the composer, a tale of intrigue (after the 'Arabian Nights' Entertainment').

BARBER OF SEVILLE, THE (It., *Il Barbiere di Siviglia*), operas by (1) Rossini, produced in Rome, 1810, with libretto by C. Sterbini; (2) Paisiello, produced at St Petersburg, 1782, with libretto by G. Petrosellini – this version achieving international success but being superseded by Rossini's. The plot is that of Beaumarchais' French play, the cunning barber-factotum of the title being Figaro: the plot of Mozart's 'THE MARRIAGE OF FIGARO' is a sequel. See ALIABIEV.

BARBER-SHOP SINGING (U.S.), the singing of home-made arrangements of sentimental songs by amateur male quartets; a 'Society for the Preservation and Encouragement of Barber-Shop Singing in America' was founded in 1938. (Cp. the reputation of English barber-shops in Shakespeare's time for impromptu music-making.)

BARBIER VON BAGDAD, DER, see THE BARBER OF BAGHDAD.

BARBIERE DI SIVIGLIA, see THE BARBER OF SEVILLE.

BARBIERI, FRANCISCO (ASENJO) (1823–94), Spanish composer, also singer, instrumentalist, and writer on music; composed Spanish comic operas of ZARZUELA type, including 'The Little Barber of Lavapies'.

BARBIROLLI, JOHN (really Giovanni Battista ....; b. 1899), English condutor of Italian and French parentage, formerly cellist. In 1936 succeeded Toscanini with New York Philharmonic-Symphony Orchestra; returned to Britain as conductor of the HALLÉ Orchestra (Manchester) 1943-68; also conducted opera. Also (1961–7) conductor of Houston (Texas) Symphony Orchestra. Also arranger – e.g. of orchestral 'Elizabethan Suite' from 16th-century composers. Knighted 1949. Wife is Evelyn Rothwell (b. 1911), oboist.

BARCAROLLE (Fr., from It.), boating-song, especially of the kind associated with Venetian gondoliers; song or instrumental piece suggestive of this, in swaying 6/8 time (e.g. the famous one in Offenbach's 'THE TALES OF HOFFMANN').

BARDWELL, WILLIAM (b. 1915), English composer, trained in London and (under Nadia Boulanger) in Paris: has written three Chinese cantatas and 'Little Serenade' (for piccolo, xylophone, and mandoline) in style suggestive of Far Eastern music. Other works include 'Diablotins' (Fr., Imps) for string quartet.

BARITONE, (1) man's voice of a range intermediate between tenor and bass; (2, of 'families' of instruments) indication of a range below the 'tenor' type, e.g. *baritone* SAXHORN, *baritone* SAXOPHONE; (3) name used in brass bands as abbreviation for *baritone saxhorn*. See also BARYTONE.

BARNBY, JOSEPH (1838–96), English conductor (especially choral), organist, and composer (part-song 'Sweet and Low', etc.). Principal of Guildhall School of Music, London; knighted 1892.

BARNETT, JOHN (original surname Beer; 1802–90), English composer (a relative of Meyerbeer), whose works include opera 'The Mountain Sylph', operettas, symphony; uncle of John Francis Barnett.

BARNETT, JOHN FRANCIS (1837–1916), English composer and pianist, nephew of John Barnett, who studied partly in Germany; made a completed version of Schubert's symphony no. 7 from the composer's sketched-out score.

BAROCCO, BAROCK (It., Ger.), see BAROQUE.

BAROQUE, term borrowed from architecture (where it has connotations of 'twisting', 'elaborate, heavy, involved construction') and used to describe characteristics of musical style roughly contemporaneous with this in the 17th and first half of the 18th centuries – applied, e.g., to Monteverdi, Purcell, and J. S. Bach, though the liberality of such application makes precise definition awkward. (Cp. ROCOCO.) The term *baroque organ* is applied to the type of this period, more brilliant in tone and less heavy than 19th-century type, with lighter wind-pressure and greater reliance on MUTATION stops. (This is a 20th-century use of the word *baroque*. In the 18th century the word meant 'uncouth, odd, rough, and antiquated in taste'.)

BARRAGE (Fr.), the use of chords played BARRÉ on the guitar.

BARRAINE, ELSA (b. 1910), French composer, pupil of Dukas; works include two symphonies, theatre and film music.

BARRAUD, HENRY (b. 1900), French composer of orchestral works, opera 'Numantia' (libretto by S. de Madariaga), ballet 'The Astrologer in the Well', symphony for strings, piano concerto, etc.; also critic.

BARRÉ (Fr.), (chord on guitar, etc.) played with one finger laid like a rigid bar across all strings, raising the pitch of all these equally.

BARREL-ORGAN, automatic organ in which projections on a hand-rotated barrel bring into action the notes required – i.e. a genuine pipe-organ, though limited to a number of pre-set tunes like a musical box; formerly used in some English churches. Not a HURDY-GURDY or STREET PIANO.

BARTERED BRIDE, THE (Cz., *Prodaná Nevěsta*), comic opera by Smetana, produced in Prague, 1866. Libretto by K. Sabina, about a village intrigue.

BARTLETT, ETHEL (b. 1900), English pianist associated with her Scottish husband, Rae Robertson (1893–1956), in a two-piano team; resident U.S.A. Many works by British and other composers were written for them.

BARTÓK, BÉLA (1881–1945), Hungarian composer, settled in U.S.A., 1940, dying there a poor man. From youth, a virtuoso pianist. Cultivated and developed Hungarian national musical style; partly in association with Kodály, collected and edited Hungarian folk-songs, showing them to be different from the gipsy music borrowed by Liszt, Brahms, etc. Active in investigating other folk-music too. His own works – often atonal and cultivating extreme dissonance, especially in his middle life – include opera 'BLUEBEARD'S CASTLE', mime-plays 'The Wooden Prince' and 'THE MIRACULOUS MANDARIN'; much piano music including 'MIKROKOSMOS', 'Out of Doors', and works for children; orchestral Dance Suite; Concerto for orchestra; 'Music for Strings, Percussion, and Celesta', three piano concertos, violin concerto, viola concerto (posthumous, edited by T. Serly), six string quartets, trio 'CONTRASTS', songs and folk-song-arrangements. See also CANTATA.

BARYTONE, obsolete stringed instrument resembling viola da gamba but having sympathetic strings like the viola d'amore. Haydn wrote extensively for it, because his patron, Prince Nicholar Esterházy, played it.

BASIC SET, term used in TWELVE-NOTE technique for the note-row or series (comprising all twelve notes within the octave) in its original chosen order – i.e. not in an order arrived at by using the row backwards, or upside-down, or both (see INVERSION, RETROGRADE).

BASS, (1) the lowest male voice; (2) the lowest note or part in a chord, a composition, etc.; (3) the lower regions of musical pitch generally – especially in antithesis to TREBLE; (4, of a 'family' of instruments) having low range, e.g. *bass* CLARINET, *bass* SAXOPHONE; *bass flute*, misnomer for alto FLUTE; (5) colloquial abbreviation for DOUBLE-BASS, or (in brass and military bands) for the bombardon (see TUBA); (6, *bass clef*), clef written and indicating F below middle C as the top line but one of the staff (and so sometimes also called *F clef*); it is normally used for bass voice, for most lower-pitched instruments, for the left-hand part of piano music, etc. See also following entries.

BASS DRUM (or 'long drum'), large shallow drum of low but indefinite pitch; used in the symphony orchestra, the military band (where it may be carried), dance-band (the drum-stick usually worked by pedal), etc.

BASS FIDDLE, colloquial term for DOUBLE-BASS. (For an eccentric use, see GRAINGER.)

BASSE (Fr.), bass; *basse chantante* equals BASSO CANTANTE.

BASSET-HORN, instrument of same type as clarinet but lower in pitch (down to the F at the bottom of the bass staff). Used, e.g., by Mozart in 'THE CLEMENCY OF TITUS'; also by R. Strauss ('Symphonies for Wind', 1943–5) but otherwise very rare since Mozart's day. It is a TRANSPOSING INSTRUMENT in F. The origin of its name is said to be from a South German term for 'small bass', the basset-hound being so named after its voice.

BASSO (It.), bass. So *basso cantante* ('singing'), a bass voice suitable for lyrical rather than dramatic parts in opera; *basso continuo*, see CONTINUO; *basso ostinato* equals GROUND BASS; *basso profondo* (not *profundo*), a bass voice of unusually low range. (The word *basso* has not been taken into English, though U.S. publicity is fond of it as sounding 'grander' than *bass*.)

BASSOON, bass woodwind instrument found in the orchestra and military band, occasionally also as soloist and in chamber music; having a double reed, thus related to the oboe. Compass from the B♭ below the bass stave upwards for about three and a half octaves. The *double-bassoon*, rarely encountered before the 19th century, has a compass an octave lower: it is often called contra-bassoon, but this is an illegitimate and undesirable offspring of 'bassoon' and It. *contrafagotto* – in modern Italian *controfagotto*. (The obsolete *Russian bassoon* was not a bassoon at all but a kind of straightened-out SERPENT.)

BASTIEN AND BASTIENNE, opera by Mozart (aged 12), produced in Vienna, 1768. Libretto by F. W. Weiskern, about a pair of pastoral lovers separated and reunited.

BATE, STANLEY (1913–59), English composer, pupil of Vaughan Williams in London, Hindemith in Berlin, N. Boulanger in Paris; resident 1942–54 in U.S.A., also visiting Brazil. Works include four symphonies, three piano concertos, and harpsichord concerto, ballets (one on *Troilus and Cressida*), 'Six Studies for an Infant Prodigy' and other piano works. Also pianist. At one time married to P. Glanville-Hicks.

BATH, HUBERT (1883–1945), English composer of film music, opera on Du Maurier's *Trilby*, etc.

BATON (Fr.), stick used by conductor to indicate time and expression.

BATTERY, collective term for percussion instruments.

BATTLE OF VITTORIA, BATTLE SYMPHONY, see WELLINGTON'S VICTORY.

BATTUTA (It.), (1) beat; (2) bar; *ritmo di tre battute*, literally 'rhythm of three bars', i.e. let the main accent fall at the beginning of every three bars.

BAUDRIER, YVES (b. 1906), French composer, pupil of D'Indy but chiefly self-taught; one of the 'YOUNG FRANCE' group, championing the idea of a 'personal message' in music. Works include symphony, symphonic poems, songs; composer of film music and lecturer on this.

BAX, ARNOLD (EDWARD TREVOR) (1883–1953), English composer – not Irish, but stayed frequently in Ireland and was much influenced by its literature and lore. Also visited Russia, 1910. Knighted 1937; Master of the King's (later Queen's) Music, 1942. Works, tending to an expansive POST-ROMANTIC idiom, include seven symphonies; 'THE GARDEN OF FAND', 'TINTAGEL', and other symphonic poems; 'Overture to a Picaresque Comedy', violin concerto, cello concerto, 'Concertante for orchestra with piano (left hand)'; music for choir and for chamber groups; 'Hardanger' for two pianos; many piano solos (see COHEN, HARRIET). Contributor to 'A GARLAND FOR THE QUEEN'.

BAYREUTH, a Bavarian town where a festival theatre was built to Wagner's designs. It opened in 1876 with 'The Ring' and has remained devoted to his music.

BAZZINI, ANTONIO (1818–97), Italian violinist and composer of 'The Dance of the Goblins' (Fr., *La Ronde des Lutins*) for violin and piano; also opera, six string quartets, etc.

BEACH, MRS H.H.A., style of name used as a composer by Amy Marcy Beach (born Chaney; 1867–1944), whose works include a 'Gaelic Symphony', a piano concerto, Mass, etc. – the first American woman to achieve a reputation as composer of such music.

BEAR, THE, nickname of Haydn's symphony no. 82 in C, 1786, of which the last movement suggests a captive bear dancing to a bagpipe.

BEARD, PAUL (b. 1901), English violinist, leader of the BBC Symphony Orchestra from 1936 to 1962.

BEAT, (1) rhythmic pulse ('the waltz has three beats to the bar'), or the physical action corresponding to this ('watch the conductor's beat') – see UP-BEAT, DOWN-BEAT; (2, acoustics) appreciable regular increase and decrease of loudness caused by discrepancy in vibrations of adjacent notes sounded together (a phenomenon which is made use of, e.g. in piano-tuning); (3) (obsolete word for) APPOGGIATURA; (4) ornament found in old music, probably meaning something similar to MORDENT.

BEATRICE AND BENEDICK (Fr., *Béatrice et Bénédict*), opera by Berlioz, produced in Baden-Baden, 1862. Libretto by composer, after Shakespeare's *Much Ado About Nothing*. (There is no reason why Shakespeare's spelling of his hero's name should not be retained in English references to Berlioz's work.)

BEBUNG, see CLAVICHORD.

BÉCARRE (Fr.), equals NATURAL, the sign ♮.

BECK, CONRAD (b. 1901), Swiss composer; in Paris, 1923–32, and in touch there with Roussel and Honegger. Works include six symphonies, viola concerto, theatre music, oratorios, four string quartets. Musical director of Basle radio.

BECKEN (Ger.), cymbals.

BECKUS THE DANDIPRATT, concert-overture by M. Arnold, published 1948; 'dandipratt' is an old word for urchin.

BEDFORD, HERBERT (1867–1945), English composer (also author, painter); married the singer Liza Lehmann. Works include unaccompanied songs and music for military band.

BEECHAM, ADRIAN (b. 1905), English composer of three unperformed operas, cantata 'Ruth', songs in Spanish and English, etc.; son of Thomas Beecham.

BEECHAM, THOMAS (1879–1961), English conductor; knighted 1916 and later that year became baronet in succession to his father, Sir Joseph Beecham (1848–1916, manufacturing chemist and patron of music and ballet). First London orchestral season, 1905–6; important opera seasons, 1910, 1911 (first English performances of R. Strauss's 'ELEKTRA' and 'SALOME', etc.); founder-conductor in 1932 of London Philharmonic Orchestra which parted company with him in 1940; founder-conductor of Royal Philharmonic Orchestra, 1946. Friend and champion of Delius; pioneer also of Sibelius's works in Britain. Also arranger – e.g. editing some of Delius's works, and creating ballet score of 'THE GODS GO A-BEGGING' from Handel.

BEES' WEDDING, THE, see SONGS WITHOUT WORDS.

BEETHOVEN, LUDWIG VAN (1770–1827), German composer, born in Bonn; son and grandson of musicians. Published a piano piece at the age of 12; worked shortly afterwards as pianist, organist, viola-player. Went to Vienna, 1792 (to study with Haydn, but did not stay with him) and remained and died there. Many love-affairs (see IMMORTAL BELOVED), but never married. Brought up as Roman Catholic but came to hold unorthodox Deistical views. From 1801, developed deafness, becoming total by about 1824 – after composition of symphony no. 9 ('CHORAL') but before the last three quartets. Vastly extended the form and scope of the symphony (he wrote nine, not including 'WELLINGTON'S VICTORY'; no. 3 is the

'EROICA') – and also of the piano concerto (he wrote five, no. 5 being the so-called 'EMPEROR'), the string quartet (sixteen and 'GREAT FUGUE'), the piano sonata (thirty-two). Other works include opera 'FIDELIO' (see also 'LEONORA'); ballet 'The Creatures of PROMETHEUS'; Mass (*Missa solemnis*) in D and a smaller Mass in C; oratorio 'CHRIST ON THE MOUNT OF OLIVES'; violin concerto, triple concerto (piano, violin, cello); CHORAL FANTASIA; theatre music – see 'EGMONT', 'CORIOLANUS', 'KING STEPHEN', 'CONSECRATION OF THE HOUSE'; 'NAME-DAY' overture; 'EQUALI' for trombones; ten violin sonatas (no. 9, 'KREUTZER'); 'ARCHDUKE' and 'GHOST' piano trios; songs; piano pieces including 'DIABELLI' and 'PROMETHEUS' variations. The so-called JENA symphony is not by him.

BEGGAR'S OPERA, THE, work of BALLAD OPERA type, with words by John Gay set to tunes then current, produced in London, 1728. Musical arrangements by Pepusch. Later musical arrangements include those of F. Austin (1920, record London run of 1,463 performances), Dent (1944), Britten (Cheltenham, 1948, libretto adapted by Tyrone Guthrie), and Bliss (film, 1953). See also 'CARNIVAL OF LONDON', 'POLLY', and 'THE THREEPENNY OPERA'.

BEGLEITUNG (Ger.), accompaniment.

BEINUM, EDUARD VAN (1901–59), Dutch conductor – of the Concertgebouw Orchestra (Amsterdam) from 1931; and of the Los Angeles Philharmonic Orchestra from 1956.

BEL CANTO (It., beautiful singing), term used – often vaguely – by teachers, 'authorities' on singing, etc., with reference to the finely cultivated voice, particularly implying suitability to the agile yet smooth voice-production demanded in the operas of Bellini, Donizetti, etc.

BELL, (1) heavy resonating vessel in hollow cup-shape found in churches, etc., and rung either directly by hand-ropes or by CARILLON; (2) orchestral instrument usually in the form of a free-hanging tube ('tubular bell') struck by hand with small hammer – a set of such bells sometimes spanning as much as an octave (see also GLOCKENSPIEL); (3) the open end of a wind instrument, at the opposite extremity to the mouthpiece. See also following entries.

BELL ANTHEM, nickname for Purcell's 'Rejoice in the Lord alway' (*c.* 1682–5), alluding to bell-like descending scales in the introduction (for strings).

BELL RONDO (It., *Rondo alla campanella*), the finale of Paganini's violin concerto in B minor (*c.* 1824), with bell-like effect. Liszt's 'La Campanella' for piano (1838, revised 1851) is based on it.

BELLINI, VINCENZO (1801–35), Italian composer of opera, pupil of Zingarelli. Visited London and Paris, 1833; wrote his last completed opera, 'THE PURITANS', for performance in Paris, and died near there. The other operas he composed in his short life – making great demand on agility and refinement of voice – include 'The Capulets and the Montagues' (based on *Romeo and Juliet*), 'The Sleep-Walker' (see 'SONNAMBULA'), and 'NORMA'.

BELLY, the upper surface (i.e. that lying directly under the strings) of a stringed instrument.

BELSHAZZAR'S FEAST, (1) suite by Sibelius drawn from his incidental music to a play by H. Procope (1906); (2) work for baritone, chorus, and orchestra by Walton (words arranged by Osbert Sitwell, chiefly from the Bible), first performed in Leeds, 1931.

BÉMOL (Fr.), equals FLAT, the sign ♭.

BEN, BENE (It.), well, very.

BEN-HAIM, PAUL (b. 1897), German-born Israeli composer; changed his surname from Frankerburger after emigrating to Palestine 1933. Works include two symphonies, piano concerto, chamber music, settings of Biblical Hebrew texts.

BENDA, JIŘI ANTONÍN (1722–95), Bohemian oboist, keyboard-player, and composer, one of a family of many musicians. Worked in Germany (known there as Georg Benda) and died there. Notable for his melodramas (in the technical sense; see MELODRAMA); wrote also symphonies, operas, church music, etc.

BENEDICITE, Latin word by which is known the 'Song of the Three Holy Children' originally found in the Septuagint. In English this forms one of the canticles of the Anglican church. It is combined with a poem by J. Austin (1613–69) in Vaughan Williams's cantata 'Benedicite' (first performed 1929).

BENEDICT, JULIUS (1804–85), German-born composer (also conductor) who settled in England 1835, becoming naturalized; knighted 1871. Works include two symphonies, two piano concertos, and operas in Italian and English including 'THE LILY OF KILLARNEY', formerly a favourite of the British public.

BENEDICTUS, (1) part of the Mass (starting '*Benedictus qui venit*', 'Blessed is he that cometh'); (2), canticle sung during Anglican morning service and based on Luke i. 68ff.

BENI MORA, 'oriental suite' for orchestra by Holst, 1910, after a holiday in Algeria when Holst heard a native flute-player repeat a four-note phrase for two and a half hours – an effect simulated in the score, but not literally.

BENJAMIN, ARTHUR (1893–1960), Australian composer and pianist resident in London; also lived in Vancouver and visited the West Indies (cp. his 'JAMAICAN RUMBA, and other pieces). His music often demonstrates a light-hearted touch, e.g. in his comic operas 'THE DEVIL TAKE HER' and 'PRIMA DONNA'. Also composed operas 'A TALE OF TWO CITIES' and 'Tartuffe' (posthumously produced), symphony, piano concerto, songs and piano pieces, ballet, film music, etc.

BENNETT, JOHN (*c.* 1570–?), English composer of madrigals (contributor to THE TRIUMPHS OF ORIANA) and church music, etc.

BENNETT, RICHARD RODNEY (b. 1936), English composer of operas

'The Ledge', 'THE MINES OF SULPHUR', 'A Penny for a Song', horn concerto, piano pieces, cantata 'Nocturnall upon S. Lucies day' (Donne) for voice and percussion, etc.; pupil of H. Ferguson and (in Paris) of Boulez. Also pianist.

BENNETT, ROBERT RUSSELL (b. 1894), American composer – also arranger of 'popular' music, e.g. 'symphonic pictures' drawn from the scores of 'musicals' by Gershwin, Kern, etc.); pupil of N. Boulanger in Paris. Works include opera, six symphonies including 'Symphony in D for the Dodgers' (Brooklyn Dodgers baseball team), 'Water Music' for string quartet, film music.

BENNETT, WILLIAM STERNDALE (1816–75), English composer and pianist, pupil of Mendelssohn at Leipzig; friend of Schumann, who dedicated his 'Symphonic Studies' (for piano) to him. Professor at Cambridge; knighted 1871. Works include cantata 'The May Queen', four piano concertos, overture 'The Naiads', piano pieces, and songs.

BENTZON, JØRGEN (b. 1897), Danish composer, pupil of C. Nielsen and Karg-Elert; has written mainly chamber music, including 'Racconti' (one-movement works using three to five instruments suggesting narrative, hence this Italian title). Other works include 'A Dickens Symphony'. Cousin of Niels Viggo Bentzon.

BENTZON, NIELS VIGGO (b. 1919), Danish composer and pianist, cousin of preceding; composes in TWELVE-NOTE system, on which he has written a book. Works include ballet 'The Courtesan'; symphonic variations for orchestra; three string quartets; three sonatas and many other piano works.

BENVENUTO CELLINI, opera by Berlioz, produced in Paris, 1838. Libretto by L. de Wailly and A. Barbier, vaguely after Cellini's autobiography (*c.* 1560). See also ROMAN CARNIVAL.

BEQUADRO (It.), NATURAL, the sign ♮.

BERCEUSE (Fr.), cradle-song, lullaby; instrumental piece suggestive of this.

BERENICE, opera by Handel, produced in London, 1737. Libretto by A. Salvi; Berenice is the wife of an ancient Egyptian king. The well-known minuet occurs in the overture.

BEREZOVSKY, NIKOLAI (also spelt Berezowsky; 1900–53), Russian-born composer who settled in U.S.A., 1922. He was also conductor, violinist, viola-player (soloist in first performance of his viola concerto, 1941). Other works include four symphonies, oratorio 'Gilgamesh' (text from Babylonian poem of 1750 B.C.), chamber music, children's opera 'Babar the Elephant' (1953).

BERG, ALBAN (1885–1935), Austrian composer; born, worked, and died in Vienna; pupil of Schoenberg, whose methods he developed. Used a free-atonal idiom combined with very closely worked structures (passacaglia, variations, etc.) in opera 'WOZZECK', completed 1921; shortly afterwards turned to strict TWELVE-NOTE technique, e.g. in Chamber Concerto (piano, violin, wind), completed 1925.

Other works include 12-note opera, 'LULU'; string quartet and (also for string quartet) 'Lyric Suite'; songs with orchestra and with piano; violin concerto 'in memory of an angel' (i.e. Manon Gropius, 18-year-old daughter of Mahler's widow by her second marriage), written shortly before his own death and not performed till after it (1936).

BERG, (CARL) NATANAEL (1879–1957), Swedish composer of symphonic poems, operas to his own librettos, piano concerto, etc.

BERGAMASCA (It., also in other languages as *bergamasque*, *bergomask*, etc.), originally the name of a dance associated with the neighbourhood of Bergamo, now a term used by composers with only the vaguest picturesque significance – e.g. by Debussy in 'Suite Bergamasque' for piano (composed at intervals between 1890 and 1905) which includes 'Clair de lune'.

BERGER, ARTHUR VICTOR (b. 1912), American composer, pupil of Piston, N. Boulanger (in Paris), and others; works include Serenade for chamber orchestra, music for wind quartet and for string quartet, songs. Also critic, and author of a book on Copland.

BERGER, JEAN (b. 1909), German-born composer resident in France and then (from 1941) in U.S.A. – naturalized 1943. Has written 'Brazilian Psalm' and other works for choir; cantata 'The Blood of Others'; 'Caribbean Concerto' for harmonica and orchestra, etc.

BERGER, THEODOR (b. 1905), Austrian composer, pupil of F. Schmidt; has written 'The Elements' (cycle of symphonic poems), two string quartets, etc.

BERGERETTE (Fr.), light French song cultivating an idealized pastoral style (like Dresden-china shepherdesses.) From Fr. *berger*, shepherd.

BERGSMA, WILLIAM (b. 1921), American composer, pupil of Hanson; has composed symphony, a 'symphony for chamber orchestra', 'The Fortunate Island' for orchestra (after visit to W. Indies), 'Tangents' and other works for piano, opera 'The Wife of Martin Guerre', etc.

BERIO, LUCIANO (b. 1925), Italian composer, pupil of Dallapiccola; has employed spatial effects, e.g. in 'Circles' (text by E. E. Cummings) for voice, harp, and 2 percussion; has also written electronic music, and works allowing free choice by performers (see INDETERMINACY) – e.g. 'Tempi Concertati' (It. concerted movements) for flute and chamber ensemble, in which certain groups of notes enclosed in rectangles may be played in any order.

BÉRIOT, CHARLES (AUGUSTE) DE (1802–70), Belgian violinist and composer, chiefly for his instrument. Toured much; first visited London, 1826.

BERKELEY, LENNOX (RANDAL FRANCIS) (b. 1903), English composer who took up music only after leaving Oxford University; then became pupil of N. Boulanger in Paris. Collaborated with Britten in 'Mont Juic', orchestral suite of Catalan dances. Has written operas including 'NELSON' and 'A DINNER ENGAGEMENT'; two symphonies; two concertos for piano, one for two pianos; many piano solos; 'Four Poems of St Teresa' for contralto and orchestra, 'Staba Mater' for six voices and orchestra, and a few other works to texts with Roman Catholic associations; film music. Contributor to 'A GARLAND FOR THE QUEEN'.

BERLIN, IRVING (originally Israel Baline; b. 1888), Russian-born composer, resident in U.S.A. from 1893. Composer of popular songs markedly successful from 'Alexander's Ragtime Band' (1911) and including the now perennial 'I'm Dreaming of a White Christmas' (from film *Holiday Inn*, 1942); his musical play 'Call Me Madam' (1950) features an ocarina.

BERLIN PHILHARMONIC ORCHESTRA, orchestra founded 1882; conductor since 1955, Herbert von Karajan (succeeding Furtwängler).

BERLIOZ, (LOUIS) HECTOR (1803–69), French composer; learnt guitar, and had general musical training at Paris Conservatory, but became proficient neither on piano nor on any orchestral instrument – yet a great master and innovator in orchestration (on which he wrote a book) also noted as conductor and music critic. Nearly all his works have some literary or other extra-musical allusion (typical ROMANTIC trait; cp. SCHUMANN). His love for the English Shakespearian actress Harriet Smithson is expressed in his 'FANTASTIC SYMPHONY', 1830; he married her in 1833 and separated from her in 1842. Other works include operas 'BENVENUTO CELLINI', 'BEATRICE AND BENEDICK', 'THE TROJANS'; choral works including 'THE DAMNATION OF FAUST' (in which occurs his arrangement of the 'RÁKÓCZI MARCH'), 'THE CHILDHOOD OF CHRIST', and Requiem; symphony 'ROMEO AND JULIET'; 'HAROLD IN ITALY' for viola and orchestra; 'Lélio' (intended sequel to the 'Fantastic Symphony') for reciter, singers, and orchestra; 'ROMAN CARNIVAL', 'THE CORSAIR', 'KING LEAR', and other overtures; songs with orchestra and with piano.

BERNAC, PIERRE (real surname Bertin; b. 1899), French baritone, particularly well known in recitals of French songs – often formerly accompanied by Poulenc.

BERNERS, LORD (Gerald Hugh Tyrwhitt-Wilson; 1883–1950), English composer (also painter, author, diplomat). Works include ballets 'The Wedding Bouquet' (words by Gertrude Stein, stage-settings of Berners' own design) and 'THE TRIUMPH OF NEPTUNE'; 'Valses Bourgeoises' for piano duet, and songs. Tended to an ironic touch and the use of French titles.

BERNSTEIN, LEONARD (b. 1918), American composer who also appears (sometimes simultaneously) as pianist and conductor; pupil of Piston and others; permanent conductor of the New York Philharmonic Orchestra since 1957. Works include 'JEREMIAH' SYMPHONY; symphony 'THE AGE OF ANXIETY', Symphony no. 3 ('Kaddish'); opera 'Trouble in Tahiti'; operetta 'Candide' (after Voltaire), 'musicals' 'On the Town' (based on ballet 'FANCY FREE') and 'West Side Story'; songs, chamber music, 'Chichester

Psalms' (in Hebrew) for Chichester Cathedral (choir and orchestra). Notably influenced by jazz. Also famous television expositor of music, etc.

BERWALD, FRANZ ADOLF (1796–1868), Swedish composer and violinist who studied in Germany; little appreciated in his lifetime, only no. 2 ('Sérieuse') of his six symphonies receiving performance. Also wrote opera 'Estrella di Soria', violin concerto, chamber music, etc., in an individual ROMANTIC style.

BEST, WILLIAM THOMAS (1826–97), English organist (chiefly at St George's Hall, Liverpool) and arranger of many works, especially for the organ.

BETHLEHEM, 'choral drama' by Boughton, produced in Glastonbury, 1916. Libretto from the medieval Coventry play.

BETROTHAL IN A MONASTERY, THE, see DUENNA.

BIBALO, ANTONIO (b. 1923), Italian composer (also pianist), resident in Norway; has written opera 'The Smile at the Foot of the Ladder' (after Henry Miller), orchestral and piano works, etc.

BIBER, HEINRICH JOHANN FRANZ VON (1644–1704), Austrian violinist, musical director of the Archbishop of Salzburg's court, and composer of violin sonatas and chamber music; also opera and church music. Reputedly the first to employ SCORDATURA.

BIGGS, E. (EDWARD GEORGE) POWER (b. 1906), English-born concert organist, resident in U.S.A.; also editor of organ music.

BILLINGS, WILLIAM (1746–1800), one of the earliest American-born composers, but a tanner by trade; wrote 'fuguing tunes' (with primitive IMITATION), words and music of hymns, music to American patriotic songs, etc. Also concert promoter. See COWELL, SCHUMAN.

BILLY BUDD, (1) opera by Britten, produced in London, 1951; libretto by E. M. Forster and E. Crozier, after Melville's novel of the English navy at the time of the mutiny of the Nore (1797); (2) opera by Ghedini, produced in Venice, 1949; libretto by Quasimodo, after the same source.

BINARY, in two sections; *binary form*, classification used of a simple movement (e.g. in an early 18th-century keyboard suite) which is in two sections, the first modulating to another key and the second returning to the original key. (Cp. TERNARY.) The above form developed historically into SONATA-FORM, an alternative name for which is, accordingly, *compound binary form*.

BINCHOIS, GILLES (EGIDIUS) (*c.* 1400–60), Netherlands composer of chansons, motets, etc., who worked at the court of Burgundy.

BINET, JEAN (1893–1960), Swiss composer, pupil of Bloch and others; lived for a time in U.S.A. He composed orchestral and chamber music, ballets, incidental music to *The Merry Wives of Windsor*, etc.

BIRDS, THE (It., *Gli Uccelli*), orchestral suite by Respighi, first performed 1927, based on 17th- and 18th-century pieces.

BIRMINGHAM SYMPHONY ORCHESTRA (properly City of Birmingham

Symphony Orchestra), orchestra founded 1920, becoming full-time 1944; musical director from 1960, Hugo Rignold.

BIRTWISTLE, HARRISON (b. 1934), English composer, pupil of R. Hall; works, with some affinity to medieval idiom, include 'Refrains and Choruses' for wind quintet; 'Music for Sleep' for child singers and instrumentalists; 'Tragoedia' for 10 players (the wind-instrumentalists also playing claves); opera 'Punch and Judy'.

BIS (Fr., twice), word actually used in French where the English use 'encore'; *bisser*, to encore.

BISBIGLIANDO (It., whispering), repeating the notes softly and quickly, as a special effect in playing the harp.

BISCROMA (It.), demisemiquaver (U.S., thirty-second-note).

BISHOP, HENRY (ROWLEY) (1786–1855), English composer, chiefly of operas; also 'adapted' (i.e. did artistic violence to) Mozart's and other operas. Prominent as conductor; knighted 1842, the first musician to receive knighthood at the hands of a British sovereign. His opera 'Clari, or The Maid of Milan' (1823) includes, 'Home, Sweet Home' used in a recurrent way anticipating the later devices of LEADING-MOTIVE and THEME-SONG.

BITONALITY, the use of two keys (see TONALITY) simultaneously; e.g. by Stravinsky (a famous early use in 'PETRUSHKA,' 1911), Holst, Milhaud.

BIZET, GEORGES (first names really Alexandre César Léopold; 1838–75), French composer, born in Paris, pupil of Halévy, whose daughter he married after Halévy's death. At 19 won prize for an operetta, 'Doctor Miracle'; later composed operas including: 'THE PEARL-FISHERS', 'THE FAIR MAID OF PERTH', 'IVAN THE TERRIBLE' (not performed till 1946), and 'CARMEN' – at first only a moderate success; Bizet died three months after its first performance. His work, marked by its clarity and melodic gifts, was later championed (e.g. by Nietzsche) as a counterblast to Wagner. It also includes incidental music to Daudet's play 'THE GIRL FROM ARLES' (*L'Arlésienne*); symphony (written at 17 but never performed till 1935); suite 'CHILDREN'S GAMES' (originally for piano duet).

BJÖRLING, JUSSI (1911–60), Swedish tenor, eminent in Italian opera at Metropolitan Opera House (New York) and elsewhere.

BLACHER, BORIS (b. 1903), German composer born of Russian parents in China; since 1953 director of the (West) Berlin High School of Music. Works include 'Romeo and Juliet', 'Prussian Fairy Tale', and other operas, oratorio 'The Grand Inquisitor' (after Dostoyevsky's *Crime and Punishment*), two piano concertos, orchestral 'Variations on a Theme of Paganini' (see PAGANINI). Is particularly interested in rhythmical organization (following Stravinsky) and has evolved a system of 'variable metres' by which variable bar-lengths are planned according to mathematical relationships.

BLANÍK (Smetana), see 'MY COUNTRY'.

BLASEN (Ger.), to blow; *Bläser*, wind instruments, wind-players;

Blasinstrument(e), wind instrument(s); *Blasmusik*, music for wind.

BLECH (Ger.), brass (section of an orchestra); *Blechmusik*, brass band, music for brass.

BLECH, HARRY (b. 1910), English conductor, formerly violinist; founder-conductor of London Mozart Players (chamber orchestra), 1949, O.B.E., 1962.

BLESSED DAMOZEL, THE, cantata by Debussy, 1887–8, on a French translation ('La Damoiselle Élue') of Rossetti's poem.

BLEST PAIR OF SIRENS, cantata by C. H. H. Parry, first performed 1887. Words from Milton's 'At a Solemn Music'.

BLISS, ARTHUR (b. 1891), English composer, pupil of C. Wood, Stanford, Vaughan Williams, and Holst. BBC director of music, 1941–5; knighted, 1950; Master of the Queen's Music, 1953. Works include ballets 'CHECKMATE' and 'MIRACLE IN THE GORBALS'; opera 'The Olympians' (with libretto by J. B. Priestley); cantata 'Mary of Magdala', orchestral 'Meditations on a theme by John Blow'; piano concerto, two-piano concerto (arranged from earlier work for piano, tenor, and strings), violin concerto; 'Music for Strings'; 'A COLOUR SYMPHONY'; piano sonata; clarinet quintet and other chamber music; 'Seven American Poems' and other songs. Wrote one of the first important film scores, *The Shape of Things to Come* (1935); also music to other films, including an arrangement of 'THE BEGGAR'S OPERA' for the filmed version. Contributor to 'A GARLAND FOR THE QUEEN' (1953). His early Stravinsky-influenced tendency towards irony and experiment yielded to a more conservative and forthright (often martial) idiom.

BLITHEMAN, WILLIAM (?–1591), English organist (at the Chapel Royal, London), and composer of church music and keyboard pieces; teacher of J. Bull.

BLITZSTEIN, MARC (b. 1905), American composer (pupil of N. Boulanger and Schoenberg) and pianist. Has composed music expressing militantly democratic and pro-labour ideas – e.g. operas 'The Cradle Will Rock' and 'No for an Answer', symphonic poem 'Freedom Morning' (dedicated to U.S. Negro Troops of Second World War), etc.; also opera 'Regina', piano concerto and piano solos, 'AIRBORNE SYMPHONY'. See also 'THE THREEPENNY OPERA'.

BLOCH, ERNEST (1880–1959), Swiss-born American-naturalized composer, pupil of Knorr in Frankfurt. Went to U.S.A., 1916, but returned to Switzerland 1930–8. Much of his work has specific Jewish associations – e.g. 'SHELOMO' (Solomon) for cello and orchestra; 'SACRED SERVICE' (*Avodath hakodesh*); 'BAAL SHEM' for violin and piano, 'ISRAEL' SYMPHONY. Other works include opera 'MACBETH'; rhapsody 'America'; symphony, piano quintet (1923, introducing quarter-tones); four string quartets; 'Scherzo Fantasque' and 'Concerto Symphonique' both for piano with orchestra.

BLOCK (percussion instrument), see TEMPLE BLOCK, WOOD BLOCK.

BLOCKFLÖTE (Ger.), RECORDER.

BLOCKX, JAN (1851–1912), Belgian composer of music mainly with Flemish nationalist associations – operas and cantatas with Flemish words, overture 'Rubens', etc.

BLOMDAHL, KARL-BIRGER (1916–68), Swedish composer (also conductor), pupil of Rosenberg, making use of TWELVE-NOTE technique. Works include three symphonies (no. 3 called 'Facets'), violin concerto, cantata 'In the Hall of Mirrors', chamber music, piano pieces, and operas 'Aniara' (set on a space-ship) and 'Herr von Hancken'. Musical director of the Swedish radio, 1965.

BLONDEL (DE NESLE), 12th-century French TROUVÈRE (minstrel) of whom some songs survive; according to legend he discovered (by singing and being answered) the place where Richard Cœur de Lion was held captive.

BLOW, JOHN (1649–1708), English composer, pupil of H. Cooke and others; teacher of Purcell; organist of Westminster Abbey, 1668–1679 (Purcell succeeding him) and again, 1695–1708. Works include English and Latin anthems, services, odes on the death of Purcell, and on other occasions (ten for New Year's Day); keyboard pieces and songs; masque 'VENUS AND ADONIS'. See BLISS.

BLUE DANUBE, THE (Ger., *An der schönen blauen Donau*, 'By the beautiful blue Danube'), waltz by Johann Strauss the younger, composed 1867; originally with chorus.

BLUE NOTE, a note of the scale (especially the third and seventh) characteristically flattened in JAZZ and in light and serious music indebted to jazz idiom. See also BLUES.

BLUEBEARD'S CASTLE (Hung., *A Kékszakállú Herceg Vára*, 'Duke Bluebeard's Castle'), opera by Bartók, produced in Budapest, 1918. Libretto by B. Balázs, giving a modern psychological interpretation of the old legend.

BLUES, type of slow, sad American Negro song, becoming widely known about 1911; strictly (*12-bar blues*) in three lines of four bars each, the second line exactly or nearly repeating the first, and the whole following a set chord-sequence. (Term also used loosely, e.g. by Copland, as indication of mood only.) See also BLUE NOTE.

BLUMENTHAL, JACOB (1829–1908), German composer who settled in England, became pianist to Queen Victoria, and wrote many drawing-room songs and piano pieces.

BOATSWAIN'S MATE, THE, comic opera by Smyth, produced in London, 1916. Libretto by composer (after W. W. Jacobs's story). For three singers; the ex-boatswain's-mate unsuccessfully courts a determined widow.

BOCCHERINI, LUIGI (1743–1805), Italian composer and cellist. By invitation of the Spanish ambassador in Paris, visited Spain in 1768–9; and was there again from 1797 until dying there in poverty and lacking a patron. Works include four cello concertos, twenty symphonies, 125 string quintets (from one of which comes 'the' Boccherini minuet), 102 string quartets, and much other chamber music; Spanish opera 'Clementina'; church music.

BOEHM, see also BÖHM (alternative spelling).

BOEHM, THEOBALD (b. 1793 or 1794; d. 1881), German flutist, composer for his instrument, and inventor. His key-mechanism (replacing finger-holes) spread from the flute to oboe, clarinet, and bassoon.

BOEHM SYSTEM, woodwind key-mechanism; see THEOBALD BOEHM.

BOËLLMANN, LÉON (1862–97), French organist (latterly at St Vincent de Paul's Church, Paris) and composer, principally for organ; also wrote symphony, symphonic variations for cello and orchestra, etc.

BOELZA, IGOR FEDOROVICH (b. 1904), Russian musical scholar, professor at Moscow University; also composer of five symphonies, film music, etc.

BOHÈME, LA (Fr., Bohemian Life, in artistic sense), Italian operas based on Murger's French novel *Scènes de la Vie de Bohème* – (1) by Puccini, produced in Turin, 1896; libretto by G. Giacosa and L. Illica; (2) by Leoncavallo, produced in Venice, 1897; libretto by composer. The two were composed contemporaneously, but the latter missed Puccini's success.

BOHEMIAN GIRL, THE, opera by Balfe, produced in London, 1843. Libretto by A. Bunn: the high-born heroine is abducted by gipsies as a child and finally, of course, restored.

BÖHM, GEORG (1661–1733), German organist and composer of a Passion, chorale preludes, etc.; from 1698 at Lüneburg, where J. S. Bach, as a boy chorister at another church, apparently came to know his music.

BÖHM, THEOBALD, see BOEHM.

BOÏELDIEU, FRANÇOIS ADRIEN (1775–1834), French composer, pupil of Cherubini and others. Wrote piano concerto, chamber music, and especially operas – including 'The White Lady' (Fr., *La Dame blanche*) after two novels of Scott, containing some Scottish tunes, and 'THE CALIPH OF BAGHDAD'. Also conductor, e.g. at St Petersburg.

BOITO, ARRIGO (1842–1918), Italian composer (opera 'MEPHISTOPHELES', etc.) and librettist, e.g. for Verdi's 'Otello' and 'Falstaff'.

BOLERO, Spanish dance, usually with a triplet on the second half of the first beat of bar; accompaniment includes dancers' voices and castanets. Ravel's purely orchestral '*Bolero*', 1928, is for ballet, not for dancing a real bolero.

BOLSHOI THEATRE, Moscow's principal opera and ballet theatre; the present building opened in 1856. (*Bolshoi* means *large*, *great*.)

BOMBARD, name given to the larger instruments of the obsolete SHAWM family.

BOMBARDA (It.), EUPHONIUM.

BOMBARDE, a SIXTEEN-FOOT reed stop on the organ.

BOMBARDON, (1) name given in brass and military bands to the two types of bass TUBA used in those bands; (2) organ stop similar to BOMBARDE.

BOND, CARRIE JACOBS (1862–1946), American composer of 'The End of a Perfect Day' (which sold over five million copies) and similar popular sentimental songs.

BONES, percussion instrument used in black-faced minstrel shows, etc.; a pair of small bones held between the fingers and clicked together.

BONGO (usually *bongos*, a pair of them), small Cuban drum struck with the fingers and used in some modern dance bands for rumbas, etc.

BONNER, EUGENE MACDONALD (b. 1899), American composer and critic; studied in U.S.A., England, France; works include operas in English and French, orchestral and chamber music.

BONONCINI, GIOVANNI (or Buononcini; 1670–1747), Italian composer and cellist, one of a family of musicians; worked in Rome, Vienna, Berlin, and (1720–32) London, where he rivalled Handel for a time, leaving eventually when plagiarism was proved against him. Works include operas, Masses, funeral anthem for the Duke of Marlborough. Died in poverty in Vienna.

BOOGIE-WOOGIE, style of fast jazz piano-playing characterized by OSTINATO bass in BROKEN octaves; popularized in U.S.A. from about 1938. Also abbreviated to *boogie*.

BORIS GODUNOV, opera by Mussorgsky, produced (in revised and cut version) in St Petersburg, 1874; afterwards edited and altered by Rimsky-Korsakov, in which form it became known also outside Russia; the complete authentic work was produced in Leningrad, 1928. A version has also been made by Shostakovich which (unlike Rimsky-Korsakov's) respects the composer's harmonies but provides new orchestration. Libretto by composer, after Pushkin's drama of the historic tsar (d. 1605).

BORODIN, ALEXANDER (PORPHYREVICH) (1833–87), Russian composer – also professor of chemistry, so could spare little time for music. Illegitimate son of a prince; pupil of Balakirev; one of the 'nationalist' group of composers known as THE MIGHTY HANDFUL. Works include opera 'PRINCE IGOR' (unfinished; completed by Rimsky-Korsakov and Glazunov), which includes the 'Polovtsian Dances'; three symphonies (no. 3 unfinished, but two movements of it advanced enough to be completed by Glazunov); symphonic poem 'IN THE STEPPES OF CENTRAL ASIA'; two string quartets; songs.

BØRRESEN, AXEL EINAR HAKON (b. 1876), Danish composer, pupil of Svendsen; works include operas, MELODRAMA (in technical sense), ballet 'Tycho Brahe's Dream', orchestral and church music.

BORTNIANSKY, DMITRI STEPANOVICH (1752–1825), Russian composer who studied in Italy, returned to Russia and became director of the court church choir, which he reformed. Composed chiefly church music, but also Italian operas.

BOSCOVICH, ALEXANDER URIAH (b. 1908), Rumanian-born Israeli composer who emigrated to Palestine, 1937. Works include violin concerto, oboe concerto, 'Semitic Suite' for orchestra or piano, songs.

BOSMANS, HENRIETTE (1895–1952), Dutch composer of concert-piece for violin and orchestra, chamber music, songs (many in French), etc.; pupil of Pijper.

BOSSI, (MARCO) ENRICO (1861–1925), Italian composer and concert organist; works include organ concerto and many organ solos, also operas, oratorios, etc.

BOSTON SYMPHONY ORCHESTRA, an orchestra founded in Boston, Mass., 1881. Koussevitzky, whose conductorship (1924–49) made it especially famous, was succeeded by Charles Munch, from whom Erich Leinsdorf took over in 1962.

BOTTESINI, GIOVANNI (1822–89), Italian double-bass virtuoso who appeared as soloist in London and elsewhere; also composer and conductor.

BOTTICELLI PICTURES, see THREE BOTTICELLI PICTURES.

BOUCHE FERMÉE (Fr.), with the mouth closed, i.e. (as instruction to singers) humming.

BOUFFE, see OPERA.

BOUGHTON, RUTLAND (1878–1960), English composer (also conductor and writer on music). In emulation of Wagner and Bayreuth, organized a festival operatic centre (not only for his own works) at Glastonbury, 1914–25; it opened with his 'THE IMMORTAL HOUR' which later ran for 216 successive performances in London. None of his later stage works – including 'ALKESTIS' and 'BETHLEHEM' – achieved such success. He favoured an accessible traditionally-based English style, expressed also e.g. in ballets, choral works, and songs (some to leftist political words).

BOULANGER, LILI (JULIETTE MARIE OLGA) (1893–1918), French composer, pupil of her sister Nadia and others; first woman to win the 'Rome Prize', principal French award to young composers. Works include cantata 'Faust and Helen' (after Goethe), psalms with orchestra.

BOULANGER, NADIA (JULIETTE) (b. 1887), French composer (orchestral works, songs, etc.), conductor, and especially teacher of distinguished musicians from many countries, especially U.S.A. (e.g. Copland, Piston, V. Thomson). Among her British pupils are Berkeley and Cole. Sister of LILI BOULANGER.

BOULEZ, PIERRE (b. 1925), French composer, pupil of Messiaen; extended the methods of TWELVE-NOTE technique to the 'organizing' (in mathematical relationships) of rhythms, volume, etc., and has also employed spatial effects. Works include piano pieces (often of great complexity, with some choice of order left to performer); 'Le Marteau sans maître' ('The Hammer without a Master') for contralto and chamber orchestra; 'Pli selon pli' ('Fold upon fold') for orchestra with soprano. In the 1960s became internationally known symphonic and operatic conductor, e.g. at Bayreuth Festival.

BOULT, ADRIAN (CEDRIC) (b. 1889), English conductor, studied in Germany; made his début 1919. Musical director of BBC, 1930–42; formed and conducted BBC Symphony Orchestra, 1930–49, then chief conductor of London Philharmonic Orchestra till 1957. Knighted 1937.

BOURDON, a SIXTEEN-FOOT organ stop of stopped DIAPASON type.

BOURGEOIS, LOUIS (*c.* 1510–*c.* 1561), French musician who contributed harmonizations (including that of the 'Old Hundredth') to Calvin's Genevan Psalter, 1551.

BOURGEOIS GENTILHOMME, LE (Fr., The Tradesman as Gentleman), (1) play by Molière (1670) with incidental music by Lully; (2) incidental music by R. Strauss to a shortened version of Molière's play, intended to precede the original version of Strauss's 'ARIADNE IN NAXOS'.

BOURGUIGNON, FRANCIS DE (b. 1890), Belgian composer (also pianist, formerly accompanist to Melba) and critic; works, some using polytonality, include piano concertos, songs, chamber music.

BOURNEMOUTH MUNICIPAL ORCHESTRA, see BOURNEMOUTH SYMPHONY ORCHESTRA.

BOURNEMOUTH SYMPHONY ORCHESTRA, the successor in 1954 to the former Bournemouth Municipal Orchestra, founded in 1893 under Sir Dan Godfrey's conductorship. Conductor 1954–60, Charles Groves, then Constantin Silvestri.

BOURRÉE (Fr.), dance-movement (found e.g. in the classical SUITE) in quick double time beginning with an up-beat.

BOUTIQUE FANTASQUE, see FANTASTIC TOYSHOP.

BOW, stick with horsehair stretched across it, used to set in vibration the strings of the violin and related instruments, also the viols; *Tourte bow*, name for the ordinary modern kind of bow (after François Tourte, inventor, 1747–1835), with stick curved inward to the hair. The earlier type, with outward-curving stick, was suitable, in association with the earlier type of BRIDGE, for playing four-string chords if necessary, as in J. S. Bach's unaccompanied violin sonatas; but the modern term 'Bach bow' sometimes refers not to the historic bow but to a 20th-century invention associated with the violinist Telmányi, supposedly suitable for Bach's music. See also BOWING.

BOWEN, YORK (1884–1961), English pianist and composer (also played violin and horn); composer, generally in conservative Romantic style, of three piano concertos, many piano solos, etc.

BOWER, JOHN DYKES (b. 1905), English organist (at St Paul's Cathedral, London, from 1936) and editor of Bach's organ works, etc. Hon.D.Mus., Oxford.

BOWING, the marking of music for stringed instruments to show which notes should be played to which stroke (up or down) of the bow.

BOWLES, PAUL (FREDERIC) (b. 1911), American composer, pupil of

N. Boulanger, Sessions, and others; studied folk-music in Spain and Latin America. Works include orchestral 'Danze Mexicana', operas, chamber music, theatre, and film scores. Also novelist.

BOYCE, WILLIAM (1710–79), English composer and organist; D.Mus., Oxford. Boy chorister at St Paul's Cathedral, London, later a pupil of Greene and (1755) Master of the King's Band; organist of the Chapel Royal, 1758. Works include church and stage music, eight symphonies, songs including 'Heart of Oak'; editor of a notable collection of English cathedral music.

BRAGA, GAETANO (1829–1907), Italian cellist, composer of popular vocal 'Serenade', also of operas, etc.

BRAHAM, JOHN (real surname Abraham; 1777–1856), English tenor, the original male lead in Weber's 'OBERON'; sang also on the Continent; composer of songs including the once very popular 'The Death of Nelson'.

BRAHMS, JOHANNES (1833–97), German composer, also pianist; born in Hamburg, where as a youngster he played in sailors' taverns; pupil of Marxsen. In 1853 met Joachim, Liszt, Schumann, and others who became interested in him; visited Vienna 1862, settled there 1863 (also died there). Never married. Entirely devoted to composition from 1864, but did not write the first of his four symphonies till 1875. Composed no opera, and did not follow widely prevalent Lisztian ideal of PROGRAMME MUSIC, but developed the forms of Beethoven's period and showed notable rhythmic originality. Works include two piano concertos, violin concerto, double concerto (violin and cello); 'ACADEMIC FESTIVAL' and 'TRAGIC' overtures; 'Variations on the ST ANTHONY CHORALE' (orchestra or two pianos), formerly known as 'Variations on a theme of Haydn'; variations on themes by Handel and by PAGANINI for piano, and many other piano works; chamber music; songs (including 'FOUR BIBLICAL SONGS') and part-songs (see 'LOVE-SONG WALTZES'); choral works including 'A GERMAN REQUIEM' and 'ALTO RHAPSODY'.

BRAIN, DENNIS (1921–57), English player of the horn; début 1938; after 1945 appeared with the Royal Philharmonic and Philharmonia Orchestras; works by Britten ('Serenade for tenor, horn, and strings'), Hindemith, and others were written for him. Was also organist. Died in car crash.

BRANDENBURG CONCERTOS, six works by J. S. Bach, 1721, for varying instrumental combinations, no two alike; dedicated to the Margrave of Brandenburg. They are works of the CONCERTO GROSSO type, though nos. 1, 3, and 6 have no fixed smaller group contrasting with the larger.

BRANLE, BRANSLE, French dance-movement in 2/2 time, something like the gavotte; it is called *brawl* in Shakespeare.

BRANNIGAN, OWEN (b. 1908), English bass singer, well known in Britten's and other operas, and in concerts; O.B.E., 1964.

BRASS, collective term for musical instruments made of brass or other metals and blown directly through a cup-shaped or funnel-shaped mouthpiece. (This excludes e.g. saxophone, because the air is actuated through a reed and not directly; it excludes flute, even if made of metal, because it has no such mouthpiece. See WOODWIND.) Normal brass instruments of the symphony orchestra are four horns, two or three trumpets, two tenor and one bass trombone, and one tuba; *heavy brass*, inexact and unhelpful term for trombones and tuba. See also the following entry.

BRASS BAND, combination of BRASS instruments only (MILITARY BAND has woodwinds too) with or without percussion; in Britain made up of a fairly rigid combination of cornets, flugelhorn, tenor and baritone saxhorns, euphoniums, trombones, and 'bombardons' – see TUBA.

BRATSCHE (Ger., pl. *-en*), viola.

BRAVO (It., brave, fine), interjection used to express approval – invariable in English-speaking countries, but *brava*, *bravi*, *brave* in Italian for a female performer, male performers, female performers, respectively.

BRAVURA (It.), courage, swagger; *bravura passage*, one calling for a bold and striking display of an executant's technique.

BRAWL, see BRANLE.

BREAK, (1) a change in tone-quality encountered on some voices and wind-instruments in passing between different REGISTERS; (2) a short solo passage, usually improvised, in a concerted jazz piece – i.e. a CADENZA; (3, verb) of the voice, to undergo that change in quality and compass which comes to a young person's voice in puberty (better spoken of as *to change*, as *break* suggests that something has been destroyed and lost).

BREAM, JULIAN (ALEXANDER) (b. 1933), English guitarist (encouraged by Segovia) making début at age 12; also lutenist. Britten and others have written works for him.

BREIT (Ger.), broadly, grandly – an indication of manner of performance, not (except incidentally) of speed.

BREVE, note which originally signified 'short' but has now (with the advent of still shorter notes) come to be the longest current – though it is now rare. It is notated 𝅜 and has a time-value equivalent to two semibreves. (The U.S. name is *double-whole-note*, a semibreve being considered – following German practice – as a whole-note.) This has apparently no connexion with the expression *alla breve*, which indicates that, in a bar nominally of four beats, the tempo is so fast that the bar is to be considered as having two beats only (falling on what would normally be the first and third beats).

BREVIS (Lat.), short; *missa brevis*, see MISSA.

BRIAN, HAVERGAL (b. 1876), English composer of twenty-six symphonies (some using voices; No. 2, 'Gothic'), opera, songs, etc.; also writer on music. Mainly self-taught.

BRIDGE, (1) on a violin, viol, guitar, etc. the supporting piece of wood which holds the strings up from the belly of the instrument, and transmits their vibrations to the body of the instrument; (2) in a composition, a section (usually *bridge passage*) the main function of which is to link together (sometimes partly by a change of key) two passages more important than itself.

BRIDGE, FRANK (1879–1941), English composer (pupil of Stanford, teacher of Britten), chiefly of chamber music – at first on traditional harmonic lines, later determinedly 'modern' – and songs; also wrote suite 'The Sea', and other orchestral music. No relation of Frederick Bridge.

BRIDGE, (JOHN) FREDERICK (1844–1924), English organist (Westminster Abbey), choral conductor, composer of church music, author of textbooks; knighted 1897. No relation of Frank Bridge.

BRIDGEWATER, (ERNEST) LESLIE (b. 1893), English pianist and composer of piano concerto and much light music, also stage and film scores.

BRIGG FAIR, 'English rhapsody' by Delius (being variations on a Lincolnshire folk-song) for orchestra; first performed, 1908. It is dedicated to Grainger, who acquainted Delius with the song.

BRIGHT, DORA (1863–1952), English pianist (apparently the first to give a recital entirely of English music), and composer – three operas, two piano concertos, etc.

BRILLANT, BRILLANTE (Fr., It.), brilliant (as a direction for performance, particularly in solo music).

BRINDISI (It.), toast, drinking-song.

BRINDLE, REGINALD SMITH (b. 1917), English composer (also critic), resident in Italy; pupil of Pizzetti and Dallapiccola. Works, in TWELVE-NOTE technique, include 'Cantata da Requiem'; 'Homage to H. G. Wells', for orchestra; quintet for clarinet, piano, and strings.

BRIO (It.), spirit, dash; *con brio*, spiritedly.

BRITTEN, (EDWARD) BENJAMIN (b. 1913), English composer; also pianist (noted particularly as accompanist to Peter Pears) and conductor, chief creator of Aldeburgh Festival and English Opera Group. Pupil of Frank Bridge (from age 12) and later of Ireland; much influenced (e.g. in vocal setting) by Purcell, and has stylistic links also with Mahler and Stravinsky. In U.S.A. and Canada, 1939–42. Unusually successful opera 'PETER GRIMES', 1945, was followed by 'THE RAPE OF LUCRETIA' and 'ALBERT HERRING' (operas with small cast, chamber orchestra, no chorus), 'BILLY BUDD' (all-male), 'GLORIANA', and (again small-scale) 'THE TURN OF THE SCREW'; 'LET'S MAKE AN OPERA!' for children; 'NOYE'S FLUDDE', 'CURLEW RIVER', 'The Burning Fiery Furnace' and 'The Prodigal Son' (all for church performance), 'A MIDSUMMER NIGHT'S DREAM'; ballet 'THE PRINCE OF THE PAGODAS'; editions of 'THE BEGGAR'S OPERA' (with the tunes very freely treated and of Purcell's 'DIDO AND AENEAS'. Concert works include 'SIMPLE

SYMPHONY', 'SINFONIA DA REQUIEM', Cello Symphony (cello and orchestra), choral 'WAR REQUIEM' and 'SPRING SYMPHONY', 'CANTATA ACADEMICA' (see CANTATA); three 'CANTICLES'; song-settings of Rimbaud ('LES ILLUMINATIONS'), Michelangelo, Donne, Pushkin, etc. (see SERENADE and NOCTURNE); two string quartets; folk-song arrangements. See also YOUNG PERSON'S GUIDE. O.M., 1965.

BROKEN CHORD, a chord of which the notes are not all played simultaneously, but one after the other (or a few followed by another few). Similarly *broken octaves*, a passage of alternate notes an octave apart – especially in piano-writing.

BROKEN CONSORT, an old English term for an ensemble of mixed strings and wind.

BROMAN, STEN (b. 1902), Swedish composer of Concerto for orchestra, an 'Academic Festival' overture, two string quartets, etc.; also critic and viola-player.

BROTT, ALEXANDER (b. 1915), Canadian violinist, conductor, and composer of violin concerto, orchestral suite 'From Sea to Sea' (descriptive of Canada), chamber music, etc. Father of BORIS BROTT.

BROTT, BORIS (b. 1945), Canadian conductor; associate conductor, Toronto Symphony Orchestra, then (1964–7) joint conductor of NORTHERN SINFONIA ORCHESTRA. Son of ALEXANDER BROTT.

BRUCH, MAX (1838–1920), German composer; also conductor – of Liverpool Philharmonic Society, 1880–3. Works include three violin concertos (no. 1 is well-known), 'KOL NIDREI' for cello and orchestra; also three symphonies, operas, choral works.

BRUCKNER, ANTON (1824–96), Austrian composer; also organist – played at Royal Albert Hall, London, 1871. At first church choirboy; went to Vienna and studied with Sechter (with whom Schubert had intended to study) and from 1868 settled in Vienna, becoming professor at the Conservatory there. Heard Wagner's 'TRISTAN AND ISOLDE', 1865, and became his fervent disciple: wrote, however, no operas but nine symphonies (no. 3 nicknamed his 'Wagner' symphony; no. 4, 'ROMANTIC'), not including two unnumbered early works later rejected by him. No. 9 (only three out of four movements finished) is dedicated 'to God' – Bruckner always retaining devout Roman Catholicism and certain unsophisticated 'country' ways. Symphonies nos. 7, 8, 9 use WAGNER TUBAS. There are important differences between the shortened published versions of his symphonies and the 'authentic' texts published after his death. Other works include four Masses, Te Deum, string quintet.

BRÜLL, IGNAZ (1846–1907), Austrian pianist and composer of ten operas, two piano concertos, etc.

BRUNEAU, (LOUIS CHARLES BONAVENTURE) ALFRED (1857–1934), French composer of operas (two with librettos by Zola, whose political and social ideas he shared), three choral symphonies, etc.; also writer on music.

BRUSSILOVSKY, YEVGENI (b. 1905), Russian composer, dismissed from Moscow Conservatory as academically poor, but studied in Leningrad under M. Steinberg. Researched into folk-music of Kazakhstan, and wrote three operas and other music based on Kazakh themes; also ballet, six symphonies, etc.

BRUSTAD, BJARNE (b. 1895), Norwegian composer; also violinist, viola-player, and conductor. Works include opera 'Atlantis' (and an orchestral piece based on this); orchestral 'Variations sérieuses' on a theme of Corelli; capriccios (duets) for violin and viola, making some use of bitonality.

BRUSTWERK (Ger.), CHOIR ORGAN.

BUCK, DUDLEY (1839–1909), American composer and organist who studied in Germany; wrote opera 'Deseret', choral works, chamber music, etc.

BUCK, PERCY CARTER (1871–1947), English organist, composer, professor of music at London University, and writer on musical and near-musical subjects.

BUFFO, BUFFA (It.), comic; *basso buffo*, *tenore buffo*, comic bass, comic tenor (in opera). (So also *buffo* by itself is sometimes found, e.g., in the list of singers required for an Italian opera, and then indicates a comic bass.) So also *opera buffa* – literally 'comic opera', but see OPERA.

BUFFOON, THE, short title of 'The Buffoon Who Outwitted Seven Other Buffoons', ballet with music by Prokofiev, produced in Paris, 1921. (Russian title *Shut*; French spelling of this, *Chout*.)

BUGLE, brass instrument without valves and so producing only one HARMONIC SERIES (normally in B♭), used by armies, etc., both as a band instrument, and to signal movements, etc. *Key bugle*, *keyed bugle*, *Kent bugle* – see OPHICLEIDE.

BÜHNENWEIHFESTSPIEL, see 'PARSIFAL'.

BULL, JOHN (1563–1628), English composer and organist – at Chapel Royal, London; first professor of music at Gresham College, London, 1596. Left England 1613; in 1617 became cathedral organist at Antwerp, where he died. Wrote notable pieces for virginals (one of them the probable source of 'God Save The Queen'; and see PARTHENIA), also music for organ and viols, and church music.

BULL, OLE (1810–80), Norwegian violinist, composer (two violin concertos, etc.), and enthusiast for Norwegian folk-music; gave Grieg early encouragement.

BULLOCK, ERNEST (b. 1890), English organist, composer (choral and organ works, fanfares for state occasions, etc.), director of the Royal College of Music 1953–60; knighted 1951.

BÜLOW, HANS GUIDO VON (1830–94), German pianist, music-editor, and conductor – reckoned the first 'virtuoso' conductor; disciple of Liszt and Wagner, but enthusiast also for Brahms. Married Liszt's daughter, who afterwards left him for Wagner. Died in Cairo.

BUONONCINI, see BONONCINI.

BURIAN, EMIL FRANTIŠEK (b. 1904), Czech composer (also singer, author, playwright, producer); inventor of 'voice band', an ensemble of voices using vowels as concords, consonants as discords (demonstrated 1928). Works include operas, ballets, chamber music.

BURKHARD, PAUL (b. 1911), Swiss composer of 'Casanova in Switzerland', 'O My Papa!', and other operettas, etc.; conductor for the Swiss radio.

BURKHARD, WILLY (1900–55), Swiss composer (also pianist and conductor); pupil of Karg-Elert and somewhat influenced by Hindemith. Works include 'The Vision of Isaiah', and other Protestant oratorios; three symphonies; Toccata for four wind instruments with percussion and strings; Mass; opera 'The Black Spider'.

BURLEIGH, HENRY THACKER (1866–1914), American (Negro) baritone, composer, and arranger of Negro spirituals; pupil of Dvořák.

BURLETTA (It.), a musical farce.

BURNEY, CHARLES (1726–1814), English author of a famous history of music and other books; also organist and composer.

BURT, FRANCIS (b. 1926), English composer, pupil of Ferguson and (in Berlin) of Blacher; has also worked in Rome. Works include 'Iambics' for orchestra, two string quartets, opera 'Volpone' (after Ben Jonson).

BUSCH, ADOLF (GEORG WILHELM) (1891–1952), German-born violinist who as anti-Nazi, took Swiss nationality; died in New York. Well known as soloist, leader of Busch String Quartet, and partner of Rudolf SERKIN (who became his son-in-law). Also composer. Brother of Fritz Busch.

BUSCH, FRITZ (1890–1951), German-born conductor who, as anti-Nazi, settled in Denmark; noted also as opera-conductor at Glyndebourne. Died in London. Brother of Adolf Busch, no relation of William Busch.

BUSCH, WILLIAM (1901–45), English pianist and composer of piano concerto, cello concerto, songs, and piano pieces, etc. No relation of Adolf or Fritz Busch.

BUSH, ALAN (DUDLEY) (b. 1900), English composer (also pianist, conductor, writer on music, and teacher); studied under John Ireland, and also in Berlin. Communist sympathies give clues to many of his works including operas 'WAT TYLER' and 'MEN OF BLACKMOOR' (both produced in East Germany), piano concerto (with male chorus declaiming leftist text in finale), 'DIALECTIC' for string quartet. Has also written violin concerto, cantata 'THE WINTER JOURNEY', piano works, etc. Maintains a tonal style but sometimes with harmonic systematizations of his own. No relation of Geoffrey Bush. See also INTERLUDE.

BUSH, GEOFFREY (b. 1920), English composer, formerly Salisbury Cathedral choirboy. Works include 'The Spanish Rivals', and other operas, two symphonies, overture 'Yorick' (in memory of Tommy

Handley), piano concertino on themes by T. A. Arne, and songs. No relation of Alan Bush.

BUSONI, FERRUCIO (BENVENUTO) (1866–1924), Italian pianist and composer; travelled widely; from 1894 lived mainly in Berlin (was himself of a German mother) and died there. Made wider appeal as a pianist, piano-teacher, and arranger (e.g. editions for piano of J. S. Bach's organ works) than as composer. Works, showing an anti-ROMANTIC tendency (he detested Wagner) and an eclectic idiom, include operas 'ARLECCHINO', 'DOCTOR FAUST', and 'TURANDOT'; piano concerto (using male choir); violin concerto; many piano solos, 'Fantasia Contrappuntistica' (It., contrapuntal fantasia) for two pianos, based on J. S. Bach's 'THE ART OF FUGUE'.

BÜSSER, PAUL HENRI (b. 1872), French composer, pupil of Gounod, and others, also conductor. Works include seven operas, church and organ music, and orchestrations of piano pieces by Debussy.

BUTTERFLY, BUTTERFLY'S WING(s), unauthorized nicknames for Chopin's Study in G flat for piano, op. 25, no. 9.

BUTTERWORTH, ARTHUR (b. 1923), English composer of symphony sinfonietta, chamber music, etc.; also orchestral trumpeter.

BUTTERWORTH, GEORGE (SAINTON KAYE) (1885–1916), English composer; collected English folk-songs and shows their influence in, e.g., 'A SHROPSHIRE LAD' and 'The Banks of Green Willow' for orchestra; also wrote songs and choral pieces; killed in action as a soldier.

BUXTEHUDE, DIDERIK (1637–1707), Danish organist and composer; from 1668 organist at Lübeck, Germany, and therefore better known by the German form of his name as Dietrich Buxtehude. Wrote organ and harpsichord pieces, also church cantatas, etc. Much esteemed in his own day; visited by Bach and Handel as young men, influencing them both.

BYRD, WILLIAM (1543–1623), English composer; organist of Lincoln Cathedral, 1563, of the Chapel Royal (jointly with Tallis), 1572. Jointly with Tallis, held from Queen Elizabeth a monopoly of music-printing. Roman Catholic; composed for both his own and the Anglican church. Works, mainly in serious vein and mainly church music, include Masses for three, four, and five voices; more than 200 Latin motets (seventeen in 'CANTIONES SACRAE', 1575); five Anglican services (one incomplete); also madrigals, rounds, and other secular vocal music, many pieces for virginals (some contributed to PARTHENIA), and IN NOMINES for viols.

BYZANTINE MUSIC, the music of the liturgical chant of the Eastern Orthodox Churches.

C

C, note of the scale. So C FLAT (C♭), DOUBLE-FLAT (C♭♭), NATURAL (C♮), SHARP (C♯), DOUBLE-SHARP (C)𝄪; *C major*, *C minor*, etc. – see MAJOR. So also *in C*, either (1) in the key of C (major, understood), or (2) indication of a non-transposing instrument in cases where otherwise a TRANSPOSING INSTRUMENT might seem to be indicated: thus, e.g. *trumpets in C* (to differentiate from trumpets in B♭, in A, etc.). So also *middle C*, the C situated about the middle of the piano, and notated on the line below the treble staff; *cello C*, the C below the bass staff (tuning of the cello's lowest note); *C clef*, any one of the clefs which indicate the position of the middle C – e.g. the ALTO and TENOR clefs, and the obsolete SOPRANO clef. For *C melody saxophone*, see SAXOPHONE.

CHM, choirmaster (in certain musical diplomas).

CABALETTA (It.), (1, e.g. as in Rossini) short operatic song in simple style; (2, e.g. as in Verdi) the final quick section of an aria or duet made up of several sections.

CABEZÓN, ANTONIO DE (1510–66), Spanish organist, harpsichordist, and composer (music for organ, for VIHUELA, etc.), musician at the Spanish court; he was blind, apparently from birth. Wrote variations, etc., of noted originality.

CACCIA (It.), hunt; for *oboe da caccia*, see OBOE; for *corno da caccia*, see HORN.

CACCINI, GIULIO (1545–1618), Italian composer (and lutenist) whose opera 'Eurydice' (1600) is one of the earliest operas; as a pioneer of a newly expressive type of music (cp. MONTEVERDI) he called his collection of madrigals and canzonets (1602) '*Nuove musiche*', i.e. new music(s).

CACHUCHA, a lively Spanish dance (from Andalusia) in 3/4 time.

CADENCE, a progression of chords (usually two) giving an effect of closing a 'sentence' in music. Thus *perfect cadence*, progression of dominant chord to tonic chord; *plagal cadence*, subdominant to tonic; *imperfect cadence*, tonic (or other chord) to dominant; *interrupted cadence*, dominant to submediant (or to some other chord suggesting a substitution for the expected tonic chord); *Phrygian cadence*, progression (deriving from the Phrygian MODE) which, in the key of C major, leads to the chord of E major (and correspondingly with other keys). Note that (1) the last three definitions are subject to differences between authorities; (2) the *feminine cadence* is not a specific kind of harmonic progression, as the above, but any cadence in which the final chord comes on a weaker beat than its predecessor (instead of, as normally, the other way round).

CADENZA (It., cadence; but pronounced as English and used in different sense), solo vocal or instrumental passage, either of an improvised nature or in some other way suggesting an interpolation in the flow of the music – particularly, today, in concertos for solo instrument and orchestra. In these, however, genuine improvisation has for 150 years been very rare, cadenzas being written out in full instead by the composer, the actual performer, or a third person (often a previous performer).

CADMAN, CHARLES WAKEFIELD (1881–1946), American composer of 'Pennsylvania Symphony' (orchestration includes iron plate banged), an opera based on American Indian themes, songs (including 'At Dawning'), etc.

CAGE, JOHN (b. 1912), American composer (also pianist), pupil of Schoenberg. Has written for 'orthodox' instruments and for his invention, the 'PREPARED PIANO'; is especially noted for 'music' which seems to involve the abdication of the composer, e.g. his 'Imaginary Landscape' for twelve radio sets, first performed in 1951, requiring 24 performers (two to each set) and conductor – dynamics, and the ratio of sound to silence, being stipulated but the result obviously depending on chance. See ALEATORY.

CAISSE (Fr.), drum; *grosse caisse*, bass drum; *caisse claire*, side drum; *caisse roulante* or *caisse sourde*, tenor drum.

CALANDO (It.), getting weaker and slower.

CALDARA, ANTONIO (1670–1736), Italian composer who settled in Vienna, 1716, where he died; works include more than seventy operas, also oratorios, chamber music, church music.

CALIFE DE BAGHDAD, LE, *see* THE CALIPH OF BAGHDAD.

CALINDA, LA, orchestral piece by Delius (excerpt from his Negro opera 'KOANGA'); a dance taking its name from an actual Negro dance imported by African slaves to the American continent.

CALIPH OF BAGHDAD, THE, opera by Boïeldieu, produced in Paris 1800. Libretto by C. H. d'A. de Saint-Just: the Caliph assumes a disguise to learn people's real feelings about him.

CALLAS, MARIA (original surname Kalogeropoulou; b. 1923); American-born soprano of Greek parentage, at first having career mainly in Italy, then of highest international reputation. Specialist in Rossini-Donizetti-Bellini, and also sings title-role of 'TOSCA', etc. Formerly used surname Meneghini Callas (Meneghini then her husband).

CAMBIATA, *see* NOTA CAMBIATA.

CAMDEN, ARCHIE (Archibald Leslie; b. 1888), English bassoonist, principal bassoonist successively of the Hallé Orchestra and of various London orchestras; notable concerto-player and recitalist.

CAMERA, DA (It.), for the room – either (1) as distinct from *da chiesa*, for the church, or (2) as implying music for a small gathering, exactly as 'chamber music' does. For *sonata da camera* see SONATA.

CAMERATA (It., society), the artistic group who worked out the idea of opera about 1600 in Florence: composer-members included CACCINI and PERI.

CAMERON, BASIL (b. 1885), English conductor who worked in U.S.A., 1932–8; in 1940 became assistant conductor of Henry

Wood's Promenade Concerts (London), with which he has remained associated.

CAMERON, JOHN (b. 1918), Australian baritone resident in Britain since 1949; has sung in opera at Covent Garden, Glyndebourne, etc.

CAMPANA, CAMPANE (It.), bell, bells.

CAMPANELLA, LA, see BELL RONDO.

CAMPIAN, see CAMPION.

CAMPION, THOMAS (also spelt Campian; 1562–1620), English composer of more than 100 songs to lute accompaniment; also of masques, etc. Wrote poems set to music by himself and others, and was also lawyer and physician.

CAMPOLI, ALFREDO (b. 1906), Italian-born violinist resident in England since childhood, making London début at 11; formerly active chiefly in light music, but since 1945 prominent in concertos, recitals, etc. – Bliss's concerto is dedicated to him.

CAMPRA, ANDRÉ (1660–1744), French composer of operas, opera-ballets, church music, etc.; in charge of music at the church of Notre Dame, Paris.

CANARIE, CANARIES, CANARY, an old dance in triple time, having a prominent dotted rhythm.

CAN-CAN, Parisian dance, sometimes supposedly salacious, in quick 2/4 time; used by Offenbach in 'ORPHEUS IN THE UNDERWORLD'.

CANCRIZANS (made-up Lat.) crab-wise. The term is used (apparently through defective observation of crabs, which move sideways) to allude to a back-to-front order of notes (i.e. RETROGRADE motion); *canon cancrizans*, a canon in which the imitating voice gives out the theme not as the first voice gave it but with the notes in reverse order.

CANNABICH, CHRISTIAN (1731–98), German composer of symphonies (adherent of the MANNHEIM school) and of operas, ballets, chamber music, etc.; also violinist and conductor.

CANNON, PHILIP (b. 1929), English composer of partly French descent, pupil of Imogen Holst. Works include opera 'Morvoren', French songs; 'Songs to Delight' (in English) for women's voices; sinfonietta, concertino for piano and strings – cultivating a lucid and often simple style.

CANON, contrapuntal composition, or section of a composition, in which a melody given by one voice (or instrument) is repeated by one or more other voices (or instruments) each entering before the previous voice has finished, so that overlapping results. A *canon at the unison* is when the 'imitating' (i.e. following) voice enters at the same pitch as the first voice; a *canon at the fifth* is when the imitating voice enters a fifth higher than the original. A *canon four in one* indicates four voices entering successively on the same melody; a *canon four in two* (or *double canon*) has two different simultaneous canons of two voices each. So also *accompanied canon*, when there are simultaneous other voices or instruments performing but not taking part in the canon; *perpetual canon*, when each voice as it comes to the end begins again (see ROUND); *canon by* AUGMENTATION, DIMINUTION, INVERSION, etc., canon in which the theme is treated in the imitating voice in one of those ways.

CANTABILE (It.), in a 'singing' fashion; flowingly and clearly.

CANTATA (It., a sung piece), an extended choral work with or without solo voices, and usually with orchestral accompaniment. This is the normal meaning of the term, as used elsewhere in this book: but occasionally, as in Bach, the term may imply simply solo voice(s) without chorus. The term is much more rarely used as an actual title than its counterpart, SONATA – but Stravinsky has composed a *Cantata* (two solo singers, female chorus, five instrumentalists) to old English texts, 1952, and Bartók a *Cantata Profana* (subtitle 'The Enchanted Stags', on a legend symbolizing a plea for political freedom) for two soloists, chorus, and orchestra, 1930. Britten's *Cantata Academica* (in Latin) was written for the 500th anniversary of Basle University, 1960.

CANTATRICE (It.), woman singer.

CANTE FLAMENCO, CANTE HONDO or (*jondo*), see FLAMENCO, HONDO.

CANTELLI, GUIDO (1920–56), Italian conductor who won the approval of Toscanini and made notably successful appearances in London (from 1950) and elsewhere; appointed principal conductor of the Scala (Milan) a week before his death in an air crash.

CANTERBURY PILGRIMS, THE, (1) cantata by Dyson (words, modernized from Chaucer's 'Canterbury Tales'), first performed 1931 (the overture, also called separately *At the Tabard Inn*, dates from 1946); (2) titles of operas (also after Chaucer) by Stanford, de Koven, and Julius Harrison.

CANTICLE, (1) a hymn with biblical words, other than from the Psalms, used in Christian liturgy (distinct from ANTHEM, not on a liturgically obligatory text); so, analogously (2) a concert work with a religious or quasi-religious text – term used, e.g. as title of three works by Britten.

CANTILENA (It.), a smooth song-like melodic line.

CANTILLATION, unaccompanied chanting in free rhythm – term used particularly of Jewish liturgical chanting.

CANTIONES SACRAE (Lat., sacred songs), title sometimes formerly applied to collections of Latin motets (e.g. one composed by Tallis and Byrd, 1575); title also of a cantata by J. Gardner (words in English, from the Bible) first performed 1952.

CANTO (It.), song; melody; *marcato il canto*, bring out the melody; *col canto*, let the tempo of the accompaniment be accommodated to that of the soloist's tune; *canto fermo*, same as CANTUS FIRMUS.

CANTOR (Lat., singer), (1) director of music in a German Lutheran church – e.g. J. S. Bach's position at St Thomas's, Leipzig; (2) the leader of the chanting in a synagogue.

CANTORIS (Lat., of the singer, i.e. of the precentor), that section of the choir in a cathedral, etc., which is stationed on the north (i.e. precentor's) side of the chancel; opposite of DECANI.

CANTUS (Lat.), (1) song, melody; *cantus firmus* (pl. *cantus firmi*), fixed song, i.e. the 'given' melody borrowed from religious or secular sources which 14th–17th century composers used as a basis of works by setting other melodies in counterpoint against it – similarly, a melody given to a student, even today, to set a counterpoint against; (2) in, e.g., the 16th century, the upper voice-line of a choir.

CANZONA, CANZONE (It.), (1) any song; e.g. 'Canzone del salce', the Willow Song from Verdi's 'OTELLO'; (2) specifically, a type of medieval Italian poem, and hence a musical setting of this; (3, developed from preceding) type of short instrumental piece, especially of the 16th to early 18th centuries, often less pronouncedly polyphonic than the RICERCAR.

CANZONET (Anglicized from It. *canzonetta*), term used *c.* 1600 for a light song for one or more voices, and later (e.g. Haydn's English canzonets) for an English solo song not from an opera.

CANZONETTA (It.), little song, light song. See CANZONET.

CAOINE, see KEEN.

CAPELLA, incorrect spelling for CAPPELLA.

CAPLET, ANDRÉ (1878–1925), French composer; also conductor – at Boston, U.S.A., 1910–14; friend of Debussy, some of whose work he arranged for orchestra. His compositions include unaccompanied Mass, song cycles, symphonic poem after Poe's 'The Masque of the Red Death'.

CAPPELLA (It.), chapel; *a cappella*, *alla cappella*, in the chapel style, i.e. unaccompanied (of choral music). Sometimes encountered in incorrect spelling *capella*.)

CAPRICCIO, CAPRICE (It., Fr.), term applied – *caprice* being also used as English – to various types of lively, light piece; and specifically to a 17th-century keyboard work in lively fugal style. See also following entries.

CAPRICCIO, opera by R. Strauss, produced in Munich, 1942. Styled 'a conversation piece in one act' (two hours). Libretto by Clemens Krauss, in which a poet and a musician are rival suitors to a young widowed countess; set in the 18th century.

CAPRICCIO ESPAGNOL (Italian-plus-French), see SPANISH CAPRICE.

CAPRICCIO ITALIEN (Italian-plus-French), see ITALIAN CAPRICE.

CAPRIOL, suite for strings by Warlock (see HESELTINE), 1926, also arranged for full orchestra; in six movements based on old French dances from Thoinot Arbeau's *Orchésographie*, a book on dancing, 1589. ('Capriol' is an imaginary character in the book.)

CARAFA, MICHELE ENRICO (full surname Carafa di Colobrano; 1787–1872). Italian opera-composer who settled in France. See MASANIELLO.

CARDEW, CORNELIUS (b. 1936), English composer, also guitarist, pupil of Howard Ferguson, later associated with Stockhausen; works include 'Octet 1961' with diagrammatic notation and free choice for performers: 'free use may be made of notes apart from those provided'. See INDETERMINACY. Has also written more conventional music for piano, string trio, etc.

CARDILLAC, opera by Hindemith, produced at Dresden, 1926. Libretto by F. Lion; it was later revised – the text extensively, the music rather less. Title is the name of the hero, a 17th-century French goldsmith.

CAREY, HENRY (*c.* 1690–1743), English composer (also poet and playwright); wrote words and music of 'Chrononhotonthlogos' (burlesque of pompous tragedy) and other stage pieces including 'True Blue'; also composed cantatas and songs. Wrote words and a tune (not the best-known one) of 'Sally in our alley'.

CARILLON (originally Fr.), (1) set of bells, e.g., in a tower, on which tunes are played either by heavy manual and pedal keyboards or mechanically; (2) bell-like organ stop; (3) title of recitation with orchestra by Elgar (1914, based on a bell-like short theme) with words by E. Cammaerts, a tribute to Belgium (a traditional home of carillon, 1).

CARISSIMI, GIACOMO (1605–74), Italian composer and church musician who wrote early examples of oratorio (e.g. 'JEPHTHA'); also cantatas, masses, vocal duets, etc.

CARMELITES, THE, English title for 'Les Dialogues des Carmélites', opera by Poulenc, produced (in Italian) at Milan, 1957; libretto by G. Bernanos, about nuns guillotined in 1794.

CARMEN (Lat.), song; the plural is *Carmina* – see CARMINA BURANA.

CARMEN, Bizet's most successful opera, produced in Paris, 1875. Libretto by H. Meilhac and L. Halévy. Title from the name of the heroine, a gipsy working in a cigarette factory. The opera's well-known habanera is taken from a song by YRADIER.

CARMINA BURANA, cantata with mimed action by Orff, first performed in Frankfurt, 1937. Title and words from a collection of medieval Latin verse (with old French and Old German interpolations) on love and liquor. Title is the Latin for 'Songs from Beuron' where the text was found in a monastery.

CARNAVAL (Fr.), see CARNIVAL (and similarly for other titles beginning with this word, except 'Le Carnaval Romain' – see 'ROMAN CARNIVAL').

CARNEVAL (Ger.), see CARNIVAL. (The use of this German title for the work by Dvořák of which the original Czech title is *Karneval* is common but absurd in English-speaking countries.)

CARNIVAL, (1) concert-overture (Cz., *Karneval*) by Dvořák, 1891, second of the cycle of three overtures originally given the collective title 'Nature, Life, and Love' (no. 1 being 'AMID NATURE' and no. 3 'OTHELLO'); (2) set of twenty-one piano pieces by Schumann, 1834–5, subtitled 'dainty scenes on four notes' (Fr., *Carnaval*:

scènes mignonnes sur quatre notes), these notes representing the four letters A, S (i.e. 'Es', the German symbol for E♭), C, and H (German name for the note B); the word ASCH makes up the home-town of the girl Schumann was then in love with, and also uses the only 'musical' letters in his own name (see also PAPILLONS); (3) orchestral version of the preceding, arranged by Glazunov and others, and used for ballet, 1910; (4) concert-overture by Glazunov, 1894.

CARNIVAL IN PARIS (Fr., *Carnaval à Paris*), 'episode for orchestra' by Svendsen, published 1879.

CARNIVAL JEST FROM VIENNA (Ger., *Faschingsschwank aus Wien*), piano work in five sections by Schumann, 1839, described by him as a 'grand romantic sonata'.

CARNIVAL OF AIX (Fr., *Le Carnaval d'Aix*), piece for piano and orchestra by Milhaud, 1927 – based on his music for the ballet 'Salade', 1924. Aix-en-Provence is Milhaud's birthplace.

CARNIVAL OF ANIMALS (Fr. *Le Carnaval des animaux*), 'grand zoological fantasy' for two pianos and orchestra by Saint-Saëns, 1886 (but the composer permitted no public performances in his lifetime); fourteen movements, of which no. 11 is 'Pianists' and no. 13 'The Swan'.

CARNIVAL OF LONDON (Fr., *Le Carnaval de Londres*), orchestral work by Milhaud, 1937, on themes from his version (to French words) of 'THE BEGGAR'S OPERA'.

CARNIVAL OF VENICE, variations for violin and piano by Paganini (1829 or before) on a popular Venetian tune, 'O mamma mia'; the theme was also used for variations by later composers, and an opera with this title (Fr., *Le Carnaval de Venise*) by A. Thomas was produced in 1857.

CAROL, a seasonal religious song for use by ordinary people, not trained singers – most commonly, though not necessarily, for Christmas. 'A Carol Symphony' by Hely-Hutchinson (1929) is based on traditional Christmas carols.

CARPENTER, JOHN ALDEN (1876–1951), American composer of orchestral suite 'Adventures in a Perambulator', two symphonies (no. 2 incorporating Algerian tunes), ballet 'Krazy Kat', etc.; combined music with a business career.

CARR, EDWIN (b. 1926), New Zealand composer of viola concerto, overture 'Mardi Gras', dances for two pianos, etc.; pupil of Frankel in London and Petrassi in Rome.

CARRILLO, JULIÁN (1875–1965), Mexican composer of three operas, masses, symphonies, etc., of 'normal' musical structure; also deviser of harps and other instruments producing intervals of quarter-, eighth-, and sixteenth-tones, and composer of more than fifty works for them.

CARTER, ELLIOTT (b. 1908), American composer of ballet 'Minotaur', symphony, concerto for English horn, suite for four saxophones, etc.; pupil of Piston and N. Boulanger, and inclining to NEO-CLASSICAL outlook. Is also critic.

CARUSO, ENRICO (1873–1921), Italian tenor who made his first public appearance in 1894 in Naples (where he was born and died); appeared in Britain from 1902, U.S.A. from 1903. One of the first artists whose enormous success owed much to the gramophone.

CARVALHO, ELEAZAR DE (b. 1915), Brazilian conductor, also composer – operas, symphony, etc. Formerly played double-bass and tuba in naval bands and cabarets.

CARWITHEN, DOREEN (b. 1922), English composer of overture 'Odtaa' (after Masefield's novel), symphony, piano concerto, chamber music, etc.

CASA, LISA DELLA, see DELLA CASA.

CASADESUS, ROBERT (MARCEL) (b. 1899), French pianist, noted as soloist and also forming two-piano team with his wife Gaby (Milhaud wrote for them 'The Ball at Martinique'); also composer of piano concertos, symphonies, etc.

CASALS, PAU (Catalan form of first name, formerly used Spanish form Pablo; b. 1876), Spanish cellist (also pianist, conductor, and composer, e.g. of oratorio 'The Manger') who made his first London appearance in 1898. Has won unsurpassed reputation, particularly in J. S. Bach's unaccompanied cello works, and has received high state honours from many countries. Since 1940 has lived outside Spain in protest against Franco's government. Founder-conductor of annual festival at Prades in the French Pyrenees (from 1950). Resident in Puerto Rico since 1956. See also THIBAUD.

CASELLA, ALFREDO (1883–1947), Italian composer and pianist; pupil of Fauré in Paris. Works include operas, symphonies, 'Puppets' (*Pupazzetti*) for piano duet, many piano solos; chamber music including a Concerto for string quartet and a Serenata for five instruments – this being one of several works showing a light, somewhat ironic touch. Wrote also oratorio 'The Desert Challenged' (idealizing Mussolini's conquest of Ethiopia) and other works with topical links; and ballet 'The Jar' (*La Giara*, after a Pirandello play).

CASSA (It.), drum; *gran cassa*, bass drum; *cassa rullante*, tenor drum.

CASSADÓ, GASPAR (1897-1966), Spanish cellist (pupil of Casals), resident in Italy; also composer and arranger of many works for cello.

CASSATION (derivation uncertain), 18th-century type of composition (e.g. by Mozart) in several movements and DIVERTIMENTO style.

CASSE-NOISETTE, see NUTCRACKER.

CASTANETS, percussion instruments of two hollowed-out wooden surfaces rhythmically clicked together by the fingers of Spanish dancers; in the orchestra the clicking pieces of wood are often mounted for convenience at the end of a small stick, which is shaken.

CASTELNUOVO-TEDESCO, MARIO (1895–1968), Italian composer, pupil of Pizzetti and exponent of a predominantly lyrical and intimate idiom; settled in U.S.A., 1939, when banned as a Jew from Italian cultural life. Works include operas, oratorio 'The Book of Jonah', two violin concertos, guitar concerto, song-settings of Shakespeare, music for the synagogue.

CASTRATO (It., castrated), male singer who had sexual organs modified to allow development of a powerful voice in soprano or contralto range. (Such singers were found in Continental churches in the 17th and 18th centuries and were particularly prominent in opera, Handel's operas for instance being written for their participation.)

CASTRO, JUAN JOSÉ (b. 1895), Argentinian composer and conductor, pupil of d'Indy in Paris. Wrote opera 'Proserpina and the Stranger' (in Spanish) which won a Verdi memorial prize but provoked stormy controversy when produced at Milan, 1952; also opera on Lorca's play 'Blood Wedding', piano concerto, orchestral works, etc.

CAT'S FUGUE, nickname of one of D. Scarlatti's so-called 'sonatas' for harpsichord (no. 30 in Kirkpatrick's catalogue; published 1738). Its theme of oddly rising intervals is thought to have been suggested by the steps of a cat on the keyboard: Prof. E. J. Dent, having failed to induce a cat to confirm this hypothesis, suggested another possible origin in the cat's nocturnal cry.

CATALANI, ALFREDO (1854–93), Italian composer who studied in Paris and composed 'La Wally' and other successful operas; also Mass, symphonic poem 'Hero and Leander', etc.

CATCH, type of ROUND with tricky, amusing (sometimes bawdy) words, cultivated by Purcell and other English composers of his time and up to the 19th century.

CAVALIERI, EMILIO DE' (*c.* 1550–1602), Italian composer, in service to the Medici family at Florence; wrote dramatic pieces to be performed in concert form (immediate forerunners of opera); also composed 'The Representation of Soul and Body' – type of 'morality play' set to music, now reckoned the first oratorio (but using costumes and action).

CAVALLERIA RUSTICANA (It., Rustic Chivalry), opera by Mascagni, produced at Rome, 1890. Libretto by G. Menasci and G. Targioni-Tozzetti: a tale of revenge in a Sicilian village. It is in one act, the well-known Intermezzo being played with the curtain up at a point in the middle when the stage is empty of characters.

CAVALLI, PIETRO FRANCESCO (1602–76), Italian composer of more than thirty operas, also of church music; worked in Venice as church singer (at first under Monteverdi) and organist.

CAVATINA (It.), (1) operatic song in 'regular' form and in one section (not like the classical 'da capo' ARIA in 3 sections); hence (2) short and rather slow song-like instrumental movement – title e.g. of a famous piece (originally for violin and piano) by Raff, and of the slow movement of Rubbra's string quartet no. 2.

CAVENDISH, MICHAEL (*c.* 1565–1628,) English composer of church music, madrigals (one of 'THE TRIUMPHS OF ORIANA'), ayres, etc.

CEBELL, dance of the gavotte type, found in old English music.

CECILIA, Christian saint executed in Sicily under the Roman Empire in the 2nd or 3rd century A.D. for professing Christianity; now called the patron saint of music (commemorated annually on 22 November) though her connexion with music is purely legendary and dates only from the 16th century, apparently through the mis-reading of a Latin text.

CÉDEZ (Fr., yield), hold the tempo back (usually implying that a return to the previous tempo will shortly follow).

CELESTA (It., but pronounced as English; Fr. form, *céleste*), instrument looking like small upright piano but having hammers striking metal bars giving bell-like sound; used, a few years after its invention in Paris, by Tchaikovsky in the 'Dance of the Sugar-Plum Fairy' (in 'NUTCRACKER') and afterwards by various composers, usually for 'picturesque' effect in the orchestra. Rare in other musical groups, but see TATE. Its compass is from Middle C upwards for four octaves.

CELIBIDACHE, SERGIU (b. 1912), Rumanian conductor, trained in Germany; principal conductor, Berlin Philharmonic Orchestra, 1945–51; has toured widely.

CELLIER, ALFRED (1844–91), English composer, especially of operettas – including 'Dorothy' (1886), with a record London run; also organist and conductor.

CELLO (It.; see end of entry), bowed four-stringed instrument, one of the family (of which the principal member is the violin) which superseded the viols in the 17th and 18th centuries; has compass from C two octaves below middle C, upwards for more than three octaves. The five-stringed cello sometimes demanded e.g. by Bach is now obsolete. (The word *cello* is abbr. from *violoncello*, meaning a small violone, this being a large viol; hence it is frequently given the apostrophe, as '*cello*. But it may be accepted, without the apostrophe, as now having become a standard English word on its own, like 'piano', since no 'really English' alternative for it has been recognized. But see GRAINGER.)

CEMBALO (It.), literally a dulcimer (cp. CIMBALOM) but used as abbr. for *clavicembalo*, i.e. keyed dulcimer, i.e. HARPSICHORD. (Used also in German; its use in English is affected.)

CENDRILLON, see CINDERELLA.

CENERENTOLA, LA, see CINDERELLA.

CESTI, MARC' ANTONIO (1618–69), Italian composer and Franciscan monk holding church and court musical posts; pupil of Carissimi. Works include operas, solo cantatas, motets.

CHABRIER, (ALEXIS) EMMANUEL (1841–94), French composer, also pianist and conductor; originally civil servant; visited Spain, 1882, and afterwards wrote orchestral rhapsody 'ESPAÑA'. Its leaning towards exuberance and humour is also evident in some of his songs. Wrote also 'Joyous March' for orchestra, piano and two-piano works, opera 'Le Roi malgré lui' (King despite himself), etc. In late life suffered melancholic near-madness.

CHACONNE, piece (originally for dancing) in slow 3-beat time, in which a given theme is repeated over and over again in the bass (i.e. a ground bass). Such a piece may be vocal (e.g. 'When I am laid in earth' in Purcell's 'DIDO AND AENEAS') or instrumental, e.g. the Chaconne which forms the final movement of Bach's Partita no. 2 in D minor for violin alone (*c.* 1720). In the latter the theme is harmonically implied even at those points when it is not actually present. See PASSACAGLIA.

CHACONY, term formerly used in England, e.g. by Purcell for CHACONNE.

CHADWICK, GEORGE WHITEFIELD (1854–1931), American composer of three symphonies, five string quartets, etc., reckoned a pioneer in establishing a distinctively American type of symphonic composition; pupil of Rheinberger in Germany.

CHAGRIN, FRANCIS (real name Alexander Paucker; b. 1905), Rumanian-born composer resident in England; founder in 1943 of the Committee (now Society) for the Promotion of New Music, London. Works include piano concerto, piano solos, much film music. Also conductor.

CHAILLY, LUCIANO (b. 1920), Italian composer of 'The Proposal' (after Chekhov), 'Trial by Tea-Party' (Procedura penale) and other operas, also of piano and chamber works, etc.; pupil of Hindemith.

CHALIAPIN(E), see SHALIAPIN.

CHALUMEAU (Fr.), (1) an obsolete instrument, forerunner of the clarinet; (2) the lowest register of the clarinet, with a distinctively 'dark' tone-colour.

CHAMBER MUSIC, music intended for a room (in fact, called by Grainger 'room music', very sensibly), as distinct from a large hall, theatre, church, bandstand, ballroom, etc.; hence, particularly, music calling for 'intimate' presentation, having only a few performers, and treating all these as soloists on equal terms. Conventionally, works for one or two performers only are excluded. (The term is not a precisely defined one; see also following entries. There is every reason for including in it the appropriate kind of vocal music, e.g. madrigal-singing with one or two voices to each part.) Note that Hindemith gave the actual title Chamber Music (Ger. *Kammermusik*) to each of a set of seven compositions for various instrumental combinations, 1922–30.

CHAMBER ORCHESTRA, an orchestra small in size, and therefore capable of playing in a room (or anyway a small hall), but not merely a string orchestra. See preceding entry.

CHAMBER OPERA, term sometimes used for an opera with few singers and a small orchestra (e.g. 'THE RAPE OF LUCRETIA' and some others of Britten) – not a good term, because by analogy with CHAMBER MUSIC such a work should be capable of being performed in an ordinary room, not a theatre; but that is not so.

CHAMBER SONATA, see SONATA.

CHAMBER SYMPHONY, title of two works by Schoenberg which use only a few players and treat them as soloists (cp. CHAMBER MUSIC). No. 1 (1906) he scored also (1935) for normal orchestra; no. 2, begun 1906, was put aside, completed in U.S.A., and first performed 1940. There are also works of this title by Schreker, Leibowitz and others.

CHAMINADE, CÉCILE (1857–1944), French composer (pupil of Godard) and pianist, performing much in England; mainly known for her light piano pieces but also wrote opera, ballet, orchestral suites, etc.

CHANGE-RINGING, the British practice of ringing church bells by teams of which each member pulls the rope controlling one bell; thus with three bells the number of available *changes* (i.e. variations of the order of pulling) is 6 (3×2×1), with four bells it is 24 (4×3×2×1), etc.

CHANGING NOTE, see NOTA CAMBIATA.

CHANSON (Fr.), song; in particular a type of song for several voices, sometimes with instruments, current in France from 14th to 16th century – during the latter part of which period Italy and England had the corresponding but different form of the MADRIGAL. The *chanson de geste*, however, was a type of heroic verse chronicle set to music and current in the 11th and 12th centuries.

CHANT, (1, Eng.) see ANGLICAN CHANT, PLAINSONG; (2, Fr.) song, singing.

CHANTY, see SHANTY.

CHAPEL ROYAL, the English court chapel (i.e. a corporate body, not a building), with records going back to 1135; many leading English musicians have been associated with it as choirboys, choir-men, or organists.

CHAPEL-MASTER, the director of music in a church – made-up English equivalent for *maître de chapelle*, *Kapellmeister*, *maestro di cappella* (Fr., Ger., It.). But the German sense is much wider: see KAPELLE, KAPELLMEISTER.

CHAPÍ, RUPERTO (full surname Chapí y Lorento; 1851–1909), Spanish composer who for a time lived in Rome; wrote ZARZUELAS, also a symphony and other orchestral works, piano pieces, etc.

CHARACTERISTIC PIECE, CHARAKTERSTÜCK (Eng., Ger.), a musical representation of a mood, a place, etc.

CHARPENTIER, GUSTAVE (1860–1956), French composer, pupil of Massenet; wrote notably successful opera 'LOUISE' and unsuccessful sequel 'Julien'. Expressed his sympathy for the socially under-privileged both in these works and in founding a music school for working-class girls. Wrote also orchestral 'Impressions of Italy', songs, etc.

CHARPENTIER, MARC-ANTOINE (1634–1704), French composer, pupil of Carissimi in Rome; held church posts in France and wrote Masses and other church music, and also operas, ballets, incidental music to plays by Molière (with whom he worked) and Racine, etc.

CHASINS, ABRAM (b. 1903), American composer of Russian parentage, pupil of R. Goldmark; works include 'Rush Hour in Hong-Kong' (for piano, from a suite of Chinese pieces; later orchestrated), also two piano concertos, etc. Musical director of a New York radio station.

CHASSE (Fr.), hunt; *La Chasse* (nickname of a Haydn symphony), see HUNT; *cor de chasse* (hunting-horn), see HORN.

CHASSEUR MAUDIT, LE, see ACCURSED HUNTSMAN.

CHAUSSON, ERNEST (1855–99), French composer, pupil of Massenet and then of Franck, stylistically bridging the gap between that generation and Debussy's. Works include 'POEM' for violin and orchestra; piano quartet; 'concerto' for violin and piano with string quartet; 'Poème de l'amour et de la mer' (Poem of love and the sea) for voice and orchestra, and many songs.

CHÁVEZ, CARLOS (b. 1899), Mexican composer (also conductor, musical organizer, and folk-song researcher) who studied in Europe and New York. Has used Mexican native instruments, writing for an ensemble of them, e.g. in 'Xochipili-Macuilxochitl' (name of the Aztec god of music). Other works include six symphonies; 'H.P.' (i.e. horse-power) and other ballets; piano pieces. Cultivates a Mexican national idiom.

CHECKMATE, ballet with music by Bliss, produced in Paris, 1937. (A game of chess between Love and Death.)

CHEF D'ATTAQUE (Fr., leader of the attack), an orchestra's first violinist (Eng., leader; U.S., concertmaster).

CHEF D'ORCHESTRE (Fr.), conductor.

CHEMINÉE DU ROI RENÉ, LA, see KING RENÉ'S CHIMNEY.

CHERKASSKY, SHURA, professional name of Alexander (for which Shura is a diminutive) Isaacovich Cherkassky (b. 1911), Russian-born pianist, naturalized American; has toured widely as concerto-player and recitalist.

CHERUBINI, (MARIA) LUIGI (CARLO ZENOBIO SALVATORE) (1760–1842), Italian-born composer, permanently in Paris from 1788 and head of the Paris Conservatory from 1822; met Beethoven, who admired his music and whose 'FIDELIO' was a 'rescue opera' influenced by Cherubini's 'Faniska'. Wrote various other operas in French and Italian including 'IPHIGENIA IN AULIS', 'Medea', 'Lodoiska', and 'The Water-Carrier' (French title 'Les Deux Journées', i.e. The Two Days); also symphony, chamber music, two Requiems and other church music.

CHEST (of viols), a set of various sizes – usually six instruments in all – such as in the 16th century were often stored together in a chest or cupboard, and for which composers often wrote as an ensemble.

CHEST VOICE, that 'register' of the voice which gives the feeling to the singer of coming from the chest – i.e. the lower register, contrasted with HEAD VOICE.

CHEVREUILLE, RAYMOND (b. 1902), Belgian composer of ballet

'Cinderella', three symphonies, various concertos, 'Prayer of Those Condemned to Death' for narrator and orchestra, six string quartets, 'Lilliputian Music' for four flutes, etc.

CHIESA, DA (It.), for the church (as opposed, e.g., to *da camera*, for the room); for *sonata da chiesa*, see SONATA.

CHILD, WILLIAM (1606–97), English composer, particularly of church music, including about twenty-five services; court musician to Charles II.

CHILD AND THE SPELLS, THE (Fr., *L'Enfant et les sortilèges*), opera by Ravel, produced in Monte Carlo, 1925. Libretto by Colette: fantasy in which objects of furniture, etc., come to life. ('The Child and the Apparitions' has been used as a title when the opera has been produced in U.S.A.)

CHILD OF OUR TIME, A, oratorio by Tippett, first performed 1944. Text (by the composer) forms a specifically modern plea for the oppressed, with special reference to the Nazi persecutions, and the music incorporates Negro spirituals to parallel the traditional chorales in Bach's PASSIONS.

CHILDHOOD OF CHRIST, THE (Fr., *L'Enfance du Christ*), oratorio by Berlioz, first performed 1854. Words by the composer.

CHILDREN'S CORNER, suite of six piano pieces by Debussy, 1906–8, dedicated to his daughter. No. 1 is 'Doctor GRADUS AD PARNASSUM'; titles of the other pieces, as of the whole suite, are in English (as Debussy conceived it), no. 2 being 'Jimbo's (i.e. Jumbo's) Lullaby' and no. 6 'The Golliwogg's (*sic*) Cakewalk'.

CHILDREN'S GAMES (Fr., *Jeux d'enfants*), suite of twelve pieces by Bizet for piano duet, 1871; he afterwards made an orchestral suite of five, and five more were later orchestrated by Karg-Elert.

CHILDREN'S OVERTURE, A, orchestral work by Quilter, published 1914, based on nursery-rhyme tunes and originally designed for the play 'Where the Rainbow Ends' (to which Quilter wrote the music) though it was not in fact so used.

CHIMNEY OF KING RENÉ, THE, see KING RENÉ'S CHIMNEY.

CHINESE BLOCK, see WOOD BLOCK.

CHINESE PAVILION, see JINGLING JOHNNY.

CHISHOLM, ERIK (1904–65), Scottish composer – also pianist, conductor, and teacher: professor at the University of Capetown from 1946. Works include two piano concertos, no. 2 subtitled 'The Indian' (indebted to Indian music); trilogy of short operas called 'Murder in Three Keys' (1, 'Black Roses'; 2, 'Dark Sonnet'; 3, 'Simoom'); also symphonies, chamber music, etc.

CHITARRA (It.), guitar.

CHITARRONE (It., big guitar), large lute-like instrument much in use in 17th and 18th centuries; similar to but not identical with THEORBO.

CHIUSO (It.), closed; (of horn notes), 'stopped' by the placing of the hand in the bell.

CHOCOLATE SOLDIER, THE (Ger., *Der tapfere Soldat*, The Valiant Soldier), operetta by O. Strauss, produced in Vienna, 1908. Libretto by L. Jacobson and R. Bernauer, based on Shaw's 'Arms and the Man'.

CHOIR, (1) a body of singers, especially in a place of worship (*chorus* or *choral society* being more used in other contexts); (2) part of a church where singers are seated; (3) usual abbreviation for CHOIR-ORGAN.

CHOIR-ORGAN (or simply *Choir*), division of an organ (a manual and the equipment controlled by it) having predominantly soft stops and suitable for accompanying a choir. (Originally *chair-organ*, i.e placed behind the organist's chair or stool.)

CHOKE CYMBALS, see CYMBAL.

CHOPIN, FRÉDÉRIC FRANÇOIS (French form of Polish *Fryderyk Franciszek*; 1810–49), Polish composer and pianist of partly French descent. Born at Zelazowa Wola, near Warsaw; studied in Warsaw; settled in Paris, touring from there (e.g. to England and Scotland). Never revisited Poland (under Russian occupation) but was keen patriot and student of Polish literature. Never married; met 'George Sand' (real name Aurore Dudevant) 1838, and lived with her till 1847; suffered from consumption, gave his last public concert in 1848, and died in Paris. Works – nearly all for piano, and equally remarkable for harmonic imagination and for use of piano technique – include three sonatas (no. 2, in B♭ minor, including a funeral march), four scherzos, twenty-five preludes, twenty-seven studies, nineteen nocturnes, fourteen waltzes, ten polonaises, at least fifty-five mazurkas (these and some other works influenced by Polish folk-music), four ballades; also two piano concertos, sonata for cello and piano, songs, etc. Contributor to the HEXAMERON. See also 'LES SYLPHIDES'.

CHOPSTICKS, anonymous short quick-waltz tune for piano, playable with two outstretched forefingers, or with the little fingers if the hand is held vertically like a chopper. Variations have been written on it by, e.g., Borodin, Rimsky-Korsakov, and Liszt. The French and German names for it mean 'cutlets' – thus the reference is to chopping (not to chopsticks in the Chinese sense).

CHORAGUS, musical office-holder at Oxford University, subordinate to professor – office revived 1926, after lapsing.

CHORAL, (1, Eng.) relating to a choir or chorus; see CHORAL FANTASIA, CHORAL SYMPHONY; (2, Ger.) equals CHORALE (in the sense of traditional congregational hymn-tune).

CHORAL FANTASIA, the name generally given to Beethoven's Fantasy, op. 80, for piano, chorus, and orchestra (the words, by C. Kuffner, in praise of music) – first performed 1808. It appears to have been used as a kind of study for Beethoven's Ninth Symphony (see next entry).

CHORAL SYMPHONY, either (1) a symphony in the normal sense but using a chorus as well, or (2) a work of symphonic dimensions but written for voices alone, e.g. Bantock's 'Atlanta in Calydon' (Swinburne), first performed 1912. The first of these two senses is much the commoner. 'The Choral Symphony', in common usage, is Beethoven's symphony no. 9 in D minor, first performed 1824, having three purely orchestral movements followed by a setting of Schiller's 'Ode to Joy' for four solo singers, chorus, and orchestra; among other examples (in the first sense) are Mahler's SYMPHONY OF A THOUSAND and Vaughan Williams's SEA SYMPHONY.

CHORALE, (1) Ger. *Choral*, i.e. type of traditional German metrical hymn-tune for congregational use, e.g. '*Ein' feste Burg*' (A Stronghold Sure) by Luther, adapted from plainsong; this, like many other chorales, was made use of by Bach. So *chorale-prelude*, instrumental piece (usually for organ) based on a chorale. (The English word *chorale* is mock-foreign and synthetic, but useful in avoiding 'choral prelude', suggesting a choral work.) For *Passion chorale*, see PASSION. (2) a choir or choral society – French word, also used in the title of some U.S. choirs.

CHORD, any simultaneous combination of notes – but sometimes defined as any simultaneous combination of not less than three notes. (Whether the notes form a CONCORD or discord is irrelevant: the term *chord* is not related to these.) See also following entries.

CHORD ORGAN, type of ELECTRONIC organ in which the right hand plays a short piano-like keyboard and the left operates a set of buttons producing pre-selected chords (approximately as on the left-hand side of a PIANO-ACCORDION). See HAMMOND ORGAN.

CHORDING, (1) (satisfactory or unsatisfactory) intonation of a chord by several performers, e.g. a choir; (2) in composition, the spacing of the intervals in a chord; (3, U.S.) the provision of chords, e.g. on a guitar, to accompany a melody.

CHORD-SYMBOL, type of simple harmonic notation used e.g. by guitarist in playing modern dance music: e.g. C7 means a chord of the minor 7th on C (i.e. C–E–G–B♭) but no stipulation is made as to which note should form the bass. Cp. FIGURED BASS.

CHOREOGRAPHIC POEM, a composition for the use of ballet presumably on the analogy of SYMPHONIC POEM – description used by Ravel of his 'LA VALSE'.

CHOROS, see VILLA-LOBOS.

CHORUS, (1) a substantial body of singers not all singing separate parts; (2) colloquial term for the REFRAIN of a song, in which a chorus (in the first sense) often joins; (3) term figuratively used for a group of instruments, or organ stops, used in the manner of a chorus (i.e. not as soloists but as contributing a mass of sound).

CHOUT, see BUFFOON.

CHRIST ON THE MOUNT OF OLIVES (Ger., *Christus am Oelberge*), oratorio by Beethoven, first performed 1805. F. X. Huber's words were replaced in Victorian England by a new text and title as 'Engedi, or David in the Wilderness' (by H. Hudson), in view of 'the objectionable (*sic*) nature of the German libretto'.

CHRISTMAS CONCERTO, name given to Corelli's Concerto Grosso in G minor, op. 6, no. 8, for strings and continuo, 1712 – intended for church use, inscribed 'made for Christmas night', and having a 'Pastorale' at the end. (The name also applies to Torelli's Concerto Grosso in G minor, op. 8, no. 6, of 1708.)

CHRISTMAS ORATORIO, work for soloists, chorus, and orchestra by Bach, 1734, in the form of six cantatas – the first for performance on Christmas Day and the others to follow on particular days up to Epiphany. Text, the Christmas story from the Bible, with commentary.

CHRISTMAS SYMPHONY (Haydn), see LAMENTATION SYMPHONY.

CHRISTOFF, BORIS (b. 1919), Bulgarian bass who trained in Rome and won international eminence in opera after the Second World War.

CHRISTOPHER COLUMBUS (Fr., *Christophe Colomb*), opera by Milhaud, produced (in German) in Berlin, 1930. Libretto (in French) by Paul Claudel. The opera uses a cinema screen – e.g. to show images of tropical landscapes when Columbus reads Marco Polo's Travels.

CHROMATIC, pertaining to intervals outside the diatonic (major or minor) scale; *chromatic scale*, ascending or descending by semitones; *chromatic compass*, see COMPASS. So also *chromatic progression*, a chord-progression which involves departure from the prevailing diatonic scale; *chromaticism*, tendency of a piece or a composer towards the use of intervals outside the prevailing diatonic scale, and thus often towards a plentiful use of modulation (but the term is not used to cover ATONAL music, etc.). So also *chromatic* HARMONICA, *chromatic* HARP. And see following entry.

CHROMATIC FANTASIA AND FUGUE, by Bach for harpsichord, 1720–23, the fantasia being notable for CHROMATIC progressions.

CHURCH CANTATA, cantata written for actual performance during church service, though not forming part of the liturgy – e.g. those by Bach.

CHURCH MODES, see MODE; the term is a misleading one since, though the modes persisted in church use and are to be heard, e.g. in plainsong and in 16-century church music, they were by no means specially ecclesiastical and are found equally in the secular music (whether folk-music or works by known composers) of the period.

CIACCONA (It.), equals CHACONNE.

CIKKER, JAN (b. 1911), Czechoslovak composer of 'Resurrection' (after Tolstoy), 'Mr Scrooge' (after Dickens) and other operas; also orchestral, chamber, and piano works.

CILÈA, FRANCESCO (1866–1950), Italian composer chiefly of operas (including 'ADRIENNE LECOUVREUR') in the prevailing Italian idiom of the day, typified by Puccini; also of cello-and-piano sonata, piano solos, etc.

CIMAROSA, DOMENICO (1749–1801), Italian composer, chiefly of operas (more than sixty); pupil of Sacchini and Piccinni. Held court posts in St Petersburg and then Vienna, where 'THE SECRET MARRIAGE' was produced, 1792; this won wide fame for its combination of dramatic and musical values, in a style near Mozart's. Said to have been condemned to death in Naples for pro-French-Revolutionary sentiment, but reprieved and banished: died in Venice on way back to Russia. Other works include church music.

CIMBALOM (Hung.), Hungarian dulcimer (having horizontal strings struck with hammers) used in Hungarian popular music and in certain works indebted to this – e.g. Kodály's opera 'HÁRY JÁNOS' (and the suite drawn from it).

CINDERELLA, title of various stage works based on Perrault's fairy-tale, e.g.: (1) opera by Rossini, produced at Rome, 1817 ('La Cenerentola', libretto by J. Ferretti); (2) opera by Massenet, produced at Paris, 1899 ('Cendrillon', libretto by H. Cain); (3) opera by Wolf-Ferrari, produced at Venice, 1900 ('Cenerentola', libretto by M. Pezzè-Pescolato); (4) ballet, with songs, by Prokofiev, produced in Moscow, 1945 (*Zolushka*, i.e. the Ash-Girl).

CINEMA ORGAN, organ (normally a UNIT ORGAN) designed to what was conceived to be the taste of cinema audiences, and therefore incorporating 'freak' stops such as xylophone, motor-horns, etc.

CIPHER(ING), the continuous sounding, through a mechanical mishap, of a note on the organ.

CIRY, MICHEL (b. 1919), French composer of three symphonies, two piano concertos, choral works, etc.; pupil of N. Boulanger; is also a music-engraver.

CIS (Ger.), C sharp; *Cisis*, C double-sharp.

CITOLE, see CITTERN.

CITTERN (also *cither*, *cithern*), obsolete plucked wire-stringed instrument with strings set in pairs tuned to the same note (like lute) but built with flat back (like guitar). An earlier name is *citole* – despite D. G. Rossetti's poem 'The Blessed Damozel', which implies that the two are different; a *gittern*, however, is apparently not a cittern but an old English name for a guitar (or something very like it).

CLAIR DE LUNE (Fr., Moonlight), piano piece by Debussy (later subjected to multifarious arrangements): see BERGAMASCA.

CLARABELLA, see CLARIBEL.

CLARI (opera), see BISHOP.

CLARIBEL, CLARIBEL FLUTE (or *clarabella*), an 8-FOOT organ stop of flute-like tone.

CLARIBEL, pen-name of Mrs Charlotte Alington Barnard (1830–69), composer of 'Come Back to Erin' and other favourite Victorian songs.

CLARINET, woodwind instrument with single reed and normally a wooden (exceptionally a metal) body, in use since mid-18th century; constituent of symphony orchestra, military band, dance band, etc.

Also favoured as solo instrument and in chamber music – *clarinet trio*, *clarinet quartet*, trio or quartet incorporating clarinet; *clarinet quintet*, string quartet plus clarinet. Standard orchestral sizes of clarinet are those in B♭ (lowest note, D below middle C) and in A, a semitone lower, both being TRANSPOSING INSTRUMENTS with upward range of more than three octaves. Other instruments found are the *bass clarinet* in B♭, an octave below the standard B♭ (and bass clarinet in A, rare); high clarinet in E♭, a fourth above the standard B♭ (and high clarinet in D, rare); clarinet in C (not a TRANSPOSING INSTRUMENT), now virtually disused; *alto clarinet* (very rare; similar to BASSET-HORN); *double-bass clarinet* (also called *pedal clarinet*), very rare, an octave below bass clarinet.

CLARINO (It.), name used of a type of 17th-18th-century trumpet part – see TRUMPET.

CLARIONET, obsolete spelling of CLARINET.

CLARKE, JEREMIAH (*c*.1659–1707), English composer, pupil of Blow; organist, e.g. at St Paul's Cathedral, London. Disappointed in love, he shot himself. Composed church and stage music, choral setting of 'Alexander's Feast' (Dryden), etc., and also of harpsichord pieces among which occurs 'The Prince of Denmark's March' – see TRUMPET VOLUNTARY, under which title (sometimes with a misattribution to Purcell) it is widely known.

CLÀRSACH (Gael.), ancient small Celtic harp, revived in the 20th century for folksong accompaniment.

CLASSIC(AL), CLASSICISM, terms indicating, according to context, (1) a style supposedly notable for masterly compactness of form, moderation in the use of resources, and avoidance of undue emotionalism – used in opposition to ROMANTIC(ISM); so *the Vienna Classics*, i.e. Haydn, Mozart, and Beethoven; (2) a style or work that is 'accepted', 'standardized', and 'old' (opposite to 'modern'); so *the classical suite* (e.g. Bach's) and *the classical concerto* (e.g. Mozart's); (3) a style or work that is supposedly 'heavy' (opposite to 'light' or 'popular') – e.g. 'I don't like classical music'. See also NEO-CLASSIC and the following entry.

CLASSICAL SYMPHONY, title of symphony no. 1 by Prokofiev, first performed 1918; its Haydn-size orchestra and modernized Haydnesque idiom (but with a gavotte instead of the customary minuet of Haydn's period) allude with delicate humour to the first sense given in the preceding entry.

CLAVECIN (Fr.), harpsichord; *claveciniste*, harpsichord-player (term also used for a French composer for the harpsichord in the days of that instrument's pre-eminence, e.g. Couperin).

CLAVES (Sp.), a pair of wooden sticks beaten together to mark the rhythm in Latin-American dance music, etc., see BIRTWISTLE.

CLAVICEMBALO (It.), harpsichord. (The term literally means 'keyed dulcimer' and is normally abbreviated to *cembalo*.)

CLAVICHORD, soft-toned keyboard instrument having strings hit by metal 'tangents'; much used from 16th to 18th centuries as a solo instrument (not loud enough, e.g. for concertos for which a harpsichord was used), and revived in the 20th century for old music. (Since the tangents remain in contact with the string while it is vibrating – unlike the hammers of a piano or the quills of a harpsichord – it is possible by 'shaking' the individual notes of a keyboard to produce a kind of vibrato effect, in Ger. *Bebung*.)

CLAVICYTHERIUM, rare and obsolete instrument of harpsichord type with strings perpendicular, as in the upright piano.

CLAVIER, term originally French and meaning keyboard, or manual (of an organ); taken into German, where an alternative spelling is *Klavier*, and there having its meaning extended to include a piano or any keyboard instrument; used in English for contexts in which a definite choice between different keyboard instruments is not implied – e.g. 'Bach's clavier concertos' (intended for harpsichord, but now more often played on piano); 'THE WELL-TEMPERED CLAVIER' (intended by Bach as suitable for harpsichord or clavichord). See also following entries.

CLAVIERBÜCHLEIN, see LITTLE CLAVIER BOOK.

CLAVIERÜBUNG (Ger., Clavier Exercise), title of a work by Bach (who borrowed the title from Kuhnau) in three sections (1731, 1735, 1739), consisting of works for harpsichord (including the ITALIAN CONCERTO) and organ. THE GOLDBERG VARIATIONS, 1742, were also headed *Clavierübung* and may be regarded as the fourth section of the work.

CLAVIOLINE, trade-name of a type of ELECTRONIC keyboard instrument, similar to SOLOVOX but without octave-coupling.

CLAY, FREDERIC (1838–89), English composer of 'I'll sing thee songs of Araby' and other favourite Victorian ballads; also of stage music and cantatas.

CLEF, sign which fixes the location of a particular note on the staff – and hence the location of all other notes; placed normally at the beginning of each line of music and at any point where a new clef cancels the old. The TREBLE clef fixes the note G above middle C; the ALTO and TENOR fix middle C; the BASS fixes the F below middle C. Other clefs are obsolete, but the SOPRANO lingered well into the 19th century.

CLEMENCY OF TITUS, THE (It., *La Clemenza di Tito*), opera by Mozart, produced at Prague, 1791; libretto by C. Mazzolà, after Metastasio – extolling imperial magnanimity, and so suiting an opera composed for the coronation of the Austrian Emperor as King of Bohemia. (Previous operas on this plot were composed by Gluck and by Hasse – Mozart heard the latter in 1770.)

CLEMENS NON PAPA, nickname given to Jacob Clement (d. before 1588), Flemish composer of Latin church music, psalms in Flemish, songs, etc. (The nickname, formerly thought to mean 'Clement not the Pope', i.e. Clement VIII, was probably designed to avoid confusion with a Flemish poet, Clemens Papa, of the composer's home town of Ypres.)

CLEMENTI, MUZIO (1752–1832), Italian composer and pianist who, showing great gifts as a child, was taken to England by Peter Beckford, M.P., and thereafter lived mainly there; died at Evesham. Composed mainly for piano, pioneering a new (non-harpsichord) technique. Works include more than sixty sonatas (some with illustrative intent, e.g. one called '*Didone abbandonata*', 'The Forsaken Dido') and famous collection of studies, 'GRADUS AD PARNASSUM'; also symphonies, chamber music, etc. Also entered the piano-manufacturing trade.

CLEMENZA DI TITO, LA, see THE CLEMENCY OF TITUS.

CLÉRAMBAULT, LOUIS NICOLAS (1676–1749), French composer of cantatas, harpsichord and organ pieces, etc.; church organist in Paris.

CLEVE, HALFDAN (b. 1879), Norwegian composer of five piano concertos, songs with orchestra, etc.; also pianist.

CLEVER GIRL, THE (Ger., *Die Kluge*), opera by Orff, produced in Frankfurt, 1943; libretto by composer, after a fairy-tale by Grimm about a peasant's clever daughter.

CLIFFORD, HUBERT (JOHN) (1904–59), Australian-born composer (symphony, light orchestral music, film music, etc.) resident in England; formerly on BBC staff.

CLOAK, THE (It., *Il Tabarro*), one-act opera by Puccini, produced in New York, 1918, with the other two one-act operas ('SISTER ANGELICA' and 'GIANNI SCHICCHI') which follow it to form what Puccini called his Triptych (*trittico*). It is under a cloak that a husband reveals to his wife the body of her lover whom he has killed.

CLOCK, THE, nickname of Haydn's symphony no. 101 in D – from the clock-like ticking at the opening of the slow movement.

CLOSE, a cadence; *full close*, perfect cadence; *half-close*, imperfect cadence. (See CADENCE.)

CLOSE HARMONY, harmony in which the notes of a chord lie near together – this sometimes implying, e.g. in popular *close-harmony trios*, etc., that the supporting harmonizing notes keep as near to the melody as possible without any particular logic of harmonic PROGRESSION.

CLUSTER, a group of adjacent notes on the piano keyboard played together, e.g. with the forearm flat – demonstrated in public by Cowell (aged 15) in 1912; Ives was independently using the same idea at the same time (see CONCORD SONATA). The usual U.S. term is *tone-cluster*, for which the English would be *note-cluster* (see TONE, 5).

CLUTSAM, GEORGE HOWARD (1866–1951), Australian-born composer (especially of stage works), pianist, and critic who settled in England 1889; 'edited' (i.e. mauled) Schubert's music for the musical play 'LILAC TIME'.

CLUYTENS, ANDRÉ (1905–67), Belgian-born conductor resident in France: active in opera, e.g. at the Bayreuth Wagner Festival, and at concerts.

COATES, ALBERT (1882–1953), English composer and conductor, born in Russia of English parents; conducted in Russia both before and after the 1917 Revolution, but lived from 1919 mainly in London until going as conductor in 1946 to South Africa, where he died. Works include operas 'Samuel Pepys', 'Pickwick' (London, 1936), and 'Van Hunks and his Devil' (Capetown, 1952); also orchestral and piano works.

COATES, ERIC (1886–1957), English composer of light songs (e.g. 'Bird Songs at Eventide'), light orchestral pieces (e.g. 'The Three Bears', 'The Three Elizabeths'), etc.; originally viola-player.

COCKAIGNE, concert-overture by Elgar, first performed 1901. Subtitled 'In London Town' and punning 'Cockaigne' (imaginary land of idle luxury) and 'cockney'.

CODA (It., tail), in musical analysis, a section of a movement considered to be added at the end as a rounding-off rather than as a structural necessity. Thus in SONATA-FORM, the coda (if there is one) occurs only after both principal subjects have been recapitulated in the tonic key. (As with all such terms of analysis, the meaning here given is of value only as an approximation: Beethoven's codas, for instance, have great importance in his musical design and do not strike the listener as 'stuck on' at the end.) See also CODETTA.

CODETTA (It., little tail), in musical analysis, a rounding-off passage which does for a section of a movement what a CODA does for a movement.

COFFEE CANTATA, nickname for a humorous cantata by Bach, about 1732 (now sometimes given as comic opera) alluding to the contemporary craze for coffee. Known also by its opening words, '*Schweiget stille, plaudert nicht*' (Ger., Be silent, do not chatter).

COGLI, see CON.

COHEN, HARRIET (1895–1967), English pianist for whom several British composers have written music expressly – e.g. Fricker (piano concerto) and particularly Bax, of whose works she has been the leading exponent. While her right hand was incapacitated through injury Bax wrote for her his 'Concertante for Orchestra with Piano (Left Hand)', 1950. C.B.E., 1938.

COI, COL, see CON.

COLAS BREUGNON, see THE MASTER OF CLAMECY.

COLE, HUGO (b. 1917), English composer, pupil of R. O. Morris, Howells, and (in Paris) N. Boulanger. Works, cultivating an approachable and lyrical idiom, include operas for children, horn concerto, oratorio 'Jonah', string quartets, oboe quartet. Also critic.

COLEMAN, EDWARD (?–1669), English singer, lutenist, and composer of stage music, songs, etc.; wrote part of the music to 'THE SIEGE OF RHODES'.

COLERIDGE-TAYLOR, SAMUEL (1875–1912), English composer, born in Croydon of an English mother and W. African father; pupil of Stanford. Wrote works inclining to exotic and picturesque associations (cantatas 'HIAWATHA' and 'A Tale of Old Japan', Symphonic Variations on an African Air, etc.) but also violin concerto, string quartet and other chamber music, many piano solos, etc.

COLL', COLLA, COLLE, see CON.

COLLINGWOOD, LAWRANCE (ARTHUR) (b. 1887), English composer (operas 'MACBETH' and 'The Death of Tintagiles', etc.) and conductor, especially of opera; C.B.E., 1948.

COLLINS, ANTHONY (1892–1964), English composer and conductor (originally viola-player), at one time resident in U.S.A. Works include film music, two symphonies, violin concerto, and an orchestration of Schubert's GRAND DUO. See also HEMING.

COLORATURA (It.), term applied to an agile, florid style of vocal music or to its performance; *coloratura soprano*, soprano with voice suited to this.

COLOUR (of musical tone), see TONE-COLOUR. See also following entries.

COLOUR SYMPHONY, A, symphony by Bliss, 1922 – the movements headed Purple, Red, Blue, and Green, and interpreting these in the light of heraldic associations found by the composer in an old book.

COLOUR-ORGAN, term used in English for the light-projecting instrument specified in Skriabin's 'PROMETHEUS', 1911.

COME (It.), like; *come prima*, as at first, as at the opening, etc.; *come sopra*, as above.

COMEDY ON THE BRIDGE (Cz., *Komedie na mostě*), opera by Martinu, produced on the Prague radio, 1937; afterwards staged. Libretto, by composer (after V. K. Klicpera), mocks frontier restrictions.

COMMODO, mis-spelling for COMODO.

COMMON CHORD, see TRIAD.

COMMON METRE (in hymns), the metre of a four-line stanza having eight, six, eight, and six syllables per line.

COMMON TIME, four crochets (U.S., quarter-notes) to the bar, written 4/4 or c. (The latter sign is not a 'C' for common time, but derives from an obsolete way of indicating time-values.)

COMMUNITY-SINGING, singing by the public at a meeting, a sporting event, etc. So *community songs*, those suitable for such occasions.

COMODO (It., easy), easily-flowing, leisurely.

COMPASS, the range of a voice or instrument from the highest to the lowest note obtainable; *chromatic compass*, the range in which a complete CHROMATIC scale is playable (said of instruments which for part of their compass are not chromatic, e.g. trombone which has gaps at the lower end of its range.)

COMPOSITION, (1) a piece of music, considered as the result of a deliberate individual creative act – term therefore not usually applied (*a*) to a folk-tune, which may have reached its present shape through oral tradition and untutored adaptation, and (*b*) to a musical work not thoroughly original but ARRANGED from some other work; (2) the art of making pieces of music. Neither of these senses has any connexion with the use of the word in the following entry.

COMPOSITION PEDAL, COMPOSITION PISTON, foot-operated or hand-operated lever on the organ bringing into action a pre-selected group of stops simultaneously.

COMPOUND TIME, any musical metre not classifiable as SIMPLE TIME, in which the beat-unit divides into two. Thus 12/8 is a compound time, because the unit of beat is ♩. (the bar having four of these) and this divides not into two but into three, ♪♪♪ (The term is, however, now more academic than practical: it is of no use in analysing, say, a score by Stravinsky, or in classifying a RUMBA in which the beat is of non-uniform length.)

COMTE ORY, LE, see COUNT ORY.

COMUS, (1) masque with words by Milton, originally produced 1643 with music by H. Lawes; (2) work in which Milton's words were adapted, and new music was provided by T. Arne, 1739; (3) ballet with music arranged by Lambert from Purcell, some of Milton's words being spoken, produced 1942. Another ballet, entitled 'The Masque of Comus' with music arranged by Ernest Irving from Handel and Lawes, was produced in 1946.

CON (It.), with; *cogli*, *coi*, *col*, *coll'*, *colla*, *colle*, with the. (In general, see next word of phrase.) *Con brio*, with spirit; *colla parte*, the tempo and expression of the accompaniment to be accommodated to that of the soloist; *clarinetti coi flauti*, the clarinets to play the same notes as the flutes.

CONCERT, a substantial performance of music before an audience (other than in conjunction with a stage performance, or as part of a religious service or similar ceremony, etc.); a performance by one or two, however, is called not concert but *recital*, and the latter term is sometimes extended a little. See also following entries.

CONCERT BAND, American type of band of woodwind, brass, and percussion instruments (similar to, but not identical with, British MILITARY BAND) for which works have been expressly written by Hindemith, Schoenberg, and various American composers.

CONCERT-OVERTURE, see OVERTURE.

CONCERTANT (Fr.), in a concerted form, with interplay between instruments – term used e.g. by Stravinsky, 'Duo Concertant' (1932) for violin and piano, avoiding terms 'sonata' or 'suite'; so also (feminine form) *concertante*, as in F. Martin's 'Petite Symphonie Concertante' for harp, harpsichord, piano and two string orchestras (1945). See also following entry.

CONCERTANTE, (1, Fr.) see preceding entry; (2, It.) in a concerted form; *sinfonia concertante*, term used for a work for solo instrument(s) and orchestra with the implication that the form followed is nearer that of the symphony than of the concerto. Similarly *concertante* by itself, though not a noun in Italian, is arbitrarily used by some modern British composers (e.g. Bax, Rawsthorne, Fricker) to indicate a piece using solo instrument(s) and orchestra not carrying the formal implications of a concerto.

CONCERTED, pertaining to a performance by several people on more or less equal terms; so a *concerted number* (more usually called 'ensemble') in an opera.

CONCERTGEBOUW (Du., concert-building), name of an Amsterdam concert-hall, opened 1888, and of its resident orchestra. Bernard Haitink has been principal conductor since 1961 – till 1964, jointly with Eugen Jochum.

CONCERTINA, hexagonal-bodied instrument with bellows, similar to ACCORDION in principle but having only studs (never a piano-like keyboard) for the fingers. Popular for informal occasions (and even sometimes penetrating the concert-hall) in the last century, it has now been almost entirely superseded by the accordion.

CONCERTINO, (1) a little (and usually rather light) CONCERTO, in the first sense given below; (2) in older usage, the smaller group of instruments in a CONCERTO GROSSO.

CONCERTIZE (U.S., chiefly promoters' jargon), to give concerts, to make a concert tour.

CONCERTMASTER (U.S.), the first violinist of an orchestra (following German term *Konzertmeister*) – Eng., leader.

CONCERTO (It., a concert, a concerted performance), (1) a work using and contrasting solo instrument(s) and orchestra – generally in three movements, and generally keeping to certain structural principles of which Mozart is regarded as the classic exponent (*this is the 'standard' meaning*); (2) an orchestral work in several movements, with or without solo instruments (*this, actually the earlier sense, is exemplified in Bach's* BRANDENBURG CONCERTOS; see also CONCERTO GROSSO, *in which 'concerto' itself has a special meaning*); (3) term used apart from this by composers for exceptional reasons of their own – e.g. Bach's 'ITALIAN CONCERTO', which, though for a single player, employs an effect of instrumental contrast between the two manuals of a harpsichord; Bartók's 'Concerto for Orchestra', so called because of the solo functions filled by individual orchestral instruments.

CONCERTO GROSSO (It., great concerto), (1) type of orchestral work prevalent in 17th and 18th centuries usually (but not always) having an interplay between the larger body of instruments ('concerto' or 'ripieno') and a smaller group ('concertino') – as distinct from the modern concerto, in which only one soloist (rarely more, and anyway not a group) provides the contrast with the orchestra; (2) title used for certain 20th-century works based broadly on 17th- and 18th-century models – though Bloch's Concerto Grosso No. 1, for example, has only piano soloist instead of a concertino. (See NEO-CLASSIC.)

CONCORD, a chord which seems harmonically at rest; its opposite, *discord*, seems jarring, thus requiring a RESOLUTION to another chord. What constitutes a concord is not something fixed: throughout history composers have tended to admit more and different chords as concords, and in, e.g., much TWELVE-NOTE music, the ideas of concord and discord need not have any structural relevance for the composer.)

CONCORD SONATA, piano sonata no. 2 by Ives (inscribed 'Concord, Mass., 1840–60'), completed 1915, first performed 1938. The movements are I, Emerson; II, Hawthorne; III, The Alcotts; IV, Thoreau; and the music, in Ives's characteristically experimental vein, uses such devices as CLUSTERS of notes by laying a strip of wood on the keyboard.

CONCRETE MUSIC (Fr., *musique concrète*), type of quasi-musical organization of sound, originated chiefly by Pierre Schaeffer at the Paris radio station in 1948–9: musical and other sounds are recorded and, if desired, electronically distorted, and then assembled into a time-structure – the 'composer' thus working with recorded sound only, and the final work similarly existing only as recorded sound. See also ELECTRONIC.

CONDUCT, to direct a performance with the motions of a baton or the hands (but formerly, e.g. in early 19th-century England before the advent of the baton, *to conduct* was simply to be in charge of the performance, usually while also playing the piano or organ). So *conductor*, etc.

CONDUCTUS, in medieval music, a type of secular vocal composition having one 'given' part (CANTUS FIRMUS) to which other parts were set in counterpoint: the 'given' part being either specially composed or taken from some other secular work, not from plainsong.

CONJUNCT MOTION, see MOTION.

CONSECRATION OF THE HOUSE, THE (Ger., *Die Weihe des Hauses*,) title of a German play to which Beethoven wrote an overture and incidental music, 1822. The play, by C. Meisl, was adapted from an earlier play, Kotzebue's *The Ruins of Athens*, to which Beethoven had also written an overture and incidental music.

CONSECUTIVE, term applied to harmonic intervals of like kind succeeding one another. E.g., C struck with the E above, and then F struck with the A above (each of these pairs forming the interval of a THIRD) would give *consecutive thirds*. The sounding of *consecutive fifths* (see FIFTH) was avoided for about five centuries before 1890 as a musically poor effect – with certain very rare and deliberate exceptions; consecutive fifths are therefore still banned in academic training today, based on formerly current idiom. *Consecutive octaves* come under a similar ban in strict PART-writing, since two voices singing consecutive octaves would not be singing real parts at all, but just the same tune at an octave's distance. But in writing for an orchestra or piano, for instance, consecutive octaves are recognized as necessary; and in any case the operation of the ban on 'consecutives' is hinged with various tricky points of definition and qualifications. *Hidden fifths* are consecutive fifths not actually present but thought to be implied, and therefore equally liable to academic disapproval.

CONSERVATOIRE, -TORIUM, -TORY, school of musical training – originally in Italian, *conservatorio*, meaning an orphanage where children were 'conserved' and given musical and other training. (*Conservatoire* should be regarded as French; *conservatory* is unexceptionable English; *conservatorium* is the German form and is used also in Australia.) See also PARIS CONSERVATOIRE ORCHESTRA.

CONSOLE, the part of an organ actually at the player's command – manuals, pedals, stops, pistons, etc.

CONSONANCE, equals CONCORD.

CONSORT, old English word for a group of instruments; *whole consort*, all-wind or all-string; *broken consort*, mixed wind and string.

CONSTANT, MARIUS (b. 1925), Rumanian-born composer who settled in France after the Second World War and has worked much for the French radio as composer and conductor. Works include 'The Flute-Player', (radio 'cartoon', on the 'Pied Piper' story), also suite drawn from this; small-scale opera 'Pygmalion' (not on Shaw's play); violin concerto, 'Three Complexes' for piano and double-bass, woodwind trio, ballet 'Paradise Lost'.

CONSUL, THE, opera by Menotti, produced in New York, 1950. Libretto by the composer: the action takes place in a modern totalitarian state, from which escape to a 'free' country is made impossible by red tape at that country's consulate (the consul himself never appears).

CONTES D'HOFFMANN, LES, see TALES OF HOFFMANN.

CONTINENTAL FINGERING, see FINGERING.

CONTINUO (It., abbr. of *basso continuo*), a type of bass-line which was written (particularly about 1650–1750) for a keyboard instrument playing an accompaniment or taking part in an ensemble, and which required a special interpretation. Given only a single bass-note, the player had to work out for himself the correct harmonies to play above this note: he was commonly, but not always, helped by figures giving a kind of shorthand indication of the harmonies required (see FIGURED BASS). To *play the continuo*, therefore, is not to play a particular kind of instrument; it is to play on any keyboard instrument from this particular kind of bass. (It was customary for the actual bass-notes, though not the harmonies above, to be sounded also by, e.g., cello and double-bass. The historic English equivalent for continuo is 'thorough-bass', i.e. 'through-bass'; but 'continuo' has now acquired standard usage in English.)

CONTRA-, CONTRE-, KONTRA-, Italian, French, and German prefixes signifying (of an instrument) 'lower in pitch', usually about an octave lower. So, e.g., *contrebasse*, *Kontrabass*, French and German terms for DOUBLE-BASS; *contre-basson*, *Kontrafagott*, French and German terms for double-bassoon (see BASSOON). The Italian terms for these instruments are usually given in non-Italian musical contexts as *contrabasso* and *contrafagotto*: correct modern Italian, however, gives *contrabbasso* and *controfagotto*. The practice of introducing *contra-* as an element of made-up English words (contrabass, contrabassoon) is unnecessary and illogical: the true linguistic counterpart of this prefix is 'counter-' (as in COUNTER-TENOR), and the correct usage here is 'double-', e.g. double-bassoon.

CONTRABASSO, CONTRABBASSO, CONTRAFAGOTTO, see preceding entry.

CONTRALTO, lower type of female voice. See also ALTO.

CONTRAPUNCTUS (made-up Lat.), a counterpoint; used by Bach instead of 'fugue' as a heading for movements in his 'THE ART OF FUGUE'.

CONTRAPUNTAL, pertaining to COUNTERPOINT.

CONTRASTS, trio by Bartók, 1938, for clarinet, violin, and piano – the violinist using two instruments, one of normal tuning (G, D, A, E) and the other tuned G♯, D, A, E♭.

CONTRE-, see CONTRA.

CONTREDANSE, see COUNTRY DANCE.

CONTROFAGOTTO (It.), double-BASSOON.

CONVERSE, FREDERICK SHEPHERD (1871–1940), American composer, pupil of Rheinberger (in Munich) and others. Works include four operas, six symphonies (no. 6 posthumously performed), 'Flivver 10,000,000' for orchestra (celebrating the manufacture of the ten millionth Ford car), choral and piano works.

COOKE, ARNOLD (ATKINSON) (b. 1906), English composer, pupil of Hindemith and follower of his methods. Works include opera 'Mary Barton' (after Mrs Gaskell), oboe concerto, clarinet concerto, much chamber and piano music, children's and other songs.

COOKE, BENJAMIN (1734–93), English composer (pupil of Pepusch) and organist; wrote church music, glees and other vocal pieces, organ works, etc.

COOKE, DERYCK (VICTOR) (b. 1919), English musicologist who has worked extensively for the BBC and who made a completion of Mahler's Symphony No. 10.

COOKE, HENRY (*c.* 1615–1672), English bass singer and composer of church music, songs, part of the music to 'THE SIEGE OF RHODES', etc.

COOPER, JOHN (*c.* 1570–1627), English composer, player of the lute and other instruments; changed name to Giovanni Coperario (or Coprario) while studying in Italy and retained this on returning. Composed masques, music for lute and for organ, anthems, madrigals, etc., author of 'Rules how to Compose'. Teacher of the brothers Lawes.

COPERARIO, see preceding entry.

COPERTO (It.), covered, e.g. of drums muffled with a cloth to give a muted effect.

COPLAND, AARON (b. 1900), American composer, pupil of R. Goldmark and (in Paris) N. Boulanger; also pianist, lecturer, and writer, prominent in general championing of American music. Born in Brooklyn. His work variously shows an indebtedness to jazz ('Music for the Theatre', 1925), to cowboy songs and similar indigenous American tunes (ballets 'RODEO' and 'APPALACHIAN SPRING'), and to Latin-American music ('EL SALÓN MÉXICO', clarinet concerto); but elsewhere it is sometimes completely abstract, fiercely dissonant, and devoid of 'popular' influences – e.g. piano variations, piano sonata. Other works include opera 'The Tender Land', three symphonies, 'QUIET CITY' (orchestral suite), 'A LINCOLN PORTRAIT' (with narrator), piano quartet and other chamber music, film scores.

COPPÉLIA, ballet with music by Delibes, produced at Paris, 1870. (Subtitled 'or, The Girl with Enamel Eyes' – a girl deceiving a toymaker into thinking her one of his own dolls come to life.)

COPRARIO, see COOPER, JOHN.

COQ D'OR, LE, French title of Rimsky-Korsakov's 'THE GOLDEN COCKEREL'; since this is a Russian work, there is no point in English-speaking countries in using the French title.

COR (Fr.), HORN; *cor anglais*, see ENGLISH HORN; *cor de chasse* (hunting-horn), see HORN; *tenor cor*, see MELLOPHONE.

CORDA (It.; pl. *corde*), a string. So, in piano-playing, *una corda* (one string) – instruction to play with soft pedal, this pedal achieving its effect (on grand pianos) by causing the hammers to hit only one instead of three strings to each note. The terms *tre corde* or *tutte le corde* (three strings, all the strings) cancel this, indicating that the soft pedal is not to be used.

CORELLI, ARCANGELO (1653–1713), Italian violinist, composer chiefly for his instrument, of which he was one of the first great exponents. In service as musician to a cardinal at Rome. More than anyone else, established the form of the CONCERTO GROSSO; among his examples in this form is the so-called CHRISTMAS CONCERTO. See also FOLÍA.

CORIOLANUS (Ger., *Coriolan*), overture by Beethoven, 1807, to a play (not related to Shakespeare's) by H. von Collin.

CORNELIUS, PETER (1824–74), German composer (also critic), pupil of Liszt and admirer of Wagner; wrote 'THE BARBER OF BAGHDAD' and other operas, some notable songs and part-songs, etc.

CORNEMUSE (Fr.), BAGPIPE.

CORNET, (1), an obsolete instrument: see CORNETT. (2), brass wind instrument with three valves, resembling trumpet but squatter in appearance, of wider bore, and easier to play; a TRANSPOSING

INSTRUMENT in B♭, with compass from E below middle C upwards for about two and a half octaves – can be switched to becoming an instrument in A, half a tone lower. It 'arrived' in 1820s, i.e. before valved trumpet, so found a ready use in being the only brass instrument of its pitch capable of fully chromatic use; but it has now been generally driven out of the symphony orchestra by the valved trumpet (except when called for specially – e.g. Lambert, 'THE RIO GRANDE' where no trumpets are used, and M. Arnold, 'BECKUS THE DANDIPRATT' which uses trumpets as well). It has also been driven out of dance music, but was used in early jazz. It is still a basic instrument in the brass band (where a smaller, higher *soprano cornet* in E♭ is also used) and most military bands.

CORNET-À-PISTONS (Fr.), equals CORNET (2).

CORNETT, obsolete wood or ivory wind instrument having cup-shaped mouthpiece (like modern brass) but finger-holes (like modern woodwind); used e.g. by Bach to reinforce the choral soprano parts in church music, as trombones would reinforce the lower vocal parts. The OPHICLEIDE and SERPENT are of the same family. (In modern spelling the word would be *cornet*, but the old spelling is kept to distinguish it from CORNET (2) above.)

CORNISH, see CORNYSHE.

CORNO (It.), HORN; *corno inglese*, ENGLISH HORN; *corno di bassetto*, BASSET HORN. ('Corno di Bassetto' was Bernard Shaw's pseudonym as a music critic.)

CORNOPEAN, organ stop of soft but trumpet-like tone.

CORNYSHE, WILLIAM (also Cornish and other spellings; *c.* 1465–1523), English composer of songs (including a setting of Skelton), church music, etc.; in service as musician, actor, and master to Henry VII and to Henry VIII whom he accompanied to the Field of the Cloth of Gold, 1520 (cp. FAYRFAX, SERMISY).

CORONATION CONCERTO, nickname for Mozart's piano concerto in D, K.537, performed by him at coronation festivities for the Emperor Leopold II at Frankfurt, 1790 (composed 1788).

CORONATION MASS, (1) nickname for Mozart's Mass in C, K.317 (1779), apparently through some association with the annual crowning of a statue of the Virgin; (2) nickname (reason unknown) for Haydn's Mass in D minor – see NELSON MASS.

CORONATION OF POPPAEA, THE (It., *L'Incoronazione di Poppea*), opera by Monteverdi, produced in Venice 1642; libretto by G. F. Bussenello, on Nero's expulsion of his wife in favour of his mistress, Poppaea.

CORSAIR, THE, concert-overture by Berlioz (Fr., *Le Corsaire*), 1831. Not after Byron's poem, but after Fenimore Cooper's novel *The Red Rover* – title of overture was originally 'Le Corsaire Rouge'.

CORTÈGES, 'fantasy overture' by Rawsthorne, 1945; uses what might be march-rhythms of different kinds, but no interpretative clue is given on the score.

CORTOT, ALFRED (1877–1962), Swiss-born pianist resident in France – noted as soloist and chamber-music player (see THIBAUD) and also as conductor; was a champion of Wagner's music in France. Edited piano works and wrote about them.

COSÌ FAN TUTTE, opera by Mozart, produced at Vienna, 1790. Libretto by L. da Ponte, mocking women's vows of fidelity. Title literally means 'So do all women'; sub-title is 'or, The School for Lovers' (*La Scuola degli amanti*), which might make a suitable title in English.

COSTA, MICHAEL ANDREW AGNELLUS (1808–84), Italian-born composer-conductor who settled in London, 1821, and achieved leading position as conductor. Knighted 1869. Composed operas, oratorios, symphonies, etc.

COUNT ORY (Fr., *Le Comte Ory*), opera by Rossini, produced in Paris, 1828. Libretto by E. Scribe and C. G. Delstre-Poirson: the Count is a medieval suitor whose amorous pursuit leads him to disguise himself as a hermit and then as a female pilgrim.

COUNTERPOINT, The simultaneous combination of two or more melodies to make musical sense, one melody then being spoken of as *the counterpoint of* or *in counterpoint to* another. So *double counterpoint*, when two melodies, one above the other, can exchange position; similarly *triple*, *quadruple counterpoint* (etc.), where three, four (etc.) melodies can take up any positions relative to each other: all these are kinds of *invertible counterpoint*, as practised in FUGUE. A certain academic discipline abstracted from 16th-century practice is called *strict counterpoint*; *free counterpoint* denotes counterpoint not bound by this.

COUNTER-SUBJECT, see FUGUE.

COUNTER-TENOR, a rare male voice higher than tenor, current in England in Purcell's and Handel's time and revived in the 20th century in concerts and opera; called male ALTO in, e.g., Anglican cathedral usage.

COUNTRY DANCE, kind of dance originating in England (e.g. the 'Sir Roger de Coverley') and cultivated e.g. by Mozart and Beethoven, who called it *Kontretanz* – based on Fr. *contredanse* (counter-dance), derived by false etymology from the English word.

COUP D'ARCHET (Fr.), stroke of the bow, the attack with the bow.

COUP DE GLOTTE (Fr.), stroke of the glottis, a method of vocal 'attack' counselled by some teachers of singing.

COUPERIN, French family of musicians (see below). The surname alone is taken to refer to François Couperin.

COUPERIN, CHARLES (1638–79), French organist (in Paris) and composer; father of François Couperin.

COUPERIN, FRANÇOIS (1668–1733), called 'Couperin le grand' (the great), French composer, also harpsichordist and organist; pupil of his father (see preceding entry). Held official post under Louis XIV. Composed over 200 harpsichord pieces, some with picturesque titles; concertos, organ pieces, works for viols, church and other vocal music. Wrote famous book on harpsichord-playing. Nephew of Louis Couperin.

COUPERIN, LOUIS (*c.* 1626–1661), French organist (in Paris) and composer. Brother of Charles Couperin and uncle of François Couperin (see preceding entries).

COUPLE (verb), on the organ, to contrive that the stops normally controlled by one manual are available also on another manual (or on pedals); or that the striking of one note should also cause the sounding of the same note an octave higher or lower. Henee *coupler*, mechanism for this. Similarly sometimes on a harpsichord and on some ELECTRONIC instruments, e.g. SOLOVOX.

COUPLER, see preceding entry.

COUPLET (Fr., not the same meaning as in English), (1) stanza of a poem, the music being repeated for each successive stanza – an operatic song may take the form of *couplets*; (2) forerunner, e.g. in Couperin's works, of what in RONDO form is called the 'episode'.

COURANTE (Fr.), dance in triple time occurring in the classical SUITE.

COVENT GARDEN, usual name for the London theatre whose official title has been 'the Royal Opera House, Covent Garden' since 1892 (previously the 'Royal Italian Opera House'). It has had its own resident opera and ballet companies since 1946. The latter became the Royal Ballet in 1957. Since 1961 the Opera's musical director has been Georg Solti.

COW-BELLS, as percussion instrument, specified e.g. in R. Strauss's ALPINE SYMPHONY with picturesque intent.

COWELL, HENRY (DIXON) (1897–1966), American composer and pianist, given to musical experiment; developed the idea of CLUSTERS of adjacent notes played e.g. with forearm on the piano, and extended this to orchestral technique also; co-inventor of the RHYTHMICON, electrical instrument reproducing predetermined rhythms, and composed for this in association with other instruments. Prolific composer for orchestra, band and various instrumental groups; works (some with synthesized titles like Synchrony, Tocanta) include thirteen symphonies, 'Hymns and Fuguing Tunes' (after BILLINGS), opera, works for piano in both conventional and unconventional techniques. Also writer on music and teacher.

COWEN, FREDERIC (HYMEN) (1852–1935), English composer and conductor, born in Jamaica; works include operas, six symphonies (no. 3, 'Scandinavian'), and about 300 songs.

COW-HORN, brass instrument (roughly of HORN type, but valveless) made to imitate the sound of a rustic horn and used in Britten's SPRING SYMPHONY.

COX, DAVID (VASSALL) (b. 1916), English composer (pupil of Howells) and member of BBC music staff; works, mainly vocal, include choral suite 'Of Beasts' (words from a medieval bestiary).

COX AND BOX, operetta by Sullivan, produced in London, 1867.

Libretto by F. C. Burnand. Cox and Box are alternate tenants (day and night) of the same lodgings.

CRAFT, ROBERT (LAWSON) (b. 1923), American conductor, particularly associated with Stravinsky and with Stravinsky's enthusiasms, e.g., Webern.

CRAWFORD, ROBERT (b. 1925), Scottish composer, pupil of Gál and Frankel; works include sinfonietta, string quartet, quintet for wind and strings.

CRAXTON, HAROLD (b. 1885), English pianist, teacher, and editor of piano music.

CREATION, THE (Ger., *Die Schöpfung*), oratorio by Haydn, first performed in Vienna, 1798. Composed to German translation of English text by 'Lidley' (unknown) after Genesis and Milton's 'Paradise Lost'. See also CREATION MASS.

CRÉATION DU MONDE, LA, see CREATION OF THE WORLD.

CREATION MASS, nickname (because of a quotation in it from 'THE CREATION'), for Haydn's Mass in B♭, 1801.

CREATION OF THE WORLD, THE (Fr., *La Création du monde*), ballet (a long way after Genesis) with music by Milhaud, using jazz idiom; produced in Paris, 1923.

CREATURES OF PROMETHEUS, THE, see under PROMETHEUS.

CRESCENDO (It., growing), increasing in loudness.

CRESPIN, RÉGINE (b. 1927), French soprano, internationally noted in Wagner and as Puccini's Tosca, etc.

CRESTON, PAUL (real name Joseph Guttoveggio; b. 1906), American composer, also organist. Works include five symphonies (no. 3 on Gregorian chant), saxophone concerto, concertino for marimba, fantasia for trombone and orchestra.

CROCE, GIOVANNI (1558–1609), Italian composer (and priest), pupil of Zarlino; in charge of music at St Mark's, Venice. Wrote motets, psalms, madrigals, etc.

CROCHE (Fr.), quaver (U.S., eighth-note). ('M. Croche' was an imaginary person under whose name Debussy wrote music criticism.)

CROFT, WILLIAM (1678–1727), English organist (at Westminster Abbey, 1708) and composer of songs, harpsichord pieces, stage music, etc., and much church music including hymn-tune 'St Anne' ('O God our Help in Ages Past').

CROOK, detachable section of the tube of horns, trumpets, etc., made in various sizes so as to give a different basic key to the instrument when fitted. (A player in Mozart's time, seeing 'horn in D' specified, would fit a 'D crook', giving a HARMONIC SERIES with D as the fundamental. The use of VALVES, general from about 1850, has almost eliminated the necessity for changing crooks, but on e.g. an ordinary trumpet in B♭ there is a mechanism which in effect can change the instrument to one having an 'A crook'.)

CROON (particular usage, especially in 1930s), to sing softly and sentimentally through a microphone, as in dance bands.

CROSS, JOAN (b. 1900), English operatic soprano (also teacher and opera producer); created some of Britten's leading opera roles. C.B.E., 1951.

CROSS-FINGERING, fingering the ascending or descending scale (on woodwind instruments) in a way that goes against the normal order of lifting up and putting down successive fingers.

CROSSE, GORDON (b. 1937), English composer, pupil of Wellesz and (in Italy) Petrassi. Works include 'Meet my folks!', 'Ahmet the Wood-seller' and others involving child singers and instrumentalists; also 'Symphonies' (see SYMPHONY) for chamber orchestra, 'Elegy for small orchestra', opera *Purgatory*, etc.

CROSSLEY-HOLLAND, PETER (CHARLES) (b. 1916), English composer (cantata 'The Sacred Dance', etc.), performer on the (medieval) minstrel's harp, and authority on oriental music.

CROSS-RELATION(S), the relation set up when, for instance, the notes A♮ and A♭ occur simultaneously or in immediate succession in different PARTS – that is, a special effect of harmony in which the parts are not unanimous in whether they treat a particular note as sharp, natural, or flat. (*Cross-relation*, the standard American term, is better than *false relation*, more usual in Britain.)

CROTCH, WILLIAM (1775–1847), English composer; child prodigy as organist and composer whose later works (oratorio 'Palestine', church and organ music, etc.) did not fulfil his exceptional early promise. Professor at Oxford, 1797, and first principal of the Royal Academy of Music, 1822.

CROTCHET, the note ♩ (U.S., *quarter-note*) considered as a time-value, equivalent to half a minim or 2 quavers. Its rest is notated 𝄽 or 𝄾

CROUCH, FREDERICK NICHOLLS (1808–96), English composer who emigrated to U.S.A., 1849; wrote 'Kathleen Mavourneen' and other songs, also operas.

CROWD (string instrument), equals CRWTH.

CROWN IMPERIAL, march by Walton for coronation of George VI, 1937 (title from William Dunbar's poem 'In Honour of the City', earlier set as cantata by Walton).

CRUCIFIXION, THE, oratorio by Stainer (text written, and selected from the Bible, by J. S. Simpson), first performed 1887.

CRUFT, ADRIAN (FRANCIS) (b. 1921), English composer (also double-bass player), pupil of Jacob and Rubbra. Works include Partita for small orchestra, concert-overture 'Actaeon', church music and songs.

CRWTH (Welsh; equivalent to English *crowd* as musical instrument), obsolete British stringed instrument shaped like a lyre but played with a bow, surviving longest in Wales; an ancestor of the violin family. (Sometimes misleadingly called 'bowed harp'.)

CSÁRDÁS (Hung.), Hungarian dance in sections *lassú* (slow) and *friss* (quick). *Die Csárdás-Fürstin*, see GIPSY PRINCESS.

CUCKOO, toy instrument, used e.g. in the TOY SYMPHONY formerly ascribed to Haydn.

CUÉNOD, HUGUES (b. 1902), Swiss tenor of unusually high range; noted in recitals (including medieval music) and in opera.

CUI, CÉSAR ANTONOVICH (1853–1918), Russian composer of French descent; general in the Russian army; critic, propagandist for 'national' Russian music, and member of the group of composers called THE MIGHTY HANDFUL. Works include ten operas, many piano pieces and songs. Completed Dargomizhsky's 'THE STONE GUEST' and made one of the several completions of Mussorgsky's 'SOROCHINTSY FAIR'.

CUIVRE, CUIVRÉ, (Fr.) brass, brassy (the latter used e.g. in horn-playing to signify a 'forced', ringing tone); *cuivres*, brass instruments.

CUNDELL, EDRIC (1893–1961), English conductor, composer, and principal of the Guildhall School of Music, London, 1938–59. C.B.E., 1949.

CUNNING LITTLE VIXEN, THE (Cz. *Přihody Lišky Bystroušky*), opera by Janáček, produced in Brno, 1924; libretto by R. Těsnohlídek, using both human and animal characters.

CUPID AND DEATH, masque with words written by J. Shirley, 1653, with music conjecturally by C. Gibbons; revived 1659, with music (certainly) by C. Gibbons and M. Locke.

CURLEW, THE, song-cycle by Warlock, 1923, to four linked poems by Yeats; accompaniment for flute, English horn, and string quartet.

CURLEW RIVER, opera (styled 'parable for Church Performance') by Britten, first performed at Orford (Suffolk), 1964. Libretto by William Plomer, based on medieval Japanese play.

CURTAL(L), old English name for BASSOON.

CURZON, CLIFFORD (MICHAEL) (b. 1907), English pianist, pupil of Schnabel, Landowska, and N. Boulanger; London début at age 16; various overseas appearances. Also harpsichordist. C.B.E., 1958.

CYCLE, (1) name given to a set of works, especially songs, intended to be performed as a group and often linked musically or by other means; (2) term used in the expression *cycle of fifths*, the 'chain' by which (given 'equal TEMPERAMENT') a succession of perfect fifths upwards or downwards will lead back to the original note again (at a higher or lower octave) after passing through all the other eleven notes of the chromatic scale. See also CYCLIC FORM.

CYCLIC FORM, (1) form of a work in which a theme does duty (often in new guise) in more than one movement – e.g. Franck, Symphony; Elgar, Symphony no. 1; (2, obsolete; see CYCLE, 1) form of any work with more than one movement.

CYMBAL, percussion instrument consisting of a plate of metal either struck with drumstick (single stroke or roll) or clashed against another cymbal. The so-called *ancient cymbals* or *antique cymbals* (specified e.g. in Debussy's AFTERNOON OF A FAUN) are tuned to definite pitch. Ordinary cymbals are of no definite pitch – but nevertheless one of them may sound higher than another, and three so differing are used e.g. by Nono, 'Epitaph for Lorca'. *Choke cymbals* are two ordinary cymbals mounted face to face on a rod (e.g. in dance bands) and struck with side-drum stick.

CYTHERN, see CITTERN.

CZARDAS, incorrect spelling of CSÁRDÁS.

CZERNY, CARL (1791–1857), Austrian pianist and composer of an enormous number of piano studies; also of many other piano works (e.g., fantasies on popular operatic and other tunes of the day) and of church music, etc. Contributor to the HEXAMERON. Pupil of Beethoven and himself a famous teacher – e.g., of Liszt.

D

D, note of the scale. So D FLAT (D♭), DOUBLE-FLAT (D♭♭), NATURAL (D♮), SHARP (D♯), DOUBLE-SHARP (D𝄪); *D major*, *D minor*, etc. – see MAJOR. So also *in D*, either (1) in the key of D (major, understood), or (2) indication of a TRANSPOSING INSTRUMENT on which the note written C sounds as D (and correspondingly with other notes) – e.g. *trumpet in D*, or (colloquially) a *D trumpet*, now obsolete but used by Purcell, Handel, etc.

D., abbr. of DEUTSCH (in Schubert's works).

d, symbol in TONIC SOL-FA notation for the first degree (tonic) of the scale, pronounced *doh*.

D.C., abbr. of *da capo*; see DA.

DIM., abbreviation of (1) DIMINUENDO; (2, mainly in dance-band harmony, etc.) DIMINISHED.

DIV., abbreviation of DIVISI or 'divided'.

D.MUS., abbr. of DOCTOR OF MUSIC.

d' (Fr., It.), of (before a vowel); see under second word of phrase.

DA (It.), from; *da capo* (abbr. D.C.), repeat from the beginning. So also *da capo al fine*, *da capo al segno* (repeat) up to the occurrence of the word 'fine' (end), or up to the sign indicating this (e.g. 𝄐 – see PAUSE). Similarly *dal segno*, (repeat) from a specified sign, instead of repeating right from the beginning. (For *da capo* aria, see ARIA.)

DAL, see preceding entry.

DALAYRAC, NICOLAS (also spelt d'Alayrac; 1753–1809), French composer of songs, string quartets, and especially operas – over fifty of them, including 'All for love' (*Tout pour l'amour*) on *Romeo and Juliet*.

DALCROZE, see JAQUES-DALCROZE.

DALE, BENJAMIN JAMES (1885–1943), English composer and teacher;

won attention with piano sonata at 17, and later wrote cantata 'Before the Paling of the Stars', much music for one or more violas, etc.

DALLAPICCOLA, LUIGI (b. 1904), Italian composer (also pianist and teacher), practitioner of TWELVE-NOTE composition. Works include operas 'Night Flight', THE PRISONER, JOB; ballet 'Marsyas'; piano concerto, orchestral and choral works; music for piano (including 'Annalibera's Musical Notebook', for his 8-year-old daughter) and for three pianos; songs (some in German) with orchestral, piano, and other accompaniments.

DAMASE, JEAN-MICHEL (b. 1928), French pianist and composer of piano concerto, sarabande for string orchestra, ballet 'The Diamond-Cruncher', etc.; also of several works for harp – his mother being a harpist.

DAMNATION OF FAUST, THE (Fr., *La Damnation de Faust*), cantata by Berlioz, 1846; since 1893 also occasionally staged as opera. Words by composer and A. Gandonnière, after Goethe.

DAMOISELLE ÉLUE, LA, see BLESSED DAMOZEL.

DÄMPFER (Ger.), MUTE.

DAMPING PEDAL, soft pedal (of piano).

DAMROSCH, WALTER (1862–1950), German-born conductor who went with his father (Leopold Damrosch, 1832–85, also a conductor) to settle in U.S.A. in boyhood; champion of Wagner, and commissioned Tchaikovsky's Symphony No. 6. Was himself composer of operas including 'Cyrano' (after Rostand's *Cyrano de Bergerac*), and 'The Man Without a Country'; also of choral works, etc.

DANCE BAND (in modern sense) instrumental group which in the 1930s was generally established as being composed of three basic sections – saxophones (some players doubling clarinets), brass (trumpets and trombones), and 'rhythm' (piano, drums, guitar, and double-bass usually playing pizzicato). From the 1950s formal full bands were displaced in popular leadership by 'pop groups' based on electronically amplified guitars of differing types, with percussion.

DANCE OF THE HOURS, ballet music from Act 3 of Ponchielli's opera 'LA GIOCONDA'.

DANCE-POEM, description sometimes given by composers to a substantial orchestral work intended for ballet and having narrative interest (cp. CHOREOGRAPHIC POEM, SYMPHONIC POEM).

DANCES OF GALÁNTA, orchestral suite by Kodály, 1934, based on tunes in a collection of gipsy music from Galánta (a small Hungarian market town).

DANCO, SUZANNE (b. 1911), Belgian soprano, appearing in opera at Edinburgh Festival, Covent Garden, etc.; also noted recitalist.

DANSE (Fr.), dance.

DANSE MACABRE, orchestral work by Saint-Saëns, 1874; inspired by medieval idea of skeletons' dance; quotes DIES IRAE.

DANTE SONATA, usual short name for Liszt's piano work, 'After a reading of Dante' (Fr., *Après une lecture du Dante*), labelled by him as a 'Fantasia, quasi sonata'. Played by Liszt in 1839; revised and given its present form 1849. Arranged by Lambert for piano and orchestra and used for ballet, 'Dante Sonata', 1940.

DANTE SYMPHONY, work by Liszt, first performed 1857. Two movements, 'Inferno' and 'Purgatorio', ending with the MAGNIFICAT sung by a women's chorus. (Liszt wrote two alternative versions of this ending.)

DANZA (It., Sp.), dance.

DAPHNIS AND CHLOE, ballet with music by Ravel (using a chorus), produced in Paris, 1912. (The two orchestral suites drawn from it do not comprise the whole.) An ancient Greek story of pastoral love.

DAQUIN, LOUIS CLAUDE (also spelt d'Acquin; 1694–1772), French composer of harpsichord pieces (including 'The Cuckoo'), church music, etc.; organist from boyhood, holding post at French royal chapel from 1739.

DARGASON, English folk-tune used as a COUNTRY DANCE and incorporated into Holst's 'ST PAUL'S SUITE'.

DARGOMIZHSKY, ALEXANDER SERGEYEVICH (1813–69), Russian composer, 'nationalist' in musical ideas and associated with the group known as THE MIGHTY HANDFUL, though not a member. Composed 'THE RUSSALKA', 'THE STONE GUEST', and other operas, also various orchestral and vocal works including satirical and other songs.

DARKE, HAROLD (EDWIN) (b. 1888), English organist (at St Michael's, Cornhill, London, since 1916) and composer chiefly of cantatas, church and organ music, and songs; pupil of Stanford.

DARNTON, (PHILIP) CHRISTIAN (b. 1905), English composer who studied partly in Germany. Works include operas, cantata 'Jet Pilot', three symphonies, piano concerto. Also writer on music.

DART, (ROBERT) THURSTON (b. 1921), English harpsichordist, organist, and conductor; professor of music at Cambridge, then (1964) at London University.

DAUGHTER OF THE REGIMENT, THE (Fr., *La Fille du régiment*), opera by Donizetti, produced in Paris, 1840. Libretto by J. H. V. de Saint-Georges and J. F. A. Bayard: the heroine, brought up as a regimental 'mascot', turns out to be of noble (if illegitimate) parentage.

DAVID, FÉLICIEN (CÉSAR) (1810–76), French composer (also theatre conductor); travelled in Near East, arranged oriental melodies for piano, and won noted success with orchestral descriptive work 'The Desert'. Also composed operas, twenty-five string quintets, etc.

DAVID, FERDINAND (1810–73), German violinist and composer – mainly for violin, including five concertos.

DAVIDSBÜNDLER (Ger.), members of the (imaginary) League of David formed by Schumann in opposition to a Philistine attitude to art; hence Schumann's 'Davidsbündler-Tänze' (-Dances) for piano, 1837, revised 1850.

DAVIE, CEDRIC THORPE (b. 1913), Scottish composer (pupil of Vaughan Williams and Kodály), also organist, professor at St Andrews University and writer on music. Composed music for Edinburgh Festival revival (1949) of old Scottish play, *The Three Estates*; other works include piano concerto and many pieces with Scottish associations.

DAVIES, PETER MAXWELL (b. 1934), English composer, pupil of Petrassi in Italy; shows debt to medieval musical techniques e.g. in 'St Michael' Sonata for seventeen instruments; 'PROLATION' for orchestra; cycle of medieval carol-settings and instrumental pieces, 'O Magnum Mysterium'. Has also written String Quartet with an element of performers' improvisation, pieces for child performers, etc.

DAVIES, (HENRY) WALFORD (1869–1941), English musical educator – professor at University of Wales, and first widely popular BBC talker on music; also organist (St George's Chapel, Windsor) and composer of 'SOLEMN MELODY', oratorio 'Everyman', church music, etc. Knighted 1922; Master of the King's Music, 1934.

DAVIS, COLIN (b. 1927), English conductor, formerly clarinettist; musical director of Sadler's Wells Opera 1959–65, appointed principal conductor of BBC Symphony Orchestra from 1967. C.B.E., 1965.

DAVY, JOHN (1763–1824), English composer of song 'The Bay of Biscay', much theatre music, etc.; also organist.

DAVY, RICHARD (d. after 1514), English composer of many motets, part-songs, etc.; organist of Magdalen College, Oxford, 1490–92.

DAWSON, PETER (1882–1961), Australian bass who appeared in opera (Covent Garden, 1909) but became best known in light songs of English 'ballad' type – some of which (e.g. 'Boots' and other Kipling settings) he himself composed under name J. P. McCall.

DE (Fr.), of (for names and phrases beginning thus, see under second word).

DEAD MARCH, any funeral march, especially 'the Dead March in Saul', i.e. from Handel's oratorio 'Saul', 1739.

DEATH AND THE MAIDEN (Ger., *Der Tod und das Mädchen*), title of song by Schubert, 1817; hence nickname of Schubert's string quartet in D minor, 1826, the second movement of which uses part of the song as a theme for variations.

DEATH AND TRANSFIGURATION (Ger., *Tod und Verklärung*), symphonic poem by R. Strauss, first performed 1890.

DEBORAH AND JAEL (It., *Dèbora e Jaele*), opera by Pizzetti, produced at Milan, 1922. Libretto by composer, after the Bible.

DEBUSSY, CLAUDE-ACHILLE (really named Achille-Claude; 1862–1918), French composer, also noted as critic; born near Paris, worked and died in Paris; visited Russia 1872 and elsewhere later. Worked out new outlook on harmony and musical structure, of which the name IMPRESSIONISM reveals its kinship with contemporary visual art; he has affinity also with such poets as Verlaine and Baudelaire, whom he set. Was first pro- then anti-Wagner; his opera 'PELLÉAS AND MÉLISANDE' is unlike any predecessor though seemingly indebted to Mussorgsky for cultivation of natural speech-inflexions. Achieved first marked success with 'THE AFTERNOON OF A FAUN', 1894; had already composed cantata 'THE BLESSED DAMOZEL'. Also wrote 'IBERIA', 'THE SEA', 'NOCTURNES', and other works for orchestra; two books of piano preludes (with picturesque titles) and other piano works including 'Suite bergamasque' (see BERGAMASCA) and 'CHILDREN'S CORNER'; string quartet, violin sonata, cello sonata; music to 'KING LEAR' and 'THE MARTYRDOM OF ST SEBASTIAN'. See also CLAIR DE LUNE.

DECANI (Lat., of the dean), that section of the choir in a cathedral, etc., which is stationed on the south (i.e. dean's) side of the chancel; opposite of CANTORIS.

DECRESCENDO (It., lessening), becoming softer.

DEERING, see DERING.

DEFESCH, WILLIAM (1697–1758), Belgian organist, violinist, cellist, and composer who settled in London, 1731; wrote Mass, oratorios, concertos, songs, etc.

DEGREE, classification of a note with reference to its position in the scale. Thus the notes of the scale of C major (upwards, C–D–E–F–G–A–B–C) are called the 1st, 2nd (etc.) degrees of the scale, returning eventually to the 1st degree, i.e. C. The alternative names for the 1st–7th degrees (major or minor scale) are TONIC, SUPERTONIC, MEDIANT, SUBDOMINANT, DOMINANT, SUBMEDIANT, LEADING-NOTE. Other names are used in the TONIC SOL-FA system.

DEHORS (Fr. outside), sounding prominently – term applied to a melody, etc., which the composer intends should 'stand out' from its surroundings.

DEL MAR, NORMAN (RENÉ) (b. 1919), English conductor; conductor of B.B.C. Scottish Orchestra, 1960–65.

DEL MONACO, MARIO (b. 1915), Italian tenor, known (e.g. in title-role of Verdi's 'OTELLO') at Covent Garden, the Scala, Milan, and the Metropolitan, New York.

DELALANDE, MICHEL RICHARD (1657–1726), French composer and church organist; in service to Louis XIV. Works include ballets and instrumental pieces as well as motets with instrumental accompaniment and other church music. (The name is usually given as Lalande, but Delalande is correct.)

DELANNOY, MARCEL (FRANÇOIS GEORGES) (b. 1898), French composer, formerly painter and architect, and mainly self-taught in music. Works include operas, ballets (among them a contribution to 'JEANNE'S FAN'), symphony, string quartets, songs.

DELDEN, LEX VAN (b. 1919), Dutch composer of chamber and choral music, children's ballets, 'In Memoriam' for orchestra (for the 1953 Dutch flood victims), six symphonies, etc.; also critic.

DELIBES (CLEMENT PHILIBERT) LÉO (not Délibes; 1836–91), French composer, also organist, pupil of Adam. Works include ballets 'COPPÉLIA' and 'SYLVIA' (notably full of musical substance); 'LAKMÉ' and other operas; also Mass, songs, etc.

DELIUS, FREDERICK (baptized Fritz Albert Theodor, 1862–1934), English composer of German descent; born in Bradford. Settled 1889 in France, dying at his home at Grez-sur-Loing near Fontainebleau. Became blind and largely paralysed: FENBY, his amanuensis from 1928, took down some late compositions, e.g. 'SONGS OF FAREWELL', from dictation. Evolving highly personal, somewhat IMPRESSIONIST idiom (related to both Grieg and Debussy), Delius also wrote 'IRMELIN', 'KOANGA', 'A VILLAGE ROMEO AND JULIET', and three other operas; choral-orchestral works including 'APPALACHIA', 'A MASS OF LIFE', 'REQUIEM', 'SEA DRIFT'; orchestral works including 'ON HEARING THE FIRST CUCKOO IN SPRING', 'BRIGG FAIR', 'PARIS', and two pieces called 'Dance Rhapsody'; two wordless choral 'AQUARELLES'; three violin sonatas, violin concerto, piano concerto; many songs (English, French, German, Danish, Norwegian texts), etc.

DELLA CASA, LISA (b. 1919), Swiss soprano, active in opera (especially noted in Mozart and R. Strauss) and in recital.

DELLER, ALFRED (GEORGE) (b. 1912), English counter-tenor, noted in works by Purcell and others written for his type of voice; Britten and others have written specially for him.

DELLO JOIO, NORMAN (b. 1913), American composer (also pianist, organist, and teacher), pupil of B. Wagenaar and Hindemith; influenced by and makes use of Gregorian chant, e.g., in 'New York Profiles' and 'Variations, Chaconne, and Finale' for orchestra. Has also written opera 'The Trial at Rouen' (about Joan of Arc), ballets, harmonica concerto, piano works, etc.

DELVINCOURT, CLAUDE (1888–1954), French composer of mime-cantata 'Lucifer'; dance-poem 'The Offering to Siva', string quartet, etc.; director of the Paris Conservatory.

DEMESSIEUX, JEANNE-MARIE-MADELEINE (b. 1921), French organist, pupil of Dupré; noted recitalist, visiting Britain from 1948. Also composer.

DEMUTH, NORMAN (1898–1968), English composer (former choirboy at St George's Chapel, Windsor), teacher, and writer on music. Works include ballet 'Planetomania', two symphonies, concerto for alto saxophone and military band.

DENT, EDWARD JOSEPH (1876–1957), musicologist, opera translator, professor of music at Cambridge; made an arrangement of 'THE BEGGAR'S OPERA', edited various works by Purcell, etc. Also composer. See also CAT'S FUGUE.

DENZA, LUIGI (1846–1922), Italian composer of 'Funiculi, funiculà' and about 500 other songs; also opera, etc. Settled in London 1879, teaching; died there.

DER (Ger.), (1) the (masc. sing.); (2) of the (fem. sing.).

DERING, RICHARD (also Deering; *c.* 1580–1630), English organist, in service to Charles I's queen; composed church music, canzonets, fancies for viols, etc.; previously studied in Italy.

DES, of the (Fr., pl.; Ger., masc. and neut. sing.).

DESCANT (1) medieval term – see DISCANT. (2) additional part sung (sometimes improvised) above a given melody, e.g. above a hymn-tune; *descant recorder*, see RECORDER.

DESK, an orchestral music-stand; in the strings of an orchestra each desk is shared by two players, so that *first desk only* is an instruction that the particular passage is to be played by the first *two* players only.

DESMOND, ASTRA (b. 1898), English mezzo-soprano who sings in many languages; also writer on the songs e.g. of Grieg and Sibelius. C.B.E., 1949.

DESPRÉS, JOSQUIN (*c.* 1450–1521), Flemish composer – this name, also spelt (by himself) Desprez, being the French version of a Flemish name. Pupil of Ockeghem, and singer at the Papal chapel in Rome. Composed Masses, motets, Stabat Mater, and other church music; also CHANSONS. His work is notable for an expressiveness new at that time – see MUSICA RESERVATA.

DESSAU, PAUL (b. 1894), German composer; works include opera 'The Trial of Lucullus' (libretto by Brecht), in which a piano having metal-covered hammers is used; also music to Brecht's plays, film music, orchestral works. Also conductor. Lived in France and U.S.A. 1933–45.

DÉTACHÉ (Fr.), detached – an instruction to bow the violin, etc., in a particular way. It is the opposite of *lié* (bound) but does not imply *staccato*.

DETT, ROBERT NATHANIEL (1882–1943), American (Negro) composer, conductor, teacher, writer; Canadian-born; pupil of N. Boulanger and others. Works include oratorios, suites for piano, choruses and songs, deriving some influence from Negro folk-music.

DEUTEROMELIA, see PAMMELIA.

DEUTSCH, OTTO ERICH (1883–1967), Austrian musicologist who settled in England after Hitler took Austria, but returned to Austria in 1952; compiled a complete thematic catalogue of Schubert's works (published 1951). These works may now be referred to by their 'Deutsch' (or 'D.') numbers.

DEUTSCHER TANZ, see GERMAN DANCE.

DEUTSCHES REQUIEM, EIN, see GERMAN REQUIEM.

DEUTSCHLAND ÜBER ALLES, see EMPEROR'S HYMN.

DEUX (Fr.), two.

DEVELOPMENT, the section of a movement (e.g. in SONATA-FORM) between the intial statement of themes and their final recapitulation, during which the themes are 'developed', i.e. expanded, modified, combined, broken up, etc.

DEVIL IN MUSIC, see TRITONE.

DEVIL'S TRILL, THE, nickname for a violin sonata in G minor by Tartini, composed about 1714, and having a famous trill in the last of four movements; said to be modelled on a sonata played to Tartini by the Devil appearing in a dream.

DEVIL TAKE HER, THE, comic opera by Benjamin, produced in London, 1931. Libretto by A. Collard and J. B. Gordon: variation on the theme of the dumb wife cured, the devil being later called on to take her – and obliging.

DI (It.), of; for phrases beginning thus, see next word of phrase.

DIABELLI, ANTON (1781–1858), Austrian composer (pupil of Haydn) and publisher. Wrote mainly for the piano, including a waltz on which fifty invited composers each wrote one variation, and Beethoven wrote thirty-three uninvited.

DIABOLUS IN MUSICA, see TRITONE.

DIALECTIC, title of string quartet by A. Bush, 1929. (Title presumably with reference to dialectic as process of fruitful struggle between opposites, according to the Marxist beliefs of the composer.)

DIAMOND, DAVID (LEO) (b. 1915), American composer, pupil of N. Boulanger in Paris. Works – inclined to polyphony and use of the MODES – include six symphonies, violin concerto, 'Rounds' for string orchestra, music to Shakespeare's 'ROMEO and JULIET', choral works, piano pieces, film music.

DIAPASON, the 'basic' tone of the organ, 'open' or 'stopped' according to whether the ends of the pipes are clear or plugged, the 'open' being the louder. Normally of eight-FOOT length: *double diapason*, of sixteen-foot length – see DOUBLE (2). (Other English uses of the term are obsolete, but see following entry.)

DIAPASON NORMAL (Fr.), a standard indication of pitch: A=435 vibrations per second. The now accepted international standard is different: see FREQUENCY.

DIAPHONE, type of organ-stop in which added vibratory apparatus assists loudness.

DIAPHONY, medieval form of combining two melodies; see ORGANUM.

DIATONIC, pertaining to a given major or minor key (opposite of CHROMATIC); so *diatonic scale*, any one of the major or minor scales; *diatonic harmony*, harmony made up predominantly from the resources of the prevailing key, without much use of notes outside its scale; similarly *diatonic discord*, discord arriving from clashes within the key itself.

DIBDIN, CHARLES (1745–1814), singer (at first choirboy), composer, theatrical manager, publisher, author of novels and other literary works. In 1789 he instituted 'table entertainments' at which he recited, sang, and accompanied. Composed 'Tom Bowling' and many other sea songs, and over 100 stage pieces including *Lionel and Clarissa*.

DICHTERLIEBE, see POET'S LOVE.

DICHTUNG (Ger.), poem; *symphonische Dichtung*, SYMPHONIC POEM.

DIXTION, correct and clear enunciation in singing. (This is the recognized meaning in musical contexts, but properly the term should refer to literary skill in using words.)

DIDO AND AENEAS, opera by Purcell, produced in London in 1689 or 1690. Libretto by N. Tate, after Virgil's account of Dido's abandonment by Aeneas and her ensuing suicide. (Purcell's only fully operatic stage work.) See CHACONNE.

DIEPENBROCK, ALPHONS (1862–1921), Dutch composer, mainly of vocal music – Mass, church music, songs (Dutch, German, and French), etc. – also of incidental music to plays. Mainly self-taught. Was also critic.

DIEREN, BERNARD VAN (1884–1936), Dutch-born composer and writer on music, resident in Britain from 1909. Cultivated an individual and often intricate idiom; wrote many songs and several unusual works, e.g. symphony (with voices) on Chinese themes, and a setting for voices and piano of De Quincey's 'Murder as one of the Fine Arts'.

DIES IRAE (Lat., Day of Wrath), a section of the Requiem Mass, the plainsong tune of which is quoted e.g. in Berlioz's FANTASTIC SYMPHONY, Saint-Saëns' DANSE MACABRE, and various works of Rakhmaninov including 'Rhapsody on a Theme of Paganini' for piano and orchestra.

DIES NATALIS, setting by Finzi, 1940, of a Christmas poem by Traherne; for high voice and strings.

DIFFERENTIAL TONE, see RESULTANT TONE.

DIMINISH, (1) to 'lessen' certain intervals; see DIMINISHED; (2) to subject a melody to DIMINUTION.

DIMINISHED, term applied to a type of INTERVAL regarded as a 'lessened' version of a certain other interval. In practice this is a useful term only for (1) *diminished 5th*, e.g. , one semitone less than perfect 5th, and (2) *diminished 7th*, e.g. , one semitone less than minor 7th. In effect the latter sounds as  i.e. as major 6th: but it is distinctive by the intermediate harmony it is presumed to carry, namely 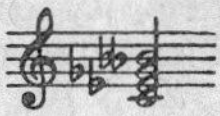, otherwise  (and various other notations); this chord is the *diminished 7th chord* on C, referred to in dance bands, etc., as *C diminished* (abbr. *C dim.*).

DIMINUENDO (It., lessening), becoming gradually softer.

DIMINUTION, the treatment of a melody in such a way as to decrease (usually halving) the time-values of its notes (used e.g. in some fugues).

D'INDY, see INDY.

DINNER ENGAGEMENT, A, comic opera by Berkeley, produced in Aldeburgh, 1954. Libretto by Paul Dehn, the dinner being given by (relatively) impoverished English nobility.

DIOCLESIAN (properly *The Prophetess, or The History of Dioclesian*), play by T. Betterton for which Purcell wrote the music, 1690.

DISCANT, a developed form of the type of medieval part-writing called ORGANUM. The most reliable medieval theorists describe it as essentially a homophonic, measured style.

DISCORD, see CONCORD (of which it is the opposite).

DISJUNCT MOTION, see MOTION.

DISSONANCE, discord (see CONCORD); *Dissonance Quartet*, nickname for Mozart's string quartet in C, K.465 (1785), opening with a passage in which there is a pronounced use of dissonance.

DITAL HARP, obsolete 19th-century English harp-like instrument in which a 'dital' (finger-key, cp. pedal) raised the pitch of some strings, and other strings were played against a finger-board as on a lute.

DITTERSDORF, CARL DITTERS VON (Ditters originally his surname; 1739–99), Austrian violinist and composer, in service to various noble patrons; friend of Haydn and Mozart. Composed symphonies, string quartets, church music, etc.; also operas, including one on 'The Marriage of Figaro' (probably before Mozart's) and one on *The Merry Wives of Windsor* (1797).

DIVERSIONS, alternative term for VARIATIONS.

DIVERTIMENTO (It., an amusement), a not-too-serious work, usually for a small instrumental group, in several movements (e.g. by Mozart).

DIVERTISSEMENT (Fr., an amusement) (1) a musical paraphrase on familiar tunes, or some similar light instrumental work; (2) a danced entertainment of the type of BALLET (1), but being merely a suite of dances not unified by any fundamental idea or connecting story.

DIVINE POEM, THE (Rus., *Bozhestvennaya poema*), orchestral work by Skriabin, also called his symphony no. 3. First performed in Paris, 1905. Illustrates the composer's theosophical ideas and has an explicit literary source. The three movements are entitled 'Struggles – Delights – Divine Play'. Cp. 'POEM OF ECSTASY'; 'PROMETHEUS'.

DIVISI (It.), divided – term used e.g. of the first violins or other string group of the orchestra when they temporarily split into two or more smaller bodies playing different parts.

DIVISION VIOL, see VIOL.

DIVISIONS (1) obsolete term for VARIATIONS because the splitting of the time-values of notes was formerly a common way of making variations; (2) obsolete term for long vocal runs, as in Handel.

DIXIELAND, name given to a style of jazz-playing based on the 'classic' jazz of the pre-1914 era in New Orleans – unsentimental, rather naïvely syncopated, and using small bands of a particular instrumental combination.

DO, the note C (in Latin countries, and formerly elsewhere); cp. DOH.

DOBBS, MATTIWILDA (b. 1925), American (Negro) soprano of high range, the first Negro to win international reputation in opera – Covent Garden, Glyndebourne, the Scala (Milan), etc.

DOBROVEN, ISSAY ALEXANDROVICH (also spelt Dobrowen; 1894–1953), Russian-born composer (pupil of Taneyev) pianist (pupil of Godowsky), and internationally known conductor and opera producer – latterly resident in Sweden; died in Norway.

DOCTOR FAUST, opera by Busoni; completed after Busoni's death by Jarnach and produced in Dresden, 1925. Libretto by composer, on the Faust legend but not based on Goethe's drama.

DOCTOR GRADUS AD PARNASSUM, see GRADUS AD PARNASSUM.

DOCTOR OF MUSIC, the highest musical degree (British, Commonwealth and American; not awarded elsewhere). Abbr. *D.Mus.*, *Mus.D.*, or *Mus.Doc.*

DODECAPHONIC (Gk., *dodeka*, 12), pertaining to the TWELVE-NOTE method of composition. Similarly *dodecaphony*, *-ist*, etc.

DODGSON, STEPHEN (b. 1924), English composer, pupil of R. O. Morris and others. Works include symphony; piano quartet; capriccio for clarinet, harp, and string trio.

DOH, in TONIC SOL-FA, the spoken name for the first degree (tonic) of the scale, written **d**. Cp. DO.

DOHNÁNYI, ERNÖ (he used the German form, Ernst von; 1877–1960), Hungarian pianist and composer of two piano concertos, 'Variations on a Nursery Theme' (same as 'Twinkle, twinkle') for piano and orchestra, two symphonies, three operas, etc. More 'German' in style than his 'nationalist' Hungarian contemporaries, Bartók and Kodály. From 1948 resident in U.S.A.

DOKTOR FAUST, see DOCTOR FAUST.

DOLCE (It.), sweet(ly); *dolcezza*, sweetness.

DOLENTE (It.), sorrowful(ly).

DOLES, JOHANN FRIEDRICH (1715–97), German composer of church music, songs, etc.; pupil of Bach, and appointed in 1756 as Bach's successor in his Leipzig post.

DOLLY, suite of six children's pieces for piano duet by Fauré, 1893; orchestrated for ballet by Rabaud, 1896.

DOLMETSCH, surname of a Swiss (anglicized) family famous for the authentic interpretation of old music and for the revived manufacture of old instruments. See next entry.

DOLMETSCH, CARL (b. 1911), English (French-born) player of the recorder (also of violin and viols); since 1940 director of the Haslemere Festival devoted to old music and founded by his father, Arnold Dolmetsch (1858–1940). Also craftsman, active especially in making recorders in his family's workshops.

DOMESTIC SYMPHONY, see SYMPHONIA DOMESTICA.

DOMINANT, the 5th note of the scale, in relation to the keynote: thus if the key is C (major or minor), the dominant is G. So *dominant seventh*, chord of the (minor) 7th on the dominant (in this case G, B, D, F) resolving normally on the TONIC chord (in this case C major or minor). So also *secondary dominant*, term sometimes encountered as translation of Ger. *Wechseldominante* (literally 'exchange dominant'), meaning 'the dominant of the dominant', e.g. the note D in key C (major or minor).

DOMRA, Russian plucked instrument, usually three-stringed, with convex back like mandolin; made in several sizes and used for folk music, etc. Cp. BALALAIKA.

DON CARLOS, opera by Verdi, produced in Paris, 1867. Libretto (in French) by F. J. Méry and C. du Locle, after Schiller: Don Carlos is the son of Philip II of Spain.

DON GIOVANNI, opera by Mozart, produced (in Italian) in Prague, 1787. Original title, *Il Dissoluto Punito, o sia Il Don Giovanni* ('The Rake Punished, or, Don Giovanni'). Libretto by L. da Ponte, dealing with some of the loves of the character more familiarly known as Don Juan, who is eventually dragged down to hell by a statue. (Cp. 'THE STONE GUEST' and 'ZAMPA'.)

DON JUAN, symphonic poem by R. Strauss, first performed 1889; after a poem by Lenau (1802–50).

DON PASQUALE, comic opera by Donizetti, produced (in Italian) in Paris, 1843. Libretto partly by the composer: Don Pasquale is an old man who loves a young girl and is outwitted.

DON QUIXOTE, symphonic poem by R. Strauss, first performed 1896. After Cervantes, and styled 'fantastic variations on a theme of knightly character'.

DONA NOBIS PACEM (Lat., Give us peace), part of the Mass; also title of cantata by Vaughan Williams (further text from the Bible, Whitman, and John Bright) first performed 1936.

DONATONI, FRANCO (b. 1927), Italian composer of concerto for kettledrums with strings and brass; also of symphony for strings, ballet 'The Fishing Lantern' (*La Lampara*) etc.

DONIACH, SHULA (b. 1905), Russian-born (woman) pianist and composer resident in Britain; has visited Israel and writes works to Hebrew texts in purposefully Hebraic style, etc. – including 'Voices of Jerusalem' for two voices and chamber ensemble.

DONIZETTI, GAETANO (1797–1848), Italian composer; after 1844 suffered mental illness and paralysis. Composed more than sixty operas in a style of characteristic Italian lyricism but also with humour. Some are in French (e.g. 'DAUGHTER OF THE REGIMENT') but most in Italian – including 'DON PASQUALE', 'THE ELIXIR OF LOVE', 'LUCIA DI LAMMERMOOR'. The theory that he was the grandson of a Scot named Don(ald) Izett has been discounted.

DONNA DIANA, comic opera by Rezniček, produced at Prague, 1894. Libretto by composer, after a Spanish comedy; title from the heroine, daughter of the mayor of Barcelona.

DOPO (It.), after(wards).

DOPPEL (Ger.), double. See also DOPPELSCHLAG.

DOPPELSCHLAG (Ger.), equals TURN (musical ornament).

DOPPIO (It.), double; *doppio movimento*, at double the speed (of the preceding section).

DORATI, ANTAL (b. 1906), Hungarian-born, American-naturalized conductor of Minneapolis Symphony Orchestra, 1949–60; BBC Symphony Orchestra, 1963–6. Musical director of the Royal Opera, Stockholm, from 1966. Also composer; arranged the music of J. Strauss the younger for the ballet 'Graduation Ball'. Composed oratorio 'The way of the Cross' (on text by Claudel).

DORIAN MODE, the MODE represented by the white keys of the piano beginning on D.

'DORIAN' TOCCATA AND FUGUE, nickname for a certain Toccata and Fugue in D minor (not the familiar one) by Bach; given because, although in fact in D minor, it was originally written without key-signature, as a work in the Dorian mode and ending on D would be.

DOT, mark in musical notation (1) placed above note, indicating STACCATO; (2) placed after note, indicating that the time-value of the note is to be extended by half; similarly a *double dot* indicates that the time-value is to be extended by half as much again – e.g., ♩..=♩‿♪‿𝅘𝅥𝅯 (But before the double dot was invented, by Leopold Mozart, the single dot might indicate prolongation by an amount greater than half, even by three-quarters – i.e., as much as the double dot now conveys; the performer deduced from the musical context which interpretation was intended.)

DOUBLE, (1) twofold – so DOUBLE BAR; *double chant*, form of ANGLICAN CHANT covering two verses of a psalm for each repetition, instead of one; *double choir*, *double chorus*, choir with a twofold multiplicity of voices (usually two choirs of four parts making eight voice-parts in all); *double concerto*, concerto either with two solo instruments (e.g. Brahms's) or two orchestras (e.g. Martinů's); *double* COUNTERPOINT; DOUBLE-FLAT; *double fugue*, FUGUE with two subjects; DOUBLE-HANDED; *double* HORN; *double organ*, obsolete term for an organ with two manuals, or simply with one manual of full range; DOUBLE-SHARP. So also *double octaves*, *double thirds*, etc. (in piano playing) octaves or thirds played simultaneously in both hands. (2) prefix meaning 'sounding (about) an octave lower'. (This meaning arises because a pipe doubled in length sounds an octave lower: see FOOT.) So DOUBLE-BASS; *double*-BASSOON; *double* DIAPASON. So also *double-bass clarinet*, *double-bass saxophone*, lowest and extremely rare members of the CLARINET and SAXOPHONE families. (3, verb) term alluding to (a) duplication of a melody by several performers: so, e.g., 'the voice-part is doubled by the clarinet and, an octave lower, by the bassoon'; (b) duplication of instruments by one player: so, e.g., 'Berlioz's Fantastic Symphony demands two flutes, the second doubling piccolo', i.e. the second player to play piccolo instead of flute when required. (4, Fr.), a variation, especially in the form of an ornamented version of the theme (cp. DIVISION). See also the following entries.

DOUBLÉ (Fr.), a TURN (musical ornament).

DOUBLE BAR, double perpendicular line marking the end of a composition or of a major division of it; usually but not always placed coincidentally with the single bar-line, and sometimes equipped with 'repeat' marks – see REPEAT. See also BAR.

DOUBLE-BASS, the largest and lowest bowed stringed instrument of the orchestra – also used in dance bands (mainly pizzicato), and occasionally introduced into the military band for concerts; used occasionally in chamber music, very rarely solo. The standard modern instrument has four strings, and a compass from E just over an octave below the bass stave, upwards for nearly three octaves; but five-string instruments, with an extra string sounding B below bottom E, are also found. (In shape and origin, and also in the underhand method of bowing still sometimes seen, the instrument shows its kinship with the VIOLS rather than with the violin and the other modern orchestral stringed instruments.)

DOUBLE-FLAT, indication (notated ♭♭) of the lowering of the pitch of a note by two semitones. (Cp. FLAT.) Its use is necessitated by the 'grammar' of harmony, even though the resultant note, e.g. on the piano, will always have an alternative simpler name – e.g. A♭♭ is G♮, i.e. G natural.

DOUBLE-HANDED (of an instrumentalist) capable of playing two different instruments. (See DOUBLE, 3. But the term does not usually refer to a player skilled merely on different sizes of the 'same' instrument, e.g. flute and piccolo, but to such wider skill as will enable him e.g. to play in a light orchestra on, say, the violin or saxophone as required.)

DOUBLE-SHARP, indication (notated 𝄪) of the raising of the pitch of a note by 2 semitones. (Cp. SHARP.) Its use is necessitated by the 'grammar' of harmony, even though the resultant note, e.g. on the piano, will always have an alternative simpler name – e.g. F𝄪 is G♮, i.e. G natural.

DOUCE(MENT), see DOUX.

DOUX, DOUCE(MENT), sweet(ly).

DOWLAND, JOHN (1563–1626), English lutenist and composer, serving the king of Denmark (1598–1606) and other such patrons; achieved international reputation and had his music published in eight capitals. Became Roman Catholic but later Protestant again. Works are chiefly solo songs with lute, and lute solos; also wrote 'Lachrimae, seven passionate pavans . . . for lute, viols, or violins', etc. Father of Robert Dowland.

DOWLAND, ROBERT (1586–1641), English lutenist (at Charles I's court, succeeding his father, John Dowland), composer, and publisher of an international collection of AYRES.

DOWN IN THE VALLEY, opera by Weill, first performed at Indiana University, 1948. Libretto by A. Sundgaard, a tale of American folk-ballad type: the score incorporates five U.S. folk-songs, and the remainder is composed in that style.

DOWN-BEAT, the downward motion of the conductor's stick or hand, especially as indicating the first beat of the bar; (term therefore also used for) the first beat of the bar, whether or not the piece is being 'conducted'. Cp. UP-BEAT.

DOWN-BOW, the motion of the bow of a stringed instrument when pulled by the player – the opposite (pushing) motion being an *up-bow*.

DOWNES, RALPH (b. 1904), English organist (noted in recital) and designer of organs, e.g. at the Royal Festival Hall; also composer. Worked in U.S.A., 1928–35.

DRAGHI, GIOVANNI BATTISTA (1640–1710), Italian harpsichordist, composer of harpsichord pieces, songs, etc.; settled in London, becoming organist to Charles II's wife, and died there.

DRAGONETTI, DOMENICO (1763–1846), Italian double-bass player who won exceptional fame as a soloist; was also a composer for his instrument, and a friend of Beethoven; settled in London and died there.

DRAMATIC (soprano, tenor, etc.) having powerful voice and a style suitable for forceful operatic roles.

DRAME (Fr.), drama; *drame lyrique*, lyric drama – term used e.g. by Debussy to describe 'PELLÉAS AND MÉLISANDE'.

DRAMMA (It.), drama; *dramma per musica* (drama through music), term frequently used for 'opera' in the 17th and 18th centuries; *dramma giocoso*, comic drama, i.e. (in musical contexts) comic opera – description given by Mozart to 'DON GIOVANNI', despite its non-comic elements.

DRDLA, FRANTIŠEK (1868–1944), Czech violinist and composer chiefly for his instrument, but also of operettas, songs, etc. Known as Franz Drdla.

DREAM OF GERONTIUS, THE, oratorio by Elgar, first performed at Birmingham, 1900. Text, Cardinal Newman's poem (abridged) on a vision of the soul's fate after death.

DREIGROSCHENOPER, DIE, see THE THREEPENNY OPERA.

DRESDEN, SEM (1881–1947), Dutch composer; pupil of Pfitzner, but influenced more by French than by German music. Works, some making use of Dutch folk-music, include two piano concertos, two violin concertos, cantatas (one with brass band), chamber music. Also writer on music, conductor (especially choral), and formerly director of The Hague Conservatory.

DRIGO, RICCARDO (1846–1930), Italian composer of songs, ballet 'Harlequin's Millions' (source of a popular 'Serenade'), etc.; also conductor, holding posts in St Petersburg and elsewhere.

DROIT(E) (Fr.), right, right hand; *main droite* or *m.d.*, with the right hand (e.g. in piano music).

DRONE, pipe(s) sounding note(s) of fixed pitch continuing as a permanent bass on various forms of BAGPIPE; hence, similar effect (*drone bass*) in other forms of music.

DRUM, percussion instrument of many varieties, all having a skin which is stretched over a hollow space and struck – usually with a stick, but cp. BONGO. The KETTLEDRUMS (also called *timpani*) and some TOM-TOMS are tuned to definite notes; most other drums (e.g. BASS, SIDE, TENOR drums) are not. So *drum-head*, the stretched skin which is beaten; *drum-roll*, quick succession of strokes on the drum, the instrument's nearest approach to a sustained sound. See also following entries.

DRUM MASS, nickname for Haydn's Mass in C, 1790, in which kettledrums are unusually prominent.

DRUM-ROLL SYMPHONY, nickname for Haydn's symphony no. 103 in E♭, opening with kettledrum-roll.

DRY RECITATIVE, see RECITATIVE.

DRYSDALE, LEARMONT (1866–1909), Scottish composer of operas (one on Euripides' *Hippolytus*), cantatas, orchestral works, songs, etc., much of this music having Scottish associations.

DU (Fr.), of the.

DUBENSKY, ARKADY (or Arcady; b. 1890), Russian-born violinist and composer who settled in U.S.A., 1921; works include Fugue for eighteen violins, Fantasia on a Negro theme for tuba and orchestra, etc.

DUBOIS (FRANÇOIS CLÉMENT) THÉODORE (1837–1924), French composer of operas, church music, orchestral works, etc. Director of Paris Conservatory 1896–1905, being obliged to resign after the young Ravel had been scandalously excluded – by a jury on which Dubois sat – from entering a fourth time for the French ROME PRIZE.

DUCASSE, ROGER-, see ROGER-DUCASSE.

DUE (It.), two.

DUENNA, THE, play by Sheridan with songs by the elder and younger LINLEY and other composers. On this are based the operas 'The Duenna' by Gerhard (B.B.C. radio production, 1949) and by Prokofiev – libretto (in Russian) by composer and M. Mendelson-Prokofiev, produced in Prague, 1946. The latter is known in Russian as 'The Betrothal in the Monastery' but Sheridan's title is also sanctioned.

DUET, a combination of two performers (sometimes with accompaniment, as is usually implied e.g. by *vocal duet*), or a work for such a combination; *piano duet*, two performers on one piano.

DUETTINO (It.), a little duet.

DUETTO (It.), duet.

DUFAY, GUILLAUME (b. before 1400; d. 1474), Franco-Flemish composer, also singer – in Papal choir at Rome, 1428–37; also canon of the Church. In 1440s, in service to the court of Burgundy. Noted teacher, e.g. of Okeghem. Works include Masses (one on 'L'HOMME ARMÉ'), other church music (some with accompanying instruments), and CHANSONS.

DUKAS, PAUL (1865–1935), French composer – also editor of old music, critic, and teacher. Works – in a very clear texture, tinged with prevailing influences of IMPRESSIONISM – include opera 'ARIADNE AND BLUEBEARD', dance-poem 'THE PERI', descriptive orchestral work 'THE SORCERER'S APPRENTICE', and many piano works. Is said to have been the first major French composer to write a piano sonata.

DUKE, VERNON, see DUKELSKY.

DUKE BLUEBEARD'S CASTLE, see BLUEBEARD'S CASTLE.

DUKELSKY, VLADIMIR (b. 1903), Russian-born composer (pupil of Glière) who settled in New York, 1922. Works include three symphonies, piano concerto, orchestral 'Ode to the Milky Way', etc.; has also written, as *Vernon Duke*, 'April in Paris' and other dance tunes, light theatre music, etc.

DULCIANA, type of soft organ stop.

DULCIMER, instrument (old, but still in use for traditional music e.g. in Eastern Europe) in which strings stretched over a soundboard are struck with hammers; the Hungarian type, sometimes seen in the concert-hall, is the CIMBALOM. (Dulcimer is also commonly but wrongly, used in U.S.A. for a folk instrument of the ZITHER type, i.e. plucked.)

DUMBARTON OAKS CONCERTO, concerto in E♭ for fifteen instruments by Stravinsky, 1938 – title taken from the Washington, D.C., estate of the patron who commissioned it, where also it was first performed. (Title-page of score prints 'Dumbarton Oaks 8-v-38' and then in larger type 'Concerto en mi♭', etc.: 'Concerto' is therefore the real title, 'Dumbarton Oaks' having no more claim to substantive use than has the date.)

DUMKA (Rus., Cz.; pl. *dumky*), a lament of Ukraïnian folk-origin, a movement in which slow and fast tempos alternate – term used by Dvořák, e.g. *dumka* movements in his string sextet and piano quintet. 'Dumky Trio', nickname for Dvořák's piano trio, opus 90, 1891, made up of six thematically independent *dumka* movements in different keys.

DUMKY, see preceding entry.

DUNAYEVSKY, ISAAC (1900–55), Russian composer who also trained as violinist (pupil of Akhron); achieved chief success with popular Soviet songs. Also wrote operettas, ballets, symphonic suite on a Chinese theme, string quintet, etc.

DUNCAN, (ROBERT) TODD (b. 1903), American Negro singer, noted in Negro and other songs and also in opera – e.g. Gershwin's 'PORGY AND BESS'.

DUNHILL, THOMAS FREDERICK (1877–1946), English composer (pupil of Stanford), teacher, and writer on music. Wrote operetta 'Tantivy Towers' (words by A. P. Herbert), many songs; also ballets, symphony, 'Elegiac Variations' in memory of Parry, children's cantatas, chamber music.

DUNI, EGIDIO ROMUALDO (1709–75), Italian-born composer (pupil of Durante) who settled in France, 1757, and died there. Wrote chiefly opera, in both French and Italian: notable practitioner of the OPÉRA-COMIQUE.

DUNSTABLE, JOHN (?–1453), English composer (also mathematician and astrologer) of European repute; spent some time on the Continent. Works, displaying notable melodic invention within smoothly consonant contrapuntal style, include motets and other church music, and three-part secular songs.

DUO (It.), two performers, or a work written for them; *duo-pianist* (U.S.), member of a duo playing on two pianos (not two people on one piano).

DUODECUPLE SCALE (Lat., *duodecim*, 12), a scale of twelve notes, i.e. the ordinary European scale considered as having twelve notes all of equal value as in TWELVE-NOTE music. (This term avoids the use of CHROMATIC, which has harmonic implications foreign to twelve-note practice.)

DUPARC, HENRI, style of name used by Marie Eugène Henri Foucques-Duparc (1848–1933), French composer, pupil of Franck, prevented by illness from working after 1885. Noted for his fourteen songs – two originally with orchestra, and six others with later orchestrated accompaniment – in a warmly-harmonized style often seeming to foretell IMPRESSIONISM. Remainder of his work totals two orchestral pieces, one motet.

DUPLE TIME, time in which the primary division is into 2 or 4 – e.g. 2/4, 4/4 – as distinct particularly from TRIPLE TIME (primary division into 3). Note especially that 6/4 indicates a bar of two dotted minims (𝅗𝅥.+𝅗𝅥.) while 3/2 indicates a bar of three minims (𝅗𝅥+𝅗𝅥+𝅗𝅥) – giving different accents although both total six crotchets.

DUPLET, a pair of notes of equal time-value, written where the number of beats is not capable of simple division by two – e.g. two notes occupying a bar of 3/8, written ♩♩ (with 2 above) (One of the notes may, of course, be replaced by a rest.)

DUPLEX-COUPLER PIANO, see MOÓR.

DUPRÉ, MARCEL (b. 1886), French organist (pupil of Widor) and composer of many organ works, also two symphonies, etc. Noted recitalist. Director of the Paris Conservatory, 1954.

DUR (Ger., hard), equals MAJOR.

DURANTE, FRANCESCO (1684–1755), Italian composer, mainly of

church music; noted as theorist and teacher. Taught Pergolesi, Paisiello, and others.

DURCHFÜHRUNG (Ger., a through-leading), equals DEVELOPMENT.

DURCHKOMPONIERT (Ger., through-composed), term used of a work, especially a song, composed in a continuous form, not repeating itself in successive stanzas – opposite of STROPHIC. (Term also sometimes used to mean 'fully worked out', 'really composed', etc., as distinct from something that seems to proceed merely in patches.)

DUREY, LOUIS (b. 1888), French composer, influenced by Satie; one of the group of 'SIX', but later left it. Works include chamber music, songs, unpublished opera. After Second World War, became 'PROGRESSIST' – writing music deliberately of 'mass' appeal in accordance with Communist doctrine.

DURUFLÉ, MAURICE (b. 1902), French organist and composer, pupil of Dukas and others. Works include Requiem, organ pieces, and three dances for orchestra, but has composed very sparingly.

DUSÍK, see DUSSEK.

DUSK OF THE GODS, alternative translation ('Twilight of the Gods' is more usual) for Wagner's *Götterdämmerung*; see RING.

DUSSEK, Western-Europeanized form of surname used by Jan Ladislav Dusík (1760–1812), Czech pianist and composer. Wrote chiefly for the piano, but also chamber music, theatre music, etc. Pupil of C.P.E. Bach and friend of Haydn. Lived variously in Paris, Hamburg, London, and elsewhere, dying near Paris.

DUTILLEUX, HENRI (b. 1916), French composer of symphony, piano sonata, two-piano works, ballet 'The Wolf', etc. Has worked much for the French radio. Pupil of Büsser and others.

DVOŘÁK, ANTONÍN (1841–1904), Czech composer; 1866–73, viola-player in Czech National Theatre orchestra, conducted by Smetana, who influenced him; 1874, became friend of Brahms. Wrote cantata 'THE SPECTRE'S BRIDE' for use in England, which he visited nine times (Mus.D., Cambridge, 1891). Director of Prague Conservatory, 1891; director of the National Conservatory in New York, 1892–5, composing the 'AMERICAN' string quartet and the symphony no. 9 in E minor ('FROM THE NEW WORLD') at this time. Until recently this was known as no. 5 and the previous four symphonies were numbered in a chronologically wrong order; in addition there are four earlier symphonies of his which remained unpublished at the composer's death and were not numbered. Current practice is to number all chronologically – 1 in C minor ('The Bells of Zlonice'). 2 in B♭, 3 in E♭, 4 in D minor, 5 in F, 6 in D, 7 in D minor, 8 in G, Wrote also SLAVONIC DANCES and SLAVONIC RHAPSODIES in a Czech 'national' style which also appears in, but does not dominate, his other works. These include piano concerto, violin concerto, cello concerto in B minor (and another early cello concerto), cycle of three concert-overtures (see CARNIVAL); ten operas including ARMIDA' and 'THE RUSALKA'; Mass, Requiem; four piano trios, fourteen works for string quartet, a piano quintet, etc. (see 'AMERICAN' QUARTET and DUMKA); piano pieces and many songs and part-songs.

DYKES, JOHN BACCHUS (1823–76), English composer of many hymn-tunes and other church music; was also Anglican clergyman.

DYNAMICS, the gradations of loudness and softness in music.

DYSON, GEORGE (1883–1964), English composer of 'THE CANTERBURY PILGRIMS' and other choral works; also of chamber music, church music, etc. Director of the R.C.M., 1937–52; knighted 1941.

DZERZHINSKY, IVAN (b. 1909), Russian composer (also pianist), pupil of Gnessin. Works include 'Quiet Flows the Don' and 'Virgin Soil Upturned' (from Sholokhov's novels) and other operas; also two piano concertos, orchestral works, theatre and film music, etc.

E

E, note of the scale. So E FLAT (E♭), DOUBLE-FLAT (E♭♭), NATURAL (E♮), SHARP (E♯), DOUBLE-SHARP (E𝄪); *E major*, *E minor*, *etc.* – see MAJOR. So also either (1) in the key of E♭ (major, understood), or (2) indication of a TRANSPOSING INSTRUMENT on which the note written C sounds as E♭ (and correspondingly with other notes) – e.g. the small *clarinet in E♭*, or (colloquially) an *E♭ clarinet*.

E (It.), and.

EAGLES, see SOLOMON ECCLES.

EASDALE, BRIAN (b. 1909), English composer of 'The Sleeping Children' and other operas, piano concerto, film music, etc. Pupil of Armstrong Gibbs and Jacob.

EAST, MICHAEL (*c.* 1580–1648), English composer of madrigals (one in 'THE TRIUMPHS OF ORIANA'), anthems, viol music, etc.

EBERLIN, JOHANN ERNST (1702–62), German organist and composer of church and organ music, etc.

EBONY CONCERTO, work by Stravinsky for clarinet (slang, 'ebony stick') and dance band, augmented by harp; written for Woody Herman's band, and first performed 1946.

ECCLES, JOHN (*c.* 1660–1735), English composer of masque 'The Judgement of Paris' to Congreve's words, also of much other stage music (see SEMELE), songs, etc. Master of the King's Band, 1700. Son of Solomon Eccles.

ECCLES, SOLOMON (also known as Eagles; 1618–83), English musician who burnt his music and instruments on becoming a Quaker about 1660, and later accompanied George Fox to W. Indies.

ECHO ORGAN, a manual (and the apparatus it controls) found on certain large organs, suitable for echo effects – having soft stops, and sometimes pipes at a distance from the main body of pipes.

ECLOGUE, short poem, especially a pastoral dialogue – term sometimes taken over from poetic to musical usage, e.g. as title of the first movement of Ireland's 'Concertino Pastorale' for strings, 1939.

ÉCOLE D'ARCUEIL, see SATIE.

ÉCOSSAISE (Fr.), sort of COUNTRY DANCE cultivated e.g. by Beethoven and Schubert. (Although meaning 'Scottish' it is apparently not of Scottish origin, nor identical with SCHOTTISCHE.)

EDMUNDS, CHRISTOPHER MONTAGUE (also known as Chris Edmunds; b. 1899), English composer (pupil of Bantock), organist, and principal of the Birmingham School of Music since 1945. Works include orchestral and chamber music, and educational pieces.

EDWARDS, RICHARD (*c.* 1523–1566), English composer, also playwright and poet; wrote words of madrigal 'In going to my naked bed', and probably the music of it – as he certainly did to other verse of his own.

EGDON HEATH, symphonic poem by Holst, first performed 1928 – after Hardy's description of a Dorset landscape in *The Return of the Native*.

EGGE, KLAUS (b. 1906), Norwegian composer, pupil of Valen and others. Works, sometimes making use of Norwegian folk-music, include two piano concertos, two symphonies, and chamber music.

EGK, WERNER (b. 1901), German composer of operas, including 'Peer Gynt' (after Ibsen), 'Irish Legend' (after Yeats), 'THE GOVERNMENT INSPECTOR' (after Gogol), and 'Betrothal in Santo Domingo', and of ballet 'A Summer Day' (on themes of Kuhlau and Clementi), orchestral 'French Suite' (based on Rameau), violin concerto, etc.; also conductor. Mainly self-taught.

EGMONT, play by Goethe – for a revival of which, in 1810, Beethoven wrote incidental music, comprising overture (in concert performance combined with 'Triumph Symphony' from the end of the play), four entr'actes, two songs, music for the heroine's death, and one 'MELODRAMA' (in the technical sense). Meulemans has also written an overture to this play (1944).

EICHHEIM, HENRY (1870–1942), American composer (also violinist) who travelled in Japan, China, etc., and incorporated the effects of Oriental music – and sometimes Oriental instruments themselves – into such works as 'Nocturnal Impressions of Peking' and 'Korean Sketch' for chamber orchestra.

EIGHTEEN-TWELVE (1812), concert-overture by Tchaikovsky, 1882, commemorating Napoleon's retreat from Moscow and incorporating the 'Marseillaise', the Tsarist Russian national anthem, and other material. Scoring includes, optionally, cannon and military band.

EIGHT-FOOT (organ stop, etc.), see FOOT.

EIGHTH-NOTE, U.S. term (following the German 'Achtel') for QUAVER, a semibreve being considered as a whole-note.

EIN, EINE (Ger.), one, a. See next word of phrase and also the following entry.

EINE KLEINE NACHTMUSIK (Ger., A Little Night-Music, i.e. a little serenade), work for strings – quintet or small orchestra – by Mozart, 1787. Cp. SERENADE.

EINEM, GOTTFRIED (VON) (b. 1918), Swiss-born Austrian composer of operas including 'Danton's Death' and 'The Trial' (after Kafka), ballet 'Princess Turandot', Concerto for orchestra, Serenade for double string orchestra, chamber music, etc. Was pupil of Blacher, and also studied jazz seriously; formerly opera coach and conductor.

EINLEITUNG (Ger.), introduction, prelude, etc.

EINSTEIN, ALFRED, see KÖCHEL.

EISLER, HANNS (1898–1962), German composer, pupil of Schoenberg; in U.S.A. 1933–48, then returned to (East) Germany. Works, many linked to his Marxist beliefs, include opera 'Goliath', 'German Symphony' (including voices); chamber music; 'Newspaper Cuttings' for voice and piano; film music (and a book on this in English, 1947).

EISTEDDFOD (Welsh), type of Welsh national music festival, or a local emulation of this – or, as in Australia, any competitive music festival, no connexion with Wales being then implied. (Pl. *eisteddfodau* reserved for specifically Welsh contexts.)

EK, GUNNAR (b. 1900), Swedish composer. Works, some with themes from folk music, include three symphonies, 'Swedish Fantasy' for orchestra, choral works, songs, organ music.

EL (Sp.), the. See next word of phrase.

ELECTRA, see ELEKTRA.

ELECTRIC, term used with reference to musical instruments in two senses: (1) where electricity is used to facilitate the use of mechanical parts, e.g. *electric action* on an organ, not affecting the quality of the note produced; (2) where the use of electronic devices such as valves and photo-cells actually determines or affects the quality of the note produced – for this, see ELECTRONIC, which is the better word, although *electric guitar* (see GUITAR) is a standard term.

ELECTROCHORD, trade name of a piano-like ELECTRONIC instrument, in which the sound is picked up electrically, modified (with some controlled variation possible), and heard through loudspeakers.

ELECTRONE, trade name of a type of ELECTRONIC organ. See ORGAN.

ELECTRONIC, term used in music to denote the use of electronic devices (e.g. valves, photo-cells) in the production of sound. Thus an *electronic instrument* usually denotes one which is modelled on some conventional musical instrument but either produces the sound entirely by electronic means (e.g. HAMMOND ORGAN), or produces the sound 'naturally' and then modifies it electronically (e.g. the ELECTROCHORD and the so-called 'electric GUITAR'). The term *electronic music*, however, normally refers not to these but to a type of 'advanced' music (the subject of pioneering chiefly in Germany in the 1950s) in which composers work with sounds electronically produced under laboratory conditions. These sounds are then recorded on tape, and the work is composed as a tape-recording. The process differs from CONCRETE MUSIC in starting with laboratory sound, not sound from the outside world.

ÉLÉGIE, ELEGY (Fr., Eng.), a song of lamentation, especially for the dead, or an instrumental work of similar intention or mood.

ELEGY FOR YOUNG LOVERS, opera by Henze, produced (in German) at Schwetzingen (Germany), 1961; the libretto (originally in English) by W. H. Auden and Chester Kallman concerns a self-centred poet, writer of the 'Elegy' of the title.

ELEKTRA, opera by R. Strauss, produced in Dresden, 1909. Libretto by H. von Hofmannsthal, after Sophocles.

ELGAR, EDWARD (1857–1934), English composer, all but self-taught; Roman Catholic, but was much associated with the Three Choirs Festival (based on Anglican cathedrals). The ENIGMA VARIATIONS and 'THE DREAM OF GERONTIUS' established him, 1899–1900. Had already written song-cycle 'SEA PICTURES'. Later wrote oratorios 'THE APOSTLES' and 'THE KINGDOM' (intended as the first two parts of an uncompleted trilogy); cantata 'THE MUSIC MAKERS'; two symphonies, symphonic study 'FALSTAFF', overtures 'COCKAIGNE' and 'IN THE SOUTH', recitation with orchestra 'CARILLON'; Introduction and Allegro for Strings; violin concerto, cello concerto, chamber music, etc. The SEVERN SUITE for brass band is one of his few post-1919 works. Knighted 1904; Order of Merit, 1911; Master of the King's Music, 1924; baronet, 1931. Evolved a forthright style which won recognition as 'national' (though not indebted to folk-song), and unashamedly wrote 'popular' works such as the five 'POMP AND CIRCUMSTANCE' marches.

ELIAS, German title of Mendelssohn's ELIJAH.

ELIJAH, oratorio by Mendelssohn, first performed at Birmingham, 1846. Words from the Bible.

ELISIR D'AMORE, L', see THE ELIXIR OF LOVE.

ELIXIR OF LOVE, THE (It., *L'Elisir d'amore*), comic opera by Donizetti, produced in Milan, 1832. Libretto by F. Romani: the 'elixir' is a quack-doctor's dose of cheap wine.

ELIZALDE, FEDERICO (b. 1908), Spanish composer and conductor (also pianist), born in the Philippines; studied under Bloch, Falla, and others. Conducted dance bands and, later, symphony orchestras. Works include opera 'Paul Gauguin', piano concerto, violin concerto.

ELLINGTON, DUKE, professional name of Edward Kennedy Ellington (b. 1899), American (Negro) pianist, dance-band leader, and composer of dance music and also of concert works in, or indebted to, the jazz idiom.

ELMAN, MISCHA (German spelling of Russian *Misha*; 1891–1967), Russian-born violinist who visited U.S.A. from 1908 and afterwards settled there (U.S. citizen, 1923), maintaining high international reputation.

ELSNER, JOSEPH (XAVER) (1769–1854), German-Polish composer (twenty-seven operas, etc.), teacher of Chopin at Warsaw Conservatory.

EMBOUCHURE (Fr., used also in English), the position and application of the lips to the mouthpiece of a wind instrument. (In French the word also means the mouthpiece itself.)

'EMPEROR' CONCERTO, nickname (not Beethoven's title) for Beethoven's piano concerto no. 5 in E♭, 1808.

EMPEROR JONES, opera by Gruenberg, produced in New York, 1933. Libretto by composer, after O'Neill's play: Jones is an American Negro railwayman, who after committing murder becomes 'emperor' of a Caribbean island.

'EMPEROR' QUARTET, nickname for Haydn's string quartet in C, op. 76, no. 3 (*c.* 1799), of which the slow movement takes Haydn's own 'Emperor's Hymn' (see next entry) as a theme for variations.

EMPEROR'S HYMN, patriotic hymn by Haydn, 1797, adopted as national anthem in Austria – and later (to words 'Deutschland über Alles') in Germany. See preceding entry.

EN SAGA, see SAGA.

ENCHAINEZ (Fr.), link (them) together – i.e. let the next movement follow its predecessor without a break.

ENCHANTED LAKE, THE (Rus., *Volshebnoe ozero*), symphonic poem by Liadov, 1909 – descriptive, but with no explicit story.

ENCORE (Fr., again), term used in English (though not in French) to mean 'perform it again', or, loosely, to mean 'perform some more'; hence (noun) a repetition or extra piece in response to such demand. (For the current French term, see BIS.)

ENESCO, GEORGES, form of name adopted (primarily for use in France) by George Enescu (1881–1955), Rumanian violinist and composer (also pianist and conductor). Studied in Vienna, and later in Paris with Fauré and Massenet; afterwards mainly resident in France. Distinguished teacher, e.g. of Menuhin. Works include opera, three symphonies, two Rumanian Rhapsodies for orchestra, piano and violin solos.

ENFANCE DU CHRIST, L', see THE CHILDHOOD OF CHRIST.

ENFANT ET LES SORTILÈGES, L', see THE CHILD AND THE SPELLS

EN-GEDI, OR DAVID IN THE WILDERNESS, see CHRIST ON THE MOUNT OF OLIVES.

ENGLISH FINGERING, see FINGERING.

ENGLISH HORN, woodwind instrument of oboe type, but standing a fifth lower than the oboe, and written as a TRANSPOSING INSTRUMENT a fifth higher than sounding; compass from the E below middle C upwards for about two and a half octaves. Used rarely before the 19th-century ROMANTICS but often thereafter in the orchestra – but still rarely in chamber music, as solo instrument, etc. More usually in Britain called *cor anglais*: but the translated form *English horn* is more sensible, is accepted American usage, and corresponds also to use in other languages – Italian *corno inglese*, etc. The Italian name was known before the French and the supposed derivation from Fr. 'anglé' (angled) is wrong: the instrument seems to be called *horn* because of its curved shape and *English* possibly because of its being known from England – Purcell specifies a 'tenor hoboy', i.e. tenor oboe.

ENGLISH OPERA GROUP, an opera company (not full-time) founded 1947 with Britten as its main musical promoter. It performs the small-scale operas of Britten (i.e. those with small orchestras), and other composers' similar work, at the Aldeburgh Festival (Suffolk) and elsewhere.

ENGLISH SUITE, title of six suites for harpsichord by Bach, composed about 1725 – so called apparently because, like Purcell's suites and unlike Bach's own FRENCH SUITES, they have preludes for first movements; and because (according to an inscription over the 1st suite on an early MS. copy) they were 'composed for the English', i.e. presumably for some English patrons.

ENHARMONIC, description of the difference between, e.g., F♮ and E♯, or D♯ and E♭ – i.e., on the piano and other fixed-note instruments, a difference only of notation, not of pitch; and on other instruments, and voices, possibly a very small change of pitch also, as may be required to adjust to new harmony. Hence *enharmonic change*, the change of a note in a performer's part e.g. from D♯ to E♭; and similarly, *enharmonic modulation*, involving such a change, as in the two top notes bracketed here:

ENIGMA VARIATIONS, usual name for Elgar's 'Variations on an Original Theme, for Orchestra', first performed 1899; the word 'enigma' does not occur on the title-page but heads the actual music-type. Each variation 'portrays' a person identified in the score only by initials or a nickname – in one case by three asterisks. No. 9 ('Nimrod', i.e. a hunter, in German *Jaeger*) depicts Elgar's friend A. J. Jaeger of Novello's, his publishers; no. 14 (finale) 'E.D.U.', which quotes some previous variations, represents the composer himself. The naming of the variations is not the only 'enigma': Elgar said that a well-known tune (it has never been identified) 'goes with' his theme.

ENSEMBLE (Fr., together), (1) the quality of teamwork in performance ('their ensemble was poor'); (2) an item in opera for several soloists, with or without chorus; (3) a group of performers – the term implying no fixed number, but not a group so numerous and regularly-constituted as to deserve the name of orchestra or choir.

ENTFÜHRUNG AUS DEM SERAIL, DIE, see SERAGLIO.

ENTR'ACTE (Fr.), interval (U.S., intermission) in a play, opera, etc., or the music to be played in it; cp. ACT TUNE, INTERMEZZO.

ENTRY OF THE LITTLE FAUNS (Fr., *Marche des petits faunes*), piece by Pierné forming part of his ballet 'Cydalise and the Satyr', produced in 1923.

EPICEDIUM (Latinized form of Gk.), dirge; used by Purcell in 'The Queen's Epicedium', Latin elegy for Queen Mary, 1695.

EPISODE, a section in a piece of music considered to have a subordinate role: in particular, (1) in a RONDO, a contrasting section between recurrences of the main theme; (2) in a FUGUE, a section occurring between entries of the subject.

ÉPONGE (Fr.), sponge; *baguettes d'éponge*, drumsticks with sponge head.

EQUAL TEMPERAMENT, see TEMPERAMENT.

EQUAL VOICES, voices of the same kind. (Hence a piece of music 'for equal voices', e.g. for three trebles, as in some school music.) Cp. the following entry.

EQUALI (old It. pl., equal; see preceding entry), instrumental pieces for instruments of the same kind, especially funeral pieces for four trombones, e.g. by Beethoven (1812).

ERBSE, HEIMO (b. 1924), German composer and formerly opera-producer; pupil of Blacher; works include chamber music, ballet, operas.

EREDE, ALBERTO (b. 1909), Italian conductor (pupil of Weingartner), active especially in opera; appeared at Glyndebourne, etc.; at Metropolitan Opera, New York, from 1950.

ERLANGER, CAMILLE (1863–1919), French composer of 'The Polish Jew' and other operas, songs, piano works, etc.

ERLANGER, FRÉDÉRIC D' (1868–1943), French-born composer (also banker, and French baron), naturalized in England. Composed operas including 'Tess' (after Hardy's *Tess of the d'Urbervilles*), violin concerto, etc. No relation of Camille Erlanger.

ERNST (Ger.), serious. (But for Brahms's 'Vier ernste Gesänge' see FOUR BIBLICAL SONGS.)

ERNST, HEINRICH WILHELM (1814–65), Moravian violinist; composer of concertos, etc., for his instrument.

'EROICA' SYMPHONY, name given by Beethoven to his symphony no. 3, 1803–4 – 'Heroic Symphony to celebrate the memory of a great man', i.e. Napoleon. To him, as a liberator, the work was originally dedicated, the inscription being altered when Beethoven learnt with scorn that Napoleon had taken the title of Emperor. See also PROMETHEUS.

'EROICA' VARIATIONS, see 'PROMETHEUS'.

ERWARTUNG, see EXPECTATION.

ESCALES, see PORTS OF CALL.

ESCHER, RUDOLF (b. 1912), Dutch composer (also critic), pupil of Pijper. Was early attracted to French IMPRESSIONISM, and has written symphony in memory of Ravel, French songs, etc.; also concerto for string orchestra, piano solos, etc. Is also poet and painter.

ESPAÑA (Sp., Spain), orchestral rhapsody by Chabrier, first performed 1883, making exuberant use of Spanish tunes.

ESPANSIVA (It., expansive), title ('Sinfonia espansiva') of C. Nielsen's symphony no. 3, composed 1910–11.

ESPLÁ, OSCAR (b. 1886), Spanish composer, influenced by Spanish folk-music; has written ballets, symphonic poems, violin sonata, many piano works, etc. Also writer on music. Settled in Belgium.

ESPOSITO, MICHELE (1855–1929), Italian pianist, conductor, and composer of 'Irish Symphony', overture to Shakespeare's 'Othello', chamber music, etc.; long resident in Dublin.

ESTHER, oratorio by Handel; words by S. Humphreys, after Racine. Originally done as a masque (i.e. with action and costumes) in private, 1720, with the title 'Haman and Mordecai'; expanded and given in concert form in London, 1732, thus becoming the first English oratorio.

ESTINTO (It., extinct), as soft and lifeless as possible.

ESTUDIANTINA (Sp.), piece in the light-hearted manner associated with students.

ET (Fr., Lat.), and.

ETON COLLEGE MANUSCRIPT, a large choir-book in the Library of Eton College, dating from about 1500.

ÉTOUFFEZ (Fr.), damp down, stop the tone, etc. – direction used, e.g. when the sound of a cymbal or harp-string is to be cut short.

ÉTUDE, see STUDY.

ETWAS (Ger.), moderately, somewhat.

EUGENE ONEGIN (Rus., *Evgeny Onegin*), opera by Tchaikovsky, produced in Moscow, 1879. Libretto by composer and K. S. Shilovsky, after Pushkin: named after its caddish, though intendedly tragic, hero.

EUPHONIUM, brass instrument (mainly used in the brass band and military band), equivalent to the tenor TUBA; a TRANSPOSING INSTRUMENT in B♭.

EURHYTHMICS, a system of expressing the rhythmical aspects of music by bodily movement, invented by JAQUES-DALCROZE, who set up an institute for this in Germany in 1910.

EURYANTHE, opera by Weber, produced in Vienna, 1824. Libretto H. von Chezy: the medieval heroine, whose reputation for chastity is challenged and vindicated, gives her name to the work.

EUSEBIUS, see FLORESTAN.

EVANS, GERAINT (b. 1922), Welsh baritone, chiefly noted in opera (Papageno in 'THE MAGIC FLUTE', title-role of 'WOZZECK' etc.): Covent Garden début, 1948. C.B.E., 1959.

EVENING AND TEMPEST, name given to one of a set of three symphonies by Haydn – see MORNING.

ÉVENTAIL DE JEANE, L', see JEANNE'S FAN.

EXERCISE, (1) instrumental study of no artistic value, e.g. a *five-finger exercise* for piano; (2) in the 18th century, a short, keyboard work: D. Scarlatti's early sonatas were published under the Italian equivalent of this name; (3) the composition which candidates are obliged to write for certain university degrees in music.

EXPECTATION (Ger., *Erwartung*), a 'monodrama' (i.e. stage piece for one character) by Schoenberg, composed 1909 but not performed till 1924. In it a woman finds the body of her lover.

EXPOSITION, (1) that part of a SONATA-FORM or similar movement in which the main themes are initially stated before they undergo DEVELOPMENT; (2) in a FUGUE, the initial statement of the subject in all the 'voices' in turn.

EXPRESSIONISM, term borrowed from painting and applied to literature, drama, and music – involving the expression of the artist's state of mind by means of external symbols not necessarily in normal relation to each other. (The precise significance of this in music is somewhat vague, but the term is sometimes applied, e.g. to Schoenberg, especially as conveying the opposite of IMPRESSIONISM, as practised by Debussy.)

EXTEMPORIZE, equals IMPROVISE.

EXTENSION ORGAN, equals UNIT ORGAN.

EXTRAVAGANZA (It., *stravaganza*, anglicized), 19th-century English type of stage entertainment with music, in the form of farce or burlesque, often harnessing new words to known tunes.

F

F, note of the scale. So F FLAT (F♭), DOUBLE-FLAT (F♭♭). NATURAL (F♮) SHARP (F♯), DOUBLE-SHARP (F𝄪); *F major*, *F minor*, etc. – see MAJOR. So also *in F*, either (1) in the key of F (major, understood), or (2) indication of a TRANSPOSING INSTRUMENT on which the note written C sounds as F, and correspondingly with other notes – e.g. *trumpet in F*, or (colloquially) an *F trumpet*. So also *F-clef*, clef indicating the position of the F below middle C – the BASS clef being now the only such clef used.

f, symbol in TONIC SOL-FA notation for the fourth degree (subdominant) of the scale, pronounced *fah*.

f, abbr. of *forte* (It., loud); hence, as indications of increasingly greater loudness, *ff*, *fff*, etc. – sometimes in even greater aggregations.

f-HOLE, name given to a hole approximately in the shape of an *f*, of which there are two cut in the belly of a violin, etc., for the sake of the sound.

F.R.A.M., F.R.C.M., F.R.C.O., F.R.M.C.M., Fellow of the Royal Academy of

Music; College of Music; College of Organists; Manchester College of Music.

F.T.C.L., Fellow of Trinity College of Music, London.

FZ (abbreviation of It. *forzando*), less frequently encountered equivalent of *sf* – see SFORZANDO.

FA, the note F (in Latin countries, and formerly elsewhere); cp. FAH.

FABURDEN, FAUXBOURDON, term having various meanings, especially in church music – originally a style of composition in a particular harmonic idiom, with the melody at the top; in modern usage the term signifies (1) a four-part harmonization of a hymn having the tune in the tenor, or (2) a treble part added above a hymn-tune, i.e. a DESCANT. (The term literally means 'false drone'; *faburden* is a good English form, but the French term is also used in English.)

FAÇADE, 'entertainment' by Walton (first publicly performed 1923) for reciter and six instrumentalists, to satirical poems by Edith Sitwell declaimed in notated rhythm; also the title of two orchestral suites and a ballet (produced 1931) with music arranged from this.

FACILE (Fr., It.), easy. So *facilità* (It.), ease, fluency; also a simplified version, e.g. of a solo passage written for virtuoso performers and brought within more modest capacities.

FADO (Port.), type of Portuguese folk-song, mainly urban and properly having a particular rhythm and binary form.

FAGOTT, FAGOTTO (Ger., It.), BASSOON.

FAH, in TONIC SOL-FA, the spoken name for the fourth degree (subdominant) of the scale, written f. Cp. FA.

FAIR AT SOROCHINTSY, THE, see SOROCHINTSY FAIR.

FAIR MAID OF PERTH, THE (Fr., *La Jolie Fille de Perth*), opera by Bizet, produced in Paris, 1867. Libretto by J. H. Vernoy de St-Georges and É. Adenis, after Scott's historical novel of 15th-century Scotland.

FAIR MAID OF THE MILL, THE (Ger., *Die Schöne Müllerin*), song-cycle by Schubert, 1823, to twenty poems by W. Müller about a fruitless courtship.

FAIRFAX, see FAYRFAX.

FAIRY QUEEN, THE, an adaptation of Shakespeare's *A Midsummer Night's Dream, produced* 1692, for which Purcell wrote the music.

FALKNER, (DONALD) KEITH (b. 1900), English bass singer, director of the Royal College of Music from 1960.

FALL, LEO (1873–1925), Austrian composer of 'The Dollar Princess' and other operettas.

FALL RIVER LEGEND, ballet with music by M. Gould, produced in New York, 1948. Fall River is where the Lizzie Borden parricide case took place in 1892; the ballet deals with her psychological motivations, and the score alludes to hymns, etc., of that period.

FALLA, MANUEL DE (1876–1946), Spanish composer, also pianist. Won first major success with opera 'Life is Short' (*La vida breve*), produced 1913; later wrote ballets 'THE THREE-CORNERED HAT' and 'LOVE, THE SORCERER'. Much influenced by Spanish folk-music in these and other works – e.g. 'NIGHTS IN THE GARDENS OF SPAIN', and 'Fantasia Bética' (i.e. Andalusian Fantasy) for piano; but less so in some other works including puppet-opera 'MASTER PETER'S PUPPET SHOW', and harpsichord concerto, the latter showing NEO-CLASSICAL tendency. Other works include songs, various piano pieces, and a few works for guitar (see HOMAGE). From 1938 resident in Argentina, where he died: his opera 'La Atlántida' (i.e. the fabled continent of Atlantis) was completed after his death by E. Halffter.

FALSE RELATION(S), English term of which the American equivalent is the more sensible – see CROSS-RELATION(S).

FALSETTO (It.), kind of singing (or speech) produced by adult males in a register higher than their normal utterance: this is the standard type of voice-production used by the male ALTO voice and is sometimes specified (generally as comic effect, e.g. imitating women) in other voices.

FALSTAFF, works by several composers, after Shakespeare, including (1) opera by Verdi, produced at Milan, 1893 – libretto by A. Boito, based on *The Merry Wives of Windsor*; (2) symphonic study by Elgar, first performed, 1913 – after *King Henry IV* and *King Henry V*. See also THE MERRY WIVES OF WINDSOR.

FAMILY, term used to group instruments of similar nature and tone-quality – even if there are significant differences in shape (e.g. the saxophone family) or even if they do not all carry the same name (e.g. the 'violin family' of violin, viola, cello, and double-bass).

FANCIULLA DEL WEST, LA, see GIRL OF THE GOLDEN WEST.

FANCY, term used in England in the 16th and 17th centuries for FANTASY (2).

FANDANGO (Sp.), Spanish dance in triple time, probably of South American origin; accompanied normally by guitar, castanets, etc.

FANFARE, (1) a flourish for trumpets (or other instruments imitating them), usually by way of a proclamation or introduction; so *fanfare* TRUMPET, instrument designed for such ceremonial purpose; (2) (Fr.), a brass band.

FANTAISIE, FANTASIA, FANTASIE (Fr., It., Ger.), see FANTASY.

FANTASTIC SYMPHONY (Fr., *Symphonie Fantastique*), symphony by Berlioz, 1830, subtitled 'Episodes in the life of an artist' – with a programmatic basis derived from Berlioz's own despairing love for the actress Harriet Smithson.

FANTASTIC TOYSHOP, THE (Fr., *La Boutique fantasque*), ballet with music arranged by Respighi from the 'SOIRÉES MUSICALES' and other pieces by Rossini; produced in London, 1919.

FANTASY (or, borrowed from Italian, *fantasia*), term of various musical meanings, but nearly always associated with the idea of the 'free' play of the composer's imagination, as distinct from adherence to 'set' forms. Notable senses are – (1) a mood-piece or character-piece of a 19th-century ROMANTIC kind, e.g. Schumann's 'Fantasy-pieces' (Ger., *Fantasie-Stücke*) for piano, 1837; (2) a contrapuntal piece, normally in several sections, for one player (keyboard) or several (e.g. viols) current in the 16th and 17th centuries; an alternative name in this sense was *fancy*, and the spelling *phantasy* was used when the form was revived in 20th-century English chamber music; (3) a piece compounded of known tunes; so *fantasy on*, e.g. an opera, i.e. built from tunes contained in the opera; (4) term used in the phrase *free fantasy* or *free fantasia* as a synonym for DEVELOPMENT, e.g. in SONATA-FORM.

FARANDOLE (Fr.), a dance of Provence, accompanied by pipe and tabor – properly in 6/8 time, which the so-called *farandole* in Bizet's THE GIRL FROM ARLES is not, though it is based on an authentic Provençal tune.

FAREWELL SYMPHONY, nickname of Haydn's symphony no. 45 (in the unusual key of F♯ minor), 1772, in which the music of the last movement ends in such a way that the players may leave their stands one after the other, only two violins eventually remaining. This is said to have been a hint to Haydn's patron, Prince Esterházy, that the orchestra deserved a holiday.

FARJEON, HARRY (1878–1948), English composer of operettas, piano concerto, songs, etc.

FARMER, JOHN, English 16th–17th century organist and composer – dates unknown, but moved from a Dublin organistship to London in 1599. Noted for madrigals; wrote also psalm tunes, a musical treatise, etc.

FARNABY, GILES (*c.* 1560–*c.* 1600), English composer, living in London. Wrote music for virginals, including pieces with picturesque titles, e.g. 'A Toy', 'Giles Farnaby's Dream'; also canzonets, madrigals, psalm tunes.

FARRANT, RICHARD (d. 1580 or 1581), English organist (St George's Chapel, Windsor) and composer of anthems and other church music; also of incidental music for plays which he produced with choirboys.

FARRUCA, energetic Andalusian dance – used, e.g., by Falla for the Miller's Dance in 'THE THREE CORNERED HAT'.

FARWELL, ARTHUR (1872–1952), American composer, pupil in Europe of Humperdinck, Pfitzner, and Guilmant; studied American Indian music and derived some influence from it. Composed symphonic, choral, and chamber works, etc., and was also teacher and critic.

FASANO, RENATO (b. 1902), Italian conductor, also pianist, composer, and since 1960 director of the St Cecilia Conservatory, Rome; founder-conductor of the Virtuosi di Roma, chamber ensemble specializing in old Italian music, in 1947.

FASCHINGSSCHWANCK AUS WIEN, see CARNIVAL JEST FROM VIENNA.

FAURÉ, GABRIEL (URBAIN) (1845–1924), French composer (also organist); director of the Paris Conservatory, 1905–20, teacher of Ravel and others. Cultivated delicately-balanced idiom expressed mainly in small forms – wrote many piano solos, 'DOLLY' for piano duet, many songs, including song-cycle 'La Bonne Chanson', and other song-cycles; also two piano quartets, and other chamber music. Wrote also Requiem; orchestral works including 'PAVANE' (with optional chorus); Ballade for piano and orchestra (originally for piano alone); incidental music to 'PELLÉAS AND MÉLISANDE', and other music for the French and English stage.

FAUST, opera by Gounod, produced in Paris, 1859. Libretto by J. Barbier and M. Carré, after Goethe's drama. For other works on the Faust legend (all after Goethe, unless stated), see THE DAMNATION OF FAUST, DOCTOR FAUST, MEPHISTOPHELES, and the following entries. Incidental music has also been written to Goethe's play itself, e.g. by Diepenbrock.

FAUST, opera by Spohr, produced in Prague, 1816. Libretto by J. K. Bernard – without reference to Goethe's *Faust*, at that time not complete.

FAUST OVERTURE, A, orchestral work by Wagner, 1839, referring to Goethe's drama but intended for independent concert performance (originally conceived as the first movement of a symphony on Faust).

FAUST SYMPHONY, A, symphony by Liszt (with choral ending), after Goethe; first performed 1857, revised 1880. In three movements respectively on Faust, Gretchen, and Mephistopheles, the final chorus however being non-Mephistophelian.

'FAUST', EPISODES FROM LENAU'S, two orchestral works by Liszt, first performed 1861 – the second is the MEPHISTO WALTZ, no. 1. After a German poem on Faust by Lenau (1802–50).

'FAUST', SCENES FROM GOETHE'S, concert work by Schumann (overture and six other numbers) for soloists, chorus, and orchestra, completed 1853.

FAUXBOURDON, see FABURDEN.

FAVOLA D'ORFEO, LA, see ORPHEUS.

FAYRFAX, ROBERT (1464–1521), English composer of motets, Masses, and songs; organist of St Albans Cathedral. As a member of the Chapel Royal, attended Henry VIII to his meeting with Francis I of France on the Field of the Cloth of Gold, 1520, when the English and French choirs sang together. Cp. SERMISY.

FEIERLICH (Ger.), solemnly, exaltedly.

FEINBERG, SAMUEL EVGENYEVICH (1890–1962), Russian composer and pianist, pupil of Skriabin and Miaskovsky; has written songs, many piano solos, three piano concertos, with some debt to Russian folk-music.

FELDPARTIE, FELDPARTITA (Ger.), 'field suite', i.e. suite for open-air performance by a military band – cp. PARTITA. (Haydn wrote six.)

FEMININE, term used in certain musical contexts to imply (unjustly?) relative weakness – so, e.g., the 'second subject' in SONATA-FORM is sometimes said to have feminine character as being less assertive than the first subject. So also *feminine cadence*, *feminine ending*, in which the final chord is reached on a 'weak' beat of the bar instead of a strong beat as usual – e.g. the end of 'The Vicar of Bray'. (Where the final chord on a weak beat merely repeats a chord first reached on a strong beat, e.g. at the end of 'What shall we do with the drunken sailor?', the ending still remains 'masculine'.)

FENBY, ERIC (WILLIAM) (b. 1906), English composer who acted as amanuensis to the blind and paralysed Delius from 1928, taking down some of his late works from dictation. Also arranger of Delius's music (see, e.g., AQUARELLE) and himself a composer – overture 'Rossini on Ilkla Moor', etc.

FERGUSON, HOWARD (b. 1908), Northern-Irish composer, pianist, and teacher, resident in London. Works, cultivating straightforward and predominantly lyrical style, include Partita for orchestra, octet for wind and strings (also for string orchestra, as a 'Serenade'), five Bagatelles and other piano solos; songs including cycle 'Discovery' (poems by Denton Welch).

FERMATA (It.), the PAUSE, 𝄐

FERNANDEZ, OSCAR LORENZO (1897–1948), Brazilian composer and conservatory director. Works, in an idiom recognized by his compatriots as national, include opera 'Malazarte' (Master of the Evil Arts), and other music indebted to Brazilian folk-lore – e.g. 'Batuque' (Brazilian dance) for orchestra; also chamber music, piano solos, songs, etc.

FERRABOSCO, surname of Italo-English musical family, principally the two following.

FERRABOSCO, ALFONSO (1543–88), Italian composer of motets, madrigals, etc.; intermittently resident in London, for a time court musician to Elizabeth I, but returned finally to Italy, 1578. Father of the following.

FERRABOSCO, ALFONSO (1575–1628), English composer of Italian descent (son of preceding); court musician to James I, composer of masques, ayres, fantasies for viols, etc.

FERRIER, KATHLEEN (1912–53), English contralto – noted in recital (Bruno Walter accompanied her), oratorio, etc., and opera; many works of Britten, including the title-role of 'THE RAPE OF LUCRETIA', were written for her. C.B.E., 1953. Achieved unique reputation, particularly in Britain; died of cancer.

FERROUD, PIERRE OCTAVE (1900–36), French composer, pupil of Schmitt, killed in a motor accident in Hungary; also critic. Works include symphony, piano solos, opera 'Surgery' (i.e. dentistry, after a Chekhov story). Contributed to 'JEANNE'S FAN' (ballet).

FESCH, see DEFESCH.

FESTIN DE L'ARAIGNÉE, LE, see THE SPIDER'S BANQUET.

FESTING, MICHAEL CHRISTIAN (1680–1752), English violinist and composer, pupil of Geminiani, member of the King's band and director of the Italian Opera in London. Wrote cantatas, symphonies, works for violins, etc.

FÊTES (Debussy), see NOCTURNES.

FÉVRIER, HENRI (1875–1957), French composer of eight operas (including 'Gismonda' produced at Chicago, 1919), songs, etc.; pupil of Massenet and Fauré.

FIBICH, ZDENĚK (1850–1900), Czech composer (also conductor and critic) who studied in Leipzig and Paris. Composed operas, including 'The Tempest' (after Shakespeare); MELODRAMAS (in the technical sense); many piano works; symphonic poems; orchestral serenade 'At Twilight' of which the well-known 'POEM' is a movement.

FIDDLE, violin – term used either colloquially or referring to the violin's function as a folk or 'popular' instrument. (In the scherzo of Mahler's symphony no. 4 a solo violin with its strings tuned a tone higher than normal is directed to play 'like a fiddle' – *wie ein Fidel* – indicating 'folk' manner.) So *bass fiddle*, colloquial term for double-bass – but see GRAINGER for an eccentric use.

FIDDLE FUGUE, nickname for an organ fugue in D minor by Bach, arranged from an earlier (1720) version for violin solo.

FIDEL (Ger.), see FIDDLE.

FIDELIO, *or Married Love* (Ger., *Fidelio, oder Die Eheliche Liebe*), Beethoven's only opera, with libretto by J. Sonnleithner. Produced in Vienna, 1805; revised version, 1806; further-revised version, 1814, with new overture now known as 'Fidelio'. See also GAVEAUX and LEONORA. ('Fidelio' is the male name assumed by the heroine, Leonora, in her rescue of her husband from prison.)

FIELD, JOHN (1782–1837), Irish pianist and composer, pupil of Clementi in London; settled in St Petersburg in 1803, toured Europe from there, and died in Moscow. Invented the name and style of the NOCTURNE, taken over by Chopin. His work, admired e.g. by Schumann and Liszt, includes twenty nocturnes for piano, seven piano concertos, and chamber music.

FIERY ANGEL, THE (Rus., Ognenny Angel), opera by Prokofiev, composed 1919–27, first staged at Venice, 1955; libretto by the composer, after Bryusov's novel, involves witchcraft and religious hysteria in the 16th century. (The opera is also known as 'The Flaming Angel', 'The Angel of Fire', etc.)

FIFE, term historically meaning a kind of high-pitched flute; but today's military 'drum and fife' band includes low-pitched flutes as well as high ones – none, however, identical with the orchestral flute and piccolo.

FIFTEENTH, organ stop of DIAPASON tone sounding two octaves

above the note played – i.e. fifteen steps (of the diatonic scale) above, counting both the extreme notes.

FIFTH, an interval in melody or harmony, reckoned as taking five steps in the (major or minor) scale – counting the bottom and top notes. A *perfect fifth* is the distance e.g. from C up to G; a semitone less gives the *diminished fifth* (e.g. C up to G♭), and a semitone more gives the *augmented fifth* (e.g. C up to G♯). (For *consecutive fifths* and *hidden fifths*, 'prohibited' intervals in certain types of composition, see CONSECUTIVE.)

'FIFTHS' QUARTET, nickname for Haydn's string quartet in D minor (no. 2 of op. 76, 1797–8), because of the opening melodic leaps of a fifth. The minuet movement is known as the 'Witches' Minuet' (Ger., *Hexenmenuett*) from its eerie character.

FIGARO, see THE MARRIAGE OF FIGARO. (As a character, he also occurs in 'THE BARBER OF SEVILLE'.)

FIGLIA DEL REGGIMENTO, LA, title given in Italian usage to Donizetti's French opera 'THE DAUGHTER OF THE REGIMENT'.

FIGURE, a short musical phrase, especially one that is recognizable and repeated.

FIGURED BASS, a particular kind of CONTINUO bass, practised especially in the 17th and 18th centuries, and also used today, e.g. in academic training and as a kind of harmonic shorthand. Figures with a bass-note indicate the distance above that bass-note of the other notes which are to be sounded. E.g. if the key is C major, and the bass-note is C, the figure 5 would indicate G, and 5♯ would indicate G♯: but the choice of the particular octave in which this G or G♯ is to be placed is left to the musicianship of the performer. Various abbreviations and other conventions are also used. (The 'CHORD-SYMBOLS' used in modern dance music, though similar in being a kind of shorthand, are not the same. They are named after chords – major, minor, augmented, etc. – irrespective of which note of these chords comes in the bass; *figured-bass* symbols are invariably relative to a particular bass note.)

FILLE DU RÉGIMENT, LA, see THE DAUGHTER OF THE REGIMENT.

FIN (Fr.), end.

FINAL, (1, Eng.) the note on which the modal scale ends (see MODE), analogous to the keynote of the major or minor scale; (2, Fr.) FINALE.

FINALE (It., final; but used in English as follows), (1) the last movement of a work in several movements; (2) an ensemble ending an act of an opera – so *first finale*, *second finale*, etc., referring to Acts I, II, etc.

FINE (It.), end – term sometimes occurring in the middle of music as notated, in conjunction with some instruction at the end of the music-type to go back to an earlier point and proceed from there to the point where *fine* occurs.

FINE, IRVING (b. 1914), American composer, pupil of N. Boulanger in

Paris; also conductor. Works, tending to NEO-CLASSICISM, include Toccata Concertante for orchestra, Partita for wind quintet.

FINGAL'S CAVE, see HEBRIDES.

FINGER, GOTTFRIED (or Godfrey; 17th–18th centuries), Moravian composer who worked in England under James II's patronage until 1702, then in Germany; wrote operas and other stage music, some of it in English, and various instrumental pieces.

FINGERING, (1) the use of the fingers in playing an instrument; (2) the indication on paper of which fingers are to be used for which notes – so (in piano-playing) *Continental fingering*, numbering the thumb as 1 and the other fingers as 2–5, as opposed to (obsolete) *English fingering*, in which the thumb was signified by + and the other fingers as 1–4.

FINLANDIA, orchestral work by Sibelius, first performed 1900 – of patriotic intent, but not using folk-music as material.

FINZI, GERALD (1901–56), English composer, mainly of vocal works including 'Let Us Garlands Bring' (song-cycle to poems by Shakespeare), and 'DIES NATALIS' (high voice and strings). Also wrote clarinet concerto, etc. Contributor to 'A GARLAND FOR THE QUEEN'.

FIORITURA (It., a flowering; pl. *-re*), 'decoration' of a melody by ornaments – sometimes added by the performer, e.g. in 17th- and 18th-century Italian opera.

FIPPLE, the obstructive block of wood which canalizes the air in the instrumental species called the *fipple flute* – of which the chief example is the RECORDER.

FIREBIRD, THE (Rus., *Zhar Ptitsa*), ballet (after a Russian fairy-tale) with music by Stravinsky, produced in Paris, 1910; source of orchestral suite 1911, and of revised versions of this in 1919 and 1947. See also LIADOV.

FIREWORKS MUSIC (otherwise *Music for the Royal Fireworks*), suite by Handel for wind band, performed 1749 at the official London celebration of the Peace of Aix-la-Chapelle. Afterwards Handel added string parts, and the work is now normally given (in excerpts) in arrangements (especially that of Harty) for full modern symphony orchestra.

FIRST, term implying in an orchestra (e.g. *first trombone*) a position of leadership as well as (usually) a part higher in pitch; but in a choir (e.g. *first basses*) implying only a higher-pitched part, not leadership. See also following entries.

FIRST INVERSION, see INVERSION.

FIRST SUBJECT, see SONATA-FORM.

FIRST-MOVEMENT FORM, term sometimes used for SONATA-FORM.

FISCHER, EDWIN (1886–1960), Swiss pianist, also conductor (and simultaneous conductor-pianist, particularly in Bach); noted teacher, and also writer on music. International career; resident mainly in Germany and Switzerland.

FISCHER, FRIEDRICH ERNST, see FISHER, F. E.

FISCHER-DIESKAU, DIETRICH (b. 1925), German baritone, of unsurpassed authority in recitals of German song from the 1950s; has also a very large operatic repertory – from the Count in THE MARRIAGE OF FIGARO to the central figure of ELEGY FOR YOUNG LOVERS.

FISHER, F. E. (full name and dates unknown), presumed English composer, also violinist and cellist, active in London between 1748 and 1773. Works include trio-sonatas (two violins and keyboard continuo). May be identical with Friedrich Ernst Fischer, a German composer known to have worked in Holland.

FISHER, SYLVIA (GWENDOLINE VICTORIA) (b. 1910), Australian soprano, singing with the Covent Garden Opera, English Opera Group, etc.

FISTOULARI, ANATOLE (b. 1907), Russian-born conductor ('prodigy' conductor at 7) who has worked much in England and U.S.A., but served in French army in Second World War; much associated with ballet.

FITELBERG, GRZEGORZ (1879–1953), Polish composer (symphony, violin sonatas, etc.), and conductor of Polish radio orchestra; father of Jerzy Fitelberg.

FITELBERG, JERZY (1903–51), Polish composer of two piano concertos, two violin concertos, five string quartets, etc.; from 1940 resident in U.S.A., dying there. Shows influence of Stravinsky.

FITZWILLIAM VIRGINAL BOOK, early 17th-century English collection of 297 pieces for virginals by various (mainly English) composers in manuscript; named after Viscount Fitzwilliam (1745–1816), into whose hands it came. Published 1899.

FIVE, THE, see MIGHTY HANDFUL.

FIVE TUDOR PORTRAITS, 'choral suite' by Vaughan Williams for contralto, baritone, chorus, and orchestra, to poems by Skelton; first performed 1936.

FLAGEOLET, obsolete high six-holed wind instrument (of RECORDER type) used e.g. in Handel's 'ACIS AND GALATEA'; *double flageolet*, instrument of two such pipes side by side, often seen in 'pastoral' illustrations. The terms *flageolet-notes* (Eng.), *flageolets* (Fr.), *Flageolette* (Ger.), meaning HARMONICS on a stringed instrument, refer to the supposed resemblance of these thin-sounding notes to those of the flageolet.

FLAGSTAD, KIRSTEN (MARIE) (1895–1962), Norwegian dramatic soprano internationally celebrated for stage performances of Wagner's heroines – gradually retiring from these, however, during early 1950s; also known in some other opera roles (e.g. Dido in Purcell's 'DIDO AND AENEAS') and in recital, particularly in German and Norwegian songs.

FLAM, two-note figure in side-drum playing, in the rhythm ♫. –*open flam* or *closed flam* according to whether the first or second note falls on the accented beat.

FLAMENCO (Sp.), type of Spanish, particularly Andalusian, song (*cante flamenco*), with various sub-types named after districts – *malagueña*, *sevillana*, etc.; often danced to. (The term is properly applied only to songs of more recent origin than the '*cante* HONDO', and is less predominantly sad.) So also *flamenco style* in guitar-playing, indicating a suitably forceful style different (and with different finger-technique) from the 'classical' style.

FLAMING ANGEL, THE, see FIERY ANGEL.

FLAT, term indicating a lowering in pitch – either (1) indeterminately, as when a singer is said to sing flat, by mistake; or (2) precisely by a semitone, as represented by the sign ♭; so 'B♭' (B flat), the note a semitone lower than B♮ (B natural); so also, e.g., C♭ – a notation which is sometimes called for through adherence to the 'grammar' of music, though on e.g. the piano the note is identical with B♮ (B natural). So DOUBLE-FLAT; *flat keys*, those having flats in their key-signatures; *in three flats*, in the key of E♭ major or C minor, the key-signature of which is three flats (and similarly with other keys); *flattened seventh* (U.S., *flatted seventh*), the lowering of the seventh degree of the scale by a semitone. See also next entry.

FLAT TWENTY-FIRST, in a MIXTURE stop on the organ, a rank sounding three octaves less one tone above the note struck. (The interval of three octaves less one tone equals twenty-one steps of the diatonic scale with the top note flattened.)

FLATTERZUNGE (Ger.), flutter-tongue (see TONGUE).

FLAUTANDO, FLAUTATO (It.), direction to player of the violin, etc., to bow over the finger board in order to produce a thin, special tone supposedly like that of a flute (It., *flauto*).

FLAUTO (It., pl. *-i*), flute. Since the period of Haydn this has meant the ordinary side-blown FLUTE, i.e. the transverse flute (*flauto traverso*); its small size is the *flauto piccolo*, or little flute – commonly called PICCOLO. However, in preceding periods *flauto* alone may mean the RECORDER, Bach for instance writing *flauto traverso* in full (or just *traverso*) when he wants not the recorder but the side-blown flute; similarly *flauto piccolo* in Bach (the word *traverso* omitted) means a small-size recorder, not the 'piccolo' of current usage. For *flauto d'amore*, see under FLUTE.

FLAUTIST, see FLUTIST.

FLEBILE (It.), tearful, plaintive.

FLEDERMAUS, DIE (Ger., The Bat), operetta by J. Strauss the younger, produced in Vienna, 1874 – Strauss's most successful stage work. Libretto by C. Haffner and R. Genée: the 'bat' has the flimsiest connexion with the plot, being merely the fancy-dress costume used by one of the characters on a previous occasion. The work has been given in Britain, U.S.A., and elsewhere under many titles – 'The Gay Rosalinda' (after the leading lady), 'The Merry Countess', 'Champagne Sec', etc. – and filmed as 'Oh, Rosalinda!' (1955).

FLEXATONE, instrument which is a kind of superior version of the 'musical SAW'; like the saw it has a steel blade which is put under varying tension (by thumb-pressure) to produce different notes, but it is shaken (not bowed) to make it vibrate. A part of it, imitating an Armenian folk-instrument, occurs in Khachaturian's piano concerto (first performed 1937).

FLICORNO, name of a family of brass instruments similar to SAXHORN family, used in Italian military bands.

FLIEGENDE HOLLÄNDER, DER, see FLYING DUTCHMAN.

FLIES, J. BERNHARD, see WIEGENLIED.

FLIGHT OF THE BUMBLE-BEE, THE, orchestral interlude occurring in Rimsky-Korsakov's opera 'The Legend of Tsar Saltan' (1900), in which a prince turns into a bee and stings his villainous aunts. Has been arranged and misarranged as a virtuoso display for various solo instruments.

FLOOD, THE, 'musical play' by Stravinsky for singers, speakers and orchestra, produced on American television, 1962; text from the York and Chester miracle plays. See also NOYE'S FLUDDE.

FLORID, term descriptive of melody that is full of ORNAMENTS – whether such are written in by composer or, as common e.g. in 17th- and 18th-century Italian opera, intended to be added at the taste of the performer.

FLOS CAMPI (Lat., flower of the field), suite by Vaughan Williams for viola, small orchestra, and wordless chorus, first performed 1925; based on the Song of Solomon.

FLOTHUIS, MARIUS (b. 1914). Dutch composer, influenced by Pijper but mainly self-taught; also critic. Has written concertos for piano, violin, flute, horn; Capriccio for string orchestra; string quartet, songs, etc.

FLOTOW, FRIEDRICH VON (1812–83), German composer who studied in Paris, and worked there and in Vienna and elsewhere. Wrote operas in French, Italian, and German – the German ones including 'MARTHA' and 'Alessandro Stradella' (see STRADELLA). Composed also ballets, chamber music, etc.

FLOURISH, (1) a fanfare; (2) decorative musical figuration.

FLOYD, CARLISLE (b. 1926), American composer, also university teacher; works include operas 'Susannah', 'Wuthering Heights,' 'The Passion of Jonathan Wade' and 'Markheim'; piano pieces, etc.

FLUE-PIPE, organ pipe into which the air is made to enter directly, as into a flute or recorder (not striking a vibrant tongue or REED, as in a reed-pipe).

FLÜGEL (Ger., wing), a grand piano (i.e. a wing-shaped piano) or a harpsichord so shaped. See also FLUGELHORN.

FLUGELHORN, type of brass instrument with valves, made in various sizes. (Properly *Flügelhorn*, in German, but in British brass-band usage spelt and pronounced with simple 'u'.) The one used in British brass bands is the alto in B♭, having the same compass as the cornet in B♭: neither this nor other sizes of the instrument are commonly found in other types of musical combination, but one occurs in Vaughan Williams's Ninth Symphony. – Cp. SAXHORN.

FLUTE, (1) general name for various types of woodwind instruments without reeds, including nose-blown and other primitive instruments; *English flute*, *German flute*, old English names for the instruments now respectively called RECORDER and simply 'flute' – see next definition; (2) a type of side-blown woodwind instrument (see preceding definition) coming into standard use in the 18th century and mechanically improved since then (now sometimes made of metal, not wood): used in the orchestra and military band, also occasionally as solo instrument and in chamber music. Compass from middle C upwards for about three octaves. Other sizes of this instrument in current use are (a) the PICCOLO; (b) the various sizes used in a military 'drum and fife' band; (c) the *alto flute*, pitched a fourth or fifth lower than the standard instrument, and sometimes miscalled the *bass flute* – specified in some works by e.g. Ravel and Stravinsky, and functioning as a TRANSPOSING INSTRUMENT in G. Long obsolete is the *flûte d'amour* or *flauto d'amore* (Fr., It.,) pitched a minor third below the standard flute. The *concert flute* is a name for the standard-sized flute to distinguish it from other sizes. (3, obsolete usage, e.g. 17th-century), RECORDER.

FLUTE-À-BEC (Fr., beaked flute), RECORDER.

FLUTIST, player of the flute. (This is the older and obvious term, the current American musical usage, and fully recognized by English dictionaries: it has a clear superiority over the Italian-derived *flautist*, though the latter is in commoner musical usage in Britain.)

FLUTTER-TONGUE, see TONGUE.

FLYING DUTCHMAN, THE (Ger., Der Fliegende Holländer), opera by Wagner, produced in Dresden, 1843; libretto by composer; about the legendary accursed sailor redeemed by love.

FOERSTER, JOSEF BOHUSLAV (1859–1951), Czech composer who worked for some time in Hamburg and Vienna; also critic. Composed Masses, religious cantatas, biblical opera; also other operas (one on *The Merchant of Venice*), five symphonies, songs, and choral works.

FÖLDES, ANDOR (b. 1913), Hungarian pianist, pupil of Dohnányi, resident chiefly in U.S.A. since 1939; also composer and author.

FOLÍA, LA (Sp., also *La Follia*, It.), the name originally of a dance ('The Folly') of Portuguese origin, and hence the name of a particular tune used for the dance. This tune enjoyed an extraordinarily wide currency, especially in Renaissance times and especially as the subject of variations. It is particularly known from a set of variations written on it by Corelli in a sonata for violin and harpischord, 1700.

FOLK-MUSIC, -SONG, -TUNE, terms implying that the work concerned has been transmitted aurally among 'the people' from one generation to the next, and can be ascribed to no particular composer. As this definition suggests, (1) a folk-song must be, or have been, 'popular', but not every 'popular' song is a folk-song; (2) folk-song flourishes among a 'primitive' population, where music does not generally take a written form; (3) because of aural transmission, a folk-song is likely to exist in several differing versions. Folk-song, although 'national' in character, has tended to show wide international similarities: in particular it has preserved the MODES longer than normal 'composed' music. But it is arguable that certain 'composed' and written-down songs, e.g. Stephen Foster's, have in a sense become folk-songs – i.e. they have been transmitted aurally, they circulate in several versions, and the composer's name is unknown to many who know the songs. (Note that the above definition of folk-songs, etc., does not necessarily coincide with the use of parallel words in other languages: e.g. *Volkslied* (Ger.) takes in a wider variety of traditional popular song.)

FONTANE DI ROMA, see THE FOUNTAINS OF ROME.

FOOT, unit of length used to measure the length of a vibrating air-column; hence, a measure of pitch – because, e.g., an air-column eight feet long vibrates twice as fast as an air-column sixteen feet long, and so sends out a note one octave higher. Hence – *8-foot C*, the C two lines below the bass stave, sounded by a vibrating air-column (e.g. an open organ-pipe) approximately eight feet long; *16-foot C*, the C below this; *4-foot C*, the C above 8-foot C, and so on in proportion. So organ stops are classified by what sound will issue if the note representing 8-foot C is struck. An *8-foot stop* will sound the note itself; a *16-foot stop* will sound the note an octave below, a *32-foot stop* the note two octaves below; a *4-*, *2-*, *1-foot stop* will sound the note one octave, two octaves, three octaves, respectively above 8-foot C. These stops will have similar effects on all other notes, and thus by simultaneous use of several stops the player can sound a melody in various octaves at choice. (This terminology is sometimes used, by analogy, of other instruments, as when a double-bass is said to provide '16-foot tone' to a cello part, i.e. doubling the cello part an octave below.)

FOOTE, ARTHUR WILLIAM (1853–1937), American organist and composer of cantatas (one on Longfellow's *Hiawatha*), orchestral suites, organ and piano works, etc. Also teacher and writer of textbooks.

FORCE OF DESTINY, THE (It., *La Forza del destino*), opera by Verdi, produced (in Italian) at St Petersburg, 1862. Libretto by F. M. Piave – a tale of tragic intrigue in which a curse takes its long-range effect.

FORD, THOMAS (?1580–1648), English lutenist and composer of ayres (with lute), madrigals, anthems, dances, etc.; musician to Charles I.

FORGOTTEN RITE, THE, 'prelude' for orchestra by Ireland, 1913; no explanation of the title is given on the score, but it is known to be connected with the Channel Islands.

FORLANA, FORLANE (It., Fr.), old Italian dance in 6/8 time.

FORM, the layout of a piece of music considered as a succession of sections. A simple song may thus be said to have a *form* consisting of, say, one line, another line, the first line repeated, then another line; while a more involved piece may be said to have a *form* corresponding to one of various basic types –see, e.g., BINARY, TERNARY, FUGUE, PASSACAGLIA, RONDO, SONATA-FORM, VARIATIONS; or such a piece may be said to be 'free' in form, i.e., unrelated to such a 'set' type. Note that *form* as thus conventionally defined takes in only the 'horizontal' aspects of music and not the 'vertical' (harmony, counterpoint), and does not deal fully with rhythm; it would be better (and more analogous to terminology in, e.g., painting) if *form* were to be defined as taking in these also, i.e. as concerned with the totality of significant relationships between notes.

FORMALISM, a supposed fault in composition for which Russian composers have been denounced by Soviet officialdom at various times – e.g. Prokofiev, Shostakovitch, and others in 1948; the apparent implication is that the music concerned has been over-intellectually conceived with undue emphasis on 'form' as distinct (supposedly) from 'content'. There usually seems an added implication that the music is over-discordant and uncritically pursues modernity for its own sake.

FORTE, FORTISSIMO (It.), loud, very loud (abbr. *f*, *ff*; quite commonly *fff* and even greater aggregations are used to indicate still greater loudness).

FORTEPIANO, an early Italian name meaning the same as PIANOFORTE. Its use in English to denote the late 18th-century piano is arbitrary and affected. (*Fortepiano* is, however, the standard Russian word for the normal instrument.)

FORTNER, WOLFGANG (b. 1907), German composer (also conductor and teacher); since Second World War, influenced by TWELVE-NOTE method. Works include Lutheran church music; Latin oratorio 'The Sacrifice of Isaac' (with forty solo instruments including 'jazz trumpets' and 'jazz trombones'); concertos for various instruments; organ works; opera 'Blood Wedding' (after Lorca's play).

'FORTY-EIGHT, THE', or '*Forty-Eight Preludes and Fugues*' see THE WELL-TEMPERED CLAVIER.

FORZA DEL DESTINO, LA, see THE FORCE OF DESTINY.

FOSS, LUKAS (surname originally Fuchs; b. 1922), German-born American composer; after study in Paris, settled in U.S.A., 1937, and became pupil of Hindemith. Also pianist (formerly with Boston Symphony Orchestra). Works include operas 'The Jumping Frog' (after Mark Twain) and (for television) 'Griffelkin'; biblical cantata (for one voice) 'The Song of Songs'; 'Recordare' for orchestra (after Gandhi's assassination); two piano concertos, symphony. In 1957 formed a chamber ensemble employing improvisation on principles somewhat analogous to those of jazz.

FOSTER, ARNOLD (WILFRID ALLEN) (b. 1898), English composer and conductor, much associated with the revival and arrangement of English folk-music; pupil of Vaughan Williams.

FOSTER, STEPHEN COLLINS (1826–64), American composer, almost entirely self-taught. Composed mainly songs to his own words, including 'The Old Folks at Home', 'Camptown Races', and other 'plantation songs' (i.e. of the black-faced minstrel-show type) which became among the world's best-known songs – often with some alteration of the original tunes; also 'drawing-room' songs, e.g. 'Jeanie with the Light Brown Hair'. Died poor and an alcoholic.

FOUNTAINS OF ROME (It., *Fontane di Roma*), an orchestral work by Respighi in four sections each 'depicting' a different fountain; first performed 1917. Cp. PINES OF ROME.

FOUR BIBLICAL SONGS, song-cycle for bass and piano by Brahms, 1896, his last work but one. ('Four Serious Songs' is a literal translation of the Ger. *Vier ernste Gesänge*, but a less revealing one.) The piano accompaniment has been orchestrated, e.g. by Sargent.

FOUR BOORS, THE, see THE SCHOOL FOR FATHERS.

FOUR SAINTS IN THREE ACTS, opera (in four acts) by V. Thomson, produced in Hartford, Conn., 1934 – with all-Negro cast. Libretto by Gertrude Stein, with saints (far more than four) and without normal 'plot'.

FOUR SEASONS, THE (It., *Le Quattro Stagioni*), a set of four concertos by Vivaldi, published 1725, for violin and orchestra 'depicting' birds, storms, falls on the ice, etc., as indicated on score. (Also the title of H. Hadley's symphony no. 2. See also 'THE SEASONS', by Haydn.)

FOUR SERIOUS SONGS, see FOUR BIBLICAL SONGS.

FOUR TEMPERAMENTS, THE, (1) title of symphony no. 2, 1902, by C. Nielsen (Dan., *De fire temperamenter*), each of the 'temperaments' having one movement; (2) title of Hindemith's Theme and Variations for piano and strings, 1940, each 'temperament' taking charge for one variation. (The reference is to the 'temperaments' thought in medieval times to be the dominant factor in a man's character – choleric, phlegmatic, melancholic, sanguine.)

FOUR-FOOT (organ stop, etc.), see FOOT.

FOURNIER, PIERRE (b. 1906), French cellist, internationally prominent as soloist and (e.g. at the Edinburgh Festival) in chamber music.

FOURNITURE (Fr.), equals FURNITURE (organ stop).

FOURTH, an interval in melody or harmony, reckoned as taking four steps in the (major or minor) scale, counting the bottom and top notes. Hence, *perfect fourth*, the distance, e.g., from C up to F; one semitone more gives the *augmented fourth*, e.g. C up to F♯. (The *diminished fourth*, one semitone less than the perfect, is little used, being virtually equivalent – e.g. on the piano – to the major THIRD: but note its inclusion, as F♯–B♭, in the so-called 'mystic chord' which SKRIABIN compounded entirely of various fourths.)

FRA DIAVOLO, *or The Inn at Terracina* (Fr., . . . *ou L'Hotel de Terracine*), comic opera by Auber, produced in Paris, 1830. Fra Diavolo (It., Brother Devil), is a character modelled on a celebrated Italian brigand and renegade monk who died in 1806.

FRACTIONAL TONE, equals MICROTONE.

FRANÇAIX, JEAN (b. 1912), French composer (also pianist), pupil of N. Boulanger and others; had a piano suite published at 9. Works, cultivating clarity (and often brevity) of style, and influenced by Stravinsky, include piano concertino (1934) and concerto (1936); symphony for strings, 'Beach', and other music for ballet; Serenade for twelve instruments (also used as ballet with title 'A la Françaix'), chamber music; operas.

FRANCESCA DA RIMINI, (1) 'symphonic fantasy' by Tchaikovsky, first performed 1877 – after Dante, who narrates her tragic love and her fate in hell (Tchaikovsky originally intended an opera on this subject); (2) title of operas on this subject by Goetz, Rakhmaninov, Zandonai, and others, and of a symphonic poem by H. Hadley.

FRANCESCATTI, ZINO (b. 1905), French violinist (father Italian-born); made public appearances from age 5. For a time pursued legal studies, but became internationally known virtuoso.

FRANCK, CÉSAR AUGUSTE (1822–90), Belgian composer, son of a German mother; studied at Paris Conservatory and settled in Paris in 1844. Was also organist (eventually at the church of Ste Clotilde, Paris) and noted teacher. Exponent of cyclic form (use of the same theme in more than one movement or section of a work), e.g. in Symphonic Variations for piano and orchestra, violin sonata. Also evolved notably individual harmonic language, much given to CHROMATICISM. Other works include Symphony; 'THE ACCURSED HUNTSMAN', 'THE JINNS', and other symphonic poems; piano quartet and other chamber music; piano and organ works; many songs; religious cantatas including 'The Beatitudes' and 'The Redemption'; three operas (one unperformed and unpublished).

FRANCŒUR, FRANÇOIS (1698–1787), French violinist, court musician, and composer of operas, ballets, violin sonatas, etc.

FRANKEL, BENJAMIN (b. 1906), English composer, also noted teacher; formerly café pianist, dance-band violinist and orchestrator, etc. Has composed several works with Jewish allusions, e.g. violin concerto (in memory of 'the six million', i.e. Jews whose deaths were caused by the Nazis). Other works include 'Mephistopheles' Serenade and Dance' (for the National Youth Orchestra), three symphonies, string trio, four string quartets, much film music.

FRANZ, ROBERT, pen-name of Robert Franz Knauth (1815–92), German composer, chiefly of more than 250 songs – also of church music, etc. Through deafness and a nervous disease, ceased to compose in 1868.

FRASER-SIMSON, HAROLD (1878–1944), English composer of light opera 'Toad of Toad Hall', musical comedy 'The Maid of the Mountains', children's songs to A. A. Milne's poems, etc.

FRAUENLIEBE UND -LEBEN, see WOMAN'S LOVE AND LIFE.

FREDERICK THE GREAT (Friedrich II, 1712–86), King of Prussia, amateur flutist and composer – especially of music with prominent flute parts. While C. P. E. Bach was in his service, J. S. Bach visited him in 1747 and later dedicated to him 'THE MUSICAL OFFERING'.

FREE COUNTERPOINT, see COUNTERPOINT.

FREE FANTASIA, name sometimes given to the DEVELOPMENT section of a movement, e.g. in SONATA-FORM.

FREISCHÜTZ, DER (Ger., The Marksman with Magic Bullets), opera by Weber, produced in Berlin, 1821, with libretto by F. Kind; the rustic hero is involved in black magic.

FRENCH HORN, see HORN.

FRENCH OVERTURE, see OVERTURE.

FRENCH SIXTH, type of 'augmented sixth' chord (see AUGMENTED) distinguished by the intermediate intervals of the chord – e.g. (reading upwards) D♭, F, G, B. (Cp. GERMAN SIXTH, ITALIAN SIXTH – the reason for the names is not known.)

FRENCH SUITE, title given to each of six suites for harpsichord by Bach, composed about 1722; unlike Bach's 'ENGLISH SUITES' they have no preludes, but the supposition that they represent a characteristically French style has not been universally accepted.

FREQUENCY, term in acoustics for the number of complete vibrations undergone by an air-column or a resonating body in one second. As frequency increases, the pitch of the note sounded is raised, so pitch can be defined by frequency: by international agreement, 1939, the A commonly used for tuning (i.e. that above middle C) is fixed at a frequency of 440. See PITCH.

FRESCOBALDI, GIROLAMO (1583–1643), Italian composer and organist – at Antwerp, then (1608–28) at St Peter's, Rome, where a chronicler reports an audience of 30,000 listening to him. Wrote toccatas, fugues, ricercari, etc., for organ and harpsichord, influencing German and other music; also motets, madrigals, etc.

FRET, name given to each of the strips of wood or metal fixed on the fingerboard of, e.g., guitar, viols, lute (but not the violin family). The player presses his finger against a fret to shorten the length of string vibrating. So *fretted* instruments, those fitted with frets.

FRETTA (It.), haste; *non in fretta*, not hurrying the pace. Cp. AFFRETTANDO.

FRICKER, PETER RACINE (b. 1920), English composer, pupil of R. O. Morris and Seiber; formerly also orchestrator for dance bands, etc.; director of music at Morley College (London), then (1965) professor of music at Santa Barbara, California. Writes in a highly dissonant idiom (indebted both to Bartók and to TWELVE-NOTE methods) using very close-worked counterpoint. Works include three symphonies; 'Prelude, Elegy and Finale' for strings; two piano concertos; two violin concertos (no. 1 with chamber orchestra, no. 2

properly 'Rapsodia Concertante'); two string quartets, wind quintet; songs and piano works.

FRICSAY, FERENC (1914–63), Hungarian conductor, pupil of Kodály. Conductor of West Berlin Radio, later operatic musical director in W. Berlin (1951–2, 1961–3) and Munich.

FRID, GEZA (b. 1904), Hungarian pianist and composer of a piano concerto (with chorus), string quartets, etc.; resident in Holland.

FRIML, RUDOLF (b. 1879), Czech composer who settled in U.S.A., 1906, and won success with 'Rose Marie' and other musical plays; also composer of a piano concerto, etc., and himself a pianist.

FROBERGER, JOHANN JACOB (1617–67), German organist and composer for organ and harpsichord; pupil of Frescobaldi; visited England, 1622.

'FROG' QUARTET, nickname of Haydn's string quartet in D, op. 50, no. 6 (1787), with a 'croaking' theme in the finale.

'FROM A HOUSE OF THE DEAD' (Cz., *Z Mrtvého domu*), opera by Janáček, produced in Brno (posthumously) 1930; text by composer, after Dostoievsky's novel of a Siberian prison-camp. (Also known as 'From *the* house', etc., the Czech language having no definite or indefinite article.)

FROM BOHEMIA'S FIELDS AND GROVES (or 'Meadows and Forests', etc.), see MY COUNTRY.

FROM MY LIFE (Cz., *Z mého zivota*), title of the first of Smetana's two string quartets; in E minor, 1876. The high E in the finale depicts 'the fatal whistling in my ear in the highest register which in 1874 announced my deafness'. (The German title *Aus meinem Leben* is only a translation from Czech, and there is no point in its use outside German-speaking countries.) The quartet has been arranged for full orchestra by G. Szell – in this version, first performed 1941.

FROM THE NEW WORLD (Cz., *Z nového svéta*), subtitle of Dvořák's symphony in E minor, composed in U.S.A. and first performed in New York, 1893; no. 9, but formerly called 'no. 5' (see DVOŘÁK). Some of its tunes allude to idioms of U.S. Negro folk-music, but without any direct quotation.

FROTTOLA (It., pl. *-e*), light Italian song for several voices with the melody at the top, flourishing about 1500; set to poems of one particular metre of which successive stanzas were sung to repetitions of the same music.

FRUMERIE, GUNNAR DE (b. 1908), Swedish pianist and composer; works include Symphonic Variations (on a Swedish folk-tune), two piano concertos, two violin concertos, opera, piano solos. Sometimes writes in classic dance-forms – saraband, etc.

FRY, WILLIAM HENRY (1813–64), American composer – opera 'Leonora', 1845, reckoned the first notable American opera. Also critic.

FUGA, FUGE (It., Ger.), equal FUGUE. (The Italian orginal means 'flight'.)

FUGATO (It.), fugued, i.e. suggestive of the style of FUGUE though not actually constituting a fugue.

FUGHETTA (It.), a little FUGUE.

FUGUE a type of contrapuntal composition for a given number of PARTS or 'voices' (so called, whether the work is vocal or instrumental). Hence *fugue in three voices, a four-part fugue*, etc. The essential feature of a fugue is the entries of all the voices successively in IMITATION of each other. The opening entry is in the tonic key and is called the *subject*; the imitative entry of the next voice, in the dominant, is called the *answer*; similarly with the entries of subsequent voices (if any) alternately. Commonly there are several complete entries of all voices (with the order changed) in the course of a fugue; the complete entries are separated by *episodes*. Commonly also each voice having announced the *subject* or *answer* passes to another fixed thematic element called the *countersubject* – the countersubject being heard in the first voice simultaneously with the answer in the second voice, etc. But the great masters of fugue such as Bach (see, e.g., 'THE ART OF FUGUE' and 'THE WELL-TEMPERED CLAVIER') do not confine the fugue to a strict pattern, though time-wasting academic theorists have done so. For a further distinction, see ANSWER. See also preceding and following entries.

FUGUING TUNE, type of 18th-century American hymn-tune, practised and perhaps originated by Billings – in which there is occasional primitive IMITATION between parts.

FULEIHAN, ANIS (b. 1901), Cyprus-born American composer; settled in U.S.A. 1914. Also pianist and conductor. Works include two-piano concerto, THEREMIN concerto, 'Three Cyprus Serenades' for orchestra, ballets, chamber works, songs in English and French. After the Second World War, became director of the Beirut (Lebanon) conservatory.

FULL ANTHEM, anthem (in the Anglican church) sung by the full choir throughout, without soloists.

FULL ORCHESTRA, an orchestra of the four usual sections (strings, woodwind, brass, percussion) and of normal concert-hall strength.

FULL ORGAN, direction that the organ should be played at full strength. Owing to the construction of the instrument and of the human ear, this does not necessarily imply the use of all the stops.

FULL SCORE, see SCORE.

FULLER, DONALD (b. 1919), American composer, pupil of B. Wagenaar, Copland, and Milhaud. Works include symphony; songs; sonatina for oboe, clarinet, and piano.

FUNDAMENTAL, FUNDAMENTAL NOTE, the primary or 'parent' note of the HARMONIC SERIES.

FUNEBRE, FUNÈBRE (It., Fr.), of a funeral. So *marcia funebre, marche funèbre*, funeral march.

FUNERAL MARCH OF A MARIONETTE (Fr. *Marche funèbre d'une*

marionette), work of humorous intent by Gounod – piano solo and piano duet versions published 1873, orchestral version later.

FUNERAL MARCH SONATA, nickname for Chopin's piano sonata in B♭ minor, completed 1839, having a funeral march as its third movement.

FUOCO (It.), fire; *con fuoco*, with fire.

FÜR (Ger.), for.

FURIANT (Cz.), quick Czech dance with changing rhythms – though some of Dvořák's movements so entitled do not change in rhythm. (The word is not connected with 'fury'.)

FURNITURE, type of MIXTURE stop on the organ.

FURTWÄNGLER, WILHELM (1886–1954), German orchestral and operatic conductor, chiefly in Berlin and Vienna, touring widely elsewhere; first visited London 1924. Also composer of two symphonies, etc.

FUTURISM, attempt, particularly by the Italian poet Marinetti and by RUSSOLO, at 'a great renovation of music through the Art of Noises' – first mooted 1909 and persisting in Italy at least until the 1920's. Special 'noise instruments' (e.g. exploders, thunderers, and whistlers) were invented, composed for, and performed on.

FUX, JOHANN JOSEPH (1660–1741), Austrian composer of eighteen operas, much church music, etc.; organist; and especially known as theorist and author of a highly influential treatise on counterpoint called 'GRADUS AD PARNASSUM'.

G

G, note of the scale. So G FLAT (G♭), DOUBLE-FLAT (G♭♭), NATURAL (G♮), SHARP (G♯), DOUBLE-SHARP (G𝄪); *G major*, *G minor*. MAJOR, so also *in G*, either (1) in the key of G (major, understood), or (2) indication of a TRANSPOSING INSTRUMENT on which the note written C sounds as G (and correspondingly with other notes) – e.g. *horn in G* (obsolete), *alto flute in G*; note, however, that the bass trombone is sometimes spoken of as being 'in G' because G is its FUNDAMENTAL, but the music for it is written at the pitch at which it sounds. So also *G-clef*, clef indicating the position of G above middle C, i.e. the TREBLE clef; *G-string*, string of an instrument tuned to the note G, especially the lowest string of a violin. (For the so-called 'Air on the G string' see AIR.)

G.P., abbr. of GENERAL PAUSE.

GABRIELI, ANDREA (*c.* 1510–86), Italian composer, pupil of Willaert at St Mark's, Venice, where he later became chief organist. Works include motets, madrigals, organ pieces. Pupils included Giovanni Gabrieli (his nephew). No relation of Domenico Gabrieli.

GABRIELI, DOMENICO (*c.* 1655–90), Italian cellist and composer of eleven operas, etc. No relation of the more famous Gabrielis, Andrea and Giovanni.

GABRIELI, GIOVANNI (1557–1612), Italian composer, pupil of his uncle (Andrea Gabrieli) whom he succeeded as chief organist of St Mark's, Venice, 1585. Works include 'Sacred Symphonies' and other church music for voices with instruments, often using antiphonal groups; music for brass ensembles; organ works. Teacher of Schütz.

GADE, NIELS VILHELM (1817–90), Danish composer (opera, choral works, eight symphonies, overture 'Echoes from Ossian', etc.) and conductor. Studied at Leipzig and was much influenced by Mendelssohn, though Danish 'national' traits exist in his earlier works.

GAGNEBIN, HENRI (b. 1886), Belgian-born composer of Swiss parents resident in Switzerland, and head of the Geneva Conservatory since 1925. Has composed oratorios, symphony, etc.

GAILLARD (Fr.), equals GALLIARD.

GÁL, HANS (b. 1890), Austrian-born composer and musicologist, resident in Scotland from 1938; lecturer at Edinburgh University, 1945. Works include two symphonies, 'Pickwickian Overture', piano concerto, violin concerto, eight German operas.

GALANT (Fr., Ger.), courtly – term used of an 18th-century style distinguished by formal elegance and clarity (rather than by intense feeling), practised e.g. by C. P. E. Bach and influencing e.g. Mozart.

GALANTIEREN, GALANTERIES (Ger., Fr.), in the classical SUITE, those numbers (e.g. minuet, polonaise) whose inclusion was optional, not obligatory.

GALILEI, VINCENZO (1520–91), Italian composer of vocal and instrumental music; lutenist; musical theorist; contributor to the current of ideas from which opera eventually resulted. Father of the astronomer Galileo Galilei.

GALLIARD, lively dance at least as old as the 15th century, usually but not always in 3/2 time; often contrasted with, and sometimes built from the same musical material as, a PAVAN (which is slower); obsolete, but revived e.g. by Vaughan Williams in JOB.

GALLIERA, ALCEO (b. 1910), Italian operatic and orchestral conductor, touring much. Also composer – of ballet 'The Wise and Foolish Virgins', etc.

GALOP, a 19th-century ballroom dance in quick 2/4 time.

GALUPPI, BALDASSARE (1706–85), Italian composer, chiefly of operas, but also of harpsichord sonatas, etc. Visited London and St Petersburg; in service at St Mark's, Venice, from 1748. (Browning's poem 'A Toccata of Galuppi's' refers to him; but the exact work is unidentified, if not imaginary.)

GAMBA (It., leg), (1) abbr. for *viola da gamba*; (2) organ stop imitating this instrument's tone.

GAMELAN, native Indonesian instrumental ensemble using string, wind, and varied percussion instruments.

GAMME (Fr.), scale.

GAMUT, (1) compass, range (also metaphorically); (2, various obsolete senses) the G at the bottom of the bass clef; the written system of HEXACHORDS; the musical scale (like French *gamme*).

GANZ (Ger.), whole, complete(ly); hence *Ganze*, abbreviation of GANZETAKTNOTE.

GANZ, RUDOLPH (b. 1877), Swiss-born composer of orchestral and other music who settled in U.S.A.; also conductor (of the St Louis Symphony Orchestra, 1921–7).

GANZETAKTNOTE (Ger.), semibreve (U.S., whole-note) – literally meaning a note lasting a whole bar or measure.

GAPPED, (of a scale) having some intervals of more than a tone's distance, unlike the normal major or minor scales; e.g. the PENTATONIC scale.

GARDEN OF FAND, THE, symphonic poem by Bax, first performed 1920. Fand is a figure of Irish legend; her garden in this work is the sea.

GARDINER, HENRY BALFOUR (1877–1950), English composer who trained in Germany. Composed little, but works include Symphony, 'Shepherd Fennel's Dance' (after T. Hardy) for orchestra, chamber music, 'Noel', and other piano pieces. Was also noted promoter of music by other British composers.

GARDNER, JOHN (LINTON) (b. 1917), English composer. Works include symphony, orchestral variations on a theme of C. Nielsen; choral work 'CANTIONES SACRAE' and unaccompanied secular motet 'A Latter-Day Athenian Speaks'; opera 'The Moon and Sixpence' (after W. Somerset Maugham); ballet 'Reflection'; variations for brass quartet; works for military band. Formerly on the musical staff of Covent Garden Opera.

GARLAND FOR THE QUEEN, A, set of choral pieces by (in order) Bliss, Bax, Tippett, Vaughan Williams, Berkeley, Ireland, Howells, Finzi, Rawsthorne, and Rubbra in honour of the coronation of Queen Elizabeth II, 1953. Texts by poets of the composers' choice. The work was suggested by 'THE TRIUMPHS OF ORIANA'.

GASPARD DE LA NUIT, set of three piano pieces by Ravel, 1908; the title (Gaspard of the Night) was taken from a set of prose-ballads by A. Bertrand, subtitled 'Fantasies in the manner of Rembrandt and Callot'. No. 1 is 'Ondine' (water-nymph seducing young men to their death); no. 2, 'Le Gibet' (The Gibbet); no. 3, 'Scarbo' (name of a diabolic creature).

GASPARINI, FRANCESCO (1668–1727), Italian composer of more than fifty operas, also of oratorios, church music, etc.; pupil of Corelli.

GASSMANN, FLORIAN LEOPOLD (1723–74), Bohemian composer, chiefly of operas; pupil of 'Padre Martini'; worked at court in Vienna.

GASTEIN SYMPHONY, supposed lost symphony written by Schubert at Gastein (Austria), 1825. The sonata in C for piano duet (see GRAND DUO) is thought by some authorities to be an arrangement of it.

GATTY, NICHOLAS COMYN (1874–1946), English composer of six operas (including 'The Tempest' and 'Macbeth' after Shakespeare), chamber music, etc.; also critic.

GAUL, ALFRED ROBERT (1837–1913), English composer of religious cantatas including 'The Holy City', formerly very well known.

GAUNTLETT, HENRY JOHN (1805–76), English lawyer and church musician; composer of 'Once in Royal David's City' and many other hymns (apparently thousands).

GAVAZZENI, GIANANDREA (b. 1909), Italian composer, conductor, and writer on music; works include several for orchestra called 'Concerto di Cinquandò' ('Cinquandò' being the name of his grandfather's house).

GAVEAUX, PIERRE (1761–1825), French composer (also tenor); wrote about thirty operas including 'LEONORA, or Wedded love', to a libretto which was the principal source of the libretto of Beethoven's 'FIDELIO'.

GAVOTTE, old dance in 4/4 time beginning on the third beat of the bar; sometimes (but not always) a constituent of the classical SUITE, and occasionally revived in modern times – e.g. by Prokofiev in his 'CLASSICAL SYMPHONY'.

GAY, JOHN (1685–1732), English poet and playwright, particularly known for having written the words of 'THE BEGGAR'S OPERA' to popular tunes of the day.

GAYANEH, ballet with music by Khatchaturian, produced 1942 – named after its collective-farm heroine, the virtuous wife of a villain. Contains the 'Sabre Dance'.

GAZZA LADRA, LA, see THE THIEVING MAGPIE.

GEBRAUCHSMUSIK, see UTILITY MUSIC.

GEDACKT, GEDACT, end-stopped type of organ pipe of soft tone. (The term means 'covered'; in modern German, *gedeckt*).

GEDALGE, ANDRÉ (1856–1926), French composer of operas, three symphonies, etc.; influential teacher at Paris Conservatory, where his pupils included Ravel and Milhaud.

GEDDA, NICOLAI (b. 1925), Swedish-born tenor of Russian and Swedish descent, prominent in opera and operetta in many languages (Covent Garden début, 1959) and on records.

GEIGE (Ger., pl. *-en*), fiddle, violin.

GEISHA, THE, operetta by S. Jones, produced in London, 1896. Libretto, set in Japan, by 'Owen Hall' (i.e. J. Davis) and H. Greenbank. It was afterwards produced in many countries and languages, apparently helping to set a fashion for oriental operatic subjects.

'GEISTER' TRIO, see 'GHOST' TRIO.

GEMINIANI, FRANCESCO (1687–1762), Italian violinist, composer (violin sonatas, trios, and works of CONCERTO GROSSO type, etc.), and author of a famous treatise on violin-playing. Pupil of Corelli. After 1714 lived partly in England, and died in Dublin.

GEMSHORN, soft-toned organ stop usually of 4-FOOT pitch.

GENÉE, (FRANZ FRIEDRICH) RICHARD (1832–95), German conductor (especially at Vienna), composer of many operettas and librettist of others – see e.g. FLEDERMAUS.

GENERAL PAUSE (abbr. G.P.), a rest of one or more bars for all performers – i.e. complete silence. Note that this does not correspond to the usual English meaning of 'pause' – see PAUSE, English and German meanings.

GENTLE SHEPHERD, THE, ballad opera set to traditional airs selected by the librettist, Allan Ramsay, and produced in Edinburgh, 1728. One of the first BALLAD OPERAS. It has a conventional pastoral plot.

GENZMER, HARALD (b. 1909), German composer of concertos for various instruments (one for trautonium), septet with harp, two piano sonatas, etc. Influenced by Hindemith.

GERHARD, ROBERTO (b. 1896), Spanish composer, resident in Britain since 1938; pupil of Pedrell and Schoenberg; some of his works use TWELVE-NOTE technique. Has written opera 'THE DUENNA' (after Sheridan; for radio), ballets, music to many radio plays and feature programmes; 'Pedrelliana' (after works of Pedrell) for orchestra, two symphonies, violin concerto, a setting of Edward Lear's 'The Akond of Swat' for mezzo-soprano and two percussionists, 'Concerto for eight instruments, including accordion, without orchestra; arrangements of old Spanish music, etc.

GERMAN, EDWARD, pen-name of Edward German Jones (1862–1936), English composer; also violinist and theatre conductor. Cultivated light, melodious, and theatrically effective style; wrote 'MERRIE ENGLAND', 'TOM JONES', and other operettas, and music to various plays including Shakespeare's *Henry VIII* and Anthony Hope's *Nell Gwynn* (dances from these now heard independently). Also composed two symphonies, Welsh Rhapsody, etc., and completed Sullivan's 'The Emerald Isle'.

GERMAN DANCE, type of slow waltz, cultivated e.g. by Mozart and Schubert.

GERMAN FLUTE, obsolete name for the ordinary (side-blown) flute, as distinct from the RECORDER, formerly known as the 'English flute'.

GERMAN REQUIEM, A (Ger., *Ein deutsches Requiem*), work for soloists, chorus, and orchestra by Brahms; first complete performance, 1869. Texts from Luther's translation of the Bible; title of the work therefore distinguishes it from Roman Catholic Requiem to prescribed Latin text.

GERMAN SIXTH, type of 'augmented sixth' chord (see AUGMENTED) distinguished by the intermediate intervals of the chord – e.g. (reading upwards) D♭, F, A♭, B. (If the B is re-named C♭ then the chord becomes also a 'minor seventh' chord, i.e. the dominant seventh in the key of G♭ – an ambiguity useful in modulation.) Cp. FRENCH SIXTH, ITALIAN SIXTH – the reason for the names is not known.

GERMANI, FERNANDO (b. 1906), Italian organist (also composer and music-editor); held post at St Peter's, Rome, 1948–59, and is a much-travelled recitalist.

GERSHWIN, GEORGE (1898–1937), American pianist and composer of many popular songs; extended his range (especially in applying jazz idioms to concert works) in 'RHAPSODY IN BLUE' (1924), piano concerto, 'Cuban Overture', 'AN AMERICAN IN PARIS', opera 'PORGY AND BESS', piano preludes. (The orchestration of 'Rhapsody in Blue' is by F. Grofé; of the other works, by Gershwin himself.) Studied with R. Goldmark but was mainly self-taught. Died after an unsuccessful brain operation.

GERTLER, ANDRÉ (b. 1907), Hungarian-born violinist who settled in Belgium. Toured with Bartók at the piano. Specializes in modern works.

GES (Ger.), G flat.

GESCHÖPFE DES PROMETHEUS, DIE see PROMETHEUS.

GESTOPFT, stopped (notes on the horn). (See STOP.)

GESUALDO, CARLO (*c.* 1560–1615), Italian prince who was also a composer and lutenist; wrote madrigals employing very adventurous and 'prophetic' harmony, and also songs to religious words, etc. Gained notoriety by having his wife and her lover assassinated in 1590.

GETEILT (Ger., in older spelling *getheilt*), divided; see DIVISI.

GEVAERT, FRANÇOIS AUGUSTE (1828–1908), Belgian theorist (author of treatises on orchestration, etc.), director of the Brussels Conservatory, composer, and musical editor.

GHEDINI, GIORGIO FEDERICO (1892–1965), Italian composer of operas including 'BILLY BUDD'; 'The Golden Flea', 'THE HAPPY HYPOCRITE' (after Max Beerbohm); concertos for string orchestra (in clear, NEO-CLASSICAL style), church music, etc.; also editor of old Italian music.

'GHOST' TRIO, nickname (from 'mysterious' slow movement) for Beethoven's piano trio in D, op. 70, no. 1 (1808).

GIANNEO, LUIS (b. 1897), Argentinian composer of violin concerto, sinfonietta, piano pieces (some of them for children), songs, etc. Has utilized American-Indian themes.

GIANNI SCHICCHI, one-act comic opera by Puccini, produced in New York, 1918 – along with 'THE CLOAK' and 'SISTER ANGELICA', two other one-act operas which precede it and with which it forms Puccini's 'triptych' (It., *trittico*). Libretto by G. Adami: Schicchi, a medieval Florentine rogue, is the hero.

GIANNINI, VITTORIO (1903–66), American composer of operas 'The Taming of the Shrew' (after Shakespeare), 'Beauty and the Beast';

also symphonies and 'Frescobaldiana' for orchestra, based on Frescobaldi's organ works.

'GIANT' FUGUE, nickname for a fugue in D minor by Bach contained in Part III of the 'CLAVIERÜBUNG' – from the giant-like strides of a figure in the pedals.

GIARDINI, FELICE DE (1716–96), Italian violinist, opera manager, and composer, long resident in London; collaborated with Avison in oratorio 'Ruth'. Died in Moscow.

GIBBONS, CHRISTOPHER (1615–76), English composer of fantasies for strings, church music, and (with Locke) music for the masque 'CUPID AND DEATH'. Private organist to Charles II, organist of Westminster Abbey. Son of Orlando Gibbons.

GIBBONS, ORLANDO (1583–1625), English composer, also virginalist and organist; his father William, brothers Edward, Ellis, and Ferdinando, and son Christopher were also musicians. Choirboy at King's College, Cambridge; later organist of Chapel Royal and Westminster Abbey. Works include about forty anthems and other church music; notably expressive madrigals ('The Silver Swan', etc.); IN NOMINES and other works for viols; keyboard pieces (see PARTHENIA).

GIBBS, (CECIL) ARMSTRONG (1889–1960), English composer of many songs in an accepted, recognizably 'English' vein – many of them to poems by de la Mare; also of 'La Belle Dame Sans Merci' and other cantatas, comic opera 'The Blue Peter', waltz 'Dusk', church music, etc.

GIBSON, ALEXANDER (b. 1926), Scottish conductor, former musical director of Sadler's Wells Opera, conductor of Scottish National Orchestra since 1959.

GIESEKING, WALTER (WILHELM) (b. 1895–1956), German pianist (though born in France). Made début in 1915 and afterwards toured widely; of high international reputation, particularly in French music. Was also composer.

GIGA (It.), equals JIG.

GIGLI, BENIAMINO (1890–1957), Italian tenor; made début 1914. Had operatic career but later maintained his exceptional celebrity chiefly by recitals of operatic excerpts, etc., and by records.

GIGOUT, EUGÈNE (1844–1924), French organist and composer, especially for organ; pupil of Saint-Saëns.

GIGUE (Fr.), equals JIG.

GILBERT, HENRY FRANKLIN BELKNAP (1868–1928), American composer, pupil of MacDowell; made use of Negro, American-Indian, and Creole melodies – Creole in, e.g., ballet 'The Dance in Place Congo'.

GILELS, EMIL (b. 1916), Russian pianist; won international prizes in Vienna (1936) and Brussels (1938) and after the Second World War appeared in Britain and U.S.A.

GILES, NATHANIEL (*c.* 1558–1633), English organist (of the Chapel Royal, 1596) and composer of madrigals and much church music.

GILLIS, DON (b. 1912), American composer (also trumpeter, trombonist, teacher, and conductor); cultivates easy, sometimes jazzy, style and has written seven symphonies and 'Symphony no. 5½' (also called 'A Symphony for Fun' and used for ballet).

GILSON, PAUL (1865–1942), Belgian composer, also teacher and critic. Works include two Flemish operas, Fantasy on Canadian Themes for orchestra, many songs.

GIMEL, see GYMEL.

GINASTERA, ALBERTO (b. 1916), Argentinian composer of music which often has nationalist characteristics – e.g. ballet 'Panambi' (on an American-Indian legend), 'Argentinian Concerto' for piano and orchestra; other works include overture to Goethe's 'Faust', operas 'Don Rodrigo' and 'Bomarzo'. Lived in U.S.A., 1945–6.

GIOCONDA, LA, opera by Ponchielli, produced in Milan, 1876. Libretto by Boito, after Victor Hugo. 'La Gioconda', literally 'the joyful girl', is the name of a street-singer, the heroine. The opera is unrelated to da Vinci's portrait or to D'Annunzio's play (1898), similarly named. Act III contains the 'Dance of the Hours' (ballet).

GIOCOSO (It.), merry, playful, humorous.

GIOIELLI DELLA MADONNA, I, see THE JEWELS OF THE MADONNA.

GIORDANELLO, see GIUSEPPE GIORDANI.

GIORDANI, GIUSEPPE (*c.* 1753–1798), Italian composer of operas, ballets, church music, concertos, songs, etc. – the song 'Caro mio ben' (My very dear one) is ascribed to him. Never left Italy, but was formerly confused with Tommaso Giordani (no relation). Known also as Giordanello.

GIORDANI, TOMMASO (*c.* 1730–1806), Italian composer (no relation of Giuseppe Giordani) who worked in Dublin (where he died) and London. Composed or contributed items to more than fifty operas, Italian and English; wrote songs for Sheridan's *The Circle* on its first production.

GIORDANO, UMBERTO (1867–1948), Italian composer of 'ANDRÉ CHÉNIER', 'Fedora', and other operas of the Italian 'realistic' kind (see VERISMO).

GIPPS, RUTH (b. 1921), English composer, pupil of Vaughan Williams and others: works include two symphonies, cantata 'Golden Market', chamber music. Also conductor, oboist, and pianist.

GIPSY BARON, THE (Ger., *Der Zigeunerbaron*), operetta by J. Strauss the younger, produced in Vienna, 1885. Libretto by I. Schnitzer. The hero is a young Hungarian landowner regarded by the gipsies as their chief – and eventually made a real baron. See RÁKÓCZI MARCH.

GIPSY PRINCESS, THE, English title commonly used for *Die Csárdás-*

fürstin (Ger., Princess Csárdás), operetta by Kalman, produced in Vienna, 1921.

GIRL FROM ARLES, THE (Fr., *L'Arlésienne*), play by Alphonse Daudet, 1872, for which Bizet wrote incidental music: the second of the two suites drawn from this is an arrangement made by Guiraud after Bizet's death.

GIRL OF THE GOLDEN WEST, THE, opera by Puccini, produced in New York, 1910. Set in California at the time of the Gold Rush. The Italian title *La Fanciulla del West* omits 'golden'; but the title of D. Belasco's play – on which the opera libretto was based by G. Civinini and C. Zangarini – is used in English also for the opera.

GIS, GISIS (Ger.), G sharp, G double-sharp.

GISELLE, *or The Wilis* (Fr., . . . *ou les Wilis*), ballet with music by Adam, produced in Paris, 1841. The Wilis are the spirits of maidens who die before their intended marriages.

GITTERN, old English name for an instrument, apparently the same as guitar (not the same as CITTERN).

GIULIO CESARE, see JULIUS CAESAR.

GIUSTO (It.), strict, just, proper; hence such expressions as *allegro giusto*, meaning either (1) allegro with a special attention to keeping a strict beat, or (2) a moderate (neither too fast nor too slow) allegro.

GLAGOLITIC MASS, Mass by Janáček for chorus, organ, and orchestra, 1927. Glagolitic is an obsolete Slav ecclesiastical language; the form of Mass written in it has not been used ecclesiastically since the 15th century, but has patriotic Czech associations.

GLANVILLE-HICKS, PEGGY (b. 1912), Australian-born composer, resident in U.S.A.; pupil of Vaughan Williams, Wellesz, and N. Boulanger; is also critic. Works include piano concerto, chamber music, opera 'The Transposed Heads'. Formerly married to Stanley Bate.

GLASS HARMONICA, obsolete instrument consisting of glass vessels of various sizes, rubbed with damped finger (or operated mechanically) – written for, e.g. by Mozart. Also called the 'musical glasses'.

GLASSER, STANLEY (b. 1926), South African composer, pupil in London of Seiber and Frankel. Works include cantata with recitation 'The Vision of Nongquase' (on a S. African tribal legend); Sinfonietta Concertante for orchestra; chamber music.

GLAZUNOV, ALEXANDER (KONSTANTINOVICH) (1865–1936), Russian composer of eight symphonies (all by 1906), plus one (1909) unfinished, first performed in Moscow 1948; concertos for piano (two), for violin, for saxophone; overture 'CARNIVAL'; ballets including 'THE SEASONS', piano pieces, songs, etc. Cultivated a Romantic idiom without the musical 'nationalism' of his teacher, Rimsky-Korsakov. Became director of the St Petersburg (later Leningrad) Conservatory but left in 1928 and settled in Paris, where he died.

GLEBOV, IGOR, see ASAFIEV.

GLEE, short choral composition, properly in several sections and for unaccompanied male voices; flourished in Britain about 1750–1830. (Cp. PART-SONG.) Hence *glee club* – term used in U.S. for choir cultivating short works of various types.

GLI (It.), the (masc. pl.).

GLIÈRE, REINHOLD (MORITZOVICH) (1875–1956), Russian composer of Belgian descent; pupil of Arensky, Taneyev and Ippolitov-Ivanov; professor at the Moscow Conservatory. Works include 'Shah-Senem' (based on folk-music of Azerbaijan) and other operas; 'The Red Poppy' and other ballets; three symphonies (no. 3, 'Ilya Murometz'); concerto for coloratura soprano and orchestra; chamber music; many songs and piano pieces.

GLINKA, MIKHAIL IVANOVICH (1804–57), Russian composer, the first whose music won general acceptance outside Russia; shows various 'nationalist' traits in his works. Regarded therefore as the 'father' of Russian music. Studied piano with Field; visited Italy and Germany before bringing out operas 'IVAN SUSSANIN' (1836) and 'RUSSLAN AND LUDMILLA'; made other trips abroad later, dying in Berlin. Also composed 'Jota aragonesa' and other works in imitation-Spanish style; chamber music for strings and for wind; many piano pieces and songs.

GLISSANDO (mock-It. from Fr. *glisser*, to slide) sliding up and down the scale, i.e. making a quick uninterrupted passage up or down the scale, e.g. on the piano, harp, xylophone, trombone. The effect of PORTAMENTO on stringed instruments is not comparable since it implies only the smooth linking of two notes, not the deliberate sounding of the notes in between.

GLOCKE(N) (Ger.), bell(s) – referring, in orchestral scores, to tubular bells. (See BELL.)

GLOCKENSPIEL (Ger., play of bells), percussion instrument of tuned metal bars giving small bell-like sound: played with keyboard or (more usually) small hammers held in hand. (The term is also used, though more rarely, for a chime of real bells played mechanically or by hand, i.e. a CARILLON.)

GLORIANA, opera by Britten, produced in London, 1953, in honour of the coronation of Queen Elizabeth II. Libretto by W. Plomer; Gloriana is Elizabeth I.

GLOTTE, COUP DE, see COUP DE GLOTTE.

GLUCK, CHRISTOPH WILLIBALD (VON) (1714–87), German composer, born in Bavaria but possibly of Bohemian origin; travelled much – London, 1745; Paris, 1773–9, where his followers opposed those of Piccinni; settled and died in Vienna. Was consciously an operatic reformer, stressing importance of subordinating music to dramatic needs – and also dispensing with 'dry RECITATIVE'; his 'ALKESTIS' (1767) has a famous preface expounding his ideas. This opera, like its predecessor 'ORPHEUS', was originally in Latin; both were later revised, with French texts. Other operas include

'IPHIGENIA IN AULIS', 'IPHIGENIA IN TAURIS', and 'ARMIDA', all in French. Wrote in all more than forty-five stage works; also instrumental pieces, etc.

GLYNDEBOURNE, a small opera house in the Sussex countryside founded by John Christie, the owner of the estate in which it stands. International short summer seasons there opened in 1934.

GNECCHI, VITTORIO (1876–1954), Italian composer of operas, including 'La Rosiera', 1910, with an early use of quarter-tones. His earlier opera 'Cassandra' aroused controversy when it was suggested that R. Strauss plagiarized it in 'Elektra'.

GNESSIN, MIKHAIL FABIANOVICH (1883–1957), Russian composer, pupil of Rimsky-Korsakov and Liadov; travelled in Western Europe and Palestine. He composed many works with Jewish associations including operas 'The Youth of Abraham' and 'The Maccabees'; also symphonic poems, chamber music, Jewish folk-song arrangements, etc.

GOBBI, TITO (b. 1915), Italian baritone, making début 1938; well known in opera (Rigoletto; Falstaff; Scarpia in 'TOSCA', etc.) and has appeared in many films. Also opera producer.

GOD SAVE THE KING (QUEEN), British national anthem; author and composer unknown, though a keyboard piece by Bull (in the minor key) has some relationship to the tune. Generally adopted in the mid-18th century. (Tune also set to various other words – e.g. U.S., 'My Country, 'Tis of Thee', 1831.)

GODARD, BENJAMIN LOUIS PAUL (1849–95), French composer, also violinist. Works include 'Jocelyn' (from which the well-known 'Berceuse' comes) and seven other operas; also orchestral works, over 100 songs, etc.

GODOWSKY, LEOPOLD (1870–1938), Polish-born pianist who became American, 1891; made and performed many virtuoso-style transcriptions of famous orchestral and other works. Was also composer, e.g., of the 'Triakontameron' (thirty piano pieces each composed on a different day).

GODS GO A-BEGGING, THE, ballet with music arranged by Beecham from various works of Handel, produced in London, 1928.

GOEDICKE, ALEXANDER FEDOROVICH (1877–1957), Russian pianist, teacher, and composer of operas, piano concerto, trumpet concerto, folk-song arrangements, etc.

GOEHR, ALEXANDER (b. 1932), English (German-born) composer, pupil of R. Hall and (in Paris) of Messiaen. Works include Symphony (previously and misleadingly called Little Symphony) for small orchestra, violin concerto, cantatas 'Sutter's Gold' and 'The Deluge', also 'A Little Cantata of Proverbs' (text by Blake) and opera 'Arden Must Die'. Son of WALTER GOEHR.

GOEHR, WALTER (1903–60), German-born conductor, resident in Britain from 1933; also composer (pupil of Schoenberg), especially of radio, theatre, and film music. He is among the composers who have made orchestral arrangements of Mussorgsky's 'PICTURES AT AN EXHIBITION'. Father of ALEXANDER GOEHR.

GOETZ, HERMANN (1840–76), German composer of opera 'THE TAMING OF THE SHREW', symphony, piano concerto, chamber music, songs, etc.; settled in Switzerland and died there.

GOLDBERG, SZYMON (b. 1909), Polish-born violinist resident in Holland, where he has his own chamber orchestra.

GOLDBERG VARIATIONS, usual name for Bach's thirty variations for harpsichord (with two keyboards) on an original theme; written for his pupil, J. G. Goldberg, whose noble patron required music as a solace for insomnia. See QUODLIBET.

GOLDEN COCKEREL, THE (Rus., *Zolotoy Petushok*), Rimsky-Korsakov's last opera; at first banned by censorship, then produced (only after the composer's death) in St Petersburg, 1909. Libretto by V. I. Bielsky, after Pushkin: title from a magic 'weathercock' which gives warning of danger to the city. The work is a satire on stupid despotism.

GOLDEN SONATA, nickname (not the composer's) for Purcell's sonata in F for two violins, viola da gamba, and harpsichord (or organ), no. 9 of a set of 10 published posthumously in 1697. (The set is called 'Sonatas of Four Parts', but see PURCELL.)

GOLDMARK, CARL (1830–1915), Austro-Hungarian composer who trained in Vienna and eventually settled there. Works include operas ('The Cricket on the Hearth', after Reade; 'The Winter's Tale', after Shakespeare; etc.): two symphonies, one called 'RUSTIC WEDDING'; two violin concertos, piano music, and songs. Uncle of Rubin Goldmark.

GOLDMARK, RUBIN (1872–1936), American composer, nephew of preceding; pupil of Dvořák, teacher of Gershwin. Wrote orchestral works – one on 'Hiawatha' – chamber music, piano pieces, etc.

GOLDSCHMIDT, BERTHOLD (b. 1903), German-born composer (pupil of Schreker) resident in England since 1935. Works include opera 'Beatrice Cenci' (after Shelley); ballet 'Chronica'; piano concerto, two piano sonatas, etc. Also conductor.

GOLESTAN, STAN (1876–1956), Rumanian composer who studied with d'Indy, Dukas, and Roussel in Paris, and remained there. Works include symphony, 'Rumanian Concerto' for violin and orchestra, chamber music. Also critic.

GOLLIWOGG'S CAKEWALK, see CHILDREN'S CORNER.

GONDOLIERS, THE, *or, The King of Barataria*, operetta by Sullivan, produced in London, 1889. Libretto by W. S. Gilbert (his last successful collaboration with Sullivan). Title from the heroes, two Venetian boatmen who despite their own equalitarian views find themselves jointly reigning as king.

GONG, percussion instrument (also called 'tam-tam') of oriental origin – bronze disk struck with hammer. Possibly first used orchestrally by Gossec in 1791. Normally considered as of indefinite pitch, but

Puccini requires tuned gongs in 'TURANDOT' and modern composers sometimes ask for several of differing (though still indefinite) pitch.

GOOD-HUMOURED LADIES, THE, ballet with music arranged by Tommasini from the keyboard works of D. Scarlatti; produced in Rome, 1917.

GOODMAN, BENNY (b. 1909), American clarinettist who became eminent in the jazz sphere (led his own band from 1933) and afterwards became noted soloist with orchestra, chamber-music player, etc.; works such as Copland's clarinet concerto and Bartók's 'CONTRASTS' were written for him.

GOOSSENS, EUGENE (1893–1962), English conductor and composer (also violinist), son and grandson of conductors of the same name (of Belgian descent). Took conducting posts in U.S.A. and then (1947–56) in Sydney, also becoming director of the State Conservatorium there. As conductor, noted pioneer of new music. His own works include operas 'JUDITH' and 'DON JUAN DE MAÑARA', two symphonies, piano pieces and chamber music (string octet also arranged as Concertino for string orchestra). Brother of Leon Goossens (and also of Sidonie and Marie Goossens, harpists). Knighted 1955.

GOOSSENS, LÉON (b. 1896), English oboist, noted soloist for whom concertos and other works have been written by his brother Eugene Goossens and others.

GOPAK, Russian folk-dance in quick 2/4 time. (In English sometimes also written as *hopak*.)

GORDON, GAVIN (MUSPRATT) (b. 1901), Scottish bass singer, actor, opera producer – and composer e.g. of 'THE RAKE'S PROGRESS' and other ballets.

GOSS, JOHN (1800–80), English organist (St Paul's Cathedral, London, 1838) and composer, chiefly of church music. Knighted 1872. No relation of John Goss (1894–1952), English baritone.

GOSSEC, FRANÇOIS JOSEPH (1734–1829), Belgian composer, from 1751 living in France (where he died); also musical organizer and teacher. Wrote symphonies, pioneering the form in France; also many operas and ballets, chamber music, works for outdoor performance celebrating the French Revolution, etc. Innovator in orchestration and the massed use of instruments.

GOTOVAC, JAKOV (b. 1895), Yugoslav composer of 'Ero the Joker' and other operas, choral works, songs with orchestra and with piano, etc.; makes use of folk-music idiom. Is also conductor. Studied in Vienna.

GÖTTERDAMMERUNG, see RING.

GOTTSCHALK, LOUIS MOREAU (1829–69), American pianist, the first such to win international standing as a virtuoso. Also composer of virtuoso-style piano pieces and of two operas and various orchestral works.

GOUDIMEL, CLAUDE (*c.* 1510–1572), French composer, at first of

Roman Catholic church music; then, after becoming a Protestant, of psalm-tunes, etc., for Protestant use. Also wrote secular songs. Killed in the 'St Bartholomew' massacre of Protestants.

GOULD, MORTON (b. 1913), American composer and conductor (also pianist). Associated with 'popular' music, but works include three symphonies; four 'American Symphonettes' (*sic*) from no. 2 of which comes 'Pavanne' (*sic*); concerto for tap dancer and orchestra; ballet 'FALL RIVER LEGEND'.

GOUNOD, CHARLES (FRANÇOIS) (1818–93), French composer, pupil of Halévy and others at the Paris Conservatory, where he won the 'Rome Prize' and so spent three years in Rome; afterwards church organist in Paris. At one time intended to become a priest. Had great success with opera 'FAUST', 1857. Also conductor; first conductor of what is now Royal Choral Society, during the years 1870–75 spent in London. Later concentrated on religious music, e.g. oratorio 'THE REDEMPTION'. Other works include opera 'ROMEO AND JULIET' and twelve other operas; nine masses and other church music; many songs; three symphonies; several miscellaneous pieces including a 'Meditation' on the first prelude of Bach's 'THE WELL-TEMPERED CLAVIER' (the so-called 'AVE MARIA'), and the 'FUNERAL MARCH OF A MARIONETTE'. Cultivated an immediately effective style, often chromatically inclined, which has slumped in favour since his death.

GOVERNMENT INSPECTOR, THE, opera by Egk, produced in Schwetzingen (Germany), 1957; libretto ('*Der Revisor*') by composer, after Gogol's Russian play satirizing officialdom.

GOW, NATHANIEL (1763–1831), Scottish musician (son and father of other musicians); was trumpeter, violinist, publisher, song-composer, etc. Wrote tune of song 'Caller Herrin'' – the words were fitted later.

GOYESCAS (Sp., Goya-esque works), (1) two sets of piano pieces (seven in all) by Granados, suggested by Goya's paintings and first performed 1914; (2) opera by Granados, produced in New York 1916, partly based on the preceding and having a plot of love and killing in a Goya-esque setting; libretto (in Spanish) by F. Periquet.

GRABU, LOUIS (d. after 1694), French violinist and composer; Master of the King's Music to Charles II, 1665; composer of music to Dryden's 'Albion and Albanius' and other stage works.

GRACE-NOTE, equals ORNAMENT.

GRADUS AD PARNASSUM (Lat., Steps to Parnassus – the mountain sacred to the Muses), (1) a treatise on counterpoint by Fux, 1725; (2) a collection of piano studies by Clementi, 1817. It is to the latter that Debussy pays humorous homage in 'Doctor Gradus ad Parnassum' (see CHILDREN'S CORNER).

GRAENER, PAUL (1872–1944), German composer of operas (one about W. F. Bach), orchestral works, etc.; also conductor. Lived in London 1896-1908.

GRAESER, WOLFGANG (1906–28), Swiss mathematician, scientist, and musical scholar who scored Bach's 'THE ART OF FUGUE' for orchestra and wrote a book on the work.

GRAINGER, PERCY ALDRIDGE (1882–1961), Australian-born composer and pianist; lived 1900–15 in London and thereafter in U.S.A. (naturalized). Pupil in Germany of Busoni; friend of Grieg. Collected and edited English folk music and based some compositions on it. Also wrote choral works, many short orchestral pieces (e.g. 'Country Gardens', 'Handel in the Strand'); usually published his work in several different (and often unconventional) instrumental versions. Used deliberately anglicized vocabulary, e.g. 'louden' (crescendo), 'middle-fiddle' (viola), 'bass fiddle' – to mean cello, not double-bass, which term he retained. See also LONDONDERRY AIR.

GRAN CASSA (It.), BASS DRUM.

GRAN MASS, mass by Liszt for the inauguration of a church at Gran, Hungary, 1856.

GRANADOS, ENRIQUE (full surname Granados y Campina; 1867–1916), Spanish composer (pupil of Pedrell), also pianist and conductor; his seven operas include 'GOYESCAS', partly based on piano works of the same name. Wrote also other piano music, orchestral works, and songs, cultivating Spanish 'nationalist' idiom. Died when the ship on which he was returning from New York was torpedoed by a German submarine.

GRAND CHŒUR (Fr.), equals FULL ORGAN.

GRAND DUKE, THE, *or*, *The Statutory Duel*, operetta by Sullivan – his last (unsuccessful) collaboration with W. S. Gilbert as librettist – produced in London, 1896. The Grand Duke loses his title through a type of duel with playing-cards.

GRAND DUO, name given to a sonata in C by Schubert (1824) for piano duet. It is thought by some to be an arrangement by Schubert of his lost 'GASTEIN' symphony; and accordingly orchestral arrangements of it have been made by Joachim and by A. Collins.

GRAND JEU (Fr.), FULL ORGAN.

GRAND OPERA, imprecise term sometimes meaning all-sung opera (without spoken dialogue) and also used by laymen to distinguish 'serious' opera from, e.g., operetta.

GRAND PIANO, see PIANO.

'GRANER' MASS, GRANER MESSE (Eng., Ger.), equals GRAN MASS (*Graner* being the German adjective from the place-name Gran).

GRAUN, CARL HEINRICH (1704–59), German composer (also tenor singer), musical director to Frederick II of Prussia from 1740. Earlier influenced by Lotti at Dresden, and later himself visited Italy. Wrote Italian and German operas, chamber music, and church music including notably successful cantata 'The Death of Jesus' – see PASSION.

GRAVE (It., heavy, grave), in slow tempo.

GRAVICEMBALO (It., corruption of *clavicembalo*), harpsichord.

GRAZIA, GRAZIOSO (It.), grace, graceful(ly).

GREAT, usual abbreviation for GREAT ORGAN.

GREAT C-MAJOR SYMPHONY, name for Schubert's symphony no. 9 in C (in some editions called no. 7 – see SCHUBERT), written 1828 but never performed in the composer's lifetime. The title distinguishes the symphony from the shorter no. 6 in the same key, and alludes both to its quality and its unusual length: it takes nearly an hour in performance.

GREAT FUGUE (Ger., *Grosse Fuge*), fugue by Beethoven for string quartet, op. 133 (1825), originally designed as last movement of Quartet in B♭, op. 130; but Beethoven gave this work a new finale and issued the fugue separately.

GREAT ORGAN (or simply *Great*), chief and most powerful division of an organ (a manual and the equipment controlled by it). No connexion with Great Organ Mass.

GREAT ORGAN MASS, nickname for Haydn's Mass in E♭, 1766, with an important organ part. Better called 'Great Mass with Organ', avoiding suggestion of a connexion with 'Great Organ'. Cp. LITTLE ORGAN MASS.

GREAT SERVICE, see SERVICE.

GRECHANINOV, ALEXANDER TIKHONOVICH (1864–1956), Russian composer (pupil of Rimsky-Korsakov) resident in France from 1925, in U.S.A. from 1939. Works, in a traditional Russian idiom, include operas, five symphonies, many songs, music for children, music for the Russian Orthodox and the Roman Catholic church – and 'Missa Oecumenica', 1944, designed to embrace musically both Eastern and Western Christianity.

GREENBERG, NOAH (1919–66), American conductor and musical editor, specializing in medieval and Renaissance music; founder of New York Pro Musica (performing ensemble), 1952.

GREENE, MAURICE (1695–1755), English composer of songs, church music, etc.; also organist.

GREENSLEEVES, old English tune mentioned by Shakespeare and found with several sets of words; *Fantasia on Greensleeves*, orchestral work by Vaughan Williams adapted from his opera 'Sir John in Love' (produced 1929).

GREGORIAN CHANT, type of PLAINSONG associated with Pope Gregory I (otherwise St Gregory; *c.* 540–*c.* 604) and now standard in the Roman Catholic Church.

GREGORIAN TONE, name given to each of eight melodies of Gregorian chant (each in a different MODE) prescribed by the Roman Catholic Church for the psalms. TONUS PEREGRINUS is additional to these.

GRETCHANINOV, see GRECHANINOV.

GRÉTRY, ANDRÉ ERNEST MODESTE (1742–1813), Belgian composer who studied in Italy and in 1767 settled in France (where he died). Was one of the chief composers of OPÉRA-COMIQUE: he wrote dozens of works of this type, including 'Zémire and Azor' (on the tale of Beauty and the Beast) and 'Richard Cœur de Lion'. The latter is the source of an aria quoted in Tchaikovsky's 'THE QUEEN OF SPADES' as an evocation of this period.

GRIEG, EDVARD HAGERUP (1843–1907), Norwegian composer whose Scottish great-grandfather's name was Greig; also pianist, particularly as accompanist to his wife (and cousin) Nina, who sang his songs. Encouraged by Ole Bull, went to study in Leipzig; later, pupil of Gade in Copenhagen. Became 'nationalist' in music. At Ibsen's request, wrote music for 'PEER GYNT'. Wrote no symphony, no opera, but works include piano concerto, 'HOLBERG SUITE' for strings, music to Bjørnson's 'SIGURD JORSALFAR'; choral works; 'Bergliot' (text by Bjørnson) for reciter and orchestra; three violin sonatas, many songs and piano works, various Norwegian folk-music arrangements. Had Norwegian government pension. Often visited Britain; Hon. D.Mus., Cambridge, 1894.

GRIFFES, CHARLES TOMLINSON (1884–1920), American composer – pupil of Humperdinck, in Germany, but mainly influenced by French IMPRESSIONISM. Overworked, through poverty, and died of pneumonia. Composed 'The Pleasure Dome of Kubla Khan' (after Coleridge) for orchestra; music to a Japanese mime play; 'THE WHITE PEACOCK' for piano (later orchestrated) and other piano music.

GROSSE CAISSE (Fr.), equals BASS DRUM.

GROSSE FUGE, see GREAT FUGUE.

GROSSE TROMMEL (Ger.), equals BASS DRUM.

GROSSES ORCHESTER (Ger.), equals FULL ORCHESTRA.

GROUND, term sometimes used for GROUND BASS.

GROUND BASS, bass theme which is persistently repeated while upper parts proceed; hence, e.g., in 17th-century England 'DIVISIONS on a ground', i.e. a piece in variation-form constructed by this means. Cp. CHACONNE.

GROVE, GEORGE (1820–1900), English musical scholar (also engineer, biblical commentator, magazine editor, etc.), first director of the Royal College of Music (1883–94); founder and first editor (1879–89) of *Grove's Dictionary of Music and Musicians*. Knighted 1883.

GROVE'S DICTIONARY (not *Groves'*), see GROVE, GEORGE.

GROVÉ, STEFANS (b. 1922), South African composer of Elegy for Orchestra, chamber music, piano solos, etc.; holds a college musical post in Baltimore.

GROVEN, EIVIND (b. 1901), Norwegian composer of choral music, symphonic poems, etc.; strongly influenced by Norwegian folk music (on which he is an authority). Disliking the use of the 'tempered scale' (see TEMPERAMENT), he has invented an organ 'with automatically controlled non-tempered intervals.

GROVES, CHARLES (b. 1915), English conductor – formerly of Bournemouth Municipal (now Symphony) Orchestra; from 1963, of Royal Liverpool Philharmonic Orchestra. C.B.E. 1968.

GROVLEZ, GABRIEL (MARIE) (1879–1944), French pianist, conductor, and composer of an 'Almanac of Images' and other piano works; also of songs, two operas, etc.

GRUENBERG, LOUIS (1884–1964), Russian-born American composer and pianist (brought to U.S.A. at age 2); piano pupil of Busoni in Vienna. Much influenced by jazz and Negro music: his works include 'EMPEROR JONES' and other operas, also violin concerto, symphonic poems, 'Jazzberries' for piano.

GRUENTHAL, JOSEPH, see TAL.

GRUPPETTO (It.), equals TURN (type of ornament).

GUARNERI, GUARNERIUS, Italian family (the second name is the Latinized form) of 17th- and 18th-century makers of violins, etc. The founder, Andrea Guarneri, was a pupil of Amati. Giuseppe Antonio Guarneri (1698–1744) is known as Giuseppe Guarneri del Gesù.

GUARNIERI, CAMARGO (MOZART) (b. 1907), Brazilian composer, pupil of Koechlin in Paris, professor at São Paolo Conservatory. Also conductor. Works, making use of Brazilian folk-music, include two symphonies; 'Brazilian Dance', etc., for orchestra; piano and violin concertos; chamber music. (Modestly refrains from using his middle name.)

GUASTAVINO, CARLOS (b. 1914), Argentinian composer and pianist. Works include many songs and pieces for one and two pianos; also 'Cantilena' for guitar, orchestral and choral works, etc.

GUI, VITTORIO (b. 1885), Italian conductor who in 1928 founded in Florence the orchestra from which eventually arose the *Maggio Musicale* (Musical May) Festival there. Noted conductor of opera, e.g. at Glyndebourne; and is also composer (symphonic poems, songs to his own words, etc.), and critic.

GUIDO D'AREZZO (*c.* 990–*c.* 1050), Italian monk (long resident in Arezzo, hence the name) and musical theorist. Inventor of two devices greatly facilitating the practice of music: (1) the names 'ut', 're', 'mi', etc. (ancestors of modern 'do', 're', 'mi') as indication of the relative positions of the notes of the scale – 'ut' to be either G, C, or F, bottom notes of the HEXACHORDS then used; (2) the 'Guidonian hand', an aid to memory whereby the tips and joints of the fingers are given the names of the various notes.

GUILLAUME TELL (Fr.), see WILLIAM TELL.

GUILMANT, FÉLIX ALEXANDRE (1837–1911), French organist in Paris and composer of two 'symphonies' for organ and orchestra, many organ solos for recital and church use.

GUION, DAVID (WENDEL FENTROSS) (b. 1895), American pianist (pupil of Godowsky), composer, and arranger of 'Turkey in the Straw', and other traditional American tunes.

GUIRAUD, ERNEST (1837–92), American-born French composer (eight operas, one unfinished and completed by Saint-Saëns) and teacher. Wrote recitatives for Bizet's 'CARMEN'; arranged the second suite from Bizet's 'L'Arlésienne' (see THE GIRL FROM

ARLES); revised 'THE TALES OF HOFFMANN', left unfinished by Offenbach.

GUITAR, plucked, fretted string instrument: it exists in various types of which the principal one came to other European countries from Spain and is therefore sometimes called 'Spanish guitar'; now normally with six strings, with compass from E below the bass stave upwards for more than three octaves. There is some solo music written for it, mainly by Spanish and Latin-American composers – also concertos, e.g. by Villa-Lobos, Castelnuovo-Tedesco. It is used very occasionally in chamber music and in the symphony orchestra. An *electric guitar* is a guitar connected to electrical apparatus modifying and amplifying the sound as in dance bands, etc., where guitars of other types (notably *bass guitar*, with function analogous to plucked double-bass) are also found. See also HAWAIIAN GUITAR.

GUNDRY, INGLIS (b. 1905), English composer, pupil of Vaughan Williams and others; works include 'The Partisans', 'Avon', and other operas, ballet, orchestral and chamber music, songs.

GUNG'L, JOSEPH (1810–89), Austro-Hungarian bandmaster and composer of marches, dances, etc.: visited U.S.A., 1849.

GURIDI, JESÚS (b. 1886), Spanish (Basque) composer, using Basque themes; studied in Paris and elsewhere. Works include operas, organ music, folk-song arrangements.

GURLITT, CORNELIUS (1820–1901), German pianist, organist, and composer of much educational piano music; also opera. Great-uncle of Manfred Gurlitt.

GURLITT, MANFRED (b. 1890), German conductor and composer of operas (one on the 'WOZZECK' story used by Berg), orchestral and chamber works, etc. Settled in Japan 1939. Great-nephew of Cornelius Gurlitt.

GURNEY, IVOR (BERTIE) (1890–1937), English composer (also poet), chiefly of songs, some to his own words; cultivated an individually lyrical style within the English song-writing tradition. Also composed piano and orchestral music. War injuries led to his becoming insane, 1922.

GURRELIEDER, see SONGS OF GURRA.

GUSLA, ancient Slavonic one-string bowed instrument, distinct from Gusli.

GUSLI, Russian instrument of zither type used in folk-music; 'played' by Sadko in Rimsky-Korsakov's opera of that name, the effect being simulated in the orchestra.

GUT (Ger.), good, well, markedly.

GYMEL (from Lat. *gemellus*, twin), type of late medieval vocal music in TWO PARTS, making considerable use of thirds and sixths, and chiefly practised in England.

GYROWETZ, ADALBERT (Germanized form of Czech name Jirovec; 1763–1850), Bohemian composer, some of whose symphonies (he wrote more than sixty) were performed under Haydn's name in

Paris. Visited London 1789–92; court conductor at Vienna from 1804. Composed German and Italian operas, MELODRAMAS, about sixty string quartets, church music, etc.

H

H, German note-symbol; see B.

HARM., direction to stringed instruments that certain notes are to be played as 'harmonics'. See HARMONIC (noun).

H.M.S. PINAFORE, *or*, *The Lass that Loved a Sailor*, operetta by Sullivan, produced in London, 1878. Libretto by W. S. Gilbert, with the action aboard an English warship.

HAAS, KARL (b. 1900), German-born musicologist and conductor (also viola-player) resident in Britain since 1939; in 1943 founded London Baroque Ensemble, specializing in unfamiliar music for small combinations of instruments.

HAAS, MONIQUE (b. 1916), French pianist, internationally noted; her husband is the composer MIHALOVICI.

HÁBA, ALOIS (b. 1893), Czech composer (pupil of Novák and Schreker), sometimes using quarter-tones with special instruments to play them – and also, less frequently, using sixth-tones; works include operas, orchestral and chamber music, songs with guitar, solos for ordinary piano and for quarter-tone piano. Brother of Karel Hába.

HÁBA, KAREL (b. 1898), Czech violinist, viola-player, and composer, pupil of his brother Alois Hába; sometimes uses quarter-tones. Works in normal tonal system include violin concerto, cello concerto, septet.

HABANERA, Cuban dance with singing, introduced into Spain. The word comes from Habana (i.e. Havana), Cuba; whence the French equivalent term, *havanaise*. (For the example in Bizet's 'Carmen', see YRADIER.)

HADLEY, HENRY KIMBALL (1871–1937), American composer and conductor who studied in Vienna; works include operas, four symphonies (no. 2, 'The Four Seasons'), choral works, more than 100 songs.

HADLEY, PATRICK ARTHUR SHELDON (b. 1899), English composer of 'La Belle Dame Sans Merci' and other choral works, orchestral and chamber music, incidental music for Sophocles' *Antigone*, etc., Professor at Cambridge, 1946–63.

HAENDEL, GEORG FRIEDERICH, see HANDEL.

'HAFFNER' SERENADE, nickname of a serenade composed by Mozart, 1776, for a marriage in the Haffner family of Salzburg. See also 'Haffner' Symphony.

'HAFFNER' SYMPHONY, nickname for Mozart's symphony no. 35 in

D, arranged from a serenade (not that of the preceding entry) written for the Haffner family of Salzburg in 1782.

HAGEMAN, RICHARD (1882–1966), Dutch-born composer who settled in U.S.A. 1907; also operatic and concert conductor. Works include opera and many songs including 'Do not go my love' (text by Tagore).

HAHN, REYNALDO (1875–1947), Venezuelan-born French composer who went to Paris in infancy, entered Conservatory there at 11 (pupil of Massenet and others), and became conductor. Wrote operas (one on *The Merchant of Venice*), operettas, music for plays (including Sacha Guitry's *Mozart*), chamber music, songs (including 'If my songs had only wings').

HAIEFF, ALEXEI (b. 1914), Russian-born composer resident in New York from age 17; pupil of N. Boulanger and others. Works, showing some influence of Stravinsky, include piano concerto, chamber music, ballet 'Beauty and the Beast'.

HAIRPINS, colloquial name for the signs < and > indicating respectively crescendo and diminuendo.

HALB(E) (Ger.), half; *Halbe*, *Halbenote*, minim (U.S., half-note).

HALE, ADAM DE LA (or Halle; *c.* 1240–*c.* 1286), French minstrel (TROUVÈRE) known as 'The Hunchback of Arras'. Works include motets, secular songs, and 'Robin and Marion' (Fr., *Le Jeu de Robin et de Marion*) which is regarded as a forerunner of comic opera.

HALÉVY, JACQUES FRANÇOIS (FROMENTAL ELIAS) (original surname Levy; 1799–1862), French composer: was a pupil of Cherubini in Paris and also studied in Italy. Works include 'THE JEWESS' and more than thirty other operas, usually of a spectacular kind – mostly in French, but one in Italian on Shakespeare's *The Tempest*. Also composed ballets (see 'MANON LESCAUT'), cantatas, etc. After his death, his daughter married his ex-pupil, Bizet.

HALF-CLOSE, imperfect CADENCE.

HALFFTER, ERNESTO (full surname Halffter Escriche; b. 1905), Spanish composer of partly German descent, resident in Portugal; also conductor. Works include Sinfonietta; opera 'The Death of Carmen'; chamber music. See also FALLA. Brother of Rodolfo Halffter.

HALFFTER, RODOLFO (full surname Halffter Escriche; b. 1900), Spanish composer of partly German descent, resident in Mexico; also writer on music. Works include violin concerto, ballets, piano solos. Brother of Ernesto Halffter.

HALF-NOTE, U.S. term (following the German *Halbenote*) for MINIM, a semibreve being considered as a whole-note.

HÄLFTE, DIE (Ger., the half), direction indicating that a passage is to be played by only half the normal number of instruments, e.g. half the first violins.

HALKA, opera by Moniuszko, produced in Vilna, 1854. Regarded as the chief Polish national opera. Libretto by W. Wolski. Named after the humbly-born heroine who drowns herself when her aristocratic lover leaves her with child.

HALL, RICHARD (b. 1903), English composer who uses TWELVE-NOTE technique. Works include four symphonies, orchestral fantasy, 'The Sheep Under the Snow' (on a folk-tune); organ works; music for bamboo pipes. Is also organist and college teacher.

HALLE, ADAM DE LA, see HALE.

HALLÉ ORCHESTRA, orchestra founded in Manchester in 1857 by the German-born pianist and conductor Carl Halle, 1819–95, who became Sir Charles Hallé. Barbirolli was its conductor 1943–68, then appointed 'conductor laureate for life'.

HALLELUJAH CHORUS, the chorus consisting mostly of the one re-repeated word, 'Hallelujah', at the end of Part II of Handel's 'MESSIAH'. (This is what the term now refers to, though other works have similar choruses.)

'HALLELUJAH' CONCERTO, nickname for Handel's organ concerto in B♭ (no. 3 of his second set, published 1740), because it contains a phrase also occurring in the 'Hallelujah Chorus'.

HALLÉN, JOHAN ANDREAS (1846–1925), Swedish composer of operas in German and Swedish, symphonic poems (one on 'The Isle of the Dead', the painting which also prompted a work by Rakhmaninov), etc.; also conductor and critic.

HALLING (Norw.), a Norwegian acrobatic solo-dance for men, in 2/4 time, cultivated by Grieg and other Norwegian composers.

HALM, see KINSKY.

HALVORSEN, JOHAN (1864–1935), Norwegian composer, also violinist and conductor; married a niece of Grieg. As a young violinist, worked in Aberdeen. Compositions – strongly influenced by Grieg – include two symphonies, violin concerto, stage music.

HAMAN AND MORDECAI, see ESTHER.

HAMBRAEUS, BENGT (b. 1928), Swedish composer, also organist; has worked much in Germany and has written ELECTRONIC music – also 'Spectogram' for soprano, flute, and percussion, etc.

HAMERIK, ASGER (1843–1923), Danish composer, pupil of Gade and Berlioz; in U.S.A., 1872–98. Works include seven symphonies (no. 6 'Spirituelle', i.e., light), four operas, two choral trilogies. Father of Ebbe Hamerik.

HAMERIK, EBBE (b. 1898), Danish composer and conductor. Studied with his father (Asger Hamerik) and abroad. Works include 'The Travelling Companion' (after Hans Andersen) and other operas; orchestral 'Variations on an Old Danish Folk-Tune'; woodwind quintet.

HAMILTON, IAIN (b. 1922), Scottish composer, pupil of Alwyn. Originally apprenticed as engineer. Works, tending to abstruse and unusually dissonant (sometimes TWELVE-NOTE) idiom, include two symphonies (no. 1 prompted by Rostand's play *Cyrano de Bergerac*), piano concerto, concerto and other works for clarinet, 'Sonata notturna' for horn and piano, cantata 'The Bermudas' (text by Marvell).

HAMLET, various works after Shakespeare, including (1) opera by A. Thomas, produced in Paris, 1868 (libretto, J. Barbier and M. Carré); (2) symphonic poem by Liszt, 1858, composed as a prelude to the play; (3) overture-fantasia by Tchaikovsky, 1888; (4) incidental music by Tchaikovsky to the play, 1891 – shortened version of the preceding, plus other movements adapted from his earlier works; (5) opera by Searle, produced in Hamburg, 1968.

'HAMMERKLAVIER' SONATA, nickname for Beethoven's piano sonata in B♭, op. 106 (1815–19). The nickname has small justification: the word is merely an ostentatiously German substitute (hammer keyboard) for the Italian 'pianoforte', and this was not the only sonata to which Beethoven applied it.

HAMMOND, JOAN (HOOD) (b. 1912), New-Zealand-born soprano; spent early years in Australia; made operatic début in Vienna, then appeared (1938) in London, continuing to specialize in operatic music.

HAMMOND ORGAN, type of ELECTRONIC organ (the sounds produced electrically but simulating those of a pipe-organ), usually with two manuals and pedal keyboard; invented in U.S.A., 1934. (Trade name, after its inventor, who also invented the SOLOVOX. The Hammond Company also makes the 'CHORD ORGAN'.)

HANDEL, GEORGE FRIDERIC (form of name adopted in England by Georg Friederich Händel or Haendel, 1685–1759), composer; born at Halle, Germany; first visited England 1710, and was naturalized there in 1727. Precocious musical activity, at first against his father's wish. Violinist in Hamburg Opera orchestra, 1703. Visited Italy, 1706–10. Wrote Italian operas for London, including 'RINALDO' (his first there), 'BERENICE' 'JULIUS CAESAR' 'ORLANDO', and 'XERXES'. 'Invented' English biblical oratorio with 'ESTHER', 1732; other oratorios include 'SAUL', 'ISRAEL IN EGYPT', 'MESSIAH', 'SAMSON', 'BELSHAZZAR', 'JUDAS MACCABAEUS', 'SOLOMON', 'SUSANNA', 'THEODORA', and (last) 'JEPHTHA'. (See ORATORIO.) Other vocal works include 'ACIS AND GALATEA', 'SEMELE', and 'ALEXANDER'S FEAST'; four coronation anthems including 'ZADOK THE PRIEST'. Noted harpsichordist and organist; played his organ concertos as intermissions in oratorio. Wrote for orchestra his WATER MUSIC, FIREWORKS MUSIC, and works of CONCERTO GROSSO type (for strings alone and for wind and strings); composed also 'THE HARMONIOUS BLACKSMITH' (later so called), other harpsichord pieces, etc. Worked within the prevailing style of his time, based on Italian vocal line. Made some unacknowledged 'borrowings' from other composers, and also reused parts of his own works. Became partially blind, 1751; totally so, 1753. Died in London. (See also KERL.)

HAND-HORN, the 'natural' HORN (i.e. without valves): incapable of a continuous scale, it could produce only the notes of the HARMONIC

SERIES, plus a few others obtained by putting the hand in the bell.

HANDL, JACOB (1550–91), Austrian church musician working finally in Prague; composer of motets, Masses, etc.

HANS HEILING, opera by Marschner, produced in Berlin, 1833. Libretto by E. Devrient (originally written for Mendelssohn). Named after a gnome king who unsuccessfully courts a human girl.

HANSEL AND GRETEL (Ger., *Hänsel und Gretel*), opera by Humperdinck, produced in Weimar, 1883. Libretto by A. Wette, the composer's sister, after the brothers Grimm: the two children of the title defeat a witch. (The spelling and pronunciation 'Hansel' without the German *ä* has become standard in English.)

HANSLICK, EDUARD (1825–1904), Austrian music critic, author of influential treatise *The Beautiful in Music*; champion of Brahms and opponent of Wagner, who pilloried him as Beckmesser in 'THE MASTERSINGERS'.

HANSON, HOWARD (b. 1896), American composer; worked in Rome 1921–24 as recipient of an American prize; from 1924, director of the Eastman School of Music, Rochester, N.Y. Also conductor. Works, some alluding to his Swedish descent, include five symphonies (no. 1 'Nordic', no. 4 'Requiem' – in memory of his father; no. 5 'Sinfonia Sacra'), piano concerto, opera, chamber music, songs.

HANUŠ, JAN (b. 1915), Czechoslovak composer of 'The Servant of Two Masters' (after Goldoni), 'The Torch of Prometheus' and other operas; also of four symphonies, wind quintet, etc.

HAPPY HYPOCRITE, THE, opera by Ghedini, produced in Milan, 1956; libretto ('*L'Ipocrite felice*') by Franco Antonicelli, after Max Beerbohm's story of a rake reformed.

HARDANGER FIDDLE (Norw., *hardingfele*), Norwegian folk-instrument of violin type, but with four SYMPATHETIC strings as well as the usual four. Named after a region of Norway where it is used. A concerto for it has been written by Geirr Tveitt.

HARDELOT, GUY D', pen-name of Helen Rhodes, *née* Guy (1858–1936), born at Hardelot, France – English composer of 'Because' and other genteelly sentimental and enormously successful songs.

HARMONIC (adjective) (1) relating to harmony; hence the *harmonic minor* scale (see MINOR) used in harmonizing; hence also the HARMONIC SERIES (see below), being the series of tones (*harmonic tones*) from which the system of harmony has historically sprung; (2) relating to the HARMONIC SERIES itself; hence, e.g. the *harmonic flute* stop on an organ, producing 4-FOOT tone from an 8-FOOT pipe pierced at half-length – i.e. using the second tone of the HARMONIC SERIES.

HARMONIC (noun), harmonic tone (see preceding entry), i.e. one of the tones of the HARMONIC SERIES. The lowest such tone, or 'fundamental', is called the *first harmonic*, the next lowest the *second harmonic*, etc. But in such phrases as 'playing in harmonics' on stringed instruments, the allusion is to harmonics with the exclusion of the first – since the first is the 'normal' sound requiring no special directions. To obtain these harmonics other than the first, it is necessary to set the string vibrating not as a whole length but in fractional parts of its length. (See HARMONIC SERIES.) A violinist, etc., does this by placing a finger lightly at a given point of a vibrating string: when the string is an open string (i.e. not otherwise fingered) then the result is called a *natural harmonic*, but when the string is a stopped string (one finger used for stopping and another for 'lightly placing') then the result is an *artificial harmonic*. The harmonics obtainable on the harp (also by 'lightly placing' the finger on a vibrating string) are in this sense 'natural' harmonics.

HARMONIC SERIES, the set of tones (called *harmonic tones* or simply *harmonics*) produced by a vibrating string or air-column, according to whether this is vibrating as a unit through its whole length or in aliquot parts ($\frac{1}{2}$, $\frac{1}{3}$, $\frac{1}{4}$, etc.). Vibration of the whole length gives the lowest ('fundamental') tone, or 'first harmonic'. The other tones, or 'upper partials', i.e. the second, third, fourth, and higher harmonics, are at fixed intervals above the fundamental – an octave above it, then a perfect fifth above that, and so on, decreasingly, ad infinitum. E.g. if the fundamental is the C in the bass stave, the series will begin as follows:

no. in harmonic series	1	2	3	4	5	6	7	8	9	*etc*
proportion in which string or air column is vibrating	Whole	$\frac{1}{2}$	$\frac{1}{3}$	$\frac{1}{4}$	$\frac{1}{5}$	$\frac{1}{6}$	$\frac{1}{7}$	$\frac{1}{8}$	$\frac{1}{9}$	*etc*

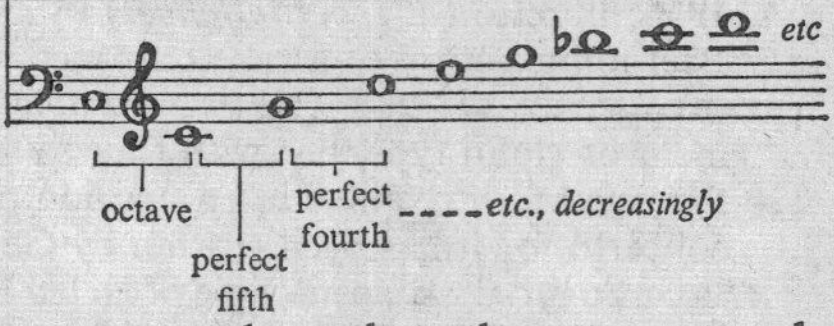

etc

octave

perfect fifth

perfect fourth ----*etc., decreasingly*

(Not all of these, however, correspond exactly to the notes as tuned in modern European scales.) The importance of the series lies in the following points (among others): (1) the basic technique of brass instruments is to produce the various harmonics by varying the mode of blowing; on, e.g., a bugle this one harmonic series yields all the notes available, while on, e.g., a trumpet and trombone the range is made more complete by use of valves and slide respectively; (2) the use of the upper partials also forms an important device in string-playing (see preceding entry); and these tones are used also on woodwind instruments – in the simplest instance, 'blowing harder' on a tin-whistle to produce a higher octave means the use of the second harmonic; (3) every note of normal musical instruments consists not of a 'pure' tone (like that of a tuning-fork) but of a blend of the 'fundamental' and certain upper partials, the precise blend differing between instruments. In fact this difference in blend determines the difference between tone-colours of instruments.

HARMONICA, name given to various types of musical instruments – especially, today, to the instrument also called 'mouth organ', i.e. small wind-instrument with metal reeds (one to each note), made in various sizes, most often with range upwards from about middle C, the superior models having chromatic compass. The instrument has mainly been used informally, e.g. by children, but works by e.g. Milhaud and Vaughan Williams have been written for Larry Adler, its most notable exponent. (Cp. REED ORGAN.) The name was also given to an instrument consisting of musically tuned glasses (now obsolete): see GLASS HARMONICA.

HARMONIE (Fr.), (1) harmony; (2) wind band (not a purely brass band, which in Fr. is *fanfare*). Also in German, in both senses; hence the two following entries.

HARMONIEMESSE, German name (see preceding entry) for Haydn's WIND-BAND Mass.

HARMONIEMUSIK (Ger.), music for wind instruments (see HARMONIE).

HARMONIOUS BLACKSMITH, THE, nickname for a set of variations in Handel's suite for harpsichord in E (1720). Although the regular strokes of the theme may suggest a blacksmith's hammering, the nickname is not Handel's, is not contemporary with him, and is not derived from any circumstances connected with the composition of the work (legends to the contrary notwithstanding).

HARMONIUM, small portable instrument of the REED-ORGAN family, in which pedals actuate a bellows which drives air through the reeds. Mainly used as a substitute in humble circumstances for the organ as an accompaniment to hymns, etc.; very occasionally elsewhere, e.g. in some 'Bagatelles' (with two violins and cello) by Dvořák.

HARMONY, the simultaneous sounding of notes in a way that is musically significant. (COUNTERPOINT is concerned with the simultaneous combination of melodies, not individual notes; but counterpoint and harmony represent overlapping types of relationships between notes, and a composer considers both relationships together.)

HAROLD IN ITALY, work by Berlioz, 1834, for viola and orchestra – but called a 'symphony'. After Byron's *Childe Harold.* Written for Paganini, who wanted a viola work for himself, but rejected by him as giving the soloist too little prominence.

HARP, plucked stringed instrument of ancient origin, of which the chief modern development (*double-action harp*, from early 19th century) now has a compass from B below the bass clef upwards for nearly 7 octaves. It is much used in orchestral music, less in chamber music, solos, and accompaniment of voices. Its strings in their basic position give the scale of C♭ major (i.e. for practical purposes, B major) which is modified by the use of seven pedals – one raising all the notes C♭ to either C♮ or C♯ as desired, the other pedals doing similarly for all the D♭'s, all the E♭'s, etc. Despite the pedal action the basic tuning of the harp is thus DIATONIC; a *chromatic harp* (giving a CHROMATIC scale) was also in use in the 19th and early 20th centuries. (Simpler and smaller harps, more or less after ancient models, are also still found, e.g. in accompanying folk-music. See also AEOLIAN HARP and DITAL HARP.)

'HARP' QUARTET, nickname for Beethoven's string quartet in E♭, op. 74 (1809), with harp-like pizzicato arpeggios in the first movement. It is a somewhat absurd nickname, because it might be taken for a descriptive name: on the analogy of e.g. 'piano quartet' a 'harp quartet' ought to be a work for harp and three bowed instruments.

HARP STOP, a contrivance on a harpsichord damping the strings so that the resulting tone resembles the rather thin tone of a harp.

HARP-LUTE, another name for the DITAL HARP.

HARPSICHORD, keyboard instrument with strings plucked mechanically – as distinct from the piano, in which the strings are struck, and from CLAVICHORD, where the process is again different. Prominent *c.* 1550–1800 as solo and ensemble instrument, and revived after 1900 for new works (e.g. concerto by Falla) and for performing old music authentically. Two manuals are commonly found, and are actually required sometimes for contrast, e.g. in Bach's ITALIAN CONCERTO; there is sometimes a pedal keyboard too as on the organ. The player has little control of tone-quality by means of touch, but has at his disposal certain STOPS and COUPLERS. Cp. SPINET and VIRGINALS.

HARRIS, ROY ELLSWORTH (b. 1898), American composer; took no professional training until after he was 20, but later studied with N. Boulanger in Paris; has held various university teaching posts. Works – sometimes using 'folk' material, and sometimes the old MODES, but always 'modern' in spirit – include seven symphonies of which no. 4 ('Folk Song') is for chorus and orchestra, incorporating various traditional tunes. Other works include concertos for piano, for two pianos, for accordion; 'Elegy and Paean' for viola and orchestra (with electrically amplified piano); various 'occasional' works and chamber music.

HARRIS, WILLIAM HENRY (b. 1883), organist of St George's Chapel, Windsor, since 1933, and composer of church music, cantatas, etc. Knighted 1954.

HARRISON, JULIUS (ALLEN GREENWAY) (1885–1963), English composer, conductor, and writer on music; works include Mass, orchestral 'Worcestershire Suite', songs including 'Cavalier Songs'.

HARRISON, LOU (b. 1917), American composer of opera 'Rapunzel' (after William Morris), Mass, three orchestral suites, works for percussion instruments alone, ballets, etc.; pupil of Cowell and Schoenberg. Also critic.

HARRISON, PAMELA (b. 1915), English composer, pupil of Jacob.

Works include symphonic poem 'Evocation of the Weald'; chamber music and songs.

HARSÁNYI, TIBOR (1898–1954), Hungarian composer, pupil of Kodály, but resident in Paris since 1923 and predominantly French in musical outlook. Works include symphony, violin concerto, nonet, stage works.

HARTMANN, JOHAN PETER EMILIUS (1805–1900), Danish composer of operas including 'Little Kirsten' (after Hans Andersen), ballet 'A Folk-Tale' (with Gade, his son-in-law), symphonic poems on Nordic subjects, choral works, etc. Director of the Copenhagen Conservatory.

HARTMANN, KARL AMADEUS (1905–63), German composer. Dissociated himself from the Nazis. Pupil of Scherchen and Webern. Works, with ATONALIST leanings, include eight symphonies, two string quartets, 'pacifist' opera 'Simplicius Simplicissimus'. Also organizer of notable concerts of modern music in Munich ('Musical Viva').

HARTY, (HERBERT) HAMILTON (1879–1941), Northern Irish conductor (Hallé Orchestra, 1920–33) and composer of an Irish Symphony, violin concerto, cantata 'The Mystic Trumpeter', many songs, etc. Also pianist and organist. Made modern orchestral arrangements of excerpts from Handel's FIREWORKS MUSIC and WATER MUSIC which have become standard. Knighted 1925.

HARWOOD, BASIL (1859–1949), English cathedral organist and composer of church music, cantatas, organ concerto, etc.

HÁRY JÁNOS, opera by Kodály, produced in Budapest, 1926; orchestral suite drawn from this, first performed 1927. The opera contains traditional Hungarian tunes, and the libretto (by B. Paulini and Z. Harsányi) concerns the folk-hero whose name forms the title (in Hungarian fashion, i.e. with surname first).

HASLER, see HASSLER.

HASSAN, play by Flecker to which Delius wrote incidental music, 1920, including the now well-known 'Serenade'.

HASSE, JOHANN ADOLPH (1699–1783), German composer, also tenor singer; pupil of Porpora and A. Scarlatti in Italy. Wrote dozens of Italian operas, one on the libretto afterwards used by Mozart in 'THE CLEMENCY OF TITUS'; also church music, harpsichord works, etc. Director of the Dresden Court Opera; afterwards lived mainly in Vienna and in Venice, where he died.

HASSLER, HANS LEO (also Hasler; 1564–1612), German composer, pupil of A. Gabrieli in Venice; also organist at various churches and courts. Wrote church music, organ works, German songs including the original tune made familiar by Bach as the 'Passion' chorale, 'O Sacred Head'.

HATTON, JOHN LIPTROT (1809–86), English singer, pianist, organist, theatre conductor, and composer of 'Simon the Cellarer', 'To Anthea', and about 300 other solo songs; also of part-songs, church music, stage music, etc.

HAUBENSTOCK-RAMATI, ROMAN (b. 1919), Polish-born composer, resident in Israel 1950–7, later in Paris and Vienna. Works include electronic music; 'Interpolation' for flute and recorded tape; 'Recitative and aria' for harpsichord and orchestra; 'Credentials' (text from Beckett's 'Waiting for Godot') for voice and eight instrumentalists – whose written parts are divided into square 'fields' which can be played vertically or horizontally. See INDETERMINACY.

HAUER, JOSEF MATTHIAS (1883–1959), Austrian composer who arrived at a form of TWELVE-NOTE technique independently of Schoenberg and seemingly a little before him (from 1912; books 1925, 1926); he postulated forty-four combinations (called tropes) of the twelve notes of the octave. Works, using this method, include piano concerto, violin concerto, chamber music, cantata 'The Way of Humanity'.

HAUNTED BALLROOM, THE, ballet with music by G. Toye, produced in London, 1934.

HAUTBOIS (Fr.), oboe – the actual word (literally meaning 'high wood') from which 'oboe', really an Italian word, is derived.

HAUTBOY, obsolete English term (from preceding entry) for oboe. An alternative spelling was *hoboy*.

HAVANAISE (Fr.), equals HABANERA.

HAWAIIAN GUITAR, type of guitar differing from normal (a) by distinctive tuning of strings; (b) by the fact that the strings are 'stopped' not with the fingers but with a small metal bar (called 'a steel') forming a movable 'NUT' going right across all strings. The particular intervals of the tuning can therefore be reproduced at any pitch by sliding the steel, making possible the sliding thirds which are characteristic of the instrument (e.g. in commercialized 'Hawaiian'-style dance music, popular before 1939–45 war).

HAYDN, surname of two composers, brothers (below). The surname alone alludes to the first.

HAYDN, (FRANZ) JOSEPH (1732–1809), Austrian composer (not, despite some writers, of Croatian descent). Born at Rohrau; cathedral choirboy in Vienna; became pupil of Porpora; married an unappreciative wife, 1760. Took post with Hungarian noble family of Esterházy, 1761–90, first at Eisenstadt (Austria) then at Eszterháza (Hungary). Achieved European reputation there, especially for his symphonies and string quartets: he established the now 'classical' concept of both these types. Visited Britain 1791–2 and 1794–5 – presenting in London the last twelve (see SALOMON) of his 104 catalogued symphonies (for a previous set see PARIS), and also other works; received honorary Oxford degree. Handel's oratorios in London influenced him towards his own 'THE CREATION' and 'THE SEASONS', written on his return to Vienna, where he died. Nicknames have been given to many of his symphonies (e.g. BEAR, CLOCK, DRUM-ROLL, FAREWELL, LONDON, OXFORD, PHILOSOPHER, SURPRISE) and to his Masses (e.g. NELSON MASS, WIND-BAND MASS), in which he characteristically combines cheerfulness and devotion. Wrote also cello concerto (see KRAFT), various other concertos, eighty-four string quartets, 125 trios with BARYTONE; more than twenty Italian and German operas (e.g. 'ARMIDA', 'THE WORLD OF THE MOON', 'Deceit Outwitted' – It. 'L'Infedeltà delusa'); songs, some in English; EMPEROR'S HYMN; 'THE SEVEN LAST WORDS'; etc. (Very prolific throughout unusually long career.) See TOY SYMPHONY for a work ascribed, mistakenly, to him. Brother of Michael Haydn.

HAYDN, (JOHANN) MICHAEL (1737–1806), Austrian composer of much church music, also of symphonies, chamber music, operas, etc. (See TOY SYMPHONY). Also organist. In service to the Archbishop of Salzburg from 1762, dying in Salzburg. Brother of Joseph Haydn.

HEAD, MICHAEL (b. 1900), English singer, pianist, and composer – especially of songs which he sings to his own accompaniment.

HEAD VOICE, that 'register' of the voice which gives the feeling to the singer of vibrating in the head – i.e. the higher register, contrasted with CHEST VOICE.

HEBRIDES, THE, overture by Mendelssohn, born of his visit there, 1829; later revised, and first performed 1832 in London. (Also called 'Fingal's Cave').

HECKELCLARINA, instrument of the clarinet type invented by the German firm of Heckel for the playing of the 'shepherd's pipe' part in act 3 of Wagner's 'TRISTAN AND ISOLDE' – now more usually played on the English horn.

HECKELPHONE, bass instrument of the oboe type (see OBOE) made by the German firm of Heckel; an octave lower in pitch than the oboe; used e.g. by R. Strauss and, under the name 'bass oboe', by Delius, but rare.

HEGER, ROBERT (b. 1886), German composer of symphonic poem 'Hero and Leander', violin concerto, cantata 'Song of Peace', etc.; influenced by R. Strauss. Also conductor.

HEIFETZ, JASCHA (German spelling of Russian Yasha, diminutive of Jacob; b. 1901), Russian-born violinist, boy prodigy; first appeared in U.S.A. 1917, becoming naturalized there 1925; continued touring, with immense reputation. Commissioned violin concertos from Gruenberg and Walton.

HEILLER, ANTON (b. 1923), Austrian composer and organist; works – mainly church music, apart from a chamber symphony – include five Masses, Te Deum, many motets.

HEIMKEHR AUS DER FREMDE, DIE, see SON AND STRANGER.

HELDENLEBEN, EIN, see A HERO'S LIFE.

HELDENTENOR, see HEROIC TENOR.

HELICON, form of tuba passing round the player's body, e.g. the SOUSAPHONE. (Rare in Britain, common in U.S.A.) The name is from its helical (i.e. spiral) shape, not from the ancient Mt Helicon, sacred to the Muses.

HELLER, STEPHEN (1814–88), Hungarian pianist, and composer

chiefly for the piano – sonatas, fantasies, studies, pieces with 'romantic' titles, etc.

HELY-HUTCHINSON, (CHRISTIAN) VICTOR (1901–47, South African-born pianist, conductor, teacher, and composer, educated in England; worked in S. Africa, then (from 1926) in England. Finally BBC Music Director, 1944–7. Works include 'A Carol Symphony' (see CAROL), chamber music, children's song and other songs.

HEMIDEMISEMIQUAVER. the note 𝅘𝅥𝅱 (U.S., sixty-fourth-note) considered as a time-value, equivalent to half a demisemiquaver. Its rest is notated 𝅁 .

HEMING, MICHAEL SAVAGE (1920–42), English composer of a 'Threnody' for orchestra – unfinished; completed by A. Collins as 'Threnody for a Soldier Killed in Action', this being Heming's own fate.

'HEN' SYMPHONY, nickname for Haydn's symphony no. 83 in G minor (1786) – bestowed by someone who eccentrically detected a hen's clucking in the oboe figure of the first movement.

HENKEMANS, HANS (b. 1913), Dutch composer, pupil of Pijper and influenced by Debussy; also pianist. Has written works for piano and for piano and orchestra; also symphony, flute concerto, etc.

HENRIQUES, (VALDEMAR) FINI (1867–1940), Danish composer, pupil of Svendsen; also violinist, pupil of Joachim. Works include operas, ballet 'The Little Mermaid' (after Hans Andersen), two symphonies, piano solos.

HENRY V (1387–1422), king of England, amateur composer; the vocal compositions bearing the name 'Roy Henry' in the OLD HALL MANUSCRIPT are usually considered to be by him; a case has also been made for Henry IV, but Henry VI is now considered ineligible.

HENRY VIII (1491–1547), king of England, amateur composer, some of whose vocal music survives; but the motet 'O Lord the Maker of All Things', formerly attributed to him, is really by W. Mundy.

HENSCHEL, GEORGE (originally Isidor Georg Henschel; 1850–1934), German-born baritone, pianist, composer, and conductor who was naturalized British 1890 and knighted 1914. Conductor of the newly founded Boston Symphony Orchestra 1881–4; as singer accompanying himself, broadcast and recorded until his seventies. Composed two operas, songs in German and English, much piano music, etc.

HENSEL, FANNY, see MENDELSSOHN-BARTHOLDY, FANNY.

HENZE, HANS WERNER (b. 1926), German composer (pupil of Fortner) resident in Italy since 1953; has employed, but has now abandoned, TWELVE-NOTE technique. Works include operas 'Boulevard Solitude' (see 'MANON'), 'King Stag', 'The Prince of Homburg', 'ELEGY FOR YOUNG LOVERS', 'The Bassarids' and 'THE YOUNG LORD'; cantata 'Novae de infinito Laudes' (words by Giordano Bruno; Lat., 'New praises of the infinite'); 'Undine' and other ballets; five symphonies; 'Ode to the West Wind' (after Shelley) for cello and orchestra; 'Dance Marathon' for jazz band and symphony orchestra.

HER FOSTER-DAUGHTER, see JENUFA.

HERBERT, VICTOR (1859–1924), Irish-born composer (also cellist, conductor) who settled in New York, 1886, and wrote many successful operettas including 'Naughty Marietta' and 'Babes in Toyland'; also serious operas, symphonic poem 'Hero and Leander', etc.

HERO'S LIFE, A (Ger., *Ein Heldenleben*), symphonic poem by R. Strauss, 1898, with autobiographical connotation – the section 'The Hero's Works of Peace' quoting some of Strauss's previous compositions.

HÉRODIADE, see HERODIAS.

HERODIAS (Fr., *Hérodiade*), opera by Massenet, produced in Brussels, 1881. Libretto by P. Milliet and 'Henri Grémont' (i.e., G. Hartmann), after a tale by Flaubert: a variation of the story of Salome, who here begs for John the Baptist's life to be saved and afterwards kills herself. Cp. SALOME.

HEROIC TENOR, tenor capable of 'heavy' dramatic roles in opera, especially (as translation of Ger. *Heldentenor*) in Wagner.

HEROLD, (LOUIS JOSEPH) FERDINAND (1791–1833), French composer of 'ZAMPA', 'The Pré aux Clercs' (referring to a famous duelling-ground) and many other operas; also two symphonies, etc. Also pianist and opera chorus-master.

HERRMANN, BERNARD (b. 1911), American composer, pupil of B. Wagenaar and others; also conductor, especially for radio. Works include symphony, violin concerto, opera 'Wuthering Heights', cantata 'Moby Dick', string quartet, and music for 'Citizen Kane' and other films.

HERVÉ, pen-name of Florimond Ronger (1825–92), French composer of operettas, many parodying historical subjects or literary works (one on *The Knights of the Round Table*); also of ballets, a symphony with voices on *The Ashanti War*, many songs, etc.

HERZ, HENRI (really Heinrich; 1806–87), Austrian pianist-composer who settled in Paris and wrote eight piano concertos and other works in brilliant 'virtuoso' style. Contributor to the HEXAMERON.

HESELTINE, PHILIP, see WARLOCK.

HESS, MYRA (1890–1965), English pianist, pupil of Matthay; promoted and directed National Gallery Concerts in London during the Second World War; D.B.E., 1941. Her piano transcription of a chorale from Bach's church cantata no. 147, under the name 'Jesu, joy of man's desiring', has made this among the most widely-known of Bach's works.

HEURE ESPAGNOLE, L', see THE SPANISH HOUR.

HEXACHORD, obsolete (11th-17th centuries) grouping of notes not by octaves (eight notes) but by sixes – Greek *hex*, 6. The 'hard', 'natural', and 'soft' hexachords ascended respectively from G, C, and F, using what are now the white notes of the piano. Cp. GUIDO D'AREZZO.

HEXAMERON, variations contributed by Liszt, Thalberg, Herz, Pixis, Czerny, and Chopin on a march from Bellini's 'THE PURITANS', 1831; with linking passages by Liszt. (From Greek for 'six days' – cp. 'Decameron', ten days – alluding to the six composers. Cp. also GODOWSKY.)

HEXENMENUETT, see FIFTHS QUARTET.

HIAWATHA, three cantatas by Coleridge-Taylor, first performed together in 1900: 'Hiawatha's Wedding Feast', 'The Death of Minnehaha', 'Hiawatha's Departure'. Words from Longfellow's 'Hiawatha', narrative poem of American-Indian life.

HIDDEN FIFTHS, see CONSECUTIVE.

HILL, ALFRED (1870–1960), Australian composer, also violinist and conductor; studied in Leipzig; spent some time in New Zealand and used Maori folk-lore for cantata 'Hinemoa' and song 'Waiata Poi', etc. Also composed seventeen string quartets, 'Overture of Welcome' (players of orchestra entering successively), etc.

HILL, EDWARD BURLINGAME (b. 1872), American composer and teacher: works include three symphonies, violin concerto, 'Music for English horn and orchestra'.

HILL-BILLY SONG, type of traditional song of the (white) American country-dwellers of the Appalachian Mountains, etc.

HILLER, FERDINAND (1801–85), German pianist (pupil of Hummel), conductor, teacher, and composer – many piano pieces, also operas and three symphonies.

HILLER, JOHANN ADAM (1728–1804), German composer (also flutist and singer) and conductor; cantor at St Thomas's, Leipzig (Bach's old position). Wrote church music, instrumental works, and 'The Devil is at Large' (*Der Teufel ist los*) – the first of that type of opera known as SINGSPIEL.

HILTON, JOHN (*c.* 1560–1608), English organist (of Trinity College, Cambridge) and composer of anthems, madrigals, etc. Contributor to 'THE TRIUMPHS OF ORIANA'. See also next entry.

HILTON, JOHN (1599–1657), English organist (of St Margaret's, Westminster) and composer of church music, 'Ayres or Fa-Las' (in this case, works of BALLET type), etc. Was also compiler and part-composer of 'Catch that Catch Can' – collection of rounds, catches, and canons, etc. He was possibly a son of the John Hilton who died in 1608.

HIMMEL, FRIEDRICH HEINRICH (1764–1819), German composer of operas (in German and Italian), church music including anthem 'Incline thine ear', piano works, etc.

HINDEMITH, PAUL (1895–1963), German composer – formerly violinist and viola-player (soloist in first performance of Walton's viola concerto, 1929); teacher in Berlin from 1927. Banned by Nazis as musically 'degenerate' (though not Jewish); taught in Turkey from 1933, settled in U.S.A. 1939. Noted teacher and theoretician. Composed for almost every type of musical medium, and (in his earlier period) much music of deliberately functional intent (see UTILITY MUSIC), e.g. for pianola, and a musical game for children; his piano work 'LUDUS TONALIS' is also didactic. His earlier work was in a dissonant idiom verging on atonality, e.g. in the works labelled 'CHAMBER MUSIC' (*Kammermusik*); later he adopted an 'advanced' but strictly tonal idiom backed by his own theoretical writings. Composed operas 'MATHIS THE PAINTER' (on the life of the painter Grünewald) and 'The Harmony of the World' (on the life of the astronomer Kepler): he based a symphony on each of these. Other works include opera 'CARDILLAC', oratorio 'The Unending'; 'NOBILISSIMA VISIONE' and other ballets; 'Symphonic Metamorphoses of Themes of Weber' (see METAMORPHOSIS); Symphony in E♭ and many other orchestral works; 'THE FOUR TEMPERAMENTS' for piano and strings; 'Funeral Music' for viola and strings, on the death of George V; six string quartets, many sonatas for various instruments; songs including cycle 'The Life of Mary' (*Das Marienleben*).

HISTOIRE DU SOLDAT, L', see THE SOLDIER'S TALE.

HOBOKEN, ANTHONY VAN (b. 1887), Dutch musicologist, living in Switzerland; has compiled a definitive catalogue of Haydn's works of which the first volume was published in 1957.

HOBOY, see HAUTBOY.

HOCKET (Fr., '*hoquet*', hiccup), in medieval church music, the insertion of rests into vocal parts, even in the middle of words – often for expressive purposes.

HODDINOTT, ALUN (b. 1929), Welsh composer of symphony, clarinet concerto, Four Welsh Dances, chamber music, oratorio 'Job', cantata 'Rebecca', etc. Was helped in training by Arthur Benjamin.

HODGSON, PETER (b. 1928), English composer of two symphonies, bassoon concerto, quartet for flute and strings, etc.; pupil of H. Ferguson and others.

HODIE, see THIS DAY.

HØFFDING, FINN (b. 1899), Danish composer and teacher. Has written opera 'The Emperor's New Clothes' and orchestral work 'It's A True Story', both after Hans Andersen; also four symphonies, other operas, wind quintet, 'Dialogues' for oboe and clarinet, etc. Was somewhat influenced by C. Nielsen.

HOFFMANN, ERNST THEODOR AMADEUS (1776–1822), German Romantic novelist and essayist, influencing e.g. Schumann; also composer of opera 'Undine' and other works – and adopting the name 'Amadeus' in homage to Mozart, replacing 'Wilhelm'. Hero of Offenbach's 'THE TALES OF HOFFMANN'.

HOFMANN, JOSEF (really Józef Kazimierz Hofmann; 1876–1957), Polish-born pianist, pupil of Anton Rubinstein; composer of symphony, five piano concertos, and other works – some under the name 'Michel Dvorsky'. Public performer from the age of 6; first visited U.S.A., 1887, later becoming naturalized and dying there.

HOHLFLÖTE (Ger., hollow-sounding flute), type of 8-FOOT organ stop in wood or metal.

HOLBERG SUITE, suite composed by Grieg for piano, then arranged for strings (1884); bicentenary tribute, in the form of a pastiche of old dance-movements, to Ludvig Holberg (1684–1754), Norwegian dramatist.

HOLBORNE, ANTHONY (?–1602), English composer who published a book of dances and other music for viols in 1599.

HOLBROOKE, JOSEPH (CHARLES) (on some scores Josef; 1878–1958), English composer of operatic trilogy 'The Cauldron of Annwen' and other operas; orchestral variations on 'Three Blind Mice'; 'Byron' and other symphonic poems. Also pianist, conductor, and polemical writer on music.

HÖLLER, KARL (b. 1907), German composer of 'Variations on a Theme of Sweelinck' and other orchestral works in somewhat conservative style; also chamber music, etc.

HOLLINGSWORTH, JOHN ERNEST (1916–63), English conductor – Associate Conductor at the Henry Wood Promenade Concerts (London) from 1949; active also as ballet conductor at Covent Garden.

HOLLINS, ALFRED (1865–1942), English organist (blind from birth) and composer for his instrument; earlier a pianist, playing concertos, etc.

HOLMBOE, VAGN (b. 1909), Danish composer, pupil of Toch, Høffding, and others; influenced by Bartók. Works include three string quartets, eight symphonies, and ten 'chamber concertos'.

HOLST, GUSTAV (THEODORE) (originally von Holst; 1874–1934), English composer of partly Swedish descent, pupil of Stanford, at various times pianist, trombonist, teacher (especially at Morley College, London), and conductor – of Boston Symphony Orchestra, 1922. Interested in oriental philosophy, and made various settings of the Hindu scriptures in his own translations. Bold harmonic experimenter, e.g. in polytonality; finally cultivated a markedly austere style, e.g. in 'EGDON HEATH' for orchestra. Other works include operas 'At the Boar's Head' (after Shakespeare's *Henry IV*) 'THE PERFECT FOOL', and 'SĀVITRI'; 'THE PLANETS', 'BENI MORA', etc. for orchestra; 'ST PAUL'S SUITE' for strings; choral 'HYMN OF JESUS' and a 'First Choral Symphony' (words by Keats; there is no second); music for military and brass band; songs (four for voice and violin), etc. Father of Imogen Holst.

HOLST, IMOGEN (b. 1907), English musical educationist, conductor, and composer (overture, folk-song arrangements, songs, etc.); influenced by Britten. Author of books on her father (preceding).

HOMAGE, HOMMAGE (Eng., Fr.), terms used by a composer especially in the expression 'homage to' (or *hommage à*) another composer, usually implying a quotation from that other composer's work or an evocation of his style. So Falla's 'Homage' (Sp. *Homenaje*) for guitar, inscribed 'For the grave of Debussy'. Cp. also ULYSSES.

HOMAGE MARCH (1) by Wagner (Ger., *Huldigungsmarsch*), originally for military band, 1864 (for King Ludwig II of Bavaria), later orchestrated; (2) by Grieg – see SIGURD JORSALFAR.

HOMAGE TO THE QUEEN, ballet with music by M. Arnold, produced in London to celebrate the coronation of Elizabeth II, 1953.

HOME, SWEET HOME, see BISHOP, who composed it.

HOMENAJE, see HOMAGE.

HOMMAGE, see HOMAGE.

HOMME ARMÉ, L' (Fr., The Armed Man), title of an old French secular song used by Dufay, Palestrina, and more than twenty-five other composers of the 15th, 16th, and early 17th centuries as a CANTUS FIRMUS in their Masses. Such Masses are accordingly known by this name.

HOMOPHONY (from Gk for same-sounding), term used as opposite of POLYPHONY – i.e. signifying that (as for instance in an English hymn-tune) the PARTS move together, presenting only a top-melody and chords beneath, as distinct from the contrapuntal interplay of different melodies simultaneously. So also *homophonic*; and cp. MONOPHONY.

HONDO (Sp., deep), term used in the expression *cante hondo* (deep song), type of sad Andalusian song characteristically using some intervals smaller than a semitone.

HONEGGER, ARTHUR (1892–1955), Swiss composer, though born in France and largely resident there. Pupil of Widor and d'Indy. Was one of the 'SIX' (group of composers) but developed his own distinctive style, often heavily dissonant and with marked declamatory elements. Collaborated with Ibert in opera 'The Eaglet' (*L'Aiglon*): other stage works include 'ANTIGONE', 'KING DAVID', 'JUDITH', 'JOAN OF ARC AT THE STAKE'. He composed five symphonies – no. 2 for strings plus optional trumpet; no. 3 'Liturgical', no. 5 'di tre re' – see RE. Other works include three 'symphonic movements' – 'PACIFIC 231', 'RUGBY', and no. 3 (non-programmatic); MONOPARTITA for orchestra; 'Dance of the Goat' for flute; piano solos; French and British film music; 'Christmas Cantata' (in English, French, German, and Latin).

HOOK, JAMES (1746–1827), English organist and composer – working in both capacities at Vauxhall Gardens, London, 1774–1820; wrote musical plays, concertos, sonatas, cantatas, catches, and over 2,000 songs including 'The Lass of Richmond Hill'.

HOPAK, see GOPAK.

HOPKINS, ANTONY (surname changed from Reynolds in boyhood; b. 1921), English composer. Is also pianist, and noted as radio commentator on music. Works, tending to light and often humorous style, include operas 'Lady Rohesia', 'The Man from Tuscany', and 'THREE'S COMPANY'; ballet 'Café des Sports'; musical play 'Johnny the Priest'; 'Scena' for soprano and strings (later arranged for three voices and full orchestra).

HOPKINSON, FRANCIS (1737–91), American statesman, writer, and amateur composer – e.g. of the song 'My Days Have Been So Wondrous Free', the first published composition by a native-born American.

HORENSTEIN, JASCHA (Ger. spelling of Rus. *Yasha*, dim. of Jacob) (b. 1898), Russian-born, Vienna-trained conductor, noted in Bruckner and Mahler; settled in Switzerland.

HORN, (1) type of wind-instrument descended from primitive use of an animal's horn for blowing through. The term now applies especially to the coiled brass orchestral instrument which was developed (particularly in France, whence the name *French horn*) from the earlier *hunting horn* or *hand horn*. This earlier instrument, without valves or keys, yielded to the player only the notes of the HARMONIC SERIES, like a bugle, plus a few obtainable by the insertion of the hand in the bell of the instrument. The particular harmonic series sounded depended on the length of the instrument's tube: from about 1700 CROOKS were inserted into the instrument to vary the length of the tube and thus to make the harmonic series available at various different pitches. But only from about 1850 did the modern horn, with VALVES to secure a chromatic range of notes, become standard. It is normally today a TRANSPOSING INSTRUMENT in F, with compass from B below the bass staff upwards for about three and a half octaves; also used is the *double horn*, which can be switched from a horn in F (as normal) to a horn in high B♭. Orchestral horn parts assume that the odd-numbered players specialize in the higher notes, the even-numbered in lower: four horns are usual, six or eight sometimes met. The instrument is also standard in the military (not the brass) band; a few concertos have been written for it, e.g. by R. Strauss, or for its valveless predecessor, e.g. by Mozart. (2) term used colloquially in the brass band to mean not the above instrument (not used in the brass band) but the tenor SAXHORN; and used as jazz slang to mean a trumpet, a trombone, even a saxophone. (3) *English horn*, see under ENGLISH.

HORN, CHARLES EDWARD (1786–1849), English singer and composer of many songs including 'Cherry Ripe'; also of oratorios and music for plays. Settled in U.S.A., 1833, dying there. Son of Karl Friedrich Horn.

HORN, KARL FRIEDRICH (1762–1830), German-born pianist, organist, composer of piano music, etc.; settled in England, 1782, and died there. An early participant in the 19th-century revival of Bach. Father of C. E. Horn.

HORN SIGNAL, SYMPHONY WITH THE, nickname for Haydn's symphony no. 31 in D, 1765 – from the slow movement with its horn-calls. Four horns are used instead of the two normal at that period.

HORNEMAN, CHRISTIAN EMIL (1841–1906), Danish composer of opera 'Aladdin', orchestral and piano music, songs, etc.

HORNPIPE, lively English dance formerly (e.g. in Purcell) with three beats in the bar, now (as in the well-known 'Sailor's Hornpipe' and as in Sullivan's 'RUDDIGORE') with two beats in the bar. Named because originally accompanied by pipe made from animal's horn.

HOROSCOPE, ballet with music by Lambert, produced in 1938; the characters are astrological entities. (An orchestral suite is drawn from the score.)

HOROVITZ, JOSEPH (b. 1926), Austrian-born composer-conductor-pianist resident in England since 1938; pupil of Jacob and N. Boulanger. Works include 'Alice in Wonderland' and other ballets; operas 'The Dumb Wife' and 'Gentleman's Island'; clarinet concerto. Formerly assistant musical director of the 'Intimate Opera' company.

HOROWITZ, VLADIMIR (b. 1904), Russian-born pianist; début 1922. Came to U.S.A. 1928 and settled there, earning highest reputation. Contracted nervous ailment; ceased to give concerts, 1950, though continued to make records. Married to Toscanini's daughter, Wanda.

HORSLEY, CHARLES EDWARD (1822–76), English pianist, organist, and composer especially of oratorios (pupil of Mendelssohn); went to Australia 1862 and later to U.S.A., where he died.

HOT, lively, exciting (of jazz, etc.) – international but now faded term (Joe Daniels and his Hot Shots, Quintette du Hot Club de France, etc.).

HOTTER, HANS (b. 1909), German baritone (formerly church organist) noted in Wagner (e.g. as Sachs in 'Die Meistersinger'); also opera producer, e.g. of 'THE RING' at Covent Garden.

HOUSE OF THE DEAD, see FROM A HOUSE OF THE DEAD.

HOVHANESS, ALAN (b. 1911), American composer of Armenian descent; also conductor and organist. Works, much influenced by ancient Middle Eastern music, mainly have Armenian titles – piano concerto (with strings) entitled 'Lousadzak' (The Coming of Light), also two other piano concertos and other works for various solo instruments with strings; also piano solos, ballet 'Ardent Song', etc.

HOWELLS, HERBERT (NORMAN) (b. 1892), English composer (pupil of Stanford), teacher, and former cathedral organist. Compositions include choral works to religious texts – Requiem, 'HYMNUS PARADISI', 'Missa Sabrinensis' (Lat., Severn Mass), etc.; also orchestral works, two piano concertos, music for piano solo, string quartet, brass band, etc.; church music. Follows a conservatively inclined idiom but with distinctive individual chromaticism. Contributor to 'A GARLAND FOR THE QUEEN'.

HUCBALD (*c.* 840–*c.* 930), French monk and author of a musical treatise in Latin about the MODES, DIAPHONY, etc.

HUDSON, GEORGE (?–?) English 17th-century violinist and composer, in service to Charles II; wrote part of the music to 'THE SIEGE OF RHODES'.

HUGH THE DROVER, *or, Love in the Stocks*, opera by Vaughan

Williams, produced in London, 1924. Libretto by H. Child: the scene is a Cotswold village at the time of the Napoleonic Wars. Styled 'a Romantic ballad opera', but see BALLAD OPERA.

HUGHES, ARWEL (b. 1909), Welsh composer of opera 'Menna' (on a Welsh legend) and other works of Welsh inspiration; also of a Prelude for orchestra, etc. Pupil of Vaughan Williams. Also conductor – of BBC Welsh Orchestra since 1950.

HUGHES, HERBERT (1882–1937), Northern Irish composer, arranger of Irish folk-songs, critic, etc. Father of Spike Hughes.

HUGHES, SPIKE (really Patrick Cairns Hughes; b. 1908), English composer (radio music, folk-song arrangements, etc.), and writer on music and other things; has had extremely varied musical career, at one time as dance-band leader. Of Irish descent; son of Herbert Hughes.

HUGUENOTS, THE (Fr., *Les Huguenots*), Meyerbeer's most successful opera, produced in Paris, 1836. Libretto by E. Scribe and E. Deschamps, culminating in the St Bartholomew Massacre, 1572.

HULLAH, JOHN PYKE (1812–84), English composer of songs including 'O that we two were maying', opera 'The Village Coquettes' (libretto by Dickens), etc.; singing-teacher and writer of textbooks.

HUMFREY, PELHAM (or Humphrey; 1647–74), English composer who studied in France and Italy and was in service to Charles II. Wrote music to plays including Shakespeare's *The Tempest*, also church music, vocal solos and duets, etc. One of Purcell's teachers.

HUMMEL, JOHANN NEPOMUK (1778–1837), German pianist (pupil of Mozart) and composer (pupil of Haydn and others), touring extensively as performer. Wrote concertos and other works for piano, and also operas, church music, etc.

HUMORESK, HUMORESQUE (Ger., Fr., the latter also used as Eng.), type of instrumental composition supposedly of a wayward or capricious nature – term used e.g. by Schumann and Dvořák.

HUMPERDINCK, ENGELBERT (1854–1921), German composer; friend and assistant to Wagner; also teacher (for some time in Spain) and critic. Composed operas including 'HANSEL AND GRETEL' and 'Kings' Children' (Königskinder); also incidental music to various plays, choral works, 'Moorish Rhapsody' for orchestra, etc.

HUMPHREY, PELHAM, see HUMFREY.

HUNGARIAN FANTASIA, see HUNGARIAN RHAPSODY.

HUNGARIAN RHAPSODY, title given by Liszt to each of nineteen piano pieces in Hungarian gipsy style – nos. 1–15 were composed by 1852, and others about thirty years later. Some were afterwards orchestrated, and on no. 14 is based Liszt's 'Hungarian Fantasia' (properly 'Fantasia on Hungarian Popular Themes') for piano and orchestra, 1852.

HUNT, THE, nickname for Haydn's symphony no. 73 in D, 1781 – from the music of the horns and oboes in the finale, a movement originally taken from one of Haydn's operas.

'HUNT' QUARTET, nickname for Mozart's string quartet in B♭, K. 458 (1784), because the opening suggests hunting-horns.

HUNTING-HORN, instrument used for giving signals while hunting, from which evolved the orchestral HORN.

HURDY-GURDY, term applied wrongly to any instrument worked by turning a handle (e.g. BARREL-ORGAN, STREET PIANO) and correctly only to one such instrument, a kind of portable, mechanical viol called in French *vielle*. One hand turns a handle actuating a rosined wheel which acts as a bow; the other hand stops the strings not directly (as e.g. on a violin) but by means of a tiny piano-like keyboard. In addition there are one or two freely vibrating strings, giving a DRONE bass. Haydn and others wrote for this instrument.

HURLSTONE, WILLIAM YEATES (1876–1905), English composer and teacher cut off by early death: wrote Fantasy-Variations on a Swedish Air, for orchestra, also chamber music, etc.

HUSA, KAREL (b. 1921), Czechoslovak composer of orchestral and chamber works – including 'Evocations of Slovakia' for clarinet, violin, and cello; pupil of Honegger and N. Boulanger; resident in Paris and later in U.S.A.

HYDRAULIS, ancient instrument, also called *water-organ*, much used under the Romans; precursor of the organ. Water was used to maintain a constant pressure on the air fed to the pipes.

HYMN, a song of praise to a deity, saint, etc.; especially (in Protestant churches) such as has words specially written, not taken directly from the Bible, and is sung congregationally. Also an extended composition to words supposedly of a hymn-like nature – see following entries.

HYMN OF JESUS, THE, work for two choruses, semi-chorus, and orchestra by Holst, 1917; text from the Apocryphal 'Acts of St John'.

HYMN OF PRAISE (Ger., *Lobgesang*), symphonic cantata by Mendelssohn, first performed 1840. One choral movement (religious text) is preceded by three orchestral and the whole is numbered as Mendelssohn's 2nd symphony.

HYMN TO ST CECILIA, setting for unaccompanied chorus by Britten (who was born on St Cecilia's Day) of a poem by W. H. Auden, 1942. Cp. ODE FOR ST CECILIA'S DAY; see also CECILIA.

HYMN TO THE SUN, an aria sung by the Queen of Shemakhan in Rimsky-Korsakov's opera 'THE GOLDEN COCKEREL'.

I

I (It.), the (pl.) – see next word of phrase.

IBERIA, (1) four sets each of three piano pieces by Albéniz, representing various parts of Spain; first performed complete 1909 (five of the pieces were later orchestrated by Arbós); (2) orchestral work by Debussy, first performed 1910, being the second part of his 'IMAGES' for orchestra. It is in three movements suggestive of aspects of Spain.

IBERT, JACQUES (FRANÇOIS ANTOINE) (1890–1962), French composer, pupil of Fauré; director of the French Academy in Rome from 1937. Collaborated with Honegger in opera 'The Eaglet' (*L'Aiglon*) and with nine other composers in 'JEANNE'S FAN'. Other works, often tending to a light style, include 'Angélique' and other operas; symphonic poem after Wilde's *The Ballad of Reading Jail*; orchestral suite 'PORTS OF CALL' (*Escales*); Divertissement, arranged from his music to the play *The Italian Straw Hat*; Concertino da Camera for alto saxophone and eleven instruments; 'The Little White Donkey' and other piano works.

IDÉE FIXE, term used by Berlioz, e.g. in the FANTASTIC SYMPHONY, for what is usually called MOTTO THEME.

IDOMENEO, see IDOMENEUS.

IDOMENEUS, KING OF CRETE, *or*, *Ilia and Idamantes*, opera by Mozart, produced in Munich (in Italian), 1781. Libretto by G. B. Varesco: a story of love and sacrifice taking place after the Trojan War, Idamantes being the son of Idomeneus and the lover of Ilia. (The story is based on Virgil, the usual title *Idomeneo* being an italianization of the king's Latin name.)

IDYLL, literary term for a peaceful, pastoral work – transferred to music e.g. in Wagner's SIEGFRIED IDYLL.

IFIGENIA, see IPHIGENIA.

ILLUMINATIONS, LES, cycle of nine songs by Britten, 1939, for high voice and strings, to French poems by Rimbaud evocative of various sights and sounds.

ILLUSTRATIVE MUSIC, music describing, evoking, or otherwise alluding to a non-musical source, e.g. a poem, novel, play, picture, landscape, or an explicit emotional experience. (The more usual, but confusing, term for this is 'programme music'.)

IMAGES, title given by Debussy to two series of works – (a) two sets each of three piano pieces (1905, 1907), and (b) three orchestral works of which 'IBERIA' was completed in 1908, 'Dances of Spring' (*Rondes de Printemps*) in 1909, and 'Gigues' (originally 'Gigues Tristes', i.e. Sad Jigs) in 1912 – the orchestration of 'Gigues' being by Caplet.

IMITATION, a composers' device in part-writing: one voice repeats (if not literally, then at least recognizably) a figure previously stated by another voice. CANON and FUGUE employ imitation according to strict and regular patterns.

IMMORTAL BELOVED (Ger., *Unsterbliche Geliebte*), a form of address used by Beethoven in a famous love-letter which he dated 'Monday 6 July' (not specifying a year). The identity of the woman has long been puzzled over. It now appears that she was Josephine von

Brunswick, and that the year was 1812. She had a child, surmised to be Beethoven's, in 1813.

IMMORTAL HOUR, THE, opera by Boughton, produced in Glastonbury, Somerset, 1914. Libretto by composer, on Celtic legend as drawn from plays and poems of 'Fiona Macleod' (i.e. William Sharp).

IMPERIAL (Fr., *L'Impériale*), nickname for Haydn's symphony no. 53 in D, about 1773 – presumably named, somewhat arbitrarily, from its 'Largo maestoso' opening.

IMPERIAL MASS, another nickname for Haydn's NELSON MASS.

IMPRESARIO, THE (Ger., *Der Schauspieldirektor*), play with overture and other music by Mozart (and usually classed as one of his operas), produced in Vienna, 1786. Words by G. Stephanie, satirizing the relationships of impresario and female singers.

IMPRESSIONISM, term borrowed from painting (applied e.g. to Monet, Degas, Whistler, and used to describe the works e.g. of Debussy and Ravel in so far as they seem to interpret their titles not in a narrative or dramatic way (like the ROMANTICS) but as though an observer were recording the impression on him at a given instant.

IMPROMPTU, short piece of music (usually for piano, e.g. by Schubert, Chopin) seeming to suggest improvisation.

IMPROVISATION, see IMPROVISE.

IMPROVISE (or 'extemporize'), to perform according to spontaneous fancy, not from memory or from written copy – though often a performer improvises 'on' (i.e. round about) a given tune. Hence *improvisation*: this term is sometimes also used as title of an actual written-down piece presumably intended to convey the spirit of genuine improvisation.

IN, term with various musical usages including (1) indication of a conductor's beat – so e.g. *in* 2, meaning that two beats will be actually given to each bar, although the composer may have indicated two or four or six, etc.; (2) indication of the division of forces in an orchestra – so e.g. *in* 4, applied to the violas, would indicate that the viola-players are to be divided into four sections each playing a different PART; (3) indication of key, e.g. *symphony in C minor*; (4) indication of (a) the basic key in which a wind instrument is pitched, and sometimes also of (b) the transposition it consequently requires (see TRANSPOSING INSTRUMENT). Only usage can show whether or not the additional meaning (b) is implied. E.g. *horn in F* means not only that the instrument is basically pitched in F (if blown, without depressing any valves, it will produce a HARMONIC SERIES basically related to the key of F major), but also that it is a TRANSPOSING INSTRUMENT sounding a fifth lower than written – the note written as C sounds as F, etc. Thus here both the meanings (a) and (b) are implied. But a bass trombone is sometimes said to be *in G* because of its basic harmonic series, but it is not a transposing instrument, being written at the pitch it sounds.

IN MODO DI (It.), in the manner of.

IN NATURE'S REALM, alternative English name for Dvořák's overture 'AMID NATURE'.

IN NOMINE, type of 16th- and 17th-century English polyphonic composition for viols or virginals, based on a plainsong melody, nearly always the melody called 'Gloria tibi trinitas'. Taverner wrote a Mass based on this plainsong melody, and afterwards transcribed for virginals the part of his Mass beginning 'In nomine domini' ('In the name of the Lord'); he therefore, following a practice then quite normal, used the words *In Nomine* as a title for the transcription. Later composers, apparently regarding this example as a kind of prototype, also gave the title *In Nomine* to their works based on the plainsong 'Gloria tibi trinitas', though the form has no connexion with the words except through Taverner's example.

IN THE SOUTH, concert-overture by Elgar, subtitled 'Alassio', the Italian town where he composed it (1904). The word 'Moglio' above a clarinet phrase in the score is the name of a nearby village.

IN THE STEPPES OF CENTRAL ASIA, usual English title for the work actually entitled simply 'In Central Asia' (Rus., *V srednei Azii*), 'orchestral picture' by Borodin, 1880, representing the approach and passing of a caravan; composed to accompany a *tableau vivant*.

INCREDIBLE FLUTIST, THE, ballet with music by Piston, first performed 1938, the flutist being a charmer of snakes and human beings. A concert suite drawn from it was first given in 1940.

INDETERMINACY, the principle, employed by some modernist composers from the 1950s, of leaving elements of the performance either to pure chance (see ALEATORY) or to the decision of the performer. For examples, see BERIO and STOCKHAUSEN.

INDIAN QUEEN, THE, so-called 'opera' by Purcell, produced in London, 1695 (the last of its five acts is by D. Purcell). It was in fact an adaptation, with music, of a play by Dryden and R. Howard on the rivalry of Mexicans and Peruvians – 'Indian' thus meaning American-Indian.

INDY, (PAUL MARIE THÉODORE) VINCENT D' (1851–1931), French composer, pupil and follower of Franck; enthusiast for Wagner; joint founder of the Schola Cantorum (a Paris musical academy, originally for the study of church music), 1894; later taught also at Paris Conservatory. Works include 'Fervaal' and five other operas; 'SYMPHONY ON A FRENCH MOUNTAINEER'S SONG' and two other symphonies; orchestral variations 'Istar' (after a Babylonian epic); triple concerto for flute, cello, piano, and orchestra; songs, folk-song arrangements, piano works, much chamber music.

INEXTINGUISHABLE, THE, see THE UNQUENCHABLE.

INFANTINO, LUIGI (b. 1921), Italian operatic tenor; appearances at the Scala, Milan, and Metropolitan, New York, etc.

INGEGNERI, MARC' ANTONIO (*c.* 1545–1592), Italian composer, choirmaster of Cremona Cathedral; teacher of Monteverdi. Works include Masses and other church music (some formerly attributed to Palestrina) and madrigals.

INGHELBRECHT, DESIRÉ ÉMILE (1880–1965), French conductor and composer of ballet 'El Greco', chamber music, 'La Nursery' for piano duet, etc.

INGLESE (It.), English. For *corno inglese* see ENGLISH HORN.

INSTRUMENT, MUSICAL, an object (other than the organs of the body) used for the production of musical sound by the application of mechanical energy – or, as in ELECTRONIC instruments, by the application of electrical impulses. The usual classification of instruments is into *wind, strings*, and *percussion* (in which, respectively, vibrations are set up in an air-column, a string, and a membrane or other surface). Wind-instruments are divided, e.g. in the orchestra, into WOODWIND and BRASS (between which there is a difference in method of sound-production, more important than differences in materials used). Note that this classification is one of practical convenience and is not technically exhaustive: the piano, for instance, uses strings but is also 'percussive' in mechanism – and yet is not normally spoken of as a stringed or percussion instrument. See also INSTRUMENTATION.

INSTRUMENTATION, the writing of music for particular instruments – term used particularly with reference to a composer's necessary knowledge of what is practicable, and what sounds well, on different instruments. Cp. ORCHESTRATION, which properly applies to scoring for groups and not primarily to the qualities of individual instruments.

INTENDANT (Ger.), superintendent, administrative director – especially of an opera house or other kind of theatre.

INTERLUDE, piece of music inserted between other pieces (e.g. organ passage between the verses of a hymn) or between non-musical events, e.g. between the acts of a play. (Occasionally also used as a musical title without such implications, e.g. in A. Bush's 'Lyric Interlude' for violin and piano, 1944.)

INTERMÈDE (Fr.), INTERMEZZO.

INTERMEZZO (It.), something 'in the middle', hence (specifically musical meanings) – (1) instrumental piece in the middle of an opera, e.g. that performed while the stage is left empty in Mascagni's 'CAVALLERIA RUSTICANA'; (2) short concert-piece – term used e.g. by Brahms for some piano works; (3, obsolete) short comic opera, e.g. Pergolesi's 'THE MAID AS MISTRESS' originally played between the acts of an early 18th-century serious opera. See also the following entry.

INTERMEZZO, opera by R. Strauss, produced in Dresden, 1924. Libretto by composer, based on an episode (i.e. 'intermezzo' in a non-musical sense) in his own life, and having as hero an opera-conductor whose peace is interrupted when his wife suspects him of infidelity.

INTERNATIONAL(E), socialist anthem composed by P. Degeyter (1848–1932), formerly also the national anthem of the U.S.S.R. (till 1944); its title refers to an international socialist organization which (according to the English version of the song) 'unites the human race'. See THESE THINGS SHALL BE.

INTERRUPTED CADENCE, see CADENCE.

INTERVAL, the 'distance' between two notes, in so far as one of them ig higher or lower than the other. Thus the interval from C to the G above it is a 'fifth', to the A above it a 'sixth', etc. (These are calculated by counting upwards, and by including in the count the notes at both extreme ends.) The names 'fifth', 'sixth', etc., are themselves further defined – see PERFECT, MAJOR, MINOR, AUGMENTED, DIMINISHED. Intervals above an octave ('eighth') are called *compound intervals*, being 'compounded' of so many octaves plus a smaller interval. Thus the interval from C to the next G above it but one (twelve notes, counting the extremes) is called a twelfth and is a compound interval made of an octave (C–C) and a fifth (C–G).

INVENTION, name given by Bach to a type of short keyboard work in two-part counterpoint; fifteen of these are included in his LITTLE CLAVIER BOOK, 1720, for the instruction of his son W. F. Bach. The term has also been applied by Bach's editors to similar pieces in three-part counterpoint in the same collection (called by Bach himself 'symphonies') and has been occasionally used also by later composers.

INVERSION, see INVERT.

INVERT, to turn upside-down; thus (1) a chord not in its 'root position' is said to be in one or other *inversion* – see POSITION (3); (2) two melodies in counterpoint may be mutually *inverted* by the upper becoming the lower and vice versa (counterpoint capable of making sense under this treatment is called *invertible counterpoint* and forms the stuff of, e.g., FUGUE); (3) a single melody may be *inverted* by being performed 'upside-down', i.e. with all its successive intervals applied in the opposite direction. Thus an upward interval of a major third (say D–F♯) when inverted would be replaced by a downward interval of a major third (D–B♭) – or by an upward interval of a minor sixth which would produce the same note (D–B♭) though in a higher octave. A melody so inverted is called the *inversion* of the original – often abbreviated to *I* in the theory of TWELVE-NOTE technique.

INVISIBLE CITY OF KITEZH, THE, workable abbreviation for 'The Legend of the Invisible City of Kitezh and of the Maid Fevronia' (Rus., *Skazkanie o nevidimom gradie Kitezhe i devie Fevronie*), opera by Rimsky-Korsakov, produced in St Petersburg, 1907. Libretto by V. I. Bielsky, combining two Russian legends – of the miraculous rescue of Kitezh from the Tartars, and of St Fevronia.

INVITATION TO THE DANCE (not 'to the Waltz'), piano piece by Weber (Ger., *Aufforderung zum Tanz*), in the form of a waltz with slow introduction and slow epilogue, 1819. Orchestrated e.g. by Berlioz and by Weingartner; used for the ballet 'Le Spectre de la rose', 1911.

IOLANTA, opera by Tchaikovsky, produced in St Petersburg, 1892. Libretto (after Hans Andersen) by M. I. Tchaikovsky, the composer's brother: the name-part is that of a blind medieval princess, having no connexion with 'Iolanthe'.

IOLANTHE, *or The Peer and the Peri*, operetta by Sullivan, produced in London and New York on the same day, 1882. Libretto by W. S. Gilbert, on the interaction of Fairyland and the House of Lords. The term *Peri*, usefully borrowed to rhyme with fairy, is derived from Persian mythology: cp. 'THE PERI', 'PARADISE AND THE PERI'.

IONIAN MODE, the MODE which may be represented by the white keys of the piano from C to C.

IPHIGENIA IN AULIS, operas after Euripides by several composers including – (1) Gluck (Fr., *Iphigénie en Aulide*), with libretto by F. L. L. du Roullet, indebted to Racine; produced in Paris, 1774; (2) Cherubini (It., *Ifigenia in Aulide*), with libretto by F. Moretti; produced in Turin, 1788 – Cherubini's last Italian opera, after which he settled in Paris. The plot of these operas has its sequel in 'Iphigenia in Tauris'.

IPHIGENIA IN TAURIS, operas after Euripides (see also preceding entry) by various composers including (1) Gluck (Fr., *Iphigénie en Tauride*) with libretto by N. F. Guillard; produced in Paris 1779; (2) Piccinni, with libretto by A. du C. Dubreuil; produced in Paris, 1781. (Supporters of Gluck and Piccinni clashed over the two operas.)

IPPOLITOV-IVANOV, MIKHAIL (1859–1935), Russian composer, pupil of Rimsky-Korsakov; director of the Moscow Conservatory. Studied folk music, e.g. of Georgia, and wrote orchestral 'Caucasian Sketches', and other regionally-titled works – also two symphonies, operas, many songs, etc. Completed Mussorgsky's unfinished opera 'The Marriage'.

IRELAND, JOHN (NICHOLSON) (1879–1962), English composer, pupil of Stanford; also pianist and formerly organist. Destroyed his works up to 1908. Published no opera, no ballet, no symphony, but piano concerto and various orchestral works (e.g. 'THE FORGOTTEN RITE', 'MAI-DUN', 'A LONDON OVERTURE', 'SATYRICON', Concertino Pastorale for strings); sonata, and many other works for piano. Cultivated a personal idiom within the Romantic tradition and often linked with the depiction of places. Also wrote many songs, including 'Sea Fever'; cantata 'THESE THINGS SHALL BE'; three piano trios, etc. Contributor to 'A GARLAND FOR THE QUEEN'.

IRIS, opera by Mascagni, produced in Rome, 1898. Libretto, set in Japan, by L. Illica – the joint librettist, later, for Puccini's 'MADAME BUTTERFLY'.

IRMELIN, opera by Delius, composed 1890–92, produced posthumously in Oxford, 1953. Libretto by composer, named after the nobly-born herione. The '*Prelude to Irmelin*' is a later work, composed 1932 and based on themes from the opera.

IRVING, ROBERT (AUGUSTINE) (b. 1913), English conductor, especially of ballet; at Covent Garden, then with New York City Ballet.

ISAAC, HEINRICH (*c.* 1450–1517), Flemish (Germanized) composer, holding posts with the Medici and other noble families, and living in Austria and Italy; died in Florence. Composed church music; instrumental works; songs in French, Italian, German, and Latin: the well-known tune 'Innsbruck' which he harmonized was probably now his own composition.

ISAACS, EDWARD (1881–1953), English pianist and composer chiefly for the piano; blind from 1925. Director of the Manchester Tuesday Midday Concerts.

ISLAMEY, fantasy for piano by Balakirev, evoking an 'oriental' atmosphere and prompted by a visit to the Caucasus; first performed 1869. Orchestrated by Casella, 1908.

ISLE OF THE DEAD, THE, a picture by the German painter Arnold Böcklin (1827–1901), which prompted Rakhmaninov's symphonic poem of the same name (1909) and a few other musical works.

ISORHYTHMIC (from Gk, equal-rhythmed), term applied to certain medieval motets, e.g. by Machaut, of which the rhythms are repeated according to a strict scheme not corresponding to repetition in the melody.

ISRAEL IN EGYPT, oratorio by Handel, with words from the Bible, first performed in London, 1739; predominantly choral, and includes famous double (i.e. eight-part) choruses. Incorporates unacknowledged 'borrowings' from KERL.

'ISRAEL' SYMPHONY, work for orchestra with five solo voices by Bloch, first performed in New York, 1916; originally to have been called 'Fêtes juives', and refers to Jewish religious festivals.

ISTESSO TEMPO, L' (It.), at the same tempo, i.e. preserving the same pace although the unit of beat may have changed – say from 2/4 to 6/8, in which case the old ♩ would be the new ♩.

ITALIAN CAPRICE, orchestral work by Tchaikovsky, composed in 1879 in Italy, based on tunes heard there. (Original title 'Capriccio Italien' is bastard Italian-plus-French.)

ITALIAN CONCERTO, work for harpsichord with two manuals by Bach, published 1735 (see CLAVIERÜBUNG); the contrast of loud and soft tone between the keyboards suggests the contrast implicit in the name CONCERTO.

ITALIAN GIRL IN ALGIERS, THE (It., *L'Italiana in Algeri*), comic opera by Rossini, produced in Venice, 1813. Libretto by A. Anelli, the heroine easily outwitting the Sultan who holds her prisoner.

ITALIAN OVERTURE, see OVERTURE.

ITALIAN SERENADE, work by Wolf for string quartet, 1887; he later made an arrangement for orchestra and intended to add two more movements to this.

ITALIAN SIXTH, type of 'augmented sixth' chord (see AUGMENTED) distinguished by having a major third (and no other note) between the notes forming the sixth – e.g. (reading upwards) C, E, A♯. (Cp. FRENCH, GERMAN sixths.) The reason for the names is not known.

ITALIAN SONG-BOOK (Ger., *Italienisches Liederbuch*), Wolf's song-settings, 1890–6, of forty-six Italian poems in German translation.

'ITALIAN' SYMPHONY, Mendelssohn's symphony no. 4 in A major and minor; commemorating a visit to Italy, and first performed 1833. See SALTERELLO.

ITALIENISCHES LIEDERBUCH, see ITALIAN SONG-BOOK.

ITURBI, JOSÉ (b. 1895), Spanish conductor and pianist (sometimes simultaneously). Resident in U.S.A.; held conductor's post in Rochester (N.Y.), 1935–44. Several film appearances.

IVAN SUSSANIN, opera by Glinka, produced in St Petersburg, 1836. Libretto by G. F. Rosen: originally staged as 'A Life for the Tsar'. *Ivan Sussanin* (the name of its historic 17th-century peasant hero) was Glinka's own intended title, and is now used for the opera in Russia – where it is now given with an altered plot, substituting the national leader Minin for Tsar Michael.

IVAN THE TERRIBLE, (1) opera by Bizet, with libretto by A. Leroy and H. Trianon about the Russian Tsar; composed, 1865, withdrawn, thought lost, recovered 1944 and produced in Württemberg, 1946; (2) title sometimes given to Rimsky-Korsakov's opera 'THE MAID OF PSKOV'.

IVANHOE, Sullivan's only 'serious' opera, produced in London, 1891. Libretto by J. R. Sturgis, after Scott's novel. (See also MARSCHNER.)

IVES, CHARLES (EDWARD) (1874–1954), American composer of music which, all written before 1920, anticipates later devices, e.g. POLYTONALITY, POLYRHYTHM, quarter-tones. Was organist and choirmaster and had business career, his work being little recognized until his 'CONCORD' piano sonata was played in 1939 and his symphony no. 3 in 1946. Works include five symphonies, 'Three Places in New England' for orchestra, and songs.

J

JACK, the vertical strip of wood carrying the plectrum that plucks the string of a harpsichord, virginals, etc.; as the finger-key is depressed, the jack moves up and the string is plucked.

JACKSON, WILLIAM (1730–1803), English organist and composer of church music; also of operas, harpsichord pieces, etc. Was organist of Exeter Cathedral and is known as 'Jackson of Exeter'.

JACKSON, WILLIAM (1815–66), English organist and composer

(church music, glees, etc.); active in Yorkshire and known as 'Jackson of Masham'.

JACOB, GORDON (PERCIVAL SEPTIMUS) (b. 1895), English composer, pupil of Stanford and C. Wood; noted also as teacher and as authority on orchestration. Works, inclined to a conservatively melodious style, include 'Passacaglia on a Well-known Theme' ('Oranges and Lemons'); two symphonies, three suites, etc., for orchestra; concertos for various instruments; chamber music and choral works. Also arranger, e.g. of popular tunes in comic style, and of music for ballet. C.B.E., 1968.

JACOBI, FREDERICK (1891–1952), American composer, also conductor; pupil of Bloch and others; studied American-Indian music and wrote string quartet and other works making use of it; also symphony, Jewish liturgical music, etc.

JACOBSON, MAURICE (b. 1896), English composer, pupil of Stanford and Holst; also pianist, musical arranger, and music-publishing executive. Works, in a broadly traditional idiom, include cantata 'The Hound of Heaven', and other vocal music; orchestral works; ballet 'David'; various educational pieces.

JACQUES, REGINALD (b. 1894), English conductor – e.g. of his own string orchestra, and (1932–60) of London Bach Choir; also musical arranger, educationist, and formerly organist.

JADASSOHN, SALOMON (1831–1902), German composer of four symphonies, two piano concertos, etc.; also conductor and author of textbooks. Pupil of Liszt.

JAHRESZEITEN, DIE, see SEASONS.

JAM SESSION, informal improvised performance by jazz musicians.

JAMAICAN RUMBA, piece for two pianos by Benjamin, published 1938 after a visit to Jamaica; arranged also for many other combinations.

JAMES, PHILIP (b. 1890), American conductor, organist, professor, and composer of 'Station WGZBX' for orchestra (satirical suite of which the last movement is called 'Mikestruck'), choral and organ works, etc.

JANÁČEK, LEOŠ (1854–1928), Czech composer; also choral conductor; studied Czech folk-song and speech which greatly influenced his musical idiom. Works include 'JENŮFA', 'KATYA KABANOVÁ', 'THE CUNNING LITTLE VIXEN', 'THE MAKROPOULOS AFFAIR', 'FROM A HOUSE OF THE DEAD', and six other operas; GLAGOLITIC MASS, and many other choral works; Sinfonietta, 'Taras Bulba', and other orchestral works; song cycle 'The Diary of One who Vanished'; folk-song arrangements. Visited England in 1926.

JANEQUIN, see JANNEQUIN.

JANISSARY MUSIC, term for the effect produced by using triangle, cymbals, and bass drum, e.g. in Mozart's overture to 'THE SERAGLIO' – imitating Turkish music as played by the janissaries, infantry forming the Sultan's bodyguard.

JANNEQUIN, CLEMENT (also spelt Janequin; *c.* 1475–*c.* 1560), French composer of long dramatic CHANSONS in four parts with, e.g. representation of bird-song; also of other songs, and Masses and other church music. Possibly a pupil of DESPRÉS.

JANSSEN, WERNER (b. 1899), American conductor (who has given some notable 'first performances') and composer: works, often with characteristic American 'popular' flavour, include 'New Year's Eve in New York' and 'Louisiana Suite' for orchestra, and much film music.

JAQUES-DALCROZE, ÉMILE (1865–1950), Swiss (Austrian-born) inventor of 'EURHYTHMICS' (system of expressing the rhythmical aspects of music by bodily movement); also composer of operas, etc.

JARNACH, PHILIPP (b. 1892), French-born Spanish (Catalan) composer with a German mother; trained chiefly in Paris; taught in Zürich, Berlin, etc. Studied also with Busoni and completed Busoni's unfinished 'DOCTOR FAUST'. Himself composed Sinfonia Brevis and other orchestral works, unaccompanied violin sonatas, etc.

JÄRNEFELT, ARMAS (1869–1958), Finnish-born conductor and composer, naturalized Swedish in 1910. Introduced Wagner's music to Finland. Works include PRAELUDIUM and Berceuse for orchestra, choral music, songs. His sister married Sibelius.

JAZZ, term used at least from 1914 for a type of American popular music originating among Negroes of New Orleans and taken over also by whites; also used generally for various types of dance music indebted to this (though purists reserve the term for such music as retains the original flavour and the original basis of improvisation). The jazz idiom, characterized by certain syncopations over strongly reiterated rhythms, has influenced e.g. Lambert, Stravinsky, and Milhaud, as well as many American composers. Cp. BLUE NOTE, BLUES, RAGTIME.

JEANIE DEANS, opera by MacCunn, produced in Edinburgh, 1894; libretto by J. Bennett, after Scott's *The Heart of Midlothian.* Named after the heroine, who secures from George II a pardon for her wronged half-sister.

JEANNE D'ARC AU BÛCHER, see JOAN OF ARC AT THE STAKE.

JEANNE'S FAN (Fr., *L'Éventail de Jeanne*), ballet to which movements of the music were contributed by Auric, Delannoy, Ferroud, Ibert, Milhaud, Poulenc, Ravel, Roland-Manuel, Roussel, and Schmitt – originally (1927) for piano, performed privately; later orchestrated.

JEANS, SUSI (b. 1911), Austrian-born organist and harpsichordist, resident in England, specializing in old music; originally Susi Hock, she married the physicist Sir James Jeans (author of book *Science and Music*).

JEJÍ PASTORKYNA, see JENŮFA.

JELINEK, HANNS (b. 1901), Austrian composer, mainly self-taught, but studied briefly with Schoenberg, Berg, and Schmidt. Compositions, in TWELVE-NOTE technique (and supplemented by a treatise on this) include 'Symphonia brevis' for orchestra, 'Twelve-note primer' for piano, song-setting (with orchestra) of Goethe's 'Prometheus'.

JEMNITZ, ALEXANDER (Hungarian form, *Sándor*; b. 1890), Hungarian composer, conductor, and writer on music; pupil of Reger and Schoenberg. Works include 'Overture for a Peace Festival'; harp sonata; various piano and organ works.

'JENA' SYMPHONY, name given to a symphony found at Jena, Germany, in 1909, and thought by some to be an early work of Beethoven's; but, despite the inscription '*par Louis van Beethoven*', it was shown in 1957 to be by J. F. Witt.

JENKINS, JOHN (1592–1678), English composer in service to various noble families. Wrote fantasias for viols, church music, songs, and rounds; also sonatas for two violins (then something of a new instrument) with bass viol and keyboard.

JENSEN, ADOLF (1837–79), German pianist and composer, particularly of piano music and songs; also of an opera, cantatas, etc. Pupil of Liszt.

JENŮFA, opera by Janáček, produced in Brno, 1904. Libretto by composer, after a play by G. Preissova; originally titled 'Her Foster-daughter' (Cz., *Jeji Pastorkyňa*). Named after the heroine, whose illegitimate baby is drowned by Jenůfa's foster-mother.

JEPHTHA, (1) Latin oratorio by Carissimi (words from the Bible) for six voices and organ, composed by 1650; one of the earliest oratorios – each 'character' sings, and there is a narrator; (2) oratorio by Handel, first performed in London, 1752; words by T. Morell, after the Bible.

'JEREMIAH' SYMPHONY, symphony no. 1 by Bernstein, first performed 1944; with mezzo-soprano solo in the last movement, to words from the Book of Jeremiah.

JEREMIÁŠ, JAROSLAV (1889–1919), Czech composer of oratorio 'John Huss', etc.; pupil of Novák and brother of Otakar Jeremiáš.

JEREMIÁŠ, OTAKAR (b. 1892), Czech composer, pupil of Novák, brother of preceding. Works include opera 'The Brothers Karamazov' (after Dostoyevsky), cantata 'Songs of My Country', Choral Fantasia (with orchestra), etc. Also conductor.

JESU, JOY OF MAN'S DESIRING, see HESS.

JEUNE FRANCE, LA, see YOUNG FRANCE.

JEUX D'ENFANTS, see CHILDREN'S GAMES.

JEW'S HARP, primitive instrument held in the mouth, having a strip of metal 'twanged' (i.e. set vibrating) by the finger, the player eliciting different notes by altering the shape of the cavity of the mouth. (Reason for the name unknown; apparently not a corruption of 'jaw's harp'.)

JEWELS OF THE MADONNA, THE (It., *I Gioielli della Madonna*), opera by Wolf-Ferrari, produced in Berlin (in German), 1911. Libretto, originally in Italian, by E. Golisciani and C. Zangarini. Blood-and-thunder plot, like CAVALLERIA RUSTICANA, and likewise containing popular orchestral intermezzo.

JEWESS, THE (Fr., *La Juive*), opera by Halévy, produced in Paris, 1835. Libretto by E. Scribe (originally written for Rossini): the 'Jewess' executed by order of a 15th-century Cardinal turns out to be the Cardinal's own daughter.

JIG, type of dance usually in 6/8 or 12/8 time; and often constituting the last movement of an 18th-century suite, in which it was usually built in BINARY form.

JINGLING JOHNNY, obsolete military-band percussion instrument shaped like a tree or pavilion (hence other name, *Chinese pavilion*) and hung with bells which were shaken.

JINNS, THE (Fr., *Les Djinns*), symphonic poem by Franck, 1884, after verses about these oriental demons by Hugo.

JIRÁK, KAREL BOLESLAV (b. 1891), Czech composer, pupil of Novák; also conductor. Has written five symphonies, Overture to a Shakespearean Comedy, three string quartets, many song-cycles, etc. Resident in U.S.A. since 1947.

JOACHIM, JOSEPH (1831–1907), Hungarian violinist and composer, living mainly in Germany; visited Britain aged 13 and many times thereafter. Friend of Brahms, whose violin concerto is dedicated to him; himself composed three violin concertos, overtures to *Hamlet* and *King Henry IV*, etc. See also GRAND DUO (Schubert), which he orchestrated.

JOAN OF ARC AT THE STAKE (Fr., *Jeanne d'Arc au bûcher*), play by P. Claudel with some spoken parts (including Joan's) and some sung; music by Honegger – his most widely performed stage work. Produced at Basel, 1938.

JOB, (1) oratorio by C. H. H. Parry (words from the Bible), first performed 1892; (2) 'masque for dancing' (in effect a ballet) with music by Vaughan Williams, produced in London, 1931 (after Blake's illustrations to the Book of Job); (3) opera (but called a 'mystery play') by Dallapiccola, after the Bible, produced in Rome, 1950.

JOCELYN, opera by Godard, produced in Brussels, 1888. Libretto by P. A. Silvestre and V. Capone, after Lamartine: Jocelyn is a seminarist tempted by earthly love. The work is now remembered by the leading tenor's 'Berceuse'.

JODEL, see YODEL.

JOHANSEN, DAVID MONRAD (b. 1888), Norwegian composer of violin sonata, cantatas on Old Norse texts, and other works of 'nationalist' character; took official post under Nazi occupation of Norway.

JOHN OF FORNSETE, English 13th-century monk, conjecturally the composer of 'SUMMER IS ICUMEN IN'.

JOHNNY STRIKES UP (Ger., *Jonny spielt auf*), opera by Křenek, in a jazz-influenced style; produced in Leipzig, 1927, and afterwards translated into eighteen languages. Libretto by composer: Johnny is a Negro jazz violinist.

JOHNSON, HUNTER (b. 1906), American composer of ballet 'Letter to the World', symphony, piano concerto, piano sonata, etc.

JOHNSON, JOHN (*c.* 1540–95), English lutenist and composer of songs and lute music; attached to the court of Elizabeth I.

JOHNSON, ROBERT (*c.* 1490–*c.* 1560), Scottish priest and composer who fled to England from religious persecution; wrote Latin motets, English church music, also secular vocal works. See also following entry.

JOHNSON, ROBERT (*c.*1583–1633), English lutenist, serving Charles I and James I; composed solo songs (including two from *The Tempest*), catches, viol music, etc. See also preceding entry.

JOHNSTONE, MAURICE (b. 1900), English composer of orchestral works, brass band works (including a symphonic poem on Shakespeare's *Tempest*), etc.; formerly also BBC musical administrator.

JOIO, NORMAN DELLO, see DELLO JOIO.

JOLIE FILLE DE PERTH, LA, see THE FAIR MAID OF PERTH.

JOLIVET, ANDRÉ (b. 1905), French composer, pupil of Varèse and others; one of the former group called 'YOUNG FRANCE'. Has been influenced by oriental music. Works include opera, symphony, concertino for piano and trumpet, works for MARTENOT, piano solos, oratorio 'The Truth About Joan [of Arc]'. Musical director of the Comédie Français, Paris. See also LESUR.

JOMELLI, NICCOLÒ (1714–74), Italian composer, pupil of Leo; wrote oratorios, church music, etc., but especially operas – more than fifty. Was a pioneer of the use of the orchestral crescendo. Much admired in Germany, and was for long resident in Stüttgart.

JONES, DANIEL (b. 1912), Welsh composer of five symphonies (he was apparently the first Welsh composer to have a symphony performed), eight string quartets, opera 'The Knife', oratorio 'St Peter', music to *Under Milk Wood* (dramatic poem by his friend Dylan Thomas); also of a sonata for three kettle-drums (typifying his interest in the formal properties of rhythms) etc. O.B.E., 1968.

JONES, ROBERT (?–? 1617), English lutenist, in service to various patrons; composed mainly songs with lute, but also anthems, and a madrigal in 'THE TRIUMPHS OF ORIANA'.

JONES, SIDNEY (1861–1946), English composer of 'THE GEISHA' and other operettas; also conductor.

JONGEN, JOSEPH (1873–1953), Belgian composer of symphonic poems, piano concerto, quartet for saxophones, piano and organ works, etc. Director of the Brussels Conservatory, 1920–39. Brother of Léon Jongen.

JONGEN, LÉON (b. 1885), Belgian composer and pianist; director of the Brussels Conservatory since 1939, succeeding his brother Joseph Jongen. Works include operas, 'Rhapsodia Belgica' for violin and orchestra, piano solos.

JONGLEUR (Fr., juggler), medieval wandering minstrel who was singer, instrumentalist (chiefly on a form of fiddle), acrobat, juggler, etc.

JONGLEUR DE NOTRE DAME, LE, see OUR LADY'S JUGGLER.

JONNY SPIELT AUF, see JOHNNY STRIKES UP.

JORDÁ, ENRIQUE (b. 1911), Spanish conductor; from 1948 to 1954 worked in Capetown.

JOSEPH, the best-known opera by Méhul, produced in Paris, 1807; libretto by A. Duval, after the Bible.

JOSEPHS, WILFRED (b. 1927), English composer of Requiem for baritone, chorus and orchestra (text is the KADDISH), two symphonies, piano sonata, music for child performers, music for theatre and television, etc.; was a dentist before becoming full-time musician.

JOSHUA, oratorio by Handel (words by T. Morell, after the Bible), first performed in London, 1748.

JOSQUIN DES PRÉS, see DESPRÉS.

JOSTEN, WERNER (b. 1885), German-born composer who settled in U.S.A., 1920. Works include ballets, choral and orchestral works, two pieces for strings and piano called 'Concerto Sacro' – prompted by Grünewald's altar-painting at Isenheim (cp. MATHIS THE PAINTER).

JOTA, northern Spanish dance in quick triple time, traditionally with castanets.

JOUBERT, JOHN (b. 1927), South African composer who studied in London under H. Ferguson and others, and took teaching post at University College, Hull, 1950. Works include Te Deum, violin concerto, ballet 'Vlei Legend', opera 'Silas Marner' (after George Eliot) and radio opera 'Antigone', cycle of Latin unaccompanied motets 'Pro Pace' (for peace), octet for strings and wind.

JOYCE, EILEEN (b. about 1912), Australian pianist who was 'discovered' by Grainger, studied in Germany, and settled in England – winning great popularity. Is also harpsichordist. Daughter of an itinerant labourer, she claims not to know her exact birth-date.

JUBILATE (DEO), Latin name for Psalm 100, as used in church services (in English, 'O be joyful in the Lord') and as occasionally set for concert and ceremonial purposes, as an expression of rejoicing.

JUDAS MACCABAEUS, oratorio by Handel (words by T. Morell, after the Bible), first performed in London, 1747.

JUDITH, works based on the Apocryphal Book, including – (1) oratorio by T. Arne (words by I. Bickerstaffe) first performed in London, 1761; (2) oratorio by C. H. H. Parry, first performed, 1888; (3) opera by Honegger, produced in Monte Carlo, 1926 – expanded from his music to a play by R. Morax, 1925; (4) one-act opera by E. Goossens, produced in London, 1929; libretto by Arnold Bennett.

JUGGLER, see JONGLEUR.

JUIVE, LA, see THE JEWESS.

JULIUS CAESAR, operas in Italian by (1) Handel, produced in London, 1724 – properly 'Giulio Cesare in Egitto', i.e. in Egypt; libretto by N. Haym; (2) Malipiero, produced in Genoa, 1936; libretto by composer, after Shakespeare.

JULLIEN, LOUIS GEORGES MAURICE ADOLPHE ROCH ALBERT ABEL ANTONIO ALEXANDRE NOÉ JEAN LUCIEN DANIEL EUGÈNE JOSEPH-LE-BRUN JOSEPH-BARÊME THOMAS THOMAS THOMAS-THOMAS PIERRE CERBON PIERRE-MAUREL BARTHÉLEMI ARTUS ALPHONSE BERTRAND ÉMANUEL DIEUDONNÉ JOSUÉ VINCENT LUC MICHEL JULES-DE-LA-PLANE JULES-BAZIN JULIO-CÉSAR (1812–60), French conductor, more than anyone else responsible for the establishment of promenade concerts in London; also composer of quadrilles and other light music, and of opera 'Peter the Great'. (That his name was as above is alleged in a contemporary magazine article; another source gives his surname as originally 'Julien' and his baptismal names simply as 'Louis Antoine'. He was anyway known by his surname only.) He became insane shortly before his death.

JUNGE LORD, DER, see YOUNG LORD.

JUNGFERNQUARTETTE, see RUSSIAN QUARTETS.

JUON, PAUL (1872–1940), Russian composer (pupil of Taneyev and Arensky) who settled in Germany; wrote two symphonies, two violin concertos, chamber music, etc.

'JUPITER' SYMPHONY, nickname given in many different countries to Mozart's last symphony, no. 41 in C (K.551): the name has no authority, only convenience. The dates of composition of this and the two preceding symphonies span less than seven weeks in 1788.

JURINAC, SENA (really Srebenka; b. 1921), Yugoslav soprano who has appeared with Vienna State Opera, at Glyndebourne, etc.

JUST INTONATION, the adoption in performance of the 'natural' non-tempered scale (see TEMPERAMENT). This is theoretically possible on voices, bowed-string instruments, etc., in which the pitch of the notes is not mechanically fixed.

K

K., abbreviation (1) of KÖCHEL (in cataloguing Mozart's works), and (2) of KIRKPATRICK (in cataloguing D. Scarlatti's).

KB., abbreviation of Ger. *Kontrabass*, i.e. double-bass.

K.V., see KÖCHEL.

KABALEVSKY, DMITRI (BORISOVICH) (b. 1904), Russian composer, generally in Soviet-approved neo-Tchaikovsky style; pupil of Miaskovsky. Is also pianist and writer on music. Has composed operas including 'THE MASTER OF CLAMECY' (the overture is also known as 'Colas Breugnon') and 'The Family of Taras' (on a story of the Nazi occupation of Russian territory); three piano concertos and other concertos for violin and cello; four symphonies, songs (including nursery rhymes), etc.

KADDISH, Jewish mourners' prayer, in Aramaic (similar to Hebrew); set in Bernstein's Symphony no. 3 and Josephs' Requiem.

KAISERQUARTETT (Ger.), see EMPEROR QUARTET.

KAJANUS, ROBERT (1856–1933), Finnish conductor, friend of Sibelius and specializing in his music; also composer of symphonic poems, etc.

KALINNIKOV, VASSILY SERGEYEVICH (1866–1901), Russian composer of two symphonies, songs, stage music, etc.

KALKBRENNER, FRIEDRICH WILHELM MICHAEL (1785–1849), German pianist who settled in Paris; noted performer and teacher; also composer of three piano concertos, many studies, etc.

KALLIWODA, JOHAN VÁCLAV (or in German, Johann Wenzel; 1800–66), Bohemian violinist and composer of seven symphonies and other orchestral works once frequently performed; also of opera, string quartets, etc.

KÁLMÁN, EMMERICH (1882–1953), Austrian composer, particularly of operettas including 'THE GIPSY PRINCESS'; latterly lived in France and U.S.A., and died in Paris.

KAMINSKI, HEINRICH (1886–1946), German composer of music to religious texts using modal style; also of opera, Concerto for Orchestra, 'Triptych' for voice and organ, etc.

KAMINSKI, JOSEPH (b. 1903), Polish-born Israeli violinist and composer who emigrated to Palestine, 1936; works include concertino for trumpet and 'Comedy Overture'.

KAMMER (Ger.), chamber; hence *Kammermusik*, *Kammersymphonie*, etc. (See under CHAMBER.)

KAPELLE (Ger.) chapel; hence, the musical establishment of a prince's private chapel; hence again, any established musical institution, e.g an orchestra. Cp. Kapellmeister.

KAPELLMEISTER (Ger., chapel-master), musical director, originally of a prince's private chapel; term later used also for a 'resident conductor', e.g. of an orchestra. Hence *Kapellmeistermusik*, 'conductor's music' (abusive term for) empty music composed by someone who has a conductor's familiarity with mere technique, but has nothing more.

KARAJAN, HERBERT VON (b. 1908), Austrian conductor; début, 1927. Conductor of the Berlin Philharmonic Orchestra, 1955; musical director of the Vienna State Opera, 1957–64; has also frequently conducted in London. Is also opera producer.

KAREL, RUDOLF (1880–1945), Czech composer, pupil of Dvořák; wrote symphonic poems 'The Ideal' and 'Demon', also operas, violin concerto, etc. Died in a Nazi concentration camp.

KARELIA, overture and orchestral suite by Sibelius, 1893, evocative of the province of Karelia in the south of Finland.

KARG-ELERT, SIGFRID (real name Karg; 1877–1933), German composer, also pianist and organist; now known chiefly for his many organ works. Wrote also symphony, string quartets, many songs, etc.

KARYNX, primitive horn of ancient Gallic culture, sometimes in a doubly bent form with upraised bell.

KASSERN, TADEUSZ ZYGFRYD (1904–57), Polish composer who also studied law; works include sinfonietta, concerto for strings, piano sonatas, and choruses. Died in New York.

KASTALSKY, ALEXANDER DMITRIEVICH (1856–1926), Russian composer, pupil of Tchaikovsky and Taneyev; active in church music before and after the 1917 Revolution. Also composed patriotic choral works, opera, etc.

KÁT'A KABANOVÁ, see KATYA KABANOVÁ.

KATCHEN, JULIUS (b. 1926), American pianist, resident in Paris; has toured widely, and has also conducted.

KATERINA ISMAILOVA, opera by Shostakovich, produced in Leningrad, 1934 under the title 'Lady Macbeth of the Mtsensk District'; new title was first used in Moscow production later in the same year. Libretto by A. G. Preis and the composer (after a story by Leskov), centring on a woman who kills her husband and father-in-law. The work was banned under Stalin and brought out in a revised version in Moscow, 1963.

KATYA KABANOVÁ (in Czech properly spelt *Kát'a* ...), opera by Janáček, produced in Brno, 1921. Named after the tragic heroine, whose husband is mother-ridden: libretto by composer, after V. Cervinka's translation of Ostrovsky's play *Storm*.

KAY, ULYSSES (SIMPSON) (b. 1917), American composer, pupil of Hanson and Rogers: works include Sinfonietta, oboe concerto, piano and organ pieces.

KAZOO, children's musical instrument into which one hums to produce an effect rather superior to that of comb-and-paper.

KEEL, (JAMES) FREDERICK (1871–1954), English baritone singer, song-composer, and editor of Tudor-period songs and of folk-songs.

KEEN (Ir., *Caoine*), an Irish funeral song accompanied by wailing; to wail thus.

KEISER, REINHARD (1674–1739), German composer, also director of the Hamburg Opera, and afterwards for some time in Copenhagen. Wrote more than 100 operas, some with mixed German and Italian words; more than anyone else, established Hamburg as an opera centre. Also composed oratorios, a 'St Mark PASSION', etc.

KELER-BÉLA, pen-name of Adalbert von Keler (1820–82), Hungarian violinist, bandmaster, conductor, and composer chiefly of dances and marches.

KELL, REGINALD (b. 1906), English clarinettist, resident 1948–57 in U.S.A., where he has recorded with his own wind ensemble.

KELLEY, EDGAR STILLMAN (1857–1944), American composer (also organist and critic) who studied in Germany. Studied Chinese music and wrote an orchestral suite on Chinese themes. Other works include 'Gulliver' Symphony (after Swift), operettas, string quartets.

KELLY, MICHAEL (1762–1826), Irish tenor, friend of Mozart; took part in the first performance of 'THE MARRIAGE OF FIGARO'; was himself the composer of music for many London stage pieces.

KEMPE, RUDOLF (b. 1910), German conductor, formerly oboist; director of the Munich Opera 1952–4; noted Wagner conductor at Covent Garden; principal conductor, Royal Philharmonic Orchestra, 1961–3, and again from 1964.

KEMPFF, WILHELM (b. 1895), German pianist, formerly director of a musical academy at Stuttgart; also composer of symphonies, one-act opera 'King Midas', etc.

KENT BUGLE, see OPHICLEIDE.

KENTNER, LOUIS (b. 1905), pianist born at Karvinna (then in Hungary, now in Czechoslovakia) who studied in Budapest and settled in England, 1935. Noted exponent of Liszt; gave first performance of Bartók's Piano Concerto no. 2; partner of Menuhin (his brother-in-law) in recitals.

KERL, JOHANN CASPAR (also Kerll; 1627–93), German organist and composer, chiefly in Munich and Vienna. Studied in Italy, wrote Italian operas – also church music, etc. Handel 'borrowed' some of his music and incorporated it into, e.g. 'ISRAEL IN EGYPT'.

KERLE, JACOB VAN (*c.* 1531–91), Flemish composer of church music, long in service to the Bishop of Augsburg; his work was performed with approval at the Council of Trent, 1562–3, when propriety in church music was discussed. Died in Prague.

KERLL, see KERL.

KERN, JEROME (DAVID) (1885–1945), American composer of many popular songs of marked individuality – especially in 'Show Boat' and other musical plays, and in films of similar nature. Composed also a few other works including 'Portrait of Mark Twain' for orchestra.

KERTESZ, ISTVÁN (b. 1929), Hungarian-born, German-naturalized conductor; musical director of Cologne Opera House and (1965–8) principal conductor of the London Symphony Orchestra.

KETÈLBEY, ALBERT WILLIAM (1875–1959), English composer of 'In a Monastery Garden' and other popular light orchestral pieces; formerly theatre conductor.

KETTING, PIET (b. 1905), Dutch pianist and composer (pupil of Pijper; also influenced by Schoenberg). Works include symphony, string quartets, settings of Shakespeare and other songs.

KETTLEDRUM, cauldron-shaped drum originally from the Orient, and originally smaller and more delicate-sounding than now; in modern form, tuned to a definite pitch, normally by handles on the rim. Two such drums were normal in the symphony orchestra up to Beethoven, and later composers have used three or (rarely) more. The drum rests on a stand, the skin facing upwards; the tone-quality may be varied according to the drumsticks used and the point of impact. A cloth on the drum may be used to give the effect of a mute. Mechanically tuned drums, using pedals, and commonly called *pedal drums*, have also come into wide use in the 20th century; they (1) make tuning quicker, allowing rapid changes in the middle of a movement, and (2) allow the use of a glissando (drum struck, then pedal depressed – e.g. in Bartók's Concerto for Orchestra). The kettledrum is standard also in the mounted military band – one slung each side of a horse. (In all contexts *kettledrum* is preferable to *timpani*, the Italian term: this is a plural form of which the singular is not commonly used in English, though *timpano* is perfectly good Italian.)

KEY, (1) a lever, e.g. on piano, organ, or a woodwind instrument, depressed by finger or foot to produce a note. (2) a classification of the notes of a scale, the most important note being called the *key-note* and the others functioning in relation to it. If the keynote is C, then the key may be either C major or C minor, according to whether the major or minor scale is used basically in the music concerned (see MAJOR); notes outside the 'basic' scale are said to be foreign to the key. The sharps and flats appertaining to the key used are displayed in a KEY-SIGNATURE; other sharps, flats, and naturals occurring 'casually' in the music are written as ACCIDENTALS. The major and minor keys were the only two types of note-ordering generally used in Western music in approximately 1600–1900; earlier, the MODES prevailed, and later certain composers began to dispense with key altogether (see ATONALITY).

KEYBOARD, a continuous arrangement of keys – see KEY (1) – either for the fingers, as on the piano, or for the feet, as on the 'pedal keyboard' of an organ. So also *keyboard of light*, instrument throwing colours on a screen in Skriabin's PROMETHEUS'. The term, *keyboard* is also used as a general term for a 'keyboard instrument' – especially in such contexts as 'Bach's keyboard works' where the works may be suitable for more than one type of keyed instrument.

KEY-BUGLE, see OPHICLEIDE.

KEYED BUGLE, see OPHICLEIDE.

KEYED TRUMPET, see TRUMPET.

KEYNOTE, see KEY (2).

KEY-SIGNATURE, the indication in written music of the number of sharps or flats in the prevailing key, such indication normally being placed at the beginning of each line of music (or at any point when the key-signature is changed). Thus flat-signs on the lines or spaces in the staff denoting B, E, and A indicate that these notes are to be played as B♭, E♭, and A♭ – unless an indication to the contrary is given by an ACCIDENTAL. Thus the key of E♭ major or C minor is indicated, since only these have all these three notes flat (and no others). Thus it is the 'natural' form of the minor scale which is used to determine key-signature. See MAJOR.

KHACHATURIAN, ARAM (ILICH) (b. 1903), Russian (Armenian) composer, pupil of Gnessin and Miaskovsky; aged 20 before he began professional study. Works, often influenced by Armenian folk-music include piano concerto (with a part for FLEXATONE, imitating

Armenian folk-instrument), violin concerto, cello concerto, three symphonies; ballets 'GAYANEH' and 'Spartacus'; music to Lermontov's play 'MASQUERADE'; choral, piano, and chamber works. For 'Sabre Dance' see GAYANEH.

KHOROVOD (Rus.), type of traditional Russian round dance with singing; one of the sections (based on a Russian folk-tune) of Stravinsky's 'THE FIREBIRD' is so named.

KHOVANSKY AFFAIR, THE (Rus. *Khovanschhina*), unfinished opera by Mussorgsky; as completed by Rimsky-Korsakov, it was produced in St Petersburg, 1886. A later completion, more faithful to the composer's harmonic originality, has been made by Shostakovich. Libretto, by Mussorgsky and V. V. Stassov, about the princes of the Khovansky family at the time of Peter the Great.

KHRENNIKOV, TIKHON NIKOLAYEVICH (b. 1913), Russian composer, pupil of Shebalin; works include two symphonies, piano concerto, operas. As secretary-general of the Union of Soviet Composers, took part in denouncing Prokofiev and other musicians for 'FORMALISM' in 1948.

KIENZL, WILHELM (1857–1941), Austrian composer encouraged by Liszt and associated with Wagner; composed operas including 'The Preacher' (*Der Evangelimann*), and also many piano pieces and songs.

KIKIMORA, work by Liadov styled 'legend for orchestra' and published 1910. Kikimora is a malevolent goblin – the name is etymologically related to Fr. *cauchemar*, nightmare.

KILADZE, GRIGORI VARFOLOMEYEVICH (1903–62), Russian (Georgian) composer who worked in manual trades as a young man; later pupil of Shcherbachev and others. Works, some influenced by Georgian folk-music, include operas, ballets, 'Heroic Symphony', and other orchestral works.

KILPINEN, YRJÖ (1892–1959), Finnish composer enjoying a state grant to enable him to compose; he wrote hundreds of songs in Finnish, Swedish, and German, also other works including a sonata for viola da gamba.

KINDERSCENEN, see SCENES OF CHILDHOOD.

KINDERTOTENLIEDER, see SONGS ON THE DEATH OF CHILDREN.

KING, CHARLES (1687–1748), English composer of church music, organist of St Paul's Cathedral, London; pupil of Blow and Clarke.

KING, MATTHEW PETER (1773–1823), English composer of many stage works, solo songs, piano sonatas, etc.

KING, ROBERT (17th century), English composer of songs, stage music, etc.; member of Charles II's band, 1680.

KING, WILLIAM (1624–80), English organist, priest, and composer of church music and songs.

KING ARTHUR, *or The British Worthy*, 'opera' by Purcell, produced in London, 1691. It was actually a spectacular play by Dryden for which Purcell wrote extensive music. King Arthur and some of the other characters do not sing.

KING CHRISTIAN II, play by G. Paul for which Sibelius wrote incidental music, 1898; concerns the 16th-century Danish king.

KING DAVID (Fr., *Le Roi David*), 'dramatic psalm' by Honegger – basically an oratorio with spoken narration. Words by R. Morax, after the Bible. First performed, as a stage work, in Mézières, Switzerland, 1921.

KING LEAR, play by Shakespeare, music for which includes – overture by Berlioz, 1831; overture and incidental music by Balakirev, 1861; incidental music by Debussy, 1904, only two fragments surviving. (The incidental music formerly ascribed to Haydn is now thought spurious.)

KING PRIAM, opera by Tippett, produced in Coventry, 1962. Libretto, by the composer, treats the Homeric story of Greek and Trojan leaders.

KING RENÉ'S CHIMNEY (Fr., *La Cheminée du Roi René*), wind quartet by Milhaud, 1939, referring to a street in Aix-en-Provence (the composer's birthplace) commemorating a 15th-century king.

KING ROGER (Pol., *Król Roger*), opera by Szymanowski, produced in Warsaw, 1926. Libretto by composer and J. Iwaskiewicz, about a 12th-century king of Sicily.

KING'S HENCHMAN, THE, opera by Deems Taylor, produced in New York, 1927; libretto by Edna St Vincent Millay, a variation of the TRISTAN AND ISOLDE legend set in 10th-century England.

KING STEPHEN, play by A. von Kotzebue for which Beethoven wrote the overture and incidental music, 1811. It refers to Stephen I of Hungary, canonized in 1083.

KING THAMOS (Ger., *Thamos, König in Aegypten* – i.e. in Egypt), play by Baron T. P. von Gebler for which Mozart wrote incidental music, 1773, revised and added to in 1779.

KINGDOM, THE, oratorio by Elgar, first performed 1906; text from the Bible. See APOSTLES.

KINSKY, GEORG (1882–1951), German musicologist who catalogued Beethoven's works; the definitive edition, revised by Hans Halm, was issued in 1955.

KIPNIS, ALEXANDER (b. 1896), Russian-born bass resident in U.S.A., with high reputation in Russian and German songs.

KIRBYE, GEORGE (*c.* 1565–1634), English composer of madrigals (one in 'THE TRIUMPHS OF ORIANA'), motets and other church music, viol pieces, etc.

KIRCHNER, LEON (b. 1919), American composer, pupil of Bloch, Schoenberg, and Sessions; works, in highly dissonant idiom, include piano concerto, piano sonata, string quartet. Is also pianist.

KIRKPATRICK, RALPH (b. 1911), American harpsichordist (also performer on piano and clavichord) whose biography of D. Scarlatti incorporated a catalogue of Scarlatti's works which has become standard. Thus these works are referred to by their 'Kirkpatrick' or 'K' numbers. (This has superseded the LONGO numbering.)

KIRNBERGER, JOHANN PHILIPP (1721–83), German violinist, composer, and important theorist; pupil of Bach.

KISTLER, CYRILL (1848–1907), German composer of many operas (one about the rogue also portrayed by R. Strauss in 'TILL EULENSPIEGEL'), orchestral music, etc.

KIT, very small type of violin formerly used by dancing-masters.

KITCHEN DEPARTMENT, humorous term for the percussion section of an orchestra.

KITEZH, see THE INVISIBLE CITY OF KITEZH.

KITHARA, ancient Greek plucked string instrument, in shape similar to lyre, but – unlike the lyre – plucked with the fingers and not with a plectrum, and used for solos as well as for accompanying voices.

KJERULF, HALFDAN (1815–68), Norwegian composer who studied in Leipzig. His works, including choruses, male voice quartets, and songs were among the first to bring the flavour of Norwegian folksong into the concert-hall.

KLAVIER (Ger.), piano, harpsichord, or other keyboard instrument – also spelt *clavier*. For Bach's 'Das wohltemperierte Klavier', see THE WELL-TEMPERED CLAVIER. See also following entries.

KLAVIERAUSZUG (Ger.), a piano 'reduction' – i.e. the score of an orchestral or similar work arranged for piano.

KLAVIERÜBUNG, see CLAVIERÜBUNG.

KLEBE, GISELHER (b. 1925), German composer, pupil of Blacher and others; uses TWELVE-NOTE technique. Works include two symphonies, one of them for forty-two strings; sonatas for violin and for two pianos; 'Roman Elegies' (text by Goethe) for reciter with instruments operas, 'The Robbers' (on Schiller's play), 'Alkmene', 'Figaro seeks a divorce' (sequel to 'THE MARRIAGE OF FIGARO'), 'Jacobowsky and the Colonel' (after Franz Werfel's play). Has also written ELECTRONIC music.

KLECKI, see KLETZKI.

KLEIBER, ERICH (1890–1956), Austrian-born conductor, especially noted in opera (gave first performance of Berg's 'WOZZECK'); expelled by Nazis from Germany and became an Argentinian citizen in 1938. Returned after the war to East Germany and became director of the Berlin State Opera; left for West Germany, 1955.

KLEIN (Ger.), little; *kleine Flöte* (little flute), piccolo; *kleine Trommel* (little drum), side drum. See also next entry.

KLEINE NACHTMUSIK, EINE, see EINE KLEINE NACHTMUSIK.

KLEMPERER, OTTO (b. 1885), German-born conductor, internationally noted in opera and concerts; expelled by Nazis and became American citizen. Also composer of Mass, etc.

KLENAU, PAUL (AUGUST) VON (1883–1946), Danish composer and conductor who lived much in Germany; works include operas (one about Rembrandt), oratorios, and an orchestral piece called 'Bank Holiday – Souvenir of Hampstead Heath'.

KLENOVSKY, NIKOLAI SEMENOVICH (1857–1915), Russian composer

of ballets, choral music, etc.; also conductor. Pupil of Tchaikovsky. Not to be confused with Paul Klenovsky.

KLENOVSKY, PAUL, the pseudonym under which Henry Wood made an orchestral arrangement (1929) of Bach's organ Toccata and Fugue in D minor.

KLETZKI, PAUL (also spelt in Polish fashion, Klecki; b. 1900), Polish-born – now Swiss – conductor who trained partly in Berlin and has repeatedly visited Britain. Also composer of orchestral and chamber music.

KLUGE, DIE, see THE CLEVER GIRL.

KNIGHT, JOSEPH PHILIP (1812–87), English clergyman who composed 'Rocked in the cradle of the deep' and other songs.

KNIPPER, LEV (KONSTANTINOVICH) (b. 1898), Russian composer, pupil of Glière and, in Berlin, of Jarnach. Works include operas (one on Voltaire's *Candide*), fourteen symphonies and a 'Turkmenian Suite' for orchestra, violin concerto, popular choruses.

KNORR, IWAN (1853–1916), German composer of operas, chamber music, etc.; teacher in Leipzig of Quilter and C. Scott.

KOANGA, opera by Delius, produced (in German) in Elberfeld, 1904; revised after Delius's death by Beecham and Edward Agate and produced in London, 1935. Libretto by C. F. Keary, Koanga being an African chief transported as a slave to America. See also BANJO and CALINDA.

KOCH, ERLAND VON (b. 1910), Swedish composer of ballet 'Cinderella', violin concerto, songs, etc.

KÖCHEL, LUDWIG VON (1800–77), Austrian scholar who compiled a catalogue of Mozart's works which has become standard. Such works are now referred to as 'K. . . .' (followed by a number). The German usage is sometimes 'K.V.', for *Köchel-Verzeichnis*, i.e. Köchel Index. The current modern revision of this catalogue, 1937, was made by Alfred Einstein (1880–1952).

KODÁLY, ZOLTÁN (1882–1967), Hungarian composer. Collected and edited Hungarian folk-songs, partly in collaboration with Bartók; developed a strongly national idiom based on these songs, but less harsh and explosive than Bartók's. Achieved a national status as composer, particularly with his 'PSALMUS HUNGARICUS' and his opera 'HÁRY JÁNOS'. Other works include two other operas; Concerto for Orchestra, Symphony, 'DANCES OF GALÁNTA', variations on Hungarian folksong 'The Peacock', and other orchestral works; 'Dances of Marosszek' for piano (afterwards orchestrated); Missa Brevis, and other choral works; chamber music, songs, etc.

KOECHLIN, CHARLES (1867–1950), French composer, pupil of Massenet and Fauré; also writer of textbooks, etc. Works, in an eclectic but not 'revolutionary' style, include symphony, Rhapsody on French Songs and other orchestral pieces; three string quartets, songs, piano solos.

KOETSIER, JAN (b. 1911), Dutch conductor and composer, resident in Germany. Has written symphony, organ works, etc.

KOFFLER, JOZÉF (1896–1942), Polish composer using TWELVE-NOTE technique; wrote three symphonies, piano solos, ballet, etc. Died in the Nazis' massacre of the Warsaw ghetto.

KÖHLER, (CHRISTIAN) LOUIS HEINRICH (1820–86), German composer of much educational piano music, and of opera and other works; also pianist and conductor.

KOL NIDREI (Heb., All the vows), work for cello and orchestra by Bruch, published 1881; 'after Hebrew melodies'. The title refers to a prayer associated with the annual Jewish Day of Atonement.

KONDRACKI, MICHAL (b. 1902), Polish composer, pupil of Szymanowski and (in Paris) of Dukas and N. Boulanger. Works include opera and ballet, piano concerto, cantatas.

KONDRASHIN, KYRIL (PETROVICH) (b. 1914), Russian conductor; on staff of Bolshoi Theatre, Moscow, 1943–56, afterwards conductor of the Moscow Philharmonic Orchestra.

KONTRABASS (Ger.), double-bass; similarly *Kontrabassposaune*, double-bass trombone, etc.

KONTRAFAGOTT (Ger.), double-bassoon.

KONZERTMEISTER (Ger.), leader of an orchestra; U.S., concertmaster.

KORBAY, FRANCIS ALEXANDER (really Ferencz Sándor Korbay; 1846–1913), Hungarian singer, also pianist, who settled and taught in London (dying there); arranged Hungarian gipsy songs, with English words.

KORCHMAREV, KLEMENTY ARKADIEVICH (b. 1899), Russian composer of operas (including 'Ten Days That Shook the World', on the 1917 Russian Revolution', piano music, choral symphony 'Holland' (on Dutch revolutionary poems), etc.

KOREAN TEMPLE BLOCK, see TEMPLE BLOCK.

KORNETT (Ger.), equals CORNET (modern), or the ancient instrument – see CORNET.

KORNGOLD, ERIC WOLFGANG (1897–1957), Austrian-born composer, naturalized in U.S.A., 1943. Child prodigy: at age 13, wrote piano sonata played by Schnabel. Later works include 'The Dead City' and other operas, violin concerto, piano (left-hand) concerto; also much film music – in Hollywood after 1935. Was also conductor.

KOSTELANETZ, ANDRÉ (b. 1903), Russian-born conductor who settled in U.S.A., 1922, and, with his own orchestra, won fame in succulent arrangements of light music.

KOTZWARA, FRANZ (Germanized form of original name Koczwara; ?–1791), Czech-born violinist, double-bass player, and composer who settled in London; committed suicide there. His imitative fantasia 'The Battle of Prague', for piano with optional additional instruments, formerly enjoyed great popularity.

KOUSSEVITZKY, SERGE, form of name used by Sergey Alexandrovich

Kussevitsky (1876–1951), Russian-born conductor who settled in U.S.A.: conductor of the Boston Symphony Orchestra, 1924–49. Encouraged young composers, partly by means of the Koussevitzky Music Foundation, which continues after his death.

KOVAL, MARIAN (b. 1907), Russian composer, pupil of Gnessin and Miaskovsky; also critic. Works include cantatas, song-cycles, and operas – including 'The Wolf and the Seven Goats', for children.

KOVEN, (HENRY LOUIS) REGINALD DE (1859–1920), American composer, educated at Oxford and elsewhere in Europe. Wrote 'The Canterbury Pilgrims' and other operas – including 'Robin Hood', for a London performance of which he composed the song 'Oh, Promise Me'; also operettas, ballets, piano music, songs, etc.

KOZELUCH, LEOPOLD (Germanized form of original name Koželuh; 1752–1818), Czech composer who settled in Vienna; was one of the precursors of the 'classical' symphonic style (i.e. that of Haydn), and one of the first to compose specifically for the piano as distinct from the harpsichord. Wrote also operas, oratorio 'Moses in Egypt', etc.

KRAFT, ANTON (1752–1820), Bohemian-Austrian cellist and composer, member of Haydn's orchestra at Eszterháza. Composed chiefly cello music; but the suggestion that 'Haydn's' cello concerto was really composed by Kraft is now thought erroneous.

KRAKOWIAK, Polish dance in quick 2/4 time from the Cracow region.

KRAUS, LILI (b. 1908), Hungarian-born pianist, pupil of Bartók, Kodály, and Schnabel; noted as soloist, and formerly as duettist with Syzmon Goldberg. After internment by the Japanese in the Second World War, was naturalized British while on tour in New Zealand.

KRAUSS, CLEMENS (1893–1954), Austrian conductor; friend and noted interpreter of R. Strauss; librettist of Strauss's opera 'CAPRICCIO'.

KREBS, JOHANN LUDWIG (1713–80), German organist and composer of church music, keyboard works, etc.; a favourite pupil of Bach.

KREIN, ALEXANDER ABRAMOVICH (1883–1951), Russian composer of ballet, patriotic cantatas, etc., and also of works with Jewish associations – e.g. operas 'The Youth of Abraham' and 'The Maccabees'. Brother of Grigory Krein.

KREIN, GRIGORY ABRAMOVICH (1879–1955), Russian composer, brother of preceding; pupil of Glière and (in Leipzig) of Reger. Works include two piano concertos, much chamber music. Father of Julian Krein.

KREIN, JULIAN GRIGORIEVICH (b. 1913), Russian composer, son of preceding. Studied with Dukas in Paris, later returning to Russia. Works include symphonic prelude 'Destruction' for orchestra, various piano pieces.

KREISLER, FRITZ (1875–1962), Austrian violinist of enormous fame; also composer of string quartet, operettas, and especially of violin pieces some of which he fathered on various 17th- and 18th-century composers (admitting his 'fraud' in 1935). See PUGNANI.

KREISLERIANA, cycle of piano pieces by Schumann, 1838, dedicated to Chopin – referring to the character of the eccentric musician, Kreisler, created in the writings of E. T. A. HOFFMANN.

KREJČÍ, IŠA (b. 1904), Czech composer, pupil of Novák and Jirák; works include opera 'The Tumult at Ephesus' (after Shakespeare's *The Comedy of Errors*), sinfonietta, nonet and other chamber music.

KRENEK, ERNST (b. 1900), Austrian-born composer of partly Czech descent, resident in U.S.A. since 1938. Pupil of Schreker; married (formerly) to Mahler's daughter Anna. Discarded the Czech spelling (as Křenek) of his name. Showed jazz influence in very successful opera 'JOHNNY STRIKES UP', 1927; later adopted TWELVE-NOTE technique, but some works (e.g. piano concerto no. 3, symphony no. 5) are in a free-atonal idiom. Other works include Symphonic Elegy (for strings, in memory of Webern), opera 'The Golden Ram' (modernistic treatment of the legend of the Golden Fleece), and various works with specifically American associations – orchestral variations on folk-tune 'I wonder as I wander', choral 'Santa Fé Time-Table' (on names of railway stations), etc. Has written a piece for ELECTRONIC MUSIC (with voices added). Is also teacher and writer of textbooks, e.g. on Machaut.

KREUTZER, RODOLPHE (1766–1831), French violinist and composer of nineteen violin concertos, over forty operas, etc.; friend of Beethoven. See Kreutzer Sonata.

KREUTZER SONATA, nickname for Beethoven's sonata in A (1803) for violin and piano, dedicated to Rodolphe Kreutzer.

KŘIČKA, JAROSLAV (b. 1882), Czech composer of operas, overture to Maeterlinck's *The Blue Bird*, song-cycles, etc.; also conductor. Was 'involuntarily retired' in Czechoslovakia, 1945.

KRIEGER, JOHANN PHILIPP (1649–1725), German composer, partly trained in Italy. Wrote Masses and other church music, instrumental suites, etc.

KRIPS, HENRY (b. 1914), Austrian-born conductor, resident in Australia from 1948; brother of Josef Krips.

KRIPS, JOSEF (b. 1902), Austrian conductor, pupil of Weingartner; former chief conductor of Vienna State Opera. Associated with London Symphony Orchestra 1951–4. Brother of Henry Krips.

KUBELÍK, JAN (1880–1940), Czech violinist (also composer) who toured much; father of Rafael Kubelík.

KUBELÍK, (JERONYM) RAFAEL (b. 1914), Czech conductor – active in concerts and opera in Prague, later touring widely and in 1950 appointed orchestral conductor in Chicago; 1955–8, musical director of Covent Garden Opera. Also composer of two symphonies, etc. Son of Jan Kubelík, husband of ELSIE MORISON.

KUBIK, GAIL (b. 1914), American violinist, conductor, and composer – pupil of Piston and N. Boulanger. Works include three symphonies, two violin concertos (no. 1 withdrawn), cantata 'In Praise of Johnny Appleseed', music for film cartoon *Gerald McBoing Boing*.

KUHLAU, FRIEDRICH (1786–1832), German flutist and composer who settled in Denmark and wrote Danish operas, piano works, etc. Died in Copenhagen.

KUHNAU, JOHANN (1660–1722), German composer and organist, Bach's immediate predecessor in Leipzig. Wrote harpsichord works including so-called 'Biblical Sonatas', which are early examples of 'ILLUSTRATIVE music'; also motets and other church music.

KULLAK, THEODOR (1818–82), German composer of much educational piano music; also of piano concerto, etc.

KUNST DER FUGE, DIE, see THE ART OF FUGUE.

KUNZ, ERICH (b. 1909), Austrian baritone, member of the Vienna State Opera since 1941; has also appeared at Glyndebourne, etc.

KURTZ, EFREM (b. 1900), Russian-born conductor, resident in U.S.A. (naturalized 1944) and later in Switzerland; 1955–7, joint conductor of Liverpool Philharmonic Orchestra with John Pritchard. Wife is ELAINE SHAFFER, flutist.

KUULA, TOIVO (1883–1918), Finnish composer of cantatas, orchestral music, etc., in a Finnish national style; also conductor. Pupil of Busoni and Sibelius. Was murdered.

KVAPIL, JAROSLAV (b. 1892), Czech composer of three symphonies, cantata 'The Lion-Hearted' (on movement for Czechoslovak independence in the First World War), etc.; also pianist and organist.

L

L, indication (in numbering D. Scarlatti's keyboard works) of a reference to LONGO's catalogue. But see also KIRKPATRICK.

l, symbol in TONIC SOL-FA notation for the sixth degree (sub-mediant) of the scale, pronounced *lah*.

L.G.S.M., Licentiate of the Guildhall School of Music.

L.H., left hand (e.g. in piano-playing).

L.R.A.M., Licentiate of the Royal Academy of Music.

L.T.C.L., Licentiate of Trinity College (of Music), London.

L' (Fr., It.), the.

LA, the note A (in Latin countries, and formerly elsewhere); cp. LAH.

LA (Fr., It., Sp.), the.

LA FORGE, FRANK (b. 1879), American pianist, voice-teacher, and composer chiefly of songs.

LA HALE, LA HALLE, see HALE.

LABROCA, MARIO (b. 1896), Italian composer of symphony, a Stabat Mater, etc.; pupil of Respighi and G. F. Malipiero. Also critic. Musical director of the Italian Radio.

LAC DES CYGNES, LE, see SWAN LAKE.

LADMIRAULT, PAUL ÉMILE (1877–1944), French composer of piano works, operas, church music, etc.; his music often has specifically Breton associations.

LADY MACBETH OF THE MTSENSK DISTRICT, see KATERINA ISMAILOVA.

LADY NEVILL'S BOOK, see MY LADY NEVILL'S BOOK.

LAH, in TONIC SOL-FA, the spoken name for the 6th degree (submediant) of the scale, written l. Cp. LA.

LAJTHA, LÁSZLÓ (b. 1892–1963), Hungarian composer (also pianist) who has worked in France and Switzerland. Followed Bartók in collecting and editing Hungarian folk-music. Works include seven symphonies, ten string quartets, ballets; also writer on music.

LAKMÉ, opera by Delibes, produced in Paris, 1883. Libretto by E. Gondinet and P. Gille, the title-role being that of the daughter of a Brahmin priest, in love with a British officer.

LALANDE, MICHEL RICHARD DE, see DELALANDE.

LALO, (VICTOR ANTOINE) ÉDOUARD (1823–92), French composer, also viola-player; composed little until his forties. Works include 'SPANISH SYMPHONY' (*Symphonie espagnole*) and other works for violin and orchestra; opera 'The King of Ys' (*Le Roi d'Ys*), ballet 'Namouna'; chamber music and songs.

LAMBERT, CONSTANT (1905–51), English conductor (particularly of ballet), composer, arranger (e.g. of ballet 'COMUS'), and writer on music. Works – influenced by jazz in, e.g., 'THE RIO GRANDE' and piano concerto – also include 'Summer's Last Will and Testament' (baritone, chorus, and orchestra), 'HOROSCOPE' and other ballets, orchestral 'AUBADE héroïque', songs, film music.

LAMENT, a piece of music signifying grief especially at a death; and, specifically, a type of piece for bagpipes played at Scottish clan funerals.

'LAMENTATION' SYMPHONY, nickname for Haydn's symphony no. 26 in D minor, composed about 1765; so called because certain themes resemble plainsong melodies sung in Roman Catholic churches in the week before Easter (see next entry). Sometimes the form 'Lamentatione' – bastard Latin-*cum*-Italian – is encountered. The work is also called 'Christmas' Symphony – it is not known why.

LAMENTATIONS, the Lamentations of the prophet Jeremiah, traditionally sung (in plainsong or to other settings) in Roman Catholic churches in the week before Easter. See also THRENI.

LAMOUREUX ORCHESTRA, a Paris orchestra founded 1881 by Charles Lamoureux (1834–99), violinist and conductor. Markevich became its conductor in 1957.

LANCEN, SERGE (b. 1922), French pianist and composer, chiefly of piano music – concerto, concertino, solos, often in a light vein.

LANCERS, a type of quadrille which became popular in the second half of the 19th century.

LAND OF HOPE AND GLORY, see POMP AND CIRCUMSTANCE.

LANDI, STEFFANO (*c.* 1590–*c.* 1655), Italian composer of church music and operas; also singer in the Papal choir.

LANDINI, FRANCESCO (or Landino; 1325–97), Italian organist, lutenist, and composer (also poet); blind from early childhood. Wrote concerted vocal music of various kinds, and was an exponent of ARS NOVA. Born, lived, and died in Florence. See LANDINO.

LANDINO, alternative form of LANDINI's surname; *Landino sixth*, a type of cadence characteristically found in his music. In this the leading-note falls to the submediant before rising from that note to the tonic; i.e. the 6th degree of the scale is inserted between the 7th and the 8th. Thus this term does not refer to 'a sixth' in the harmonic sense but to the melodic insertion of the 6th degree of the scale.

LÄNDLER (sing. or pl.), type of dance in triple time originating in rural Austria and being a slow variant of the waltz. Beethoven and Schubert wrote examples.

LANDOWSKA, WANDA (1877–1959), Polish-born harpsichordist and authority on old music, etc.; long resident in France, then from 1941 in U.S.A. Falla's harpsichord concerto was written for her.

LANDRÉ, GUILLAUME (LOUIS FRÉDÉRIC) (b. 1905), Dutch composer, pupil of his father (below) and of Pijper. Works, favouring CYCLIC FORM, include three symphonies and a 'Sinfonia Sacra' in memory of his father, violin concerto, much chamber music; also opera 'Jean Lévecq' (after Maupassant's 'The Return'), etc. Also critic.

LANDRÉ, WILLEM, form of name used by Guillaume Louis Frédéric Landré (1874–1948), Dutch composer of French descent, father of Guillaume Landré (above). Wrote operas, cantatas, 'Little Suite on the Notes E–F' for orchestra, etc. Also critic.

LANGSTROTH, IVAN SHED (b. 1887), American composer of orchestral, chamber, and (especially) organ works; pupil of Humperdinck in Berlin.

LANIER, NICHOLAS (or Laniere; 1588–1666), English composer, the most prominent of a musical family of that surname. Master of the King's Music to Charles I and Charles II; Italian-influenced, is said to have introduced the recitative to England. Was also singer and painter. Composed masques and songs.

LANNER, JOSEPH (FRANZ KARL) (1801–43), Austrian violinist, orchestra-leader, and composer of over 200 waltzes and other light music; the chief rival of Johann Strauss the elder.

LAPARRA, RAOUL (1876–1943), French composer primarily of Spanish-influenced music, e.g. opera 'La Habanera'; he was his own librettist. Killed in an air-raid.

LARA, ISIDORE DE, pen-name of Isidore Cohen (1858–1935), English singer, concert organizer, and composer of operas in English (including 'The Light of Asia', produced 1892) and in French.

LARGAMENTE (It.), broadly – term usually denoting a spacious and deliberate style rather than a clear indication of slow tempo. Cp. LARGO, from which it is derived.

LARGE, the note of the largest time-value in the notation which grew up in the Middle Ages and gave rise to the present notation. It was divisible into either two or three 'longs'.

LARGHETTO (It., a little largo), direction indicating a speed not quite as slow as LARGO.

LARGO (It., broad), slow; but cp. LARGAMENTE. For the work referred to as 'Handel's Largo', see XERXES.

LARK ASCENDING, THE, 'romance' by Vaughan Williams for violin and orchestra after a poem by Meredith; composed 1914 but not performed till 1921.

'LARK' QUARTET, nickname of Haydn's string quartet in D, op. 64, no. 5, composed 1789 – from the high-soaring violin part at the opening.

LARSSON, LARS-ERIK (b. 1908), Swedish composer, pupil of Berg in Vienna – but not himself a TWELVE-NOTE composer. Has written three symphonies, opera 'The Princess of Cyprus', etc.

LASSO, see LASSUS.

LASSÚ (Hung.), the slow section of a CSÁRDÁS.

LASSUS, ROLAND DE (Italianized form, Orlando di Lasso; 1530–94), Flemish composer. Choirboy in Mons, his birthplace; afterwards choirmaster at the church of St John Lateran, Rome, and then worked in Antwerp before taking service at the Bavarian court in Munich. He settled there (travelling to Italy, however) and died in Munich. His works, all for two or (usually) more voices, number more than 2000 and include madrigals and similar works to French, German, and Italian poetry, as well as much religious music – masses, motets, miscellaneous biblical settings in Latin, settings of various texts in Italian, etc. Was preoccupied with such religious settings towards the end of his life; latterly suffered from mental depression.

LAST SAVAGE, THE, opera by Menotti, produced in Paris, 1964. Libretto (originally in Italian) by composer, satirizing modern civilization.

LASZLÓ, MAGDA (b. 1912), Hungarian soprano (though born in what was then Rumania); member of the Budapest Opera, but then went in 1945 to live in Italy, becoming noted there (and elsewhere) particularly in modern music by Dallapiccola and others.

LAUDA, LAUDE (It.), a song of praise; *lauda spirituale* or *laude spirituale* (pl., *laudi spirituali*), type of Italian religious song for several voices, having its own distinctive poetry and sung (14th–18th centuries) by a religious confraternity called the *laudisti*. This type of work is reckoned a forerunner of ORATORIO.

LAUDA SION (Lat., Praise, O Zion), a Roman Catholic hymn (SEQUENCE) for the feast of Corpus Christi, sung either to traditional plainsong or to other settings.

LAUDI, see LAUDA.

'LAUDON' SYMPHONY, nickname for Haydn's symphony no. 69 in C,

1778, composed in honour of the Austrian field-marshal so named.

LAVOLTA, English name for an old dance featuring a leap (It., *volta*). One is included in Britten's 'GLORIANA'.

LAWES, HENRY (1596–1662), English composer in service at court; celebrated in a sonnet by Milton, having set Milton's 'COMUS'. Wrote coronation anthem for Charles II, songs (some to poems by Herrick), church music; collaborated in the music to 'THE SIEGE OF RHODES', the first English opera, 1656. Brother of William Lawes.

LAWES, WILLIAM (1602–45), English composer of masques, songs, music for viols, etc.; pupil of J. Cooper. Musician to Charles I; killed while fighting on Royalist side in the Civil War. Brother of Henry Lawes.

LAWRENCE, MARJORIE (FLORENCE) (b. 1908), Australian mezzo-soprano resident in U.S.A. Well known in opera and concerts, and continued career even after developing poliomyelitis in 1941.

LE (Fr. masc. sing., It. fem. pl.), the.

LE FLEM, PAUL (b. 1881), French composer, pupil of d'Indy and Roussel. Works include a symphony, a dance-drama on Shakespeare's *Macbeth*, chamber music, etc. Also critic and choral conductor.

LE FLEMING, CHRISTOPHER KAYE (b. 1908), English composer of choral works, educational piano music, etc., and musical educationalist.

LE GALLIENNE, DORIAN (1916–63), Australian composer, pupil in England of Howells, Benjamin, and Jacob. Works include Sinfonietta, incidental music to plays, piano solos, songs. Also critic.

LE SUEUR, see LESUEUR.

LEAD, see LEADER.

LEADER, the directing member of an ensemble, e.g. a string quartet or café band. But as applied to an orchestra, *leader* in Britain means the principal violinist (U.S., concertmaster) as the chief performer, whereas in U.S.A. it is an alternative term for conductor. Similarly with *to lead*.

LEADING SEVENTH, term which is in fact an abbreviation for 'chord of the minor seventh built on the leading-note' – e.g., in C major, the chord B, D, F, A, (reading upwards). This is characteristically produced by the harmonica, sucked.

LEADING-MOTIVE, English equivalent term for Ger. *Leitmotiv* (not *-motif*) – a theme used (particularly in Wagner's operas) recurrently to denote an object, an aspect of character, etc. (For an anticipation of the device, see BISHOP.)

LEADING-NOTE, the seventh degree of the major scale, so called because it seems to lead upwards to the TONIC a semitone above it. In the minor scale this note (e.g. B♮ in the key of C minor) is commonly used in ascending but not in descending.

LECLAIR, JEAN MARIE (1697–1764), French violinist and composer – and, in his twenties, a ballet-master. For a time played in the Paris

Opéra orchestra, and himself wrote operas and ballets as well as twelve violin concertos and other violin music. Visited Holland to meet Locatelli, and shortly after a second visit there was murdered near his home in Paris.

LECOCQ, ALEXANDRE CHARLES (1832–1918), French composer, also organist. From 1868 successful with dozens of operettas including 'Madame Angot's Daughter' (*La Fille de Mme Angot*) from which the ballet 'Mam'zelle Angot' (1947) is derived, and 'Giroflé-Girofiá'.

LEDGER LINE, short line written above or below the staff to accommodate notes outside the staff – as in the following:  (This is the correct spelling, but *leger line* is also encountered.)

LEEUW, TON DE (b. 1926), Dutch composer, pupil of Messiaen (in Paris) and Badings; also pianist and critic. Works include piano concerto, symphony for strings and percussion, orchestral 'Funeral Music for Willem Pijper', radiophonic oratorio 'Job', opera 'The Dream', chamber works.

LEFÉBURE, YVONNE (b. 1904), French pianist, pupil of Cortot and others, prominent in new music; she also lectures, writes, etc.

LEFÉBURE-WÉLY, LOUIS JAMES ALFRED (1817–69), French organist, performing from age 8, and composer chiefly of organ works.

LEGATO (It., bound together), smoothly, not STACCATO – as a direction for performance.

LEGEND OF THE INVISIBLE CITY OF KITEZH AND OF THE MAID FEVRONIA, see THE INVISIBLE CITY OF KITEZH.

LÉGER (Fr, light; *légèrement*, lightly; *musique légère*, light music.

LEGER LINE, see LEDGER LINE.

LEGG(I)ERO, LEGG(I)ERAMENTE (It.), light, lightly. (The current Italian form omits the 'i', which was formerly correct usage.)

LEGNO (It.), wood; *bacchetta di legno* (instruction to drummer to use) wooden-headed drumstick; *col legno*, with the wood – instruction to string player to hit the string with the back of the bow instead of with the hair, producing a dry and rather grotesque sound (an effect used, e.g., in Saint-Saëns's 'DANSE MACABRE').

LEHÁR, FERENCZ (Germanized as Franz, but surname not Léhar; 1870–1948), Hungarian composer, for a time violinist and military bandmaster; wrote a violin concerto, etc., but mainly many successful Viennese operettas including 'The Count of Luxembourg', 'Frederica', 'The Land of Smiles', 'THE MERRY WIDOW'.

LEHMANN, LIZA, form of name used by Elizabetta Nina Mary Frederika Lehmann (1862–1918), English soprano and composer. Works include 'In a Persian Garden' (words from Fitzgerald's translation of Omar Khayyam) and other song-cycles, and opera 'The Vicar of Wakefield' (after Goldsmith).

LEHMANN, LOTTE (b. 1885), German-born operatic and concert

soprano, naturalized in U.S.A.; also novelist and autobiographer.

LEIBOWITZ, RENÉ (b. 1913), French (Polish-born), composer, conductor, and noted theoretician, pupil of Ravel, Schoenberg and Webern. Works include piano and choral music, Chamber Symphony, and 'The Explanation of Metaphors' for speaker, two pianos, harp, and percussion.

LEICHT (Ger.), (1) light; (2) easy.

LEIGH, WALTER (1905–42), English composer of light opera 'The Jolly Roger' and other theatre music, concertino for harpsichord and strings, etc.; pupil of Hindemith. Killed in action in Libya.

LEIGHTON, KENNETH (b. 1929), English composer, pupil of Petrassi in Rome. Works include violin concerto, viola concerto (with harp, strings, and kettledrums), cello concerto, orchestral 'Primavera Romana' (It., Roman Spring), etc.; also pianist and university teacher.

LEINSDORF, ERICH (b. 1912), American conductor, born and trained in Vienna; conducted opera at the Metropolitan, New York, from 1938; became conductor of the Boston Symphony Orchestra, 1962.

LEITMOTIV, see LEADING-MOTIVE.

LEKEU, GUILLAUME (1870–94), Belgian composer, pupil of Franck and d'Indy. Works include piano quartet and cello sonata, both completed by d'Indy after Lekeu's early death from typhoid; also orchestral 'Fantasy on two Angevin Airs', symphonic study on *Hamlet*, etc.

LEMARE, EDWIN HENRY (1865–1934), English organist who performed much in U.S.A. and died in Los Angeles; composed much organ music including two solo 'symphonies'.

LEMMINKÄINEN'S HOMECOMING, orchestral work by Sibelius referring to one of the heroes of the Kalevala (Finnish national epic); it is no. 3 of four pieces about Lemminkäinen, nos. 1 and 2 being unpublished and no. 4 being 'THE SWAN OF TUONELA'.

'LENINGRAD' SYMPHONY, nickname for Shostakovich's symphony no. 7, glorifying the spirit of besieged Leningrad and partly composed there, 1941.

LENT, LENTO (Fr., It.), slow.

LEO, LEONARDO (1694–1744), Italian composer working in Naples. His comic operas, some in Neapolitan dialect, are considered (with Pergolesi's) pioneers of their type. Wrote, or contributed numbers to, about seventy operas in all; other works include oratorios, church music, harpsichord pieces.

LEONCAVALLO, RUGGIERO (1858–1919), Italian composer of 'PAGLIACCI' (The Clowns), his only successful opera – in a vivid and melodramatic vein. Before this worked as café pianist, etc. Was encouraged by Wagner and, acting as his own librettist, wrote various other operas including 'LA BOHÈME' which failed where Puccini's on the same subject succeeded. Other works include operettas, symphonic poem 'Serafita'.

LEONI, LEONE (16th–17th century), Italian church musician (at

Vicenza cathedral, 1588), composer of Masses, motets (some with instruments), etc.; also composed madrigals. Dates of birth and death unknown.

LÉONIN (also Leoninus, Lat.), French composer active about 1160–1180 as church musician in Paris: wrote a cycle of two-part settings for all the principal church feasts of the year.

LEONORA, (1) the name of the heroine of Beethoven's opera FIDELIO – hence Beethoven's Leonora Overtures nos. 1, 2, and 3 (the numbering, formerly thought chronologically deceptive, is now considered correct). Each of these was in its time put forward as the overture to the opera, but all were eventually superseded for this purpose by the overture now actually called 'Fidelio'. The 'Leonora' overtures are now heard as concert pieces; and no. 3, the best-known, is also sometimes performed (without any authority from Beethoven) during the opera 'Fidelio' as an orchestral interlude before the last scene. (2) title of the opera by Gaveaux (*Leonora, or Wedded Love*), produced in Paris in 1798, from the libretto of which (by J. N. Bouilly) the plot of Beethoven's 'FIDELIO' derives. (3) name used (with reference to Beethoven's use) in the title of Liebermann's opera *Leonora* 40/45 (produced in Basel, 1952, with libretto by composer) in which, as in 'FIDELIO', love triumphs over officialdom, this time in the Second World War. (4) see FRY.

LEONORE; 'LEONORE 40/45', see preceding entry. (The name is the German form of Leonora.)

LEROUX, XAVIER NAPOLÉON (1863–1919), French composer, pupil of Massenet; also critic. Works include opera 'The Tramp' (Le Chemineau) using French peasant songs; also other operas, church music, songs, etc.

LES (Fr.), the.

LESCHETIZKY, THEODOR (Germanized form of *Teodor Leszetycki;* 1830–1915), Polish piano teacher mainly active in St Petersburg and Vienna; developed a famous 'method', and taught Paderewski and other noted pianists. Also composer of operas, piano solos, etc.

LESSON, term used in 17th-18th centuries for a short keyboard piece or a set of such pieces (i.e. a SUITE). Cp. EXERCISE.

LESUEUR, JEAN FRANÇOIS (1760–1837), French composer who wrote church music using orchestra and then, when this met disapproval, wrote spectacular operas and French Revolutionary pieces using enormous forces. In court service to Napoleon and then to Louis XVIII. Taught Berlioz and Gounod.

LESUR, DANIEL JEAN YVES (b. 1908), French composer of orchestral music, 'The Inner Life' for organ, piano solos, songs, etc. Also pianist and organist. With Baudrier, Jolivet, and Messiaen formed the 'YOUNG FRANCE' group, and collaborated with Jolivet in a ballet, 'The Child and the Monster'.

LET'S MAKE AN OPERA!, Britten's 'entertainment for young people' (his own description) produced in Aldeburgh, 1949. It incorporates a miniature opera, 'The Little Sweep' – about a maltreated boy chimney-sweep of the mid-19th century – most of the roles in which are for children. This opera is rehearsed in the first section of the 'entertainment' and performed, with the audience's vocal participation, in the second.

LEVANT, OSCAR (b. 1906), American pianist, composer of piano concerto, etc.; friend and noted interpreter of Gershwin. Also actor, radio comedian, author of autobiography *A Smattering of Ignorance*, etc.

LEVERIDGE, RICHARD (*c.* 1670–1758), English bass singer and composer chiefly of songs (including 'The Roast Beef of Old England') and stage music, etc.

LEWIS, ANTHONY (CAREY) (b. 1915), English composer (trumpet concerto, cantata 'A Tribute of Praise', etc.), conductor, and authority on 17th- and 18th-century English music. Pupil of N. Boulanger. Formerly with BBC, then professor at Birmingham University; from 1968 principal of R.A.M. C.B.E., 1967.

LEWIS, RICHARD (b. 1914), English tenor noted in opera (Glyndebourne, Covent Garden, etc.) and oratorio. Created the part of Troilus in Walton's 'TROILUS AND CRESSIDA'. C.B.E., 1962.

LEWKOVITCH, BERNHARD (b. 1927), Danish composer, also Roman Catholic choirmaster and organist; works include Masses, motets, five piano sonatas.

LEY, HENRY GEORGE (1887–1962), English organist and composer (songs, church music, etc.); Precentor (i.e. musical director) of Eton College 1926–45.

LEYGRAF, HANS (b. 1920), Swedish pianist – from age 9; studied partly in Germany and Austria. Also conductor, and composer of a piano-concertino, string quartet, piano solos, etc.

LIADOV, ANATOL KONSTANTINOVICH (1855–1914), Russian composer of symphonic poems 'BABA YAGA', 'THE ENCHANTED LAKE', and 'KIKIMORA', and of other works for orchestra and piano in Russian 'nationalist' style; also collector and arranger of folk-songs, and conductor. Was originally invited to compose the music for 'THE FIREBIRD', but owing to his characteristic dilatoriness Stravinsky undertook it.

LIAPUNOV, SERGEY MIKHAILOVICH (1859–1924), Russian pianist and composer in 'nationalist' style; friend of Balakirev, and collector of folk-songs. Wrote two piano concertos, Rhapsody on Ukrainian themes for piano and orchestra, piano solos, etc.

LIBRETTO (It., booklet), the text of an opera – or sometimes of an oratorio or other non-stage work. Plural *libretti* (It.) or *librettos* (as anglicized word).

LICENZA (It.), license, freedom; *con alcuna licenza* (or *con alcune licenze*, plural), with some freedom(s) as to performance, or as to the construction of a work (when it does not follow 'strict' pattern).

LIDHOLM, INGVAR (b. 1921), Swedish composer of chamber music. Concerto for string orchestra, piano sonata, etc.; studied in London with Seiber, 1954, thenceforward using TWELVE-NOTE method, in e.g. Concertino for flute, oboe, English horn, and cello (without orchestra).

LIE, SIGURD (1871–1904), Norwegian composer, also violinist and conductor, who before dying of tuberculosis wrote symphony, many songs, violin sonata, etc.

LIEBE DER DANAE, DIE, see THE LOVE OF DANAE.

LIEBERMANN, ROLF (b. 1910), Swiss composer, who uses TWELVE-NOTE technique in a free and individual style; works include operas 'Leonora 40/45' (see LEONORA), 'Penelope', and (in English, after Molière's play) 'SCHOOL FOR WIVES'; also concerto for jazz band and symphony orchestra, etc. Administrator of Hamburg State Opera since 1959.

LIEBESLIEDER WALZER, see LOVE-SONG WALTZES.

LIEBESTRAUM (Ger., a dream of love; pl. *-träume*), title given by Liszt to his piano arrangements (1850) of three of his songs. *Liebestraum* no. 3 is the well-known one.

LIEBLICH (Ger.), lovely; *Lieblich Gedackt* (organ stop), same as GEDACKT.

LIED (Ger., pl. *Lieder*), song; specifically, in the non-German-speaking world, the type of song with piano composed by, e.g., Schubert, Schumann, and Wolf. The term is dubiously applied also to songs not in German but of a similar kind, e.g. by Grieg. For the term *Lieder Recital* instead of 'song recital' there is no excuse unless the programme is exclusively of German song. See also the following entries.

LIED(ER) OHNE WORTE, see SONGS WITHOUT WORDS.

LIED VON DER ERDE, DAS, see SONG OF THE EARTH.

LIEDER EINES FAHRENDEN GESELLEN, see SONGS OF A WAYFARER.

LIEDERKRANZ, LIEDERKREIS (Ger.), song-CYCLE, *Liederkreis* is used as the actual title of two cycles by Schumann, to poems by Heine and by Eichendorff (both 1840).

LIEDERTAFEL (Ger., song-table – referring to origin in drinking-gatherings), male-voice choir in German or German-descended communities, e.g. in U.S.A. and South Australia.

LIER, BERTUS VAN (b. 1906), Dutch cellist, conductor (pupil of Scherchen), critic, teacher, and composer (pupil of Pijper). Works include three symphonies, 'The Dyke' for orator and orchestra, stage music, unaccompanied cello sonata.

LIFE FOR THE TSAR, A, see IVAN SUSSANIN.

LIGATURE, (1) a slur-mark indicating a group of notes all sung to the same syllable (term sometimes also used in instrumental music when the SLUR indicates that notes are to be phrased together); (2) on the clarinet, saxophone, etc., the metal band which secures the reed to the mouthpiece.

LIGETI, GYÖRGY (b. 1923), Hungarian composer who left Hungary in 1956, afterwards living in Vienna and Cologne. Works, in 'advanced' idiom, include 'Apparitions' for orchestra, 'Articulation' for recorded tape. Also writer on music and teacher.

LIGHT, term applied to music supposedly not requiring the listener's full concentration; *light orchestra*, orchestra providing this. So also *light opera*, imprecise non-technical term sometimes used by laymen in opposition to *grand opera* (also imprecise), and not clearly distinguishable from *operetta*.

LILAC TIME, operetta distortedly based on the life of Schubert and distortingly using his music. The score used in the London production, 1923, was by H. Berté and G. H. Clutsam (after a German original, 1916); the American one, called 'Blossom Time', was by S. Romberg.

LILBURN, DOUGLAS (GORDON) (b. 1915), New Zealand composer, partly trained in London. Works include 'Aotearoa' for orchestra (Maori name for New Zealand), three symphonies, string trio and other chamber music, piano solos.

LILY OF KILLARNEY, THE, opera by Benedict, produced in London 1862 (and long a favourite in Britain); libretto by J. Oxenford and D. Boucicault, after the latter's play *The Colleen Bawn.*

LINCOLN PORTRAIT, A, work for narrator and orchestra by Copland, on sayings of Abraham Lincoln, first performed 1942.

LINEAR COUNTERPOINT, term – senseless, because all counterpoint is a matter of lines – sometimes used for a type of 20th-century counterpoint (e.g. Stravinsky's) held to be musically valid through the value of the separate lines themselves and not through their mutual harmonization.

LINLEY, THOMAS (1732–95), English composer, especially for the stage; composed the song 'Here's to the Maiden' for Sheridan's *The School for Scandal.* Was also singing-teacher and concert-promoter. Father of Elizabeth Ann Linley, singer, who married Sheridan. See also next entry.

LINLEY, THOMAS (1756–78), English composer of opera 'The Cady of Baghdad', etc., and, with his father (see preceding entry), of music for Sheridan's *The Duenna.* In boyhood, studied in Italy, met Mozart there and became his firm friend; met early death by drowning.

LINKE HAND (Ger.), left hand.

'LINZ' SYMPHONY, nickname for Mozart's symphony no. 36 in C, K.425, composed in Linz and first performed there in 1783.

LIPATTI, DINU (1917–50), Rumanian pianist, pupil of Cortot; and composer, pupil of N. Boulanger and Dukas. Wrote various works for piano (including sonatina for left hand) and two pianos, etc., and before early death had attained highest international rank as pianist. Settled in Switzerland and died there.

LIPKIN, MALCOLM (b. 1932), English composer of 'Sinfonia di Roma' (of Rome), two violin concertos, etc.

LIRA (It.), (1) lyre; (2) the VIELLE in its medieval sense (bowed-string instrument, not the 'hurdy-gurdy'; (3) term used in various compound names, e.g. *lira da braccio* (... for the arm), type of bowed-string instrument developed in the 16th century, without the 'waist' of a violin; *lira da gamba* (for the leg), a larger relation of this; *lira organizzata*, superior type of hurdy-gurdy composed for by Haydn.

LISZT, FERENCZ (Germanized as Franz; 1811–86), Hungarian pianist and composer. As child prodigy pianist, visited France and Britain. Lived with the Countess d'Agoult 1833–44, one of their children (Cosima) later becoming Wagner's wife. From 1848 lived with the Princess Sayn-Wittgenstein, whose eventual effort to secure a divorce from her husband failed; Liszt separated from her in 1861, never married, and in 1865 took minor orders in the Roman Catholic Church and was referred to as 'the Abbé Liszt'. He revisited London in 1886. He consistently aided new composers from Berlioz to Grieg, and made Weimar a highly important centre when he was court musical director there 1848–59. His piano works include a sonata (pioneering one-movement form), also DANTE SONATA, twenty HUNGARIAN RHAPSODIES, 'MAZEPPA' (also for orchestra), and other pieces with allusive titles; and many operatic paraphrases, transcriptions of other composers' works, etc. Arranged Schubert's 'WANDERER FANTASY' in a version for piano and orchestra. Also composed 'THE PRELUDES', 'ORPHEUS', 'HAMLET', 'DANTE SYMPHONY', 'FAUST SYMPHONY', 'Episodes from Lenau's FAUST', etc., for orchestra; four 'MEPHISTO WALTZES'; 'MALEDICTION' for piano and orchestra; 'GRAN MASS', 'VIA CRUCIS' and other church works; more than 70 songs in French, German, Italian, Hungarian, and English (Tennyson's 'Go not, happy day'); and much else. See also LIEBESTRAUM. Was a bold harmonic innovator, especially in late years. His 'Hungarian' music is chiefly of a gipsy, not an authentically peasant, character.

LITANY, an extended form of Christian prayer for help, often set to music; and the term is sometimes used allusively in the titles of instrumental pieces.

LITOLFF, HENRY CHARLES (1818–91), French pianist, composer, and publisher; he was born in London of an Alsatian father and settled eventually in Paris. Works include operas, piano solos, and five works for piano and orchestra called symphony-concerto (*concerto symphonique*), from the fourth of which comes the well-known scherzo.

LITTLE CLAVIER BOOK FOR ANNA MAGDALENA BACH (Ger., *Clavierbüchlein für A.M.B.*), an instructional book of keyboard pieces, some with words, compiled by J. S. Bach for his second wife.

LITTLE NIGHT MUSIC, A, see EINE KLEINE NACHTMUSIK.

LITTLE ORGAN BOOK (Ger., *Orgelbüchlein*), a compilation by Bach of forty-six chorale preludes for the organ, 1717.

LITTLE ORGAN MASS, Mass in B♭ composed by Haydn about 1770 – short in length and, like the 'GREAT ORGAN MASS', with a solo organ part.

'LITTLE RUSSIAN' SYMPHONY, see 'UKRAINIAN' SYMPHONY.

LITTLE SWEEP, THE, see 'LET'S MAKE AN OPERA!'.

LITUUS (Lat.), ancient Roman military wind-instrument of trumpet type, used by cavalry. The word is also found in later usages, e.g. (exceptionally) in Bach's church cantata no. 118 (*c.* 1737) in which the exact type of wind instrument meant is uncertain.

LIVERPOOL PHILHARMONIC ORCHESTRA, see ROYAL LIVERPOOL PHILHARMONIC ORCHESTRA.

LIVIABELLA, LINO (1902–64), Italian composer of opera 'The Shell' (*La Conchiglia*), after R. L. Stevenson's *The Bottle Imp*; also of 'Monte Mario' and 'The Conqueror' (symphonic poems).

LLOYD, CHARLES HARFORD (1849–1919), English organist (e.g. of the Chapel Royal) and composer of church and organ music, cantatas, etc.

LLOYD, GEORGE (b. 1913), English composer of operas 'Iernin', 'The Serf' and 'John Socman', all on British history or legend; also of five symphonies and a few other works. Pupil of Farjeon.

LOBGESANG, see HYMN OF PRAISE,

LOCATELLI, PIETRO (1693–1764), Italian violinist and composer, pupil of Corelli in Rome, settled in Amsterdam and died there. Works include sonatas, studies, and other works for violin; also trios, works of CONCERTO GROSSO type, etc.

LOCK, see LOCKE.

LOCKE, MATTHEW (also Lock; *c.* 1630–1677), English composer, in service to Charles II, 1661; also author of pamphlet defending his own 'modern' style. Works include masques 'CUPID AND DEATH' (with C. Gibbons), opera 'THE SIEGE OF RHODES' (with others), songs, church music, works for viols. Apparently not the composer of the music to 'MACBETH' long attributed to him.

LOCO (It., place), indication that music is to be performed at the pitch written, cancelling the instruction '*8va sopra*' (i.e. '*ottava* ...') or '*8va bassa*' indicating that music is to be played respectively an octave higher or an octave lower than written.

LOCRIAN MODE, a MODE that could be represented by the white keys of the piano beginning on B, if it were not rejected as unusable in practice. (Unlike the other MODES, it would not include a note a perfect fifth upward from its 'final', B.)

LODER, EDWARD (JAMES) (1813–65), English composer of operas including 'The Night Dancers', 'Raymond and Agnes'; songs including 'The Brooklet' (translation of the poem set by Schubert as 'Wohin?' in 'THE FAIR MAID OF THE MILL'), string quartets, etc.

LOEFFLER, CHARLES MARTIN (TORNOW) (1861–1935), Alsatian-born violinist-composer who spent boyhood partly in Russia (his orchestral 'Memories of My Childhood' has Russian musical elements) and settled in U.S.A., 1881. Composed other orchestra works including 'A Pagan Poem' (after Virgil) with piano, English horn, and three trumpets; also cantatas, chamber music, songs, etc.

LŒILLET, JEAN BAPTISTE (1680–1730), Belgian composer, flutist, oboist, and harpsichordist, who worked much in London and died there. Wrote music for flute, recorder, and other instruments, and helped to popularize the flute (a new instrument compared to the recorder) in England.

LOEWE, (JOHANN) CARL GOTTFRIED (1796–1869), German composer, also organist; visited London, 1847. Noted for songs, especially ballads on dramatic poems, e.g. 'Edward' and 'The Erl King' (see BALLAD, 2) wrote also operas, oratorios, piano music, etc. Had a six-week trance in 1864 and died after a similar attack.

LOGROSCINO, (BONIFACIO) NICOLA (1698–*c.* 1765), Italian composer the exact date of whose death is unknown; wrote dozens of operas, some in collaboration with other composers. Was one of the first to compose elaborate operatic finales. Also wrote church music.

LOHENGRIN, opera by Wagner, produced in Weimar, 1850; libretto by composer. Lohengrin, Knight of the Holy Grail with personal swan-drawn transport, is incidentally the son of PARSIFAL.

LÖHR, HERMANN (FREDERIC) (1872–1944), English composer of 'Where My Caravan Has Rested' and other popular English drawing-room songs.

LONDON, GEORGE (b. 1921; original surname Burnstein), American (Canadian-born) baritone who came to Europe in 1949, afterwards joining the Vienna State Opera.

LONDON OVERTURE, A, orchestral work by Ireland, 1936; has a prominent phrase said to originate from a bus-conductor's intonation of 'Piccadilly!'

LONDON PHILHARMONIC ORCHESTRA, an orchestra founded by T. Beecham in 1932, but becoming self-governing in 1939. Principal conductor from 1967, Bernard Haitink.

'LONDON' SYMPHONY, nickname for Haydn's last symphony, no. 104 in D, first performed 1795 during Haydn's second visit to London. A curious nickname, because all Haydn's last twelve symphonies were written for London and first performed there. See also next entry.

LONDON SYMPHONY, A, title of Vaughan Williams's symphony no. 2 (but, in conformity with his practice, not numbered by him), first performed 1914; revised version first performed 1920. Quotes the Big Ben chimes and is an evocation of London. See NOCTURNE. (See also preceding entry.)

LONDON SYMPHONY ORCHESTRA, an orchestra founded in 1904, self-governing from the beginning; principal conductor from 1968, André Previn.

LONDONDERRY AIR, Irish folk-tune which was first brought into print in 1855; it has since been variously arranged (e.g. by Grainger as 'Irish Tune from County Derry') and fitted with various tiresome words.

LONG, obsolete time-value of a note, in the system of notation which grew up in the Middle Ages and was superseded by the present one; a long could equal either a half or a third of a 'large' and was itself divisible into either two or three 'breves'.

LONG, MARGUERITE (MARIE CHARLOTTE) (1874–1966), French pianist associated with many modern French composers; also noted teacher. Among works dedicated to her is Ravel's piano concerto (not the one for left hand).

LONGO, ALESSANDRO (1864–1945), Italian pianist who compiled a catalogue of D. Scarlatti's keyboard works, these being referred to as 'Longo No. . . .' or 'L. . . .' (followed by a number). This catalogue and system of numbering have been superseded by those of KIRKPATRICK.

LOPATNIKOV, NIKOLAY LVOVICH (b. 1903), Esthonian-born Russian pianist and composer who settled in Germany, 1920, and became pupil of Toch; in U.S.A. since 1939. Works, showing some traditional Russian influences as well as those of Stravinsky and Hindemith, include violin concerto, two piano concertos, two symphonies, opera 'Danton', violin and piano sonata with side-drum *ad lib.*

LORIOD, YVONNE (b. 1924), French pianist, noted especially in performing the works of Messiaen and other modern French composers.

LORTZING, (GUSTAV) ALBERT (1801–51), German composer, almost entirely of operas and operettas, with his own librettos; his 'TSAR AND CARPENTER' (*Zar und Zimmermann*) is still popular in Germany. Also conductor and, on occasion, tenor singer.

LOS ANGELES, VICTORIA DE (b. 1923), Spanish soprano noted in opera and recital; sometimes accompanying herself on the guitar in Spanish traditional songs.

LOTTI, ANTONIO (*c.* 1667–1740), Italian composer of church music, oratorio, etc.; also of opera. Was church singer and organist, becoming chief organist of St Mark's, Venice, from 1704 till death.

LOUD PEDAL, misleading name for the sustaining pedal of the piano – see PIANO.

LOUIS FERDINAND, PRINCE, form of name used by Prince Friedrich Christian Ludwig of Prussia (1772–1806), amateur composer of chamber music, etc.; praised by Beethoven, who dedicated to him his piano concerto no. 3.

LOUISE, opera by G. Charpentier, produced in Paris, 1900. Libretto by composer; 'realistic' opera (cp. Italian 'VERISMO') which put the slums of Paris on the stage. The heroine is a seamstress.

LOURE (Fr.), a type of rustic French bagpipe; and hence a French dance, usually in moderate 6/4 time. Hence also *louré* (derived from a technique of bagpipe-playing), a kind of bowing on the violin, etc.

in which several notes are taken in one stroke of the bow but are slightly detached from one another.

LOURÉ, see preceding entry.

LOURIE, ARTHUR VINCENT (b. 1892), Russian-born composer who settled first in France (1921), then in U.S.A. (1941). Works, some with Roman Catholic allusions, include 'Kormchaya' (Rus., Helmswoman, i.e. the Virgin Mary) for orchestra; string quartets, settings of poems by Tolstoy and Mayakovsky.

LOVE FOR THREE ORANGES (Rus., *Liubov k trem apelsinam*), opera by Prokofiev, produced in French in Chicago, 1921. Libretto, in Russian, by composer, after an Italian play by Gozzi: satirical fable, some of the actors impersonating an audience, the main action being thus a 'play within a play'. The prince who loves the three oranges finds his princess in the third. An orchestral suite drawn from this includes a march also well-known in a piano arrangement.

LOVE IN A VILLAGE, opera with music collected and arranged by T. Arne, produced in London, 1761; the music is by sixteen other composers as well as Arne himself, the work being a PASTICCIO. Modern revivals include one with the music edited by Oldham, produced in Aldeburgh, 1952.

LOVE OF DANAE, THE (Ger., *Die Liebe der Danae*), opera by R. Strauss, completed 1940 but not performed until 1952 in Salzburg. Libretto by H. von Hofmannsthal and J. Gregor, on Danae's preference for Midas over Jupiter.

LOVE OF THE THREE KINGS, THE (It., *L'Amore dei Tre Ré*), third and most successful opera by Montemezzi, produced in Milan, 1913; libretto by S. Benelli on a medieval story about a blind king.

LOVE POTION, THE, alternative English title for Donizetti's '*L'Elisir d'amore*'; see ELIXIR OF LOVE.

LOVE, THE MAGICIAN, see next entry.

LOVE, THE SORCERER (Sp., *El Amor brujo*), ballet with music by Falla, first performed 1915, later revised; written for a ballerina who can sing as well as dance. A suite for orchestra (properly with contralto) is drawn from it. (Title commonly translated 'Love, the Magician'; *brujo* is actually a 'male witch', and the ballet is about a girl malevolently haunted by a dead lover.)

LOVE-SONG WALTZES (Ger., *Liebeslieder-Walzer*), a set of eighteen waltzes by Brahms 'for piano duet and [four] vocal parts *ad lib.*', 1869; fifteen more, called 'New Love-Song Waltzes' (1875) were designated as 'for four voices and piano duet'.

LUALDI, ADRIANO (b. 1885), Italian composer of operas including 'The Moon of the Caribbees' (after Eugene O'Neill) with some unorthodox orchestration – e.g. 'the two lowest strings of a double-bass, untuned'; also of string quartet, songs, etc. Is director of the Florence Conservatory, conductor, and critic.

LUCAS, LEIGHTON (b. 1903), English conductor, noted in ballet and in French music; also composer (film music, a Latin Requiem Mass, orchestral works, etc); formerly ballet-dancer.

LUCIA DI LAMMERMOOR, LUCY OF LAMMERMOOR, opera by Donizetti, produced in Naples, 1835. Libretto by S. Cammarano, after Scott; set in Scotland about 1700. After slaying her husband the heroine has a famous 'mad scene'.

LUDAS TONALIS (Lat., the play of notes), piano work by Hindemith, first performed 1944. It comprises a prelude, twelve fugues separated by eleven interludes, and a postlude which is the INVERTED (upside-down) version of the prelude. Intended as studies in both composition and piano technique.

LUENING, OTTO (b. 1900), American composer who studied in Munich and Zürich; works include opera, 'Evangeline', 'Pilgrim's Hymn' for orchestra, and a 'Concerto for light, movement, sound, and voice' (a dance work for tape-recorder and orchestra). Is also conductor and university professor.

LUIGINI, ALEXANDRE CLÉMENT LÉON JOSEPH (1850–1906), French violinist, conductor, and composer of orchestral piece called 'Egyptian Ballet' and other light orchestral music; also of operas, etc.

LUISA MILLER, opera by Verdi, produced in Naples, 1849. Libretto by S. Cammarano, after Schiller: the setting is the Tyrol, and the three acts are respectively headed Love, Intrigue, and Poison.

LULLY, JEAN-BAPTISTE (originally Giovanni Battista Lulli; 1632–87), Italian-born composer who was taken in boyhood to France and first worked there as a scullion, then as a violinist. Went into service of Louis XIV, 1652; naturalized French, 1661; achieved the supreme musical position at court, 1662. Himself a dancer, collaborated with Molière in comedy-ballets including 'LE BOURGEOIS GENTILHOMME'; from 1673 wrote operas including 'ALKESTIS' and 'ARMIDA'. Wrote also church music, dance music, etc., and established the 'French OVERTURE'. A brilliant intriguer; obtained a monopoly of opera production in France; made a fortune by speculation; injured his foot with the long staff he used for beating time on the floor, and died of the resulting abscess.

LULU, opera by Berg, with libretto by composer; almost completed, but only Acts I and II (of three) published; first staged in Zürich, 1937. An orchestral suite from it had been previously performed. Its 'heroine', a prostitute, typifies female sexuality.

LUMBYE, HANS CHRISTIAN (1810–74), Danish composer of galops and other dance music, etc., and conductor of such works in Copenhagen.

LUNGO, LUNGA (It.), long.

LUR, prehistoric Scandinavian large bronze horn of which several specimens have been found.

LUSINGANDO, LUSINGHIERO (It.), flatteringly, i.e., alluringly.

LUSTIG (Ger.), cheerful.

LUSTIGE WITWE, DIE, see THE MERRY WIDOW.

LUSTIGEN WIEBER VON WINDSOR, DIE, see THE MERRY WIVES OF WINDSOR.

LUTE, fretted stringed instrument plucked with the fingers, much in use 1400–1700 for solos, song accompaniment, and ensembles; it had isolated orchestral use even as late as Bach's 'ST JOHN PASSION', 1723. It is rarely encountered today, and then only for the playing of old music. The sizes of lutes differed, and also the tuning; but a regular feature was the tuning of strings in pairs (called 'courses') in unison or octaves. Hence *lutenist* (more rarely *lutanist*), a player of the lute.

LUTH (Fr.), lute; *luthier*, lute-maker – and hence, today, a maker of stringed instruments in general.

LUTHER, MARTIN (1483–1546), German Protestant leader; he was skilled in music (as singer, flutist, and lutenist) and is thought to have written the music to hymns – e.g. 'A Stronghold Sure'. This cannot be proved, though he certainly wrote the words of hymns and a treatise in praise of music. See REFORMATION SYMPHONY.

LUTHIER, see LUTH.

LUTOSLAWSKI, WITOLD (b. 1913), Polish composer of orchestral 'Little Suite', 'Silesian Triptych' for voice and orchestra, children's songs, songs for massed choirs, etc.

LUTYENS, ELISABETH (b. 1906), English composer, daughter of Sir Edwin Lutyens, architect. Works include dramatic scene 'The Pit', ballet 'The Birthday of the Infanta' after Oscar Wilde; unaccompanied motet on German philosophical text by Wittgenstein, horn concerto, viola concerto, six 'Chamber Concertos' for various instrumental groups; six string quartets, songs in English and French, film music; writes in TWELVE-NOTE technique.

LVOV, ALEXIS FEODOROVICH (1798–1870), Russian composer of operas, much church music, and the pre-Revolutionary Russian National Anthem – quoted in Tchaikovsky's overture '1812' (see under EIGHTEEN).

LYADOV, LYAPUNOV, see LIADOV, LIAPUNOV.

LYDIAN MODE, the MODE represented by the white keys on the piano beginning on F.

LYMPANY, MOURA, professional name of Mrs Mary Korn (born Mary Johnstone, 1916), English pianist, pupil of Matthay. (Her mother's maiden name was Limpenny.) Was for some time resident in U.S.A., having married an American in 1951.

LYRE (Gk, *lyra*), ancient Greek stringed instrument plucked with plectrum, used to accompany singers (cp. KITHARA); term also used for similar plucked instruments of other civilizations, even if played without plectrum. See also LIRA.

LYRIC, (1, strictly) relating to vocal performance with the lyre, i.e. sung; hence *lyric drama*, occasional synonym for opera (especially in French, as *drame lyrique*); hence also *the lyric stage*, i.e. the operatic stage; (2, of a poem) not epic, not dramatic, but fairly short and expressing the writer's own feelings; hence (term taken over from poetry into music)' Lyric Piece' (Grieg), 'Lyric Suite' (A. Berg), etc.; (3, noun) the words of a song in a musical play, etc.

M

M', Names beginning thus are listed as if spelt MAC. . . .

m, symbol in TONIC SOL-FA for the third degree (mediant) of the scale, pronounced *me*.

MA., abbr. of MAJOR.

MAJ., abbr. of MAJOR.

MAN., abbr. of manual(s), in organ-playing.

M.D., right hand (in piano-playing; Fr. *main droite*; It. *mano destra*).

mf, see MEZZO.

M.G., left hand (in piano-playing; Fr., *main gauche*).

MI., abbr. of MINOR.

MIN., abbr. of MINOR.

M.M., see METRONOME.

M.MUS., abbr. of Master of Music (degree in between 'Bachelor' and 'Doctor' of Music, awarded at some universities).

M.S., left hand (in piano-playing, etc.; It., *mano sinistra*).

MS., MSS., manuscript(s).

M.-SOP., abbr. of MEZZO-SOPRANO.

MUS.B., MUS.BAC., Bachelor of Music.

MUS.D., MUS.DOC., Doctor of Music.

MUS.M., Master of Music – degree awarded in some universities, intermediate between the two preceding.

MA (It.), but.

MA MÈRE L'OYE, see MOTHER GOOSE.

MÁ VLAST, see MY COUNTRY.

MACBETH, (musical works after Shakespeare, including) (1) opera by Verdi, produced in Paris (in Italian), 1847, and later revised; libretto by F. M. Piave and A. Maffei; (2) symphonic poem by R. Strauss, first performed 1890; (3) opera by Bloch, produced in Paris, 1910; libretto by E. Fleg; (4) opera by Collingwood, produced in London 1934; libretto selected from Shakespeare.

The incidental music for a production of the play (in a mauled version by Davenant) in 1674 was formerly ascribed to Locke; he is now thought not to have written it, but it is not known who did.

MCBRIDE, ROBERT GUYN (b. 1911), American composer, showing some influence of jazz; works include ballet 'Show Piece', oboe quintet and other chamber music, orchestral 'Strawberry Jam – Home Made' (caricaturing a jam session).

MCCALL, J. P., see DAWSON, PETER.

MCCORMACK, JOHN (1884–1945), Irish-born tenor who studied in Italy, made Coven Garden début 1907, and later concentrated on recitals. Enormously popular. Naturalized American, 1917, and later created a Papal Count.

MACCUNN, HAMISH (1868–1916), Scottish composer of opera 'JEANIE DEANS' and others less successful; concert-overtures 'Land of the Mountain and the Flood', and 'The Ship o' the Fiend'; cantatas, songs, etc., many on Scottish subjects. Was also conductor, particularly of opera.

MACDOWELL, EDWARD (ALEXANDER)) (1861–1908), American composer, also pianist. Trained in France and Germany. Wrote many short piano pieces, somewhat after Grieg's manner, which have had wide popularity; also two piano concertos, 'Hamlet and Ophelia' and other symphonic poems, songs, etc. The Macdowell Colony – a peaceful working-place for composers and other artists, in New Hampshire – was organized in his memory.

MCEWEN, JOHN BLACKWOOD (1868–1948), Scottish composer of seventeen string quartets (no. 6, 'Biscay'), orchestral works including 'Grey Galloway' (no. 2 of 3 'Border Ballads'), viola concerto, etc. Principal of the R.A.M., 1924–36; knighted 1931.

MACFARREN, GEORGE ALEXANDER (1813–87), English composer of church music, many operas (one on Robin Hood), oratorios, overtures to 'Hamlet' and other plays, etc. Principal of the R.A.M., professor at Cambridge; knighted 1883.

MACHAUT, GUILLAUME DE (also Machault; *c.* 1300–1377), French composer – also poet and priest, latterly Canon of Rheims. Considered the chief exponent of ARS NOVA in France. His Mass for four voices is almost the earliest surviving polyphonic mass. Composed also other vocal music to religious and secular texts, some to a very intricate scheme of construction (see ISORHYTHMIC, a term applying to some of his work).

MACKENZIE, ALEXANDER (CAMPBELL) (1847–1935), Scottish violinist, conductor, principal of the R.A.M. (1888–1924), and composer. Works include 'Columba', 'The Cricket on the Hearth', and other operas; many vocal works of all types; three orchestral Scottish rhapsodies. Knighted 1895.

MACKERRAS, (ALAN) CHARLES (b. 1925), Australian conductor (born in U.S.A.); resident in Britain since 1947. Active in opera (Sadler's Wells, Covent Garden); appointed 'first conductor', Hamburg State Opera, 1965. Arranger e.g. of Sullivan's music for the ballet 'PINEAPPLE POLL', and of Verdi's for 'The Lady and the Fool'. See NATHAN.

MCKIE, WILLIAM (NEIL) (b. 1901), Australian-born organist, resident in Britain; organist of Westminster Abbey, 1941. Was in charge of the music at the Coronation service in 1953, and was afterwards knighted.

MACONCHY, ELIZABETH (b. 1907), English composer of Irish

parentage. Studied under Vaughan Williams, and also in Prague. Cultivates chamber music (including six string quartets) in a contrapuntal style not based on normal key-relationships; has also written symphony for orchestra, symphony for double string orchestra, viola concerto, clarinet quintet, songs, ballets, operas (including 'The Sofa').

MCPHEE, COLIN (b. 1901), American (Canadian-born) composer, pupil of Varèse; lived in Bali, became authority on its music, and has composed symphony 'Tabuh-Tabuhan' based on Balinese musical systems; also piano solos, concerto for piano and wind octet, etc.

MADAME BUTTERFLY (It., *Madama . . .*), opera by Puccini, produced in Milan, 1904 (February); successful only in a revised version three months later. Libretto by G. Giacosa and L. Illica, after D. Belasco's (American) play: the Japanese heroine is deserted by an American naval lieutenant.

MADERNA, BRUNO (b. 1920), Italian composer, pupil of Scherchen. Works include concerto for two pianos, percussion, and harps; Fantasia and Fugue on B–A–C–H, for two pianos; 'Music in Two Dimensions' using 'electronic music' (see ELECTRONIC). Also conductor, prominent in modern music.

MADETOJA, LEEVI ANTTI (1887–1947), Finnish composer of operas, three sumphonies, recitations with piano, etc.; pupil of Sibelius and d'Indy.

MADRIGAL, (1) type of contrapuntal composition for several voices, for secular use, cultivated in the 16th and 17th centuries; originating in Italy but flourishing also in England (where the BALLETT was a related type); written to words in the language of the country (not in Latin) and often of high literary merit; (2) term used also for the Italian forerunner of the above type, from the 14th century (after which the term fell out of use until revived as above); (3) term used also in various looser senses – e.g. the so-called madrigals in operettas by Sullivan and German, which pay vague homage to an older manner without reviving it. (They have, for instance, independent orchestral parts; the true madrigals, above, have no independent instrumental parts, though certainly instruments were used, when desired, to double the voice-parts.)

MAELZEL, JOHANN NEPOMUK (1770–1838), see METRONOME.

MAESTOSO (It.), majestic, dignified.

MAESTRO (It., master), title given in Italy to recognized conductors and composers (and sometimes used with an absurd looseness elsewhere). The *maestro al cembalo* was the musician who in the 18th century and thereabouts directed ensembles while playing the harpsichord; so also *maestro di cappella*, the musical director of a chapel, a prince's establishment, etc. (but not used today in such a wide sense as its German equivalent, KAPELLMEISTER).

MAESTRO DI MUSICA, IL, see THE MUSIC MASTER.

MAGGIO MUSICALE, see MAY FESTIVAL.

MAGGIORE (It.), major.

MAGIC FLUTE, THE (Ger., *Die Zauberflöte*), opera by Mozart, produced in Vienna, 1791; libretto by E. Schikaneder, probably with 'C. L. Giesecke', real name J. G. Metzler. The flute secures the passage of the hero through danger to enlightenment; the opera is one of Masonic and humanistic symbolism.

MAGNARD, (LUCIEN DENIS GABRIEL) ALBÉRIC (1865–1914), French composer of three operas, four symphonies, chamber music, etc., of a dramatic but austere type. Pupil of d'Indy; was killed (or killed himself after) defying German soldiers invading his home.

MAGNIFICAT, the hymn of the Virgin Mary as given in St Luke (Latin name, from first word of the Vulgate translation); used in Roman Catholic and Anglican services, the musical setting in the latter being often combined with a setting of the NUNC DIMITTIS. Hence Vaughan Williams's *Magnificat*, concert-setting of the words of the hymn, plus additional text; first performed 1932.

MAHAGONNY, see RISE AND FALL OF THE CITY OF MAHAGONNY.

MAHLER, GUSTAV (1860–1911), Austrian (Bohemian-born) composer; also noted conductor – Vienna State Opera, 1897–1907. Jewish, but became Roman Catholic. Attended Bruckner's university lectures and admired him, but was never a direct pupil; his own music, of an intensely expressive and chromatically-inclined type, is incidentally regarded as the forerunner of Schoenberg's and thus of TWELVE NOTE music. Most of his works have a literary or other non-musical link. Wrote nine completed symphonies notable for length, large forces used, highly individual orchestration, and some employment of PROGRESSIVE TONALITY. Nos. 2 ('RESURRECTION'), 3 and 8 ('SYMPHONY OF A THOUSAND') employ vocal soloists and chorus, no. 4 a soprano soloist. No. 10, left unfinished, was completed by Deryck Cooke and first performed entire in this form in 1964. The 'SONG OF THE EARTH', though formally a song-cycle with orchestra, is also of symphonic dimensions. Wrote also cycles, 'SONGS OF A WAYFARER' and 'SONGS ON THE DEATH OF CHILDREN', both with orchestra, and other songs; little else.

MAHOMET II, see THE SIEGE OF CORINTH.

MAI-DUN, 'symphonic rhapsody' by Ireland, 1921, alluding to the prehistoric fortification in Dorset also known as Maiden Castle.

MAID AS MISTRESS, THE (It., *La Serva padrona*), comic opera by Pergolesi, produced in Naples, 1733 (as 'intermezzo' between the acts of a serious opera). Libretto by G. A. Federico. Prodigiously successful musical setting of light-hearted intrigue: in France, set off a rivalry between champions of Italian and French opera (the so-called 'War of the buffoons') after Pergolesi's death.

MAID OF PSKOV, THE (Rus., *Pskovitianka*), opera by Rimsky-Korsakov, produced in St Petersburg, 1873; libretto by composer. Also called *Ivan the Terrible*, the 16th-century Tsar being one of the chief characters.

MAIDEN QUARTETS, see RUSSIAN QUARTETS.

MAJOR, MINOR, terms contrasting with one another and having various musical applications – (1) Scales, The major SCALE of C (i.e. treating the note C as its point of repose) is –

(and the same notes descending).

The minor scale is divided for theoretical purposes into three types. The *natural minor* scale of C is

(and the same notes descending).

The *melodic minor* scale of C is

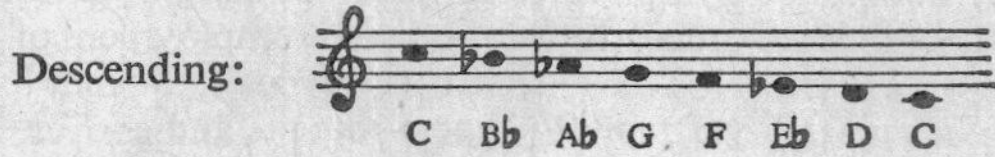

The *harmonic minor* scale of C is

(and the same notes descending).

And similarly with scales beginning on the other notes; i.e. all major scales are internally alike, the distances (INTERVALS) between successive notes being the same, although the note of starting differs. All scales belonging to one of the three types of minor scale are, similarly, alike.

(2) Keys. The KEY of C major is that in which the notes of the scale of C major are treated as 'normal', other notes entering only for special purpose. The key of C minor bears the same relation to the scale of C minor: but, though there are three types of minor scale, there is only one type of minor key (the three types of scale corres-

ponding to different aspects of it). The KEY-SIGNATURE of a minor key is determined by the *natural minor* scale (above); e.g. for C minor

it is three flats (B♭, E♭, A♭):

(3) Chords. A *major* or *minor* chord is one which, being built out of the major or minor scale, may serve to identify that scale. More particularly, the *common chord of C major*, or just *chord of C major*, or *C-major triad* means the notes C. E. G; as contrasted with the *common chord of C minor* (*chord of C minor*, *C-minor triad*), C, E♭, G. (4) Intervals. The INTERVALS second, third, sixth, and seventh are classified as either *major* or *minor*, the latter a semitone less than the former. Thus, measuring upwards from C, the major and minor intervals (in that order) are – second, C–D, C–D♭; third, C–E, C–E♭; sixth, C–A, C–A♭; seventh, C–B, C–B♭. Likewise, of course, measured upwards or downwards from any other note.

MAKROPOULOS AFFAIR, THE, (Cz. Věc Makropulos) opera by Janáček, produced in Brno, 1926; libretto by composer, after Čapek's play about a woman called Makropoulos (*this is the normal English spelling of such Greek names, though the Czech spelling is different*) who possesses an 'elixir of eternal life'. Also known as 'The Makropoulos Case'; but, although the opera is concerned with a law suit, no legal 'case' is referred to in the original title.

MAL (Ger.), time (in the sense of 1.*Mal*, first time).

MALAGUEÑA (Sp.), dance originating in Málaga, marked by singing; also instrumental piece of similar nature.

MALCOLM, GEORGE (JOHN) (b. 1917), English harpsichordist, pianist, conductor, church musician, and composer of 'Variations on a Theme of Mozart' for four harpsichords: till 1959, Master of the Music at Westminster Cathedral. C.B.E., 1965.

MALCUZYŃSKI, WITOLD (b. 1914), Polish-born pianist, pupil of Paderewski; resident successively in France, U.S.A., and Switzerland.

MALEDICTION, name applied to a Liszt piano concerto, composed apparently in the early 1840s but not published till after his death. In fact Liszt gave the name only to the opening theme of the work.

MALINCONIA (It.), melancholy.

MALIPIERO, GIAN FRANCESCO (b. 1882), Italian composer of operas including 'JULIUS CAESAR' and (after Pirandello) 'The Fable of the Changeling Son'; seven symphonies, plus a Symphony in one movement and a 'Symphony of the Zodiac'; chamber music, many songs, etc. Somewhat influenced by the old MODES, and was formerly averse from the harsher modern dissonances; but in mid-1950s (e.g. in his 'Dialogues' for various voices and instruments) approached TWELVE-NOTE technique. Is also noted as musical historian and editor of Monteverdi, Vivaldi, and other old Italian composers. Uncle of Riccardo Malipiero.

MALIPIERO, RICCARDO (b. 1914), Italian composer and critic, formerly pianist and cellist; nephew of preceding. From 1945 adopted TWELVE-NOTE method and repudiated much of his earlier works. Other than these, his music includes 'Concerto breve' for ballerina and orchestra, various other concertos, operas 'Minnie la candida' and 'La Donna è mobile' (quotation from RIGOLETTO). His 'Sinfonia Cantata' (baritone and orchestra using four languages) record his impressions of U.S.A.

MALKO, NICOLAI (properly Nikolay Andreyevich; 1888–1961), Russian-born conductor; held leading posts in Russia as conductor and teacher, but left in 1928, afterwards touring widely and settling in U.S.A., 1940. Principal conductor of the Yorkshire Symphony Orchestra, 1954; of Sydney Symphony Orchestra, 1957.

MANCINELLI, LUIGI (1848–1921), Italian composer of operas (one on *A Midsummer Night's Dream*), etc.; noted opera conductor, much at Covent Garden.

MANDIKIAN, ARDA (b. 1925), Greek singer, born in Turkey, who worked much in Britain from 1948; specializes in unusual music (opera and concert) including the fragments that remain of ancient Greek music.

MANDOLA, MANDORA, obsolete lute-like stringed instrument, related to the Mandolin.

MANDOLIN, plucked stringed instrument of Italian origin, now usually of eight strings tuned in pairs (to the same four notes as a violin) and played with plectrum. Used e.g. by Mozart to accompany a serenade in 'DON GIOVANNI' and in Mahler's 7th symphony. Also spelt *mandoline*.

MANÉN, JOAN (b. 1883), Spanish violinist and composer of operas; etc.; he edited the complete works of Paganini.

MANFRED, works based on Byron's and verse drama – (1) overture and fifteen numbers (including background music for speech) by Schumann, composed for stage performance and first given in 1852; (2) symphony by Tchaikovsky, first performed 1886 – not numbered among his other symphonies.

MANNHEIM SCHOOL, name given by modern historians to a group of mid-18th-century composers centred at the court of Mannheim (Germany) and notable for (1) the cultivation of a type of symphony forerunning the classical (Haydn-Mozart type); (2) refinement of orchestral technique – the clarinet and the controlled orchestral crescendo supposedly making here their first entry into this type of music. The founder of the school is generally considered to be J. W. STAMITZ, a Bohemian; the other members (including F. X. Richter) were all either Bohemian or Austrian, except for Toeschi, an Italian.

MANNINO, FRANCO (b. 1924), Italian composer of a piano concerto opera 'Vivì', and other works; also pianist and conductor.

MANON, opera by Massenet, produced in Paris, 1884. Libretto by H. Meilhac and P. Gille. Named after the heroine; based on Prévost's novel *Manon Lescaut*, as were also Balfe's opera 'The Maid of Artois' (1836), Henze's 'Boulevard Solitude', and 'Manon Lescaut'.

MANON LESCAUT, title of various works based on Prévost's novel (see also preceding entry), including (1) ballet with music by Halévy, 1830; (2) opera by Auber, produced in Paris, 1856 (libretto by E. Scribe); (3) opera by Puccini, produced in Turin, 1893 (libretto by M. Praga, D. Oliva, and L. Illica – though the process of writing it was so involved that the title-page names no librettist).

MANUAL, a keyboard played with the hands – especially on the organ, as opposed to a pedal-keyboard; hence *manualiter*, bogus-Latin term for 'to be played on the manuals'.

MANZONI REQUIEM, name sometimes given to Verdi's Requiem, written to commemorate the poet and novelist Alessandro Manzoni (d. 1873); first performed 1874.

MAOMETTO II, see THE SIEGE OF CORINTH.

MARACA, Latin-American percussion instrument used in rumba bands, etc., and occasionally elsewhere – e.g. in Lambert's ballet 'HOROSCOPE'. It is a gourd filled with dried seeds which rustle when the instrument is shaken – it is made of other materials to produce the same effect. Usually as plural, *maracas*.

MARAIS, MARIN (1656–1728), French bass-viol player; also composer (pupil of Lully) writing operas, music for viols, a Te Deum, etc.

MARBECK, JOHN (also Merbecke, etc.; *c.* 1510–*c.* 1585), English composer of Mass, motets, and (especially) 'The Book of Common Prayer Noted'; i.e. the first musical setting of the Anglican prayer-book. Was also organist at St George's, Windsor; compiler of the first biblical concordance in English, and theological writer; condemned to death for heresy in 1544 but pardoned.

MARCATO (It.), marked; *marcato il basso*, the bass to be played in a prominent manner.

MARCELLO, BENDETTO (1686–1739), Italian composer – also violinist, singer, writer, translator, and civil servant. Works include operas, oratorios, a CONCERTO GROSSO long ascribed to Bach, and famous setting of Italian paraphrases of the Psalms.

MARCH, a piece for marching, slow (usually 4/4) or quick (usually 2/4 or 6/8); transferred from military to other uses. See also MARCHE, MARCIA.

MARCHAL, ANDRÉ (b. 1894), French organist, from 1945 at St Eustache, Paris; noted recitalist, touring Europe, U.S.A., Australia; blind from birth.

MARCHAND, LOUIS (1669–1732), French organist, and composer chiefly for the organ and harpsichord. Toured in Germany; but the story that he left Dresden rather than face a challenge to compete at the organ with Bach is not authenticated.

MARCHE (Fr.), march; *Marche militaire*, French title used by Schubert for each of three marches for piano duet, op. 51, composed before 1824 – no. 1 being the famous one.

MARCIA (It.), march; *alla marcia*, in march-like style – term thus usually applied to 4/4, 2/4, or 6/8 rhythms (see MARCH), but exceptionally applied also to a section in 5/4 time in Wordsworth's symphony no. 4.

MARENZIO, LUCA (1553–99), Italian composer; wrote more than 200 madrigals, very successful and having much influence in England. Wrote also a Mass and other church music, but, exceptionally for an Italian of that period, never held a church appointment. Worked for a time in Warsaw, but mainly in Rome.

MARIA THERESA, nickname for Haydn's symphony no. 48 in C – in honour of the Empress of Austria who visited Eszterháza in 1773. (Usually called 'Maria Theresia', but this is a mis-spelling of her name.)

MARIMBA, Latin-American percussion instrument of African origin; a sort of large, deeper-toned XYLOPHONE played with soft-headed sticks. Milhaud wrote a concerto (1947) for marimba and vibraphone (one player).

MARINE TRUMPET, see TRUMPET MARINE.

MARINUZZI, GINO (1882–1945), Italin conductor and composer of operas, symphonic poems, etc.; editor of old Italian music. See also the following entry.

MARINUZZI, GINO (b. 1920), Italian conductor and composer (born in New York), son of preceding. Has written orchestral works, piano solos, film music, etc. Re-edited his father's opera 'The Adventures of Pinocchio'.

MARITANA, opera by W. V. Wallace, produced in London, 1845; libretto by E. Fitzball. Named after its Spanish gipsy heroine. Despite its fearsomely complex plot, once extremely popular among English-speaking audiences.

MARKEVICH, IGOR (b. 1912), Russian composer and conductor who settled in Paris; pupil of Nadia Boulanger. Works include Sinfonietta, ballets, cantata on Milton's *Paradise Lost*. In 1957 appointed conductor of the Lamoureux Orchestra (Paris), in 1965 of the U.S.S.R. State Symphony Orchestra.

MARRIAGE OF FIGARO, THE (It., *Le Nozze di Figaro*), comic opera by Mozart, produced in Vienna (in the original Italian), 1786. Libretto by L. da Ponte, based on a comedy by Beaumarchais – sequel to that on which the libretto of Rossini's 'THE BARBER OF SEVILLE' is based. Figaro, formerly a barber whose successful intrigues resulted in Count Almaviva's marriage, is now the Count's personal servant. (See also PAER and KLEBE.)

MARSCHNER, HEINRICH AUGUST (1795–1861), German composer –

also conductor, for a time assistant to Weber. Composed German Romantic operas including 'The Vampyr', 'The Templar and the Jewess' (after Scott's *Ivanhoe*), and 'HANS HEILING'; also songs, male choruses, orchestral works, etc.

MARSEILLAISE, LA, French national anthem of which Rouget de Lisle (1760–1836) wrote both tune and words in 1792; so named because it was associated with the body of Marseilles volunteers who sang it on entering Paris.

MARTELÉ, MARTELLATO (Fr., It.), hammered, i.e. strongly accented – as applied e.g. to the piano, and to a certain manner of bowing the violin and other stringed instruments.

MARTENOT, convenient English name for the instrument otherwise called 'Martenot Waves' (Fr., *Ondes Martenot*), after its French inventor, Maurice Martenot (b. 1898). It is an ELECTRONIC instrument sounding only one note at a time, played with a keyboard. Brought out in 1928, it has been considerably used as a solo and orchestral instrument – e.g. by Honegger in 'JOAN OF ARC AT THE STAKE'.

MARTHA, *or Richmond Fair* (Ger., *Martha, oder Der Markt von Richmond*), opera by Flotow, produced in Vienna, 1847. Libretto by F. W. Riese: under the name of Martha, the aristocratic heroine lets herself be bound as a servant (in jest) at the hiring fair at Richmond (presumably Surrey). The opera incorporates 'The Last Rose of Summer' (words and tune by THOMAS MOORE).

MARTIN, EASTHOPE (d. 1925, birth-date unknown), English composer of 'Come to the Fair' and other popular light songs, and of similar instrumental pieces.

MARTIN, FRANK (b. 1890), Swiss composer, who has worked much in Holland; is also pianist. From 1930 came under the influence of TWELVE-NOTE technique, but uses this in combination with 'normal' tonality in a highly individual way. In 'The Drugged Wine' (Fr., *Le Vin herbé*) for voices and instruments, used the legend on which also Wagner's 'TRISTAN AND ISOLDE' is based. His 'Petite Symphonie Concertante' (i.e., Little Sinfonia Concertante) for harpsichord, harp, piano, and two string orchestras was later also arranged for one full orchestra without soloists. Has also composed opera 'THE TEMPEST' (Ger., *Der Sturm*), after Shakespeare; oratorios 'Golgotha' and 'The Mystery of the Nativity'; various orchestral and chamber works; 'Six Monologues from *Everyman*' (voice with piano accompaniment, later orchestrated).

MARTÍN Y SOLER, VICENTE (1754–1806), Spanish composer of Italian operas (including 'Una Cosa rara', quoted by Mozart in 'DON GIOVANNI'), Russian operas, church music, etc. Died in St Petersburg, where he held a court post.

MARTINET, JEAN LOUIS (b. 1912), French composer (pupil of Koechlin and Roger-Ducasse), also conductor. Works include 'Orpheus' and other symphonic poems, variations for string quartet, choral music. Unlike most of his generation, shows some indebtedness to Ravel; but has also used TWELVE-NOTE methods.

MARTINI, GIOVANNI BATTISTA (1705–84), Italian priest, mathematician, and composer of music for church and stage, etc. Author of learned musical treatises; teacher of Mozart and other distinguished composers. Known as 'Padre' Martini.

MARTINI, GIOVANNI PAOLO, name used by Johann Paul Aegidius Schwartzendorf (1741–1816), known as 'Martini the German' (It., *Martini il Tedesco*), German organist and composer who settled in France. Now remembered for his song 'Plaisir d'amour' (Fr., Pleasure of love); wrote also operas, church music, works for military band, etc.

MARTINI IL TEDESCO, see preceding entry.

MARTINI, 'PADRE', see MARTINI, GIOVANNI BATTISTA.

MARTINON, JEAN (b. 1909), French conductor, giving London concerts from 1946, later associated with Israel Philharmonic Orchestra; also composer of opera 'Hecuba', three symphonies, etc.

MARTINŮ, BOHUSLAV (1890–1959), Czech composer, formerly violinist: resident from 1932 chiefly in France, also in U.S.A.; pupil of Suk and Roussel. Works, in an individual idiom sometimes fiercely dissonant, include 'Julietta', 'COMEDY ON THE BRIDGE', 'The Marriage' (English libretto by the composer, after Gogol's play), 'The Greek Passion' (after Kazantzakis's novel, 'Christ Recrucified'), and other operas; five symphonies, 'Double Concerto' for two string orchestras, piano and kettledrums; concertos for piano, for two pianos, for violin, for two violins; symphonic poems 'Tumult' (Fr., *La Bagarre*) and 'Half-time' (referring to a Soccer match); six string quartets and other chamber music (see THEREMIN).

MARTUCCI, GIUSEPPE (1856–1909), Italian pianist, composer (two symphonies, two piano concertos, etc.), arranger of old Italian music, conductor, director of Naples Conservatory.

MARTYRDOM OF ST SEBASTIAN, THE (Fr., *Le Martyre de St Sébastien*), mystery-play by D'Annunzio for which Debussy wrote incidental music, 1911.

MARX, JOSEPH (1882–1964), Austrian composer of many songs (some with orchestral accompaniment) in the German Romantic tradition; also of a piano quartet, 'Romantic Piano Concerto', etc.

MARZIALE (It.), martial.

MASANIELLO, name usually given in Britain to Auber's opera, 'The Dumb Girl of Portici' (Fr., *La Muette de Portici*), produced in Paris, 1829. Libretto by E. Scribe and G. Delavigne. Masaniello, a revolutionary leader, is the hero; Auber avoided using his name for the title because another opera of that title (by Carafa) had appeared two months earlier. The other title referred to the principal female character; she is dumb, and the part is traditionally taken by a dancer.

MASCAGNI, PIETRO (1863–1945), Italian composer, pupil of Ponchielli. His 'CAVALLERIA RUSTICANA' won an operatic competition in 1889 and scored a success which he never afterwards matched in other operas including 'L'Amico Fritz' (Friend Fritz), 'IRIS', and 'The Masks' (*Le Maschere*). He followed the full-blooded Italian operatic manner of the time – see VERISMO. Other works include symphony, Requiem; was also conductor and conservatory director.

MASKARAD, MASKARADE, see MASQUERADE.

MASKED BALL, A (It., *Un ballo in maschera*), opera by Verdi, produced in Rome, 1859. Libretto by A. Somma, on a plot based on the assassination of Gustav III of Sweden, 1792. But to comply with censorship the action was changed, most incongruously, to Boston (Mass.). Some later productions have put the action in Italy or, as in E. J. Dent's English version, have reverted to Sweden.

MASON, DANIEL GREGORY (1873–1953), American composer of three symphonies (no. 3, 'A Lincoln Symphony'), piano music, etc.; pupil of d'Indy. Also writer on music. Grandson of Lowell Mason.

MASON, LOWELL (1792–1872), American composer of hymns, and musical educationist. Grandfather of Daniel Gregory Mason.

MASQUE, type of English stage entertainment (related to opera and ballet) cultivated chiefly in the 17th century and intended for aristocratic audiences: it incorporated vocal and instrumental music, dancing, and spectacle. For examples see 'COMUS', 'VENUS AND ADONIS', 'ALFRED'. Anachronistically and confusingly, Vaughan Williams's 'JOB' is styled 'a masque for dancing'.

MASQUE OF COMUS, see COMUS.

MASQUERADE, (1) opera by C. Nielsen (Dan., *Maskarade*), produced in Copenhagen, 1906; libretto by V. Andersen, after Holberg, involving an 18th-century masked ball; (2) play by Lermontov (Rus., *Maskarad*) for which Khachaturian wrote incidental music, 1939. from which a suite is drawn; it deals with the licentious life of the Russian aristocracy in the early 19th century.

MASS, the principal service of the Roman Catholic Church; High Mass is sung, Low Mass said. The musical setting of the 'Proper' of the Mass, varying with the occasion, has normally been left to the traditional plainsong – except for the REQUIEM MASS, to which new settings have been frequently composed. The unvarying part, called the 'Ordinary' or 'Common' of the Mass and consisting of five sections (Kyrie, Gloria, Credo, Sanctus with Benedictus, and Agnus Dei), has been frequently set: such settings are usually called simply (e.g.) Mass in B minor (Bach), Mass in C (Beethoven's early setting) – or they may have titles (e.g. Haydn's 'NELSON' MASS) for ease of identification. See also MISSA, and the following entry.

MASS OF LIFE, A, work by Delius for four solo singers, chorus, and orchestra; first performed complete, 1909. Text from Nietzsche's

Thus Spake Zarathustra: not a Mass, but a kind of pagan counterpart to one.

MASSENET, JULES ÉMILE FRÉDÉRIC (1842–1912), French composer, pupil of A. Thomas. Wrote twenty-seven operas, in a mellifluous and sometimes rather 'light-weight' style, including 'MANON', 'The Cid', 'WERTHER', 'CINDERELLA', and 'OUR LADY'S JUGGLER.' Other works include ballets, incidental music to plays, orchestral suites, piano concerto, about 200 songs.

MASTER OF CLAMECY, THE (Rus., *Master iz Clamecy*), opera by Kabalevsky, produced in Leningrad, 1938. Libretto by V. Bragin, after R. Rolland's French novel *Colas Breugnon*, about a 16th-century Burgundian craftsman. His name is also used as an alternative title of the opera, especially for its overture, outside Russia.

MASTER OF MUSIC, degree awarded at some universities, ranking between Bachelor and Doctor of Music.

MASTER OF THE KING'S (OR QUEEN'S) MUSIC, title of a British court post, dating from Charles I's time, and now carrying a small salary and no fixed duties. It formerly implied also the directorship of the king's private band.

MASTER PETER'S PUPPET SHOW (Sp., *El Retablo de Maese Pedro*), opera by Falla, first staged in Paris 1923 (after an earlier performance in Seville in concert version). Libretto by composer, after an episode from 'Don Quixote'. Uses three human characters plus marionettes.

MASTERSINGER (Ger., *Meistersinger*, sing. and pl.), title given to members of a German guild of musicians, flourishing in the 14th-16th centuries; they were by origin merchants, etc., not aristocrats like the earlier MINNESINGERS. 'The Mastersingers' (or 'Die Meistersinger') is commonly used as a short title for 'The Mastersingers of Nuremberg'.

MASTERSINGERS OF NUREMBERG, THE (Ger., *Die Meistersinger von Nürnberg*), comic opera by Wagner, produced in Munich, 1868. Libretto by composer, dealing with a medieval guild (see preceding entry) and serving incidentally as a platform for some of Wagner's own views on art. See HANSLICK.

MATHIAS, WILLIAM (b. 1934), Welsh composer of 2 piano concertos, wind quintet, organ music, etc.

MATHIESON, MUIR (b. 1911), Scottish conductor; active in films since 1931 and instrumental in introducing a number of important composers to film work; himself a composer of film music too. Has also conducted concerts, ballet, etc.

MATHIS THE PAINTER (Ger., *Mathis der Maler*), (1) opera by Hindemith, produced in Zürich, 1938 (scheduled for Berlin, 1934, but banned by Nazis); libretto by composer, alluding to the painter Grünewald (early 16th century) and his altar-piece at Isenheim – and incidentally expounding Hindemith's own views on the artist's proper relation to society; (2) title of a symphony by Hindemith, drawn from the opera (the first movement is the overture); first performed 1934, in advance of the opera.

MATIN, LE, see MORNING.

MATRIMONIO SEGRETO, IL, see THE SECRET MARRIAGE.

MATSUDAIRA, YORITSUNE (b. 1907), Japanese composer, pupil of A. Tcherepnin. Works, with some experiments in applying TWELVE NOTE technique to traditional Japanese music, include Theme and Variations for piano and orchestra.

MATTHAY, TOBIAS (1858–1945), English pianist, and famous piano teacher, evolving a method of his own; also composer. His pupils include Myra Hess.

MATTHESON, JOHANN (1681–1784), German organist, harpsichordist, singer, and composer of operas, church cantatas, keyboard music, etc.; also noted writer on music.

MATTHEWS, DENIS (b. 1919), English pianist, noted in Beethoven; also composer (pupil of Alwyn) and occasional writer on music.

MATTINATA (It.), morning song.

MAW, NICHOLAS (b. 1935), English composer of opera 'One Man Show'; 'Scenes and arias' (concert work for three female singers and orchestra on old French texts); 'Nocturne' for mezzo-soprano and chamber orchestra; 'Essay' for organ; string quartet, etc.

MAYUZUMI, TOSHIRO (b. 1929), Japanese composer, trained in Tokyo and Paris, has written CONCRETE and ELECTRONIC music, and also music for ordinary instruments, including 'Bacchanal' for orchestra, Divertimento for ten instruments, 'Tonepleromas 55' for wind and percussion instruments and musical saw.

MAZEPPA, (1) works by Liszt for piano (final version 1847) and for orchestra (founded on the former, 1851) – alluding to the story (cp. Byron and Victor Hugo) that Mazeppa survived his punishment of being lashed naked to a wild horse, and became a Cossack chief; (2) opera by Tchaikovsky, produced in Moscow, 1884, with libretto by composer and V. P. Burenin, after Pushkin – alluding to Mazeppa's later treason to Peter the Great. Mazeppa (1644–1709) is a historical character.

MAZURKA, Polish country dance in 3/4 or 3/8 time; brought by Chopin (he wrote at least 55) into concert music.

MC. Names beginning thus are listed as if spelt MAC....

ME, in TONIC SOL-FA, the spoken name for the third degree (mediant) of the scale, written m. Cp. MI.

MEAN-TONE TEMPERAMENT, see TEMPERAMENT.

MEASURE, see BAR. (Also a term, used poetically, for a dance, etc.)

MEDIANT, name for the third degree of the scale, e.g. E in C major – so called because it stands midway between the tonic (or keynote) and dominant, i.e. between the first and fifth degrees. Cp. SUBMEDIANT.

MEDIUM, THE, opera by Menotti, produced in New York, 1946.

Libretto by composer, about a fake spiritualistic medium. Also filmed, with the score slightly altered, 1951.

MEDTNER, NICOLAS (properly Nikolay Karlovich; 1880–1951), Russian composer and pianist of German descent. Left Russia in 1921, and in 1936 settled in England, where he died. Works, conforming generally to traditional structures and a Romantic idiom, include four piano concertos, many songs in Russian and German, many piano solos (several called 'Fairy Tales').

MEFISTOFELE, see MEPHISTOPHELES.

MÉHUL, ÉTIENNE (HENRI NICOLAS) (1763–1817), French composer, encouraged by Gluck to write for the stage. Operas include 'JOSEPH' and 'The Two Blind Men of Toledo'; wrote also ballets, symphonies, patriotic (French Revolutionary) music, etc.

MEIJER, see SIGTENHORST MEIJER.

MEISTERSINGER VON NÜRNBERG, DIE, see THE MASTERSINGERS OF NUREMBERG.

MELCHIOR, LAURITZ (b. 1890), Danish (naturalized American) tenor who began as baritone; noted in Wagner's operas, and has also appeared in films.

MELISMA (Gk. song; pl. *melismata*), a group of notes sung to a single syllable. (Term also sometimes applied more loosely, to any florid vocal passage in the nature of a cadenza.) *Melismata* is also the title of a collection of English vocal pieces published by T. Ravenscroft in 1611.

MELLERS, WILFRED (HOWARD) (b. 1914), English writer on music, professor of music at York, and composer of orchestral works, Latin motets for chorus and brass, songs, cantata 'Yggdrasil', etc.

MELLOPHONE,type of brass instrument shaped similarly to an orchestral HORN and used as a kind of 'poor relation' to it (e.g. occasionally in dance bands), being easier to play. Named presumably from 'mellow'; it is also called the 'tenor cor'.

MELODIC MINOR, see MINOR.

MÉLODIE (Fr.), (1) melody; (2) a song.

MELODRAMA, term of which the current English sense (a sensational and sentimental play) is a debased meaning. As used in this book, and generally in musical contexts, it refers to the dramatic use of spoken words against a musical background – whether throughout a musical work (as in certain 18th-century examples) or forming part of a work, as in the gravedigging scene in Beethoven's 'FIDELIO'. But note that the Italian form *melodramma* means simply opera.

MELODRAMMA, see preceding entry.

MELODY, a succession of notes varying in pitch and having a recognizable musical shape. Thus the three 'dimensions' of music are often thought of as (1) melody, (2) rhythm, (3) harmony and counterpoint. The term is also used as title for certain rather simple pieces – e.g. *Melody in F*, the almost sole survivor of Anton Rubinstein's piano solos, being no. 1 of 'Two Melodies', op. 3 (1853).

MEN OF BLACKMOOR, opera by Alan Bush, produced at Weimar, 1956. Libretto by Nancy Bush (the composer's wife) on a story of a 19th-century mining community.

MENASCE, JACQUES DE (1905–60), Austrian-born pianist and composer; settled in U.S.A., 1941. Pupil of Berg but not himself a TWELVE-NOTE practitioner. Works, with some IMPRESSIONIST traits, include two piano concertos, songs, and (mainly) piano pieces.

MENDELSSOHN, name by which the composer J. L. F. Mendelssohn Bartholdy and his family (see following two entries) are customarily known. Mendelssohn was their original surname, Bartholdy being added by the composer's father.

MENDELSSOHN BARTHOLDY, FANNY CÄCILIE (also, in the French form, Cécile; 1805–47), German (amateur) pianist and composer, valued consultant of her brother (see next entry). Six of her songs were published as his, and she also wrote part-songs, piano solos, a piano trio. Married W. Hensel, painter, 1829.

MENDELSSOHN BARTHOLDY, (JAKOB LUDWIG) FELIX (1809–47), German composer; a grandson of the Jewish philosopher Moses Mendelssohn, but was brought up as a Lutheran. Brother of preceding. Noted pianist and organist; also conductor, head of Leipzig Conservatory (1843), and amateur painter. Born in Hamburg; boy prodigy, composing the overture to 'A MIDSUMMER NIGHT'S DREAM' at 17 (the other music to it later). Visited Scotland, 1829 (see 'SCOTCH' SYMPHONY, 'HEBRIDES') and afterwards revisited Britain nine times, conducting the first performance of 'ELIJAH' in 1846. Other works include operetta 'SON AND STRANGER', oratorio 'ST PAUL'; five symphonies (no. 2 'HYMN OF PRAISE', no. 3 'SCOTCH', no. 4 'ITALIAN', no. 5 'REFORMATION'); 'RUY BLAS' and other overtures; two piano concertos; violin concerto in E minor (a youthful concerto in D minor, left in MS., was resuscitated by Menuhin); string octet (later scored for full orchestra) and other chamber music; 'SONGS WITHOUT WORDS' and other piano solos; organ works, songs. Combined Romantic ardour with a classical decorousness of form; but did not fulfil all his early promise, and has suffered a severe general decline in popularity during this century.

MENGELBERG, (KURT) RUDOLF (1892–1959), Dutch composer (born in Germany) and writer on music. Works include Mass (Missa Pro Pace), Symphonic Variations for cello and orchestra, songs. Also writer on music. Cousin of Willem Mengelberg.

MENGELBERG, (JOSEF) WILLEM (1871–1951), Dutch conductor, from 1895 to 1941 with the Concertgebouw Orchestra of Amsterdam. Appeared in Britain, U.S.A., and elsewhere. Expressed sympathy with the Nazis, and did not regain influence after the Second World War.

MENNIN, PETER (originally Mennini; b. 1923), American composer, pupil of B. Rogers and Hanson. Has written six symphonies, 'Concertato' [*sic*] for orchestra (inspired by Melville's *Moby Dick*), string quartet, piano pieces, etc. Head of Juilliard School of Music, New York, 1962.

MENO (It.), less; *meno mosso*, less moved, i.e., slower. Sometimes composers unhelpfully omit *mosso* and write, e.g., *poco meno* (really 'a little less') for 'a little slower'.

MENOTTI, GIAN-CARLO (b. 1911), Italian-born composer living in U.S.A. since 1928, studying and afterwards teaching in Philadelphia. Has won international success as composer of operas (with his own librettos) in a 'realistic' vein sometimes reminiscent of Puccini's (see VERISMO). These include 'AMELIA GOES TO THE BALL', with libretto originally in Italian, and successors, nearly all in English – 'The Old Maid and the Thief', 'THE MEDIUM', 'THE TELEPHONE', 'THE CONSUL,' 'AMAHL AND THE NIGHT VISITORS' (for television), 'THE SAINT OF BLEECKER STREET', 'THE LAST SAVAGE', 'The Labyrinth' (for television), and 'Martin's Lie' (for church performance, mainly with child performers); also of 'THE UNICORN, THE GORGON, AND THE MANTICORE', sung off-stage, mimed on-stage; has also written piano concerto, etc. Acts as stage director for his operas, and directed the film of 'THE MEDIUM'. See also VANESSA. Founder of music festival at Spoleto, Italy, 1958.

MENUET, MENUETT (Fr., Ger.), MINUET.

MENUETTO, term often written in scores by German-speaking composers under the impression that it is the Italian (correctly *minuetto*) for 'minuet'.

MENUHIN, HEPHZIBAH (b. 1920), American-born pianist mainly celebrated in partnering her brother (see next entry) in recitals; resident from 1938 in Australia, later in Britain.

MENUHIN, YEHUDI (b. 1916), American violinist of international fame since boyhood; pupil afterwards of Enesco and Adolf Busch. Commissioned Bartók's unaccompanied violin sonata and in 1952 resuscitated an early MS. concerto by Mendelssohn. Brother of Hephzibah Menuhin. Also known in recent years as conductor; chief musical figure of the Bath Festival and musical director of its chamber orchestra since 1959. Hon. K.B.E., 1965. See also KENTNER.

MEPHISTO (abbr. for Mephistopheles), name used by Liszt in four 'Mephisto Waltzes' of which no. 1 (see FAUST) is the well-known one. Nos. 1 and 2, written for orchestra, were transcribed both for piano solo and for piano duet; no. 3 is for piano; no. 4 (unfinished, not published till 1952) is also for piano.

MEPHISTOPHELES (It., *Mefistofele*), opera by Boito, produced 1868; libretto by composer, after Goethe's *Faust*.

MER, LA, see SEA.

MERBECKE, see MARBECK.

MERCADANTE, (GIUSEPPE) SAVERIO (RAFFAELE) (1795–1870), Italian composer of about sixty operas; was also church musician and

(1840) director of the Naples Conservatory. Became totally blind in 1862 but continued to compose.

MERRIE ENGLAND, the most popular operetta by German, produced in London, 1902. Libretto by B. Hood – introducing Queen Elizabeth I, Essex, etc.

MERRY WIDOW, THE (Ger., *Die lustige Witwe*), first and most popular operetta by Lehár, produced in Vienna, 1905. Libretto by V. Leon and L. Stein, concerning romantic and diplomatic intrigue.

MERRY WIVES OF WINDSOR, THE (Ger., *Die lustigen Weiber von Windsor*), the most successful opera by Nicolai, produced in Berlin, 1849. Libretto by S. H. Mosenthal, after Shakespeare. (Another German opera so titled, by Dittersdorf, had appeared in 1797; Verdi's 'FALSTAFF', and Vaughan Williams's 'Sir John in Love' are founded on the same play.)

MERULO, CLAUDIO (real surname Merlotti; 1533–1604), Italian composer of music for stage and church: noted organist (at St Mark's, Venice) and organ composer.

MESSA DI VOCE (It., placing of the voice), the steady swelling and decreasing of vocal volume in one long held note.

MESSAGER, ANDRÉ (CHARLES PROSPER) (1853–1929). French composer of 'Monsieur Beaucaire' (in English) and other operas, 'Véronique' and other operettas, and of ballets (including 'The Two Pigeons'), piano duets, etc. Also distinguished opera conductor, e.g. of the first performance of Debussy's 'PELLÉAS AND MÉLISANDE' which is dedicated to him. Pupil of Saint-Saëns.

MESSE (Fr., Ger.), MASS.

MESSIAEN, OLIVIER (EUGÈNE PROSPER CHARLES) (b. 1908), French composer, and also organist and writer on music. Member of the former 'YOUNG FRANCE' group. Influenced by Indian music, and cultivates great rhythmical complexity – see 'TURANGALÎLA'. Uses almost literal orchestral imitation of bird-song in various works including 'The Awakening of the Birds' for piano and orchestra. Has also written various works with Roman Catholic associations, including church music, 'Visions of the Amen' for two pianos, 'Twenty-four Looks at the Child Jesus' for one piano: also songs, organ works, etc.

MESSIAH (not *The Messiah*), oratorio by Handel, first performed in Dublin, 1742. Words selected from the Bible by C. Jennens. Composed in under four weeks in 1741.

MESTO (It.), sad.

METÀ (It.), half.

METAMORPHOSES (Ger., *Metamorphosen*), work for twenty-three solo strings by R. Strauss, inscribed 'In Memoriam', quoting the funeral march from Beethoven's 'EROICA' symphony, and being apparently a dirge for lost Germany. First performed 1946.

METAMORPHOSIS, term used to describe the way a composer may change a theme – altering tempo and rhythm, even notes, but preserving something essential and recognizable. This device has its obvious use in ILLUSTRATIVE MUSIC, and is also used elsewhere, e.g. in some symphonies (Franck's, Elgar's no. 1). Hindemith wrote an orchestral piece called 'Symphonic Metamorphoses of [in English references usually mistranslated *on*] Themes of Weber' (1943); cp. MOTTO.

METER, U.S. spelling of Metre.

METRE, term used in prosody to cover the relationship between accented and unaccented beats, and sometimes similarly used in music – e.g. 3/8 and 6/8 being described as different kinds of *metres*. Usually the term RHYTHM is so defined as to cover this relationship along with others; but some writers define *rhythm* and *metre* as mutually exclusive, *metre* concerned with the basic unvarying pulse (as above) and *rhythm* with the actual time-patterns of notes effected by the composer with reference to this basic pulse. (For *variable metre*, see BLACHER.) The usage 'common metre', etc., with reference to hymns, alludes to the verse, not to the music. See also next entry.

METRICAL, of METRE; so (referring to the verse, not the music) *metrical psalm*, a psalm translated and versified in a regular syllabic metre, and thus singable to an ordinary hymn-tune.

METRONOME, apparatus for sounding an adjustable number of beats per minute. The one commonly in use is that patented in 1814 by J. N. Maelzel (1770–1838) who stole the invention from D. N. Winkel. There is also a pocket type consisting simply of an adjustable pendulum. A composer wishing that there should be, e.g., sixty crotchet beats a minute, writes 'M.M. [Maelzel's Metronome] ♩ = 60'. Metronome marks for early works are added by modern editors.

METROPOLITAN OPERA HOUSE (New York), the principal opera house of the United States, opened 1883; re-housed, 1966. Not state-subsidized, un-like the world's other major opera theatres.

MEULEMANS, ARTHUR (b. 1884), Belgian composer, also conductor and writer on music. Has written a great number of works including fourteen symphonies, three operas, an overture to Goethe's play 'Egmont', and much other incidental music for the theatre.

MEWTON-WOOD, NOEL (1923–53), Australian pianist (pupil of Schnabel) who settled in England and became a noted interpreter of modern composers; himself composer of a piano concerto, ballet music, etc. Committed suicide.

MEYER, see SIGTENHORST MEIJER

MEYERBEER, GIACOMO (born Jakob Liebmann Beer, the changed surname recognizing a legacy from a relative named Meyer; 1791–1864), German composer of operas in Italian, German, and especially French – including 'ROBERT THE DEVIL', 'THE HUGUENOTS', 'The Prophet', 'The African Woman' (*L'Africaine*). These are noted for spectacle and for a striking use of the orchestra.

Visited Italy; settled in Paris 1826 and died there, but was also active in Berlin from 1842 as musical director to the King of Prussia. Wrote also church music, marches, songs, etc.

MEYEROWITZ, JAN (b. 1913), German-born composer resident in U.S.A. since 1946; pupil of Casella and Respighi in Rome. Works include 'The Barrier', 'Esther', and other operas; also cantata (in English) 'The Glory Around His Head', a symphony subtitled 'Midrash Esther' (referring to Jewish biblical commentary), chamber music, etc.

MEZZO, MEZZA (It.), half. So *mezza voce*, at half voice, i.e. with moderate tone; *mezzo-forte* (abbr. *mf*), midway between loud and soft; *mezzo-soprano*, type of female voice half-way between soprano and contralto range. The form *mezzo-contralto* is sometimes encountered, denoting (finically) a little lower than mezzo-soprano.

MI, the note E (in Latin countries, and formerly elsewhere); cp. ME. For *mi contra fa*, see TRITONE.

MIASKOVSKY, NIKOLAY YAKOVLEVICH (1881–1950), Russian composer, pupil of Glière, Rimsky-Korsakov, and others. The most prolific modern composer of symphonies – he wrote twenty-seven (no. 19 is for wind-band, no. 27 was performed posthumously). Wrote also symphonic poem 'Nevermore' (after Poe), violin concerto, piano solos, songs, etc. Denounced by Soviet officialdom in 1948 for 'FORMALISM', etc., along with Prokofiev, Shostakovich, and others.

MICHELANGELI, ARTURO BENEDETTI (b. 1920), Italian pianist, touring widely; first heard in Britain 1946.

MICROTONE, an interval smaller than a semitone. (An alternative name is 'fractional tone'). Quarter-tones have been systematically exploited by A. Hába and other Czechs, and have also had occasional use in more 'orthodox' contexts, e.g. the string parts of Bloch's chamber music; see also CARRILLO, whose experiments in this field have extended to much smaller intervals.

MIDDAY, name given to one of a set of three symphonies by Haydn: see MORNING.

MIDDLE C, the note C found at approximately the middle of the piano keyboard. It is tuned to a frequency of 261.6.

MIDI, LE title of one of a set of three symphonies by Haydn: see MORNING.

MIDSUMMER MARRIAGE, THE, opera by Tippett, produced in London, 1955. Libretto by composer, applying ancient myth to modern characters (and having parallels to Mozart's 'THE MAGIC FLUTE'). A set of 'Ritual Dances' for chorus and orchestra is drawn from this.

MIDSUMMER NIGHT'S DREAM, A, play by Shakespeare to which Mendelssohn composed an overture in 1826 (when he was 17), and other incidental music including the celebrated Wedding March in

1842. Incidental music to the play has also been written by Orff. See also the following, and MIGNON.

MIDSUMMER NIGHT'S DREAM, A, opera by Britten, produced at Aldeburgh, 1960. The libretto is Shakespeare's play, abbreviated.

MIGHTY FIVE, THE, an alternative English term for THE MIGHTY HANDFUL.

MIGHTY HANDFUL, THE, English translation of Rus. *moguchaya kuchka*, term invented by Stassov, later applied to Balakirev, Borodin, Cui, Mussorgsky, and Rimsky-Korsakov. These five Russian composers took up a consciously 'nationalist' standpoint in music, drawing much on Russian history, literature, folk-music, and folklore generally. They are thus contrasted with composers thought to look more toward Western Europe, e.g. Tchaikovsky and Anton Rubinstein. (The contrast cannot be pressed too far, however: note Tchaikovsky's musical devotion to Pushkin, for instance.)

MIGNON, opera by A. Thomas, produced in Paris, 1866. Libretto by J. Barbier and M. Carré, after Goethe's *Wilhelm Meister*. The soprano air 'I am Titania' occurs with reference to a performance (within the action of the opera) of *A Midsummer Night's Dream.*

MIGNONE, FRANCISCO (b. 1897), Brazilian composer who studied in Italy. Works include opera 'The Diamond Broker' (incorporating a dance called 'Cogada' which is also given as a concert work); symphonic poem 'Four Churches'; piano solos. Some of his works are illustrative of ideas borrowed from Brazilian folk-lore.

MIGOT, GEORGES ELBERT (b. 1891), French composer, pupil of d'Indy and Widor. Has written operas, choral works to religious texts, 'Three Epigrams' and other orchestral works, solos for piano and for harpsichord – in an individual and predominantly contrapuntal idiom. Is also writer on music. His detachment from prevailing French musical fashions has earned him the name of 'The Group of One'.

MIHALOVICI, MARCEL (b. 1898), Rumanian-born composer who studied with d'Indy in Paris and settled there. Works include opera 'Phaedra' (after Seneca), ballets, orchestral works, 'Concerto quasi una fantasia' for violin and orchestra, chamber music. Wife is the pianist MONIQUE HAAS.

MIKADO, THE, *or the Town of Titipu*, operetta by Sullivan, produced in London, 1885; libretto by W. S. Gilbert. Set in an imaginary Japan, it was its creators' most successful work and has been played considerably overseas (sometimes in far-fetched adaptations); a filmed version appeared in 1936.

MIKROKOSMOS (Gk, microcosm), piano work by Bartók, composed between 1926 and 1937; it consists of 153 small pieces in the nature of technical studies, progressively arranged.

MILÁN, LUIS (*c.* 1500–*c.* 1565), Spanish player of the vihuela (Spanish form of lute), and composer of music for it; also composer of songs with lute accompaniment in Spanish, Portuguese, and Italian – including one of the first published books of songs for a single voice with accompaniment, 1536.

MILANOV, ZINKA (b. 1906), Yugoslav soprano who appeared at Salzburg Festival in 1937 and has since won international operatic fame. (Milanov is her married name; she was formerly known under her maiden name of Zinka Kunc.)

MILFORD, ROBIN HUMPHREY (1903–60), English composer, pupil of Vaughan Williams and others. Works include violin concerto, choral music to religious and other texts, chamber music, songs.

MILHAUD, DARIUS (b. 1892), French composer, born at Aix-en-Provence (see 'CARNIVAL OF AIX' and 'KING RENÉ'S CHIMNEY'); became a member of the group of composers called the 'SIX'; collaborated with nine other composers in ballet 'JEANNE'S FAN'. Associated with various important literary figures, especially Claudel (opera 'CHRISTOPHER COLUMBUS', play 'PROTEUS', and other works), and Cocteau (ballets, etc.). Visited Brazil and U.S.A., and influenced by jazz as early as 1922–3 (ballet 'THE CREATION OF THE WORLD') and also by Latin-American music (see SAUDADES; 'SCARAMOUCHE'). Notable exponent of POLYTONALITY. Very prolific composer. His other works include operas 'BOLIVAR' and 'David'; an arrangement of 'THE BEGGAR'S OPERA' in French, from which his 'CARNIVAL OF LONDON' is drawn; seven symphonies, no. 6 for wordless chorus with oboe and cello; various concertos, one for a marimba-and-vibraphone player; fifteen string quartets, of which nos. 14–15 can be played separately or together; Jewish liturgical music; many songs. In U.S.A. during Second World War, and considerably afterwards.

MILITARY BAND, a band of brass and woodwind (not brass alone – see BRASS BAND) with percussion, maintained by armies, etc., principally for performing on the march. The instruments and numbers vary considerably between countries and to a lesser extent even within them. A British band typically uses flute, piccolo, oboe, clarinets, bassoons, saxophones, horns (orchestral), cornets (sometimes trumpets), trombones, euphoniums, bombardons (see TUBA), plus percussion. Double-bass (stringed) is sometimes added when not on the march.

MILITARY SYMPHONY, nickname for Haydn's symphony no. 100 in G (first performed 1794, on Haydn's visit to London), having 'military band' effects from bass drum, cymbals, and triangle.

MILLÖCKER, KARL (1842–99), Austrian composer of 'The Beggar Student' and many other operettas; also of piano pieces, etc. Active also as theatre conductor.

MILNER, ANTHONY (FRANCIS DOMINIC) (b. 1925), English composer; pupil of R. O. Morris, Seiber, and others. Has written chiefly vocal music including unaccompanied Mass, cantata 'The City of Desolation' and other works with Roman Catholic associations; also an oboe quartet. Is also teacher, and writer on music.

MILSTEIN, NATHAN (b. 1904), Russian-born American violinist, pupil of Auer and Ysaÿe; arranger of violin pieces.

MILTON, JOHN (1563–1647), English composer, father of the poet Milton. Contributed a madrigal to 'THE TRIUMPHS OF ORIANA' and wrote other vocal music, fantasies for viols, etc.

MIME, acting without speech; a stage piece consisting of such (sometimes given with music.)

MINACCIANDO (It.), threatening.

MINES OF SULPHUR, THE, opera by Richard Rodney Bennett, produced in London, 1965; libretto, by Beverley Cross, is a ghost-story. The title is metaphorical and a quotation from Shakespeare's 'Othello'.

MINIATURE SCORE, see SCORE.

MINIM, the note 𝅗𝅥 (U.S., half-note) considered as a time-value; equivalent to two crotchets or to half a semibreve. Its rest is notated 𝄼

MINIPIANO, trade name for a type of small upright piano with a less extensive keyboard than normal.

MINKUS, LÉON (really Aloisius Ludwig Minkus; 1827–90), Austrian-born composer who settled in Russia and died there; composed mainly ballets, including a 'Don Quixote'.

MINNESINGER (Ger., sing. and pl.; also as English word), type of minstrel flourishing in guilds in 12th- and 13th-century Germany. By social origin these singers were aristocratic; the MASTERSINGERS who flourished afterwards were of the merchant class.

MINOR, term opposed to 'major' and applied to scales, keys, chords, and intervals; for all these usages see MAJOR.

MINSTREL, (1) general term applied in modern usage to a type of medieval musical performer, usually singing to his own accompaniment, and usually belonging to a guild or other recognized company; in medieval times such performers were classed more particularly (see, e.g. JONGLEUR, MASTERSINGER, MINNESINGER, TROUBADOUR, TROUVÈRE); (2) term applied to a black-faced (imitation-Negro) entertainer such as were organized into troupes in U.S.A. in the 1830s and later elsewhere. Debussy's 'Minstrels', in his second book of piano preludes, refers to these.

MINUET, MINUETTO (Eng., It.), dance in triple time of French rustic origin, 'promoted' to court use and becoming widely fashionable in the 18th century. It forms the standard third movement of the 'classical' (Haydn-Mozart) sonata, symphony, string quartet, etc., later developing with Beethoven into the SCHERZO. It is normally in AABA form, the 'B' being in contrast and called 'trio' because of the French custom (long since dropped) of writing it in only three PARTS.

MINUTE WALTZ, nickname for Chopin's waltz in D♭, opus 64, no. 1 (published 1847); it was evidently given by someone too insensitive to realize that it can be played in one minute only if taken too fast.

MIRACLE, THE, nickname for Haydn's symphony no. 96 in D – because, when Haydn directed its first performance in London in 1791, a chandelier was supposed to have fallen on a vacant space in a crowded hall, hitting no one. This account is now known to be false.

MIRACLE IN THE GORBALS, ballet with music by Bliss, first performed 1944. The 'miracle' occurs when a suicide is brought to life by a saintly 'stranger' (in the Gorbals slums of Glasgow).

MIRACULOUS MANDARIN, THE (Hung., *A csodálatos mandarin*), one-act mime-play with music by Bartók (scenario by M. Lengyel), composed 1919; produced at Cologne, 1926; source of a concert suite first performed 1928. The mandarin, though stabbed and hanged by robbers, refuses to die until the robbers' girl yields herself to him – a plot which has largely kept the work off the stage.

MIREILLE, opera by Gounod, produced in Paris, 1864. Libretto by M. Carré, after a Provençal poem. (The name is that of the heroine.) It has a tragic ending, but Gounod also provided a happy ending as an alternative.

MIRLITON (Fr.), equals KAZOO.

MIRROR CANON, MIRROR FUGUE, a canon or fugue in which two or more PARTS appear on paper simultaneously both the right way up and upside down – i.e. as if a mirror lay between them, making one the reflection of the other. (The use of the term for a piece that can be played backwards – i.e. as if a mirror could be put at the end – is sometimes encountered but is not correct.)

MISERERE, the name in the Roman Catholic Church for Psalm 50 (51 in the Hebrew and English Bibles), often set by composers; see ALLEGRI. A setting is incorporated into Act 4 of Verdi's 'Il Trovatore'.

MISSA (Lat.), Mass. So – *missa brevis*, either (1) a setting of the Mass in unusually concise musical form, or (2) a setting of the Kyrie and Gloria only, in obsolete Lutheran usage; *missa parodia*, see PARODY MASS; *missa sine nomine* ('... without a name'), Mass of entirely original material, not based on a plainsong or secular tune (term used in the 15th and 16th centuries, when the latter was the common practice, the Mass then taking the name of its source). So also *Missa solemnis*, term sometimes used by composers for a lengthy and exalted setting of the Mass – and now particularly associated with Beethoven's Mass in D (first performed, as yet incomplete, 1824), so entitled. See also next entry.

MISSA PAPAE MARCELLI, a Mass by Palestrina dedicated to Marcellus II, who became Pope in 1555.

MISURA (It.), a measure (in various senses); *senza misura*, not in strict time (e.g. of a passage in which bar-lines are omitted).

MIT (Ger.), with.

MITROPOULOS, DIMITRI (1896–1960), Greek-born American conductor – of the New York Philharmonic-Symphony Orchestra, 1949–58. Was also pianist, sometimes playing a solo and directing an orchestra at the same time; and as a composer (pupil of Busoni) wrote opera, piano music, arrangements for orchestra of organ works by Bach, etc.

MIXED CHORUS, MIXED VOICES, etc., a body comprising both male and female (adult) voices.

MIXOLYDIAN MODE, the MODE represented by the white notes on the piano from G to G.

MIXTURE, type of organ-stop simultaneously sounding two or more of the higher tones (other than octaves) of the HARMONIC SERIES. A stop sounding two such tones is said to be a mixture of two *ranks* (and so forth); and the number of ranks is indicated in organ specifications by roman figures. The *mixture* is used in conjunction with 'normal' stops to add richness to the tone.

MODAL, of the old 'modes'. See next entry.

MODE, name for each of the ways of ordering the notes of a scale. Thus in references to major and minor keys (see MAJOR), the terms *major mode* and *minor mode* may be met. But the chief use of the word is in reference to the scales prevalent in the Middle Ages. The *modes* in this sense were driven from general Western European art-music about 1600, but (*a*) survive in plainsong and much folk-song, and (*b*) have been occasionally cultivated by later composers, sometimes as a deliberate archaism. The modes can be best understood by considering scales starting from different notes on the white keys of the piano. Each corresponds to a *mode*. That from B to B (Locrian mode) was not used. The others were:

D – D, called Dorian, numbered I
E – E, called Phrygian, numbered III
F – F, called Lydian, numbered V
G – G, called Mixolydian, numbered VII

plus two more introduced in the 16th century:

A – A, called Aeolian, numbered IX
C – C, called Ionian, numbered XI

– these two foreshadowing the minor and major keys respectively. A melody in the Dorian mode will end on D, in the Phrygian on E, etc. This note is called the *final*.

The modes detailed above are called the *authentic modes*: this implies that the compass of the melody shall be within the octave marked (D to D for the Dorian, etc.). The *plagal modes* are formed from the same notes but have a compass that puts the final in the middle: e.g. in the plagal mode corresponding to the Dorian, the melody will still end on D but will have a compass from A to A. Accordingly it is called *Hypodorian* and given the number II; the other plagal modes also take the prefix *hypo-* (from the Greek for 'under') and take the even number following that of the corresponding authentic mode. Thus Hypolydian, Mode VI (F as final, but range C to C), etc.

Note that (1) the modal system thus links the *kind* of scale with the *pitch* of a scale – unlike the key-system, where major and minor scales are merely relative, to be applied at any pitch; but, of course, a modern composer using a mode can transpose it to any pitch (by the use of what are, on the piano, black notes); and older composers did this to a limited extent; (2) the names of the modes are taken from ancient Greek names, but do not correspond to Greek usage; (3) the old modes as described above are sometimes called 'church modes' or 'ecclesiastical modes' but quite unsuitably, as their use was general and not merely ecclesiastical.

MODERATO (It.), at a moderate pace. It is also used after another tempo-direction, e.g. *allegro moderato*, implying 'a moderate allegro' i.e. that the word 'allegro' is not to be taken in an extreme sense.

MODINHA, type of Portuguese (and hence Brazilian) popular song mainly flourishing in the 18th and 19th centuries.

MODO (It.), manner: *in modo di*, in the manner of.

MODULATE, to change from one key to another in the course of a composition – such a change being accomplished by 'continuous' musical means (i.e. not simply by starting afresh in another key) and having a definite validity in the structural organization of the music. Hence *modulation.*

MODULATOR, diagram used for instructional purposes in TONIC SOL-FA, for practice in sight-reading and modulation.

MOERAN, ERNEST JOHN (1894–1950), English composer, pupil of John Ireland. Works include symphony, sinfonietta, violin concerto, cello concerto, chamber music, piano solos, choral works, many songs and folk-song arrangements. Himself a collector of Norfolk folk-songs, he was influenced (especially in earlier works) by folk-music and by Delius. He spent much time in the Irish countryside, and died there suddenly.

MOESCHINGER, ALBERT (b. 1897), Swiss composer of three symphonies, orchestral variations and fugue on a theme of Purcell, piano variations on a theme of Stravinsky, much chamber music, etc.

MOHAUPT, RICHARD (1904–57), German-born composer who settled in U.S.A., 1939, but returned to Europe, 1955. Works include opera 'The Hostess of Pinsk' (on Napoleon's invasion of Russia); 'Town Piper Music' (after a painting by Dürer) for orchestra; violin concerto. Was also conductor. Died in Austria.

MOÏSE, see MOSES.

MOISEIWITSCH, BENNO (German transliteration of Rus. *Moiseivich*; (1890–1963), Russian-born pianist who settled in Britain during the First World War and was naturalized in 1937. Toured much and won celebrity in romantic music.

MOLL (Ger.), minor – in the sense *D-moll*, D minor, etc.

MOLLOY, JAMES LYMAN (1837–1909), Irish composer of 'Love's Old Sweet Song' and similar popular Victorian songs; London barrister by profession.

MOLTO (It.), much, very; so, e.g., *allegro molto* or (more rarely) *allegro di molto*, very fast.

MOMENT MUSICAL (Fr., pl. *Moments musicaux*), title given by Schubert to each of a set of six short pieces for piano, completed 1827; and afterwards used similarly by other composers.

MOMPOU, FEDERICO (b. 1893), Spanish pianist and composer, mainly for the piano but also of songs; writes in a Spanish 'national' idiom but is also influenced by French 'IMPRESSIONISM' and has lived much in Paris.

MONACO, MARIO DEL, see DEL MONACO.

MONCKTON, LIONEL (1861–1924), English composer of 'The Country Girl' and other musical comedies, etc.; collaborated with H. Talbot in 'The Arcadians'.

MONDO DELLA LUNA, IL, see THE MAN IN THE MOON.

MONIUSZKO, STANISLAW (1819–72), Polish composer who is regarded as the chief 19th-century composer of his country, after Chopin – especially through his opera 'HALKA'. Wrote other operas in a Romantic style recognized as 'national', and also many songs and much church music. Was also conductor, and formerly organist; studied in Berlin.

MONK, WILLIAM HENRY (1823–99), English organist and composer of 'Abide with Me' and other hymns, etc.; editor of *Hymns Ancient and Modern*, 1861.

MONN, GEORG MATTHIAS (1717–50), Austrian organist, and composer of the first extant symphony in four movements, with minuet, 1740 (anticipating the Haydn-Mozart type). Also composed concertos, chamber music, etc.

MONOCHORD, scientific instrument consisting of a single string with a movable bridge, used (since the time of Ancient Egypt) for showing how, by altering the ratios in which the string is vibrating, different notes may be produced. These are the notes of the HARMONIC SERIES. A musical instrument based on this principle is the TRUMPET MARINE.

MONODIC, see MONODY.

MONODRAMA, stage piece for one character, e.g. Schoenberg's 'EXPECTATION' (Ger., *Erwartung*). Berlioz's 'Lélio' is also so styled because it has only one actor – though many other performers (musicians, not actors).

MONODY (from Gk for 'single song'), term used to describe the melody-and-accompaniment style of writing (e.g. in early 17th-century Italian opera) in contrast to the earlier polyphonic style when all PARTS were held as of equal importance (none simply as accompaniment). So also *monodic*.

MONOPARTITA, hybrid term (Gk *mono-* + PARTITA) used by Honegger for a suite (1951) whose movements are linked and which is intended to form a single musical structure.

MONOPHONY (from Gk for 'single sound'), term used of music with a single line of melody (with neither harmonic support nor other melodies in counterpoints). It is sometimes used also even when a simple accompaniment is present, provided that the melody is self-sufficient. So also *monophonic*. (Cp. HOMOPHONY, POLYPHONY.)

MONOTHEMATIC, having only a single theme.

MONSIGNY, PIERRE ALEXANDRE (1729–1817), French composer, of a noble family. Wrote successful operas of the OPÉRA-COMIQUE type, including 'Rose and Colas', 'The Deserter', and 'Philemon and Baucis'. Ceased to compose in middle life, with the rise of Grétry.

MONTE, PHILIPPE DE (1521–1603), Flemish composer. Visited Italy and (briefly) England. Chapel music director to the Hapsburg emperors at Vienna and at Prague, where he died. Composed madrigals and similar works (more than 1,200 surviving), and also Masses, motets, etc.

MONTÉCLAIR, MICHEL PINOLET DE (1667–1737), French composer of operas, chamber music, etc.; in early life a church chorister, and afterwards player of double-bass and other stringed instruments in Paris.

MONTEMEZZI, ITALO (1875–1952), Italian composer of 'THE LOVE OF THE THREE KINGS' and other operas; also orchestral works, Elegy for cello and piano, etc.

MONTEUX, PIERRE (1875–1964), French conductor, noted in Stravinsky and in other modern works. Formerly with the Diaghilev ballet company, conducting the first performance of e.g. 'THE RITE OF SPRING'. Later resident in U.S.A., conducting in Boston, San Francisco, etc.; principal conductor of London Symphony Orchestra from 1961 until his death.

MONTEVERDI, CLAUDIO (1567–1643), Italian composer, notable in the history of opera, harmony, and orchestration. Choirboy at his birthplace, Cremona; afterwards held various state and church musical positions in Mantua and elsewhere – finally in Venice, where he died. Became a priest, 1632. Operas, rich in dramatic expression (and for this purpose making characteristic use of particular instruments, as in modern orchestration) include 'ORPHEUS', 'The Combat of Tancred and Clorinda', 'The Return of Ulysses' and (when he was 75 'THE CORONATION OF POPPAEA' – these have received various modern editions. Some other operas are lost. Wrote also more than 250 madrigals including a few 'madrigali spirituali' (to religious words); Masses, two settings of the Magnificat, and other vocal works with varying accompaniment – and often with 'daringly' expressive harmony. Wrote no purely instrumental works.

MONTGOMERY, (ROBERT) BRUCE (b. 1921), English composer of 'An Oxford Requiem' (texts from the Bible and Anglican Prayer Book), overture 'Bartholomew Fair' (after Ben Jonson), piano pieces, songs, much film music, etc. Writes fiction under the name 'Edmund Crispin'.

MOONLIGHT SONATA, nickname (not Beethoven's, and fitting only the first movement) for Beethoven's piano sonata in C♯ minor, op. 27, no. 2 (1801).

MOÓR, EMANUEL (1863–1931), Hungarian pianist, composer (operas, seven symphonies, etc.), conductor, and inventor of what he called the Duplex-Coupler piano (1921) with two keyboards tuned an octave apart. Settled in Switzerland and died there.

MOORE, DOUGLAS (STUART) (b. 1893), American composer; pupil of d'Indy, N. Boulanger, and Bloch; professor of music at Columbia University, New York. Works include several alluding to American history and legend – operas 'The Devil and Daniel Webster', 'Giants in the Earth', 'Ballad of Baby Doe', 'The Wings of the Dove'; orchestral works 'Pageant of P. T. Barnum' and 'Farm Journal', etc. Has also written two symphonies, chamber music, works for amateur performers, etc.

MOORE, GERALD (b. 1899), English pianist, particularly noted as song-accompanist; also writes and lectures about his work.

MOORE, THOMAS (1779–1852), Irish poet who was also a composer: wrote tune and words of 'The Last Rose of Summer' (see MARTHA). Also wrote new words (now standard) to traditional Irish tunes, e.g. 'The Minstrel Boy'.

MORALES, CRISTÓBAL (*c.* 1500–1553), Spanish composer, also priest. For a time was singer in the Papal chapel in Rome, afterwards holding cathedral music posts in Spain. Composed Masses, motets, and other church music; also secular cantatas and madrigals.

MORALITY, name given to a type of religious play current in the Middle Ages. Vaughan Williams's opera 'THE PILGRIM'S PROGRESS' is also so labelled.

MORBIDO (It.), gentle, delicate (not 'morbid'). So *morbidezza*, delicacy, etc.

MORCEAU (Fr.), a piece (of bread, music, etc.).

MORDENT, an obsolete musical ORNAMENT represented by a sign over the note. Thus: [music example] performed as [music example] This is *upper mordent*. In the *lower mordent* (sign ♆) the second note is the one below, not above, the principal note – in the above example it would be C. These two are sometimes called respectively *inverted mordent* and just *mordent*; and in German *Mordent* means only the second, the first being called *Pralltriller*.

MOREAU, JEAN BAPTISTE (1656–1733), French composer of church music, stage works, songs, etc. Teacher of both singing and composition, and held a court post under Louis XIV.

MORENDO (It.), dying – direction aimed not at the performer but at the music, which is to lose force and (if necessary) speed.

MÖRIKE-LIEDER, MÖRIKE SONGS (Ger., Eng.), usual name for a set of fifty-three songs by Wolf (1888) to words by the German poet G. F. Mörike (1804–75). He also wrote four early settings of Mörike

MORISON, ELSIE (JEAN) (b. 1924), Australian soprano who settled in Britain; formerly in Sadler's Wells Opera, later appearing at Glyndebourne, Covent Garden, etc. Husband is RAFAEL KUBELÍK.

MORLEY, THOMAS (1557–1603), English composer, pupil of Byrd; organist of St Paul's Cathedral, London, and member of the Chapel Royal. Writer of textbook, *A Plain and Easy Introduction to Practical Music*. Composed 'It was a lover and his lass' for Shakespeare's *As You Like It* (1599); also Latin and English church music, madrigals, balletts (he introduced this form to England), canzonets for two and more voices, solo songs with lute, pieces for viols and for virginals. Much of his music shows a light and sprightly character. Editor of and contributor to 'THE TRIUMPHS OF ORIANA'.

'MORNING'; 'MIDDAY'; 'EVENING AND TEMPEST', titles given respectively to three symphonies by Haydn (nos. 6–8, 1761). The music has illustrative intent, though no explicit clues are given. Haydn affixed the titles in French, the international 'polite' language of the time – *Le Matin, Le Midi, Le Soir et la Tempête*, the last being also known sometimes simply as *Le Soir*.

MORNING HEROES, 'symphony' by Bliss – work for orator, chorus, and orchestra, on texts by various authors, in memory of the composer's brother and others killed in the First World War. First performed 1930.

MORRIS, type of English folk-dance associated with Whitsuntide, the dancers wearing bells; traditionally accompanied by PIPE and tabor.

MORRIS, HAROLD CECIL (b. 1890), American pianist, composer (three symphonies, violin concerto, chamber music, etc.), and teacher.

MORRIS, REGINALD OWEN (1886–1948), English composer (symphony, violin concerto, etc.), more famous as teacher at R.C.M. and Oxford University, and as writer of textbooks, e.g. on 16th-century counterpoint.

MORTELMANS, LODEWIJK (1868–1952), Belgian composer, noted especially for Flemish songs; wrote also symphonic poems, piano works, etc.

MOSCHELES, IGNAZ (1794–1870), German-Bohemian pianist and composer (eight piano concertos, etc., now never performed); friend of Beethoven, teacher of Mendelssohn. Resident in England, teaching, 1826–46, and also conducted there.

MOSÈ IN EGITTO, see MOSES.

MOSES, opera by Rossini, originally in Italian (*Mosè in Egitto*, i.e. Moses in Egypt), produced in Naples, 1818, with libretto by A. N. Tottola; revised and enlarged version, in French (*Moïse*), produced in Paris, 1827, with libretto by G. L. Balochi and V. J. E. de Jouy.

MOSES AND AARON (Ger., *Moses und Aron*), opera by Schoenberg. The libretto, by the composer, exists complete, but he finished the music of only the first two (out of three) acts. The work was first performed posthumously on the Hamburg radio station, 1954, and first staged in Zürich, 1957.

MOSSO (It.), moving, animated.

MOSSOLOV, ALEXANDER VASSILIEVICH (b. 1900), Russian composer (also pianist), pupil of Glière. Won wide notice with orchestral piece 'Iron Foundry' (also known, unmetallurgically, as 'Steel Foundry'), 1928, incorporating a metal sheet, shaken. Expelled from Union of Soviet Composers for drunkenness, 1936; rehabilitated, and composed a harp concerto, 1939. Other works include symphonies (no. 4 for the Lermontov centenary), works based on Central Asian folk-music, and operas.

MOSZKOWSKI, MORITZ (1854–1925), Polish-German pianist and composer, dying in poverty in Paris. Composed well-known sets of Spanish dances for piano duet; also a 'Joan of Arc' symphony, piano concerto, operas, etc.

MOTET, (1, normal current use) type of church choral composition, usually in Latin, to words not fixed in the liturgy – corresponding in the Roman Catholic service to the ANTHEM (in English) in the Anglican service; (2, exceptionally), type of work related to the preceding but not exactly conforming to it – e.g. Parry's 'SONGS OF FAREWELL' (designated by the composer as *motets*) which are choral and 'serious' but not ecclesiastical; (3, medieval use) a vocal composition defined not so much by its function as by its particular form – it was based on a 'given' (not specially composed) set of words and melody to which were added one or more melodies (with other words) in counterpoint. Sometimes, even in works for church use, the 'given' melody was taken from a secular song. The motet in this sense superseded the CONDUCTUS, being in a freer style.

MOTHER GOOSE (Fr., *Ma mère l'oye*), suite by Ravel for piano duet 1908, orchestrated and given as ballet, 1915. It consists of five movements, based on fairy-tales by Perrault.

MOTIF (Fr.), term sometimes used in English for LEADING-MOTIVE and sometimes simply for 'theme', etc.; better avoided because of its ambiguities.

MOTION, term used to describe the course upwards or downwards of a melody or melodies. A single melody is said to move by *conjunct motion* or *disjunct motion* according to whether a note moves to an adjacent note or to some other note (i.e. by a 'step' or by a 'leap'). Apart from this, two melodies move by *similar motion* (in the same direction, i.e. up or down together), or by *contrary motion* (one up, one down), or by *oblique motion* (one remaining on the same note, the other not). *Parallel motion* is 'similar motion' of such a kind that the parts not only move up and down together, but do so 'in parallel', preserving the same interval between them.

MOTIV, MOTIVE (Ger., Eng.), a short recognizable melodic or rhythmic figure – term used especially to indicate the smallest possible subdivision in musical analysis, one THEME possibly having several *motives*. But the term LEADING-MOTIVE conveys a larger type of unit and a different meaning.

MOTO (It.), movement; *con moto*, with movement; *moto perpetuo* (perpetual motion), title given to a rapid piece, usually having repetitive note-patterns – also (Lat.), *perpetuum mobile*.

MOTTL, FELIX (1856–1911), Austrian conductor and arranger of orchestral music – e.g., from Gluck's stage works. Also composer of three operas.

MOTTO, MOTTO THEME, theme which, in the course of a piece of music, recurs (perhaps transformed) in the manner of a quotation – e.g. in Berlioz's 'FANTASTIC SYMPHONY' (where it is called *idée fixe*') and in Tchaikovsky's symphony no. 5. The device is related to METAMORPHOSIS of themes, but in the latter there is not a sense of quotation, only of transformation.

MOTU PROPRIO (Lat.), a type of decree issued by the Pope; in musical contexts referring particularly to that of Piux X, 1902, emphasizing the prime value of plainsong and Palestrina-period polyphony for the Roman Catholic Church, and curbing tendencies to use secular-style compositions, orchestral instruments, women's voice, etc.

MOULAERT, RAYMOND (b. 1875), Belgian composer, also musicologist. Works include 'Symphony of Waltzes', 'Symphony of Fugues', music for brass, songs (some unaccompanied).

MOULE-EVANS, DAVID (b. 1905), English composer of symphony, orchestral 'Vienna Rhapsody', overture 'The Spirit of London', songs and part-songs, etc.

MOUNT OF OLIVES, THE, see CHRIST ON THE MOUNT OF OLIVES.

'MOURNING' SYMPHONY, nickname for Haydn's symphony no. 44 in E minor (*c.* 1772). Haydn wanted its slow movement to be played at his own funeral service.

MOUSSORGSKY, see MUSSORGSKY.

MOUTH-ORGAN, see HARMONICA.

MOUTH MUSIC, English equivalent for Gaelic *port á beul*, type of wordless but articulated singing used to accompany Scottish Highland dancing when no instrument is available.

MOUTON, JEAN (*c.* 1475–1522), French composer of Masses and other church music; in service at the French court. Pupil of Josquin Després, and teacher of Willaert.

MOUVEMENT (Fr.), (1) motion; *mouvement perpetuel*, MOTO PERPETUO; *au mouvement*, *premier* (*1er*) *mouvement*, equals *a tempo*, *tempo primo* (see TEMPO); so also *mouvementé*, with movement; (2) a MOVEMENT in the sense below.

MOVABLE DOH, description of systems of sight-reading, etc., in which (e.g. in TONIC SOL-FA), *doh* represents the keynote, *ray* the note above, etc., whatever the key. (Opposite to systems wherein, as in Continental SOLFEGGIO, *do* is C, *re* is D, etc., whatever the key.)

MOVEMENT, the primary self-contained division of a large composition – usually each having a separate indication of speed, hence the name. A large composition without any such division is said to be 'in one movement'. The word is used as a title in Stravinsky's 'Movements for piano and orchestra' (short work in five sections, 1958–9).

MOVIMENTO (It.), motion (not 'movement' in the preceding sense); *doppio movimento*, at double the preceding speed.

MOZART, (JOHANN GEORG) LEOPOLD (1719–87), German violinist and author of a famous 'Method'; composer (see TOY SYMPHONY); and father of the following. Settled in Salzburg, Austria.

MOZART, WOLFGANG AMADEUS (christened Joannes Chrysostomus Wolfgangus Theophilus; 1756–91), Austrian composer, born in Salzburg. His father (see above) took him and his sister on tour to Paris, London, etc., chiefly as harpsichord prodigies, in 1763–6. He had already begun to compose (including opera 'BASTIEN AND BASTIENNE'); by 1773, he had thrice visited Italy and had entered the service of the Prince Archbishop of Salzburg. Disliked this and left it after a quarrel, 1781, settling in Vienna. Visited Prague (where 'DON GIOVANNI' and 'THE CLEMENCY OF TITUS' were produced), Berlin, and elsewhere; died, poor, in Vienna, of typhus. Other operas include 'IDOMENEUS', 'THE SERAGLIO', 'THE IMPRESARIO', 'THE MARRIAGE OF FIGARO', 'THE MAGIC FLUTE'. Wrote also twenty-one concertos for piano, one for clarinet, and various others, more than anyone else establishing the concerto form; his symphonies (including those nicknamed HAFFNER, LINZ, PRAGUE, PARIS, JUPITER) are numbered up to forty-one, but some of these are spurious and some other works of this kind are not so numbered. Composed various serenades (see HAFFNER, EINE KLEINE NACHTMUSIK); 'A MUSICAL JOKE'; twenty-four string quartets (some nicknamed, e.g. 'PRUSSIAN QUARTETS'), one clarinet quartet, six string quintets and other chamber works; sonatas for violin, and for harpsichord (or piano); Requiem (unfinished, completed by Süssmayr), seventeen Masses, some works for Masonic use, isolated arias with orchestra and songs with piano.

MOZART AND SALIERI, opera by Rimsky-Korsakov, produced in Moscow, 1898 – a setting of Pushkin's dramatic poem, based on the (false) notion that Salieri poisoned Mozart.

MOZARTIANA, suite by Tchaikovsky, 1887 – orchestration of three piano works and the motet 'Ave Verum Corpus' by Mozart.

MUDGE, RICHARD (1718–63), English clergyman and composer known by a set of six concertos (of CONCERTO GROSSO type).

MUETTE DE PORTICI, LA, see MASANIELLO.

MUFFAT, GEORG (1653–1704), German organist and composer of Scottish descent. Studied in Paris; wrote harpsichord and organ music, works of CONCERTO GROSSO type, etc.

MUFFLE, to cover the surface of a drum with a cloth, producing an effect analogous to that of a MUTE.

MULÈ, GIUSEPPE (1885–1951), Italian cellist, and composer of operas, music to Greek plays, symphonic poems, etc.

MÜLLER, PAUL (b. 1898). Swiss composer who studied partly in Paris and Berlin. Teaches in Zürich, and is also conductor. Works include viola concerto, Sinfonia for string orchestra and another Sinfonia for full orchestra; Missa Brevis and other choral works; chamber music.

MULLINER BOOK, a MS. collection of English pieces (mainly for keyboard instrument, but a few for cittern and gittern) made by Thomas Mulliner and apparently dating approximately from 1550 to 1575; published in modern notation 1951 (edited by Denis Stevens) and reckoned one of the most valuable sources of its period.

MUNCH, CHARLES (b. 1891), French (Alsatian) conductor, formerly violinist; conductor of the Boston Symphony Orchestra 1949–62. (Name originally spelt Münch.)

MUNDY, JOHN (?–1630), English composer of church music, madrigals (one in 'THE TRIUMPHS OF ORIANA'), pieces for virginals, etc. Organist of St George's Chapel, Windsor. Son of William Mundy.

MUNDY, WILLIAM (*c.* 1529–*c.* 1591), English composer of anthem 'O Lord, the Maker of All Things' (sometimes wrongly attributed to Henry VIII) and of other anthems, Latin motets, etc. Singer in the Chapel Royal but perhaps a secret Roman Catholic. Father of John Mundy.

MURADELY, VANO (b. 1908), Russian composer, pupil of Shcherbachev and Miaskovsky. Works include 'Symphony in Memory of Kirov', choral works, opera 'The Great Friendship' (1947) – this work touching off the denunciation by Soviet officialdom in 1948 of Muradely and other composers (including Prokofiev and Shostakovich) for FORMALISM and other alleged faults.

MURDER IN THE CATHEDRAL opera by Pizzetti, produced in Milan, 1958, libretto (*Assassinio nella Cattedrale*) a shortened Italian version of T. S. Eliot's play about Thomas à Becket.

MURRILL, HERBERT HENRY JOHN (1909–52) English composer of opera 'Man in Cage', 'Suite Française' for harpsichord, two cello concertos (no. 2 on a Catalan folk-song and dedicated to Casals), etc. Pupil of A. Bush. Formerly organist; director of music, BBC, from 1950 until his death.

MUSARD, PHILIPPE (1793–1859), French violinist, conductor, composer of quadrilles etc.; gave early successful promenade concerts in Paris and (1840 and afterwards) in London.

MUSETTE, (1) French type of bagpipe fashionable in Louis XIV's time through the cultivation of 'pastoral' ideal; used in the opera orchestra by Lully; (2) type of gavotte with a drone bass suggesting the above instrument.

MUSGRAVE, THEA (b. 1928) Scottish composer, pupil of N. Boulanger in Paris; works include 'Cantata for a summer's day', two piano sonatas, Sinfonia for orchestra, 'The Five Ages of Man' for chorus and orchestra with optional brass band, opera 'The Decision'.

MUSIC, the art or science of arranging sounds in notes and rhythms to give a desired pattern or effect. (Definition adapted from *Collins New Age Encyclopedia*, 1963.) See also following entries.

MUSIC FOR THE ROYAL FIREWORKS, see FIREWORKS MUSIC.

MUSIC MAKERS, THE, work for contralto, chorus, and orchestra, by Elgar, first performed 1912. Text, A. O'Shaughnessy's poem. In this score Elgar quotes some of his own earlier works.

MUSIC MASTER, THE (It., *Il Maestro di musica*), one-act comic opera satirizing the singing-master's profession; the music is commonly ascribed to Pergolesi, but in fact is not by him – apparently an altered version of 'Orazio', opera mainly by P. Auletta, with libretto by A. Palombo, produced in Naples, 1737 or earlier.

MUSICA FICTA (Lat., feigned music), in old music (up to 16th century) the practice of treating certain notes in performance as though they were marked with FLAT or SHARP signs. This practice was necessary to avoid certain harmonic anomalies that would otherwise result in polyphonic writing, and was carried out by performers according to the recognized conventions of the period. Editors of old texts for modern usage now write in the alterations necessary.

MUSICA RESERVATA (Lat., reserved music), term originating in the early 16th century of which the exact meaning is now unknown: applied to the expressive style 'founded' by Josquin Després, and to the manner of performance appropriate to it, and thought to refer to (1) the maintenance of rules governing proper musical interpretation of emotions, and (2) the 'reserving' of music to connoisseurs of the new style.

MUSICA TRANSALPINA, the first printed collection of Italian (i.e. transalpine) madrigals with English words; it had great influence on English music. Edited by Nicholas Yonge in two volumes, 1588 and 1597, the composers including Palestrina, Marenzio, and Lassus.

MUSICAL (noun), see MUSICAL PLAY.

MUSICAL BOX, toy in which pins on a rotating cylinder 'pluck' the teeth of a comb which, being of different lengths, emit different notes; several sets of pins allow several tunes.

MUSICAL COMEDY, type of English and American light entertainment, prominent in late 19th and early 20th centuries – related to OPERETTA, but often less unified musically and using more than one composer. The type of entertainment that succeeded it is more usually called MUSICAL PLAY (or merely 'musical').

MUSICAL GLASSES, equals GLASS HARMONICA.

MUSICAL JOKE, A (Ger., *Ein musikalischer Spass*), work for strings and two horns by Mozart, 1787, satirizing clumsy composition.

MUSICAL OFFERING (Ger., *Musikalisches Opfer*), work by Bach, 1747, of thirteen pieces in various contrapuntal forms, dedicated to Frederick the Great, and all using a theme given by Frederick to Bach on his visit to court that year.

MUSICAL PLAY, term for the type of light stage entertainment (largely American-influenced) which succeeded the older MUSICAL COMEDY in the mid-20th century; often abbreviated simply to 'musical'.

MUSICAL SAW, see SAW.

MUSICAL SWITCH, medley of well-known tunes, one tune being 'switched' (after a few bars only) into the text – of no musical value, its only distinction lying in ingenuity.

MUSIC-DRAMA, term used by Wagner of his operas, after 'Lohengrin', the term 'opera' itself being thought to be inadequate or inappropriate to his intended new type of drama set to continuously expressive music based on LEADING-MOTIVES (as distinct from the old division into operatic 'numbers').

MUSICOLOGY, musical scholarship – 20th-century word useful in such contexts as 'to study musicology', implying an academic discipline different from that in 'to study music'. So also *musicologist* (usually implying someone whose activity is more 'learned' than that of a mere critic), *musicological*, etc.

MUSIK, MUSIKALISCH (Ger.), music, musical; *Musikalischer Spass*, see MUSICAL JOKE; *Musikalisches Opfer*, see MUSICAL OFFERING.

MUSIKWISSENSCHAFT (Ger.), equals MUSICOLOGY.

MUSIQUE (Fr.), music; *music concrète*, see CONCRETE MUSIC.

MUSSORGSKY, MODEST PETROVICH (1839–81), Russian composer; at first army officer, later a civil servant, but studied briefly as a young man with Balakirev. (Both were members of the 'MIGHTY HANDFUL', the group of five 'nationalist' composers.) Expressed sympathy with 'the people' and showed it in various works including his masterpiece, the opera 'BORIS GODUNOV'. Evolved, partly from Russian speech-inflexion, a highly individual musical idiom misunderstood by many contemporaries – Rimsky-Korsakov 'correcting' (misleadingly) much of his work after his death and fathering on him a piece called 'Night on the Bare Mountain' (see 'ST JOHN'S NIGHT ON THE BARE MOUNTAIN' for details). His other works include unfinished operas 'THE KHOVANSKY AFFAIR', 'SOROTCHINSY FAIR', and 'The Marriage'; choral works, 'PICTURES AT AN EXHIBITION' for piano (orchestrated by others); many songs including cycle 'SONGS AND DANCES OF DEATH'. Took to drink, died after alcoholic epileptic fits.

MUSTEL ORGAN, keyboard instrument of the AMERICAN ORGAN type, invented by V. Mustel (1815–90).

MUTA (It.), change (imperative) – direction when, e.g. a player has to transfer from one instrument to another, or a drummer has to change the tuning of a drum (e.g. '*muta la in si*', change A to B).

MUTANO (It., they change), term used as the plural of MUTA.

MUTATION STOP, organ stop sounding not the note struck but one of its HARMONIC SERIES other than the octave – e.g. a stop called 'twelfth' sounding the twelfth above.

MUTE, a contrivance to reduce the volume of an instrument and/or modify its tone – on bowed instruments, a pronged damper placed at the bridge; on brass instruments, an object of wood, metal, or fibre (there are various types) placed in the bell. To depress the SOFT PEDAL of a piano or to MUFFLE a drum is also in effect to apply a mute. (So also *to mute*, as verb.)

MY COUNTRY (Cz., *Má Vlast*), cycle of six symphonic poems by Smetana, composed 1874–9 (after he had become deaf): (1) Vyšehrad (an ancient citadel); (2) Vltava (river); (3) Šárka (Bohemian Amazon leader); (4) From Bohemia's Fields and Groves (Cz. *Z Českych Luhů a Hájů*); (5) Tábor (city associated with the Hussites); (6) Blanik (legendary sleeping-place of dead Hussite heroes).

MY LADY NEVILL'S BOOK, a MS. collection of forty-two virginal pieces by Byrd, 1591 (published 1926).

MYASKOVSKY, see MIASKOVSKY.

MYSLIVEČEK, JOSEF (1737–81), Bohemian composer of Italian operas, and also of symphonies, etc.; called '*il divino Boemo*' (It., the divine Bohemian). Mozart admired him. He died in poverty in Rome.

MYSTIC CHORD, see SKRIABIN.

N

NABOKOV, NICOLAS (originally Nikolay; b. 1903), Russian-born composer who has lived in Germany, U.S.A., and (chiefly) France. Works include opera 'The Death of Rasputin', and 'Ode, or Meditation at Night on the Majesty of God, as revealed by Aurora Borealis' (cantata, also used as ballet). Also secretary-general of the (anti-Communist) Congress for Cultural Freedom.

NABUCCO (It., abbr. of 'Nabucodnosor', i.e. Nebuchadnezzar), opera by Verdi, produced in Milan, 1842. Libretto by T. Solera, after the biblical story of the Israelites' captivity in Babylon. 'With this opera [his third] my career as a composer may rightly be said to have begun' (Verdi).

NACH (Ger.), to, after; so, e.g., *E nach G* (instruction to kettledrummer) 'change the tuning of the drum from E to G'.

NACHEZ, TIVADAR (1859–1930), Hungarian violinist, editor of violin music, composer of violin concerto, etc. Settled in France and died in Switzerland.

NACHSCHLAG (Ger., after-stroke), (1) the two extra notes which conventionally close a TRILL; (2) an extra note (printed in small type) coming after a main note and robbing that main note of some of its time-value – see SPRINGER.

NACHTANZ (Ger.), 'after-dance', i.e. a quick dance normally used to follow a slow one, e.g. a galliard following a pavan.

NACHTMUSIK (Ger.), serenade (literally, 'night music') – not a normal musical term, but used in Mozart's 'EINE KLEINE NACHTMUSIK'.

NAIL FIDDLE, NAIL HARMONICA, NAIL VIOLIN, alternative names for a freak 18th-century instrument having nails of graduated sizes stroked with a violin-bow.

NAME-DAY (Ger., *Namensfeier*), concert-overture by Beethoven, 1814, celebrating the name-day of Francis II, Emperor of Austria.

NAMENSFEIER, see preceding entry.

NÁPRAVNÍK, EDUARD (1839–1916), Czech composer of four operas, four symphonies, etc.; settled in Russia 1861, becoming a leading conductor and dying there.

NARDINI, PIETRO (1722–93), Italian violinist and composer of six violin concertos, chamber music, etc.; held court posts. A leading pupil of Tartini.

NARES, JAMES (1715–83), English composer of church music, glees, harpsichord pieces, etc.; also organist.

NATHAN, ISAAC (1790–1864), English singer and composer – of stage works, songs to words by his friend Byron, etc. Settled in Australia 1841, and died there. CHARLES MACKERRAS is a descendant.

NATIONALISM, NATIONALIST, terms applied to music which (usually through elements derived from folk-music) suggests supposed national characteristics. The terms are particularly applied to the work of such 19th-century composers as Smetana, Liszt, Balakirev, and Grieg, with the implication of national 'emancipation' from the domination of German-Austrian musical concepts.

NATURAL, (1, of a note or key), not sharp or flat – designated by the sign ♮; (2, of a horn, trumpet, etc), not having valves, keys, or other mechanism, and so producing only the notes of the HARMONIC SERIES as determined by the length of the tube; (3) a type of 'harmonics' in string-playing – see HARMONIC. See also next entry.

NATURALE (It., natural), direction that a voice or instrument which has been performing in an 'abnormal' way (e.g. falsetto, muted) should return to its 'natural' manner of performance.

NAUMANN, JOHANN GOTTLIEB (1741–1801), German composer who studied in Italy with Tartini and G. B. Martini, and won wide fame in his day, especially with operas – mostly in Italian, but three in Swedish and one in Danish for Stockholm and Copenhagen. Wrote also symphonies, Masses, oratorios, etc.

NAYLOR, BERNARD (b. 1907), English composer of choral works, 'Sonnets from the Portuguese' (E. B. Browning) for voice and string quartet, etc. Pupil of Vaughan Williams, Holst, and Ireland; spent two periods as conductor in Canada. Son of Edward Naylor.

NAYLOR, EDWARD (WOODALL) (1867–1934), English composer of opera 'The Angelus', and of church music, etc.; also organist and musicologist. Father of Bernard Naylor.

NEAPOLITAN SIXTH, a type of chord – in key C, it comprises the notes F, A♭, D♭; and correspondingly in other keys. The reason for the name is uncertain – cp. ITALIAN SIXTH, but note that the

Neapolitan sixth is always relative to the prevailing key, whereas an *Italian sixth* is formed irrespective of it.

NEEL, (LOUIS) BOYD (b. 1905), English conductor, since 1952 Dean of the Royal Conservatory of Music, Toronto. Qualified originally in medicine, but turned to music, founding Boyd Neel String Orchestra in London in 1933. In 1957 the orchestra was renamed 'PHILOMUSICA of London'.

NEGRO MINSTRELS, see MINSTREL.

NEGRO QUARTET, see AMERICAN QUARTET.

NEGRO SPIRITUAL, see SPIRITUAL.

NELSON, opera by Berkeley, produced in London, 1954. Libretto by A. Pryce-Jones, mainly on Nelson's relationship with Lady Hamilton.

NELSON MASS, nickname for Haydn's Mass in D Minor, 1798, because it is supposed to signalize joy at Nelson's victory in the Battle of the Nile.

NEO–, prefix (from Greek for 'new') used, in classifying musical styles, to indicate the re-adopting (real or supposed of apparently outmoded characteristics, suitably modified for a new era. So, e.g., *neo-modal*, referring to the 20th-century revival (e.g. by Vaughan Williams) of the old MODES; *neo-Romantic*, referring to the inclination of some composers to Romanticism even after the 20th-century reaction against it; NEO-CLASSICAL (special meaning – see below).

NEO-BECHSTEIN PIANO, patented ELECTRONIC instrument (1931) in which the strings of a piano are struck by hammers, in approximately the normal way, but with electrical modification of the sound (heard through loudspeakers). The ELECTROCHORD is similar.

NEO-CLASSIC(AL), NEO-CLASSICISM, terms used of a trend in musical style manifesting itself particularly in the 1920s. Its characteristics include – preference for small rather than large instrumental forces; use of CONCERTO GROSSO technique; emphasis on contrapuntal values; avoidance of 'emotionalism'. In the hands of Stravinsky, Hindemith, and others this had analogies with Bach's rather than Mozart's (the so-called 'Viennese classical') period, and might be better labelled *neo-baroque*. See BAROQUE, CLASSIC(AL).

NEUM(E), generic name for each of the various signs in the old musical notation (superseded by the current staff notation) showing the note(s) to which a syllable of vocal music was to be sung. As surviving in plainsong notation, the *neums* give precise indication of pitch; but, originally, from the 7th century, they were only approximate reminders of the shape of the melody.

NEVEU, GINETTE (1919–49), French violinist; child prodigy, appearing in Paris at age 7, afterwards winning high international repute. Killed in an air crash.

NEVIN, ARTHUR FINLEY (1871–1943), American composer of operas, chamber music, etc.; researcher into American-Indian folk music; brother of Ethelbert Nevin.

NEVIN, ETHELBERT WOODBRIDGE (1862–1901), American composer of 'The Rosary' (sold 6 million copies in thirty years) and other popular sentimental songs; 'Narcissus' and other piano pieces, etc. Himself also a pianist. Brother of preceding.

NEW MUSIC, term with two special historical meanings – (1) in the early 17th century, the type of newly expressive music then being pioneered – see CACCINI; (2) in the period 1850–1900, the music of Liszt, Wagner, and their followers as opposed to that of, e.g., Brahms (supposedly more 'traditional' in outlook).

NEW PHILHARMONIA ORCHESTRA, London orchestra which in 1964 succeeded the disbanded Philharmonia Orchestra (founded 1945); the old one was privately run, the new self-governing.

'NEW WORLD' SYMPHONY, see FROM THE NEW WORLD.

NEW YORK PHILHARMONIC-SYMPHONY ORCHESTRA, orchestra established from the merger in 1928 of the New York Philharmonic and New York Symphony Orchestras; principal conductor since 1958, Leonard Bernstein.

NEW YORK PRO MUSICA, see GREENBERG.

NEWAY, PATRICIA (b. 1919), American soprano, noted particularly for creating the heroine's part in Menotti's 'The Consul' in New York and later in Europe.

NIBELUNG'S RING, THE, see RING.

NICHOLSON, RICHARD (*c.* 1570–1639), English organist and composer of madrigals (one in 'THE TRIUMPHS OF ORIANA'), anthem works for viols, etc. The first professor of music at Oxford, 1627.

NICHOLSON, SYDNEY (HUGO) (1875–1947), English organist, composer (chiefly of church music), and founder of what is now the Royal School of Church Music; knighted 1938.

NICOLAI, (CARL) OTTO (EHRENFRIED) (1810–49), German composer and conductor; studied in Italy and wrote Italian operas as well as (in German) 'THE MERRY WIVES OF WINDSOR'; also choral and orchestral works, etc. Founder-conductor of the Vienna Philharmonic Concerts (i.e. of the present-day Vienna Philharmonic Orchestra), 1842; in 1847 went as director of the court opera and the cathedral choir to Berlin, where he died of a stroke.

NIEDERMEYER, (ABRAHAM) LOUIS (1801–62), Swiss composer who settled in Paris, founded an influential school of church music, and died there.

NIELSEN, CARL (AUGUST) (1865–1931), Danish composer, reckoned his country's greatest and influencing many younger Danish composers; director of the Royal Danish Conservatory, 1930; also conductor, and formerly violinist. In 1891–2 composed his symphony no. 1, probably the first ever to begin in one key and end in another (PROGRESSIVE TONALTIY) – a principle much evident in his succeeding five symphonies (no. 2 'THE FOUR TEMPERAMENTS', no. 3 'Sinfonia ESPANSIVA', no. 4 'THE UNQUENCHABLE') and other works. These include concertos for flute, for clarinet, for violin;

operas 'Saul and David' and 'MASQUERADE'; chamber music (see SERENATA), organ work 'Commotio'.

NIELSEN, RICCARDO (b. 1908), Italian composer of opera 'The Incubus', chamber music, works for one and two pianos, etc., in TWELVE-NOTE technique; previously (to 1943) practised a tonal, neo-classical idiom, composing symphony, violin concerto, etc.

NIENTE (It.), nothing, so *a niente*, to nothing – term used e.g. after the sign >, indicating that the sound is gradually to die away entirely.

NIGG, SERGE (b. 1924), French composer, pupil of Messiaen; gave up TWELVE-NOTE technique in 1948–9 in favour of a deliberately 'obvious' style as preached by Communist theory (see PROGRESSIST). Works include symphonic poems 'Timur' and 'For a Captive Poet'; piano concerto, piano sonata.

NIGGER MINSTRELS, see MINSTREL.

NIGGER QUARTET, see AMERICAN QUARTET.

NIGHT ON THE BARE MOUNTAIN, see ST JOHN'S NIGHT ON THE BARE MOUNTAIN.

NIGHTINGALE, imitative toy instrument used in the TOY SYMPHONY usually (but wrongly) ascribed to Haydn.

NIGHTS IN THE GARDENS OF SPAIN (Sp. *Noches en los jardines de España*), 'symphonic impressions' by Falla for piano and orchestra in three movements; first performed 1916.

NILSSON, BIRGIT (b. 1918), Swedish soprano, internationally known as Brünnhilde in Wagner's 'RING', in the title-role of Puccini's 'TURANDOT', etc.

NIN, JOAQUÍN (full surname Nin y Castellanos; 1879–1949), Spanish pianist, editor of old Spanish music, composer of stage works, pieces for violin and for piano, etc. Born and died in Cuba. Father of Joaquín Nin-Culmell.

NIN-CULMELL, JOAQUÍN (b. 1908), Cuban-Spanish composer – but born in Berlin and now resident in U.S.A.; son of Joaquín Nin. Has written piano concerto, piano quintet, etc.

NINETEENTH, a MUTATION stop on the organ producing a note at the interval of a nineteenth (two octaves and a fifth) above the note touched.

NINTH, an interval of nine steps (counting the bottom and top notes) e.g. from C upwards for an octave and a whole-tone to D (*major ninth*) or for an octave and a semitone to D♭ (*minor ninth*). So, e.g., a *chord of the dominant ninth* – in the key of F major this would be (reading upwards), C, E, G, B♭, D; C is the dominant of F major, the B is flat according to the scale of F major, and the note D indicates the interval of the major ninth from C.

NINTH SYMPHONY (Beethoven), see CHORAL SYMPHONY.

NOBILE, NOBILMENTE (It.), noble, nobly.

NOBILISSIMA VISIONE (It., most exalted vision), orchestral suite by

Hindemith, 1938, extracted from his ballet on St Francis of Assisi (produced the same year).

NOBLE, DENNIS (1899–1966), English baritone; was church chorister, as boy and man. Studied in Italy, and won high reputation in Britain as operatic and concert soloist.

NOBLE, THOMAS TERTIUS (1867–1953), English organist who lived much in U.S.A., and died there; composer of church music, etc.

NOCES, LES, see WEDDING.

NOCHES EN LOS JARDINES DE ESPAÑA, see NIGHTS IN THE GARDENS OF SPAIN.

NOCTURNE, a night-piece: (1, generally, in Italian, *notturno*) 18th-century composition of SERENADE type for several instruments in several movements; (2) short lyrical piece, especially for piano, in one movement – a sense originated by Field and adopted by Chopin; (3) term applied at the composer's fancy – e.g. to the third movement of Vaughan William's 'A LONDON SYMPHONY', which is headed 'Scherzo (Nocturne)', and in Britten's song-cycle with orchestra (1958) entitled Nocturne. See also next entry.

NOCTURNES, a set of three orchestral pieces by Debussy, first performed complete in 1901 – (1) Clouds; (2) Fêtes; (3) Sirens. The last has a wordless female chorus.

NODE, a stationary point on a vibrating string or air-column – the vibrations taking place in opposite directions on either side of it.

NOËL (Fr., Christmas), a Christmas carol.

NOIRE (Fr., black), crotchet (U.S., quarter-note).

NON (Fr., It.), not.

NONET, a composition for nine instruments or nine voices; if the former, it will probably be in some regular several-movement form – cp. QUARTET.

NON-HARMONIC NOTE (U.S., non-harmonic tone), term used in the theory of harmony for a note that is not part of the chord with which it sounds, and therefore needs a separate 'explanation' – e.g. it may be a PASSING-NOTE or APPOGGIATURA.

NONO, LUIGI (b. 1924), Italian composer, pupil of Scherchen; follower of the TWELVE-NOTE method, especially as developed by Webern. Works, often with many percussion instruments, include 'Epitaph for Federico García Lorca' (for speaker, singers, and orchestra); 'Encountera' (*Incontri*) for twenty-four instruments; cantata 'On the Bridge of Hiroshima' for soprano, tenor and orchestra; opera 'Intollerance' (title changed from original 'Intolerance 1960').

NORÇOMBE, DANIEL (b. 1576, d. before 1626), English lutenist and composer who contributed a madrigal to 'THE TRIUMPHS OF ORIANA'. (An English viol-player of the same name active in Brussels as late as 1647 is a different man.)

NORDRAAK, RICHARD (1842–66), Norwegian composer of what is now the Norwegian national anthem; despite his short life, exerted great influence (e.g. on Grieg) in the direction of a Norwegian national style of music.

NORMA, opera by Bellini, produced in Milan, 1821. Libretto by F. Romani. Named after the heroine, a young Druidic priestess torn between love and duty.

NORTHERN SINFONIA ORCHESTRA, chamber orchestra based on Newcastle-on-Tyne, established 1961. Rudolf Schwarz has been principal conductor since 1964 – till 1967 jointly with Boris Brott.

NOTA CAMBIATA (It., exchanged note), a device in counterpoint by which an 'extra' NON-HARMONIC note is used on an accented beat. Instead of (a) below, in which the B is an auxiliary note between the two C's, the use of *nota cambiata* (b) gives the extra note D, which is thought of as a substitute for the B (hence the idea of 'exchange'). The leap from B to an accented D, both non-harmonic notes, is the essential feature; or it might have been from D to B. (The U.S. term is simply *cambiata.*)

NOTATION, the writing down of music – whether by symbols (as in ordinary STAFF notation), by letters (as in TONIC SOL-FA) or by a graphic representation of how an instrument should be fingered to produce particular notes (as in TABLATURE).

NOTE, (1) a single sound of a given pitch and duration; (2) a written sign for the preceding; (3) a lever depressed by the performer on the piano, organ, etc., to produce a sound of particular pitch. The U.S. term for the first of these is TONE.

NOTE-CLUSTER, see CLUSTER.

NOTE-ROW (U.S., *tone-row*), in TWELVE-NOTE music, the order in which the composer chooses to arrange the twelve notes comprised within the octave, this order serving as the basis for the particular composition.

NOTTURNO, see NOCTURNE.

NOVACHORD, patented ELECTRONIC instrument: it has a six-octave piano-like keyboard, manual controls varying the tone-quality, and pedals for sustaining notes and for volume control. Chords and not merely single notes can be played.

NOVÁK, VÍTĚZSLAV (1870–1949), Czechoslovak composer, pupil of Dvořák; director of the Prague Conservatory 1919–22 and long a professor there. Works, of 'nationalist' musical character, include symphonic poems, piano concerto, three string quartets, cantata 'THE SPECTRE'S BRIDE', operas, ballets, Slovak folk-song arrangements.

NOVELETTE, NOVELLETTE (Eng., Ger.), title for a short instrumental piece supposedly the equivalent of a romantic tale – term first used by Schumann, 1838 (piano work).

NOWOWIEJSKI, FELIKS (1877–1946), Polish composer of an oratorio 'Quo Vadis?' (after Sienkiewicz), operas, organ music, etc.; also conductor.

NOYE'S FLUDDE, work of operatic type (though intended for church performance with participation of the audience in traditional hymns) by Britten, first performed at Orford (Suffolk), 1958. Title is ancient spelling of 'Noah's Flood'; text is adapted from the Chester miracle play. See also THE FLOOD.

NOZZE DI FIGARO, LE, see THE MARRIAGE OF FIGARO.

NUNC DIMITTIS, text from St Luke (named from its opening words, in Latin translation) forming part of the Roman Catholic and Anglican evening service; for the latter, composers have commonly written a 'MAGNIFICAT and Nunc Dimittis' as a unified work.

NUSSIO, OTMAR (b. 1902), Swiss composer of orchestral suites using Swiss traditional tunes; also of violin concerto, etc.

NUT, (1) on a stringed instrument, the ridge over which the strings pass between the pegs and the finger-board; *movable nut*, contrivance placed on the finger-board e.g. of a ukulele, having the effect of shortening all strings equally and thus raising their pitch at choice, to facilitate playing in various keys; (2) on the bow of, e.g., a violin, the device at the heel by which the tension of the bow-strings can be regulated.

NUTCRACKER, THE (Rus., *Shchelkunchik*), ballet with music by Tchaikovsky, produced in St Petersburg, 1892 – some months after the concert suite drawn from it had already been performed. On a fairy-tale, with a battle between the Nutcracker and the King of Mice. See CELESTA.

NYSTROEM, GÖSTA (b. 1890), Swedish composer, pupil of d'Indy in Paris – where, himself a painter, his artistic outlook was influenced by Picasso, Braque, etc. Works include four symphonies (no. 4 'Sinfonia del Mare', i.e. of the sea), viola concerto, Sinfonia Concertante for cello and orchestra; stage music; songs (showing some Swedish 'national' elements) with orchestra and piano.

O

OP., abbr. of OPUS.

O (It.), or; *o sia*, see OSSIA.

O SALUTARIS HOSTIA (Lat., O Saving Victim), latter part of a Roman Catholic hymn, sung to its own plainsong melodies or to later composed settings.

OBBLIGATO (It., obligatory), term used of an instrument having a compulsory, unusual, and special role – e.g. 'song with flute obbligato' (where *obbligato* is really an adjective qualifying 'flute').

It should be noted (1) that, by contrast, 'flute ad lib.' would imply optional, not compulsory, use of the instrument; (2) that occasionally the word *obbligato* is encountered actually meaning *ad lib.* – quite wrongly; (3) that the spelling is not 'obligato'.

OBERLIN, RUSSELL (b. 1928), American counter-tenor; former member of the New York Pro Musica; sang as Oberon in Britten's 'A Midsummer Night's Dream' at Covent Garden, 1961.

OBERON, *or The Elf-King's Oath*, opera by Weber, produced in London, 1826; libretto, in English, by J. R. Planché. The story, a romance set in the days of Charlemagne, has nothing to do with the exploits of Oberon in *A Midsummer Night's Dream.*

OBLIGATO, mis-spelling for OBBLIGATO.

OBLIQUE MOTION, see MOTION.

OBOE, woodwind instrument blown through a double reed and having a compass from the B♭ below middle C upwards for more than two and a half octaves; standard in the orchestra, and used also in the military band, in chamber music, and as solo instrument. *Oboe d'amore*, similar instrument of slightly lower pitch and less pungent tone, written for e.g. by Bach and (exceptionally in modern times) by Ravel ('BOLERO') and R. Strauss; *oboe da caccia* – literally 'hunting oboe', though it is not clear why – predecessor of the ENGLISH HORN, the present 'contralto' to the oboe's soprano. Basically of the same family as the oboe is the BASSOON. Between oboe and bassoon in pitch are two different instruments each with compass approximately an octave below the oboe – the (French) *baritone oboe*, blown through a side tube like the bassoon, and the (German) HECKELPHONE, sometimes called (e.g. in Delius's scores) *bass oboe.*

OBRECHT, JACOB (latinized as Obertus; 1452–1505), Netherlandish composer who worked mainly in Flanders, but also visited Italy and died of plague there. Wrote Masses, motets, and secular songs, showing some emotional characteristics foreshadowing the expressive art of Després.

OCARINA, small keyless wind instrument with holes for fingers mainly used as a toy, and featured in the musical play 'Call Me Madam' (music by Irving Berlin). The body is shaped like an egg – or, counting the protruding mouthpiece, rather like a goose, thus possibly suggesting the name (from It. *oca*, goose ?).

OCKEGHEM, JEAN DE (or Okeghem; *c.* 1430–*c.* 1495), Flemish composer, in service to the French court; also visited Spain. Of great influence; called 'the Prince of Music' in his own day; his pupils included Després. Wrote Masses and motets, sometimes choosing a secular tune as CANTUS FIRMUS; wrote also secular songs in French in a rather lighter style.

OCTANDRE, title of a composition by Varèse (exploiting the extremes of dissonance), 1924, for eight players – seven wind instruments and double-bass. Title literally means a plant with eight stamens.

OCTAVE, the interval that is considered as having eight (Lat., *octo*) steps, counting both the bottom and top notes; according to our notation, notes an octave apart from each other have the same letter-names, the note an octave above A being also called A, etc. This naming corresponds to the fact that notes an octave apart seem to the ear like the same note sounded at different pitches, not like entirely different notes. Strictly the interval from A to the next A above is the *perfect octave*; from A up to A♭ and from A up to A♯ are respectively the *diminished* and *augmented octave*. Thus also *double octave*, two octaves; *at the octave*, (performed) an octave higher than written; *in octaves*, (performed) with each note doubled one or more octaves above or below; *octave coupler*, device on organ or harpsichord whereby the note struck is doubled an octave higher (sometimes called *super-octave coupler*, to distinguish from *sub-octave coupler* doubling at the octave below); *octave key*, finger-lever on woodwind instruments giving player access to a higher octave. For *consecutive octaves* see CONSECUTIVE.

OCTET, composition for eight instruments or eight voices; if the former, it will probably be in some regular several-movement form – cp. QUARTET. Also a group of eight performers.

OCTOBASS, a huge bowed stringed instrument, larger and pitched lower than a double-bass, invented in 1849. It failed to win acceptance.

OCTUOR (Fr.), octet.

ODE, (1) musical setting of a poem itself called 'Ode', such a setting often having a ceremonial nature – see the following; (2) term exceptionally used in music with some vaguer significance: Stravinsky's work in memory of Koussevitzky's wife, 1943, is entitled 'Ode: Elegiacal Chant'.

ODE FOR ST CECILIA'S DAY, (1) title of three choral works by Purcell (1683, 1692, and one of uncertain date, the 1683 setting in Latin and the others in English); (2) title of a setting by Handel of Dryden's poem of the same title, first performed in London, 1739. See also HYMN TO ST CECILIA.

ODE TO NAPOLEON, work by Schoenberg, 1943, for speaker (whose part is rhythmically notated at approximate pitch), strings and piano; text, by Byron, expresses loathing of despotism.

ODO OF CLUNY (?–942), French monk, appointed Abbot of Cluny in 927; he was a noted composer and teacher, and various writings on music are ascribed to him.

OEDIPUS REX (Lat., King Oedipus), 'Opera-oratorio' by Stravinsky – intended for stage presentation with restricted movement, but first performed as a concert work in Paris, 1927. The text is a Latin translation by J. Daniélou of a script by Cocteau suggested by Sophocles' Greek tragedy.

OFFENBACH, JACQUES (1819–80), French composer born at Offenbach-am-Main, Germany; statements that his original surname was Wiener, Levy, or Eberst are unsubstantiated. He was taken to Paris in boyhood and remained there, attaining tremendous success as composer of nearly ninety French operettas including 'La Belle Helène' and 'ORPHEUS IN THE UNDERWORLD', often satirizing contemporary manners, and in a sprightly musical style which became standard for this type of work. Also wrote opera 'THE TALES OF HOFFMANN'. Had early career as cellist, and later managed his own theatres; encouraged J. Strauss the younger to write operetta. Visited England and U.S.A.

OFFERTOIRE (Fr.), equals OFFERTORIUM.

OFFERTORIUM, OFFERTORY (Lat., Eng.), a plainsong or polyphonic setting of Biblical words (in Latin) occurring after the Credo in the Mass of the Roman Catholic Church while the Eucharist is being prepared and offered. Organ music supplementing or replacing this is also so called.

OGDON, JOHN (b. 1937) English pianist, joint winner in 1962 of the International Tchaikovsky Competition at Moscow (see ASHKENAZY); known for performance of Busoni's concerto and other unusual works. Also composer, e.g. of preludes for piano.

OHANA, MAURICE (b. 1914), composer of Anglo-Spanish descent, born in Casablanca and resident in Paris; works include choral settings of Spanish verse (some by Lorca) and a guitar concerto.

OHNE (Ger.), without.

OISTRAKH, DAVID (b. 1908), Russian violinist for whom Prokofiev and other Russian composers have written works specially; has made highly successful appearances in London, New York, etc., from 1955. Also conductor. His son, Igor Oistrakh (b. 1931), is also a noted violinist.

OKEGHEM, see OCKEGHEM.

OLD HALL MANUSCRIPT, a collection of 14th–15th-century church music found at St Edmund's College, Old Hall, Herts, and published 1933–9.

OLDHAM, ARTHUR (b. 1926), English composer, pupil of Britten; works include ballet 'Bonne-Bouche', an edition of the 18th century ballad opera 'LOVE IN A VILLAGE', song-cycle 'The Commandment of Love' (to religious texts).

OLIPHANT, medieval horn made of elephant's tusk or of gold, a symbol of high dignity (e.g. that of knighthood).

OMPHALE'S SPINNING WHEEL (Fr., *Le Rouet d'Omphale*), symphonic poem by Saint-Saëns, 1871 – alluding to the queen whom Hercules served as a slave for three years, spinning wool for her.

ON HEARING THE FIRST CUCKOO IN SPRING, piece by Delius for small orchestra, first performed 1913; it introduces a Norwegian folk-song, and the cuckoo is discreetly impersonated by a clarinet.

ON WENLOCK EDGE, cycle of six songs by Vaughan Williams (to poems by A. E. Housman), 1909, with accompaniment of string quartet and piano.

ONDES MARTENOT, see MARTENOT.

O'NEILL, NORMAN (1875–1934), English composer of much theatre music, including the incidental music to Barrie's *Mary Rose*; also theatre conductor. Wrote also orchestral works, chamber music, etc.

ONSLOW, GEORGE (1784–1853), French composer (mother French, father British); lived awhile in London but settled in France and died there. Wrote thirty-six string quartets and other chamber music (in part indebted to the 'Vienna Classics') which won fashionable success in England and France; also operas, etc.

OPEN, (1, *of a string*), allowed to vibrate throughout its full length, not 'stopped' by a finger pressed on it; (2, *of a pipe*), not stopped at the end – e.g. the *open diapason* of the organ, contrasted with the 'stopped diapason'; (3, *of the notes of the orchestral horn*), not 'stopped' by the placing of the hand firmly inside the bell.

OPER (Ger.), opera – also in the sense of 'opera company'; so *Staatoper*, State Opera.

OPERA, (1, *obsolete*), OPUS; (2) a company performing opera as defined below; so *Vienna State Opera*, etc.; or an opera itself, e.g. the Opéra (building) in Paris, opened in 1875; (3, *principal meaning*), type of drama in which all or most characters sing and in which music constitutes a principal element having its own unity. The first works properly so classified are those arising in Italy about 1600 (see, e.g., CACCINI, PERI), though precursors are found e.g. in the Middle Ages. Various synonyms or near-synonyms for the term *opera* are to be met, their precise significance often depending on historical context: see e.g. MUSIC-DRAMA (Wagner's term). The apparent sub-divisions of opera (see following entries) have seeming inconsistencies which are similarly to be resolved only by their differing historical contexts.

OPÉRA BOUFFE (Fr.), type of light, often satirical opera or operetta, e.g. the operettas of Offenbach. Term taken from, but not historically quite the same as, OPERA BUFFA.

OPERA BUFFA (It.), comic opera, particularly the 18th-century kind as represented by Pergolesi's 'THE MAID AS MISTRESS'. Cp. OPERA SERIA.

OPÉRA COMIQUE (Fr.), term literally signifying simply comic opera, but having two special meanings – (1), in the 18th century, a type of French comic opera with spoken dialogue, e.g. by Philidor, Mo-signy, less lofty in ideas and style than the current serious operas (generally on heroic or mythological subjects); (2), in the 19th century, any opera with spoken dialogue, whether comic or not – Gounod's 'FAUST' and Bizet's 'CARMEN' (in their original versions, without recitatives) being so classifiable. (Note that the Paris theatre called the 'Opéra-Comique' originally observed this distinction but has long ceased to do so.)

OPERA SERIA (It.), term literally signifying 'serious opera', opposite to OPERA BUFFA, but used particularly for a specific type of opera flourishing in the 18th century and lingering up to, e.g., Rossini's

'SEMIRAMIS' (1823). This type is characterized by (1) Italian libretto, (2) heroic or mythological plot, (3) much formality in music and action, (4) often, leading roles for CASTRATO singers.

OPERA-BALLET, stage work giving approximately equal importance to opera and ballet, especially those written by Lully, Rameau, and others in 17th- and 18th-century France.

OPERA-ORATORIO, work standing midway between the types 'opera' and 'oratorio' – designation applied e.g. to Stravinsky's 'OEDIPUS REX', where the action is intended to be presented on the stage but in a static manner remote from ordinary theatrical practice.

OPERETTA (It., little opera), term used for an opera of a light type whether full-length or (like some of Offenbach's) in one act. The term is virtually synonymous with 'light opera'; and cp. MUSICAL COMEDY.

OPÉRETTE (Fr.), operetta.

OPHICLEIDE, obsolete bass instrument made of metal and having keys; used in the orchestra (e.g. by Berlioz, Mendelssohn, early Verdi) as an improvement on the SERPENT, but was itself superseded about 1850 by the tuba, on which instrument the parts intended for the ophicleide are now normally played. The *key bugle* (or *keyed bugle*, or *Kent bugle*) was an instrument of related type, but roughly of bugle size and pitch; it had some use in early 19th-century bands before the advent of the cornet.

OPUS (Lat., a work; abbr. *op.*) term used, with a number, for the enumeration of a composer's works supposedly in the order of their composition; if an 'opus' comprises more than one piece, then a subdivision may be used (e.g., 'opus 49, no. 2'). Occasionally the letters *a* and *b* are used to indicate different but equally valid versions of the same work: see ST ANTHONY VARIATIONS. But confusion arises because various composers have (a) failed to number their works, (b) numbered only some and not others, (c) allowed their works to appear with numbers not representing their real order of composition – e.g. Dvořák, to satisfy a publisher's desire to present early works as recent ones.

ORATORIO, (1) type of musical composition (originating about 1600 in performances at the Oratory of St Philip Neri in Rome, hence the name) consisting of an extended setting of a religious text set out in more or less dramatic form – usually for soloists, chorus, and orchestra; not requiring scenery, costumes, or action; but sometimes originally performed in a theatre – as were Handel's oratorios; (2) term used also for a type of work similar to the above but on a non-religious – though usually 'elevated' – subject: e.g. Handel's 'SEMELE', Tippett's 'A CHILD OF OUR TIME', and certain Soviet Russian works to patriotic texts.

ORCHESTRA, a numerous body of instrumentalists – such a body, as distinct from more intimate groups, originating in early 17th-century Italian opera, afterwards altered in constitution (obsolete instruments being replaced by new ones) and made more systematic. So *symphony orchestra*, standard large orchestra of 19th and 20th centuries, able to play symphonies, etc. – as opposed, to, e.g. *chamber orchestra* (small size), *string orchestra* (strings only), *light orchestra* (of size and constitution to play light music only), *theatre orchestra* – traditionally constituted like a symphony orchestra except for being smaller numerically, but today also usually differing by regularly incorporating e.g. saxophones, not normally present in the symphony orchestra. A combination of wind instruments, or any combination for dancing to, is customarily called not an orchestra but a band; *dance orchestra* is a 20th-century grandiosity for a large dance band. Note that *philharmonic orchestra*, unlike *symphony orchestra*, is not a type of orchestra: see PHILHARMONIC. Although composers may vary both the kind and numbers of instruments used (and variety is especially noticeable in the percussion section) the following would be regarded as a normal 20th-century orchestra – (*a*, woodwind), two flutes with one piccolo, two oboes with one English horn, two (ordinary) clarinets with one bass clarinet, two bassoons with one double-bassoon; (*b*, brass), four horns, three trumpets, two tenor and one bass trombone, one tuba; (*c*, percussion), three kettledrums, one side drum, one triangle, one pair of cymbals, one bass-drum; (*d*, unclassified), two harps; (*e*, strings), about fourteen first violins, about fourteen second violins, about twelve violas, about ten cellos, about eight double-basses. This order is that conventionally followed in the (modern) printing of a score, except that there is no standard order in percussion.

ORCHESTRATION, the art of writing suitably for an orchestra, band, etc.; or of scoring for these a work originally designed for another medium. So *orchestrate*, *orchestrator*.

ORCHESTRE DE LA SUISSE ROMANDE, see ANSERMET.

ORD, BORIS (first name really Bernhard: 1897–1961), English organist, harpsichordist, and choral conductor; on Cambridge University staff.

OREFICE, GIACOMO (1865–1922), Italian composer of operas (one on Chopin's life using Chopin's music), symphony, chamber music etc.

ORFEO, see ORPHEUS.

ORFF, CARL (b. 1895), German composer, chiefly for the stage; also conductor, editor of old music, and musical educator (a specially devised educational range of percussion instruments bears his name). Works – using a strongly rhythmical, percussive, clear-textured style avoiding counterpoint – include operas 'THE CLEVER GIRL' (*Die Kluge*), 'The Moon', 'Oedipus the Tyrant', 'ANTIGONE' and others; stage work 'CARMINA BURANA'; 'Carmina Catulli' (choral setting of poems of Catullus); incidental music to *A Midsummer Night's Dream*.

ORGAN, (1) keyboard instrument in which wind is blown by a bellows through pipes to sound the notes; made in various sizes down to the medieval 'portative', i.e. portable, carried by the player. Tone is varied by the selection and combination of different stops (see STOP; FOOT) on different keyboards: a pedal keyboard, originating in Germany before 1500, has gradually become standard as well as up to five (very rarely more) manual keyboards. These five are called CHOIR, GREAT, SWELL, SOLO, and ECHO (reading upwards), but it is common to find only two (Great, Swell) or three (Choir, Great, Swell). The 19th and 20th centuries have brought not only mechanical improvements, e.g. electricity to work the bellows, but have also much increased the power and variety of organs – not necessarily with comparable artistic gain. *Extension organ* or *unit organ*, type of organ built for economy of space and expense: for its principle see UNIT ... The *cinema organ* is usually a unit organ with some 'freak' stops, e.g. piano, motor-horn. (2) term for each component tone-producing part of the instrument described above – e.g. the *Great Organ*, *Pedal Organ*, meaning the Great and Pedal keyboards plus the pipes controlled by them and the appropriate machinery; (3) term for an instrument controlled by keyboard, and imitative of the organ as described above, but pipeless – e.g. REED ORGAN, HAMMOND ORGAN (the latter being one of several patented ELECTRONIC organs). See also BARREL ORGAN.

ORGANISTRUM, equals HURDY-GURDY.

ORGAN-POINT, equals PEDAL-point.

ORGANUM (Lat.), a medieval form of PART-writing (from the 9th century) based on a plainsong which was harmonized by the addition of one, two, or three more parts. (Also called *diaphony*.)

ORGATRON, patented type of keyboard ELECTRONIC instrument (U.S.A., 1934) in which the sound, imitative of a pipe-organ, is taken electrically off vibrating reeds.

ORGEL (Ger.), organ; so Bach's *Orgelbüchlein* – see LITTLE ORGAN BOOK.

ORGUE (Fr.), organ.

ORLANDO, Italian opera by Handel, produced in London, 1733. Libretto by G. Bracciotti, after Ariosto's 16th-century epic poem, *Orlando Furioso* (i.e., mad Orlando). Remarkable for its operatic depiction of the hero's madness.

ORMANDY, EUGENE (original surname Blau; b. 1899), Hungarian-born violinist who settled in U.S.A., 1920, and became conductor; succeeded Stokowski as conductor of Philadelphia Orchestra, 1936.

ORNAMENT, one or more notes considered as an 'extra' embellishment of a melody, either – (1) inserted by the performer (e.g. the opera-singer in Handel's time) from his knowledge of current conventions without specific written instructions from the composer – see APPOGGIATURA; (2) conveyed by a sign or abbreviation, e.g. ~ (TURN), *tr.* ~~ (TRILL), or by notes in small type (see e.g., ACCIACCATURA); or (3) written in full in ordinary notation, even when it could have been conveyed by a sign – as, e.g., the turn is written out in full by Wagner and Bruckner.

ORNSTEIN, LEO (b. 1895), Russian-born pianist and composer who settled in U.S.A., 1906. Works include piano concertos, theatre music, chamber music, piano solos – at one time considered 'wildly' modern.

ORPHÉE (Fr.), see various titles beginning ORPHEUS.

ORPHEUS, operas by various composers including – (1) by Monteverdi (one of the first of all operas), produced in Mantua, 1607; libretto by A. Striggio ('La Favola d'Orfeo', The Story of Orpheus); (2) by Gluck, produced in Vienna, 1762, with Italian libretto ('Orfeo et Euridice', Orpheus and Eurydice) by R. da Calzabigi; revised version in French, produced in Paris, 1774. See also following entries.

ORPHEUS, symphonic poem by Liszt, 1854 – Orpheus, tamer of the beasts, symbolizing the power of art.

ORPHEUS, ballet with music by Stravinsky, produced in New York, 1948 – on Orpheus's quest for Eurydice, and his death.

ORPHEUS BRITANNICUS (Lat., the British Orpheus, i.e. Purcell), title of three posthumous volumes of Purcell's songs; eighteen of these have been arranged by Britten.

ORPHEUS IN THE UNDERWORLD (Fr. *Orphée aux enfers;* i.e. in Hades), operetta by Offenbach produced in Paris, 1848. Libretto by H. Crémieux and L. Halévey, satirizing modern times under cover of guying the old legend. It quotes, satirically, the famous aria 'Che farò' from Gluck's 'Orpheus'.

ORR, CHARLES WILFRED (b. 1893), English composer of songs – many to Housman's verse; also writer on music.

ORR, ROBIN (ROBERT KEMSLEY) (b. 1909), Scottish composer, pupil of Casella in Siena, N. Boulanger in Paris. Works include prelude and fugue for string quartet, songs, opera 'Full Circle'.

ORREGO SALAS, JUAN (b. 1919), Chilean composer of 'Five Castilian Songs' for voice and chamber orchestra – also of opera, ballet, symphony, etc. Is also conductor and writer on music.

ORTHEL, LEON (b. 1905), Dutch composer and pianist; pupil of J. Wagenaar, and also studied in Berlin. Has written four symphonies (no. 4 also called Sinfonia Concertante for piano and orchestra), cello concerto, violin sonata, etc. – leaning to a conservative, Romantically-inclined idiom.

OSSIA (It., from *o sia*, or it may be), (1) term used to introduce an alternative version of a musical passage, e.g. an editor's correction of an old composer's text which appears to be in error, or a composer's own simpler alternative for a passage difficult to perform; (2) term used to introduce the alternative title of an opera, etc. – for an example see 'OTELLO' (Rossini).

OSTERC, SLAVKO (b. 1895), Yugoslav composer of ballet, concerto for piano and wind instruments, chamber music, etc.; pupil of A. Hába; sometimes uses quarter-tones.

OSTINATO (It., obstinate), a persistently repeated musical figure or rhythm; so *basso ostinato*, a bass having this characteristic – i.e. a GROUND BASS. (The term *pizzicato ostinato* in the third movement of Tchaikovsky's symphony no. 4, exceptionally means only 'persistent pizzicato', not implying repetition.)

OSTRČIL, OTAKAR (1879–1935), Czech composer of operas, symphonic poems, etc.; in later works was influenced by Mahler. Also opera conductor.

OTELLO, form of name used by Italians for the character called Othello by Shakespeare: title of operas (based on Shakespeare's play) (1) by Rossini, produced in Naples, 1816, with libretto by B. de Salsa (*Otello, ossia Il Moro di Venezia*; Othello, or The Moor of Venice); (2) by Verdi, produced in Milan, 1887, with libretto ('Otello') by A. Boito. See also OTHELLO.

ÔTEZ (Fr.), take off (imperative); *ôtez les sourdines*, take off the mutes.

OTHELLO, concert-overture by Dvořák, 1892, after Shakespeare; see CARNIVAL. (See also OTELLO.)

OTTAVA (It., sometimes written 8va.), octave; so *all'ottava*, at the octave (higher); *ottava bassa*, an octave lower.

OTTAVINO (It.), the modern Italian name for the small flute, elsewhere called PICCOLO (itself signifying 'little' in Italian).

OTTERLOO, (JAN) WILLEM VAN (b. 1907), Dutch composer of three symphonies, piano and organ works, etc. Conductor of the Residentie Orchestra at The Hague since 1949.

OTTONI (It.), brass instruments.

OUR LADY'S JUGGLER (Fr., *Le Jongleur de Notre Dame*), opera by Massenet, produced in Monte Carlo, 1902. Libretto by M. Léna, ultimately after a medieval miracle play. The juggler, having nothing to offer to the Virgin but his tricks, finds that these are accepted.

OUR MAN IN HAVANA, opera by Malcolm Williamson, produced in London, 1963; libretto by Sidney Gilliat after Graham Greene's novel, bitterly satirizing espionage and 'security'.

OURS, L', see THE BEAR.

OUSELEY, FREDERICK (ARTHUR) GORE (1825–89), English organist, composer of church music, etc., professor at Oxford, clergyman, and baronet (succeeding his father).

OUVERTURE, OUVERTÜRE (Fr., Ger.), equal OVERTURE.

OVERBLOW, to blow a woodwind instrument harder, in such a way that its notes are 'stepped up' from those of its 'basic' pitch. In most such instruments the notes are 'stepped up' first of all by an octave (this representing, in the HARMONIC SERIES, the distance from the first to the second harmonic), and such instruments are said to *overblow an octave*. In the clarinet, however, the second harmonic is missing and the notes are 'stepped up' not by an octave but by a twelfth: it is therefore said to *overblow a twelfth*.

OVERSTRUNG, description of pianos in which the strings are set at two different levels, crossing – this affording greater length of string for a given size of instrument.

OVERTONE, name for any notes of the HARMONIC SERIES except the first ('fundamental').

OVERTURE, (1) piece of orchestral music preceding an opera or oratorio – since Gluck, usually musically allusive to what follows; (2) similar piece preceding a play; (3) since Mendelssohn's 'HEBRIDES', also a type of one-movement orchestral work composed for the concert-hall, and usually having a title revealing a literary, pictorial, or emotional clue. (This last type is specifically called *concert-overture*.) So *French overture*, 17th–18th-century form of (1) above, in three movements slow-quick-slow; *Italian overture*, quick-slow-quick (the form from which the symphony evolved).

OX MINUET (Ger., *Ochsenmenuett*), minuet attributed to Haydn, but really by his pupil, I. X. von Seyfried (1776–1841), who introduced it into an opera of the same name, compiled mainly from Haydn's works. (Haydn was supposed to have received an ox as payment for this minuet.)

OXFORD ELEGY, AN, work by Vaughan Williams for speaker, chorus, and small orchestra, on words from Matthew Arnold's 'The Scholar Gipsy' and 'Thyrsis' – first performed in Oxford, 1952.

'OXFORD' SYMPHONY, nickname for Haydn's symphony no. 92 in G, performed when Haydn visited Oxford University in 1791 to receive an honorary doctorate; but composed 1788 without this purpose in mind.

P

p, abbr. of *piano* (It., soft); hence, as indications of increasing degrees of softness, *pp*, *ppp*, etc. – sometimes in even greater aggregations.

PED., (1, in piano music) instruction that the sustaining pedal is to be depressed until a point when its release is indicated; (2, in organ music), indication of music to be played on the pedal keyboard.

PIZZ., abbr. of PIZZICATO.

PAAP, WOUTER (b. 1908), Dutch composer, mainly self-taught; works include 'The Art of Printing' for orator and orchestra, orchestral works, piano solos, etc. Also critic.

PACHELBEL, JOHANN (1653–1706), German organist, and composer of organ music (including preludes on Lutheran chorales), harpsichord music, etc. Teacher of Bach's elder brother Johann Christoph, who in turn was the teacher of Bach himself in his boyhood.

PACIFIC 231, 'symphonic movement' by Honegger, first performed 1924. Named after an American railway engine – but 'I have not aimed to imitate the noise of an engine, but rather to express in terms of music a visual impression and physical enjoyment' (Honegger). See RUGBY.

PACINI, GIOVANNI (1796–1867), Italian composer of more than eighty operas, some notable for their orchestral technique; also of church music, etc.

PADEREWSKI, IGNACY (JAN) (1866–1941), Polish pianist, pupil of Leschetizky in Vienna, and composer of operas, piano concerto, symphony, piano solos (including Minuet in G), songs, etc., in Romantic style. Also statesman: first Prime Minister of the newly created state of Poland, 1919 (he resigned after ten months). Died in New York.

PAER, FERDINANDO (1771–1839), Italian composer who became musical director to Napoleon, and settled in Paris, 1807. (In France the spelling Paër is used.) His forty operas include a follow-up of Mozart's 'THE MARRIAGE OF FIGARO' ('The New Figaro', 1797), and an Italian setting of the plot which had already served Gaveaux in 'LEONORA' and which was to serve Beethoven in 'FIDELIO'.

PAESIELLO, see PAISIELLO.

PAGANINI, NICCOLÒ (1782–1840), Italian violinist, called by Schumann 'the turning-point of virtuosity'; enormously successful – though, with the subsequent advance in the general level of performers' skill, his feats are no longer regarded as freakishly difficult. Was also guitarist (wrote three string quartets with guitar part) and viola-player: he commissioned, but never played, Berlioz's 'HAROLD IN ITALY'. Compositions include five violin concertos, of which apparently only four survive in full, authentic form; no. 2 in B minor has 'BELL RONDO'; variations for violin called 'THE CARNIVAL OF VENICE'; and twenty-four Capricci (i.e. studies) for violin unaccompanied. One of the latter, in A minor, is the source of (1) Brahms's 'Studies in Piano Technique: Variations on a Theme of Paganini', 1866; (2) Rakhmaninov's 'Rhapsody on a Theme of Paganini' for piano and orchestra (also in variation-form), 1934; (3) Blacher's orchestral 'Variations on a Theme of Paganini', 1947. Schumann, Busoni, and others have also transcribed his works for piano. They have a certain intense, 'demonic' quality – emphasized in his lifetime by the legends of his being inspired by the Devil, etc. Died in Nice.

PAGLIACCI (It., Clowns), opera by Leoncavallo, produced in Milan, 1892. Libretto by composer – on the interaction between a play and the real tragic 'drama' lived by the players.

PAINE, JOHN KNOWLES (1839–1906), American organist and composer (two symphonies, cantatas, etc.) who studied in Germany and later founded the musical faculty at Harvard.

PAISIELLO, GIOVANNI (1740–1816), Italian composer who worked in St Petersburg (Catherine the Great's court), Paris (under Napoleon) and Naples, where he died. Wrote more than 100 operas, including a very successful 'BARBER OF SEVILLE' (before Rossini's); also symphonies, church music, etc. Befriended and influenced Mozart. His name is sometimes spelt Paesiello.

PALESTER, ROMAN (b. 1907), Polish composer resident in France. Works – showing some influence of Stravinsky – include symphonies, violin concerto, 'Vistula' Cantata, string quartet, sonata for three clarinets.

PALESTRINA, GIOVANNI PIERLUIGI DA (*c.* 1525–1594), Italian composer who took the name Palestrina from his native town, near Rome. Was choirboy, and spent all his musical life in service of the Church; but also proved an able business-man. Became choirmaster of the Julian Chapel at St Peter's, Rome, and a member of the Papal chapel; later held other high positions. Much honoured in his lifetime, and described on his coffin as 'Prince of Music'. After his first wife died he entered the priesthood, but abandoned it and remarried. Apart from a few madrigals his works are all Latin church music for unaccompanied choir – nearly 100 Masses (including MISSA PAPAE MARCELLI and a Mass on L'HOMME ARMÉ'), motets, a Stabat Mater, psalms, etc. Posthumous veneration of him (often entailing the unjust neglect of his contemporaries) has led to various romantic legends; see next entry.

PALESTRINA, opera by Pfitzner, produced in Munich, 1917. Libretto by Pfitzner, about the composer – but on the basis of the totally unfounded legend that Palestrina, by composing his 'MISSA PAPAE MARCELLI' at direct angelic inspiration, persuaded the ecclesiastical Council of Trent (1545–63) not to ban polyphonic music.

PALLAVICINO, CARLO (*c.* 1630–88), Italian composer, chiefly of opera; worked much in Dresden where he died.

PALMGREN, SELIM (1878–1951), Finnish composer who studied in Germany and Italy with Busoni and others; also pianist and conductor. For a time lived as teacher in U.S.A. Works include many short piano pieces with 'picturesque' titles (e.g. 'Night in May') and some of Finnish nationalist significance; also five piano concertos, operas, cantatas, etc.

PAMMELIA, a collection of English rounds, catches, etc., for voices, published by T. Ravenscroft in 1609. Named from Greek for 'all-honey', and succeeded by *Deuteromelia* (also 1609; Gk *deutero-*, second).

PANATERO, MARIO (b. 1919), Italian composer, pupil of Ghedini and F. Martin; also conductor and critic. Has written stage music, concerto for flute and strings, cantata 'The Surrender of Calais' (after Froissart), etc.

PANDORA, plucked stringed instrument of lute type, surviving in the Near East.

PAN-PIPES, a series of simple short vertical pipes fixed side by side in order to give a scale when blown – an ancient, medieval, and 'folk' instrument. Papageno, as a 'child of Nature', plays one in Mozart's 'THE MAGIC FLUTE'.

PANTOMIME (from Gk for all-imitating), (1) a play in dumb-show, a mime-play – either as a self-contained work or (as in Ravel's 'DAPHNIS AND CHLOE', where the story of Pan and Syrinx is mimed) as an episode in a larger work; (2) type of English stage-entertainment presented at Christmas-time, loosely founded on a fairy-story or some similar traditional source, interspersed with songs and formerly concluded by a harlequinade.

PANTONAL(ITY), see ATONAL.

PANTOUM (Fr.), type of quatrain of Malayan origin introduced into French verse by Hugo and used by Ravel to describe what is in effect the scherzo (second of four movements) of his piano trio, 1914.

PANUFNIK, ANDREZEJ (b. 1914), Polish composer of three symphonies (No. 3, 'Sinfonia Sacra'), 'Lullaby' for twenty-nine strings and two harps (with some use of quarter-tones), Polish folk-song settings, etc.; also conductor. Left Poland in protest against political regimentation and came to England, 1954; conductor, City of Birmingham Symphony Orchestra, 1957–9.

PAPILLONS (Fr., Butterflies), twelve short dance pieces by Schumann, op.2 (1829-31); thematically connected with Schumann's 'CARNIVAL'.

PARADIES, (PIETRO) DOMENICO (or Paradisi; 1710–92), Italian harpsichordist, composer of operas, etc., as well as of harpsichord works. Lived for many years as teacher in London.

PARADISE AND THE PERI (Ger., *Das Paradies und die Peri*), cantata by Schumann, 1843, with German text translated from part of T. Moore's 'Lalla Rookh'. The Peri here is a good spirit of Persian mythology, seeking readmittance to Heaven; cp. 'THE PERI' and 'IOLANTHE'.

PARALLEL MOTION, see MOTION.

PARAY, PAUL CHARLES (b. 1886), French conductor – of the Colonne Orchestra, Paris, since 1933; also much associated with the Israel Philharmonic Orchestra, and has conducted in Britain, U.S.A., etc. Also composer of oratorio 'Joan of Arc' and a Mass for the 500th anniversary of her death; orchestral works, etc.

PARERGON (Gk, accessory work), term used by R. Strauss in his 'Parergon to the SYMPHONIA DOMESTICA' for piano (left hand) and orchestra, 1925, partly based on the same material as the other work.

PARIS CONSERVATOIRE ORCHESTRA, properly Orchestra de la Société des Concerts du Conservatoire de Paris, French orchestra founded 1828 and conducted since 1947 by André Cluytens.

PARIS: THE SONG OF A GREAT CITY, orchestral work by Delius, 1899, styled a 'Nocturne'; produced as ballet (entitled 'Nocturne'), 1936.

'PARIS' SYMPHONIES (Haydn's), a set of six symphonies composed by Haydn in or shortly after 1785, mainly for a series of concerts in Paris – nos. 82 ('THE BEAR'), 83 ('THE HEN'), 84, 85 ('THE QUEEN') 86, 87.

'PARIS' SYMPHONY (Mozart's), nickname for Mozart's symphony

no. 31 in D, composed in Paris for a performance there 1778.

PARKER, CLIFTON (b. 1905), English composer of film music – also of opera and incidental music to plays, etc. Formerly pianist.

PARKER, HORATIO (WILLIAM) (1863–1919), American composer and organist; pupil of Rheinberger in Germany. Wrote 'Hora Novissima' and other oratorios; also two operas, symphony, organ concerto, etc. D.Mus., Cambridge (England), 1902.

PARLANDO, PARLANTE (It., speaking) – either as a literal instruction (e.g. in opera), or as a direction in song indicating a near approach to a speaking tone.

PARODY MASS (or, Lat., *missa parodia*), a type of Mass flourishing in the 16th century, based on musical material taken from another work by the same or another composer. (No 'parody' in the modern sense is implied.)

PARROTT, (HORACE) IAN (b. 1916), English composer of orchestral and piano works, opera 'The Black Ram' etc., writer on music, and professor at University College, Aberystwyth.

PARRY, (CHARLES) HUBERT (HASTINGS) (1848–1918), English composer of 'BLEST PAIR OF SIRENS', 'SONGS OF FAREWELL' and other choral works, unison song 'Jerusalem', many solo settings of notable English verse; also of five symphonies, an opera, oratorios (e.g. JOB, JUDITH), much chamber music, etc. By his works and teaching, much influenced (as did Stanford) the creation of a distinctively English modern school of composers. Also writer on music, director of the Royal College of Music (1894–1918), professor at Oxford (1900–8). Knighted 1898; baronet 1903. No relation of Joseph Parry.

PARRY, JOSEPH (1841–1903), Welsh composer of hymn-tune 'Aberystwyth' (sung to 'Jesu, lover of my soul') and other hymns; also of operas, oratorios, orchestral works, etc. Of very poor origins, was sent to the R.A.M. by a fund raised in Britain and the U.S.A. (where he had spent some years). Became professor at Aberystwyth. No relation of C. H. H. Parry.

PARSIFAL, opera by Wagner, produced in Bayreuth, 1882; libretto by composer: the hero being the 'simpleton without guile' who restores a scared spear to the Knights of the Holy Grail (see also LOHENGRIN). Wagner described the work as a *Bühnenweihfestspiel*, approximately a Sacred Festival Play.

PART, (1) the music of a particular performer in an ensemble – *the tenor part*, *the flute part*, etc.; *score and parts*, expression contrasting the score (containing the music of all performers) with the music written separately for individuals; hence – (2) an individual 'strand' of music, whether or not it is actually performed by one or more; a *fugue in four parts* or *four-part fugue*, etc.; so also PART-SONG, PART-WRITING; (3) a section e.g. of an oratorio, a complete evening's work being thus divided into *parts* so that intervals can be made.

PARTE (It.), equals PART (1, 2); *colla parte*, with the (solo) part, i.e. the accompanying instrument(s) accommodating the soloist to allow some licence of tempo.

PARTHENIA (Gk, maidenhood), fanciful title given to the first book of keyboard music ever printed in England, 1611, containing pieces by Bull, Byrd, and O. Gibbons. Full title, *Parthenia, or the Maidenhead of the first music that ever was printed for the virginals.* A succeeding volume was called *Parthenia inviolata* (a pun on 'unviolated' and 'set for viols').

PARTIAL, name given to each of the notes of the HARMONIC SERIES, the lowest or 'fundamental' being the *first partial* and the others (numbered upwards consecutively) *upper partials.*

PARTIE (Fr.), (1) PART (in all senses); (2) PARTITA.

PARTITA (It.), suite – term used much in the 18th century, occasionally revived since. See also FELDPARTIE, MONOPARTITA.

PARTITION, PARTITUR (Fr., Ger.,), equal SCORE.

PARTOS, OEDOEN (b. 1907), Hungarian-born Israeli viola-player and composer who settled in Palestine 1938; works include 'In Memoriam' (Heb., *Yizkor*) for viola and orchestra, and a choral fantasy on Yemenite Jewish themes.

PART-SONG, (literally) any song written for several vocal PARTS, as distinct from a solo or unison song; but the term is chiefly applied to certain types of work (particularly in the 19th and 20th centuries) in which the highest vocal line has the chief melodic interest, the other voices (and sometimes piano) accompanying – in contrast to, e.g., the MADRIGAL, where all voices are supposed to have equal melodic importance.

PART-WRITING, the laying-out of a composition so that each part (see PART, 2) progresses euphoniously. (The U.S. term, 'voice-leading', was introduced as translation of Ger. *Stimmführung* by immigrant musicians unaware of the established English term.)

PAS (Fr.), step (in dancing, etc.); *pas d'action*, ballet scene of a dramatic nature; *pas seul*, *pas de deux*, etc., dance for one person, for two, etc.

PASHCHENKO, ANDREI FILIPOVICH (b. 1883), Russian composer of 'Eagles Rebellion' and other operas, ten symphonies, 'Requiem' (to his own text, in memory of Russian soldiers of the Second World War), etc.

PASODOBLE (Sp., double step), modern Spanish dance in quick 2/4 time – used, in a spirit of parody, in Walton's 'FAÇADE'.

PASQUINI, BERNARDO (1637–1710), Italian organist, harpsichordist, and composer of operas, harpsichord sonatas, etc.

PASSACAGLIA, piece (originally a dance) in which a theme is continually repeated – but, unlike the CHACONNE, not necessarily always in the bass.

PASSAGE, a section of a musical composition – sometimes, not always, with the implication of not having much structural importance (e.g.

when a piece is said to contain 'showy passage-work' for a soloist's display).

PASSING-NOTE, in harmony, a note which forms a discord with the chord with which it is heard, but which is 'justified' because it is melodically placed between two notes which are not discordant. E.g. the D in the two examples below: the melody appears merely to be 'passing' on the discordant D between the two notes E and C, both concordant. When, however, the discordant note occurs between two repetitions of the same concordant note, a different term is used: see AUXILIARY NOTE.

PASSION, a musical setting of the biblical story of Christ's death, properly to be sung in churches in the week before Easter. Works of this character exist as Latin motets (e.g. by Byrd and Lassus), but the term is usually reserved for larger works written in the vernacular tongue – notably those in German by Bach (ST JOHN PASSION, ST MATTHEW PASSION) and earlier by Schütz. These have a semi-dramatic form, individual singers taking the parts of Christ, Judas, etc. The so-called *Passion Chorale* (see CHORALE) is the hymn 'O Haupt voll Blut und Wunden' (usually translated 'O Sacred Head'), originally by Hassler, which Bach used prominently in both his Passions as part of the (non-biblical) commentary made by soloists and chorus on the story: other hymn-tunes are similarly incorporated. See also GRAUN; PEPPING (for one of the few modern examples); A CHILD OF OUR TIME (for a parallel).

PASSION, or (It.) *La Passione*, nickname for Haydn's symphony no. 49 in F minor, 1768, from the intensity of emotion it conveys (no religious significance).

PASTICCIO (It., a pie), operatic work with music drawn for the purpose from works by different composers – as commonly in the 18th century; see e.g., 'LOVE IN A VILLAGE'. The term might well be extended to include a complementary phenomenon – a work with music drawn from different works by the same composer, e.g., 'VIENNA BLOOD'.

PASTICHE (Fr.), (1) PASTICCIO; (2) a piece composed deliberately in the style of another composer.

PASTORAL (noun), (1) obsolete term for a stage entertainment with a rustic setting – e.g. Handel's 'ACIS AND GALATEA'; (2) title of a work by Bliss for mezzo-soprano, chorus, and small orchestra, on 'pastoral' poems by various writers; first performed 1929. See also the following entries.

'PASTORAL' SONATA, nickname (not the composer's) for Beethoven's piano sonata in D, op. 28, 1801: the last movement may seem to suggest a dance to a rustic bagpipe.

PASTORAL SYMPHONY, (1) Beethoven's own title for his symphony no. 6 in F, first performed 1808. Title goes on '... or Memories of Life in the Country (the expression of feeling, rather than painting)' – the five movements having allusive titles (e.g. no. 2, 'By the Brook', this movement having imitations of quail, cuckoo, and nightingale); (2) title of an orchestral interlude in Handel's 'MESSIAH', referring to the shepherds to whom Christ's birth was announced, and said to be based on an Italian folk-melody heard by Handel (cp. PIFFERO) – this not being a SYMPHONY in the modern sense; (3) title ('A Pastoral Symphony') of Vaughan Williams's symphony no. 3 (but, in conformity with his practice, not numbered by him); it has a wordless high voice in the last movement – first performed in 1922.

PASTOURELLE, light French song of pastoral character, cultivated especially in the 18th century.

'PATHETIC' SONATA, title given by Beethoven (in French, as 'Sonate pathétique') to his piano sonata in C minor, op. 13, composed about 1798.

'PATHETIC' SYMPHONY, name (authorized by composer) for Tchaikovsky's symphony no. 6, 1893. See DAMROSCH.

PATHÉTIQUE (Fr.), see preceding entries.

PATIENCE, *or Bunthorne's Bride*, operetta by Sullivan, produced in London, 1881. Libretto by W. S. Gilbert. Patience, the dairymaid heroine of this satire on 'aestheticism', does not become the bride of the poet Bunthorne – nor does anyone.

PATTER SONG, type of comic song (especially in opera) dependent for its effect on the rapid enunciation of syllables – usually a solo, though Sullivan has a patter-trio in 'RUDDIGORE'.

PAUKE(N) (Ger.), kettledrum(s); *Paukenmesse*, see DRUM MASS; *Sinfonie mit dem Paukenschlag* (symphony with the drum-stroke) see SURPRISE SYMPHONY; *Sinfonie mit dem Paukenwirbel*, see DRUM-ROLL SYMPHONY.

PAULUS, see ST PAUL.

PAUSA (It.), a REST (not a PAUSE, It. *fermata*).

PAUSE (Eng.), (1) the sign .., meaning that the note or rest so marked must be held longer than normally, to an extent determined by the performer's discretion – though the composer may add the words 'short' or 'long' in various languages as an additional indication; (2) term used in the phrase *general pause*, meaning a rest of one or more bars for all performers (abbr. G. P.), See also next entry.

PAUSE (Ger.), (1) a PAUSE (as in English, above); (2) a REST; (3) an interval (in a concert, etc.).

PAVAN, PAVANE (Eng., Fr.), slow stately dance dating at least from the 16th century, and mentioned in Shakespeare; it was often followed by the quicker GALLIARD. Fauré's work so entitled (1887) is for orchestra and optional chorus; Ravel's 'Pavan for a dead Infanta' (Fr., *Pavane pour une Infante défunte*), was composed for piano in 1899 and later orchestrated. (Note that *pavan*, accented on first syllable, is the authentic English form.)

PAVILLON (Fr.), the 'bell' (extremity opposite to the mouthpiece) of a horn, trumpet, etc. (Named from its pavilion-like shape.) So, as direction to brass-players, *pavillons en l'air*, with the bells held high up so as to increase the volume. But for *pavillon chinois* (i.e., Chinese), see JINGLING JOHNNY.

PAZ, JUAN CARLOS (b. 1897), Argentinian composer who uses TWELVE-NOTE technique and has also been influenced by jazz. Works include stage and orchestral music, 'Music for Trio' (clarinet, saxophone, trumpet) and other chamber music, and piano solos.

PEARL-FISHERS, THE (Fr., *Les Pêcheurs de perles*), opera by Bizet, produced in Paris, 1863. Libretto by E. Cormon and M. Carré: the scene is set in Ceylon, though the characters are called Indians.

PEARS, PETER (b. 1910), English tenor, much associated with Britten – who wrote for him the leading tenor parts in his operas and other works (e.g. 'PETER GRIMES', 'SERENADE', 'WAR REQUIEM'). Internationally distinguished also in Bach, etc.; also choral conductor, translator, and writer on musical subjects.

PEARSALL, ROBERT LUCAS (calling himself de Pearsall; 1795–1856), English composer, chiefly of vocal music – madrigals in 16th-century style, part-songs, Anglican and Roman Catholic church music, etc. Settled in Germany and died there.

PEARSON, H. H., see PIERSON.

PÊCHEURS DE PERLES, LES, see THE PEARL-FISHERS.

PEDAL, (1, in harmony) a note sustained below (i.e., at the foot of) changing harmonies: this is called a *pedal* or *pedal point* or *pedal bass*, and if it is thus sustained but not in the bass it is an *inverted pedal* (cp. INVERT, 1); (2) the lowest ('fundamental') note of the HARMONIC SERIES, especially with reference to the playing of brass instruments. (3) a foot-operated lever – see HARP, HARPSICHORD. KETTLEDRUM, ORGAN, PIANO. See also following entries.

PEDAL CLARINET, see CLARINET.

PEDAL POINT, see PEDAL (1).

PEDAL-BOARD, a keyboard played with the feet – such as is normally found on the organ, sometimes on the harpsichord, and rarely attached to a piano (see PEDAL-PIANO).

PÉDALIER (Fr.), (1) PEDAL BOARD, (2) PEDAL PIANO.

PEDAL-PIANO, a piano fitted with a pedal keyboard in addition to its ordinary one – used by organists for home practice, but also written for expressly, e.g. by Schumann and Alkan.

PEDRELL, FELIPE (1841–1922), Spanish musicologist, editor of old Spanish music; as teacher of Falla, Granados, and others, was the principal 'midwife' of the 20th-century Spanish-nationalist school of composition. Himself also composer of operas, church music, symphonic poems, etc. See GERHARD.

PEEL, (GERALD) GRAHAM (1877–1937), English composer of more

than 100 songs to poems by Housman, Masefield, etc.

PEER GYNT, play by Ibsen (named after its boasting folk-hero) for which Grieg wrote incidental music for the original production, 1876: two orchestral suites are drawn from this. An opera by Egk (1938) is also based on the play. Incidental music to the play has also been written by Saeverud (1948).

PEERSON, MARTIN (*c.* 1580–*c.* 1650), English composer of church music and other vocal music, and also works for viols and for virginals, etc.; master of the choristers at St Paul's, London.

PEETERS, FLOR (b. 1903), Belgian organist, pianist, musical editor, composer of organ concerto, organ solos, songs, etc.

PELLÉAS AND MÉLISANDE (Fr., *Pelléas et Mélisande*), play by Maeterlinck, 1892 (named from its ill-fated medieval lovers) – source of (1) opera by Debussy, almost a word-for-word setting of the play, produced in Paris, 1902; (2) incidental music to the play composed by Fauré, 1898, and by Sibelius, 1905; (3) symphonic poem by Schoenberg, composed 1902–3, first performed 1905.

PENDERECKI, KRZYSTOF (b. 1933), Polish composer of a 'St Luke Passion' (solo singers, chorus, orchestra), Canon for fifty-two string instruments and magnetic tape, etc.

PENILLION (Welsh, pl.), a type of traditional Welsh singing, in which verses (either given or improvised) are sung in counterpoint to a well-known melody played on the harp. Term used also as title of an orchestral work by Grace Williams, 1955, based on the musical ideas of traditional penillion.

PENNY WHISTLE, see TIN-WHISTLE.

PENTATONIC (from Gk *pente*, five), term used of a scale comprising only five notes – particularly that represented by the five black keys of the piano (or other notes in the same position relative to each other). This form of pentatonic scale is widely used in folk-music of many countries – Scottish, Chinese, American Negro (e.g. 'Swing Low, Sweet Chariot'), etc.

PENTLAND, BARBARA (b. 1912), Canadian composer who studied in New York; also university teacher. Works include two symphonies, three string quartets, choral pieces. Uses TWELVE-NOTE technique.

PEPPING, ERNST (b. 1901), German composer, chiefly of Protestant church music – unaccompanied motets, a 'St Matthew PASSION' etc., in a style sometimes harking back to pre-Bach models; also of orchestral and piano works.

PEPUSCH, JOHANN CHRISTOPH (also known in England as John Christopher; 1667–1752), German-born composer (also organist) who settled in London about 1700, and died there. Arranged the music for the original production of 'THE BEGGAR'S OPERA'; also composed other stage music, church music, concertos, etc., and wrote theoretical treatises.

PER (It.), by, through, for, etc.; *per archi*, for strings; *dramma per musica*, drama through music, i.e. opera.

PERAGALLO, MARIO (b. 1910), Italian composer, pupil of Casella and others; employs TWELVE-NOTE technique. Works include operas, piano concerto, violin concerto, string quartets, and 'Music for Double String Quartet'; also 'The Hill' (after E. L. Masters's 'Spoon River Anthology') and other choral works.

PERCUSSION, collective name for instruments in which a resonating surface is struck by the player – usually directly by hand or stick, but sometimes through leverage as in the type of bass-drum used in dance-bands, operated by a pedal. The piano and celesta come technically within this definition of percussion instruments but are not conventionally so classified: however, the piano is sometimes said to be 'employed as a percussion instrument' (i.e. for percussive rather than melodic effect) in such 20th-century works as Stravinsky's 'THE WEDDING'. Percussion instruments as used today in the symphony orchestra, dance band, etc., may be tuned to a definite pitch (see, e.g., KETTLEDRUM, tubular BELL, GLOCKENSPIEL, XYLOPHONE, VIBRAPHONE, MARIMBA) or may be of indefinite pitch, e.g. TRIANGLE, GONG, CASTANETS, WHIP, RATTLE, ANVIL, and the following drums – SIDE DRUM, TENOR DRUM, BASS DRUM, TABOR, TAMBOURINE, BONGO; the TOM-TOM may be of definite or indefinite pitch, the normal CYMBALS are of indefinite pitch but the so-called 'ancient CYMBAL' is not. Certain freak instruments e.g. motor-horn, iron chains are placed with the percussion section when brought (exceptionally) into the orchestra. The common British practice, in listing the members of an orchestra, of referring to 'timpani [i.e. kettledrums] and percussion' as though these were mutually exclusive is absurd: the reason for the practice is that the kettledrummer counts as the senior player and confines himself to the kettledrums, the other players taking any other instruments specified. See also Percussion Band.

PERCUSSION BAND, an assembly of percussion instruments as used in schools, normally with a piano. The percussion instruments mark various rhythms – hence the alternative name, 'rhythm band'.

PERDENDOSI (It., losing itself), direction for performance indicating 'softer and softer until dying away'.

PERFECT, (1) term used to describe the intervals of a fourth, fifth, and eighth (octave) in their 'standard' dimensions – e.g. C up to F, to G, and to C respectively. They become DIMINISHED if lessened by a semitone and AUGMENTED if enlarged by a semitone. (2) type of cadence: see CADENCE. (3) term used in the phrase 'perfect time', meaning (in medieval music) triple time. (4) term used in the phrase 'perfect pitch': see PITCH.

PERFECT FOOL, THE opera by Holst, produced in London, 1923. Libretto by composer. The work parodies the operatic manner of other composers; the title refers not to any of them, however, but to the simpleton hero.

PERGAMENT, MOSES (b. 1893), Swedish (Finnish-born) composer.

Works include piano concerto, ballets, orchestral pieces; some are linked with Jewish subjects.

PERGOLESI, GIOVANNI BATTISTA (1710–36), Italian composer, also violinist and church organist; wrote serious and comic operas, among the latter the enormously successful 'THE MAID AS MISTRESS'. (Imported into France, it provoked a quarrel between supporters of French and Italian opera – the so-called 'War of the Buffoons'.) Died of tuberculosis. Afterwards, in order to capitalize on his popularity, many works not his were ascribed to him and still commonly are – among them the opera 'THE MUSIC MASTER', concertinos for strings, the songs 'Se tu m'ami' (used by Stravinsky in 'PULCINELLA') and 'Tre giorni son che Nina'. Authentic works include a 'STABAT MATER' for female voices.

PERI, JACOPO (1561–1633), Italian composer who, as member of the Florentine artistic set called the CAMERATA, wrote what is often considered the first real opera – 'Eurydice' (1600). Also composed other operas (some in collaboration with other composers), ballets madrigals, etc. Was a priest in service to the Medici family.

PERI, THE (Fr., *La Péri*), ballet with music by Dukas – the score being described as a 'dance-poem' – produced in Paris, 1912. A peri is here a good female spirit of Persian mythology: cp. PARADISE AND THE PERI; IOLANTHE.

PEROSI, LORENZO (1872–1956), Italian priest and composer of more than thirty Masses, a series of New Testament oratorios, etc.: these had a notable but short-lived success. Suffered from mental illness.

PÉROTIN (Latinized as Perotinus), French composer active in the early 13th century; composed liturgical music showing a high degree of structural organization, in the style later known as ARS ANTIQUA.

PERPETUAL CANON, see CANON.

PERPETUUM MOBILE, see MOTO.

PERSEPHONE, stage work by Stravinsky for speaker, singers, and orchestra (styled 'MELODRAMA'); produced in Paris, 1933. Libretto, on the Greek myth, by A. Gide.

PERSICHETTI, VINCENT (b. 1915), American composer, pupil of Roy Harris. Works include four symphonies, concerto for piano duet and orchestra, ballet 'King Lear', sonatas for violin alone and for cello alone.

PESANTE (It.), heavily.

PETER AND THE WOLF (Rus., *Petya i volk*), 'musical tale for children' by Prokofiev, first performed 1936; a narrator's words are illustrated by the orchestra.

PETER GRIMES, opera by Britten, produced in London, 1945. Libretto by M. Slater, after Crabbe's poem 'The Borough'; named after its misanthropic fisherman hero.

PETERKIN, NORMAN (b. 1886), English composer of many songs; also of chamber music, etc. Self-taught. Formerly head of a music-publishing firm.

PETIT(E) (Fr.), little; *petite flûte*, PICCOLO.

PETRASSI, GOFFREDO (b. 1904), Italian composer, formerly choirboy, Works include opera 'Death in the Air', six concertos for orchestra. 'Portrait of Don Quixote' for orchestra, Introduction and Allegro for violin and eleven instruments; 'Choir of the Dead' (*Coro dei Morti*) and other choral works including 'Nonsense' (title in English) on poems by Edward Lear in Italian translation; piano works, songs, etc. Rejects the label 'neo-classical' which the harmonically and formally clear style of most of his works suggests.

PÉTROUCHKA, see next entry.

PETRUSHKA, ballet with music by Stravinsky, produced in Paris, 1911. The suite drawn from it was revised in 1947. Petruskha is a traditional Russian puppet figure: 'Pétrouchka', the French transliteration of his name, is suitable only for French usage.

PETTO, VOCE DI, equals CHEST VOICE.

PEZZO (It., pl. -*i*), a piece, a play, a musical work, etc.

PFITZNER, HANS (ERICH) (1869–1949), German composer, born in Moscow; also pianist, conductor, and writer – attacking Busoni and modernism generally, from a traditionalist German-Romantic standpoint. Works include 'PALESTRINA' and other operas, piano concerto, violin concerto, chamber music, songs (some with orchestra).

PHANTASIE, PHANTASY (Ger., Eng.), see FANTASY.

PHILADELPHIA ORCHESTRA, American orchestra established in 1900; Stokowski, whose conductorship (1912–38) made it particularly famous, was succeeded by Eugene Ormandy.

PHILHARMONIA ORCHESTRA, see NEW PHILHARMONIA.

PHILHARMONIC (from Gk, meaning friendly to harmony), term used as title of various orchestras and other musical bodies. Not that *philharmonic orchestra* merely identifies a particular orchestra; it does not also stand for a type of orchestra, as 'symphony orchestra' does: see ORCHESTRA. *Old Philharmonic pitch* and *New Philharmonic pitch* are two standards of PITCH, both now obsolete.

PHILIDOR, surname of a French musical family of whom the most important is François Philidor.

PHILIDOR, FRANÇOIS ANDRÉ DANICAN (1726–95), French composer especially of operas (see OPÉRA-COMIQUE) including 'TOM JONES'; also of a Requiem for Rameau, etc. He was also noted as a chess-player. Died in London.

PHILIPS, PETER (1561–1628), English composer of madrigals, motets, pieces for virginals, etc.; also organist. A Roman Catholic, he worked mainly in the Low Countries (then under Spanish rule) and died probably in Brussels.

PHILLIPS, MONTAGUE (FAWCETT) (b. 1885), English composer best known for his light music (operetta 'The Rebel Maid', many songs); has also written symphony, piano concerto, etc.

PHILOMUSICA OF LONDON, new name adopted by the former Boyd

Neel Orchestra (see NEEL) in 1957. It is a chamber orchestra which has specialized in 18th-century music.

PHILOSOPHER, THE, nickname for Haydn's symphony no. 22 in E♭, 1764, perhaps because it has a grave first movement instead of the customary lively one.

PHOEBUS AND PAN, commonly used title for 'The Contest Between Phoebus and Pan' (Ger., *Der Streit zwischen Phöbus und Pan*), cantata by Bach satirizing (in the character of Midas) a hostile music critic. In the 20th century it has been given as an opera.

PHRASE, a small group of notes forming what is recognized as a unit of melody; so *to phrase* and *phrasing*, terms used in regard to a performer's correctly observing the division of a melody into phrases. So also *phrase-mark*, a line linking written notes and indicating that they belong to one phrase.

PHRYGIAN CADENCE, see CADENCE.

PHRYGIAN MODE, the MODE represented by the white keys of the piano beginning on E.

PIACERE, A (It.), at pleasure, i.e. (in performance) at the performer's discretion, especially as meaning that strict time need not be observed.

PIACEVOLE (It.), agreeably, pleasantly, easily.

PIANGENDO (It., weeping), plaintive(ly).

PIANINO, a small upright piano.

PIANISSIMO (abbr. *pp*), very softly, superlative of PIANO, 1.

PIANO (It.), (1) soft, abbr. *p*; so *pianissimo* or *pp*, very soft. (2) common English word for the keyboard instrument called in Italian *pianoforte* (literally soft-loud) – the shorter term being more convenient than the longer, and no worse English. The instrument, distinguished e.g. from harpsichord and clavichord by having its strings struck with hammers, was invented shortly after 1700 (see also FORTEPIANO), and by 1800 had almost displaced the harpsichord. The modern piano is iron-framed and normally has eighty-eight keys: it is either *upright* (i.e. the strings are vertical) or *grand* (i.e. they are horizontal). It has a 'sustaining pedal' (wrongly called 'loud pedal') operated by the right foot to prolong the sound by holding off the dampers; and a 'soft pedal' (left foot) lessening the volume by causing fewer than the normal number of strings to be struck or by bringing the hammers nearer the strings before they start their movement. On a minority of pianos, there is also a centre pedal enabling selected notes to be sustained independently of others. An obsolete early form of piano is the *square piano* (oblong, box-like in shape, horizontally strung) sometimes miscalled 'SPINET' (really quite a different instrument). Used universally as a solo, accompanying, and chamber-music instrument, it has also been used (particularly in the 20th century) as an ordinary member of the orchestra and in the manner of a special percussion instrument (see, e.g., Stravinsky's 'THE WEDDING'). Instruments have also been made with double keyboards (see MOÓR), with quarter-tone tuning, etc., but none have become standard. See also PEDAL PIANO; PREPARED PIANO; STREET PIANO; and (for an experiment in harnessing the piano to electronic sound-processes) ELECTROCHORD. See also following entries.

PIANO ORGAN, see STREET PIANO.

PIANO QUARTET, see QUARTET.

PIANO QUINTET, see QUINTET.

PIANO SCORE, see SCORE.

PIANO TRIO, see TRIO.

PIANOFORTE, Italian name for the instrument more commonly called *piano* in English. The name literally means 'soft-loud', alluding to the much greater possibilities of grading volume than on the harpsichord. See PIANO.

PIANOLA, see PLAYER-PIANO.

PIATIGORSKY, GREGOR (b. 1903), Russian-born cellist who settled in U.S.A., becoming naturalized in 1942; internationally noted as soloist. Has composed and arranged works for cello.

PIBROCH (Gael., *piobaireachd*), type of Scottish Highland bagpipe music, in a kind of elaborate variation-form.

PICARDY THIRD or (Fr.) *tierce de Picardie*, the major third used at the end of a piece otherwise in the minor key, converting the expected minor chord into a major one. The effect was common up to the mid-18th century; its occasional subsequent use tends to the effect of archaism.

PICCINNI, NICOLA (or Piccini; 1728–1800), Italian composer of more than 100 operas including 'The Good Girl' (*La buona figliola*), after Richardson's *Pamela;* also of oratorios, church music, etc. Lived partly in Paris, and died there. His Paris supporters clashed with those of Gluck (both composers wrote an opera on 'IPHIGENIA IN TAURIS', for instance) though there was no personal enmity between the two men.

PICCOLO, small flute pitched an octave above the standard flute, used in the orchestra and military band. (The name is from It. *flauto piccolo*, small flute, but the current It. term is *ottavino* from the word for octave.)

PICK-MANGIAGALLI, RICCARDO (1882–1949), Czech-born composer, partly of Italian descent; naturalized Italian. Became director of Milan Conservatory. Works include operas, ballets, piano pieces.

PICTURES AT AN EXHIBITION (Rus., *Kartinki s vistavki*), piano work by Mussorgsky, 1874, giving a musical 'reproduction' of ten pictures by the Russian artist Victor Hartmann; a 'Promenade' is used as an introduction and linking passage. Orchestral versions of the work have been made by Ravel, Henry Wood, Stokowski, and Walter Goehr; also, first of all, by an otherwise unknown Russian, Tushmalov (1881).

PIERNÉ, (HENRI CONSTANT) GABRIEL (1863–1937), French organist, conductor, and composer of 'The Children's Crusade' for children's choir and orchestra, orchestral suites, operas, ballets – including 'Cydalise and the Satyr', from which comes the 'ENTRY OF THE LITTLE FAUNS'.

PIERROT LUNAIRE (Fr., Moonstruck Pierrot), (cycle of 'three times seven' songs by Schoenberg for voice, flute (also piccolo), clarinet (also bass-clarinet), violin (also viola), cello, and piano, to poems, translated into German from the French of Albert Giraud – first performed 1912.

PIERSON, HENRY HUGO (originally Pearson; 1815–73), English composer who, after resigning from his Edinburgh professorship, settled in Germany in the mid-1840's. Died there. Wrote notable songs and part-songs (including 'Ye Mariners of England'), also German operas, English oratorio 'Jerusalem', etc.

PIFA, see PIFFERO.

PIFFERARO, a player on the Piffero.

PIFFERO, type of rustic Italian wind-instrument, to whose characteristic music Handel apparently alludes in writing the word *pifa* above the music of the 'PASTORAL SYMPHONY' in 'Messiah'.

PIJPER, WILLEM (1894–1937), Dutch composer, also writer on music; pupil of J. Wagenaar. Came early under the influence of Debussy, but was later drawn towards POLYTONALITY and other 'modernisms', and to a more contrapuntal style. Works include three symphonies and the piece called 'Six Symphonic Epigrams'; five string quartets (no. 5 unfinished) and other chamber music; opera 'Halewijn', music to plays, piano pieces, etc. Also arranged Dutch folksongs. Very active as teacher, influencing most of the younger Dutch composers of his day.

PILGRIM'S PROGRESS, THE, opera by Vaughan Williams, produced in London, 1951. Officially styled 'a Morality'; libretto by composer, after Bunyan. It incorporates the composer's earlier one-act opera, 'The Shepherds of the Delectable Mountains' (London, 1922).

PILKINGTON, FRANCIS (*c.* 1562–1638), English composer, also clergyman. Composed madrigals (one in 'THE TRIUMPHS OF ORIANA'), songs with lute, anthems, lute solos, etc.

PINEAPPLE POLL, ballet with music adapted by Mackerras from the Gilbert and Sullivan operettas, produced in London, 1951. The story is based on one of Gilbert's 'Bab Ballads'.

PINES OF ROME (It., *Pini di Roma*), orchestral work by Respighi, in four linked movements, referring to the pines of four Roman sites; first performed 1924. The score includes a nightingale (on a gramophone record). Cp. FOUNTAINS OF ROME.

PINSUTI, CIRO (1829–88), Italian composer of more than 200 songs; also of opera 'The Merchant of Venice' (after Shakespeare), piano works, etc. Taught for many years in London.

PINTO, GEORGE FREDERICK (*c.* 1875–1806), English composer of songs, piano sonatas, duets for two violins, etc.; also pianist and violinist.

PINZA, EZIO (FORTUNATO) (1892–1957), Italian bass who settled in U.S.A.; after noted operatic career (Metropolitan Opera, New York, from 1926), appeared in films, Broadway 'musicals', etc.

PIPE, a hollow cylinder or cone in which air vibrates, e.g. in an organ or a blown wind-instrument; (term also used for) type of simple wind-instrument itself composed only of such a cylinder or cone without mechanism – e.g. the three-holed pipe used in English folk dancing with the TABOR, and the *bamboo pipes* (of various sizes mainly used educationally.

PIQUE DAME, German translation (not French, which would be *La Dame de Pique*) of the original title of Tchaikovsky's opera 'THE QUEEN OF SPADES'. Its use in English-speaking countries implies ignorance or snobbery.

PIRATES OF PENZANCE, THE, *or The Slave of Duty*, operetta by Sullivan, produced at Paignton (Devon), 1879, for reasons of copyright: 'official' first performance in New York the next day. Libretto by W. S. Gilbert: the pirates are all 'noblemen who have gone wrong'.

PISTON, equals VALVE (on brass instruments). Hence in French *piston* is also used as an abbreviation for *cornet-à-pistons*, i.e. the ordinary cornet.

PISTON, WALTER (b. 1894), American composer, pupil of N. Boulanger in Paris; professor at Harvard, author of important textbooks. Works, in a lithe, modern (but always basically tonal) idiom, include six symphonies, violin concerto, three string quartets, ballet 'THE INCREDIBLE FLUTIST'.

PITCH, the property according to which notes appear to be (in the conventional phrase) 'high' or 'low' in relation to each other – a property scientifically determined by the frequency of vibrations of the sound-producing agent (see FREQUENCY). So *concert pitch* is the standard of pitch to which instruments are normally tuned for performance. By international agreement of 1939, the tuning-note A (directly above middle C) is fixed at a frequency of 440; this makes middle C 261.6, and the C higher 523.2 (i.e. twice the frequency of the octave below, as is the invariable rule). But in scientific investigation it is found mathematically convenient to suppose this C to have a frequency of 512 (i.e. 2^9). Certain wind instruments are said by dealers to have *low pitch:* this means that they are built to modern concert-pitch, not to the *high pitch* (nearly a semitone higher) which is used for brass bands and was formerly used also for military bands. *Old Philharmonic* and *New Philharmonic pitch* are the names of two higher standards of pitch now obsolete. *Absolute pitch* or *perfect pitch*, term for the faculty possessed by those who on hearing a note can identify it by name: it would be better to call this not *absolute pitch* but *an absolute sense of pitch*, etc. – though in fact such a faculty of identification is really not absolute but relative (to the nearest whole-tone, semitone, etc.).

PITFIELD, THOMAS (BARON) (b. 1903), English composer of 'A Sketch-Book of Women' and other cantatas, also of piano concerto, chamber music, etc. Is also a poet (writing the texts for his own music), draughtsman, and craftsman in wood.

PIÙ (It.), more; *più lento*, slower.

PIUTTOSTO (It.), rather, somewhat.

PIXIS, JOHANN PETER (1788–1874), German pianist, composer of piano music, operas, etc.; contributor to the 'HEXAMERON'.

PIZZETTI, ILDEBRANDO (1880–1968), Italian composer of 'The Daughter of Jorio', 'DEBORAH AND JAEL', and other operas – one, MURDER IN THE CATHEDRAL, on T. S. Eliot's play; also of incidental music for plays, piano concerto, cello concerto, 'Prelude to Another Day' and other orchestral works, choral works, chamber music, etc. – all in a basically 'traditional' style. Also writer on music, and noted teacher.

PIZZICATO (It., pinched), direction that notes on bowed string instruments are to be plucked, not bowed; abbr. *pizz.* So *pizzicato tremolando*, direction used by Elgar in his violin concerto to make the orchestral string-players 'thrum' rapidly with the fingers across the strings.

PLAGAL CADENCE, see CADENCE.

PLAGAL MODES, see MODE.

PLAINCHANT, PLAINSONG, type of medieval church music which in its final form called GREGORIAN CHANT survives in Roman Catholic use today. It consists of a single line of vocal melody (properly unaccompanied) in 'free' rhythm, not divided into regular bar-lengths; it has its own system of notation. (The ritual music of the Greek church – called 'Byzantine music' – and of the Jewish synagogue, though of a somewhat similar type, is not called plainsong.)

PLANETS, THE, orchestral suite by Holst, first performed complete in 1920. Its seven movements treat their subjects from an astrological viewpoint: the last, 'Neptune, the Mystic', uses two three-part female choruses, wordless and unseen.

PLANQUETTE, ROBERT (1848–1903), French composer of 'The Bells of Corneville' and other operettas.

PLAYER-PIANO, general name for a piano fitted with the type of mechanism usually known by such trade names as 'Pianola'. By this mechanism the keys are depressed not by the fingers but by air-pressure supplied by bellows and pedals, or electrically: the air-pressure is applied through perforations on an unwinding paper roll, such perforations being arranged so that a composition is played. There is, of course, no need for the perforations to be restricted to the normal number of notes playable by two (or four) hands. Sometimes the perforations are made mechanically from an actual performance by an eminent pianist, the player-piano then reproducing (within limits) this actual performance: for this reason the alternative name *reproducing piano* is sometimes used.

PLECTRUM, small piece of wood, metal, or other material used to pluck the strings of lute, mandolin, banjo, etc.; also the part of the mechanism of the harpsichord which performs an analogous function.

PLEIN(E) (Fr.), full; *plein jeu* (full play), either (1) a type of MIXTURE stop on the organ, or (2) FULL ORGAN.

PLESSIS, HUBERT DU (b. 1922), South African composer, pupil in London of A. Bush. Has written songs to English, Afrikaans, Dutch, and German texts; also Serenade for strings, string quartet, sonata for piano duet, etc.

PLEYEL, IGNAZ JOSEPH (1757–1831), Austrian pianist, violinist, composer (symphonies, chamber music, etc.), pupil of Haydn, and founder of the piano-making firm of Pleyel in Paris. Died in Paris.

PNEUMA (Gk, breath), a type of florid passage sung to a single vowel in plainsong.

POCHETTE (Fr., pocket), small-size violin (small enough to be kept in a long pocket) formerly used by dancing-masters.

POCHETTO, POCHETTINO (It.), very slightly. (Diminutive of POCO.)

POCHISSIMO (It.), very slightly. (Superlative of POCO.)

POCO (It.), slightly. Note the difference in correct Italian between *un poco crescendo* (with a little increase in volume) and *poco crescendo* (with little increase in volume) – i.e. the difference between 'a little' and just 'little' (with its negative sense) in English. But in musical contexts the usage is often loose and the sense is usually 'a little', even without the *un*.

POEM, POEMA, POÈME (Eng., It., Fr.), term which was brought into music by Liszt in the expression SYMPHONIC POEM and which has since been somewhat extended (cp. DANCE POEM); usually implies music based on a narrative. See also following entries.

POEM, title of (1) a movement from Fibich's orchestral serenade, 'At Twilight' (Cz., *V Podrečer*), 1903; (2) work for violin and orchestra, in one movement, by Chausson, 1896 (Fr. *Poème*).

POEM OF ECSTASY, THE (Rus., *Poema ekstasa*), orchestral work by Skriabin (on 'Joy in creative activity') first performed in New York, 1908. Cp. 'DIVINE POEM' and 'PROMETHEUS'.

POEM OF FIRE, see PROMETHEUS.

POEMA, POÈME, see POEM.

POET AND PEASANT (Ger., *Dichter und Bauer*), play to which Suppé wrote the overture and other incidental music.

POET'S LOVE (Ger., *Dichterliebe*), song-cycle by Schumann, 1840, to sixteen poems by Heine.

POI (It.), then; *scherzo da capo, e poi la coda*, repeat the scherzo and then go on to the coda.

POINT, (1) the end of the bow opposite to that held by the hand; (2) see PEDAL, 1 (for *pedal-point*; *organ-point* is the same thing); (3, verb) see POINTING.

POINT D'ORGUE (Fr., organ-point), (1) pedal point (see PEDAL, 1);

(2) the PAUSE, 𝄐; (3) the place in the music – generally a pause on the second inversion of the tonic chord – at which a cadenza in a concerto begins.

POINTILLIST, term borrowed from painting (where it refers to the use of separate dots of pure colour instead of mixed pigments) and applied to music where the notes seem to be applied in isolated 'dots' rather than in normal melodic curves – e.g. certain music of Stockhausen and Nono.

POINTING, in Anglican chant, the allotting of syllables to the notes on which they are to be sung.

POLACCA (It.), equals POLONAISE.

'POLISH' SYMPHONY, nickname for Tchaikovsky's symphony no. 3, 1875; it has a finale in POLONAISE rhythm but has otherwise no claim to the name.

POLKA, a dance in 2/4 time for couples, originating in the 19th century in Bohemia.

POLLY, ballad opera with words by John Gay and musical arrangements by Pepusch – a sequel to THE BEGGAR'S OPERA. It was published 1729, but banned from the London stage as subversive of authority and not produced till 1777. Modern musical arrangements by F. Austin (London, 1922) and J. Addison (Aldeburgh, 1952).

POLO, type of Spanish dance, with song.

POLONAISE (Fr. for 'Polish'), a stately Polish dance in 3/4 time, dating at least from the 16th century: its use for concert pieces goes back at least to Bach. Chopin's thirteen examples are of an ardent, even martial, nature, apparently expressing patriotic sentiments.

POLOVTSIAN DANCES, see PRINCE IGOR.

POLYMETRICAL, combining different METRES simultaneously. So also *polymetry*.

POLYMODAL(ITY), terms which if used correctly would refer to the simultaneous sounding of several different MODES, even if all at the same pitch (i.e. all coming to rest on the same note) – e.g., if a tune in the Dorian mode ending on D was heard against a tune in one of the other modes so transposed that it also ended on D. But in fact the terms are confusingly used by some commentators (e.g. on Vaughan Williams's 'PASTORAL SYMPHONY') to allude to an effect which would be POLYTONALITY (the simultaneous use of several keys) except that the composer is using not the scales of modern keys but the scales of the old modes. Thus the essential thing pointed out by these commentators is not the simultaneous use of more than one mode, but the simultaneous use of modes (whether one or more) at different pitches. In other words the term is used by them not as a properly grammatical compound of *poly-* and *modality*, but as a Lewis Carroll portmanteau-word from *polytonality* and *modality*.

POLYPHONIC, see next entry.

POLYPHONY, term literally meaning (from Gk) any simultaneous sounding of different notes; but, as commonly used, it implies the presence of counterpoint – opposite of HOMOPHONY, where melodic interest is virtually confined to one 'line' of music, the other sounds acting as accompaniment. So *polyphonic*. The *polyphonic period*, imprecise term usually indicating the 16th and early 17th centuries, i.e. the period of (e.g.) Palestrina, Lassus, and Byrd. (The style of such a later composer as Bach is also polyphonic, but there the polyphony is governed by the harmonic scheme, whereas in the earlier period the polyphony supposedly 'comes first' and gives rise to the harmony.)

POLYRHYTHM(Y), the systematic exploitation of several rhythms performed simultaneously – especially in the 20th century, sometimes with the aid of mechanical devices, e.g. RHYTHMICON. But there are earlier examples, notably Mozart's three different simultaneous dance-rhythms in 'DON GIOVANNI'.

POLYTONAL, see next entry.

POLYTONALITY, the simultaneous use of more than one key (an effect used systematically e.g. by Holst, Milhaud). Where only two keys are involved the more precise term is 'bitonality'. See TONALITY.

POMMER, see SHAWM.

POMP AND CIRCUMSTANCE, title of five military marches by Elgar: nos. 1–4 composed in 1901–7, no. 5 in 1930. Title is a quotation from Shakespeare's *Othello*. Elgar adopted part of no. 1 in his 'Coronation Ode' (1902) with the words 'Land of hope and glory'.

PONCE, MANUEL (1882–1948), Mexican composer who studied in Italy and Germany, and (at the age of 40), under Dukas in Paris. Works include 'Southern Concerto' (Sp., *Concierto del sur*) for guitar and chamber orchestra; violin concerto (using in the second movement his own well-known song 'Estrellita'); orchestral and piano works, etc.

PONCHIELLI, AMILCARE (1834–86), Italian composer of 'LA GIOCONDA' (from which the 'Dance of the Hours' comes) and other operas; also cantatas (one in memory of Garibaldi), etc. Was also church musician.

PONS, LILY (b. 1904), French-born soprano resident in U.S.A. (naturalized 1940); famous in coloratura operatic parts, and also in lighter music.

PONTICELLO (It.), the bridge of a violin or other stringed instrument; *sul ponticello* (literally, 'on the bridge'), instruction to play with the bow as close to the bridge as possible, for the production of a special kind of 'nasal' or 'metallic' tone-quality.

POOT, MARCEL (b. 1901), Belgian composer of operas, three symphonies, symphonic poem 'Charlot' (i.e. Charlie Chaplin), chamber music, etc. Director of the Brussels Conservatory, 1949. Pupil of Dukas and others.

POPPER, DAVID (1843–1913), German–Czech cellist, composer of many works for his instrument.

PORGY AND BESS, Gershwin's only opera, produced in Boston, 1935. Libretto by D. Heyward and I. Gershwin (the composer's brother). Written for a Negro cast on a story about Negroes – Porgy (crippled) and Bess are lovers. Has stylistic borrowings from Negro spirituals and jazz, but no actual folk-songs are incorporated: references to it as a 'folk opera' should thus be treated cautiously.

PORPORA, NICCOLÒ ANTONIO (1686–1768), Italian composer; in London, his operas rivalled Handel's in popularity. Was also church musician and, especially, singing-teacher: one of the most famous ever. Haydn, as a young man, was for a time his pupil, accompanist, and valet.

PORT Á BEUL, see MOUTH MUSIC.

PORT DE VOIX (Fr., carrying of the voice), equals PORTAMENTO, in singing. (Term also used for certain 'ornaments' now obsolete.)

PORTAMENTO (It.), the 'carrying' of a sound – e.g., on a voice or a stringed instrument, the transition from one note to another higher or lower without any break in the sound.

PORTANDO (It.), carrying; *portando la voce*, PORTAMENTO (in singing).

PORTRATIVE, see ORGAN.

PORTER, COLE (1893–1964), American composer of popular songs – many for musical plays (e.g. 'The Gay Divorce', 'Kiss Me, Kate', etc.), and films. Pupil of d'Indy. Also writer of words to his own songs.

PORTER, QUINCY (1897–1967), American composer, pupil of d'Indy (in Paris), Bloch, and others; also viola-player, and professor at Yale. Works include viola concerto, two-piano concerto, symphony, string quartets.

PORTER, WALTER (*c.* 1595–1659), English composer of motets, madrigals, etc. Said to have been a pupil of Monteverdi.

PORTS OF CALL (Fr., *Escales*), orchestral suite by Ibert, 1922. Though not mentioned in the score, the three movements are understood to refer to Palermo – Tunis – Valencia.

PORTSMOUTH POINT, concert-overture by Walton, 1925, after a drawing by Rowlandson of a gay quayside scene.

POSAUNE (Ger.), trombone (in standard musical use: but also 'trumpet' e.g. in the biblical phrase 'the last trumpet').

POSITIF (Fr.), equals CHOIR-ORGAN.

POSITION, (1, *in string-playing*), term used to specify how far along the finger-board the left hand should rest in order to play a given passage – *first position* being that nearest the pegs; *second*, etc., progressively further away; (2, *in trombone-playing*), term specifying how far the slide should be pushed out (*first position* the least extended); (3, *in harmony*), the 'layout' of a chord, determining which note comes at the bottom. E.g., with the chord consisting of the notes C, E, G, B♭ (i.e. the dominant seventh chord in key F) – if the note C (regarded as the 'root' of the chord) is at the bottom, then the chord is in *root position*; if E is at the bottom then it is in the *first inversion;* if G is at the bottom, the *second inversion;* if B♭, the *third inversion*. It is solely what note is at the bottom that determines these 'positions'; the order of the other notes on top is irrelevant.

POSITIVE, obsolete (medieval) name for a fixed type of small organ, in contrast with the *portative*, a portable organ.

POSSIBILE (It.), possible; term used elliptically; e.g. *dim. possibile* or even > *possibile* – meaning that the sound is to be diminished to the faintest possible (not 'diminish as rapidly as possible').

POST-HORN, brass instrument of simple design – a long tube, made without valves or keys, and so able to produce only the notes of one HARMONIC SERIES. Built in various shapes (often, however, in a straight unbent tube) and formerly used by postillions for signalling. The well-known *Post-Horn Galop* (composed by the cornettist Koenig, 1884), for post-horn solo with accompaniment, skilfully uses the instrument's limited range of notes.

POSTLUDE, a final piece – opposite of PRELUDE, and equally imprecise, but much less commonly found.

POST-ROMANTIC(ISM), terms applied to musical styles seeming to continue on ROMANTIC lines even after the original 'wave' of romanticism in music apparently reached its climax in Wagner. The allusion is particularly to the employment of large forces and the linking of music to an emotional message and philosophical or similar ideas (e.g. in Mahler).

POT-POURRI (Fr.), term used in a musical sense for a medley of tunes with little formal cohesion between them.

POTTER, (PHILIP) CIPRIANI (HAMBLY) (1792–1871), English composer of nine symphonies, etc.; as student, was advised by Beethoven in Vienna. Principal of the Royal Academy of Music, 1832.

POULE, LA, see HEN.

POULENC, FRANCIS (1899–1963), French composer, member of the former group of 'THE SIX'; influenced by Satie; composed in a transparent, mellifluous, sometimes witty style. Also pianist, noted particularly as accompanist to Pierre Bernac. Works include piano concerto, two-piano concerto, concerto for organ with strings and kettledrums; piano solos, songs, Mass; opera 'THE CARMELITES', opera-burlesque 'The Breasts of Tiresias'; ballets – including 'Les Biches' (produced in Britain as 'The House Party'), based on popular songs. Contributor to ballet 'JEANNE'S FAN'.

POWELL, JOHN (b. 1882), American composer, also pianist. Works include 'Negro Rhapsody' for piano and orchestra, portraying the Negro; 'Natchez on the Hill' for orchestra, using U.S. folk-tunes; violin concerto; piano solos.

PRAELUDIUM (Lat.), prelude; the well-known orchestral work so entitled is by Järnefelt, first heard in Britain 1909. See also PUGNANI.

PRAETORIUS, Latinized name of several German musicians, before

1700. The most important is *Michael Praetorius* (1571–1621), composer, organist, writer on music.

'PRAGUE' SYMPHONY, nickname for Mozart's symphony no. 38 in D (K.504), first performed in Prague, 1787.

PRALLTRILLER, see MORDENT.

PRECENTOR, ecclesiastical musical dignitary – in an Anglican cathedral, the cleric in charge of the vocal music, to whom the organist is technically subordinate.

PRECIOSA, German play on a gipsy subject by P. A. Wolff, produced 1821, to which Weber wrote the overture and other music.

PRECIPITATO, PRECIPITOSO, etc., impetuously.

PRELUDE, properly a piece preceding something – e.g., preceding a fugue, or forming the first number of a suite, or forming the orchestral introduction to an act of an opera; but the term is also used for a short self-contained piece, e.g. for piano – whether quite abstract, e.g. Chopin's and Rakhmaninov's, or illustrative, e.g. Debussy's. See also following entries.

PRÉLUDE À L'APRÈS-MIDI D'UN FAUNE, see THE AFTERNOON OF A FAUN.

PRELUDES, THE (Fr., *Les Préludes*), symphonic poem by Liszt, taking its title from a poem by Lamartine, but originally the overture to an unpublished choral work and having no connexion with the poem. Composed 1848, revised several times, given final form 1854. Liszt's prefatory note suggests that life is a series of preludes to the hereafter. (Thus 'prelude' is not used here in its musical sense.)

PREPARATION, a device in harmony by which the impact of a discord is softened: the actual note which, in a chord, causes that chord to be discordant, is sounded first in the preceding chord where it does not form a discordant element. Thus a discord is said to be *prepared* – or, if the impact is not 'softened' in this way, *unprepared*.

PREPARE, (1, *in harmony*) see preceding entry; (2) to 'set' an instrument ready to produce a particular effect, e.g. double-basses in an orchestra may be instructed to *prepare low E♭*, i.e. to let down to E♭ their lowest string which is normally tuned to E♮; see also the following entry.

PREPARED PIANO, a piano in which the strings are 'doctored' with various objects (cp. PREPARE, 2) in order to produce tone-qualities other than normal. The originator of the idea is the American John Cage, whose works also call on the pianist for unusual actions – e.g. reaching over the keyboard and plucking the strings by hand.

PRESSEZ (Fr.), increase speed.

PRESTISSIMO (It.), very fast. (Superlative of PRESTO.)

PRESTO (It.), fast. In, e.g., Mozart, this approximates to the meaning 'as fast as possible'; later composers have tended to convey this meaning by *prestissimo*.

PREVITALI, FERNANDO (b. 1907), Italian conductor, formerly conductor of the Rome Radio Orchestra; has toured widely. Is also composer and writer on music.

PRICK-SONG, old English term for music that was 'pricked', i.e. written down, as distinct from traditional or improvised music.

PRIGIONIERO, IL, see THE PRISONER.

PRIMA, see following entries.

PRIMA DONNA, (1, ordinary sense) see PRIMO; (2) title of one-act comic opera by Benjamin, produced in London, 1949 (though written fifteen years before). Libretto by C. Cliffe: a servant successfully impersonates (in an amorous rather than vocal capacity) a prima donna.

PRIMO, PRIMA (It.: masc., fem.), first. So *primo*, the top part in piano duets; *prima donna*, the chief woman singer in the cast of an opera, etc. (over-use of this term giving rise to *prima donna assoluta*, the 'absolutely chief' woman); *prima uomo*, the chief male singer in an opera, etc.; *prima vista*, first sight (as in sight-reading); *tempo primo*, with the same tempo as at first; *come prima*, as at first; *prima volta*, first time.

PRIMROSE, WILLIAM (b. 1904), Scottish viola-player (originally violinist) resident in U.S.A. since 1937. Various works have been written specially for him, including Bartók's viola concerto.

PRINCE IGOR (Rus., *Kniaz Igor*), opera by Borodin, produced in St Petersburg, 1890. Libretto by composer. The work was left unfinished, and after Borodin's death was completed and scored by Rimsky-Korsakov and Glazunov. Named after its 12th-century Russian warrior hero, captured by the Polovtsians – whose dances occur in Act II.

PRINCE OF THE PAGODAS, THE, ballet (on a fairy-tale subject) with music by Britten; produced in London, 1957.

PRINCESS IDA, *or Castle Adamant*, operetta by Sullivan, produced in London, 1884. Libretto by W. S. Gilbert. Styled 'a respectful operatic per-version of Tennyson's "Princess"' – to which poem the libretto alludes by quotation and parody. The Princess heads a women's university.

PRINCIPAL, (1) the first of an orchestra's players of a particular instrument (e.g., 'principal horn'); (2) a singer who takes main parts in an opera company – thus 'principal tenor' does not mean the chief tenor, but any tenor who has attained the standing of a 'principal'; (3) an organ stop of the open DIAPASON type but sounding an octave higher; (4) see following entry.

PRINCIPALE (It.), name used of a type of 17th- and 18th-century trumpet part – see TRUMPET.

PRISONER, THE (It., *Il Prigioniero*), opera by Dallapiccola, produced at Florence, 1950 (previously on Turin radio); libretto by composer, after a short story by Villiers de l'Isle Adam, *Torture by Hope*.

PRITCHARD, JOHN (MICHAEL) (b. 1921), English conductor active at Glyndebourne, Covent Garden, the Vienna State Opera, etc.;

conductor of the Liverpool Philharmonic Orchestra, then (1962–6) principal conductor of London Philharmonic Orchestra. C.B.E., 1962.

PRIX DE ROME, see ROME PRIZE.

PRO MUSICA (NEW YORK), see GREENBERG.

PRODANÁ NEVESTA, see BARTERED BRIDE.

PROGRAMMATIC MUSIC, PROGRAMME MUSIC, music interpreting a story, picture, etc. A better term – because self-explanatory, and avoiding the confusion with 'concert programmes', etc. – is ILLUSTRATIVE MUSIC.

PROGRESSION, motion from one note or chord to the next, in accordance with a musically logical plan.

PROGRESSIST, self-description of those French composers (e.g. Durey, Nigg) who after the Second World War wrote music deliberately of 'mass' appeal in accordance with Communist doctrine on 'progressive' art.

PROGRESSIVE TONALITY, the systematic plan of beginning a movement in one key and ending it in another: a term applied by musicologists to the practice of, e.g., Mahler and C. Nielsen.

PROKOFIEV, SERGEY (SERGEYEVICH) (1891–1953), Russian composer; also pianist. Pupil of Rimsky-Korsakov and others. Lived abroad from 1918 until settling again in Russia in 1934; his former style, sometimes of a rather acid and iconoclastic kind, then became more straightforward and 'popular' – e.g. in 'PETER AND THE WOLF' and violin concerto no. 2. None the less, some of his later works, e.g. his symphony no. 6, were officially condemned for 'FORMALISM' in 1948, along with works by other leading Soviet composers, and his last opera 'The Story of a Real Man' was publicly produced only after his death, 1960. His previous operas include 'THE FIERY ANGEL', THE DUENNA' and 'WAR AND PEACE'. Also composed seven symphonies (no. 1, 'CLASSICAL SYMPHONY'), five piano concertos, two violin concertos, cello concerto, concertino (see ROSTROPOVICH), sinfonia concertante for cello and orchestra; 'CINDERELLA', 'ROMEO AND JULIET', and other ballets; songs, patriotic cantatas (e.g. 'ALEXANDER NEVSKY'); nine piano sonatas (see SVIATOSLAV RICHTER), two violin sonatas and other instrumental works; film music.

PROLATION, in old musical notation, the division of the semibreve into either three minims (*major prolation*) or two minims (*minor prolation*). The term is extended in Peter Maxwell Davies's *Prolation* for orchestra, in which a fixed set of rhythmic ratios is made 'to govern greater and smaller proportions – from periods covering hundreds of bars to the smallest "irrational" groups'.

PROMENADE CONCERT, the accepted British misnomer (since the audience do not now walk about) for a concert at which some members of the audience stand. Henry Wood's London series of

Promenade Concerts began in 1895, more than fifty years after the first of this type: see JULLIEN and MUSARD.

PROMETHEUS, Greek legendary figure alluded to in various musical works including – (1) 'The Creatures of Prometheus' (Ger., *Die Geschöpfe von Prometheus*), ballet for which Beethoven wrote the music (including overture), 1801. A theme from this was used by Beethoven in his Variations for piano in E♭ (1802), sometimes called the 'Eroica' Variations, because the theme was also used in the 'EROICA' SYMPHONY. Beethoven also used it in no. 7 of twelve Country Dances for orchestra, 1802. (2) song-settings of Goethe's poem 'Prometheus', e.g. by Schubert (1819) and Wolf (1889). (3) 'Prometheus – The Poem of Fire' (Rus., *Prometei – Poema Ognia*), symphonic poem by Skriabin, with chorus ad lib. and properly with a KEYBOARD OF LIGHT; first performed, without this, 1911.

PROPHETESS, THE, see DIOCLESIAN.

PROUT, EBENEZER (1835–1909), English organist, conductor, and composer; chiefly known as writer of musical textbooks which are ridiculed as pedantic by those ignorant of them.

PRUSSIAN QUARTETS, name (not the composer's) for Mozart's intended string quartets for the use of Friedrich Wilhelm II, king of Prussia, who was a good cellist: only three were actually written (K.575, 589, 590), 1789–90.

PSALM, properly (from Greek word) a hymn sung to a harp; applied almost exclusively to the contents of the Old Testament Book of Psalms, for which various settings (see e.g., METRICAL PSALM) exist for religious use – also a number of concert settings. (See PSALMUS HUNGARICUS.) So Psalmody.

PSALMODY, the study, etc., of the Psalms; or an arrangement of Psalms for singing.

PSALMUS HUNGARICUS (Lat., Hungarian Psalm), work for tenor, chorus, and orchestra by Kodály, 1923, on Psalm 55 in a 16th-century Hungarian translation which has come to have Hungarian national associations.

PSALTER, volume containing the Book of Psalms, often with music.

PSALTERY, ancient and medieval stringed instrument (now obsolete), plucked like a lyre and of similar shape, but with a sound-board at the back of the strings.

PSKOVITIANKA, see THE MAID OF PSKOV.

PUCCINI, GIACOMO (ANTONIO DOMENICO MICHELE SECONDO MARIA) (1858–1924), Italian composer, pupil of Bazzini and Ponchielli. In youth a church musician. Works almost entirely operatic, including (in this order) 'MANON LESCAUT' (1893), 'LA BOHÈME', 'TOSCA', 'MADAME BUTTERFLY', 'THE GIRL OF THE GOLDEN WEST'; a 'triptych' (It., *trittico*) ('THE CLOAK', 'SISTER ANGELICA,' 'GIANNI SCHICCHI') intended to form a single bill; 'TURANDOT'

(1924, unfinished). Became one of history's most successful opera-composers through a gift for 'strong' melody wedded to forceful dramatic plots (see VERISMO): was also original harmonist and orchestrator.

PUGNANI, GAETANO (1731–98), Italian violinist and composer of violin pieces, operas, etc.: the 'Praeludium and Allegro', formerly said to be arranged from Pugnani by Kreisler, was admitted by Kreisler in 1935 to be entirely the latter's own work.

PUGNO, (STÉPHANE) RAOUL (1852–1914), French pianist, organist, composer of operas, ballets, etc. Died in Moscow.

PULCINELLA, ballet with music by Stravinsky (including songs), produced in Paris, 1920. Based on music said to be by Pergolesi – but see PERGOLESI.

PULT (Ger.), desk – in the sense of an orchestral music-stand shared e.g. by two string-players; so *1. Pult*, first desk, i.e., instruction that a passage is to be played only by the first two players of that section.

PUNTA (It.), point; *punta d'arco*, (with the) point of the bow.

PURCELL, the surname alone indicates Henry Purcell – below.

PURCELL, DANIEL (*c*1663–1717), English composer of much stage music (see THE INDIAN QUEEN), also cantatas, etc. Also organist. Brother of Henry Purcell.

PURCELL, EDWARD COCKRAM, eye-catching pseudonym of Edward Purcell Cockram (d. 1932), composer of the song 'Passing By', etc.

PURCELL, HENRY (1659–95), English composer; boy chorister; pupil of Humfrey and of Blow, whom he succeeded as organist of Westminster Abbey in 1679. Said to have died through a cold caused by being locked out of his own house at night. Wrote short opera 'DIDO AND AENEAS' for a Chelsea girls' school; also semi-operas (music not altogether predominant) including 'THE FAIRY QUEEN', 'KING ARTHUR', 'DIOCLESIAN', 'THE INDIAN QUEEN', and music for various plays. Other works include 'ODES FOR ST CECILIA'S DAY' and other cantatas; songs (see ORPHEUS BRITANNICUS and EPICEDIUM); keyboard works; TRIO-SONATAS (some described as in three parts and some as in four, but identical in scoring), including the 'GOLDEN' SONATA; anthems (including 'BELL ANTHEM') and other church music. His subtlety of rhythm (especially in the treatment of English words) and harmony has contributed to his high 20th-century repute; he notably influenced Holst, Britten, and others. For the 'Trumpet Voluntary' misattributed to him, see CLARKE, JEREMIAH.

PURITANS, THE (It., *I Puritani*), Bellini's last opera, produced in Paris (in Italian) 1835. Libretto by C. Pepoli, based ultimately on Scott's *Old Mortality*. See also HEXAMERON.

Q

QUADRILLE, type of square-dance very popular in the 19th century – in four sections of thirty-two bars each, plus a final section. Operatic and other popular tunes were commonly adapted for the music. The *lancers* is a type of quadrille.

QUADRUPLE COUNTERPOINT, see COUNTERPOINT.

QUADRUPLET, a group of four notes (or notes and rests) of equal time-value, written where a group of three, five, or some other number of notes is suggested by the tune-signature, E.g. a four-note group occupying a bar of 3/4 time, written ♩♩♩♩ (4)

QUAIL, toy instrument imitating a quail used e.g. in the TOY SYMPHONY formerly ascribed to Haydn.

QUANTZ, JOHANN JOACHIM (1697–1773), German composer and flutist; taught Frederick the Great to play the flute, and remained in his service from 1741 until death. Wrote about 300 concertos for one or two flutes, many flute solos; also hymns, songs, etc. Author of a treatise on flute-playing.

QUARTER-NOTE, U.S. term (following the German *Viertel*) for CROTCHET, a semibreve being considered a whole-note.

QUARTER-TONE, half a semitone – an interval not used in Western music until the 20th century, and then only exceptionally, e.g. by Haba and other Czech composers (making use of special quarter-tone pianos) and by Bloch as an occasional melodic subtlety in string-writing. See also MICROTONE.

QUARTET, (1) a performing group of four instrumentalists or singers: where the instruments are unspecified (e.g. Amadeus Quartet) a string quartet is assumed – two violins, viola, cello); a *piano quartet* consists of piano, violin, viola, cello. (2) a piece for four performers; if instrumental, and actually entitled 'Quartet', it will probably have the character of a SONATA for four performers, in several movements.

QUARTET MOVEMENT, name given to a movement by Schubert, in C minor (1820) intended for a string quartet which was never completed.

QUARTETTSATZ (Ger.), same as preceding.

QUASI (It.), almost, as if, approximating to.

QUATTRO RUSTEGHI, I, see SCHOOL FOR FATHERS.

QUATUOR (Fr.), quartet.

QUAVER, the note ♪ considered as a time-value, equivalent to half a crotchet or two semiquavers; U.S., eighth-note. A quaver rest is notated 𝄾

QUEEN, THE (Fr., *La Reine*), nickname of Haydn's symphony, no. 85 in B♭ (one of the 'PARIS SYMPHONIES') so called perhaps because Queen Marie Antoinette liked it. Its slow movement consists of variations on a French song.

QUEEN OF SPADES, THE (Rus., *Pikovaya Dama*), opera by Tchaikovsky, produced in St Petersburg, 1890. Libretto by Modest Tchaikovsky (the composer's brother) after Pushkin. 'The Queen of Spades' is the nickname of an old Countess, with allusion to her former uncanny luck at cards. See GRÉTRY.

QUIET CITY, suite by Copland for trumpet, English horn, and strings, first performed 1941; taken from incidental music to a play so named.

QUILTER, ROGER (1877–1953), English composer, trained in Germany. Wrote chiefly song-settings of Shakespeare, Herrick, and other distinguished poets, his work having great sensibility within a narrow range. Also composed opera 'Julia', music to play *Where the Rainbow Ends*, 'A CHILDREN'S OVERTURE', etc.

QUINET, FERNAND (b. 1898), Belgian composer of orchestral works, songs, etc.; also cellist (former member of Pro Arte quartet), conductor, and director of the Liège Conservatory.

QUINT, organ stop sounding a note a fifth (Lat., *quintus*) higher than the key depressed. It is with the aid of this stop on the pedals that the effect of a thirty-two-FOOT stop is produced even without thirty-two-foot pipes – see ACOUSTIC BASS.

QUINTADENA, QUINTATÖN, types of organ stop which sound not only the note of the key depressed, but also the note a twelfth (i.e. an octave plus a fifth) higher.

QUINTET, (1) a performing group of five instrumentalists or singers; a *string quintet* adds an extra viola or cello to the standard string QUARTET, and a *piano quintet* usually adds a piano to this standard string quartet – but see 'TROUT' QUINTET for an exception; (2) a piece for five performers; if instrumental, and actually entitled 'quintet', it will probably have the character of a SONATA for five performers in several movements.

QUINTUOR (Fr.), quintet.

QUINTUPLET, a group of five notes (or notes and rests) of equal time-value, written where a group of three, four, or some other number of notes is suggested by the time-signature. E.g. a five-note group occupying a bar of 4/4 time, written 5

QUODLIBET (Lat., *quod libet*, what is desired), piece containing several different tunes put together in unusual and (usually) ingenious fashion – such as that which ends Bach's 'GOLDBERG VARIATIONS', incorporating two well-known tunes of his day.

R

r, symbol in TONIC SOL-FA for the second degree (super-tonic) of the scale, pronounced *ray*.

RALL., abbr. of RALLENTANDO.

R.A.M., Royal Academy of Music.

R.C.M., R.C.O., Royal College of Music, Royal College of Organists.

RECIT., abbr. of RECITATIVE.

RFZ. abbr. of RINFORZANDO.

R.H., right hand (e.g. in piano-playing).

RINF., abbr. of RINFORZANDO.

RIT., abbr. of RITARDANDO.

R.M.C.M., Royal Manchester College of Music.

RABAUD, HENRI (BENJAMIN) (1873–1949), French composer, pupil of Massenet and others; also conductor, and (1920–41) director of the Paris Conservatory. Works include 'Marouf, the Cobbler of Cairo' and other operas (one on Synge's *Riders to the Sea*), symphonic poems, songs, film music. Orchestrated Fauré's 'DOLLY'.

RACHMANINOV, see RAKHMANINOV (the spelling which is consistent with the standard transliteration of other Russian names).

RACKET(T), equals SAUSAGE BASSOON.

RÁCÓCZY MARCH, see RÁKÓCZI MARCH (correct spelling).

RADETZKY MARCH, march by Johann Strauss the elder, 1848, named after an Austrian field-marshal and coming to symbolize the Hapsburg monarchy.

RAFF, (JOSEPH) JOACHIM (1822–82), Swiss composer, disciple of Liszt, some of whose works he scored for orchestra. Prolific composer of symphonies with allusive titles (no. 1 'To the Fatherland', no. 3 'In the Forest', etc.), chamber music, operas, etc.; but now survives almost entirely by a certain 'CAVATINA' (violin and piano). Was also pianist and critic.

RAG, see RAGTIME.

RAGA (Hindi), the approximate equivalent in Indian music of a scale – but the term embraces much more than the mere specification of the notes used.

RAGTIME, name given to an early type of jazz, particularly associated with piano-playing, and having as its essential the constant syncopation ('ragging') of a straightforward tune. So a 'rag' is a piece of this type, e.g. 'Temptation Rag'. I. Berlin's 'Alexander's Ragtime Band' dates from 1911, and Stravinsky's 'Ragtime for eleven instruments' and 'Piano-Rag-Music' (indebted to this type of work) from 1918 and 1919 respectively.

RAIMONDI, PIETRO (1786–1853), Italian composer, also opera director and church musician (at St Peter's, Rome, 1851). Works include a serious opera and a comic opera which could be performed simultaneously and still make musical sense, and three oratorios which could similarly be performed simultaneously.

'RAINDROP' PRELUDE, nickname for Chopin's prelude in D♭, op. 28, no. 15 (1839), on the supposition that the repeated note A♭ (G♯) represents persistent raindrops.

RAINIER, PRIAULX (b. 1903), South African (woman) composer – also violinist – resident in Britain; studied with N. Boulanger in

Paris. Works include cello concerto, three string quartets, 'Barbaric Dance Suite' for piano, 'Cycle for Declamation' (unaccompanied high voice, on text by Donne).

RAKE'S PROGRESS, THE, (1) ballet with music by G. Gordon, produced in London, 1935; (2) opera by Stravinsky, produced in Venice, 1951; libretto by W. H. Auden and C. Kallman. Both works are based on Hogarth's series of paintings (1735); but in the case of the opera the connexion is distant.

RAKHMANINOV, SERGEY VASSILIEVICH (1873–1943), Russian composer and pianist. (The spellings *Rachmaninoff*, etc., are inconsistent with the now standard system of transliteration from Russian.) Wrote his piano Prelude in C♯ minor at age 20. Left Russia, 1918, disliking Soviet régime: and lived mainly in Switzerland and in U.S.A., where he died. Nevertheless he conspicuously aided the Russian anti-Nazi effort in the Second World War. He always maintained a Russian outlook and wrote in an emotional (and sometimes melancholy) Romantic style. Works include four piano concertos, Rhapsody on a Theme of Paganini for piano and orchestra (see PAGANINI), many piano solos (including transcriptions from other composers) and some two-piano works; also three symphonies, symphonic poem 'THE ISLE OF THE DEAD', three operas, choral symphony 'The Bells' (after Poe).

RÁKÓCZI MARCH, a Hungarian march dating from the early 19th century (composer unknown) but named after Prince Rákóczi, leader of a Hungarian revolt against the Austrians, 1703–11; has Hungarian patriotic associations. Best known from the orchestral arrangement by Berlioz included in his 'DAMNATION OF FAUST'; it also enters into Johann Strauss's 'THE GIPSY BARON'.

RALLENTANDO (It.), slowing down.

RAMEAU, JEAN PHILIPPE (1683–1764), French composer – also organist, harpsichordist, and writer of an important 'Treatise on Harmony' and other theoretical works. At 50, began his succession of more than twenty operas and opera-ballets, including 'The Courtly Indies, (*Les Indes Galantes*) and 'Castor and Pollux'. His champions and those of Pergolesi clashed in the so-called 'WAR OF THE BUFFOONS'. Other works include chamber music; dance music and other pieces for harpsichord; cantatas and church music.

RAMSAY, ALLAN (1686–1758), Scottish poet – see 'THE GENTLE SHEPHERD'.

RANDEGGER, ALBERTO (1832–1911), Trieste-born conductor, composer (operas, Masses, etc.), and singing-master who in 1854 settled in London; died there.

RANGSTRÖM, TÜRE (1884–1947), Swedish composer, largely self-taught: several of his works are associated with Strindberg, whom he knew. Works include four symphonies (no. 1 'In Memoriam August Strindberg'), three operas, more than fifty songs with orchestra.

RANK, a set of organ pipes – term used particularly of 'mixture' stops – see MIXTURE.

RANKL, KARL (b. 1898), Austrian-born composer (pupil of Schoenberg) and conductor, resident in Britain from 1939, Musical director of Covent Garden Opera, 1946–51; conductor of the Scottish National Orchestra, 1952–7. Works include five symphonies (no. 1 with three female singers), opera 'Deirdre of the Sorrows' (among the winners of 1951 Festival of Britain opera prizes), and songs. Appointed musical director of Australia's opera company, 1957–60.

RANT, an old English dance of a character not now known.

RANZ DES VACHES, type of Swiss tune (name means 'cow-rank') sounded vocally or on an alphorn to call the cows: incorporated e.g. into Rossini's overture to 'WILLIAM TELL', Beethoven's 'PASTORAL SYMPHONY' (last movement), and (satirically) Walton's 'FAÇADE'.

RAPE OF LUCRETIA, THE, opera by Britten, produced at Glyndebourne, 1946. Libretto by R. Duncan. The main tragedy, set in Rome, is commented on by a male and female 'chorus' (one performer each) standing outside the temporal dimension of the plot.

RAPSODIA, RAPSODIE (It., Fr.), equals RHAPSODY; *Rapsodie espagnole*, see SPANISH RHAPSODY.

RASCH (Ger.), quick.

RASIERMESSERQUARTETT, see RAZOR QUARTET.

RASUMOVSKY QUARTETS, name for Beethoven's three string quartets op. 59 (in F, E minor, and C), 1806–7, dedicated to Count Rasumovsky, Russian ambassador in Vienna – and, in compliment to him, using a traditional Russian tune in the first two, and perhaps (though it is not identifiable) in no. 3.

RATHAUS, KAROL (1895–1954), Polish-born composer who studied in Vienna, taught in Berlin, and in 1934 settled in London and afterwards in U.S.A. Works include three symphonies, four string quartets, piano concerto.

RATSCHE (Ger.), equals RATTLE.

RATTLE, ratchet-toothed noise-making device which is occasionally used as an orchestral percussion instrument, e.g. in R. Strauss's 'TILL EULENSPIEGEL'.

RAUZZINI, VENANZIO (1746–1810), Italian castrato singer and composer of vocal works in Italian and English, etc.; settled in London and then (1780) in Bath; died there. Noted teacher.

RAVEL, (JOSEPH) MAURICE (1875–1937), French composer – incidentally, not Jewish, certain commentators notwithstanding. His family moved from the Pyrenees to Paris before he was 1. Pupil of Fauré and others at the Paris Conservatory. Failed in three attempts for the French ROME PRIZE, and was unfairly barred (although he had already had works published and performed) from a fourth try. (See DUBOIS.) Notable for IMPRESSIONIST technique (more clear-cut, however, than Debussy's), mastery of orchestration, and innovations in exploiting the sonorities of the piano. Piano works include two concertos (one for left hand), sonatina, suites 'GASPARD DE LA NUIT' and 'Mirrors' (including 'ALBORADA del gracioso'); also (all later transcribed for orchestra) 'PAVAN for a Dead Infanta', 'VALSES Nobles et Sentimentales', and 'For the Grave of Couperin' (see TOMBEAU). Other works include 'BOLERO', 'SPANISH RHAPSODY', and 'LA VALSE' for orchestra; 'MOTHER GOOSE' (for piano duet, later orchestrated); operas 'THE SPANISH HOUR' and 'THE CHILD AND THE SPELLS'; ballet 'DAPHNIS AND CHLOE'; septet including harp (also called 'Introduction and Allegro') and other chamber music; songs (see SHEHERAZADE). Contributed to ballet 'JEANNE'S FAN'; orchestrated Mussorgsky's 'PICTURES AT AN EXHIBITION'. Visited England (Hon.D.Mus., Oxford, 1928) and U.S.A.; died in Paris. Refused the Legion of Honour.

RAVENSCROFT, THOMAS (*c.* 1590–*c.* 1633), English composer of metrical psalm-tunes and other church music, etc.; publisher of the vocal collections 'PAMMELIA' (with sequel 'Deuteromelia') and 'MELISMATA'; author of a musical treatise.

RAVVIVANDO (It.,) reviving, i.e., returning gradually to a previous faster tempo.

RAWSTHORNE, ALAN (b. 1905), English composer – mainly self-taught, having studied dentistry first; but also studied piano. Works, almost entirely instrumental and written in a contrapuntal texture influenced by Hindemith, include three symphonies, Symphonic Studies, overture 'STREET CORNER', fantasy-overture 'CORTÈGES'; concerto for string orchestra; two piano concertos (no. 1 originally with strings and percussion only); two violin concertos, oboe concerto, clarinet concerto; three string quartets, clarinet quartet, bagatelles and other piano solos; ballet 'Madame Chrysanthème' film music. Contributor to 'A GARLAND FOR THE QUEEN'.

RAY, in TONIC SOL-FA, the spoken name for the second degree (super-tonic) of the scale, written r. Cp. RE.

RAYMOND, *or The Queen's Secret*, opera by A. Thomas, produced in Paris, 1851. Libretto by A. de Leuven and J. B. Rosier, based on the story of *The Man in the Iron Mask*.

RAZOR QUARTET, name for Haydn's string quartet in F minor, op. 55, no. 2. When Haydn was visited in 1787 by the English publisher Bland, he exclaimed that he would 'give his best quartet for a good razor', and (Bland having supplied the razor) this is the resulting work.

RE, the note D (in Latin countries, and formerly elsewhere); cp. RAY. Honegger's symphony no. 5, first performed 1951, is subtitled *di tre re* – of the three D's, referring to the quiet emphatic note D ending each of the three movements.

READ, GARDNER (b. 1913), American composer; works include four symphonies, 'A Bell Overture', piano and organ music. Also teacher and writer on music.

READING ROTA, see SUMER IS ICUMEN IN.

REAL, term used in opposition to *tonal* in special senses; for *real answer* and *real fugue* see ANSWER, for *real sequence* see SEQUENCE.

REALISM, stylistic term of at least two meanings – (1) the use in opera of characterization and stories based on contemporary life as it is actually observed (not forgetting 'life in the raw'), as distinct from 'remote' subjects and 'refined' treatment: in this sense the term indicates a correspondence with the literary outlook e.g. of Zola, and is used e.g. of Italian opera of the Puccini-Mascagni type (see VERISMO); (2) the philosophic attitude of mind considered 'correct' for composers under Soviet officialdom – showing optimism, sympathy with 'the people', a desire to be comprehensible, an avoidance of such faults as 'FORMALISM' etc.; in this sense the term is opposed both to 'distortions' in art and to 'crude naturalism' (e.g. musical imitations of noises).

REALIZE, to work out in full and artistically such music as was originally left by its composer in a sparsely-notated condition. E.g. a 17th- or 18th-century piece might originally have a CONTINUO bass-line, might require ornaments (originally left to performers' taste), and might need written directions for performance in order to make it now intelligible: such a phrase as 'Britten's realizations of Purcell' covers all these functions. Though lacking the advantage of being self-explanatory, 'realize' is superior to 'arrange' in this context since it avoids the implication of alteration.

REBEC(K), obsolete (medieval and later) bowed instrument with three or four strings, a forerunner of the violin.

REBIKOV, VLADIMIR IVANOVICH (1866–1920), Russian composer of opera, orchestral suites, many piano pieces, etc. Made use of WHOLE-TONE scale and other harmonic novelties. Studied partly in Berlin, settled in southern Russia and taught and organized there; died in Yalta.

RECAPITULATION, a section of a composition which repeats in something like their original shape themes which were originally presented in an earlier section but have interveningly undergone 'development'. The term is particularly used in the scheme of construction called SONATA-FORM, and variants of it.

RÉCIT (Fr.), equals SWELL (organ).

RECITAL, a musical performance, usually by soloists or duettists, rarely by larger combinations.

RECITATIVE, type of speech-like singing which is written in ordinary notation but in which a certain freedom in rhythm (and sometimes also in pitch) is allowed in performance; used particularly in opera, oratorio, etc. as preliminary to a song (so 'recitative and air', etc.) and for dialogue. Its two chief kinds are *accompanied recitative* (It., *recitativo accompagnato* or *stromentato*) with normal orchestral accompaniment, and *dry recitative* (*recitativo secco*) which, e.g. in 18th-century Italian opera, had merely an accompaniment of 'punctuating' chords from a harpsichord (the bass-line sometimes also reinforced by other instruments). (The word is commonly pronounced to rhyme with 'thieve', probably on the mistaken supposition that it is French; as it is only English, it might well be made as English-sounding as 'narrative'.) Cp. SPEECH-SONG.

RECITATIVO, see preceding entry.

RECORDER, type of woodwind instrument, without reed, much used in 16th–18th centuries but ousted by the more powerfully toned 'ordinary' flute, which it resembles except for being blown at the end and held downwards instead of crosswise. The recorder itself was formerly known as the 'English flute'; and to Bach, for instance, the term 'flute' actually meant 'recorder' unless some such word as 'transverse' was added to indicate the other instrument. The recorder has been extensively revived in the 20th century, (a) to play the old music written for it; (*b*) as an inexpensive and relatively easy instrument for schoolchildren, etc. A few modern composers, e.g. Rubbra, have also written for it. It is currently made chiefly in five sizes named as follows – sopranino; descant (English) or soprano (Continental); treble (English) or alto (Continental); tenor; and bass. The size most often encountered is the descant.

RECTE ET RETRO (Lat., right way and backwards), the use of a theme performed normally, in counterpoint with that same theme performed backwards.

REDEMPTION, THE, oratorio by Gounod (words, in English, compiled from the Bible by the composer) first performed in Birmingham, 1882.

REDFORD, JOHN (?–1547), English composer, organist (St Paul's Cathedral, London), poet, and playwright; works include motets and organ music. The attribution to him of the anthem 'Rejoice in the Lord alway' is mistaken, but the true composer is unknown.

REDMAN, REGINALD (b. 1892), English composer of music to radio plays, songs to English translations of Chinese poems, choral work 'The Passion of Mary', etc. Also organist; formerly musical director of the BBC's West Region.

REED, a vibrating 'tongue' of thin cane or metal, used to set the air-column vibrating in certain types of mouth-blown wind instruments, certain organ pipes, etc. The reed may beat freely (e.g. in the harmonica, i.e. mouth-organ), or against a surface as does the single reed of a clarinet; or two reeds may beat against each other, e.g. the double reed of an oboe. So *reed stop* on an organ, controlling pipes which have reeds. See also REED-ORGAN.

REED-ORGAN, (1) general name for types of keyboard instrument using free-beating REEDS (one for each note) and no pipes, e.g., HARMONIUM, AMERICAN ORGAN; (2) name sometimes also used (by extension from the preceding) to cover generally various other instruments working on the same principle but not organ-like in appearance – e.g. ACCORDION, HARMONICA (mouth-organ).

REEL, quick dance for two or more couples – found chiefly in Scotland, Ireland, Scandinavia, and N. America.

REFICE, LICINIO (b. 1883), Italian composer chiefly of motets, Masses, and other religious music; also of symphonic poems with chorus. Is also priest and church musician.

'REFORMATION' SYMPHONY, descriptive name given by Mendelssohn to his symphony no. 5, 1830. The first and third (last) movements respectively quote the 'Dresden Amen' and the chorale 'Ein' feste Burg' (A Stronghold Sure), respectively of Roman Catholic and Lutheran associations. See LUTHER.

REFRAIN, part of a song that recurs (both words and music) at the end of each stanza.

REGAL, type of small portable keyboard instrument of REDE-ORGAN type (15th-17th centuries); in church it was employed to regulate the singing (Lat., *regolare* – hence the name). Some models could be folded shut like a book and so were named *Bible-regal*. In some later models, short pipes were added, taking the instrument strictly out of the reed-organ class.

REGER, MAX (1873–1916), German composer – also pianist, organist, conductor, and teacher. Works, tending to a thickly contrapuntal texture and rapidly modulating harmonies, include 'Variations on a Theme of Mozart' and other orchestral works; much chamber music; piano and organ pieces, songs.

REGISTER, (1) a set of organ pipes controlled by one particular stop; so *to register* a piece for the organ is to select the stops appropriate to it; (2) part of an instrument's compass appearing to have a distinct tone-quality of its own, e.g. the CHALUMEAU register of the clarinet; (3) a part of the compass of the voice giving its own distinctive sensation to the singer – see CHEST VOICE, HEAD VOICE.

REICHA, ANTONÍN (1770–1836), Bohemian composer and teacher friend of Beethoven; settled in Paris, becoming professor at the Conservatory in 1818. Himself a flutist, he composed twenty-four wind quintets as well as operas, symphonies, piano works, etc. Experimented in polytonality and other ideas developed (without reference to him) in the 20th century.

REICHARDT, JOHANN FRIEDRICH (1752–1814), German composer, musical director at the Prussian court; also writer on music. Wrote some notable German songs; also operas, incidental music to plays, etc.

REINE, LA see THE QUEEN.

REINECKE, CARL (HEINRICH CARSTEN) (1824–1910), German composer, pianist, conductor, writer on music; works include operas, three piano concertos, wind octet.

REINKEN, JOHANN ADAM (or Jan Adams; 1623–1722), German organist and composer, pupil of Sweelinck; Bach several times walked long distances to hear him in Hamburg.

REIZENSTEIN, FRANZ (b. 1911), German-born composer and pianist who settled in England 1934. Pupil of Hindemith (in Germany) and Vaughan Williams, showing influence of both. Works include cantata 'Voices of Night', radio opera 'Anna Kraus'; cello concerto, cello sonatas; two piano concertos and many piano solos (among them twelve preludes and fugues in different keys).

REJOICE IN THE LORD ALWAY, (1) anthem by Purcell – see BELL ANTHEM; (2) anthem by an unknown early 16th-century composer, sometimes misattributed to Redford.

RELATED, term used as a measure of one key's harmonic nearness to (or distance from) another. Hence, e.g. G major is more nearly related to D major (a difference of only one sharp in the key-signature, meaning that the modulation between them is of the simplest kind) than either is to A♭ major. The use of the term categorically (as when two keys are spoken of as 'related', and another two as 'not related') is inadvisable, since all keys are related at a greater or lesser remove, and the historical evolution of harmony has been to lessen the difficulty of transition between them. See also RELATIVE.

RELATIVE, term used to indicate the fact that a common key-signature is shared by one major and one minor key: e.g. E minor is spoken of as the *relative minor* of G major, and G major as the *relative major* of E minor, both having a key-signature of one sharp, and modulations between them being accordingly of a simple kind.

REPEAT (noun), a section of a composition consisting of a repetition of a previous section. To save the space of writing out the passage again, such a repetition is indicated by pairs of dots (called *repeat marks*) and a double bar –  . On reaching these the performer repeats from the previous pair of dots or (if there is none) from the beginning.

RÉPÉTITEUR (Fr., also used in Eng.), the member of a musical staff of an opera company who coaches the singers and (unseen) may also give them their cues in actual performance, sometimes actually prompting them with the words beforehand.

RÉPÉTITION (Fr.), rehearsal; *répétition générale*, final (dress) rehearsal, often (in Continental opera houses) given before a full but invited audience.

REPRISE (Fr., also used in Eng.), a re-taking-up, particularly a return to the first section of a composition after an intervening and contrasting section, or (in a musical play) the further occurrence of a song which has already been heard.

REPIANO, see RIPIENO.

REQUIEM (1, also *Requiem Mass*), the Roman Catholic Mass for the dead, in Latin, beginning with the word 'requiem' (repose); sung to plainsong or in settings by various composers – many appropriate to concert rather than church use, e.g. Berlioz's (1836–7) and Verdi's

(1873); (2) a choral work similarly appropriate to the commemoration of the dead but with a different text – e.g. Brahms's (1866–9) on biblical texts, called 'A German Requiem' (as opposed to Latin), and Delius's 'Requiem' (1914–16) to a 'pagan' text compiled by the composer from Nietzsche.

For Britten's 'Sinfonia da requiem' see SINFONIA.

RESOLUTION, the progression from a discord to a concord or to a less acute discord; so *to resolve* a discord.

RESPIGHI, OTTORINO (1879–1936), Italian composer, pupil of Rimsky-Korsakov in Russia; also conductor, teacher, and editor of old Italian music. Cultivated a traditionally melodious style and bright, sometimes vividly pictorial, orchestration. Works include orchestral suites 'THE BIRDS', 'THREE BOTTICELLI PICTURES', 'FOUNTAINS OF ROME', 'PINES OF ROME'; nine operas, two violin concertos, many songs. Arranged the music to the ballet 'THE FANTASTIC TOYSHOP' from Rossini.

REST, the notation of an absence of sound in a performer's part for a length of time corresponding to a given number of beats. So *crotchet rest*, etc.

RESULTANT TONE, name given to either of two acoustical phenomena: (*a*) when two loud notes are sounded, another note may sometimes also be heard, lower in pitch, which corresponds to the difference in vibration between the original two and is called 'differential tone'; (*b*) another note, higher than the original two, may also be heard, corresponding to the sum of their vibrations ('summational tone'). For a practical use of the former see ACOUSTIC BASS.

'RESURRECTION' SYMPHONY, nickname for Mahler's symphony no. 2 (1894): its final movement, with soprano and alto soloists and choir, is a setting of German words by Klopstock (1724–1803) in which the idea of Resurrection is central.

RETABLO DE MAESE PEDRO, EL, see MASTER PETER'S PUPPET SHOW.

RETARDATION, see SUSPENSION.

RETENU (Fr.), held back (as to speed).

RETROGRADE, term used of a theme when performed backwards – a device prominently used e.g. in the Middle Ages, in Bach's 'THE ART OF FUGUE', and in TWELVE-NOTE technique. In this last, both *retrograde* and *retrograde inversion* are standard procedures, the latter meaning that the theme is turned upside-down as well as played backwards (see INVERT).

RETURN OF LEMMINKÄINEN, THE, see LEMMINKÄINEN'S HOMECOMING.

REUBKE, JULIUS (1834–58), German pianist and composer, pupil of Liszt. Compositions, published after his early death, include organ sonata on Psalm 94 (alluding to the psalm's call for vengeance).

REUTTER, HERMANN (b. 1900), German composer – also pianist, and particularly song-accompanist. Has cultivated a great variety of styles. Works include operas, choral works (texts by Goethe and other distinguished poets), song-cycles.

REVISOR, DER, see THE GOVERNMENT INSPECTOR.

'REVOLUTIONARY' STUDY, nickname for Chopin's study in C minor, op. 10, no. 12 (1831), written after he had heard of the Russians' capture of Warsaw and supposedly expressing his patriotic anger at the news.

REVUELTAS, SILVESTRE (1899–1940), Mexican violinist, conductor, and composer of symphonic poems on Mexican subjects for orchestra, three string quartets, songs, etc. Studied partly in U.S.A.; worked in Spain on the Republican side in the Civil War; aimed at the expression of a Mexican national spirit, but not through actual quotation of folk-songs, etc.

REYER, ERNEST, pen-name of Louis Étienne Ernest Rey (1823–1909), French composer (operas, cantatas, etc.) and critic, follower and champion of Wagner.

REZNIČEK, EMIL NIKOLAUS VON (1860–1945), Austrian composer and conductor who settled in Germany and died there. Works, mainly before 1920, include 'DONNA DIANA' and other operas (one on the 'TILL EULENSPIEGEL' tale), four symphonies, Mass, Requiem.

RHAPSODY, title (not in itself denoting a particular musical form) used in the 19th and 20th centuries for a work generally in one continuous movement and usually suggestive of some kind of romantic 'inspiration'. Thus the composer may set his imagination working on some already existing theme(s): e.g. Liszt's 'HUNGARIAN RHAPSODIES', Delius's 'BRIGG FAIR' (using an English folk-tune), Rakhmaninov's 'Rhapsody on a Theme of Paganini' (see PAGANINI). Or no such allusiveness may be implied – e.g. Brahms's Rhapsodies for piano, his 'ALTO RHAPSODY' (voices and orchestra), and the following.

RHAPSODY IN BLUE, work for piano and orchestra by Gershwin (the first notable 'concert' work by a jazz composer in the jazz idiom), first performed 1924. The orchestration was by Grofé – though the orchestration of Gershwin's later 'serious' works was the composer's own.

RHEINBERGER, JOSEF (GABRIEL) (1839–1901), German organist – child prodigy, holding church post at age 7 – pianist, conductor, and composer of many organ works. Also composed operas, Masses, chamber music, etc. Distinguished teacher of organ and composition.

RHEINGOLD, DAS, see RING.

'RHENISH' SYMPHONY, name given to Schumann's symphony no. 3 in E (1850): the fourth of its five movements was prompted by the composer's witnessing the installation of a cardinal at Cologne (on the Rhine).

RHINEGOLD, THE, see RING.

RHYTHM, that aspect of music concerned not with pitch but with the distribution of notes in time and their accentuation. Hence such phrases as *a strongly marked rhythm* or (by ellipsis) *a strong rhythm*; *two-beat rhythm* (accent on every other beat); *a five-bar rhythm* (each five bars making a regular rhythmic unit); *waltz rhythm* (accent on the first of every three beats, at waltz pace); *free rhythm*, rhythm not determined by the regular incidence of bar-lines but arrived at by the performer according to the natural or conventional flow of the notes (as in plainsong). So also *a sense of rhythm*, implying a performer's ability to convey the rhythmic element of a composition intelligibly; *rhythm section* of a dance band, collective term for those instruments more concerned with giving the beat than with melody – normally piano, drums and other percussion, guitar, double-bass. For *rhythm band* see PERCUSSION BAND. The use of 'rhythm' in such dance-band jargon as *to get rhythm* and *Joe Snooks and his Rhythm*, though crudely understandable, carries the comic implication that rhythm forms a lesser element in other kinds of music.

RIBIBLE, equals REBEC.

RICERCAR(E) (It., to search), type of contrapuntal instrumental composition current in the 16th–18th centuries, usually in the strictest style of IMITATION.

RICERCATA, same as preceding entry.

RICHARDS, (HENRY) BRINLEY (1817–75), Welsh pianist (pupil of Chopin) and composer of 'God Bless the Prince of Wales', etc.

RICHTER, FRANZ XAVER (1709–87), see MANNHEIM SCHOOL.

RICHTER, SVIATOSLAV (b. 1914), Russian pianist, formerly opera coach. Played in U.S.A., 1960, U.K., 1961 and won highest international reputation; Prokofiev's piano sonata no. 9 is dedicated to him.

RIDDLE CANON, type of CANON in which the composer, as a puzzle, omits to say at what point and at what pitch the voices after the first make their entries. Anyone performing the canon must thus find out the answer for himself.

RIDERS TO THE SEA, opera by Vaughan Williams, produced in London, 1937: almost a word-for-word setting of Synge's play about an Irish fishing family. See also RABAUD.

RIEGGER, WALLINGFORD (1885–1961), American composer who studied and conducted in Germany. Employed a dissonant, rather austere style and sometimes a modified TWELVE-NOTE technique. Wrote many works for Martha Graham's and other dance companies; also three symphonies, concerto for piano and wind, three string quartets, 'Study in Sonority' for ten violins (or any multiple of ten), 'Music for brass choir' (in twenty-six independent parts).

RIENZI, *or The Last of the Tribunes* (Ger., . . . *der Letzte der Tribunen*), opera by Wagner, produced in Dresden, 1842. Libretto by composer, after Bulwer-Lytton's novel: the hero is an historical 14th-century Italian patriot.

RIES, German family of musicians, the most important being *Ferdinand*

Ries (1784–1838), friend of Beethoven, pianist, violinist, conductor, and composer of three operas, six symphonies, etc.

RIESCO, CARLOS (b. 1925), Chilean composer, pupil in U.S.A. of Copland and Diamond, and in Paris of N. Boulanger. Works include ballet 'Candelaría', violin concerto, four Dances (of Latin-American type) for orchestra.

RIETI, VITTORIO (b. 1898), Egyptian-born Italian composer, pupil of Respighi and others; settled in U.S.A., 1940. Works include opera 'Don Perlimplín, (on Lorca's play), various ballets (including 'Night Shadow', with music arranged from Bellini), five symphonies, piano solos. Favours a light, traditionally melodious (but not romantic) style.

RIGADOON, RIGAUDON (Eng., Fr.), old French dance of a lively nature in 2/4 or 4/4 time.

RIGOLETTO, opera by Verdi, produced in Venice, 1851. Libretto by F. M. Piave, after Hugo's *Le Roi s'amuse*: title not from its romantic tenor role but from its baritone hero, a tragic court jester. 'La donna è mobile' (Woman is fickle), its most famous aria, has itself been taken as an opera title by R. Malipiero.

RIMSKY-KORSAKOV, NIKOLAY ANDREYEVICH (1844–1908), Russian composer, also conductor; member of the 'nationalist' group of composers called the 'MIGHTY HANDFUL'. In early life was naval officer, and picked up much of his musical technique *after* being appointed professor at the St Petersburg Conservatory, 1871. His compositions usually have some literary or other extra-musical idea behind them, and are distinguished by rich orchestration: he wrote a textbook on orchestration with examples entirely from his own work. Wrote operas including 'THE MAID OF PSKOV', 'THE SNOW-MAIDEN', 'SADKO', 'MOZART AND SALIERI', 'The Legend of TSAR SALTAN', 'The Legend of the INVISIBLE CITY OF KITEZH', and 'THE GOLDEN COCKEREL' (this last banned for its 'seditious' satire until after his death). Other works include three symphonies (no. 2 'ANTAR'), RUSSIAN EASTER FESTIVAL Overture, suite 'SHEHERAZADE', 'SPANISH CAPRICE', piano concerto, folk-song arrangements. Also editor, orchestrator, and reviser (not always scrupulous by modern standards) of other composers' works – see, e.g., 'BORIS GODUNOV', 'THE KHOVANSKY AFFAIR', 'PRINCE IGOR', 'THE STONE GUEST'.

RINALDO, the first opera written by Handel for London; produced there 1711. Libretto, in Italian, by G. Rossi, ultimately after Tasso's 'Jerusalem Delivered', of which epic of the Crusades Rinaldo is a hero. (The opera has a famous march 'borrowed' in 'THE BEGGAR'S OPERA'.) See also ARMIDA (she is a pagan enchantress resisted by Rinaldo).

RINFORZANDO (It., reinforcing), direction that volume is to be suddenly increased on a particular note or chord or a small series of these, abbr. *Rinf.*

RING, THE, usual short title for *The Nibelung's Ring* (Ger., *Der Ring des Nibelungen*), series of four operas by Wagner – called by him a trilogy 'with preliminary evening'. The complete cycle of four was first performed complete in Bayreuth, 1876, but the first two parts had already been given separately – *The Rhinegold* (*Das Rheingold*), Munich, 1869; *The Valkyrie* (*Die Walküre*), Munich, 1870; *Siegfried*; *Twilight of the Gods* (*Götterdämmerung*). These form a single developing musical structure and unfold a continuous plot: libretto by composer, after old German legends. The 'Nibelung' of the title (member of a race of dwarfs) is Alberich, the first possessor of the magic ring.

RIO GRANDE, THE, work by Lambert for chorus, orchestra, and piano solo, first performed 1929; uses jazz idioms and jazz percussion instruments. Setting of a poem by Sacheverell Sitwell.

RIPIENO (It., replenished), term indicating (e.g., in the old CONCERTO GROSSO) the full body of performers as distinct from the solo group; so also indicating an additional 'filling-in' part. In the brass band the *ripieno cornets* (usually corrupted in writing and speech to *repiano cornets*) are those used to supplement the 'solo' (i.e., first) cornets.

RISE AND FALL OF THE CITY OF MAHAGONNY (Ger., *Aufstieg und Fall der Stadt Mahagonny*), opera by Kurt Weill, produced in Leipzig, 1930. Libretto by Brecht: 'Mahagonny' is the city of material pleasure and the opera bitterly satirizes 'capitalist' morality. An earlier version of the work was produced at Baden-Baden in 1927.

RITARDANDO (It.), becoming slower; abbr. *Rit.*

RITE OF SPRING, THE (Rus., *Vesni sviashchenni*), ballet with music by Stravinsky, produced in Paris, 1913 – and occasioning a riot between its champions and its opponents. The title was then translated for French audiences as *Le Sacre du printemps*, but there is no point in the use of this outside French-speaking countries.

RITENUTO (It.), held back (as to tempo).

RITMO (It.), rhythm; *ritmo di tre battute*, in a rhythm of three bars (i.e. three bars are treated as forming a rhythmical unit).

RITORNELLO (It., little return), a recurring passage, e.g. an instrumental passage always occurring between the verses of a song; so also a passage for full orchestra (without soloist) in a concerto, thought of as 'coming round again' even though the material is not necessarily repetitive.

RITUAL DANCES, see THE MIDSUMMER MARRIAGE.

RIVIER, JEAN (b. 1896), French composer, favouring a readily approachable and sometimes light style. Works include five symphonies, 'Provençal Rhapsody' for orchestra, piano concerto, violin concerto, string quartets, many songs.

ROBERT THE DEVIL (Fr., *Robert le Diable*), opera by Meyerbeer, produced in Paris, 1831. Libretto by E. Scribe: the hero is a son of the devil by a human woman.

ROBERTON, HUGH (STEVENSON) (1874–1952), Scottish choral

conductor – founder and conductor of Glasgow Orpheus Choir 1906 – 51; also composer and arranger of vocal music.

ROBERTSON, JAMES (b. 1912), English conductor, formerly with Sadler's Wells Opera; became musical director of New Zealand National Opera, then (1964) director of London Opera Centre (advanced training school).

ROBERTSON, RAE, see BARTLETT, ETHEL.

ROBESON, PAUL (LE ROY) (b. 1898), American (Negro) bass, of international repute particularly in Negro songs; also stage and film actor.

ROBINSON, STANFORD (b. 1904), English conductor, particularly associated with radio, opera, and choral work. Is also composer and arranger.

ROCCA, LODOVICO (b. 1895), Italian composer, pupil of Orefice; has written operas including 'The Dybbuk' (on a Hebrew play), also symphonic poems, cantata 'Ancient Inscriptions' (text from Greek epigrams), chamber music, etc.

ROCOCO, term originally alluding to fancy rock-work (Fr., *rocaille*) and applied in visual art to the predominantly diverting – rather than elevating – style of, e.g. Watteau (1684–1721) and to related styles in architecture. It has been borrowed by writers on music and applied e.g. to F. Couperin (1668–1733): in all cases the allusion is to a decorative and light art-style succeeding the massiveness and constructive ingenuity of BAROQUE.

RODEO, *or The Courting at Burnt Ranch*, ballet with music by Copland, produced 1942. Set in the Wild West and musically alluding to some traditional American songs.

RODGERS, RICHARD (b. 1902), American composer of light music – especially to musical plays, e.g. 'Oklahoma!'

RODZINSKI, ARTUR (1894–1958), American-naturalized conductor, Polish by origin though born in what is now Yugoslavia. He held posts with leading orchestras in New York, Chicago, etc.

ROGER-DUCASSE, JEAN JULES AMIABLE (1873–1954), French composer, pupil of Fauré. Works include mime-drama 'Orpheus', three motets, symphonic poems, piano solos. Completed and orchestrated the rhapsody for saxophone and orchestra which Debussy left unfinished at his death.

ROGERS, BENJAMIN (1614–98), English organist and composer of church music – including the Latin hymn still sung at dawn on May Day from the tower of Magdalen College, Oxford, where he was organist.

ROGERS, BERNARD (b. 1893), American composer, pupil of Bloch – also of Frank Bridge in London and N. Boulanger in Paris. Composer of opera 'THE WARRIOR', four symphonies and other orchestral works, religious choral works, 'Pastorale' for eleven instruments.

ROHRFLÖTE, ROHR FLUTE (Ger., Eng.), type of organ stop, the pipes being plugged at the end but having a thin tube ('Rohr') through the plug.

ROI DAVID, LE, see KING DAVID.

ROLAND-MANUEL, form of name used by Roland Alexis Manuel Lévy (b. 1891), French composer of operas, oratorio 'Joan of Arc', ballets, etc.; pupil of Roussel and Ravel, writer on Ravel and other musical subjects. Contributor to the ballet 'JEANNE'S FAN'.

ROLL, a very rapid succession of notes on a drum, approximating to a continuous sound. The technique varies between types of drum: on the side drum each hand gives a double stroke.

ROMAN, JOHAN HELMICH (1694–1758), Swedish composer of church music, twenty-one symphonies, etc.; studied in London and was influenced by Handel.

ROMAN CARNIVAL (Fr., *Le Carnaval romain*), overture by Berlioz, 1844, on material from his opera 'BENVENUTO CELLINI'.

ROMANCE, ROMANZE, ROMANZA, respectively the French (and English), German, and Italian forms of a term used with wide and vague musical significance. The slow middle movement of Mozart's piano concerto in D minor, K.466 (1785) is headed 'Romanze' (an early use); Mendelssohn's 'Songs Without Words' are called in French *Romances sans paroles* (*romance* in French may mean any non-operatic solo song); Vaughan Williams frequently employed *romance* and *romanza* as the titles of slow movements, and his single-movement work (1951) for harmonica with strings and piano is called Romance. A quality of intimacy and tenderness is often implied. The term now bears no direct relation to the following entry, despite the common origin of the words.

ROMANTIC (ISM), terms alluding to an artistic outlook discernible in European literature towards the end of the 18th century, and taken over to describe a supposedly similar outlook in music, principally in the 19th century. One of its literary aspects, that of harking back to the Middle Ages, is rarely found in musical contexts – apart from Bruckner's '*Romantic*' *Symphony* (no. 4 in E♭, 1874), a nickname bestowed after the composer's description of the opening in terms of a scene of medieval chivalry. Another literary aspect, that of cultivation of the supernatural, is evident, e.g. in Weber but not in other composers supposedly no less typed as Romantic, e.g. Chopin. The main musical implication is that the composer is more concerned with the vivid depiction of an emotional state (often linked with a narrative or some other extra-musical element) than with the creation of aesthetically pleasing structures. (Such structures must, however, be the result if not the aim of any successful method of composition). The attempt at more and more 'vividness' led to (*a*) a trend to the evocation of 'extreme' emotions, (*b*) an expansion of orchestral resources for this purpose. Romanticism is thus contrasted with CLASSICISM; it is also, less clearly, differentiated from IMPRESSIONISM. Composers such as Stravinsky, disclaiming a connexion between music and the portraying of emotions, are said to be *anti-romantic*. For a late variety of romanticism see POST-ROMANTIC.

ROMANZA, ROMANZE, see ROMANCE.

ROMBERG, ANDREAS JAKOB (1767–1821), German violinist, conductor, and composer of violin concertos, string quartets, etc.; also of a Toy Symphony (not the famous one). Cousin of Bernhard Romberg.

ROMBERG, BERNHARD (1767–1841), German cellist and composer, cousin of Andreas Jakob.

ROMBERG, SIGMUND (1887–1951), Hungarian-born composer of operettas ('New Moon', 'The Student Prince', 'The Desert Song', etc.) and other music, resident in U.S.A. from 1909.

ROME PRIZE, an award to young musicians (and artists of other fields) involving the opportunity to spend a period in Rome for study. The most famous of such prizes are those organized for French composers; Belgium and the United States have similar schemes.

ROMEO AND JULIET, play by Shakespeare, source of many operas and other musical works, including (1) opera by Gounod, produced in Paris, 1867; libretto ('Roméo et Juliette') by J. Barbier and M. Carré; (2) opera by Sutermeister, produced in Dresden, 1939; libretto ('Romeo und Julia') by Composer; (3) ballet with music by Prokofiev, produced in Moscow, 1935 (two orchestral suites have been drawn from it); (4) 'dramatic symphony' by Berlioz, with solo and choral voices, 1839; (5) overture-fantasy by Tchaikovsky, 1869–70; (6) music by Diamond for the play – composed 1947 as a concert work, but suitable also for theatre use. See also ZANDONAI and A VILLAGE ROMEO AND JULIET.

RONALD, LANDON, form of name used by Landon Ronald Russell (1873–1938), English pianist (accompanist to Melba), composer (song 'Down in the Forest', etc.), and conductor, noted in opera and with symphony orchestras in London and elsewhere. Son of HENRY RUSSELL. Knighted 1922.

RONDEAU, RONDEL, type of medieval French song with choral refrain. (For later instrumental use of 'rondeau', see RONDO.)

RONDO (properly spelt, in Italian, *rondò*), type of composition in which one section recurs intermittently (the French spelling *rondeau* was used e.g. by Bach). By Mozart's time the rondo had evolved into a standard pattern and was much used e.g. for the last movement of a sonata or concerto. A simple rondo is built up in the pattern of ABACADA ... (etc.), where A represents the recurring section (called *rondo-theme*) and B, C, D, ... represent contrasting sections, called *episodes*. (The rondo-theme can undergo some variation in its reappearances.) A combination of this with SONATA-FORM led to what is called the *sonata-rondo* (used e.g. by Mozart, Beethoven) in which the first episode (B) is originally in a key other than the tonic but later reappears in the tonic key (like the 'second subject' in sonata-form).

ROOT, the lowest note of a chord when that chord is in what is regarded as its 'basic' position – e.g. for the chord of C major (C, E, G) the root is C. See POSITION.

ROPARTZ, GUY, form of name used by Joseph Marie Guy-Ropartz (1864–1955), French composer of operas, five symphonies, organ and piano music, etc.; pupil of Massenet, Franck, and others.

RORE, CIPRIEN DE (1516–65), Flemish composer who worked in Italy (and died there) and so was known as 'Cipriano de Rore'; pupil of Willaert in Venice, then held various church and court posts. Wrote notable madrigals; also church music, instrumental fantasies, etc.

ROREM, NED (b. 1923), American composer of many songs (including nine song-cycles), 'Miss Julie' (after Strindberg) and other operas, three symphonies, two string quartets, etc. Pupil of V. Thomson and Copland. Lived in Paris 1949–55.

ROSALIA, name sometimes given to a 'real SEQUENCE' (because it occurred at the beginning of an old Italian popular song, 'Rosalia mia cara').

ROSAMUNDE, PRINCESS OF CYPRUS (Ger., ... *Fürstin von Cypern*), play by Helmine von Chézy, 1823, for which Schubert wrote three entr'actes, two ballet numbers, and various vocal numbers. The piece now known as the overture to *Rosamunde* was originally written for an earlier stage piece, *The Magic Harp*; the overture actually used at the first performance of *Rosamunde* was that already written for 'ALFONSO AND ESTRELLA' and is still known by that name.

ROSBAUD, HANS (1895–1962), Austrian conductor of special repute in modern music; lived in Switzerland, conducted first (concert) performance of Schoenberg's 'Moses and Aaron' at a few days' notice, Hamburg, 1954.

ROSE, see SOUND-HOLE.

ROSE CAVALIER, THE, see ROSENKAVALIER.

ROSEINGRAVE, English family of musicians, the most important of whom is Thomas Roseingrave (1690–1766), organist and composer of an opera, Italian cantatas, English church music, organ and harpsichord pieces, etc.; in Italy, became acquainted with A. and D. Scarlatti. Latterly lived in Ireland and died there. Pursued an individual English idiom unmoved by the prevailing influence of Handel.

ROSENBERG, HILDING (CONSTANTIN) (b. 1892), Swedish composer, also conductor; studied in Germany and France. Works, in a modern style but not opposed to Romanticism, include five symphonies – no. 4 being otherwise described as an oratorio, 'The Revelation of St John'; concertos for violin, viola, cello, trumpet; ballet 'Orpheus in Town'; tetralogy of stage oratorios after Thomas Mann's *Joseph and his Brethren*; six string quartets, piano solos, etc.

ROSENKAVALIER, DER, opera by R. Strauss, produced in Dresden, 1911. Libretto by H. von Hofmannsthal. The 'Cavalier of the Rose' is the ceremonial bearer of a rose from a gentleman to his betrothed – the bearer in this case winning the girl for himself instead.

ROSENMÜLLER, JOHANN (*c.* 1619–84), German composer who

worked for a time in Italy. Wrote Masses and other church music, suites of instrumental dances, etc.

ROSENTHAL, MANUEL (b. 1904), French composer, pupil of Ravel; also conductor, especially in France and (1946–51) in U.S.A. Works include symphonic suites 'Joan of Arc' and 'Musique de table' (a nostalgic wartime evocation of foods then unobtainable), operettas, oratorio 'St Francis of Assisi', piano solos. Favours clear style influenced by Ravel, some of whose piano works he has orchestrated.

ROSES FROM THE SOUTH (Ger., *Rosen aus dem Süden*), waltz by Johann Strauss the younger – from his operetta 'The Queen's Lace Handkerchief', 1880.

ROSSELLINI, RENZO (b. 1908), Italian composer of ballets including 'A Tale of Winter' (not after Shakespeare's *The Winter's Tale*), operas including 'A View from the Bridge', orchestral works, and music to films directed by his brother (Roberto Rossellini), etc.

ROSSETER, PHILIP (1568–1623), English lutenist and composer of ayres with lute and other accompaniment. Active at Queen Elizabeth's court.

ROSSI, LUIGI (1597–1659), Italian singer, organist, and composer – e.g. of opera 'Orpheus', the first Italian opera to be heard in Paris, 1647; also of solo cantatas, etc.

ROSSI, SALOMONE (*c.* 1570–*c.* 1630), Italian composer – Jewish, but exempted from the stigma of wearing the yellow badge otherwise then compulsory for Jews in Italy; colleague of Monteverdi at the court of Mantua. Wrote Italian madrigals, Hebrew psalms, etc.; his TRIO-SONATAS are among his notable pioneering in instrumental music.

ROSSI-LEMENI, NICOLA (b. 1920), Italian bass singer, born in Turkey (mother Russian, father Italian); began operatic career (specializing in Russian opera) in Italy; later sang in New York (1951), London, etc.

ROSSINI, GIOACCHINO (ANTONIO) (1792–1868), Italian composer, born at Pesaro. His operas appeared in various Italian cities; he visited England in 1823–4, and after 1829 lived partly in Paris, where he died. Sussessful in opera from 1810, although 'THE BARBER OF SEVILLE' (1816) was at first a failure. Other operas include 'THE SILKEN LADDER', 'TANCRED', 'THE ITALAIN GIRL IN ALGIERS', 'OTELLO', 'CINDERELLA', 'THE THIEVING MAGPIE', 'ARMIDA', 'MOSES', 'SEMIRAMIS', 'COUNT ORY', 'WILLIAM TELL' (1829, in French, after which success he lived for nearly forty more years but wrote no more operas). Other works include STABAT MATER and a few other church works; a few songs and duets (among them the collection 'SOIRÉES MUSICALES') and piano pieces, etc. For an arrangement, see 'FANTASTIC TOYSHOP'. Exploiter of the orchestral crescendo, and noted in his day for 'noisy' effects; but his lasting success is due to his musical gifts and theatrical flair.

ROSTAL, MAX (b. 1905), Austrian-born violinist who worked in Berlin and then (driven out by the Nazis) settled in England, 1934. Former infant prodigy. Noted in modern works; has also edited old music for violin, and is eminent teacher. Now resident in Switzerland.

ROSTROPOVICH, MSTISLAV LEOPOLDOVICH (b. 1927), Russian cellist who has won highest success in many countries; is also pianist (accompanist to his wife, Galina Vishnevskaya, soprano), composer, and conductor; much associated with Prokofiev, whose Cello Concertino he completed after the composer's death.

ROTA (Lat., wheel), term sometimes used for ROUND, particularly the famous 'SUMER IS ICUMEN IN', sometimes called 'the Reading Rota', becàuse its conjectural composer, John of Fornsete, was a monk of Reading Abbey.

ROTA, NINO (b. 1911), Italian composer of operas including 'The Two Shy People' (*I Due Timidi*) originally for radio; also of two symphonies, chamber music, songs (some to texts by Tagore), etc. Pupil of Pizzetti and Casella; his music has certain humorous touches. At eleven, had already composed an oratorio.

ROTHMÜLLER, (ARON) MARKO (b. 1908), Yugoslav baritone, active in opera in Zürich, London (Covent Garden), Vienna, etc. – e.g. title-roles of Berg's 'WOZZECK'. Also composer (Hebrew songs, a Divertimento for trombone with strings and kettledrums, etc.), and writer on Jewish music.

ROTHWELL, EVELYN, see BARBIROLLI.

ROUET D'OMPHALE, LE, see OMPHALE'S SPINNING WHEEL.

ROUND, type of short vocal 'perpetual CANON' in which the voices, entering in turn, all sing the melody at the same pitch (or at the octave). 'London's Burning' is a familiar example.

ROUSSEAU, JEAN-JACQUES (1712–78), Swiss philosopher resident in France: author of 'The Social Contract', etc. Also wrote on various aspects of music. Championed Italian, as against French, opera (see WAR OF THE BUFFOONS) and himself composed opera 'The Village Soothsayer' (Fr., *Le Devin du village*) in demonstration of his views; also composed songs.

ROUSSEL, ALBERT (1869–1937), French composer: had naval career until 1893, then studied with d'Indy and others. After visiting India wrote some works in an Eastern-influenced style, including opera 'Padmâvati'. His later works, some with NEO-CLASSICAL traits, include four symphonies, orchestral suite in F, comic opera 'Aunt Caroline's Will', ballets 'THE SPIDER'S BANQUET' and 'BACCHUS AND ARIADNE'; also chamber works, piano pieces, songs, etc. Contributor to the ballet 'JEANNE'S FAN'.

ROVESCIO, AL (It.,) in reverse. This may refer to either (1) a passage that can be performed backward, or (2) a type of CANON in which an upward interval in the original voice becomes a downward interval (of the same distance) in the imitating voice, and *vice versa*.

ROWLEY, ALEC (1892–1958), English pianist, educationist, and composer, favouring a conservative, recognizably English style. Works include two piano concertos, suite for strings 'The Boyhood of Christ', educational piano music, etc.

ROXOLANE, LA, nickname for Haydn's symphony no. 63 in C (about 1777), after a French song which is used in it as the subject of variations.

ROYAL LIVERPOOL PHILHARMONIC ORCHESTRA, an orchestra which became full-time in 1943; its parent society dates from 1840. The title 'Royal' was granted in 1956. Conductor since 1963 (succeeding John Pritchard), Charles Groves.

ROYAL PHILHARMONIC ORCHESTRA, a London orchestra founded by T. Beecham in 1946. It has no present link with the Royal Philharmonic Society (founded 1813). Principal conductor since 1961, Rudolf Kempe.

RUBATO (It., robbed), to be performed with a certain freedom as to time, for the purpose of giving the music suitable expression. As a noun ('he played with too much rubato') it is really short for *tempo rubato*.

RUBBRA, (CHARLES) EDMUND (b. 1901), English composer, pupil of Vaughan Williams, Holst, and others; also pianist, particularly as member of piano trio; lecturer at Oxford University. Compositions, in which English 16th-century music has had considerable influence, include seven symphonies, Sinfonia Concertante for piano and orchestra, piano concerto, viola concerto; two string quartets, Fantasia on a Theme of Machaut for recorder with string quartet and harpsichord, and other chamber music; two Masses – one Anglican, one for the Roman Catholic Church which Rubbra entered in 1948; other choral works, songs, etc. Contributor to 'A GARLAND FOR THE QUEEN'. See also CAVATINA.

RUBINSTEIN, ANTON GRIGOREVICH (1829–94), Russian pianist of great distinction, and composer of 'The Demon' and other operas, six symphonies, five piano concertos, etc. in German, rather than Russian, Romantic style. Now hardly known except for a few songs and piano pieces including 'MELODY IN F'. Brother of N. Rubinstein, below; no relation of Artur Rubinstein.

RUBINSTEIN, ARTUR (b. 1889), Polish-born pianist resident mainly in U.S.A.; internationally known virtuoso said to have played in every country except Tibet. Pupil of Leschetizky. Composer of some piano music, etc. No relation of the other Rubinsteins.

RUBINSTEIN, NIKOLAY GRIGOREVICH (1835–81), Russian pianist, founder and principal of Moscow Conservatory, and composer of piano music, etc. Brother of more famous Anton Rubinstein (above).

RUDDIGORE, *or The Witch's Curse*, operetta by Sullivan, produced in London, 1887. Libretto by W. S. Gilbert: the plot with 'Ruddigore' as the name of a family of 'bad baronets', parodies Victorian melodrama. The original spelling was *Ruddygore*, afterwards changed as offensive.

RUDHYAR, DANE, pen-name of Daniel Chennevière (b. 1895), French-born composer who settled in U.S.A., 1917. Works, in a dissonant idiom and mostly linked to his occultist beliefs, include symphonic poems ('To the Real', 'The Surge of Fire', etc.), piano pieces, songs.

RUGBY, no. 2 of Honegger's three 'SYMPHONIC MOVEMENTS'. First peformed 1928. The reference is to football, not to education or the railway junction – despite 'PACIFIC 231', its predecessor.

RUGGLES, CARL (b. 1876), American composer, also painter; cultivates an intensely individual style of harsh dissonances and atonal leanings. Works include 'Angels' for six trumpets, symphonic poems 'Men and Mountains' and 'Sun-Treader', piano concertino.

RÜHRTROMMEL (Ger., rolling drum), equals TENOR DRUM (not side drum).

RUINS OF ATHENS, THE, overture and incidental music (including a Turkish March) by Beethoven for a play by Kotzebue, produced for the opening of the German Theatre at Pest (Hungary), 1812.

RULE, BRITANNIA, see ALFRED; also SARGENT.

RUMBA, Cuban dance in 8/8 time (three beats *plus* three *plus* two) becoming established in ballroom dancing in U.S.A. and Europe about 1930. Occasional use in concert music – see JAMAICAN RUMBA.

RUNNING SET, type of dance discovered by Cecil Sharp in rural communities of the Appalachian Mountains (U.S.A.) and thought by him to be of English origin; Vaughan Williams's *The Running Set* is accordingly an orchestral arrangement of English folk-songs suitable for this type of dance.

RUSALKA, a water-sprite in Slavonic legend. *The Rusalka* is thus the title of operas by (1) Dargomizhsky, produced in St Petersburg, 1856; libretto by composer, after Pushkin; (2) Dvořák, produced in Prague, 1901; libretto by J. Kvapil.

RUSSELL, HENRY (1812–1900), English singer, organist, and composer of 'A Life on the Ocean Wave' and other songs; father of LANDON RONALD.

RUSSIAN BASSOON, obsolete bass wind instrument related not to the bassoon but to the SERPENT.

RUSSIAN EASTER FESTIVAL (Rus., *Voskresenaya*), overture by Rimsky-Korsakov, 1888, based on Russian Orthodox Church melodies and showing finally 'the unbridled pagan-religious merry-making on the morn of Easter Sunday'.

RUSSIAN QUARTETS, name for Haydn's six string quartets, op. 33, of 1781: they are dedicated to the Grand Duke Paul of Russia. They are also known as 'Gli Scherzi' from the character of their minuet movements (see SCHERZO), or the 'Maiden Quartets' (Ger., *Jungfernquartette*) for a reason unknown.

RUSSLAN AND LUDMILLA, opera by Glinka, produced in St Petersburg, 1842. Libretto by V. F. Shirkov and K. A. Bakhturin, after Puskin: named after the two lovers, eventually united despite the powers of magic.

RUSSOLO, LUIGI 1885–1947), Italian composer prominent in a movement to use noise-instruments in musical compositions – see FUTURISM.

RUST, FRIEDRICH WILHELM (1739–96), German composer who studied under C. P. E. Bach and W. F. Bach, and also in Italy. Wrote stage and church works, etc.; also forty-eight piano sonatas, which through later editorial tinkering (by his fond grandson, Wilhelm Rust, 1822–92) for a time won him repute as an important anticipator of Beethoven.

'RUSTIC WEDDING' (Ger., *Ländliche Hochzeit*), title of symphony by K. Goldmark, 1876: five illustrative movements, no. 1 a wedding march.

RUSTLE OF SPRING, no. 3 of six piano pieces (published 1909) by Sinding – now ubiquitous and almost the only work of his to be heard.

RUY BLAS, play by Victor Hugo for which Mendelssohn wrote an overture and a chorus for a production in Leipzig, 1839.

S

S., abbr. of SCHMIEDER (in numbering Bach's works).

S, symbol in TONIC SOL-FA for the fifth degree (dominant) of the scale, pronounced *soh*.

SF., abbr. of SFORZANDO.

SFP., abbreviation signifying that a SZORZANDO is to be followed by a (sudden) softness of tone.

SFZ., abbr. of SFORZANDO.

SOP., abbr. of SOPRANO.

SORD., abbr. of SORDINO.

SABATA, VICTOR DE (1892–1967), Italian conductor, active in opera (especially at the Scala, Milan) and in concerts, visiting Britain from 1947. Also composer of symphonic poems, operas, ballets, etc.

SACCHINI, ANTONIO (MARIA GASPARO) (1730–86), Italian composer who lived in London, 1773–81, and later in Paris, where he died. Wrote about forty operas, at first in Italian, then in French and influenced by Gluck's reforms. Also composed church music, string quartets, etc.

SACHER, PAUL (b. 1906), Swiss conductor, who founded the famous Basel Chamber Orchestra in 1926; also, since 1941, conductor of the Zürich chamber orchestra called the Collegium Musicum. Active in modern music, and has also conducted at Glyndebourne.

SACKBUT, an early English name for the trombone.

SACRE DU PRINTEMPS, LE, see THE RITE OF SPRING.

SACRED SERVICE, title usual in English for Bloch's setting of a

Jewish Sabbath morning service (1933) for baritone, chorus, and orchestra. The Hebrew title is 'Avodath hakodesh', and the text follows a U.S. 'Reformed' Jewish use.

SADKO, opera by Rimsky-Korsakov, produced in Moscow, 1898 – partly based on a symphonic poem of the same name by the composer, 1867. Libretto by composer and V. I. Belsky: Sadko is a bard, the setting is 10th-century, and the story is legendary in character. The work is styled an 'opera-bylina' (from a type of old Russian saga).

SADLER'S WELLS, a London theatre dating from the late 17th century; reopened 1931 for a repertory of plays and opera, plays being shortly dropped and ballet added. Sadler's Wells Opera retained its name on moving to the London Coliseum in 1968.

SAEVERUD, HARALD (b. 1897), Norwegian composer of seven symphonies, fifty 'Little Variations' (on a theme three bars long) and other works for orchestra; incidental music to Ibsen's *Peer Gynt*; many piano pieces, including 'Ballad of Revolt'. Influenced by Norwegian folk-music.

SAGA, A (Swe., *En Saga*), symphonic poem by Sibelius, 1892, revised 1901. It alludes to the nature of the Scandinavian sagas in general.

SAIKKOLA, LAURI (b. 1906), Finnish composer of four symphonies, a cantata based on the Kalevala (Finnish national epic poem), three string quartets, etc.; also viola-player.

SAINT ... Entries beginning 'Saint' or 'St' are all listed here.

ST ANNE, English hymn-tune, probably by Croft, published 1708; now usually sung to the words 'O God, our help in ages past'. By mere coincidence an organ fugue in E♭ by Bach opens with the same notes: this is therefore known in England as the 'St Anne' Fugue.

'ST ANTHONY' VARIATIONS, work by Brahms for orchestra, 1873, also issued by the composer for two pianos. Brahms took the theme from a 'Feld-partita' (suite for military band) in B♭ by Haydn, and called it 'Variations on a Theme of Haydn'; but it has since been found that the theme itself (called the 'St Anthony' Chorale) was not Haydn's own but was borrowed by him for the occasion. The present name is thus now preferred.

ST FRANCIS, see NOBILISSIMA VISIONE.

'ST JOHN' PASSION, properly *The Passion According to St John*, a setting by Bach for solo voices, chorus, and orchestra of the Passion narrative from St John's Gospel, with interpolations; first performed 1723. See PASSION; cp. 'ST MATTHEW' PASSION.

ST JOHN'S NIGHT ON THE BARE MOUNTAIN (Rus., *Ivanova noch na lisoi gore*), orchestral work by Mussorgsky, alluding to a 'witches' sabbath'; it took various forms, originating in 1867 and eventually ending as an introduction to Act III of the opera 'SOROCHINTSKY FAIR'. This last version was revised and altered by Rimsky-Korsakov, and it is his version (1908, usually called *Night on the Bare Mountain* or *Night on Bald Mountain*) that is usually performed. It is misleading to pass this off as Mussorgsky's, particularly since Mussorgsky's original has itself now become known.

'ST MATTHEW' PASSION, properly *The Passion According to St Matthew*, a setting by Bach for solo voices, chorus, and orchestra of the Passion narrative from St Matthew's Gospel, with interpolations first performed 1729. See PASSION; cp. 'ST JOHN' PASSION.

SAINT OF BLEECKER STREET, THE, opera by Menotti, produced in New York, 1954. Libretto by composer. The 'Saint' is a girl of a poor Italian-American family.

ST PAUL, oratorio by Mendelssohn, first performed at Düsseldorf, 1836; text from the Bible. Known in German as *Paulus*.

ST PAUL'S SUITE, work for string orchestra by G. Holst, 1913 – written for the orchestra of St Paul's Girls School, Hammersmith (London), where he taught. Incorporates the folk-tune called the 'Dargason'.

SAINT-SAËNS, (CHARLES) CAMILLE (1835–1921), French composer, pupil of Halévy and Gounod; able pianist from early childhood; also organist. Works include 'SAMSON AND DELILAH' and other operas; symphonic poems on Liszt's lines, e.g. 'OMPHALE'S SPINNING WHEEL'; five symphonies (no. 3 with organ), 'DANSE MACABRE', and other works for orchestra; five piano concertos, three violin concertos, two cello concertos, 'THE CARNIVAL OF ANIMALS' for two pianos and orchestra; chamber music, church music, many songs. Exceptionally long and prolific career. His direct, melodious, transparent style gained great success, now somewhat diminished. Frequently visited England; Hon.Mus.D., Cambridge, 1893.

SALAS, JUAN ORREGO, see ORREGO SALAS.

SALICET, SALICIONAL, organ stop of soft tone with some resemblance to orchestral stringed instruments.

SALIERI, ANTONIO (1750–1825), Italian composer who lived mainly in Vienna, and died there: Beethoven and Schubert were among his pupils. He intrigued against Mozart, but the idea (as expressed in Rimsky-Korsakov's opera 'MOZART AND SALIERI') that he poisoned Mozart is false. Wrote mainly Italian operas, but also six Masses, a 'PASSION' oratorio in Italian, two piano concertos, etc.

SALMO (It., pl. -*i*), psalm.

SALOME, opera by R. Strauss, produced in Dresden, 1905. Libretto a German translation of Oscar Wilde's French play – after the New Testament, but incorporating the medieval idea that Salome was in love with John the Baptist.

SALOMON, JOHANN PETER (1745–1815), German-born violinist and concert-organizer who settled in London (dying there); brought Haydn to England and commissioned what are now called the Salomon Symphonies.

SALOMON SYMPHONIES, the twelve symphonies commissioned from Haydn by J. P. Salomon (above) for Haydn's visits to England, 1791–2 and 1794–5. They were Haydn's last symphonies.

SALÓN MÉXICO, EL, work by Copland, first performed in Mexico City, 1937; based on the composer's impressions of a Mexican dance-hall, and incorporating some traditional Mexican tunes.

SALTERELLO, type of Italian dance: in its most common meaning, a lively dance incorporating jumps, the music similar to tarantella but not so smoothly flowing. The finale of Mendelssohn's 'ITALIAN' SYMPHONY is so styled. So spelt in modern Italian, but Mendelssohn apparently wrote *saltarello*.

SALZEDO, CARLOS (1885–1961), French-born harpist resident in U.S.A.; composer of works for harp and for various combinations including harp (e.g. 'Four Preludes to the Afternoon of a Telephone' for two harps). He sometimes used new effects on the instrument, e.g. percussion on the frame of the harp. No relation of Leonard Salzedo.

SALZEDO, LEONARD (LOPES) (b. 1921), English composer, pupil of Howells. Works include 'The Fugitive', 'Mardi Gras', and other ballets; six string quartets; two symphonies, film music, etc. Was also London orchestral violinist. No relation of Carlos Salzedo.

SAMAZEUILH, GUSTAVE (MARIE VICTOR FERNAND) (b. 1877), French composer of symphonic poems, chamber works, serenade for guitar, etc.; also critic. Pupil of Chausson, d'Indy, and Dukas.

SAMINSKY, LAZARE (b. 1882), Russian-born composer and conductor (pupil of Liadov and Rimsky-Korsakov), resident in U.S.A. since 1920. Works include five symphonies, music for Jewish worship, opera-ballet 'Jephtha's Daughter'. Is also writer, particularly on modern music and Jewish music, and synagogue music director.

SAMISEN, Japanese plucked-string instrument: the application of this term to a gong-like percussion instrument in Puccini's 'MADAME BUTTERFLY' is an error.

SAMMARTINI, GIOVANNI BATTISTA (1698–1775), Italian composer and organist, teacher of Gluck. Among his works (said to number 2,000) are various symphonies and string quartets which are considered as pioneering the style later developed, e.g. by Haydn and Mozart.

SAMSON, oratorio by Handel (text from poems by Milton) first performed in London, 1743. Cp. SAMSON AND DELILAH.

SAMSON AND DELILAH (Fr., *Samson et Dalila*), opera by Saint-Saëns, produced (in German) in Weimar, 1877. Libretto by F. Lemaire. At first barred, because of its biblical subject, from stage presentation in Britain. See also THE WARRIOR.

SANZOGNO, NINO (b. 1911), Italian conductor, noted e.g. at the Scala (Milan), Venice Festival, Italian radio.

SARABAND, SARABANDE (Eng., Fr.), dance coming to the rest of Europe from Spain, and forming a regular constituent of the old SUITE; it is slow and in 3/2 time.

SARASATE, PABLO MARTÍN MELITÓN (full surname Sarasate y Navascues; 1844–1908), Spanish violinist (among the most famous virtuosos of his time), who toured widely; composed many works for his instrument, among them some of more value than mere show-pieces, including a fantasy (with orchestra) in gipsy style called 'Zigeunerweisen' (see ZIGEUNER). See also SPANISH SYMPHONY.

SARDANA (Sp.), a national dance of Catalonia, properly to pipe-and-drum accompaniment.

SARGENT, (HAROLD) MALCOLM (WATTS) (1895–1967), English conductor; also pianist (pupil of Moiseiwitsch) and formerly organist. Conductor of BBC Symphony Orchestra, 1950–7, of Royal Choral Society from 1928, etc. Various tours overseas. Arranger of traditional songs, orchestrator of accompaniment to Brahms's 'FOUR BIBLICAL SONGS;'; revived and arranged the original melody of Arne's 'Rule, Britannia' (see ALFRED) of which the generally known version is corrupt. Knighted 1947.

SARKA (SMETANA), see MY COUNTRY.

SARRUSOPHONE, double-reed instrument, classified as woodwind though made of brass; invented by a French bandmaster named Sarrus, 1856, and made in various sizes. The largest (*double-bass sarrusophone*) has been stipulated in the orchestra to replace the double-bassoon, e.g. by Saint-Saëns and Delius. Various sizes have been used in some Continental military bands.

SARTI, GIUSEPPE (1729–1802), Italian composer who travelled much, wrote more than seventy operas (in Italian, French, Danish, and Russian), and died in Berlin. Other works include church music and harpsichord sonatas. In 'DON GIOVANNI' Mozart uses an air from Sarti's 'Between Two Litigants' (It., *Fra due litiganti*) as part of the hero's supper-music.

SATIE, ERIK (ALFRED LESLIE) (1866–1925), French composer; for a time worked as café pianist, etc., and at 39 became a pupil of Roussel and d'Indy. Influenced younger composers (see SIX) towards a cool, clear style and away from the lushness sometimes associated with IMPRESSIONISM. His piano solo and duets mostly have eccentric titles, e.g. 'Three Pear-Shaped Pieces'; several of these have been orchestrated by Poulenc and others. Wrote also ballets, including 'Relâche' (the word displayed by French theatres when they are closed), operettas, Mass (*Messe des pauvres*), symphonic drama 'SOCRATES'. Towards the end of his life a group of disciples (including Désormières and Sauguet) became known as the Arcueil School (*École d'Arcueil*) – named from the Paris suburb where Satie lived.

SATYRICON, overture by Ireland, 1946, headed with a quotation from the 'Satyricon' of Petronius (d.*c.* 66 A.D.). The quotation includes the phrase: 'not only to improve our learning, but to be merry . . .'

SATZ (Ger., a setting), term of several different musical applications in German, including (1) a musical setting; so *Tonsatz* ('note-setting') for composition; (2) a movement; so Schubert's isolated QUARTET MOVEMENT is called *Quartettsatz*; (3) a theme or subject – so *Hauptsatz*, main theme; *Nebensatz*, subsidiary theme.

SAUDADES, Portuguese (plural) work of uncertain origin, but carrying the implication of wistful remembrance of things past; it has been used for two sets of piano pieces by Milhaud, 'Saudades do Brasil' (... of Brazil), and for a set of songs by Warlock.

SAUGUET, HENRI, pen-name of Jean Pierre Poupard (b. 1901), French composer, pupil of Koechlin and others; also critic. Works, many in a light vein, include opera 'Marianne's Caprices'; 'The Strolling Players' (*Les Forains*), and other ballets; song-cycle 'The Fortune-Teller' (*La Voyante*) with orchestra; piano concerto, two string quartets.

SAUL, oratorio by Handel, first performed in London, 1739. Text, based on the Bible, by C. Jennens. Contains a famous 'Dead March'.

SAURET, ÉMILE (1857–1920), French violinist who taught in London (where he died), Chicago, and elsewhere; composer of two violin concertos, etc.

SAUSAGE BASSOON, freak instrument of bassoon type, the tube being doubled up many times on itself and inserted into a small box, apparently thought to resemble a sausage in shape. An alternative (and more formal) name was 'racket(t)'.

SAUTILLÉ (Fr., springing), type of bowing on the violin, etc., in which the bow springs rebounding off the string.

SAVILE, JEREMY (17th century), English composer known only for a few songs (including 'Here's a Health unto His Majesty') and part-songs.

SĀVITRI, one-act opera by G. Holst, produced in London, 1916. Libretto by composer, after an episode in the Hindu scriptures: Sāvitri is the self-sacrificing wife of a woodman.

SAVOY OPERAS, name for the operettas (or light operas) composed by Sullivan with librettos by W. S. Gilbert. From 'IOLANTHE' onward, these were first heard at the Savoy Theatre, London, built specially for them. The name is also customarily held to cover 'COX AND BOX' (libretto by F. C. Burnand, not by Gilbert) since this has remained in the D'Oyly Carte company's repertory along with Gilbert's works.

SAW, MUSICAL, a hand-saw used as a musical instrument for purposes of novel entertainment – very rare in serious composition (but see MAYUZUMI): it is held by the knees and played with a violin bow, the left hand altering the tension (and thus the pitch of the note produced) by bending the saw. See also FLEXATONE.

SAX, ADOLPHE (real first names Antoine Joseph; 1814–94), Belgian inventor of the SAXHORN and SAXOPHONE families of instruments.

SAXHORN, type of brass instrument with valves invented by A. Sax in 1845. As to nomenclature, there is a great difference between authorities and between various countries (see also FLUGELHORN, a near relation). The instruments used in brass bands in Britain, which are TRANSPOSING INSTRUMENTS, are the *tenor saxhorn* in E♭ and the *baritone saxhorn* in B♭, known simply as 'tenor horn' (or 'E♭

horn') and 'baritone': the former is also used in military bands but neither is used in the orchestra. The series of instruments may be regarded as being continued downwards in pitch by the TUBA family, including EUPHONIUM.

SAXOPHONE, name of a family of wind instruments having a reed resembling a clarinet's – and therefore classified among the WOODWIND (not 'brass') despite a metal body. Invented by A. Sax about 1840. Made in various sizes, the lower-pitched ones in S-shape or with additional curves (the *alto* exists in both S-shaped and straight forms). The most common are the *alto* (TRANSPOSING INSTRUMENT in E♭) with compass from the D♭ below middle C upwards for about two and a half octaves, and the *tenor* in B♭ a fifth lower. Both these are occasionally used in the modern symphony orchestra, and invariably in dance bands and British military bands (not brass bands). The other saxophones are rare outside the dance band, which frequently has a *baritone* (below the tenor, in E♭) and sometimes a *soprano* (above the alto, in B♭); rarer are the *bass* (lower than the baritone, in B♭) and the *sopranino* (higher than the soprano, in E♭). The saxophones are thus alternately in B♭ and E♭. The only other type to be commonly found is the so-called *C melody saxophone* (pitched between alto and tenor), not transposing, and so easier to use for playing from song-copies with piano accompaniment, etc. Note that the saxophone was not an ingredient of 'primitive' jazz (basic instruments being clarinet, cornet, and trombone); it is a 'sophisticated' addition.

SCALA, THE (or *La Scala*), the common form of reference to the Teatro alla Scala in Milan, erected 1788, and now ranking as Italy's main opera-house. It is so named because it was built on the former site of a church, Santa Maria alla Scala.

SCALA DI SETA, LA, see THE SILKEN LADDER.

SCALE, a progression of single notes upwards or downwards in 'steps'. (Cp. It. *scala*, stairway.) So *scalic* – e.g. 'a scalic figure', progressing upwards or downwards in steps. For the *major scale* and *minor scale*, see MAJOR. See also CHROMATIC, DIATONIC, PENTATONIC, WHOLE-TONE, MODE, TWELVE-NOTE.

SCAPINO, overture by Walton, first performed 1941. Based on an etching of 1622, Scapino being a comic valet in old Italian comedy.

SCARAMOUCHE, title of suite for two pianos by Milhaud: so called because the music is based on music by Milhaud for a play, *The Flying Doctor* produced in Paris, 1937, at the Théâtre Scaramouche.

SCARLATTI, ALESSANDRO (1660–1725), Italian composer who worked chiefly in Naples; reckoned the founder of the type of Italian opera which conquered all Europe in the 18th century. Composed more than 100 operas, many now lost; 600 'cantatas' for solo voice and continuo; various other cantatas, oratorios, Masses, madrigals, etc.; also chamber music. Possibly a pupil of Carissimi in boyhood.

Held various court and church posts. Father of Domenico Scarlatti.

SCARLATTI, (GIUSEPPE) DOMENICO (1685–1757), Italian composer; at first wrote Italian opera, etc., on the model of his father (see preceding entry), and was known also as a harpsichord virtuoso; but went in 1720 to Portugal and later to Spain (dying in Madrid) and there wrote the greater number of his single-movement harpsichord sonatas. These, numbering over 550, and in their time also called 'Exercises' (It., *Esercizi*), exploit with great variety the capabilities of the BINARY-FORM movement, and foreshadow later SONATA-FORM. (For a nicknamed one, see CAT'S FUGUE; for the numbering of the sonatas, see KIRKPATRICK.) Other works include a STABAT MATER and other church music. It is possible, but not proved, that he visited London in 1719.

SCENA (It., stage, scene), a solo vocal concert-piece to words of a dramatic nature, resembling a lengthy operatic extract. Also called *song-scena*. Spohr gave the designation 'in the form of a song-scena' to his violin concerto no. 8.

SCENES FROM GOETHE'S FAUST, see FAUST.

SCENES OF CHILDHOOD (Ger., *Kinderscenen*), set of thirteen short piano pieces by Schumann, 1838, with titles alluding to childhood life.

SCHAUSPIELDIREKTOR, DER, see THE IMPRESARIO.

SCHEHERAZADE, see SHEHERAZADE.

SCHEIDT, SAMUEL (1587–1654), German organist and composer especially of organ works (including hymn-tune harmonizations); reformed organ notation and did away with improvised ornaments. Wrote also vocal dance music, etc.

SCHEIN, JOHANN HERMANN (1586–1630), German composer and church musician. Works include hymns (some to his own words), instrumental dances, madrigals; shows Italian influence.

SCHELLING, ERNEST (HENRY) (1876–1939), American pianist (pupil of Paderewski and others), composer (pupil of Bruckner and others), and conductor. Works, in ROMANTIC style, include 'A Victory Ball' for orchestra; works for piano and orchestra, and for piano alone; songs. Was also active in bringing music to young audiences.

SCHELOMO, see SHELOMO.

SCHEMELLI, GEORG CHRISTIAN (*c.* 1678–?), German church musician who published the Schemelli Hymn-book.

SCHEMELLI HYMN-BOOK, usual name for the 'Musical Song-Book', published 1736 by G. Schemelli (above); its musical editor was Bach, who afterwards wrote chorale preludes on some of its hymn-tunes.

SCHENKER, HEINRICH (1868–1935), Austrian composer (pupil of Bruckner) who was mainly important as theorist: he claimed that a single type of basic musical structure underlies all the masterpieces written in the period from Bach to Brahms.

SCHERCHEN, HERMANN (1891–1966), German-born conductor, resident in Switzerland since 1932. Active in performing, and also in publishing, modern works of various schools (especially those of TWELVENOTE composers); author of textbook on conducting.

SCHERZANDO, direction that an impression of light-heartedness is to be given. Cp. SCHERZO.

SCHERZI, GLI, another name for Haydn's RUSSIAN QUARTETS. Alludes to the character of the 'minuet' movements: see SCHERZO. The title means 'The Scherzos'.)

SCHERZO (It., joke), a type of lively movement which historically – chiefly through Haydn and, especially, Beethoven – developed from the minuet as used in symphonies, string quartets, etc. Usually therefore it is in the characteristic minuet form, AABA; and the B section is called the TRIO (as in the minuet). Usually also it is in 3/4 time. The original implication of humour is by no means always maintained, but fast tempo is obligatory and sentimentality is avoided. Examples exist also of the scherzo not as a movement of a larger work, but as an independent work of its own – notably Chopin's four for piano. See preceding entries.

SCHERZOSO, equals SCHERZANDO.

SCHIBLER, ARMIN (b. 1920), Swiss composer of operas 'The Spanish Rose-Tree' and 'Feet in the Fire', symphonic variations, fantasy for viola and small orchestra, a Psalter for home use, etc. Pupil of W. Burkhard and others; admits debt to Vivaldi and Bach.

SCHICKSALSLIED, see SONG OF DESTINY.

SCHIPA, TITO (1890–1966), Italian operatic tenor – more active in recitals than stage appearances, however.

SCHLAGINSTRUMENT(E) (Ger.), percussion instrument(s).

SCHLEPPEND (Ger.), dragging; *nicht schleppend*, direction that the pace is not to be allowed to drag.

SCHLUSS (Ger.), end; *Schluss-Satz*, final section (see SATZ).

SCHLÜSSEL (Ger.), clef. (Not 'key', though in German *Schlüssel* means an ordinary key, as *clef* does in French.)

SCHMIDT, FRANZ (1874–1939), Austrian composer of oratorio 'The Book with Seven Seals' (after Revelations); four symphonies, etc., in traditional Austrian-symphonic style. Was also pianist, organist, and cellist.

SCHMIDT-ISSERSTEDT, HANS (b. 1900), German conductor; founder (1945) and conductor of Hamburg Radio Symphony Orchestra. Toured Europe, Australia, etc. Also composer of opera and orchestral works.

SCHMIEDER, WOLFGANG (b. 1901), German musicologist whose complete thematic index to Bach now provides the standard means of numbering his works. Such numbers are prefixed by 'S.' (for Schmieder) or 'BWV' (*Bach Werke-Verzeichnis* – i.e. Index to Bach's Works).

SCHMITT, FLORENT (1870–1958), French composer, pupil of Massenet

Fauré, and others; also pianist and writer on music. He cultivated a style based on French impressionism but of individual close-packed texture and sometimes incorporating unusual rhythmical experiments. Works include ballets 'The Tragedy of Salome' and 'Oriane and the Prince of Love'; choral setting of Psalm 46; Legend for saxophone and orchestra; various chamber music (including quartet for three trombones and tuba), many piano solos.

SCHNABEL, ARTUR (1882–1951), German pianist; driven from Germany by the Nazis, settled in U.S.A., died in Geneva. One of the most authoritative performers of his time, especially of Beethoven and other 'Viennese classics'; also musical editor and well-known teacher. Almost never performed modern works, but himself composed three symphonies, orchestral Rhapsody, etc., in very abstruse atonal idiom. His son Karl Ulrich Schnabel (b. 1909) is also a pianist.

SCHNEIDERHAN, WOLFGANG (b. 1915), Austrian violinist, noted as soloist, leader of a string quartet, and as a leader of the Vienna Philharmonic Orchestra; wife is IRMGARD SEEFRIED.

SCHNELL (Ger.), fast; *schneller*, faster.

SCHOBERT, JOHANN (*c.* 1720–1767), German harpsichordist and composer who lived in Paris from 1760 and died there (of eating toadstools mistaken for mushrooms). Wrote harpsichord solos and concertos, etc.; influenced Mozart, whose first four keyboard concertos were arrangements of Schobert and other composers.

SCHOECK, OTHMAR (1886–1957), Swiss composer and conductor, pupil of Reger and favouring an expansive German-romantic style. Works include violin concerto, horn concerto, operas, and many songs – with accompaniments for piano, for chamber groups, for orchestra.

SCHOENBERG, ARNOLD (1874–1951), Austrian-born composer who worked in Germany and then (driven out by the Nazis as a Jew and a composer of 'decadent' music) from 1933 in U.S.A., thereafter changing the spelling of his name from the original Schönberg. Died in Los Angeles. At first composed in POST-ROMANTIC style (e.g. in 'TRANSFIGURED NIGHT', 'Gurrelieder' – see 'SONGS OF GURRA'); by 1908, however, had developed a technique of ATONALITY (keylessness) shown e.g. in 'PIERROT LUNAIRE'; afterwards systematized this into TWELVE-NOTE technique (from about 1923) – later of great influence internationally. He himself varied in strictness of adherence to this technique, relaxing it (i.e. admitting the idea of key), e.g. in his late 'Ode to Napoleon'. Several works use 'SPEECH-SONG', invented by him (and also influential). Other works include opera 'MOSES AND AARON', monodrama 'EXPECTATION' (*Erwartung*), cantata 'A SURVIVOR FROM WARSAW', piano concerto, violin concerto, symphonic poem 'PELLÉAS AND MÉLISANDE', two CHAMBER SYMPHONIES, four string quartets, various songs and piano pieces. Also writer on music.

SCHÖNBERG, see SCHOENBERG.

SCHÖNE MÜLLERIN, DIE, see THE FAIR MAID OF THE MILL.

SCHOOL FOR FATHERS, the title by which is known in England (in E. J. Dent's translation) Wolf-Ferrari's comic opera 'I quatro rusteghi' (Italian [Venetian dialect], The four boors), produced (in German) in Munich, 1906. Libretto (in Italian) by G. Pizzolato, dealing with the comic outwitting of four unsympathetic men.

SCHOOL FOR WIVES, opera by Liebermann, after Molière's play (*L'École des femmes*); originally in one act, in English (libretto by Elisabeth Montagu), produced in Louisville, Kentucky, 1955; later expanded to three acts, with German libretto by Heinrich Strobel (*Schule der Frauen*).

SCHOOLMASTER, THE, nickname for Haydn's symphony no. 55 in E♭, 1774, perhaps from the grave character of its second movement.

SCHÖPFUNG, SCHÖPFUNGSMESSE, see CREATION, CREATION MASS.

SCHOTTISCHE (Ger. pl. Scottish), type of ballroom dance similar to polka, popular in the 19th century. The origin of the name is unknown; the dance is not the same as the ÉCOSSAISE, despite the name.

SCHRAMMEL QUARTET, type of Austrian light-music combination of two violins, guitar, and accordion (named after Joseph Schrammel, 1850–93, leader of such a quartet).

SCHREKER, FRANZ (1878–1934), Austrian composer, born in Monaco. Director of the Berlin State Music High School, 1920–32. Works include 'The Distant Sound' (*Der ferne Klang*) and eight other operas, ballet after Oscar Wilde's 'The Birthday of the Infanta', songs with orchestra; also CHAMBER SYMPHONY (1916, notable for cultivation of chamber orchestra, in contrast to the 'outsize' orchestrations then in vogue).

SCHUBERT, FRANZ, name of two composers; the famous one is *Franz Peter Schubert* (below), the other one is *Franz Schubert* (1808–78), German violinist-composer who worked in Dresden: his violin solo 'L'Abeille' (Fr., The Bee) is sometimes mistakenly attributed to his great namesake.

SCHUBERT, FRANZ (PETER) (1797–1828), Austrian composer who was born and died in Vienna, and hardly ever left it. At first a choirboy. Never held an official musical post, and gained little recognition in life. But matured early – wrote song 'Gretchen at the Spinning Wheel' (*Gretchen am Spinnrade*) at 17. Often worked very fast, once producing eight songs in a day. Composed more than 600 songs of great range and subtlety, regarded as founding the type of 19th-century German song (*Lied*). Showed high individuality also in piano pieces – including sonatas, dances, 'WANDERER' Fantasy, IMPROMPTUS, MOMENTS MUSICAUX; wrote also works for piano duet (see MARCHE MILITAIRE). His admiration for Rossini is evident e.g. in his 'Overture in the Italian style'; for Beethoven, in his string quartets (fifteen including 'DEATH AND THE MAIDEN', and also a QUARTET MOVEMENT) and symphonies – of which he never heard a performance of no. 8 ('UNFINISHED') or of no. 9 (and last) the 'GREAT C MAJOR'. (This is sometimes called no. 7, but the symphony properly so called is in E, left in skeleton form and completed e.g. by J. F. Barnett and by Weingartner. For another possible symphony see GASTEIN.) The 'TRAGIC' symphony is no. 4. Other works include 'ALFONSO AND ESTRELLA', and other operas; music to the play 'ROSAMUNDE, PRINCESS OF CYPRUS'; piano quintet ('TROUT') and other chamber music; six Latin Masses, and other church music. Unmarried. Died of typhus. For the numbering of his works, see DEUTSCH. See also LILAC TIME.

SCHULE DER FRAUEN, see SCHOOL FOR WIVES.

SCHULHOFF, ERWIN (1894–1942), Czech pianist and composer in a variety of styles – influenced by Schoenberg and also by jazz. Works include six symphonies (no. 6 'Symphony of Freedom'), concerto for string quartet and wind orchestra, many piano solos. Died in a Nazi concentration camp.

SCHULLER, GUNTHER (b. 1925), American composer, who sometimes uses TWELVE-NOTE technique; also horn-player. Works include symphony for brass and percussion; opera 'The Visitation'.

SCHULZ, SVEND (b. 1913), Danish composer, influenced by Ravel and often favouring a light style. Works include three one-act operas; three piano concertos; serenade for strings. Also conductor, especially choral, and critic.

SCHUMAN, WILLIAM (HOWARD) (b. 1910), American composer, pupil of R. Harris and others; 1945–61, head of the Juilliard School of Music, New York. His music has a modernistic (sometimes bitonal) idiom and has occasional allusions to jazz and other Americana. Works include seven symphonies (no. 5 'Symphony for Strings'); 'AMERICAN FESTIVAL OVERTURE', a 'William Billings Overture', and 'New England Triptych' (both with reference to themes by BILLINGS); 'A Free Song' and other cantatas; opera 'The Mighty Casey' (about baseball), ballet 'Undertow' (and suite drawn from it), piano concerto, violin concerto, chamber music.

SCHUMANN, CLARA (JOSEPHINE) (born Wieck; 1819–96), German pianist and composer, chiefly for piano; daughter of the composer Friedrich Wieck (1788–1873), and wife of R. Schumann (below). Made many visits to Britain; internationally noted as performer of her husband's and other works, and also as teacher.

SCHUMANN, ELISABETH (1885–1952), German-born soprano, internationally known in opera, and latterly especially in recitals of German song. Member of the Vienna State Opera; left Austria, owing to Hitler, and settled in New York, dying there.

SCHUMANN, ROBERT (ALEXANDER) (1810–56), German composer; had to abandon intended career as virtuoso pianist when he injured his hand with his own mechanical device for finger-development, 1832. Married Clara Wieck (see SCHUMANN, CLARA), 1840. Developed mental instability, in 1854 throwing himself into the Rhine; afterwards was in a mental asylum, where he died. His work shows ROMANTIC outlook and literary associations – cp. the fanciful titles (some given after composition, however) of various piano works, e.g. 'ABEGG' VARIATIONS, 'CARNIVAL', 'CARNIVAL JEST FROM VIENNA', 'KREISLERIANA', 'PAPILLONS', 'SCENES OF CHILDHOOD' (see also DAVIDSBÜNDLER). Other works include many songs (some in cycles, e.g. 'POET'S LOVE', WOMAN'S LOVE AND LIFE'); three string quartets, piano concerto, cello concerto, violin concerto (not heard till 1937, being suppressed by Clara Schumann and Joachim as unworthy); four symphonies (no. 1 'SPRING SYMPHONY', no. 3 'RHENISH'; no. 4 originally written directly after no. 1, later re-scored); cantata 'PARADISE AND THE PERI', opera 'Genoveva', 'Scenes from Goethe's FAUST', incidental music to Byron's 'MANFRED'. Also noted critic, of wide sympathies.

SCHÜTZ, HEINRICH (1585–1672), German composer; studied under G. Gabrieli in Venice and worked mainly as court composer in Dresden; influential in introducing Italian musical ideas (as to vocal declamation, concerted instrumental writing, etc.) to Germany. Worked also in Copenhagen. Works include the earliest German opera, 'Daphne' (music now lost); Italian madrigals; 'Sacred Symphonies', etc., for voices and instruments; four PASSIONS (one for each of the Gospels) and a Christmas Oratorio.

SCHWANDA THE BAGPIPER, see ŠVANDA THE BAGPIPER.

SCHWANENGESANG, see SWAN-SONG.

SCHWARTZENDORF, see MARTINI, GIOVANNI PAOLO.

SCHWARZ, RUDOLF (b. 1905), Austrian-born conductor who survived Nazi concentration camps (as a Jew) and came to Britain, 1947, as conductor of the Bournemouth Municipal Orchestra; afterwards conductor of the City of Birmingham Symphony Orchestra, BBC Symphony Orchestra, and (jointly with Boris Brott, from 1964) of Northern Sinfonia Orchestra.

SCHWARZKOPF, ELISABETH (b. 1915), German soprano active e.g. in the Vienna State Opera, at Covent Garden (from 1947), and in recital; formerly coloratura soprano, now taking more lyrical parts.

SCHWEITZER, ALBERT (1875–1965), French (Alsatian) theologian, medical missionary, and musician – organist, and writer on Bach. Awarded the Nobel Prize, 1952.

SCOOP, in singing, to glide up to a note disagreeably from below instead of attacking it cleanly.

SCORDATURA (It., mis-tuning), the tuning of a stringed instrument to notes other than the normal, for special effects – much used in the 17th century and revived in modern times; e.g. in Mahler's symphony no. 4, a solo violinist has to tune all his strings up a tone to represent the unearthly fiddling of a 'dance of death'.

SCORE, a music-copy combining in ordered form all the different PARTS allotted to various performers of a piece; so e.g. in an orchestral library, *score and parts*, meaning both the combined music-copy (for the conductor) and the separate copies containing just the music for particular instruments. So also *full score*, a score displaying every different participating voice and instrument; *short score*, a compressed version of the preceding, such as a composer may write out at first, when the outlines of his instrumentation are decided on but not the details; *open score*, a score displaying every part on a separate line – particularly for study or academic exercise, in cases when normal reasons of economy and convenience would suggest compression on to fewer staves; *miniature score* or *pocket score* or *study score*, one which reproduces all the details of a full score but is of a size more suitable for study than for a conductor's desk; *vocal score*, one giving all the voice-parts of a work but having the orchestral parts reduced to a piano part; *piano score*, one in which not only the orchestral parts but also the vocal parts (if any), are all reduced to a piano part. So also *to score*, to arrange a work for a particular combination of voices and/or instruments (whether this is part of the process of original composition, or in itself a process of arrangement of an already existing work).

SCORREVOLE (It.), scurrying, with rapid fluency.

SCOTCH SNAP, name for a rhythmic figure consisting of a short note on the beat followed by a longer one held until the next beat, e.g.,

Found in Scottish folk-music, but also elsewhere, e.g. in Hungarian folk-music, and in Purcell (as in the setting of English words like 'ruin'd').

'SCOTCH' SYMPHONY, Mendelssohn's symphony no. 3, completed 1842, dedicated to Queen Victoria, and inspired originally by the composer's visit to Scotland, 1829. No detailed scheme of allusions, however, has been discovered to be behind the music.

SCOTT, CYRIL (MEIR) (b. 1879), English composer who trained mainly in Germany and won considerable success there and in England up to about 1930 – particularly with songs and piano pieces showing an individual idiom (bold harmonic devices and an avoidance of conventional structures) which won him the unhelpful nickname of 'the English Debussy'. Has also written three operas (only one produced, in Germany); piano concerto and various other concertos; choral works; two string trios and other chamber music. Writer on music and on occultism, food reform, and other matters.

SCOTT, FRANCIS GEORGE (1880–1958), Scottish composer, pupil of

Roger-Ducasse in Paris. Has written mainly songs, of distinctively Scottish flavour, to Scottish verse; but also orchestral works, songs to English, French, and German verse, etc.

SCOTTO, RENATA (b. 1934), Italian soprano, famous in title-roles of Verdi's 'LA TRAVIATA', Puccini's 'MADAME BUTTERFLY', etc.

SCOTTISH NATIONAL ORCHESTRA, orchestra founded in 1950, succeeding a previous Scottish Orchestra; conductor since 1959, Alexander Gibson.

SCRIABIN(E), see SKRIABIN.

SCULTHORPE, PETER (b. 1929), Australian composer of 'Sun Music' for orchestra, six string quartets, etc.

SEA, THE (Fr., *La Mer*), 'three symphonic sketches' by Debussy, first performed 1905: (1) 'From dawn to midday on the sea'; (2) 'Play of the waves'; (3) 'Dialogue of the wind and the sea'.

SEA DRIFT, work by Delius, 1903, for baritone, chorus, and orchestra. Text an extract from Whitman's 'Out of the cradle endlessly rocking', itself one of a set of poems called 'Sea Drift'.

SEA PICTURES, cycle of five songs by Elgar for contralto and orchestra, 1899 – poems by various writers including (no. 2) Elgar's wife.

SEA SYMPHONY, A, title of Vaughan Williams's symphony no. 1 – which, however, was (in conformity with his practice) given no number by him. In four movements, it is a setting for soprano, baritone, chorus, and orchestra of verse by Whitman about the sea. First performed 1910.

SEARLE, HUMPHREY (b. 1915), English composer, pupil of Webern in Austria. After composing a piano concerto and other works, adopted TWELVE-NOTE technique in 1946 – but slackened the rigidity of its application in the mid-1950s. Works include trilogy using speakers and orchestra – 'Gold Coast Customs' (text, Edith Sitwell), 'The Riverrun' (James Joyce), 'The Shadow of Cain' (Edith Sitwell); operas 'The Diary of a Madman' and (after Ionesco) 'The Photo of the Colonel'; five symphonies, piano concerto no. 2, 'Poem for twenty-two solo strings', piano sonata, ballet 'Noctambules'; setting of Lear's 'The Owl and the Pussy-Cat' for speaker, flute, cello, and guitar; opera 'Hamlet'. C.B.E., 1968. Is also writer on music.

SEASONS, THE, (1) oratorio by Haydn (Ger., *Die Jahreszeiten*), first performed in Vienna, 1801; the German text is based on an English poem by James Thomson; (2) ballet with music by Glazunov, produceed 1900. See also THE FOUR SEASONS.

SEC (Fr., dry), direction that a note or chord is to be struck and released sharply.

SECCO, see RECITATIVE.

SECHTER, SIMON (1788–1867), Austrian organist, composer, and noted theorist and teacher of counterpoint. Bruckner studied with him and Schubert intended to do so (dying before he could).

SECOND (noun), an interval in melody or harmony, reckoned as taking two steps in the (major or minor) scale, counting the bottom and top notes: either a *minor second* (one semitone, e.g. C up to D♭), or *major second* (two semitones, e.g. C up to D), or *augmented second* (three semitones, e.g. C up to D♯). The last gives what is equivalent in practice to the minor third, e.g. C up to E♭, but the terms imply different harmonic contexts.) See also following entries.

SECOND (adjective), term implying the performance of a lower-pitched part (*second tenor, second trombone, second violins*, etc.) and usually – but not in choirs – also implying an inferiority in rank to the 'first' of the kind. (For *second inversion*, see POSITION.)

SECONDARY DOMINANT, see DOMINANT.

SECONDO (It., second), the lower of the two parts in a piano duet.

SECONDS, term used in the old-fashioned phrase 'to sing seconds', meaning the singing of an additional (often improvised) vocal line harmonizing with the melody.

SECRET MARRIAGE, THE (It., *Il Matrimonio segreto*), comic opera by Cimarosa, produced (in Italian) in Vienna, 1792. Libretto by G. Bertati, a comedy of intrigue based on the English play, *The Clandestine Marriage*, by Garrick and Colman.

SECRET OF SUSANNA, THE, see SUSANNA'S SECRET.

SEEFRIED, IRMGARD (b. 1919), German soprano resident in Austria, active in the Vienna State Opera, and internationally noted also as recitalist. Husband is Wolfgang SCHNEIDERHAN.

SEGNO (It.), sign; *dal segno* (or *D.S.*), from the sign, i.e. repeat the preceding passage beginning at the appropriate sign (usually 𝄋).

SEGOVIA, ANDRÉS (b. 1893), Spanish guitarist, for whom many works (e.g. by Falla, Castelnuovo-Tedesco) have been specially written.

SEGUE (It., it follows), term used as a direction to the performer to proceed with the next section without a break.

SEGUIDILLA, type of quick Spanish dance in triple time, often accompanied by castanets.

SEIBER, MÁTYÁS (GYÖRGY) (1905–60), Hungarian-born composer (formerly also cellist) resident in England from 1935; was also conductor and noted teacher. Pupil of Kodály, but later employed TWELVE-NOTE technique. Works include cantata 'ULYSSES', four string quartets, violin concerto, clarinet concertino, two orchestral suites based on old lute music, folk-song arrangements, educational piano works, film and radio music.

SELLICK, PHYLLIS (b. 1911), English pianist known as soloist and in two-piano appearances with her husband, CYRIL SMITH.

SEMELE, work by Handel, first performed 1744: it is of oratorio type, though not on a biblical subject but on Semele's love for Jupiter. Text adapted from the libretto written by Congreve for John Eccles' opera 'SEMELE', intended for performance in or about 1705, but not then given.

SEMIBREVE, the note 𝅝, considered as a time-value (U.S., whole-note); equivalent to two minims or half the (obsolete) breve. A semibreve rest is notated 𝄻

SEMI-CHORUS, a section of a choral body – not necessarily exactly half of the full chorus.

SEMIDEMISEMIQUAVER, an unusual equivalent of HEMIDEMISEMIQUAVER.

SEMI-OPERA, modern term for certain 17th- and 18th-century English stage works (particularly Purcell's, e.g. 'KING ARTHUR') in which music, although a principal element, is not so all-pervading as to justify the title of 'opera' as now understood. (In Purcell's own time the word 'opera' was freely used for these, however.)

SEMIQUAVER, the note 𝅘𝅥𝅯, considered as a time-value (U.S., sixteenth-note), equivalent to half a quaver or two demisemiquavers. A semiquaver rest is notated 𝄿

SEMIRAMIDE, SEMIRAMIS, opera by Rossini, produced in Venice, 1823. Libretto by G. Rossi (after Voltaire) about the ancient queen of Nineveh. (Semiramis is the accepted historical form, Semiramide an italianization of it.)

SEMITONE, the smallest interval commonly used in European music – on the piano, the interval between any note and the next note, higher or lower (whether this next note happens to be white or black). Cp. TONE (3).

SEMPLICE (It.), simple, simply.

SEMPRE (It.), always; *sempre più mosso*, always getting faster, i.e. getting faster and faster.

SENAILLÉ, JEAN BAPTISTE (1687–1730), French violinist and composer, pupil of Vitali in Italy; member of the orchestra at the French court. Wrote many sonatas for violin – from one of which comes the 'Allegro spiritoso' now usually heard as a bassoon (or euphonium) solo.

SENZA (It.), without.

SEPTET, (1) a performing group of seven instrumentalists or singers; (2) a composition for such: if instrumental and actually entitled 'Septet', it will probably have the character of a SONATA for seven performers, in several movements.

SEPTIMOLE, SEPTOLET, equals SEPTUPLET.

SEPTUPLET, a group of seven notes (or notes and rests) of equal time-value, written where a group of three, four, or some other number of notes is suggested by the time-signature, e.g. a seven-note group occupying a bar of 3/4 time, written 7 𝅘𝅥𝅘𝅥𝅘𝅥𝅘𝅥𝅘𝅥𝅘𝅥𝅘𝅥

SEQUENCE, (1) the repetition of a phrase at a higher or lower pitch than the original: if the intervals within it are slightly altered in the repetition so as to avoid moving out of key it is a *tonal sequence*, if they are unaltered it is a *real sequence*; (2) hymn-like composition with non-biblical Latin text, sung during the Roman Catholic High Mass or Requiem Mass; some Sequences have been set by various composers.

SERAFIN, TULLIO (1878–1968), Italian conductor, prominent in opera and in championing Italian works abroad.

SERAGLIO, THE, workably short title for Mozart's comic opera *The Abduction from the Seraglio* (Ger., *Die Entführung aus dem Serail*), produced in Vienna, 1782. Libretto by C. F. Bretzner and G. Stephanie, with a non-singing part for the benevolent Pasha who eventually releases his European captives. In 19th-century England this work was given in Italian, hence the style of title 'Il Seraglio'; but this has now no claim to good usage.

SERENADE, properly a piece of open-air evening music (cp. AUBADE), e.g. a lover's song outside his mistress's window, but now a term of the widest and vaguest significance. The classical (18th-century) use of the term indicates a piece for several instruments (often wind-instruments only) written in several movements of which the first is in SONATA-FORM and one at least of the others is a minuet. A German equivalent is *Nachtmusik* – (as in 'EINE KLEINE NACHTMUSIK'), or, for the song-type, *Ständchen*. See also the following entries.

SERENADE, title of a song-cycle by Britten for tenor with accompaniment of horn and string orchestra, first performed 1943. The words, by various poets, have a general association with evening or night.

'SERENADE' QUARTET, nickname for a famous string quartet in F, long known as Haydn's op. 3 no. 5, but now known to be by a contemporary of his (probably R. Hofstetter): its slow movement (violin melody, plucked-string accompaniment) is reminiscent of a song sung as a serenade, e.g. with guitar.

SERENADE TO MUSIC, work by Vaughan Williams for sixteen solo voices and orchestra, written in honour of Henry Wood's jubilee as a conductor and first performed 1938. Words adapted from Shakespeare's *The Merchant of Venice*.

SERENATA (It.), (1) a serenade, e.g. the popular piece by Braga so entitled, or Mozart's 'Serenata Notturna' (1776) for two orchestras, or C. Nielsen's 'Serenata in vano' (1914, depicting a 'fruitless' serenade); (2) 18th-century English term for a type of cantata approaching operatic form, e.g. Handel's 'ACIS AND GALATEA'.

SERIA, see OPERA SERIA.

SERIAL TECHNIQUE, see SERIES.

SERIES, a set of notes treated in composition not mainly as a recognizable theme, but as a kind of plastic material from which the composition is made: the order of the notes in the series is the main thing about it, and though the series can be turned upside-down, backwards, etc., a relationship to this order must be preserved. The 'note-row' in TWELVE-NOTE technique is the main example of such a series, but other serial techniques are possible.

SERIOUS SONGS (Brahms), see FOUR BIBLICAL SONGS.

SERKIN, RUDOLF (b. 1903), Austrian pianist, resident in U.S.A. Noted as soloist, and as partner of the late Adolf Busch (violinist), whose daughter he married. Is also composer, pupil of Schoenberg and others.

SERMISY, CLAUDE DE (*c.* 1490–1562), French composer (and priest); wrote more than 200 CHANSONS, also Masses, motets, etc. As a singer of the French royal chapel he attended François I at his meeting with Henry VIII at the Field of the Cloth of Gold, 1520 (cp. FAYRFAX).

SEROV, ALEXANDER NIKOLAYEVICH (1820–71), Russian composer of operas (including 'Judith' and 'The Power of Evil'), orchestral works, a STABAT MATER, etc.; champion of Wagner and opponent of the 'nationalist' school of Russian composers known as the 'MIGHTY HANDFUL'.

SERPENT, obsolete large S-shaped bass wind instrument (of the same family as the CORNETT) with finger-holes and sometimes keys; usually made of wood but sometimes of metal. It was used e.g. in military bands and in churches up to the mid-19th century. Modified versions were the so-called *Russian bassoon* and the (English) *bass horn*, from which developed the ophicleide which ousted the serpent from concert use.

SERRÉ (Fr., tightened), with increasing speed and tenseness (It., *stringendo*).

SERSE, see XERXES.

SERVA PADRONA, LA, see THE MAID AS MISTRESS.

SERVICE, term used for a musically unified setting of the Anglican canticles for morning or evening prayer, or for the Communion service; *short service* and *great service*, terms used in the 16th and early 17th centuries to distinguish between less and more elaborate settings. Note the antithesis between *service* (setting of prescribed liturgical text) and ANTHEM (to the composer's own choice of text).

SESQUIALTERA, a type of MIXTURE stop on the organ. (From Latin, expressing the ratio of 3:2 between certain lengths of pipes).

SESSIONS, ROGER (HUNTINGTON) (b. 1896), American composer, pupil of Bloch and others; lived for several years in Europe; noted teacher. Works, favouring a polyphonic texture and close-packed style, include three symphonies, violin concerto, opera 'The Trial of Luculllus', cantata 'Turn O Libertad' (Whitman), two piano sonatas.

SESTET, obsolete equivalent of SEXTET.

SEVEN LAST WORDS OF OUR SAVIOUR ON THE CROSS, THE (Ger., *Die sieben Worte des Erlösers am Kreuz*), orchestral work by Haydn in the form of seven slow movements for performance in Cadiz cathedral (1785) as 'incidental music' to a Lenten service when the 'Words' (actually sentences) were read and preached on. Haydn arranged the music later for string quartet and for piano, and later still as a cantata, the text including the 'Words' themselves.

SEVENTH, an interval in melody or harmony, reckoned as taking seven steps in the (major or minor) scale, counting bottom and top notes. The *major seventh* is the distance e.g. A up to the next G♯; one semitone less gives the *minor seventh* (e.g. A up to G♮), and one further semitone less gives the *diminished seventh* (e.g. A up to G♭). This last is virtually equivalent in practice to the major sixth (e.g. A up to F♯), but is used in a different harmonic context, and especially when the *diminished seventh chord* (e.g. A, C, E♭, G♭) is sounded or implied – see DIMINISHED.

SÉVERAC, (JOSEPH MARIE) DÉODAT DE (1873–1921), French composer, pupil of Magnard and d'Indy. Works, with many allusions to the life of his native region in southern France, include two operas, orchestral and chamber works, songs (some in the old Provençal language), many piano pieces.

SEXTET, (1) a performing group of six instrumentalists or singers; (2) a piece for six performers; if instrumental, and actually entitled *sextet*, it will probably have the character of a SONATA for six performers, in several movements.

SEXTOLET, equals SEXTUPLET.

SEXTUPLET, a group of six notes (or notes and rests) of equal time-value, written where a group of four, five, or some other number of notes would be suggested by the time-signature. E.g. a group of six notes occupying a bar of 4/4, written ♩♩♩♩♩♩ (bracketed 6)

SFOGATO (It., evaporated), direction used e.g. by Chopin to indicate an airy, delicate manner of performance.

SFORZANDO, SFORZATO (It., reinforced), direction that a note or chord is to be played in a 'forced' manner, i.e. with special emphasis. Abbr. *sf.*

SGAMBATI, GIOVANNI (1841–1914), Italian pianist (pupil of Liszt) and composer of two symphonies, various piano works, etc.; follower of the 'new music' of Liszt and Wagner.

SHAFFER, ELAINE (b. 1925), American flutist, internationally known as soloist. Husband is the conductor EFREM KURTZ.

SHAKE, see TRILL.

SHALIAPIN, FEODOR IVANOVICH (1873–1938), Russian bass singer noted in Russian opera – brought to London and Paris by Diaghilev, 1913 – and latterly in recital. After the 1917 Russian Revolution he was at first treated as a distinguished artist of the Soviet régime; but afterwards he settled abroad, and died in Paris. (The form Chaliapin(e), by which he was known outside Russia in his lifetime, is a French spelling of his Russian name; the spelling according to current English treatment of Russian names is as above.)

SHANTY, type of sailors' work-song, dating from the era of sail-power and unmechanized ships, suitable for aiding such rhythmical movements as pulling together on a rope. The spelling *chanty* is a 'literary' form introduced by theorists wishing to emphasize the probable derivation from the French imperative *chantez* (sing).

SHAPERO, HAROLD (b. 1920), American composer of a symphony, a 'nine-minute Overture', a sonata for trumpet and piano, piano solos, etc. Pupil of Křenek, Piston, Hindemith, N. Boulanger, and inclined to NEO-CLASSICAL forms.

SHAPORIN, YURY ALEXANDROVICH (1887–1966), Russian composer, pupil of Glazunov, N. Tcherepnin, and others. Works include symphony, patriotic cantatas, opera 'The Decembrists' (alluding to a Russian political conspiracy of December, 1825), piano sonatas, songs, etc. Made use of Russian folk-music.

SHARP, term indicating a raising in pitch – either (1) indeterminately, as when a singer is said to sing sharp, by mistake; or (2) precisely by a semitone, as represented by the sign ♯; so 'G♯' (G sharp), the note a semitone higher than G♮ (G natural); so also, e.g., B♯ – a notation which is sometimes called for through adherence to the 'grammar' of music, though on e.g. the piano the note is identical with C♮ (C natural). So DOUBLE-SHARP; *sharp keys*, those having sharps in their key-signatures; *in four sharps*, in the key of E major or C♯ minor, the key-signature of which is four sharps (and similarly with other keys); *sharpened fourth* (U.S., *sharped* . . .), the raising of the fourth degree of the scale by a semitone. (No connexion with SHARP MIXTURE.)

SHARP, CECIL (JAMES) (1859–1924), English musician who, after holding an organist's and other posts, concentrated on reviving English folk-songs and folk-dances – collecting, editing, performing and writing about them; regarded as the leader of the modern English folk-music revival.

SHARP MIXTURE, organ MIXTURE stop so called because it is derived from the higher tones of the HARMONIC SERIES and thus gives a penetrating, clear tone – 'sharp' being used here as the opposite of 'dull', not of 'flat' in its technical sense.

SHAW, MARTIN (FALLAS) (1875–1958), English composer (church music, songs, etc.), organist, and editor of song-books, hymn-books, etc.

SHAWM, obolete double-reed woodwind instrument, forerunner of the oboe; made in several sizes, the larger (lower-pitched) ones being called *pomner*. (Shawm and CHALUMEAU are cognate words.)

SHCHEDRIN, RODION (KONSTANTINOVICH) (b. 1932), Russian composer of ballet 'The Little Hump-Backed Horse', opera 'Not Only Love', piano concerto, songs, etc. Also pianist.

SHCHERBACHEV, VLADIMIR VASSILEVICH (1889–1952), Russian composer (though born in Warsaw); pupil of Liadov and others. Works include four symphonies, piano suite on poems by Alexander Blok (with whom he had affinities), opera, film music. Was also noted teacher.

SHEBALIN, VISSARION YAKOVLEVICH (1902–63), Russian composer, pupil of Miaskovsky. Works include five symphonies and 'dramatic symphony', 'Lenin', with singers; opera THE TAMING OF THE

SHREW; piano sonatas; music to plays and films. Made a completion of Mussorgsky's 'SOROCHINTSY FAIR'.

SHEHERAZADE, (1) symphonic suite by Rimsky-Korsakov, 1888 – Sheherazade being a sultan's wife (in the 'Arabian Nights') who tells stories to stave off her execution (the ballet set to this music, 1910, is on a scenario quite distinct from Rimsky-Korsakov's); (2) a set of three songs with orchestra, 1903, by Ravel; the poems, by Tristan Klingsor, are on oriental subjects, but despite the title (in French 'Shéhérazade') there is no direct allusion in the songs to the 'Arabian Nights' character. (The form *Scheherazade*, though common in references to Rimsky-Korsakov's work, represents merely the German spelling of the Russian title, and its use in English-speaking countries is unjustified.)

SHELOMO (Heb., Solomon), rhapsody for cello and orchestra, by Bloch, first performed 1916: the reference is to Solomon as depicted in the Bible. The form *Schelomo*, more common, represents a German spelling of the Hebrew name; *Shelomo* (accent on middle syllable) represents an English transliteration.

SHEPHERD, ARTHUR (b. 1880), American composer of two symphonies (no. 1 originally called 'Horizons' and incorporating some traditional cowboy songs), string quartets, cantatas, etc. Also conductor and university teacher.

SHEPHERD, JOHN (*c.* 1520–*c.* 1563), English composer of Latin and English church music; organist of Magdalen College, Oxford, and a member of the Chapel Royal.

SHEPHERDS OF THE DELECTABLE MOUNTAINS, THE, see THE PILGRIM'S PROGRESS.

SHIELD, WILLIAM (1748–1829), English composer, also violinist and viola-player; pupil of Avison. Master of the King's Music, 1817, and composer to Covent Garden Theatre. Wrote operas and other stage pieces, often incorporating (as was then customary in England) items by other composers; also songs, string quartets, etc. Exceptionally for his period, composed some music in 5/4 time. Also writer of musical textbooks.

SHOFAR (Heb.), wind-instrument made of a ram's horn, stipulated in the Old Testament for religious ritual and still used on the most solemn occasions in the synagogue. Simulated, with reference to this, in Elgar's oratorio 'THE APOSTLES'.

SHORT SCORE, see SCORE.

SHOSTAKOVICH, DMITRY (DMITRIEVICH) (b. 1906), Russian composer (pupil of Glazunov); also pianist. At 19, wrote very successful symphony, no. 1 (twelve others have followed, including no. 7, 'LENINGRAD' Symphony). Was denounced by Soviet officialdom for unmelodiousness, freakishness, etc., in 1936 (after his opera 'Lady Macbeth of the Mtsensk District' – see KATERINA ISMAILOVA); again denounced, for FORMALISM and other 'faults', in 1948 (after such works as his orchestral 'Poem of Fatherland'). In each case admitted his 'errors', and has endeavoured to find a style reconciling his individuality and Soviet official views on what music should be like. Similarly withdrew his Symphony No. 13 (includes setting of text by Yevtushenko), 1963. Has also composed other operas; 'The Golden Age' and other ballets; 'Songs of the Forests' and other cantatas to patriotic Soviet texts; songs and piano pieces (including three sets of preludes and fugues); concerto for piano, trumpet, and orchestra; violin concerto; eleven string quartets. piano quintet; film music, etc. Re-orchestrated Mussorgsky's 'BORIS GODUNOV' and made a completion and orchestration of Mussorgsky's 'THE KHOVANSKY AFFAIR'.

SHROPSHIRE LAD, A, orchestral rhapsody by G. Butterworth, 1912 – based on a song-cycle composed by Butterworth to poems of Housman.

SHTCHERBATCHEV, see SHCHERBACHEV.

SI, the note B (in Latin countries, and formerly elsewhere); cp. TE.

SIBELIUS, JEAN (real first names Johan Julian Christian; 1865–1957), Finnish composer who studied in Berlin and Vienna. Was enabled by a Finnish government grant to give up teaching and concentrate on composing from 1897. Married a sister of Järnefelt. Much of his work has Finnish 'national' associations, sometimes relating to the 'Kalevala' (Finnish national epic poem) – e.g. 'A SAGA', 'KARELIA' (overture and suite), 'THE SWAN OF TUONELA', 'LEMMINKÄINEN'S HOMECOMING', 'FINLANDIA', 'Pohjola's Daughter', 'TAPIOLA'. After the last-named work, first performed 1926, he published almost nothing. His seven symphonies developed a highly individual close-knit technique within the tonal system and following the main symphonic traditions; no. 7 is in one movement only. Other works include violin concerto; small orchestral pieces including 'VALSE TRISTE'; an unpublished opera; many songs in Finnish and Swedish; incidental music to A. Paul's KING CHRISTIAN II, Maeterlinck's PELLÉAS AND MÉLISANDE, H. Procope's BELSHAZZAR'S FEAST, Shakespeare's TEMPEST, and other plays.

SICILIANA (It.), type of song or instrumental piece (also *Siciliano* and, in French, *Sicilienne*) derived presumably from some Sicilian dance: much cultivated in the 18th century, it is in slow 6/8 (or sometimes 12/8 time, usually in a minor key.

SIDE-DRUM, small drum (slung slightly to one side when marching), used in the orchestra, military band, dance band, etc. It has a skin at either end of a shallow cylinder, the upper skin being struck with a pair of wooden sticks and the lower one being in contact with gut strings or wires (called snares; hence alternative name *snare drum*). These snares add a rattling effect to the tone; they an be disengaged if the composer so directs.

SIEGE OF CORINTH, THE (Fr., *Le Siège de Corinthe*), opera by Rossini, produced in Paris, 1826. It was a revised French version of Rossini's earlier Italian opera 'Mahomet II' (It., *Maometto II*) produced in Naples, 1820, with libretto by C. della Valle. The plot concerns the love of an 18th-century Mohammedan conqueror for the daughter of the Christian Governor of Corinth.

SIEGE OF RHODES, THE, opera produced in London, 1656, and reckoned the first English opera. The music (now lost) was contributed by Locke, H. Lawes, H. Cooke, Coleman, and Hudson. Libretto by W. Davenant, referring to the Turkish siege (1480–1) of the last Christian outpost then surviving in the Mediterranean.

SIEGFRIED, see RING; see also next entry.

SIEGFRIED IDYLL, work by Wagner, 1870, for small orchestra, celebrating the birth of his son Siegfried, and using themes from his opera of that name.

SIEGMEISTER, ELIE (b. 1909), American composer; his works, including symphony, 'Ozark Set' (referring to life in the Ozark Mountains), 'Sunday in Brooklyn', and other orchestral pieces, often refer explicitly to modern American life, sometimes with use of folk-tunes. Is also author of a pamphlet expounding Marxist view of music, and of other writings.

SIGHT-READING, SIGHT-SINGING, the reading or singing of music at first sight.

SIGNATURE, see KEY-SIGNATURE, TIME-SIGNATURE; *signature-tune*, piece played by a dance-band, a radio feature-programme, etc., at each performance as a means of identification.

SIGTENHORST MEIJER, BERNHARD VAN DEN (also Meyer; 1888–1953), Dutch composer who cultivated a 'national' style (but without incorporating folk-tunes); also pianist, and editor of Sweelinck's music. Wrote many piano works and songs; also much chamber music, a STABAT MATER and other choral works, etc.

SIGURD JORSALFAR (Norw., Sigurd the Crusader), play by Bjørnson for which Grieg wrote incidental music – the 'Homage March' and two other pieces (1872).

SILKEN LADDER, THE (It., *La Scala di seta*), comic opera by Rossini, produced in Venice, 1812. Libretto by G. Rossi; the ladder takes a lover to his lady's room.

SILVER BAND, a BRASS BAND with instruments coated in what looks like silver.

SILVESTRI, CONSTANTIN (b. 1913), Rumanian conductor, also composer and pianist; formerly active in Bucharest. Principal conductor of Bournemouth Symphony Orchestra from 1961.

SIMILAR MOTION, see MOTION.

SIMILE (It., similar), term indicating that a phrase, etc., is to be performed in the same manner as a parallel phrase preceding it.

SIMON BOCCANEGRA, opera by Verdi, produced in Venice, 1857 (libretto by F. M. Piave); new version, with libretto altered by A. Boito, produced in Milan, 1881. Named after the historical 14th-century Doge of Venice, its hero.

SIMPLE INTERVAL, an interval of an eighth (octave) or less; see INTERVAL.

SIMPLE SYMPHONY, a symphony for string orchestra by Britten, 1934, 'entirely based on material from works which the composer wrote between the ages of 9 and 12'. Used for a ballet, 1944.

SIMPLE TIME, a scheme of time-division in which the beat-unit is divisible by two – e.g. 4/4, in which the beat-unit is the crotchet, divided into two quavers. Cp. COMPOUND TIME.

SIMPSON, CHRISTOPHER (or Sympson; ? –1669), English player of the viola da gamba, author of musical treatises, and composer of various works for his instrument and for groups of strings. It is not certain whether he was related to Thomas Simpson (below).

SIMPSON, ROBERT (b. 1921), English writer on music (author of a book on C. Nielsen), member of BBC music staff, and composer – two symphonies, three string quartets, piano solos, etc.

SIMPSON, THOMAS (?–?), English 16th-17th-century viol-player and composer (dances, songs, etc.) who held various posts in Germany (by 1610 or earlier) and Denmark. It is not known whether he was related to Christopher Simpson (above).

SIN', see SINO.

SINDING, CHRISTIAN (1856–1941), Norwegian composer (also pianist) who studied in Germany and in 1921–2 taught in U.S.A. Besides 'RUSTLE OF SPRING' and other piano pieces, wrote three symphonies, two concertos for violin and one for piano, etc., in a Romantic style.

SINFONIA (It.), symphony; *sinfonia concertante*, term preferred by e.g. Haydn and Mozart to 'concerto' for an orchestral work with more than one solo instrument, and used by Walton and some other modern composers even with only one instrument (perhaps because it does not seem to emphasize, as 'concerto' does, the element of display). See also SYMPHONIA (the Greek form), SYMPHONY, and the following entries.

SINFONIA ANTARTICA (It., Antartic Symphony), title given by Vaughan Williams to his symphony no. 7 (but, in conformity with his practice, not numbered by him), first performed 1953. It is based on Vaughan Williams' music to the film *Scott of the Antartic* (1949); each of the five movements is prefaced by a literary quotation, the last one from Scott's Journal.

SINFONIA DA REQUIEM (It., Requiem Symphony), symphony by Britten, 1940, in three movements headed 'Lacrymosa', 'Dies Irae', and 'Requiem Aeternam' (titles of sections of the REQUIEM Mass).

SINFONIETTA, a small (and probably rather light) symphony – diminutive of SINFONIA; also (U.S.) performing name for a small orchestra, on the analogy of the special U.S. use of 'symphony' to mean 'symphony orchestra'.

SINGAKADEMIE (Ger., singing-academy), title used by certain choirs in German-speaking countries.

SINGING SAW, see SAW, MUSICAL.

SINIGAGLIA, LEONE (1868–1944), Italian composer who, untypically, wrote no opera. Works include string quartet and orchestral music – e.g. overture to Goldoni's comedy 'The Row at Chioggia' (*Le Baruffe chiozzotte*), and a suite of Piedmontese dances; the last-named was based on folk-music, which he cultivated on the suggestion of Dvořák, his teacher.

SINGSPIEL (Ger., a play with singing), type of stage entertainment, essentially a play in which songs are interpolated, popular in Germany in the late 18th century, Mozart's 'THE SERAGLIO' and 'THE MAGIC FLUTE' are couched in this form – having spoken dialogue instead of recitative, and being in the vernacular tongue instead of Italian – but their music is much more central to the drama than with earlier composers. Cp. HILLER, JOHANN ADAM.

SINO (It.; *sin*' before a vowel), until, up to; *sin' al fine*, until the end.

SISTER ANGELICA (It., *Suor Angelica*), one-act opera by Puccini, produced in New York, 1918, along with two others – 'THE CLOAK' preceding it and 'GIANNI SCHICCHI' following, making a 'triptych' (It., *trittico*). Libretto by G. Forzano: Sister Angelica is a nun and the setting is a nunnery.

SISTRUM, ancient rattle-like percussion instrument with rings which jangled on a metal frame when the instrument was shaken.

SIX, THE (Fr., *Les Six*), name given to the French composers, Auric, Durey, Honegger, Milhaud, Poulenc, and Tailleferre. It was invented in 1920 by the French critic Henri Collet (after these composers had together published an album of pieces) on the analogy of the Russian 'five' composers – see MIGHTY HANDFUL. Collet claimed that, inspired by Satie and Jean Cocteau, the 'Six' had brought a renaissance of French music. In fact the 'Six' did not remain a group, and only Honegger, Milhaud, and Poulenc achieved wide fame.

SIXTEEN-FOOT (as measurement of organ pipes, etc.), see FOOT.

SIXTEENTH-NOTE, U.S. term (following the German) for SEMIQUAVER, a semibreve being considered as a whole-note.

SIXTH, (1) an interval in melody or harmony, reckoned as taking six steps in the (major or minor) scale, counting the bottom and top notes. The *major sixth* is the distance e.g. from C up to A, a *minor sixth* (one semitone less) from C up to A♭, an augmented sixth (one semitone more) from C up to A♯. The last gives an interval which in practice is virtually the same as the diminished seventh (C up to B♭) but the harmonic context implied is different. (2) term used in the phrase 'Landino sixth' – see LANDINO. This refers to the sixth degree of the scale, not to the interval of six notes as described above.

SJÖGREN, (JOHANN GUSTAV) EMIL (1853–1918), Swedish composer and organist who studied partly in Germany and wrote works for piano, organ, choir, etc., showing certain 'nationalist' characteristics.

SKALKOTTAS, NIKOS (1904–49), Greek composer (also violinist), pupil of Schoenberg; also made use of Greek folk-music. Works include suites for piano, 'Greek Dances' for orchestra, three piano concertos, four string quartets – hardly any of this music being published in his lifetime.

SKILTON, CHARLES SANFORD (1868–1941), American composer who studied American-Indian music and made use of it in many of his works – including operas and pieces for string quartet.

SKETCH, (1) a rough draft of a composition, or a musical jotting made by a composer as a 'germ' or reminder; so Beethoven's 'Sketch-Books'; (2) a short piece usually interpreting pictorial or other extra-musical ideas.

SKRIABIN, ALEXANDER (NIKOLAYEVICH) (1872–1915), Russian composer, pupil of Taneyev and others; also virtuoso pianist, touring much. Composer of early Chopin-like piano pieces, then of larger-scale works prompted by theosophical beliefs and using a highly emotional new type of harmonic style designed to express these beliefs. Invented the so-called 'mystic chord' of ascending fourths, C–F♯–B♭–E–A–D, as a replacement for ordinary major and minor chords. Works include orchestral 'DIVINE POEM', 'POEM OF ECSTASY', 'PROMETHEUS, The Poem of Fire', ten piano sonatas, and many other piano works. Died of a tumour on the lip.

SLAATT(ER), see the following entry.

SLÅTT (Norw., pl. *Slåtter*), type of composition (originally a march, but afterwards more broadly treated) played by folk-musicians on the Norwegian HARDANGER FIDDLE; Grieg transcribed several examples, and other Norwegian composers have also written works of this kind. (The spellings *slaatt* and *slaatter* were formerly current in Norwegian.)

SLAVONIC DANCES, two sets each of eight dances by Dvořák – in folk-music vein but all 'original' – for piano duet, 1878 and 1886; also orchestrated by the composer.

SLAVONIC RHAPSODIES, three orchestral works by Dvořák (1878) in the vein of Czech folk-music, but all 'original'.

SLEEPING BEAUTY, THE (Rus., *Spyashchaya krasavitsa*), ballet with music by Tchaikovsky, produced in St Petersburg, 1890. (*The Sleeping Princess* was the title adopted by Diaghilev for his London presentation of it, 1921, to avoid possible confusion with a Christmas pantomime.) It lasts a full evening; an extract from it is given as 'Aurora's Wedding'.

SLEEPING PRINCESS, THE, see SLEEPING BEAUTY.

SLENTANDO (It.), becoming slower.

SLIDE, a device on some brass instruments for altering the length of tube (and thus the notes produced). The principal use today is on the TROMBONE. For the obsolete *slide trumpet* see TRUMPET.

SLOBODSKAYA, ODA (b. 1895), Russian soprano, active in opera and latterly in recitals (particularly of Russian songs); appeared in England from 1930, later becoming resident.

SLUR, in musical notation, a curved line grouping notes together and indicating that in performance they are to be joined smoothly together – sung in one breath, played with one stroke of the bow, etc.

SMETANA, BEDŘICH (Czech form of Frederick; 1824–84), Czech composer, also conductor and pianist; encouraged by Liszt. Took part in the unsuccessful Czech revolt against Austria, 1848, and afterwards worked for some years in Sweden; but from 1861 settled again in Prague. Became totally deaf in 1874 but continued to compose – e.g. cycle of symphonic poems 'MY COUNTRY', two string quartets (no. 1 'FROM MY LIFE'), opera 'THE KISS' and others. Previous works include operas 'THE BARTERED BRIDE' and 'Dalibor', choral works, many piano pieces. Cultivated, and is regarded as founding, a Czech national style influenced by folk-music.

SMITH, CYRIL (JAMES) (b. 1909), English pianist, noted as soloist and in two-piano appearances with his wife, PHYLLIS SELLICK; an attack of cerebral thrombosis in Russia in 1956 incapacitated him, but in 1957 he began to perform with right hand alone.

SMITH, JOHN STAFFORD (1750–1836), English organist, tenor singer, and composer of catches, glees, church music, etc.; see 'THE STAR-SPANGLED BANNER'.

SMYTH, ETHEL (MARY) (1858–1944), English composer who studied in Germany and had operas and other works performed there. Joined militant agitation for women's vote in Britain and was jailed, 1911; created Dame, 1922. Works, broadly conforming to traditional (German-influenced) idiom, include 'The Wreckers', 'THE BOATSWAIN'S MATE', and other operas; Mass; concerto for violin, horn, and orchestra; chamber music. In late years suffered from deafness and distorted hearing. Also writer of autobiographical and other books.

SNARE, SNARE DRUM, see SIDE DRUM.

SNEGUROCHKA, see THE SNOW MAIDEN.

SNOW MAIDEN, THE (Rus., *Snegurochka*), opera by Rimsky-Korsakov, produced in St Petersburg, 1887. Libretto by composer, after a play by Ostrovsky: the legendary Snow Maiden, daughter of Fairy Spring and King Frost, is sought in vain by the Sun-God.

SOAP OPERA, not an opera but a radio or television serial story of a sentimental nature, designed to sell the sponsor's product, e.g. soap.

SOAVE (It.), sweet(ly), tender(ly).

SOCRATES (Fr., *Socrate*), work for voice and orchestra by Satie, first performed 1920; called a 'symphonic drama' but not intended for the stage. Texts translated from Plato's dialogues.

SOFT PEDAL, see PIANO (2).

SOH, in TONIC SOL-FA the spoken name for the fifth degree (dominant) of the scale, written s. Cp. SOL.

SOIR (ET LA TEMPÊTE), LE, title of one of a set of three symphonies by Haydn: see MORNING.

SOIRÉES MUSICALES (Fr., musical evenings), a collection of songs and duets by Rossini, published 1835; an orchestral arrangement by Britten (1936) of five of its numbers bears the same title. Other arrangements include Respighi's in the ballet 'THE FANTASTIC TOYSHOP'.

SOKOLOV, NIKOLAY ALEXANDROVICH (1859–1922), Russian composer of three string quartets, incidental music to *The Winter's Tale*, etc., pupil of Rimsky-Korsakov.

SOL, the note G (in Latin countries, and formerly elsewhere); cp. SOH.

SOLDIER'S TALE, THE (Fr., *L'Histoire du soldat*), stage work by Stravinsky, produced in Lausanne, 1918. Text by C. F. Ramuz, after a collection of Russian tales: it deals with a soldier, the Devil, and a Princess. The work uses speech and dance but no singing, an 'orchestra' of seven, and an idiom indebted to jazz.

SOLEMN MELODY, piece for organ and strings by Walford Davies, 1908.

SOLER, ANTONIO (1729–83), Spanish friar and composer of harpsichord sonatas, church music, incidental music to plays, etc.

SOL-FA, see TONIC SOL-FA (and cp. SOLFEGGIO, SOLMIZATION).

SOLFÈGE, SOLFEGGIO, French and Italian terms for a method of ear-training and sight-reading by which the pupil names each note of a melody (*do* for C, *sol* for G, etc.) as he sings it. The Italian is the original term; the French, derived from it, is also used in a broader sense to take in the whole system of rudimentary musical instruction in which the above is a prime element. The name *solfeggio* is also given to a vocal exercise written for the above method of study.

SOLI, see SOLO.

SOLMIZATION, the designation of musical notes by a system of syllabic names – as applied to a nomenclature devised by Guido of Arezzo in the 11th century and now to a development of this. Such a development is represented by the current Italian *do*, *re*, *mi*, *fa*, *sol*, *la*, *si* (representing the notes from C up to B), paralleled in English TONIC SOL-FA by doh, ray, me, fah, soh, lah, te (though these are not fixed in pitch but relative, doh representing C in C major, D in D major, etc., the other notes ascending from it).

SOLO (It., alone), a piece or passage performed by one performer – either alone or with others in a subordinate, accompanying role. So *solo song* normally denotes a song for one singer with piano accompaniment. Plural in Italian, *soli*; in English, *solos*. The *solo organ* is a manual on some organs, having mainly stops suitable for the solo treatment of melodies. *Soloistic*, in musicologists' jargon, refers to the use of instruments in the orchestra not as contributing to massed effects but for their individual qualities.

SOLOMON, oratorio by Handel, produced in London, 1749. Text (based on the Bible) by someone now unknown.

SOLOMON, professional name used by Solomon Cutner (b. 1902), English pianist who appeared from age 8, and became internationally noted. C.B.E. 1946. Incapacitated by paralysis, *c*. 1955.

SOLOVOX, trade name of a type of ELECTRONIC instrument playing one note at a time from a piano-like keyboard which is usually mounted on or under an actual piano; can imitate the tone-qualities of various instruments. See HAMMOND ORGAN.

SOLTI, GEORG (b. 1912), Hungarian conductor (also pianist); from 1939 resident in Switzerland and then in Germany; musical director of the Frankfurt Opera, 1952; of Covent Garden, from 1961.

SOMBRERO DE TRES PICOS, EL, see THE THREE-CORNERED HAT.

SOMERVELL, ARTHUR (1863–1937), English composer of choral works, songs, etc., and musical educationist. Knighted 1929.

SOMMO, SOMMA (It.), highest; *con somma passione*, with the utmost passion.

SON (Fr.), sound; *musique de douze sons*, TWELVE-NOTE music; *sons bouchés*, 'stopped' notes on the horn (see STOP, verb, 2).

SONATA (It., a piece sounded; as distinct from *cantata*, a piece sung), type of instrumental work which, since the Haydn-Mozart era (regarded as the 'classic' era for this type of work), has usually been in three or four movements – or, following the example of Liszt's piano sonata (1852–3), in one movement deliberately conceived as equal to (and about as long as) several 'normal' movements combined. Only a work for one or two players is now normally called a sonata; a work of this type for three is called a Trio, for four a Quartet, etc., and for an orchestra a Symphony. Such terms as *violin sonata*, *cello sonata* normally assume the participation also of a piano. Characteristic of the sonata is the use (normally in the first movement and often in others too) of what is called SONATA-FORM (below(or a modification of it. Among the notable forerunners of this now standard type are D. Scarlatti's short one-movement keyboard works, now usually also called sonatas; and in the immediate paving of the way for the Haydn-Mozart sonata a chief part is ascribed to C. P. E. Bach. Earlier, the suite rather than the sonata was the prevailing type of instrumental piece in several movements; and indeed the 17th-century and early 18th-century *chamber sonata* (It., *sonata da camera*) represents virtually a suite (mainly in the form of dance-movements) for two or more stringed instruments with keyboard accompaniment, the restriction of the term to one or two players not having yet arisen. The *church sonata* (It., *sonata da chiesa*) was similar but of a 'graver' type, avoiding dance-movements. The pre-Haydn usage of *sonata* as applied to an ensemble has occasionally been revived: see e.g. PETER MAXWELL DAVIES.

SONATA-FORM, term used to describe a certain type of musical construction normally used in the first movement of a SONATA (above) and of a symphony (which is in effect a sonata for orchestra) and similar works. An alternative name is *first-movement form* – but the form is also found in movements other than first movements, just as it is also found in works not called sonatas. It may also be called *compound binary form* (see BINARY). The essential of sonata-form is the division of a movement (sometimes after an introduction) into three parts – exposition, development, recapitulation. The exposition, having its first theme in the 'home' key of the movement, moves into another key, normally presenting a fresh (second) subject in that key, and ends in that key; the next section 'develops' or expands the material already presented; the last section is basically a varied repetition of the first, but ending in the home key, normally by bringing the second subject into that key. Afterwards may follow a further section, called coda ('finishing off' the movement). The key into which the first section moves is normally the dominant (if the piece is in the major key) or the relative major (if the piece is in the minor key). It will be gathered that sonata-form consists basically in the relationship of keys: if the term is applied to keyless (ATONAL) music, then it must be with an altered significance.

SONATE (Fr., Ger.), equals SONATA.

SONATINA, SONATINE (It., Fr.), a 'little sonata', usually shorter, lighter, or easier than most sonatas; *Sonatina* is used in English.

SONG, any short vocal composition, accompanied or not – usually for one performer, but cp. PART-SONG. The word has no precise meaning, but is effectively defined in various contexts by contrast with other terms – e.g. *songs and duets* (implying vocal solos and vocal duets). In opera the word 'aria' or 'air' is more usual. When, as normally, a song repeats the same tune for successive stanzas of a poem, it is said to be 'strophic'; if not, then the clumsy term 'through-composed' (from Ger. *durchkomponiert*) is sometimes applied to it – but see STROPHIC. A *song-cycle* is a set of songs grouped by the composer in a particular order (usually with reference to the sense of the words) and intended to be so performed. The term *song* is also applied in a generalized sense to certain large-scale works – see e.g. SONG OF THE EARTH, SONG OF DESTINY (below). For *song-scena* see SCENA.

SONG OF DESTINY (Ger., *Schicksalslied*), work by Brahms for chorus and orchestra, 1871, to a poem by Hölderin.

SONG OF THE EARTH (Ger., *Das Lied von der Erde*), work by Mahler for mezzo-soprano, tenor, and orchestra, 1908 (first performed 1911, after Mahler's death); called by him a symphony, and of symphonic dimensions, but not numbered among his symphonies. Text from German translations of Chinese poems.

SONG-FORM, name sometimes given to ordinary TERNARY form as used in an instrumental slow-movement. The term is better avoided ('ternary' itself being better) because not all songs are in this form – though e.g. the old 'da capo' aria (see ARIA) and nearly every modern dance-tune is.

SONGS AND DANCES OF DEATH (Rus., *Piesni plyaski smerti*), cycle of four songs by Mussorgsky, 1875–7 – to poems by Golenishchev-Gutuzov evoking different aspects of death.

SONGS OF FAREWELL, (1) six unaccompanied short choral works by

Parry, 1916–18 (called MOTETS, though not designed for church use); texts, of a solemn nature, from the Bible, Donne, and other sources; (2) Delius's last choral-and-orchestral work, 1934, to poems of Whitman; dictated to Fenby, Delius by then being too incapacitated by paralysis to write.

SONGS OF A WAYFARER (Ger., *Lieder eines fahrenden Gesellen*), cycle of four songs by Mahler (1884); words by composer, expressing the sentiments of a young man scorned by his sweetheart.

SONGS OF GURRA (Ger., *Gurrelieder*), work by Schoenberg (1900–11) for four solo singers, three male choruses, and one mixed chorus and huge orchestra (including eight flutes and a set of iron chains). Text, a German translation from the Danish of J. P. Jacobsen: Gurra is the castle where dwells Tove, beloved of Waldemar IV, a 14th-century Danish king.

SONGS ON THE DEATH OF CHILDREN (Ger., *Kindertotenlieder*), cycle of five songs (1902) by Mahler, to poems by F. Rückert. There are alternative accompaniments for orchestra and for piano.

SONGS WITHOUT WORDS (Ger., *Lieder ohne Worte*), thirty-six pieces for piano by Mendelssohn published at intervals (1832–45) in six books. They resemble song-melodies with accompaniment. Most of the titles (e.g. 'Spring Song' and 'The Bees' Wedding' for nos. 30 and 34), are not Mendelssohn's; but among those he did name are the three 'Venetian Gondola Songs' (nos. 6, 12, 29).

SONNAMBULA, LA (It., The Sleepwalker), opera by Bellini, produced in Milan, 1831. Libretto by F. Romani, the heroine's sleepwalking habit leading her into a compromising situation.

SONORE, direction often used by composers to mean 'sonorously', apparently under the impression that it is an Italian word. It could be, however, either the French for 'sonorous' or (if written *sonor*^{e}) an abbreviation for the correct Italian *sonoramente*.

SOPRANINO (It., little soprano), name for a size of instrument higher than the soprano size – e.g. *sopranino* RECORDER, *sopranino* SAXOPHONE.

SOPRANO (It., upper), (1) the highest type of female voice, with approximate normal range from middle C upwards for two octaves; (2, *male soprano*) type of male voice of similar range, produced by castration as used for some operatic and church singers e.g. in the 18th century; (3, *soprano clef*), name of a clef (now obsolete) having middle C on the bottom line of the staff: ; (4) name given, in a 'family' of instruments (i.e. a group of different sizes) to the one with a range approximating to the soprano voice – and usually also carrying the implication of being higher than the 'normal'-sized instrument. E.g. *soprano* CORNET, *soprano* RECORDER, *soprano* SAXOPHONE; the small clarinet in E♭ is occasionally (though not commonly) called a *soprano clarinet* for the same reason.

SOR, FERDINAND (properly Ferdinando Sors; 1778–1839), Spanish guitarist; teacher of his instrument in Paris, London, and elsewhere; composer mainly for his instrument, but also of an Italian opera, produced when he was 19. Died in Paris.

SORABJI, KAIKHOSRU SHAPURJI (b. 1892), English-born composer (originally Leon Dudley Sorabji), son of a Parsi father and a Spanish-Sicilian mother; resident in England. Also a pianist and writer on music. Works (for orchestra, piano, organ, etc.) include 'Opus clavicembalisticum' for piano – in three parts, twelve subdivisions, 252 pages, taking two hours to perform – described (by the composer) as 'the most important work for piano since "THE ART OF FUGUE"'. Has banned public performance of his works.

SORCERER, THE, operetta by Sullivan, produced in London, 1877. Libretto by W. S. Gilbert. A representative of a respectable firm of 'family sorcerers' administers a love-potion to an English village.

SORCERER'S APPRENTICE, THE (Fr., *L'Apprenti sorcier*), symphonic poem by Dukas, also called a 'scherzo'; first performed 1897. It humorously illustrates Goethe's story (based on Lucian, second century A.D.) of the apprentice who finds he can start a spell but not stop it.

SORDINA, an occasionally found alternative to SORDINO.

SORDINO (It., pl. *-i*), a mute; abbr. *sord.* So *con sordini*, with mutes, put on mutes; *senza sordini*, without mutes, take off mutes. As applied to the piano, *sordini* refers to the dampers which remain in operation unless the sustaining pedal (right-hand side) is depressed; *senza sordini*, i.e. without dampers, means that this pedal is to be brought into use.

SOROCHINTSY FAIR (Rus., *Sorochintskaya yarmarka*), opera by Mussorgsky; libretto by composer, after a rustic story (with faked supernatural happenings) by Gogol. Begun 1874, the opera was left unfinished at Mussorgsky's death. Various completions have been made – e.g. by Cui, Shebalin, and (the most successful) N. Tcherepnin.

SORS, see SOR.

SOSTENUTO (It.), sustained, i.e. in a smooth manner.

SOTTO VOCE (It., under the voice), whispered, barely audible – term used of instrumental as well as vocal music.

SOUBRETTE (Fr.), type of pert female character (often a servant) sung by a light soprano voice in opera or operetta – e.g. Despina in 'COSÌ FAN TUTTE' (Mozart), Adèle in 'DIE FLEDERMAUS' (Johann Strauss the younger).

SOUND-BOARD, a wooden board on the piano and other keyboard instruments, located close to the strings, vibrating when they are struck, and serving to amplify the volume of their sound.

SOUND-HOLE, hole cut out of the upper surface of stringed instruments – the violin and related instruments having two holes shaped like an *f* and called *f*-hole, the lute and most guitars having one hole cut in an ornamented manner somewhat like a flower and called 'rose'. The purpose is that the vibrating air, which would otherwise by shut off under the upper surface, should be brought in contact with the outer air.

SOUNDPOST, piece of wood connecting vertically the upper and lower surfaces of the body of a violin and other stringed instruments. It helps to support the pressure of the strings on the bridge (and hence on the upper surface) and serves to distribute the vibrations of the strings over the body of the instrument.

SOURDINE (Fr.), a mute (cp. SORDINO); *mettez, ôtez les sourdines*, put on, take off, mutes.

SOUSA, JOHN PHILIP (1854–1933), American band-conductor and composer of marches ('The Washington Post', 'Stars and Stripes Forever', etc.), raising an accepted martial style to a new level of inventive design. Also composed 'El Capitán' and other operettas. Cp. SOUSAPHONE.

SOUSAPHONE, type of tuba (see TUBA, 1) made in a shape circling the player's body and ending in a big bell facing forward. It was associated with the band conducted by Sousa (above) and is still used in American bands; it was also used in some early manifestations of jazz.

SOUTENU (Fr.), sustained, smoothly flowing (the French equivalent of SOSTENUTO).

SOUZAY, GÉRARD (b. 1918), French baritone, with European and American reputation in French and German song; also opera singer.

SOWERBY, LEO (b. 1895), American organist, and composer of works for organ alone, and for organ with orchestra; also of two piano concertos, chamber music, etc.

SPANISCHES LIEDERBUCH, see SPANISH SONG-BOOK.

SPANISH CAPRICE, orchestral work by Rimsky-Korsakov (first performed 1887) on themes of Spanish 'folk-song' character. The usual form of the title, 'Capriccio espagnol', is bastard Italian-and-French.

SPANISH HOUR, THE (Fr., *L'Heure espagnole*), opera by Ravel, produced in Paris, 1911. Libretto by Franc-Nohain, set in a Spanish clock-maker's shop.

SPANISH RHAPSODY (Fr., *Rapsodie espagnole*), orchestral work by Ravel, 1907, using themes of Spanish national character.

SPANISH SONG-BOOK (Ger., *Spanisches Liederbuch*), Wolf's song-settings, 1890, of forty-four Spanish poems in German translation.

SPANISH SYMPHONY (Fr., *Symphonie espagnole*), work by Lalo for violin and orchestra – really a violin concerto in five movements – first performed 1875 and written for the Spanish violinist Sarasate. Has themes of Spanish national character.

SPEAKS, OLEY (1874–1948), American composer of 'On the Road to Mandalay', 'Sylvia', and other popular songs; also of church music. Himself a singer.

SPECIES, name given to each of five types of academic 'strict counterpoint' (see COUNTERPOINT), progressively more complex (called *first species*, *second species*, etc.).

SPECTRE'S BRIDE, THE, usual English title for *Svatebni kosile* (Cz., The Wedding Shift), cantatas written to a text of K. J. Erben by – (1) Dvořák, first performed (in English) in Birmingham, 1885; (2) Novák, 1913 (called by composer 'A symphony of horror').

SPEECH-SONG, type of vocal utterance midway between speech and song, originated by Schoenberg and used in the 'SONGS OF GURRA' and later works; the voice touches the note (usually notated in a special way, as ♪) but does not sustain it. The German term is *Sprechgesang*, and a voice-part employing it is designated *Sprechstimme*.

SPELMAN, TIMOTHY MATHER (b. 1891), American composer who studied in Germany. Has written symphonic poem 'Christ and the Blind Man', symphony, chamber music, piano works, many songs.

SPIANATO (It.), smoothed out, smooth.

SPICCATO (It., separated), a certain method of playing rapid detached notes on the violin and related instruments, the bow rebounding off the strings.

SPIDER'S BANQUET, THE (Fr., *Le Festin de l'araignée*), ballet with music by Roussel, first produced in Paris, 1913. (Prompted by Fabre's studies of insect life.)

SPINET, (1) wing-shape keyboard instrument of harpsichord type, but smaller – current in 16th–18th centuries, revived in the 20th for old music; see VIRGINALS; (2) incorrect name for the 'square PIANO'.

SPINTO (It.), pushed, urged on.

SPIRITO, SPIRITOSO (It.), spirit, spirited.

SPIRITUAL, name given to a type of religious folk-song of the American Negro, usually of solo-and-refrain design. Authorities also use the term *white spirituals* for similar songs among certain whites in the Southern States.

SPOFFORTH, REGINALD (1770–1827), English organist and composer, especially of glees – e.g. 'Hail, smiling morn'.

SPOHR, LOUIS (1784–1851), German violinist, conductor, and composer of seventeen violin concertos (no. 8 'in the form of a song-scena'); also of operas (one on 'FAUST'), oratorios, symphonies, much chamber music (including four 'double string quartets' and a nonet), etc., in mellifluous Romantic style. Several times visited England. The story that he used the baton in London as early as 1820 (and thus introduced it there) is unsupported by any evidence outside his own autobiography, which appears to be based on faulty memory. But that he was one of the first conductors to use the baton is a fact.

SPONTINI, GASPARO (LUIGI PACIFICO) (1774–1851), Italian composer, chiefly of operas of a heroic and historical kind – e.g. 'THE VESTAL' (Fr., *La Vestale*), composed for Paris where he had settled in 1803. As musical director to the court in Berlin, 1820–42, continued to compose operas (e.g. 'Agnes von Hohenstaufen', in German) and made notable reputation as opera conductor. Became deaf, 1848; died at his birthplace, near Ancona.

SPRECHGESANG, SPRECHSTIMME, see SPEECH-SONG.

'SPRING' SONATA, name (not the composer's) for Beethoven's notably cheerful sonata in F for violin and piano, op. 24 (1801).

'SPRING SONG', see SONGS WITHOUT WORDS.

'SPRING SYMPHONY', (1) nickname, authorized by the composer, for Schumann's symphony no. 1 in B♭, 1841; (2) title of a work by Britten, 1949, for three solo singers, mixed chorus, boys' chorus, and orchestra (on poems on or near the subject of spring). The final section introduces the tune and words of 'SUMER IS ICUMEN IN'.

SPRINGAR (Norw.), Norwegian folk-dance in 3/4 time, cultivated e.g. by Grieg and Svendsen.

SPRINGER, a musical ornament (used e.g. by Chopin) in which an extra note, notated in smaller type, robs the preceding note of part of its time-value. Thus: 

It is thus the opposite of an APPOGGIATURA (1) in which the extra note robs the following (not the preceding) note of part of its time-value. The German term for *springer* is *Nachschlag* (literally 'after-stroke').

SQUARE PIANO, see PIANO.

STAATSOPER (Ger.), State Opera (house or company).

STABAT MATER, a devotional poem in medieval Latin about the vigil of Mary by the Cross; used as an authorized hymn (see SEQUENCE, 2) in the Roman Catholic church since 1727, and even before then set by Palestrina and other composers. There are also more recent settings (e.g. by Pergolesi for women's voices, and by Berkeley) – as well as a traditional plainsong melody.

STABILE (It.), stable, firm; term used of an orchestra to denote 'permanent, regular, resident', etc.

STABILE, MARIANO (b. 1888), Italian baritone who enjoyed a particularly long career; distinguished as Falstaff (Verdi), as Scarpia in Puccini's 'Tosca', etc.

STACCATO (It., detached), a method of performance denoted by a dot over the note, and signifying that the note is to be made short – and thus detached from its successor – by being held for less than its full length; so the superlative *staccatissimo*.

STÄDTISCHE OPER (Ger.), Municipal Opera (house or company).

STAFF, the framework of lines and spaces on which music is ordinarily written; so *treble staff*, *bass staff*, the five-line framework respectively carrying the treble and bass clefs. So also *staff notation*, ordinary notation as distinct e.g. from TONIC SOL-FA notation; *Great Staff*, fictitious academic construction of eleven lines to include both the treble staff and bass staff with middle C in between. (An alternative name is *stave*, and the plural is always *staves*).

STAINER, JOHN (1840–91), English organist, editor of old music, professor at Oxford, writer on music, and composer of oratorio 'THE CRUCIFIXION' and of church music in mid-Victorian English idiom.

STAMIC, see STAMITZ.

STAMITZ, German form of surname adopted by a Czech family of musicians (originally named *Stamic*), whose chief members were (1) Jan Vaclav Stamic (or Johann Wenzel Stamitz; 1717–57), violinist and composer of violin concertos, symphonies, harpsichord sonatas, etc., who became musical director at the court of Mannheim, 1745, and is regarded as the founder of the 'MANNHEIM SCHOOL'; (2) his son Karel Stamic (or Karl Stamitz; 1745–1801), violinist and composer of symphonies, operas, etc.

STÄNDCHEN (Ger.), see SERENADE.

STANFORD, CHARLES VILLIERS (1852–1924), Irish composer, also organist and conductor. As professor at Cambridge, 1887, and teacher at the R.C.M., had much influence on the succeeding generation of British composers (pupils include Vaughan Williams, Howells, Bliss, Benjamin). Himself studied in Germany and was influenced, e.g. as to instrumental forms, by Brahms; but his music also shows his interest in Irish folk-songs, and includes direct settings of these and five orchestral 'Irish Rhapsodies'. Also composed seven operas (including 'Shamus O'Brien', 'The Critic', 'The Travelling Companion'); seven symphonies; 'The Revenge', and other cantatas; church music; many songs and part-songs, etc. Knighted 1901.

STANLEY, (CHARLES) JOHN (1713–86), English composer, pupil of Greene; cultivated the basically Handelian idiom of his time. Was also noted organist, though blind from the age of 2. Wrote organ music, concertos for strings, various vocal settings, etc.

STARK (Ger.), loud, strong.

STARKER, JÁNOS (b. 1924), Hungarian cellist who settled in U.S.A., 1948, and rapidly achieved high distinction.

STAROKADOMSKY, MIKHAIL (1901–54), Russian composer, pupil of Miaskovsky and others; composed works inclining to NEO-CLASSICISM, including concerto for orchestra – also an organ concerto (rare in Soviet music), string quartets, opera, etc.

STAR-SPANGLED BANNER, THE, the national anthem of the U.S.A., not officially adopted until 1931, although the words were written in 1814 to the tune at present in use. This tune had already been issued (in England) by John Stafford Smith, who in all probability was the composer.

STAVE, see STAFF.

STEFANO, GIUSEPPE DI (b. 1921), Italian tenor, prominent at the Scala, Milan (from 1947), and elsewhere.

STEFFANI, AGOSTINO (1654–1728), Italian composer, also priest and diplomat; became court musical director in Hanover (Handel afterwards succeeding him). Wrote notable vocal duets. some in his Italian operas; also church music, chamber music, etc. Died in Frankfurt on a diplomatic visit.

STEG (Ger.), bridge (of a stringed instrument); *am Steg*, on the bridge; see PONTICELLO.

STEIBELT, DANIEL (1765–1823), German pianist, composer (much piano music, also operas, etc.), and fashionable teacher in Paris and London. In 1808 took a court musical post in Russia, where he died.

STEINBERG, MAXIMILIAN OSSEYEVICH (1883–1946), Russian composer, pupil and son-in-law of Rimsky-Korsakov; director of the Leningrad Conservatory. His later works tended to illustrative music – e.g. symphony no. 4 called 'Turksib' (Turkestan-Siberia Railway). Wrote also ballets (including one on the same subject as R. Strauss's 'TILL EULENSPIEGEL'), string quartets, etc.

STEINBERG, WILLIAM (originally Hans Wilhelm; b. 1899), German-born conductor who after a period in Palestine settled in U.S.A., becoming conductor of the Pittsburgh Symphony Orchestra; 1958–60, musical director of the London Philharmonic Orchestra.

STENHAMMAR, VILHELM EUGEN (1871–1927), Swedish pianist, conductor, and composer – influenced by Wagner, but also using Swedish folk-music. Wrote two operas, two symphonies, two piano concertos, etc.

STERN, ISAAC (b. 1920), Russian-born American violinist, brought to U.S.A. in babyhood; has toured widely (Russia, Australia, etc.) and achieved the highest distinction.

STESSA, STESSO (It.), same.

STEVENS, BERNARD (b. 1916), English composer, pupil of R. O. Morris and others. Works, inclining to a straightforward lyrical style, include 'Symphony of Liberation' (1946), violin concerto, sinfonietta for strings, piano sonata, chamber and choral works.

STEVENS, DENIS (WILLIAM) (b. 1922), English musicologist specializing in pre-18th-century music; also conductor of such music. See MULLINER BOOK. Professor of Musicology, Columbia University, New York, from 1964.

STEVENS, (PAUL) JAMES (b. 1923), English composer, pupil of Frankel, N. Boulanger, and Milhaud. Works include three symphonies, songs, ballets. Has lived and worked much in France and Germany.

STIGNANI, EBE (b. 1907), Italian mezzo-soprano, active at the Scala, Milan, etc.; London appearances from 1937.

STILE RAPPRESENTATIVO (It.), a 'style aimed at representation' – term used by early 17th-century Italian composers of opera and oratorio, alluding to their newly invented device of RECITATIVE, based on the natural spoken inflexions of the voice.

STILL, ROBERT (b. 1910), English composer of a symphony; quintet for three flutes, violin, and cello; two sonatas for viola and piano, etc.

STILL, WILLIAM GRANT (b. 1895), American composer, the first

Negro to compose a symphony (1931) and to conduct a major symphony orchestra. Much of his work has specifically Negro associations – e.g. 'Afro-American Symphony', 'Lenox Avenue' (for chorus and orchestra, later as ballet) alluding to Harlem; opera 'Troubled Island' (i.e. Haiti). Has also written chamber music, etc.

STIMME (Ger., pl. *-en*), voice, instrumental PART,, stop (of an organ), etc. Cp. STIMMFÜHRUNG.

STIMMFÜHRUNG (Ger.), part-writing.

STOCKHAUSEN, KARLHEINZ (b. 1928), German composer; pupil of F. Martin and, in Paris, of Messiaen. Cultivates an extreme, modernist style taking Webern's TWELVE-NOTE idiom as its starting point. A principal cultivator of ELECTRONIC music, he was the first composer to have an electronic 'score' (or rather diagram) published, 1956. Later active in exploring spatial possibilities in music and a measure of free choice by performers – e.g. in 'Groups' (*Ger.*, Gruppen) for three orchestras (and three conductors); 'Cycle' (Zyklus) for one percussion-player who may vary the performance – beginning on any page and occasionally making a choice of variant staves bracketed together (see INDETERMINACY).

STOESSEL, ALBERT (1894–1943), American composer, conductor, and violinist: works include opera 'Garrick', symphonic portrait 'Cyrano de Bergerac', violin sonata.

STOKOWSKI, LEOPOLD (ANTHONY) (b. 1887), English-born conductor whose father was Polish, mother British; naturalized American 1915. Conductor of the Philadelphia Orchestra, 1914–36; appeared in Disney's 'Fantasia' and other films; transcribed for orchestra Bach's organ Toccata and Fugue in D minor and other works.

STONE GUEST, THE (Rus., *Kamennyi Gost*), opera by Dargomizhsky, begun 1866, left not quite finished at his death; completed by Cui, orchestrated by Rimsky-Korsakov, and produced in St Petersburg, 1872. It is a setting of Pushkin's play, on the same story as Mozart's 'DON GIOVANNI'.

STOP (noun), (1) a row of pipes on an organ, all put in or out of operation by one lever; or the lever itself; (2) by analogy, the mechanism used in the harpsichord for similar purpose – e.g. 'sixteen-FOOT stop' for adding tone an octave lower, 'harp stop' for simulating harp tone.

STOP (verb), (1, *stringed instruments*) to place the finger on a string, thus determining the length of the portion of the string which is to vibrate; so *double-stopping*, *triple-stopping*, this action on two, three strings at once. The opposite of a *stopped string* is an 'open string', i.e. one vibrating its full length without being shortened by the placing of a finger. Note that the phrase *double-stopping* is loosely used for 'playing on two strings', whether or not both strings are actually stopped or open (and *triple-stopping* similarly). (2, *horn-playing*) to insert the hand into the bell of the instrument, altering the pitch and tone-quality of the note. (3, *acoustics, organ-building, etc.*) to block the passage of air through one end of a pipe (thus creating a *stopped pipe* or *end-stopped pipe* as distinct from an 'open pipe'), producing a note an octave lower than would otherwise sound.

STORACE, STEPHEN (1763–96), English composer whose training in Italy served him in Italian and English operas, including 'No Song, No Supper'. Also wrote chamber music, etc. Friend and pupil of Mozart in Vienna.

STRAD, colloquial name for an instrument made by the STRADIVARI family.

STRADELLA, ALESSANDRO (*c.* 1645–1682), Italian composer of operas and cantatas with notable choral writing; also of church music, concertos for strings, etc. Of noble family. Was murdered. Legend says that he escaped from an earlier attempted assassination after an elopement, but evidence for this is lacking – though it forms the basis of an opera about him by Flotow, 1842.

STRADIVARI, STRADIVARIUS, Italian and latinized names of a family of Italian violin-makers at Cremona – principally Antonio Stradivari (1645–1737).

STRASCINANDO (It.), dragging – direction referring not so much to tempo as to one note's 'dragging' the next behind it, e.g. in singing PORTAMENTO.

STRAUS, OSCAR (not Strauss; 1870–1954), Austrian composer, pupil of Bruch; wrote Viennese operettas including 'THE CHOCOLATE SOLDIER' and 'A WALTZ DREAM' – also music to film *La Ronde*, etc. Naturalized French, 1939.

STRAUSS, surname of a family of Austrian musicians – Johann the elder, Johann the younger, Joseph, and Eduard (separately below); also of Richard Strauss (below), no relation.

STRAUSS, EDUARD (1835–1916), Austrian composer of dance music, etc., and conductor; son of Johann Strauss the elder.

STRAUSS, JOHANN (the elder; 1804–49), Austrian violinist, conductor, and composer who toured much – was in Britain in 1838 for celebrations of Victoria's coronation. Wrote waltzes, polkas, etc., but today chiefly famous for the RADETZKY MARCH. Father of Eduard Strauss (above) and Johann and Josef Strauss (below).

STRAUSS, JOHANN (the younger; 1825–99), Austrian violinist, conductor, and composer of enormously successful waltzes in noticeably artistic style – including 'THE BLUE DANUBE', 'ROSES FROM THE SOUTH', and 'TALES FROM THE VIENNA WOODS'; called 'the Waltz King'. Wrote also polkas ('Tritsch-Tratsch', 'Thunder and Lightning', etc.) and other dances; and sixteen operettas including 'The Bat' (see FLEDERMAUS) and 'THE GIPSY BARON'. Other operettas, e.g. 'VIENNA BLOOD' have been made by others from his music. Toured much (London, 1869; U.S.A., 1872). Son of Johann Strauss (above). Collaborated in a few works with his brother Josef Strauss.

STRAUSS, JOSEF (1827–70), Austrian composer of 'Village Swallows from Austria', 'Music of the Spheres', and other waltzes; also other orchestral dance-music, piano pieces, etc. Collaborated with his brother Johann in a 'Pizzicato Polka' and two other works.

STRAUSS, RICHARD (GEORG) (1864–1949), German composer, also conductor; no relation to the other Strausses. Born in Munich, later settling in Garmisch (also in Bavaria), where he died. After early leaning towards 'traditional' forms, took up and developed the 'SYMPHONIC POEM' – composing e.g. 'MACBETH', 'DON JUAN', 'DEATH AND TRANSFIGURATION', 'TILL EULENSPIEGEL', 'Thus Spake Zoroaster' (Ger., *Also sprach Zarathustra*), 'DON QUIXOTE', 'A HERO'S LIFE'. Also of the character of symphonic poems are his 'SYMPHONIA DOMESTICA' (see also 'PARERGON') and 'ALPINE SYMPHONY' (1913, his last work of this illustrative type). His early operas (e.g. 'SALOME', 'ELEKTRA', 'DER ROSENKAVALIER') have a grandiloquent, Wagner-influenced style and a tendency to 'shocking' subjects; but from 'ARIADNE ON NAXOS' (1913) there are signs of the more intimate manner that characterizes especially certain very late works – e.g. horn concerto no. 2, symphony for wind (both in neo-Mozartian style). Wrote also incidental music to Molière's *Le Bourgeois gentilhomme* (see 'ARIADNE ON NAXOS'); 'METAMORPHOSES' for strings; many songs, including 'FOUR LAST SONGS' with orchestra; various further operas including 'INTERMEZZO', 'THE CAVE OF DANAE', 'CAPRICCIO'; ballet 'The Legend of Joseph'.

STRAVINSKY, IGOR (FEDOROVICH) (b. 1882), Russian-born composer; also pianist and conductor. Pupil of Rimsky-Korsakov; left Russia 1914; lived mainly in Paris, naturalized French 1934; settled in U.S.A. 1939, naturalized there 1945. Won fame with pre-1914 ballets 'THE FIREBIRD', 'PETRUSHKA', and (using enormous orchestra and 'savage' dynamic elements) 'THE RITE OF SPRING'. Later developed NEO-CLASSICAL tendency (compact forms, small forces, aversion from 'emotion'; see SYMPHONY), though the austerity of this was modified from the 1930s. Showed interest in jazz (e.g. in 'THE SOLDIER'S TALE'); based ballet 'PULCINELLA' on music supposedly by Pergolesi; adopted a deliberate back-to-Mozart style in opera 'THE RAKE'S PROGRESS' (1951). Other works include 'SYMPHONY OF PSALMS' (with chorus), 'DUMBARTON OAKS' Concerto, 'EBONY CONCERTO' (for dance band); opera-oratorios 'OEDIPUS REX' and 'PERSEPHONE'; ballets 'APOLLO MUSAGETES', 'ORPHEUS', 'Agon'; Mass. Notable rhythmic and harmonic innovator, but long adhered to tonality; however, from the choral-and-orchestral 'Canticum sacrum' (Holy Canticle – in Latin, for St. Mark's, Venice), 1955, he adopted TWELVE-NOTE technique, with particular debt to Webern. Works since then include ballet 'AGON'; 'MOVEMENTS' for piano and orchestra; 'THRENI'; 'THE FLOOD'; 'Sacred Ballad' (in Hebrew, on the biblical story of

Abraham and Isaac) for baritone and small orchestra; 'Elegy for J. F. Kennedy'. Author of autobiographical and musical writings, some with ROBERT CRAFT. His son, Sviatoslav Soulima Stravinsky (b. 1910) is also a pianist, composer, and teacher.

STRAWINSKY, German spelling of the Russian name Stravinsky. It is used by Igor Stravinsky in the published versions of some compositions, but it is inappropriate in English-speaking usage.

STREET CORNER, overture by Rawsthorne, 1944. It is generally descriptive, but no explicit clue is offered.

STREET PIANO, type of instrument used by itinerant musicians, being basically a mechanical form of piano: a selection of tunes is available, played by the turning of a handle which operates a barrel-and-pin mechanism similar to that of a musical box. An alternative name (because the turning of the handle is similar to that of a BARREL-ORGAN) is *piano-organ*.

STRETTO (It., drawn together), (1) direction that the pace is to become faster; (2) term used of the overlapping of entries in certain examples of FUGUE or similar composition, the subject beginning in one voice before the preceding voice has finished uttering it. A *stretto maestrale* (magisterial) occurs when the full length of the subject, and not just the first part of it, is subjected to overlapping.

STRICT COUNTERPOINT, see COUNTERPOINT.

STRING(s), name given to the thin strands of wire or gut which are set in vibration e.g. on the piano (by hammers), violin (by the bow), harp and guitar (by plucking); hence the word *strings* is used for 'stringed instruments'. But in normal use 'the strings' or 'the string section' of an orchestra means only the violins (divided into first and second), violas, cellos, and double-basses – not the harp and piano which, if used, are classified separately. Similarly a *string orchestra* normally implies violins (first and second), violas, cellos, and double-basses only. The standard *string quartet* is two violins, viola, cello; *string trio*, violin, viola, cello.

STRINGENDO (It., tightening), direction to a performer to increase the 'tension' of the music – in effect, to increase speed, often as preparation for a new section of basically faster tempo than the old one.

STRINGFIELD, LAMAR (b. 1897), American composer and conductor, also flutist; works include 'From the Southern Mountains' and 'The Legend of John Henry' for orchestra, and other works alluding to American life and legend.

STROMENTO, see STRUMENTO.

STRONG, GEORGE TEMPLETON (1856–1948), American composer of cantatas, symphonic poem 'Undine', etc.; follower of Liszt. Left U.S.A. 1892 and settled in Switzerland, dying there. Was also painter.

STROPHIC, term used of a song in which the same music is repeated (exactly or almost exactly) for each successive stanza of a poem. The opposite type, in which the music progresses continually, has usually been called in English a 'through-composed song' (from Ger. *durchkomponiert*); it would be less ugly and less awkward to say 'non-strophic' or 'non-repeating'.

STRUMENTO (It., pl. *-i*), instrument. The old form *stromento* is also encountered.

STUART, LESLIE, pen-name of Thomas A. Barrett (1866–1928), English composer of 'Floradora' and other musical comedies, song 'Lily of Laguna', etc.

STUDY, an instrumental piece (usually solo) written to train or demonstrate the facility of the performer in certain specific points of technique – but sometimes having artistic value as well, e.g. the three sets (twenty-seven in all) by Chopin for piano. (The word translates the French *étude*, which is also, needlessly, used in English.) See also SYMPHONIC STUDY.

SU (It.), on; *sul G*, on the G-string; *sul ponticello* (on, i.e. near, the bridge), *sul tasto* or *sulla tastiera* (on the fingerboard) – special methods of bowing the violin and related instruments.

SUBDOMINANT, name for the fourth degree of the scale, e.g. F in key C (major or minor). It is so called because it dominates the scale to an extent subordinate to the DOMINANT or fifth degree.

SUBITO (It.), immediately; *attacca subito*, go on (to the next section) without a break.

SUBJECT, term used in musical analysis to define a group of notes which appears to form a basic element in a composition and which is given prominence by its position, by being repeated or developed, etc. In SONATA-FORM the main musical ideas (usually two) announced in the 'exposition' and then developed are called subjects; in fugue the term is more narrowly restricted – see FUGUE.

SUBMEDIANT, the sixth degree of the scale, e.g. A in the key of C major, A♭ in the key of C minor. So called because it is halfway between the keynote and the subdominant (working downwards), whereas the MEDIANT (third degree of the scale) is halfway between the keynote and the dominant (working upwards).

SUCHOŇ, EUGEN (b. 1908), Czechoslovak composer of opera 'The Whirlpool', cantata 'Psalm of the Carpathian Land', etc.

SUGGIA, GUILHERMINA (1885–1950), Portuguese cellist, internationally noted; wife of Casals 1906–12. The famous portrait of her in the Tate Gallery, London, is by Augustus John.

SUITE (Fr., a following), the most common name for an instrumental piece in several movements, other than a piece of the type of a SONATA. Its characteristic in the 17th and 18th centuries was the inclusion of the dance-forms 'allemande', 'courante', 'sarabande', and 'gigue' (these French names were widely used) with optional additions. The BINARY form characteristic of these dances was expanded in the mid-18th century into SONATA-FORM, and the suite was succeeded as the prevailing instrumental form by the sonata (and symphony, i.e. sonata for orchestra, etc.). Since then *suite* has lost a strict specification, and in the 19th and 20th centuries has often been used for a work rather lighter or more loosely connected than a work of sonata type: it may describe a set of movements assembled from an opera or ballet score, etc.

SUK, JOSEF (1874–1935), Czech composer – also violinist, for forty years in the Bohemian String Quartet. Pupil and son-in-law of Dvořák; his music carries on Dvořák's ideas with some modernization. Works (nearly all instrumental) include symphony 'Asrael'; 'Prague', and other symphonic poems; cycle of piano pieces 'Things Lived and Dreamed' (Cz., *Zivotem snem*) and other piano works.

SUL, SULLA, see SU.

SULLIVAN, ARTHUR (SEYMOUR) (1842–1900), English composer (also organist and conductor) who studied in Leipzig. Wrote much serious music – including symphony, overture 'Di Ballo' (see BALLO), religious cantata 'The Golden Legend', opera 'Ivanhoe' – but made his chief reputation in a long series of successful operettas, combining solid musical construction with apt reinforcement of verbal points. Those written with W. S. Gilbert as librettist are 'Thespis' (lost, unpublished), 'TRIAL BY JURY', 'THE SORCERER', 'H.M.S. PINAFORE', 'THE PIRATES OF PENZANCE', 'PATIENCE', 'IOLANTHE', 'PRINCESS IDA', 'THE MIKADO', 'RUDDIGORE', 'THE YEOMEN OF THE GUARD', 'THE GONDOLIERS', and, finally and unsuccessfully, 'UTOPIA LIMITED' and 'THE GRAND DUKE'. Operettas without Gilbert include 'COX AND BOX' and (unfinished) 'The Emerald Isle', completed by German. Knighted 1883. See also 'PINEAPPLE POLL' (ballet with score arranged from Sullivan's music).

SUMER IS ICUMEN IN, English 13th-century composition (probably *c.* 1240, though some say later). Remarkable because, among other things, it is the oldest known canon and the oldest-known SIX-PART composition. It has alternative words in Latin for church use. Known also as the 'Reading Rota' because its conjectural composer was John of Fornsete, monk of Reading Abbey. It is quoted in Britten's 'SPRING SYMPHONY'.

SUMMATIONAL TONE, see RESULTANT TONE.

SUOR ANGELICA, see SISTER ANGELICA.

SUPERTONIC, the second degree of the scale, e.g. the note D in key C (major or minor) – lying immediately above the TONIC (first degree).

SUPPÉ, FRANZ VON, Germanized form of name used by Francesco Ermenegildo Ezechiele Suppé-Demelli (1819–95), Austrian (Dalmatian-born) composer of Belgian descent. Wrote succession of popular operettas including 'The Beautiful Galatea', and 'Light Cavalry', overtures to plays including 'POET AND PEASANT'; Mass, etc.

SUR (Fr.), on; *sur la touche*, *sur le chevalet*, on the fingerboard, on (i.e. near) the bridge – special methods of bowing a violin and related instruments.

'SURPRISE' SYMPHONY, nickname for Haydn's symphony no. 94 in G (1791), because of the sudden loud chord in the slow movement.

SURVIVOR FROM WARSAW, A, work by Schoenberg (first performed 1948) for speaker, men's chorus, and orchestra; text by composer (in English, apart from German interpolations and a Hebrew prayer) depicting a Nazi concentration camp.

SUSANNA, oratorio by Handel, first performed 1749; text after the Apocrypha by author now unknown.

SUSANNA'S SECRET (It., *Il Segreto di Susanna*), one-act comic opera by Wolf-Ferrari, produced (in German) in Munich, 1909. Libretto by E. Golisciani: Susanna's terrible secret is that she smokes.

SUSPENSION, a device in harmony by which a note in a chord is kept sounding when that chord has been succeeded by another in which the prolonged note forms a discord. This discord is then normally resolved when the prolonged note falls to a note forming part of the new chord. If it rises instead of falling, then the process is in some textbooks called *retardation*, presumably on the linguistically pedantic ground that a thing 'suspended' must fall. The reverse process to both of these, when the note precedes the chord of which it forms a part, is called ANTICIPATION.

SUSSKIND, WALTER (properly Süsskind; b. 1913), Czech-born conductor, also composer and pianist; resident in Britain from 1939. Conductor of the Scottish (later called Scottish National) Orchestra, 1946–52; later conductor in Melbourne and (1956) Toronto.

SÜSSMAYR, FRANZ XAVER (1766–1803), Austrian composer of operas, church music, etc., and conductor. A pupil of Mozart, he completed the Requiem which Mozart left unfinished at his death.

SUSTAINING PEDAL, see PIANO (2).

SUTERMEISTER, HEINRICH (b. 1910), Swiss composer of operas, including 'ROMEO AND JULIET' and 'Raskolnikov' (after Dostoyevsky's *Crime and Punishment*); also of cantatas, piano concerto, two-piano concerto, etc. Pupil of Orff. Cultivates an unproblematic, romantically melodious idiom.

SUTHERLAND, JOAN (b. 1928), Australian soprano, resident in England; joined Covent Garden Opera Company, 1952; attained international celebrity in Donizetti's 'LUCY OF LAMMERMOOR' (Covent Garden, 1959) and similar coloratura roles, C.B.E., 1961.

ŠVANDA THE BAGPIPER (Cz., *Švanda Dudák*), opera by Weinberger, produced in Prague, 1927. Libretto by M. Kares, on a Czech folk-tale of which Švanda is the hero. (The spelling 'Schwanda' is inappropriate in English, being only the German representation of the sound of the Czech name. In English the pronunciation could be rendered Shvanda.)

SVANHOLM, SET (KARL VICTOR) (1904–64), Swedish tenor, well known in Wagner's 'heroic tenor' roles at Covent Garden and elsewhere;

began career as baritone, and was also organist; director of the Stockholm Royal Opera from 1956 until his death.

SVENDSEN, JOHAN (SEVERIN) (1840–1911), Norwegian composer, also conductor and pianist; studied in Leipzig, was associated with Liszt and Wagner, and wrote two symphonies and other music showing German influence. But wrote also four 'Norwegian Rhapsodies' and other works of Norwegian associations; also 'CARNIVAL IN PARIS' for orchestra, chamber music, etc.

SWAN LAKE (Rus. *Lebedino ozero*), ballet with music by Tchaikovsky, produced in St Petersburg, 1895. The swans are maidens transformed by a wicked magician.

SWAN OF TUONELA, THE, 'symphonic legend' by Sibelius, 1893 – originally written as a prelude to an opera, but published as one of four pieces on Finnish legendary subjects; see LEMMINKÄINEN'S HOMECOMING. Tuonela is the land of death surrounded by waters on which the swan floats, singing.

SWAN SONG (Ger., *Schwanengesang*), name given – by the publisher, not by Schubert – to a collection of fourteen songs by Schubert, published 1828 (after his death). They were not grouped by Schubert and do not form a unity like his genuine song-cycles.

SWANEE WHISTLE, crude woodwind instrument, mainly used as a toy: at one end is a recorder-type mouthpiece, at the other a slide which is worked backwards and forwards to vary the length of the tube and so produce different notes. Continued accuracy of pitch is almost impossible, and a sliding effect is characteristic; but it has been very occasionally used in the orchestra – e.g. in G. Gordon's ballet 'THE RAKE'S PROGRESS' to simulate a shaky singing voice.

SWAROWSKY, HANS (b. 1899), Austrian conductor, though born in Budapest; career was chiefly as opera conductor until he came from Vienna to be conductor of Scottish National Orchestra, 1957.

SWEDISH RHAPDOSY, see ALFVÉN.

SWEELINCK, JAN PIETERSZOON (1562–1611), Dutch composer – also organist and harpsichordist. Wrote organ works, notable for their development of the fugue, and for their pioneering of an independent part for the pedals; taught many German organist-composers. Wrote also various vocal works, some for the church.

SWELL, a device for increasing and diminishing the volume of sound on an organ, or on certain 18th-century harpsichords. See next entry.

SWELL ORGAN (or simply *swell*), name given to a section of the organ in which the pipes are set in an enclosed space; the player can consequently regulate the volume of sound through a pedal (*swell pedal*) which opens and closes a shutter. The manual controlling this (placed directly above the GREAT) is called the *swell manual*. But note that the 'swell effect' (of being able to increase and decrease volume) can usually be obtained also on the 'Choir' and 'Solo' manuals of the modern organ.

SYLPHIDES, LES, ballet with music arranged from piano works by Chopin; produced in Paris, 1909. The orchestration currently used in Britain is by Jacob. (Title is merely French for 'The Sylphs'.)

SYLVIA, ballet with music by Delibes, produced in Paris, 1876; the heroine is a mythical huntress.

SYMPATHETIC, term used in allusion to the capacity of strings and other bodies to vibrate (and thus give a note) when this note is sounded near them by some other agent. So *sympathetic strings*, e.g. on the viola d'amore, not touched by the bow but vibrating by their proximity to the bowed strings lying above them.

SYMPHONIA, Greek word taken into Latin and used in certain modern contexts as equivalent to 'symphony' – e.g. in R. Strauss's *Symphonia Domestica* (i.e. Domestic Symphony), 1904, describing with semi-realistic touches the composer's home life.

SYMPHONIC MOVEMENT, description used by Honegger for each of his three pieces 'PACIFIC 231', 'RUGBY', and finally the 'Symphonic Movement No. 3' (first performed 1933) which is not illustrative in nature.

SYMPHONIC POEM, term introduced by Liszt for an orchestral work which is approximately of the size and seriousness customarily associated with a symphony, but which is meant as an interpretation of something non-musical, e.g. a work of literature. A not quite satisfactory synonym is TONE-POEM; and cp. next entry.

SYMPHONIC STUDY, term not in standard use, but used by Elgar (more or less as an equivalent for SYMPHONIC POEM) for his 'FALSTAFF'; Rawsthorne's 'Symphonic Studies' (1939), however, form a completely abstract work, not an illustrative one (cp. STUDY). Schumann's *Symphonic Studies* (1836, revised 1852) are a set of variations for piano solo.

SYMPHONIE (Fr.), symphony; *Symphonie espagnole*, see SPANISH SYMPHONY. *Symphonie fantastique*, see FANTASTIC SYMPHONY.

SYMPHONY, term literally meaning 'a sounding-together', formerly indicating (1) an overture, e.g. to an opera; (2) the instrumental section introducing, or between the verses of, a vocal work. Occasionally such archaic meanings are revived, e.g. in Stravinsky's work entitled 'Symphonies for wind instruments' (1920), Gordon Crosse's entitled 'Symphonies for chamber orchestra'. But in general, since the time of Haydn (called, with some simplification, 'the father of the symphony'), the work has ordinarily indicated an orchestral work of a serious nature and a substantial size, in the shape of a SONATA for orchestra. Most such works are in four movements; some are in three; some are in one ('telescoping' a larger number of movements together) or five; other numbers are very rare. Symphonies may have a name (e.g. Beethoven's 'PASTORAL' symphony), or may include vocal parts (since Beethoven's 'CHORAL' symphony); but such remain the minority. A *symphony orchestra* (or, in U.S.A. just 'a symphony') is an orchestra numerous enough to play symphonies and having a repertory of 'serious' music; a *symphony concert* is one including a symphony or other work of similar type. See also following entries.

SYMPHONY OF A THOUSAND, nickname for Mahler's symphony no. 8, first performed 1910 – because of the huge forces employed (large orchestra, an extra brass group, seven vocal soloists, boys' choir, two mixed choirs).

SYMPHONY OF PSALMS, work for chorus and orchestra by Stravinsky, 1930, 'composed to the glory of God, dedicated to the Boston Symphony Orchestra'. In three movements; text from the Psalms, in Latin.

SYMPHONY ON A FRENCH MOUNTAINEER'S SONG (Fr., *Symphonie sur un chant montagnard français*), work for piano and orchestra by d'Indy, first performed 1887.

SYNCOPATION, a displacement of accent on to a beat that is normally unaccented.

SZABÓ, FERENC (b. 1902), Hungarian composer, resident in Russia 1931–45; works include Concerto for orchestra, cantatas, piano pieces.

SZALOWSKI, ANTONI (b. 1907), Polish-born composer resident in France, pupil of N. Boulanger. Works include Sinfonietta, Concertino for strings, piano sonatina.

SZELIGOWSKI, TADEUSZ (b. 1896), Polish composer of opera 'The Revolt of the Schoolboys', ballet 'The Peacock and the Girl' an orchestral 'Epitaph for Szymanowski', choral works, etc.

SZERVÁNSZKY, ENDRÉ (b. 1912), Hungarian composer, also critic and academic teacher. Works include symphony, two Divertimenti for strings and one for small orchestra, pieces for two violins, Hungarian folk-song arrangements.

SZELL, GEORG (b. 1896), Hungarian-born conductor active in various German opera houses before the Nazi régime; afterwards settled in U.S.A., conducting the orchestra at Cleveland (Ohio) from 1946. Is also composer.

SZIGETI, JOSEPH (b. 1892), Hungarian-born violinist, resident formerly in Britain and from 1925 in U.S.A. Internationally noted, e.g. in works by Bartók and Prokofiev; himself an editor of violin music.

SZYMANOWSKI, KAROL (1882–1937), Polish composer (also pianist) born in the Russian Ukraine. After study in Berlin was influenced by R. Strauss and Debussy, but later took to a simpler harmonic style with some debt to Polish folk-music. Works include operas 'Hagith' and 'KING ROGER'; two violin concertos; three Myths for violin and piano (no. 1, 'The Fountain of Arethusa'); three symphonies; 'Stabat Mater' song-settings of James Joyce, Tagore, and other poets. Died in a Swiss sanatorium.

T

t, symbol in TONIC SOL-FA for the seventh degree (leading-note) of the scale, pronounced *te*. Cp. SI.

TEN., abbr. of (1) tenor; (2) *tenuto*.

TR., abbr. of (1) TRILL; (2) TRUMPET.

TABARRO, IL, see CLOAK.

TABLATURE, a system of writing down music by symbols which represent not the pitch (as in ordinary modern notation) but the position of the performer's fingers. Such a system was formerly used for the lute and is now used (though not actually called tablature) for the ukelele.

TÁBOR, see MY COUNTRY.

TABOR, small drum used e.g. to accompany folk-dancing – the player beating the drum with one hand (not with sticks) while the other hand fingers a three-holed pipe.

TACET (Lat., is silent), indication that a particular performer or instrument has no part for considerable time, e.g. for a whole movement.

TAFELMUSIK (Ger., table-music), music suited to convivial gatherings, e.g. for performance at or after dinner.

TAGLIAVINI, FERRUCCIO (b. 1913), Italian tenor, noted in opera: début 1939. After the Second World War appeared in U.S.A. and Britain. For a time took up engineering and business.

TAILLEFERRE, GERMAINE (b. 1892), French composer (also pianist), member of the former group 'THE SIX'; she has written ballets, piano concerto, songs, etc., in an emphatically clear style.

TAL, JOSEPH (originally Gruenthal; b. 1910), Israeli composer; Polish-born, he emigrated to Palestine in 1935. Works include choreographic poem 'Exodus' for baritone and orchestra; 'Saul at Endor' (styled an 'opera concertante', i.e., a dramatic cantata): piano concerto.

TALBOT, HOWARD, pen-name of Richard Lansdale Munkittrick (1865–1928), American composer who settled in England and wrote music for 'The Arcadians' (see also MONCKTON) and other musical comedies.

TALE OF TWO CITIES, A, opera by Benjamin, produced in a BBC (sound radio) performance, 1953; staged in London 1957. Libretto by C. Cliffe, after Dickens's novel.

TALES FROM THE VIENNA WOODS (Ger., *Geschichten aus dem Wienerwald*), waltz by Johann Strauss the younger, 1868.

TALES OF HOFFMANN, THE (Fr., *Les Contes d'Hoffmann*), opera by Offenbach, produced in Paris, 1881, after the composer's death. Guiraud completed the scoring and supplied the recitatives which in most productions replace the original spoken dialogue. Libretto by J. Barbier and M. Carré. The hero represents the German Romantic writer E. T. A. HOFFMANN, and the story is drawn from his works.

TALLIS, THOMAS (*c.* 1505–1585), English composer and organist;

from 1572 joint organist with Byrd at the Chapel Royal, and from 1575 joint holder with Byrd of a State monopoly of music-printing in England. Cultivated a solemn style of great contrapuntal ingenuity, as seen e.g. in his Latin motet 'Spem in alium' in forty parts, i.e. for eight choirs each of five voices. Wrote mainly church music, in Latin (see CANTIONES SACRAE) and then in English; also some pieces for keyboard, viols, etc. The so-called 'Tallis's Canon' is an adaptation from one of a set of psalm-tunes, 1567; Vaughan Williams's 'Fantasia on a Theme of Tallis' (first performed 1910) is based on another of the same set.

TALON (Fr.), heel (of the bow of a stringed instrument), i.e. the end of the bow which is held by the player.

TAM O'SHANTER, concert overture by M. Arnold (after Burns' poem), published 1955.

TAMBOUR (Fr.), drum; *tambour de Basque*, equals TAMBOURINE.

TAMBOURINE, type of small drum struck with the fingers and rattled with the hand; it has little jingles inserted into its wooden frame. It is of Arab origin but was known in Europe before 1300; brought into the modern orchestra by Weber, Berlioz, and later composers mainly to evoke revelry, gipsies, exotic scenes, etc.

TAMBURO (It.), drum.

TAMING OF THE SHREW, title of operas (after Shakespeare's play) by several composers – notably by Goetz (produced at Mannheim, 1874, as 'Der widerspänstigen Zähmung', with libretto by J. V. Widmann) and by Shebalin (Moscow, 1955). See also CLAPP.

TAM-TAM, equals GONG. (Not the same as TOM-TOM.)

TANCRED (It., *Tancredi*), opera by Rossini, produced in Venice, 1813; libretto by R. Rossi, after Tasso, Tancred being a Christian hero of the Crusades.

TANEYEV, surname of two related Russian composers (separately, below). The surname without qualification indicates the second.

TANEYEV, ALEXANDER SERGEYEVICH (1850–1918), Russian composer of operas, orchestral works, etc., pupil of Rimsky-Korsakov; uncle of SERGEY IVANOVICH TANEYEV.

TANEYEV, SERGEY IVANOVICH (1856–1915), Russian pianist and composer of six symphonies, songs and choral works, etc.; pupil and friend of Tchaikovsky, and unsympathetic to the nationalist ideas of the 'MIGHTY HANDFUL' group of composers. Noted teacher. See preceding entries.

TANGENT, the metal 'tongue' which, on the clavichord, touches a string when a key is struck and so sounds that string. It remains in contact with the string for as long as the note sounds, unlike the hammers of the piano. (From Lat. *tangere*, touch.)

TANGO, Argentinian dance supposed to have been imported by African slaves into the American continent; taken into general use in ballroom dancing about the time of the First World War. Its characteristic rhythm is ♩.♪♩♩

TANNHÄUSER, *and the Singing Contest at the Wartburg* (Ger., . . . *und der Sängerkrieg auf der Wartburg*), opera by Wagner, produced in Dresden, 1845. (What is called the 'Paris version' refers to the revision made by Wagner for the Paris production of 1861.) Libretto by composer: Tannhäuser is a medieval minstrel torn between 'sacred' and 'profane' love.

TANSMAN, ALEXANDRE (b. 1897), Polish-born composer, naturalized French; settled in Paris, 1921. Works, in an individual but not 'revolutionary' style, include seven symphonies, seven string quartets, ballets, pieces for one and two pianos. Is also pianist and conductor.

TANTO (It.), so much; *allegro ma non tanto,* fast but not too fast.

TANTUM ERGO, name for part of a Latin hymn by St Thomas Aquinas, which is used in Roman Catholic services; it has its own plainsong melodies and has also been set afresh by various composers.

TANZ (Ger.), dance.

TAPIOLA, symphonic poem by Sibelius, 1926 – named after Tapio, the forest god of Finnish mythology.

TARANTELLA, fast Italian dance in 6/8 time with alternating major-key and minor-key sections. Named from the S. Italian town of Taranto, habitat of the tarantula: superstition declared the tarantula poisonous, and the dance was said to be the result of (or sometimes the cure for) this poison.

TARENTELLE, French form of TARANTELLA.

TÁROGATÓ, Hungarian single-reed woodwind instrument, related to the clarinet and saxophone; it has sometimes been used to perform part of the shepherd-boy's piping in act III of Wagner's 'TRISTAN AND ISOLDE'.

TARP, SVEND ERIK (b. 1908), Danish composer of chamber music, violin concertino, flute concertino, ballets, film music, etc. Makes some use of Danish folk-music.

TARTINI, GIUSEPPE (1692–1770), Italian violinist and composer, founder of a famous school for violin-playing. Travelled much in Italy, and for three years worked in Prague. Wrote concertos and sonatas (including the 'DEVIL'S TRILL') for violin; also trio sonatas, vocal works, etc. Improved the violin-bow. Also author of theoretical writings on music, and discoverer of what modern acoustics calls 'RESULTANT TONES'.

TASTO (It.), (1) the fingerboard of a stringed instrument; *sul tasto*, on the fingerboard; (2) the finger-key of a keyboard instrument: *tasto solo*, finger-key only – i.e. (in music which has a CONTINUO part) instruction to play only the single bass-note written, and not the supporting chords which a continuo-player would normally add.

TATE, PHYLLIS (MARGARET DUNCAN) (b. 1911), English composer; works include opera 'The Lodger', songs and folk-song arrangements, saxophone concerto, 'Nocturne' (poem by Sidney Keyes) for three voices and seven instruments.

TAUBER, RICHARD (originally Ernst Seiffert; 1892–1948), Austrian tenor, naturalized British. Well known in opera, recital, and (especially) Lehár's operettas, in some of which the leading tenor part was especially written for him. Was also composer of songs, etc., and occasionally conducted.

TAUSIG, CARL (1841–71), Polish pianist who settled in Germany, becoming pupil of Liszt; made arrangements for the piano of some organ works of Bach, orchestral pieces by various composers, etc. Also composer. Died of typhoid.

TAVERNER, JOHN (*c.* 1495–1545), English composer and organist: wrote chiefly church music in Latin, including eight Masses – one based on the then popular song, 'The Western Wind'. His Mass 'Gloria tibi trinitas' was the starting-point of the In Nomines for strings (see IN NOMINE) and a few other works. Highly esteemed in his own century and since. Imprisoned for (Protestant) heresy, afterwards abandoning music and becoming an active agent in the suppressing of the monasteries.

TAYLOR, (JOSEPH) DEEMS (1885–1966), American composer of operas (including 'THE KING'S HENCHMAN' and 'Peter Ibbetson'), orchestral works (including suite 'Through the Looking-Glass', after Lewis Carroll, originally for chamber-music group), etc., cultivating a straightforwardly melodious style; also writer and radio commentator on music.

TAYLOR, SAMUEL COLERIDGE-, see COLERIDGE-TAYLOR.

TCHAIKOVSKY, PIOTR ILYICH (1840–93), Russian composer, aloof from the overt nationalism of the 'MIGHTY HANDFUL' group, but nevertheless writing in a distinctively Russian style. A homosexual, left his wife a few weeks after marriage (1877); 1876–90, carried on an extensive correspondence with Nadezhda von Meck, a wealthy widow who made him a monetary allowance – but they hardly met. Visited U.S.A., 1892; England, 1893 (D.Mus., Cambridge). Developed cholera after drinking unboiled water (perhaps deliberately?) in St Petersburg, and died there a few days after the first performance of his last symphony, the 'PATHETIC'. His second symphony is nicknamed 'UKRAINIAN' (or 'Little Russian') and his third 'POLISH'; his 'MANFRED' symphony is unnumbered. Other works – notable for vivid, forceful scoring and for an often-expressed melancholy – include three piano concertos (no. 1 the popular one, no. 3 unfinished), violin concerto; orchestral works (see, e.g. MOZARTIANA, TEMPEST, ROMEO AND JULIET, HAMLET, FRANCESCA DA RIMINI, EIGHTEEN-TWELVE); 'EUGENE ONEGIN', 'THE QUEEN OF SPADES', 'IOLANTA', 'MAZEPPA' and seven other operas; ballets 'SWAN LAKE', 'THE SLEEPING BEAUTY', 'NUTCRACKER'; chamber works, songs.

TCHEREPNIN, ALEXANDER NIKOLAYEVICH (b. 1899), Russian-born composer and pianist, settled in Paris, 1921; university teacher in Chicago, 1949; married a Chinese singer. Works include operas, five piano concertos; Andante for tuba and piano, sonatina for kettledrums and piano; various piano solos. Son of Nikolay Tcherepnin.

TCHEREPNIN, NIKOLAY NIKOLAYEVICH (1873–1945), Russian composer of ballets (including 'Armida's Pavilion') symphonic poems, piano concerto, etc.; pupil and to some extent a follower of Rimsky-Korsakov. Also pianist and conductor. Made a completion of Mussorgsky's unfinished opera, 'SOROCHINTSY FAIR'. Settled in Paris, 1921, with his son (above).

TCHISHKO, OLES (b. 1895), Russian (Ukrainan) composer, also formerly conductor and singer. Has written 'Mutiny on the Battleship Potemkin' and other operas; overture 'Red Army Days'; arrangements of Ukrainian songs, and works based on them, etc.

TE, in TONIC SOL-FA, the spoken name for the seventh degree (leading-note) of the scale, written t. Cp. SI – the initial letter *t* was adopted in Tonic Sol-Fa because *s* would have brought confusion with *soh* (fifth degree).

TE DEUM, a Latin hymn of thanksgiving to God, used in the Roman Catholic Church and (in English as 'We praise thee') in the Anglican Church, etc. There is a traditional plainsong melody for it, and other settings for liturgical use; also settings by Handel and other later composers for concert or ceremonial use. Walton wrote one for the coronation of Queen Elizabeth II.

TEBALDI, RENATA (b. 1922), Italian soprano, active in opera – at the Scala, Milan, from 1946; first sang in Britain, 1950.

TEDESCO (It., fem. *-a*), German; *alla tedesca*, in German fashion – usually meaning 'in the manner of a GERMAN DANCE', but Vaughan Williams's 'Rondo alla tedesca' in his tuba concerto (1954) apparently indicates merely a rondo as in a symphonic work by German composers, e.g. by Beethoven.

TEIL (Ger.), part, section (not in the sense of a voice-part, etc. – see PART, 1 and 2).

TELEMANN, GEORG PHILIPP (1681–1767), German composer of operas, oratorios, and many other vocal and instrumental works (some for recorder); exhibits a style transitional between the periods of Bach and of Haydn, with some French influence. Held a leading church music post in Hamburg from 1721 until his death.

TELEPHONE, THE, one-act comic opera by Menotti, produced in New York, 1947. Libretto by composer. For two characters only (lovers) – plus the distracting telephone.

TELMÁNYI, EMIL (b. 1892), Hungarian violinist, resident in Denmark since 1919; inventor of a controversial 'Bach bow' (see BOW).

TEMA (It.), theme.

TEMPER(ED), see TEMPERAMENT.

TEMPERAMENT, the 'tempering' (i.e. slight lessening or enlarging) of musical intervals away from the 'natural' scale (that deducible by physical laws), in order to fit them for practicable performance. In particular the piano, the modern organ, and other fixed-pitch modern instruments are tuned to *equal temperament*, meaning that each semitone is made an equal interval. In this way the notes D♯ and E♭ are made identical, and other pairs similarly (though by physical laws they differ slightly); it is therefore equally easy to play in any key or, having started in one key, to modulate to any other. (Bach's forty-eight preludes and fugues, called 'THE WELL-TEMPERED CLAVIER', were among the first works to require some such system as this, being set in all the major and minor keys.) The previously prevalent system was *mean-tone temperament*, which gave a nearer approximation to 'natural' tuning than does equal temperament for C major and keys nearly related to it; but it was so far out for keys remote from C major that playing in them was virtually impossible, unless such devices as separate notes for D♯ and E♭ were adopted (as they were on some old organs). It is to be noted that instruments where the notes are not 'pre-set' (e.g. the violin family) can have no 'system' of temperament, since the player himself determines the pitch of the note and checks it by ear: and he may, indeed, get nearer to 'natural' intonation than a keyboard-player's fixed notes allow.

TEMPEST, THE, play by Shakespeare, to which Sibelius wrote incidental music (1926), and on which Tchaikovsky based his orchestral fantasy, 'The Tempest' (1873); it is the source also of Frank Martin's opera of the same name (Ger., *Der Sturm*), an almost literal setting of the text, produced in Vienna, 1956.

TEMPLE BLOCK (or *Korean temple block*), type of hollowed-out wooden vessel, approximately in the shape of a human head; it is struck with a stick as a percussion instrument, particularly in modern dance bands (and occasionally in the orchestra, e.g. in Gould's 'Philharmonic Waltzes'). There are generally several sizes, giving different pitches though not tuned to any one clear note.

TEMPLETON, ALEC (ANDREW) (1909–63), Welsh-born pianist, musical entertainer, and composer, resident in U.S.A.; blind from birth. Works include 'Bach goes to Town' and other jazz skits on the classics, also more serious compositions.

TEMPO (It., time), pace. (Now a naturalized English word in this sense, so plural should be *tempos*.) So also *tempo primo* or *a tempo*, direction to return to the original pace; *tempo di ...*, at the pace of (a specified dance-movement, for instance); *tempo giusto*, strict time but see GIUSTO).

TENERO, tender; *teneramente*, *tenerezza*, tenderly, tenderness.

TENOR, (1) the highest normal male voice, apart from the ALTO (which uses falsetto) – so named because, when polyphonic music emerged in the late Middle Ages, its function was to hold (Lat., *tenere*) the plainsong or other 'given' tune while the other voices proceeded in counterpoint to it; (2) name given, in 'families' of instruments, to that instrument thought to have a position parallel to that which the tenor voice has among voices – so *tenor* SAXOPHONE, *tenor* TROMBONE, etc.; the word *tenor* by itself means in a dance-band the tenor saxophone, in a brass band the tenor SAXHORN, and in obsolete English usage meant the viola; (3, *tenor clef*), type of clef (now little used, but sometimes encountered for cello, bassoon, tenor trombone) written , in which the note middle C is indicated on the top line but one of the staff. See also following entries.

TENOR COR, see MELLOPHONE.

TENOR DRUM, percussion instrument similar to side drum (and capable of similar rolls, etc.) but deeper in pitch, bigger, and without snares. Occasionally used in the orchestra, from the 19th century; also in the military band.

TENOR TUBA, see TUBA.

TENUTO (It., held), direction that a note is to be fully sustained, up to (and sometimes even over) its full written time-value.

TERNARY, in three sections; *ternary form*, classification used of a movement in three sections of which the third is a repetition (exact or near) of the first – i.e. a movement which may be represented as ABA or ABA′. Note that the term is also used even if the first section is initially stated twice (AABA or AABA′) as in the conventional 'minuet and trio', in which the 'minuet' section is given twice on its first statement but only once on its return. Cp. BINARY.

TERTIS, LIONEL (b. 1876), English viola-player who has raised his instrument to a new importance, many (chiefly British) composers writing new works specially for him; himself introduced new technical specifications for the making of the instrument – the result being the 'Tertis model' viola, in successively improved versions.

TESSITURA (It., texture), the compass of notes to which a particular singer's voice naturally inclines ('he has a high *tessitura*') though exceptional notes may be produced outside it; similarly, the general compass (not counting exceptional notes) of a vocal part.

TEYTE, MAGGIE (originally Tate; b. 1888), English soprano who became famous on the French opera stage – changing the spelling of her name to facilitate French pronunciation. Noted in recital (especially in French songs) as well as opera. Lived for a time in U.S.A. after the Second World War.

THAÏS, opera by Massenet, produced in Paris, 1894. Libretto by L. Gallet. Named after its heroine, a 4th-century courtesan who becomes a nun. The well-known orchestral 'Meditation' is an intermezzo between the second and last acts.

THALBEN-BALL, GEORGE (THOMAS) (b. 1896), Australian-born organist resident in Britain; well-known recitalist, and since 1949 Birmingham City Organist. Also composer of organ and vocal music, etc.

THALBERG, SIGISMOND (1812–71), Austrian (Swiss-born) virtuoso pianist (pupil of Hummel) and composer of piano concerto and many solos exploiting piano technique; contributor to the HEXAMERON. Wrote also operas, songs, etc.

THEME, a group of notes constituting (by repetition, recurrence, development, etc.) an important element in the construction of a piece. In some types of musical analysis it is broadly equated with SUBJECT; but it is sometimes also applied to separately recognizable elements within a subject. In the phrase *theme and variations* it refers to the whole musical statement on which the variations are based (i.e. something much longer than *theme* in most other senses). *Metamorphosis of themes.* Liszt's term for the way in which a theme can be changed in successive recurrences (say, to suit the dramatic progress of a SYMPHONIC POEM) while retaining its essence. See also next entry.

THEME-SONG, song in a musical play, film, series of radio shows, etc., recurring prominently and serving to identify a character, an idea, etc. See BISHOP for an early anticipation of this.

THEODORA, oratorio by Handel, first performed in London, 1750. Libretto by T. Morell: the heroine is a Christian martyr.

THEORBO, type of large lute, in frequent use in 17th and 18th centuries.

THEREMIN, type of ELECTRONIC instrument having an upright sensitive 'pole' which produces sound from the motion of the hand in space round it: invented by L. Theremin in Russia, 1924, and afterwards improved. Plays only one note at a time; has a range of five octaves and can produce various tone-colours; works have been composed for it by Martinů (Phantasy for Theremin, string quartet, oboe, and piano) and a few others.

THESE THINGS SHALL BE, work for baritone (or tenor), chorus and orchestra by Ireland, 1937 – a setting of J. A. Symonds' poem foreseeing the brotherhood of man on earth. Quotes the 'INTERNATIONALE'.

THIBAUD, JACQUES (1880–1953), French violinist, noted as soloist and also in chamber music (often with Cortot and Casals as pianist and cellist respectively). Killed in an air crash.

THIEVING MAGPIE, THE (It., *La Gazza ladra*), opera by Rossini, produced in Milan, 1817. Libretto by G. Gherardini: the magpie is the real perpetrator of the theft for which a maidservant is condemned to death.

THIMAN, ERIC (HARDING) (b. 1900), English organist and prolific composer – especially of organ works, church music, cantatas, etc.

THIRD (noun), an interval in melody or harmony, reckoned as taking three steps in the (major or minor) scale, counting the bottom and top notes: either a *major third* (four semitones, e.g. C up to E) or *minor third* (three semitones, e.g. C up to E♭) or *diminished third* (two semitones, e.g. C♯ up to E♭). The last of these is of little practical application, the interval being for practical performing purposes considered as a major second, e.g. D♭ to E♭. See also following entries.

THIRD INVERSION, see POSITION.

THIRD SOUND, Tartini's name (It., *terzo suono*) for the acoustical phenomenon he discovered, now known as a RESULTANT TONE.

THIRTY-SECOND NOTE, U.S. term (following the German) for DEMISEMIQUAVER, a semibreve being considered as a whole-note.

THIS DAY (*Hodie*), Christmas cantata by Vaughan Williams (for soprano, tenor, baritone, boys' chorus, mixed chorus, and orchestra) first performed 1954; text from the Bible and other sources. The Latin title, given in parentheses by the composer, refers to a Latin hymn of which the words are incorporated in the work.

THOMAS, (CHARLES LOUIS) AMBROISE (1811–96), French composer – also pianist, and director of the Paris Conservatory. Wrote 'MIGNON', 'HAMLET', 'RAYMOND', and other operas in a light, melodious style (see also CARNIVAL OF VENICE), and ballets, church music, instrumental pieces, etc.

THOMAS, ARTHUR GORING (1850–92), English composer who studied in Paris (and later with Sullivan and Bruch) and who shows some French operatic influence in operas 'Esmeralda' and 'Nadeshda'. Other works include cantata 'The Sun-Worshippers', songs. Became insane, 1891.

THOMÉ, FRANCIS (real first names Joseph François Luc; 1850–1909), French (Mauritius-born) composer of 'Simple Aveu' (Simple Avowal), piano piece later subject to multitudinous arrangements; also of operas, operettas, etc.

THOMPSON, RANDALL (b. 1899), American composer, pupil of Bloch and others; also noted teacher. Has written symphonies, choral works, opera 'Solomon and Balkis', etc., sometimes cultivating deliberately simple and diatonic style.

THOMSON, VIRGIL (b. 1896), American composer, pupil of N. Boulanger in Paris. Influenced by French 'simplicity' (as demonstrated especially by Satie) but also by characteristic musical Americanisms, e.g. revivalist hymn-tunes. Works include operas 'FOUR SAINTS IN THREE ACTS' and 'The Mother of Us All' (both to librettos of Gertrude Stein), cello concerto, 'Portraits' of various named people (some for orchestra, some for piano, some for unaccompanied violin), piano sonatas, songs in English and French, stage and film music. Also noted critic – of the *New York Herald Tribune*, 1940–54.

THOROUGH-BASS, see CONTINUO.

THREE BOTTICELLI PICTURES, usual English title for Respighi's *Trittico Botticelliano* (literally 'Botticelli Triptych') for small orchestra, musically representing 'Spring', 'The Adoration of the Magi', and 'The Birth of Venus'.

THREE'S COMPANY, one-act comic opera by Hopkins (with piano accompaniment), produced in Crewe, 1953. Libretto by M. Flanders: set in a business office. It is for three characters only, one of them a company director surnamed Three.

THREE-CORNERED HAT, THE (Sp., *El sombrero de tres picos*), ballet with music by Falla, first produced in London, 1919.

THREEPENNY OPERA, THE (Ger., *Die Dreigroschenoper*), opera by Weill, produced in Berlin, 1928, with libretto by B. Brecht – a modernization (using jazz) of the idea of 'THE BEGGAR'S OPERA'.

THRENI, term from Gk used as equivalent of LAMENTATIONS and hence employed by Stravinsky as title of his (Latin) setting of part of this ecclesiastical text, 1958.

THROUGH-COMPOSED, see STROPHIC.

THUNDER-MACHINE, a piece of theatre machinery imitating thunder and brought into a few orchestral scores, e.g. Strauss's 'ALPINE SYMPHONY'.

TIBBETT, LAWRENCE (b. 1896), American baritone, noted in opera: created the title-role in Gruenberg's 'EMPEROR JONES'. Formerly also actor. Appearances at Covent Garden and in recitals, films, etc.

TIE, a line in musical notation joining two adjacent notes of the same pitch, indicating that the sound of the first is to be prolonged continuously into the second, instead of the latter's being struck afresh. So also *to tie*, *tied note*, etc.

TIEF (Ger.), deep, low-pitched.

TIERCE DE PICARDIE, see PICARDY THIRD.

TILL EULENSPIEGEL, usual abbreviated title for 'Till Eulenspiegel's Merry Tricks' (Ger., *Till Eulenspiegels lustige Streiche*), symphonic poem by R. Strauss, first performed 1895. The hero is a traditional rogue of German folk-lore, dating at least from the 15th century: other composers have also written works based on his exploits (e.g. Alpaerts, symphonic poem; Rezniček, opera). He is sometimes referred to in English as Tyll Owlglass (literal translation of his surname).

TIMBALE (Fr.), equals KETTLEDRUM.

TIMBRE (Fr.), equals TONE-COLOUR.

TIMBREL, see TAMBOURINE.

TIME, term used in music to classify basic rhythmical patterns: thus a movement is said to be in *six-eight time* (6/8 time), having six quavers (U.S., eighth-notes) to the bar. (See next entry.) So also, e.g., *common time* (4/4); *waltz time* (3/4, with a characteristic lilt); *march time* (usually 4/4 or 6/8); *in free time*, without any regular accent. (The term is also used more loosely for 'speed'; e.g. *in quick time*.) See also DUPLE, TRIPLE *time*.

TIME-SIGNATURE, sign at the beginning of a composition or movement (and thereafter only when a change has to be indicated) conveying by means of figures the kind of beats in the bar and the number of these – e.g. $\frac{3}{2}$ indicates three minims in the bar, the figure 2 indicating minims (appropriately called half-notes in U.S. terminology, following the German practice by which a semibreve is considered a 'whole-note'). See also DUPLE, TRIPLE time.

TIMPANI (It., not *tympani*), equals KETTLEDRUMS. (The singular *timpano* is not generally used in English, though it is standard Italian.)

TINTAGEL, symphonic poem by Bax, 1917, referring to the castle on the Cornish coast. (For the ballet 'Picnic at Tintagel' see THE GARDEN OF FAND.)

TIN-WHISTLE, rudimentary six-holed keyless wind-instrument of RECORDER type but made of metal. Also called *penny-whistle*.

TIPPETT, MICHAEL KEMP (b. 1905), English composer, pupil of C. Wood and R. O. Morris – and of Boult and Sargent for conducting; influenced by the counterpoint and cross-rhythms of English 16th-century composers, and also by Hindemith. Formerly musical director at Morley College, London, and choral conductor there. Works include operas 'THE MIDSUMMER MARRIAGE' (choral-and-orchestral 'Ritual Dances' come from this) and KING PRIAM, two symphonies, Concerto for double string orchestra and Concerto for Orchestra, Fantasia Concertante on a theme of Corelli (for strings); piano concerto and piano sonata, three string quartets, song-cycles 'Boyhood's End' and 'The Heart's Assurance'; oratorio 'A CHILD OF OUR TIME', cantata 'The Vision of St Augustine'. Knighted 1966.

TOCCATA (It.), an instrumental piece, usually for one performer and usually consisting of a single rapid movement exhibiting the player's touch (It., *toccare*, to touch); but there are specimens, e.g. by Bach for harpsichord, which are in several movements, and here the term is of imprecise significance.

TOCH, ERNST (1887–1964), Austrian-born composer (also pianist) naturalized in U.S.A., 1940, and a prominent teacher and composer of film music there. Also wrote 'The Princess and the Pea' and three other operas, seven symphonies, orchestral fantasy 'Big Ben' (on the Westminster chimes), chamber music, piano solos, etc.

TOESCHI, CARLO GIUSEPPE (1724–88), see MANNHEIM SCHOOL.

TOGNI, CAMILLO (b. 1922), Italian composer, pupil of Casella and others; also pianist. Has written flute sonata, piano works, choral settings of T. S. Eliot, a Missa Brevis, etc. Adopted TWELVE-NOTE method in 1942.

TOM JONES, stage works based on Fielding's novel – (1) opera by Philidor, produced in Paris, 1765 (libretto by A. A. H. Poinsinet); (2) operetta by German, produced in Manchester, 1907 (libretto by A. M. Thompson, R. Courtneidge, and C. H. Taylor).

TOMASCHEK, JOHANN WENZEL, a Germanized form of the following name.

TOMÁŠEK, VÁCLAV JAN (1774–1850), Bohemian composer of operas, church music, etc., and especially of piano works and songs. Was himself also pianist and organist.

TOMASI, HENRI (b. 1901), French composer of operas 'Sampiero Corso' and 'The Silence of the Sea', ballets, suites for orchestra, etc.; also conductor.

TOMBEAU (Fr., tomb, tombstone), term used by some French composers for memorial works – e.g. Ravel's 'For the Grave of Couperin' (*Le Tombeau de Couperin*), for piano, 1917, four of the six movements being later orchestrated.

TOMKINS, name of an English family of musicians of whom the most important was Thomas Tomkins (1572–1656), pupil of Byrd, organist of the Chapel Royal, composer of much church music, also of madrigals and music for virginals and viols.

TOMMASINI, VINCENZO (1878–1950), Italian composer; arranged Scarlatti's music for the ballet 'THE GOOD-HUMOURED LADIES', and wrote operas, orchestral works, chamber and choral music, etc. Also writer on musical aesthetics.

TOM-TOM, oriental drum used in modern dance bands and (very rarely) in the orchestra – often found in sets of two or more, either tuned to definite notes or otherwise. (Not the same as TAM-TAM.)

TON (Fr.), term which as used in various contexts may mean 'note', 'tone' (interval of two semitones), or 'key'. Cp. next entry.

TON (Ger., pl. *Töne*), note, sound (not the interval of a 'tone', i.e. two semitones). So *Tonreihe*, note-row (see TWELVE-NOTE); *Tondichtung*, symphonic poem (this German word in fact providing the origin of the unsatisfactory English term TONE-POEM); *Tonkunst*, music (literally sound-art); *Tonkünstler*, musician(s). Cp. preceding entry.

TONADA (Sp.), tune, air. (Used e.g. as title of some works by Allende.) Cp. next entry.

TONADILLA (Sp.), type of Spanish stage entertainment employing a few singers.

TONAL, (1) of notes (so that *tonal structure* of a piece); (2) of tonality, as distinct from e.g. ATONALITY (so *a tonal composition*); (3) opposite to *real* in certain technical contexts – see ANSWER, SEQUENCE (1).

TONALITY, key – especially in the effect made on the listener by the observance of a single key, as opposed (in the 20th century) to polytonality (simultaneous use of several keys) or atonality (absence of key).

TONDICHTUNG, see TON (Ger.).

TONE, (1) quality of musical sound ('he plays with a pleasing tone'); (2) a musical sound consisting of a 'pure' note, as in acoustical analysis ('a note on the violin may be analysed as containing several different tones'); (3) the interval consisting of two semitones, e.g. from C up to D – see WHOLE-TONE; (4) one of the plainsong melodies (see GREGORIAN TONE) used for the singing of Psalms in the Roman Catholic Church; (5, U.S.) a note (in such usages as 'a chord consisting of four tones'). It is because of this last use, founded on German (see TON) and needlessly confusing, that there have arisen such American compounds as *tone-row* and *twelve-tone* (Eng., note-row, twelve-note). See also following entries.

TONE POEM, equals SYMPHONIC POEM. (The term is a 'translation' of Ger. *Tondichtung*, but is somewhat misleading – 'Sound Poem' would be better. See TON and TONE.)

TONE-CLUSTER, see CLUSTER.

TONE-COLOUR, the quality which distinguishes a note as performed on one instrument from the same note as performed on other instruments (or voices). The French word *timbre* is also used in English in this sense. On analysis the differences between tone-colours of instruments are found to correspond with differences in the harmonics represented in the sound (see HARMONIC SERIES).

TONGUE, to articulate a note on a wind instrument with a certain use of the tongue; so *single-*, *double-*, and *triple-tonguing*, making for progressively faster articulation; *flutter-tonguing*, the articulation of sound as if trilling an *r* (e.g. on the flute, where the resulting tone sounds pigeon-like, and on the trumpet).

TONIC, the first degree, or keynote, of the scale, e.g. F in the keys of F major and F minor. See also TONIC SOL-FA.

TONIC SOL-FA, English system of notation and sight-reading introduced in the 1840s by J. S. Curwen (1816–80), though partly anticipated by others. According to this the notes of the major scale are named (ascending) doh, ray, me, fah, soh, lah, te – doh being the keynote (tonic), and the other notes being thus related to the keynote of the moment, not fixed in pitch as in ordinary (STAFF) notation. Time-values are indicated by bar-lines and dots, and there is other symbolization. The chief use of the written system has been in choral music, for the training of amateurs. See SOLMIZATION.

TONKUNST, TONKÜNSTLER, see TON (Ger.).

TONUS (Lat.), (1) Gregorian tone – see TONE, 4; (2) MODE. See also next entry.

TONUS PEREGRINUS (Lat., foreign tone), (1) medieval term for what is now called the minor scale, not 'recognized' in the modal system then prevalent; (2) the plainsong sung in the Roman Catholic Church to Psalm 114, being in the above scale. See GREGORIAN TONE.

TORELLI, GIUSEPPE (1658–1709), Italian violinist and composer who held a court post in Germany; was one of the pioneer practitioners of the CONCERTO GROSSO, and also wrote other music for stringed instruments. See CHRISTMAS CONCERTO.

TORTELIER, PAUL (b. 1914). French cellist, also composer (e.g. of concerto for two cellos and orchestra). For a time lived in Israel.

TOSATTI, VIERI (b. 1920), Italian composer, pupil of Pizzetti: cultivates an 'unsophisticated' style on traditional Italian operatic models. Works include operas 'Treatment by Kindness' (*Il Sistema della dolcezza*), 'The Boxing Match', and 'Treasure Island' (after Stevenson); also orchestral pieces, songs, piano solos, etc.

TOSCA, opera by Puccini, produced in Rome, 1900. Libretto by G.

Giacosa and L. Illica, after Sardou's French play *La Tosca*. The name-part is that of an operatic prima donna.

TOSCANINI, ARTURO (1867–1957), Italian conductor, formerly cellist; his many important 'first performances' include that of Puccini's 'TURANDOT'. Having achieved highest international reputation in concerts and opera, refused to play under German or Italian fascism and settled in New York, where the National Broadcasting Company's orchestra was specially created for him (1937). Conducted always from memory (too short-sighted to read a score from the rostrum). His daughter Wanda married Horowitz.

TOSELLI, ENRICO (1883–1920), Italian composer of songs, including a famous 'Serenata', and also of operettas, chamber music, etc.

TOST QUARTETS, name given to twelve string quartets by Haydn, 1789–90 (op. 54 nos. 1–3, op. 55 nos. 1–3, op. 64 nos. 1–6) – dedicated to a violinist named Johann Tost.

TOSTI, (FRANCESCO) PAOLO (1844–1916), Italian composer and singing-master who settled in London, taught the British royal family, and was knighted (1908). Wrote 'Good-bye' and other songs in English, also songs in French and Italian.

TOUCHE (Fr.), finger-board (of stringed instruments); *sur la touche*, direction to play 'on the finger-board' (a special method of bowing).

TOUJOURS (Fr.), always, still.

TOUREL, JENNIE (b. 1910), Canadian-born singer of Russian parentage, educated in Europe, resident in U.S.A. Noted in Russian, French, and German songs, but sings also in six other languages; operatic appearances (from 1933) include creation of the role of Baba the Turk in Stravinsky's 'THE RAKE'S PROGRESS'.

TOURNEMIRE, CHARLES ARNOULD (1870–1939), French organist and composer of many organ works (also of operas, chamber music, etc.); noted recitalist. Pupil of d'Indy.

TOURTE BOW, see BOW.

TOVEY, DONALD FRANCIS (1875–1940), English pianist, composer (opera 'The Bride of Dionysus', cello concerto, chamber music, etc.), conductor, professor at Edinburgh University, and (especially) author of programme-notes (collected as 'Essays in Musical Analysis') and other writings on music. Made, with great technical skill, a conjectural completion of the final unfinished fugue in Bach's 'THE ART OF FUGUE'. Knighted 1935.

TOY(E), old English term sometimes used for a light piece for the virginals.

TOY SYMPHONY, a symphony of a simple kind in which toy instruments are employed. The best-known example is that which is usually ascribed to Joseph Haydn; it is now known to have been part of a longer work by Leopold Mozart, the toy instruments having perhaps been added by Michael Haydn. A modern one has been written by Malcolm Arnold (1957).

TRACKER ACTION, the mechanical linkage between the pipes and the keyboards in older types of organ, now generally replaced by pneumatic or electric action.

TRAETTA, TOMMASO (MICHELE FRANCESCO SAVERIO) (1727–99), Italian composer of operas notable for their dramatic use of the chorus; also of church music, etc. Pupil of Durante. Worked for a time in St Petersburg and London.

TRAGIC OVERTURE (Ger., *Tragische Ouvertüre*), concert-overture by Brahms, first performed 1887; it does not refer to any particular tragedy.

'TRAGIC' SYMPHONY, name given (by the composer) to Schubert's symphony no. 4 in C minor, 1816.

TRANCHELL, PETER (ANDREW) (b. 1922), English composer (born in India); works, in conservatively-inclined style, include opera 'The Mayor of Casterbridge' (after Hardy), musical play 'Zuleika' (after Max Beerbohm's *Zuleika Dobson*), choral works, songs (some with chamber-music accompaniment).

TRANSCRIBE, (1) to arrange a piece of music for a performing medium other than the original – or for the same medium but in a more elaborate style. The term usually implies a freer treatment than the simple verb 'to arrange' by itself; (2) to convert a piece from one system of notation to another, e.g. from medieval notation to the modern method. So also *transcription*.

TRANSFIGURED NIGHT (Ger., *Verklärte Nacht*), work by Schoenberg (op. 4, composed in 1899) for string sextet – in effect a 'symphonic poem' for this combination, after a poem by R. Dehmel about a moonlit walk by a man and a woman. An arrangement for string orchestra appeared in 1917.

TRANSITION, (1, *in analysis*) a passage serving mainly to join two passages more important than itself; (2) a change of key, particularly one of a 'sudden' kind, not going through the regularly ordered process called 'modulation' (see MODULATE).

TRANSPOSE, to write down or perform music at a pitch other than the original. So certain instruments on which the player produces a note different from the written note are called TRANSPOSING INSTRUMENTS; and, e.g. an English horn, playing a perfect fifth below the written note, is said to *transpose down a fifth*. A song is often *transposed* to a higher or lower key to suit a singer's convenience. So also a piece written in one of the old MODES may be said to be in e.g. the 'Dorian mode transposed', meaning with the same intervals as the Dorian mode but ending elsewhere than D where the Dorian ends. So also *transposing keyboard*, one on which the performer can transpose by mechanical aid – he strikes the keys as usual, but the sideways shifting of the keyboard causes strings higher or lower than normal to be struck.

TRANSPOSING INSTRUMENT (see preceding entry), an instrument on which the player produces a sound at a fixed interval above or below the note written. The chief reason for this is the convenience of a player changing between different sizes of instrument. A player of e.g. the clarinet knows that when seeing the note middle C in the music before him, he always puts down the same fingers in the same way. On the 'clarinet in C' (now rare) the note sounded is the note written, i.e. middle C; other clarinets' names indicate the note each produces instead of C. E.g., on the 'clarinet in B♭', the note written C sounds as B♭ – the instrument transposing the C (and all other notes) one tone lower; the 'clarinet in A' transposes one and a half tones below the written note; the 'clarinet in E♭', one and a half tones higher; the 'bass clarinet in B♭' an octave and one tone lower. The horn and trumpet usually work as transposing instruments (e.g., 'horn in F', 'trumpet in B♭'); but note that when a brass instrument is described as being 'in' a key this does not necessarily mean that it transposes but merely that it is built to a certain size – e.g. the normal orchestral tuba is 'in' F. See IN.

TRANSPOSITION, the process of transferring music to a pitch other than the original. See TRANSPOSE.

TRANSVERSE FLUTE, name for the ordinary flute, to distinguish it (as held cross-wise) from the recorder (of the same basic instrumental type, but held downwards).

TRAPS, collective term for the instruments and other equipment used by the drummer in a modern dance band.

TRASCINANDO (It.), dragging.

TRAUBEL, HELEN (b. 1899), American soprano, noted in Wagner's operas; did not appear in Europe till 1953. First appearance at the Metropolitan Opera House, New York, in 1939; in 1953 ceased to be employed there, on refusing to give up night-club engagements.

TRAUER (Ger.), mourning. So *Trauermarsch*, funeral march. So also Haydn's so-called *Trauersymphonie* (see MOURNING SYMPHONY); Mozart's *Maurische Trauermusik* (Masonic Funeral Music); Hindemith's *Trauermusik* (mourning music), for viola and strings.

TRAUTONIUM, trade name for a type of ELECTRONIC instrument invented in Germany in 1930; it produced only one note at a time. It may be fixed to a piano, one hand playing each instrument. Hindemith has written for it.

TRAVERSA, name occasionally found instead of TRAVERSO.

TRAVERSO, name sometimes used in old scores as abbreviation of *flauto traverso* (It.), i.e. the transverse flute – to distinguish this instrument (the ordinary flute, held cross-wise) from the recorder, held downwards.

TRAVIATA, LA (It., The Woman Gone Astray), opera by Verdi, produced in Venice, 1853. Libretto by F. M. Piave, after the younger Dumas's *The Lady of the Camellias* – the heroine being a self-sacrificing courtesan who eventually dies.

TREBLE, (1) type of high voice – the term usually being kept today to children's voices, the adult female equivalent being 'soprano';

(2) the upper part of a composition, or the upper regions of pitch generally – especially in antithesis to BASS; (3) name given to high-pitched members of certain 'families' of instruments: e.g. *treble* RECORDER, *treble* VIOL; (4, *treble clef*), clef written 𝄞 indicating the G above middle C as the next-to-bottom line of the staff. It is normally used for high-pitched instruments and for women's and children's voices; also for right-hand piano parts. It is moreover used for the tenor voice, by a convention according to which the notes are sounded an octave lower than written: occasionally, to indicate this, a figure 8 is written below the clef-sign.

TREMOLANDO (It., trembling), having the effect of a TREMOLO.

TREMOLO (It., a shaking, a trembling), (1, *in string-playing*) the rapid reiteration of a single note by back-and-forth strokes of the bow; (2, *in string-playing, and on other instruments*) the alternation between two notes as rapidly as possible; (3) term used (misleadingly) by some singing-teachers for the effect in the voice that should rightly be called VIBRATO.

Note that *tremolo*, as in (1) above, is strictly the rapid regular fluctuation of intensity, i.e. of volume; *vibrato* is a fluctuation of pitch, i.e. of the frequency of vibrations.

TREMULANT, device on the organ imparting a wobbling effect to the note through variation of the wind-pressure: an element both of TREMOLO and VIBRATO is involved.

TREPAK, lively Russian dance in 2/4 time.

TRIAD, a three-note chord consisting of a particular note plus its third and fifth above – e.g. C–E–G, which is called the 'common chord' of C major, no matter whether C remains the bass-note or is replaced by one of the other notes. Similarly C–E♭–G is the 'common chord' of C minor. So also *augmented triad*, containing the augmented fifth (e.g. C, E, G♯); *diminished triad*, containing the diminished 5th (e.g. C, E♭, G♭).

TRIAL BY JURY, operetta (but styled a 'dramatic cantata') by Sullivan, produced in London, 1875. Libretto by W. S. Gilbert, burlesquing an action for breach of promise. (It is the only Gilbert-and-Sullivan stage piece that is sung throughout, with no spoken dialogue.)

TRIANGLE, three-cornered metal-framed percussion instrument, struck with a metal stick; its tinkling sound is without definite pitch.

TRILL, a musical ornament (usually designated by *tr.* ~~ over the note) also called *shake*, consisting of the rapid alternation of the written note and the note above. Whether this note is a whole-tone or a semitone above depends on which of these notes occurs in the scale in use at the moment – unless the composer directs otherwise. See also TURN. See also following entry.

TRILLO (It.), (1) trill; *Trillo del Diavolo*, see DEVIL'S TRILL; (2) an obsolete vocal ornament in which a single note was repeated, the repetitions getting ever faster.

TRIMBLE, JOAN (b. 1915), Northern Irish pianist and composer; works include opera 'Blind Rafferty' (for television), songs, and many two-piano works for herself and her sister Valerie (b. 1917).

TRIO, (1) a combination of three performers; *string trio*, violin, viola, cello; *piano trio*, piano, violin, cello; (2) a work for three performers – if instrumental, and actually called a 'trio' it will probably have the character of a SONATA for three performers, in several movements; (3) the centre section of a minuet, so called because formerly it was conventionally written in three-PART harmony only, as for a 'trio' in the normal sense; so also when a scherzo or a march is constructed in minuet form (AABA), the 'B' section may be called a trio; (4) name given also to certain works by Bach for organ (or for harpsichord with two manuals and pedals) having three melodic PARTS but played by one performer; these are more reasonably called TRIO-SONATAS or sonatas.

TRIO-SONATA, type of composition favoured in the late 17th and early 18th centuries, usually for two violins and cello (or viola da gamba), with a keyboard instrument also playing the bass-line and supporting it with harmonies 'arranged' by the player – see CONTINUO. See also preceding entry.

TRIPLE CONCERTO, concerto with three soloists, e.g. Beethoven's (piano, violin, cello), 1805.

TRIPLE COUNTERPOINT, see COUNTERPOINT.

TRIPLE TIME, time in which the primary division is into three beats – e.g. three crochets in a bar (3/4) – as distinct particularly from DUPLE TIME (primary division into two). Note especially that 3/2 indicates a bar of three minims (𝅗𝅥+𝅗𝅥+𝅗𝅥) while 6/4 indicates a bar of two dotted minims (𝅗𝅥.+𝅗𝅥.) – giving different accents even though both total six crochets.

TRIPLET, a group of three notes (or notes and rests) of equal time-value, written where a group of two, four or some other number of notes is suggested by the time-signature. E.g., a three-note group occupying a bar of 2/4 time, written ♩♩♩ (with 3 above).

TRISTAN AND ISOLDE (Ger., *Tristan und Isolde*), opera by Wagner, produced in Munich, 1865. Libretto by composer, after the Arthurian legend. The two lovers (also known in English as Tristram and Yseult) drink a love-potion in mistake for poison, but eventually die just the same.

TRITONE, the interval of three tones (see TONE, 3), e.g. from F up or down to B. This is an awkward interval to sing, and its use in composition was formerly (in medieval and later practice) hedged round with various prohibitions. Hence the jingle, *Mi contra fa diabolus est* *in musica* (Mi against fa [the old names for these notes according to the system of HEXACHORDS] is the devil in music).

TRITTICO (It., Triptych), Puccini's name for the three contrasted one-act operas produced in a single evening in New York in 1918. See THE CLOAK, SISTER ANGELICA, GIANNI SCHICCHI.

TRITTICO BOTTICELLIANO, see THREE BOTTICELLI PICTURES.

TRIUMPH OF NEPTUNE, THE, ballet with music by Berners, produced in London, 1926. Called 'an English pantomime' and based on toy theatre designs. A concert suite is drawn from it.

TRIUMPHS OF ORIANA, THE, English collection of madrigals by various composers, edited by Morley and published in 1601; in the form (modelled on an Italian collection) of tributes, each poem ending 'Long live fair Oriana'. It is generally recognized that 'Oriana' was Elizabeth I. Among the twenty-three English composers represented in the first edition were J. Bennett, Hilton (the elder), Kirby, Milton, Morley, J. Mundy, Norcombe, Tomkins, Weelkes, Wilbye; an Italian madrigal (translated into English) by Croce was also included. Works by Bateson and Pilkington were added in later editions. See also A GARLAND FOR THE QUEEN.

TROILUS AND CRESSIDA, opera by Walton, produced in London, 1954. Libretto by C. Hassall, principally after Chaucer's (not Shakespeare's) version of the story.

TROJANS, THE (Fr., *Les Troyens*), opera by Berlioz, with libretto by composer, after Virgil's *Aeneid*. In two parts – (1) 'The Taking of Troy' (*La Prise de Troie*), produced (in German) in Carlsruhe, 1890, after Berlioz's death; (2) 'The Trojans at Carthage' (*Les Troyens à Carthage*), produced in Paris, 1863.

TROMBA (It.), trumpet (also with special significance – see under TRUMPET); *tromba da tirarsi*, slide-TRUMPET; *tromba marina*, TRUMPET MARINE.

TROMBONE, type of brass instrument with a slide varying the effective length of the tube. In any one position of the slide, the notes of the HARMONIC SERIES can be produced; and there are seven recognized positions of the slide, producing harmonic series a semitone apart. A combination of moving the slide (i.e. picking a particular series) and controlling the breath (i.e. picking a note within a series) yields a chromatic range – *tenor trombone*, from E below the bass stave upwards for about two and a half octaves; *bass trombone*, from the D♭ lower. (Below this, a few isolated 'pedal notes' can be produced: they are actually the first tones of the harmonic series in various positions, and are not usually called for.) The higher *alto trombone*, now obsolete, was written for e.g. by Mozart; the lower *double-bass trombone* was occasionally used by Wagner and a few others. The trombones, previously confined largely to church music, entered the opera orchestra in the late 18th century and the symphony orchestra shortly afterwards; now used also in military, brass, and dance bands. Solo and chamber music using them is rare. (There is also a rarely-encountered *valve-trombone*, as big as a trombone and with similar range, but having valves like a trumpet instead of a slide.)

TROMMEL (Ger.), drum; *grosse Trommel*, bass drum.

TRONCO, TRONCA (It.), broken off short (of a note, especially in vocal music).

TROPE, (1) type of musical interpolation into traditional liturgical plainsong, from about the 9th to the 15th century – the ecclesiastical SEQUENCE being a survival of this; hence *Troper*, a medieval book containing tropes; (2) term used, in quite a different sense from the above, in the form of twelve-note technique invented and practised by HAUER.

TROPPO (It.), too much; *allegro non troppo*, or *allegro ma non troppo*, fast but not too fast.

TROUBADOUR, type of itinerant poet-musician of southern France flourishing in the 11th–13th centuries, writing and singing songs in the Provençal language and moving in courtly (not popular) circles. Cp. TROUVÈRE, TROVATORE.

'TROUT' QUINTET, name for Schubert's quintet (1819) for piano, violin, viola, cello, and double-bass; the fourth of its five movements comprises variations on Schubert's song 'The Trout' (Ger., *Die Forelle*).

TROUVÈRE, the northern French counterpart of the TROUBADOUR, writing and singing his songs in Old French, not in Provençal.

TROVATORE, IL (It., The Troubadour), opera by Verdi, produced in Rome, 1853. Libretto by S. Cammarano: the hero, though eventually revealed as a nobleman's son, has been brought up by a gipsy and has become a troubadour.

TRUMPET, metal wind-instrument, cylindrically bored, used for signalling, etc., from ancient times, and regularly appearing in the orchestra from the 17th century. The modern form (from mid-19th century) has three valves, and is today either a TRANSPOSING INSTRUMENT in B♭ (which may be switched to a transposing instrument in A) with compass from E below middle C upwards for nearly three octaves, or a non-transposing instrument in C (one tone higher). It is used in the dance band as well as the orchestra; in the brass band and some military bands it is replaced by the cornet. It is occasionally used for solos and in chamber music. The *bass trumpet* is similar, but in C an octave lower, and rarely used. The so-called *Bach trumpet* is a late-19th-century type of high-pitched trumpet (sometimes made in long, straight form) with valves, suitable for playing high-pitched trumpet parts as written in Bach's and Handel's day. *Fanfare trumpets* are a set in various sizes for ceremonial purposes, made in long, straight form on which banners can be hung. Before the modern valve trumpet the normal instrument was a 'natural' (valveless, keyless) trumpet producing one 'HARMONIC SERIES' only, like a bugle; but the use of different instruments, and of changeable CROOKS (altering the instrument's total length of tube) went some way to allow a choice of different harmonic series as the music required it. In Bach's time, trumpeters specialized in high (*clarino*) or low (*principale*) parts, the name *tromba* sometimes being used for middle parts. Attempts before the valve-trumpet to enlarge the number of notes available led to the invention of various types of *slide-trumpet* (having a slide like a trombone's) and also of the *keyed trumpet* for which Haydn wrote his trumpet concerto.

TRUMPET MARINE, obsolete instrument apparently named on the 'Holy Roman Empire' principle, being neither marine nor a trumpet. It was a large single-stringed bowed instrument, one end of which rested on the floor. By the pressing of a finger at correct points on the string, notes of the HARMONIC SERIES could be obtained. This reliance on harmonics perhaps explains the name 'trumpet', though 'marine' remains baffling. The Italian name *tromba marina* is also sometimes found in English references. Cp. MONOCHORD.

TRUMPET TUNE, TRUMPET VOLUNTARY, pieces not composed for a trumpet, but imitating one – e.g. as solo for a trumpet-like stop on the organ. 'Trumpet Voluntary' was the name Henry Wood gave to a keyboard piece which he arranged for a combination of organ, brass, and kettledrums and which he followed another editor in mistakenly attributing to Purcell. Its original title was 'The Prince of Denmark's March', and it is now known to be by J. CLARKE.

TSAR AND CARPENTER, *or The Two Peters* (Ger., *Zar und Zimmermann, oder Die Zwei Peter*), opera by Lortzing, produced in Leipzig, 1837. Libretto after a French play by A. H. J. Mélesville, J. T. Merle, and E. Cantiran de Boirie; concerns Peter the Great.

TSCHAIKOWSKI, -SKY, German spellings of the name TCHAIKOVSKY.

TUBA, (1) type of bass brass valved instrument made in several sizes and shapes – when circular, called 'helicon', of which the SOUSAPHONE is a variety. The standard orchestral tuba (or *bass tuba*) is in F, with compass from the F an octave below the bass clef, upwards for about three octaves; and since its invention (1835) has become the normal lowest brass instrument of the orchestra. (Very rarely used as soloist, though Vaughan Williams has composed a concerto for it.) *Double-bass tuba* signifies a lower and much rarer instrument, used e.g. by Wagner in 'THE RING' in conjunction with the WAGNER TUBAS, of which it is not one. *Tenor tuba* signifies an instrument higher than the bass tuba – in Britain equated with the euphonium. The lowest instruments of the brass and military band, also in effect types of tuba, are called bombardons – in B♭ (lowest) and E♭; both are lower, and so bigger to look at, than the orchestral tuba. (2) powerful trumpet-like organ stop; (3) ancient Roman straight trumpet.

TUBULAR BELL, see BELL.

TUCKET, obsolete English word (found in Shakespeare) for a fanfare.

TUDWAY, THOMAS (*c.* 1650–1726), English composer of church music, organist, professor at Cambridge, and compiler of a collection of English Cathedral music.

TUNE, (1) melody, especially the upper part of a simple composition; (2) term (noun and verb) referring to correct intonation – so *in tune, out of tune, to tune a piano*, etc. ('Dancers dancing in tune' is a phenomenon observed only by Tennyson.) See also next entry.

TUNING-FORK, a two-pronged metal object set in vibration to produce a sound which serves to check the pitch of instruments and to give the pitch to voices. Its note is a 'pure' tone – not having any of the upper harmonics (see HARMONIC SERIES) which enter into the tone of normal instruments.

TURANDOT, (1) opera by Puccini, produced in Milan, 1926; completed by Alfano, Puccini having died; libretto by G. Adami and P. Simone; see GONG (2) opera by Busoni, produced in Zürich, 1917; libretto (in German) by composer; (3) play by Schiller for which Weber wrote incidental music, 1809. The source of all these is an Italian play by Carlo Gozzi (1722–1806): Turandot is a cruel Chinese princess eventually conquered by love.

TURANGALÎLA, title of a symphony by Messiaen, with a solo piano part, 1947. It is influenced (especially as to rhythm) by Indian music, to which the title refers, and 'the whole work is a love-song' (Messiaen).

TURCA, ALLA (It.), in the Turkish style – in effect having, or simulating, the percussion instruments brought to Austria (and so introduced to western Europe) by Turkish military bands in the 18th century. (Cp. JANISSARY MUSIC.) So the *Rondo alla turca* forming the last movement of Mozart's piano sonata in A (K.331), 1778 – arranged by others for various combinations.

TURCHI, GUIDO (b. 1916), Italian composer; influenced by Bartók, to whose memory he inscribed his 'Concerto Breve' (short) for string quartet or string orchestra. Other works include 'Five Comments on the *Bacchae* of Euripides' for orchestra; 'Invective' for choir and two pianos.

TURINA, JOAQUÍN (1882–1949), Spanish composer, pupil of d'Indy in Paris. Works, cultivating a distinctively Spanish national style, include symphonic poem 'The Procession of the Virgin of the Dew' (Sp., *La Procesión del Rocio*); symphonic rhapsody for piano and orchestra; 'The Bull-Fighter's Prayer' (*La Oración del torero*) for string quartet; piano solos and songs.

TURN, musical ornament normally indicated by a special mark, as follows:  played  (and various similar indications).

TURN OF THE SCREW, THE, opera by Britten, produced in Venice,

1953. Libretto by M. Piper, after Henry James's story about the ghostly possession of children.

TUSCH (Ger.), a flourish of wind instruments and drums, occasionally accorded by a German orchestra to a distinguished conductor.

TUTTI, see TUTTO.

TUTTO (It., fem. *-a*, pl. *tutti*, *tutte*), all. So, in piano works, *tutte le corde*, all the strings, i.e. not with soft pedal (see CORDA). The word *tutti*, meaning 'all the performers', is loosely used e.g. in a concerto as signifying a passage for the orchestra without the soloist – whether or not every member of the orchestra is actually playing. In choral works *tutti* can mean chorus as opposed to soloists, or full chorus as opposed to semi-chorus.

TVEITT, GEIRR (b. 1908), Norwegian composer; also pianist and writer on music. Studied in Germany, Austria, and France. Works, using an idiom influenced by Norwegian folk-music (and often linked with Norwegian literary subjects) include five piano concertos, concerto for Hardanger fiddle and orchestra, operas, choral works, chamber music.

TWELFTH, on the organ, a MUTATION stop sounding a twelfth (i.e. an octave plus a fifth) above the note depressed.

TWELVE-NOTE, term used to describe a technique of composition in which all twelve notes within the octave (i.e. the seven white and five black notes of the piano) are treated as 'equal' – i.e. are subjected to an ordered relationship which (unlike that of the major-minor key system) establishes no 'hierarchy' of notes (but see below). One such technique was invented by J. M. HAUER; but the term is now virtually confined to the technique invented by Schoenberg, described by him as a 'method of composing with twelve notes which are related only to one another'. This method works through the 'note-row' (or 'series'), in which all the twelve notes are placed in a particular order as the basis of a work. No note is repeated within a row, which accordingly consists of twelve different notes and no others. The note-row does not necessarily form a theme or part of one, but it is used as the 'tonal reservoir' from which the piece is drawn: it may be used as it stands, or transformed (see INVERT and RETROGRADE) or transposed. The total structure of the work, not merely the shape of the particular melody, must conform to the observance of the note-row. Originally twelve-note technique developed as a standardization of ATONAL music; but certain composers (e.g. Dallapiccola, F. Martin), while using twelve-note methods of construction, have allowed the resultant music to present a definitely implied relation to the major-minor key system; and, as if fore-shadowing a rapprochement from the other side, some composers who do not follow twelve-note technique have made use of complete series of all the twelve notes without repetition of any one note – e.g. Walton, violin sonata; Britten, 'THE TURN OF THE SCREW'.

TWILIGHT OF THE GODS, THE, usual translation of Wagner's '*Götterdämmerung*' – see RING.

TYE, CHRISTOPHER (*c.* 1500–*c.* 1573), English composer who became a clergyman in the newly reformed Church of England. Wrote notable church music in Latin and English, including settings of the Acts of the Apostles in his own metrical rhymed English translation. Also wrote IN NOMINES. See also ROBERT WHITE.

U

UCCELLI, GLI, see BIRDS.

UHR, DIE, German nickname (The Clock) for Haydn's 'CLOCK' Symphony.

UILLEAN PIPES, see BAGPIPES.

'UKRAINIAN' SYMPHONY, nickname for Tchaikovsky's symphony no. 2 in C minor, first performed 1873; so called from the use of folk-tunes in the first and fourth movements. More often called 'Little Russian' symphony (meaning identically the same); but 'Ukraine', as the more intelligible term nowadays, is preferable.

UKULELE (sometimes spelt ukelele), small guitar-like four-stringed instrument from the South Pacific islands (but of Portuguese origin); having some vogue since the 1920s in the U.S.A. and Europe, being cheap and easily learnt. A special notation is used – see TABLATURE.

ULYSSES, cantata by Seiber, first performed 1949; text (philosophically speculative) from James Joyce's novel. Of its five sections, no. 4 is labelled 'Homage to Schoenberg' and quotes from the last of Schoenberg's 'Six Little Piano Pieces', op. 19 (1911).

UN', UNA, UNO (It.), a. (For entries beginning thus, see under second word.)

UN, UNE (Fr.), a. (For entries beginning thus, see under second word.)

UND (Ger.), and.

UNDA MARIS (Lat., wave of the sea), organ stop similar to VOIX CÉLESTE.

'UNFINISHED' SYMPHONY name given to Schubert's symphony no. 8 in B minor, 1822. It has only two completed movements, though sketches exist for a third (Scherzo). Schubert presumably either (1) intended to complete the work later; or (2) forgot about it; or (3) actually did complete it, the two final movements having been lost. The work remained unperformed until 1865. Various attempts have been made to complete it.

UNICORN, THE GORGON, AND THE MANTICORE, THE, 'madrigal-opera' by Menotti produced in Washington 1956. Uses dancers for the action supported by chorus and orchestra. Text – a fable for modern times – by the composer.

UNION PIPES, see BAGPIPES.

UNISON, a united sounding of the same note; thus *unison song*, a song for several people all singing the same tune (not harmonizing). Expressions such as *singing in unison* are generally (but loosely) also applied to the singing of the same tune by men and women an octave apart – where 'singing in octaves' would be more strictly accurate.

UNIT ORGAN (also called *extension organ*), type of organ which saves space by having various stops 'borrow' pipes from each other. Thus an eight-FOOT stop and a four-foot stop will share pipes for the part of their range that overlaps, instead of having completely separate sets of pipes as on a 'normal' organ. Cinema organs are usually of this type.

UNPREPARED (discord), see PREPARATION.

UNQUENCHABLE, THE (Dan., *Det Uudslukkelige*), title of symphony no. 4 by C. Nielsen, 1916. The title – more usually and more awkwardly translated as 'The Inextinguishable' – comes from the composer's dictum, 'Music is life, and as such is unquenchable'.

UNSTERBLICHE GELIEBTE, see IMMORTAL BELOVED.

UP-BEAT, the upward motion of the conductor's stick or hand, especially as indicating the beat preceding the bar-line, i.e. the beat preceding the main accent; term therefore also used for the beat preceding such an accent, whether or not the piece is being 'conducted'. Cp. DOWN-BEAT.

UP-BOW, the motion of the bow of a stringed instrument when pushed by the player – the opposite (pulling) motion being a *down-bow*.

UPPER PARTIAL, see HARMONIC SERIES.

UPRIGHT PIANO, see PIANO.

UT, French name for the note C in SOLMIZATION.

UTILITY MUSIC, English equivalent for the original German form *Gebrauchsmusik*, utilized by Hindemith, Weill, and others in Germany in the 1920s to indicate music directed to a social or educational purpose and not merely constituting art for art's sake. Hindemith disowned the term in his book *A Composer's World* (1951) as a misleading and useless label.

UTOPIA LIMITED, *or The Flowers of Progress*, operetta by Sullivan, produced in London, 1893. Libretto by W. S. Gilbert, postulating a Utopia run on the lines of a British limited liability company.

V

VA., abbr. of VIOLA.

V.S., see VOLTI.

VACTOR, DAVID VAN (b. 1900), American composer, pupil of Dukas in Paris; also flutist and conductor. Has written many works incorporating solo flute; also ballet, Passacaglia and Fugue for orchestra, etc.

VALEN, FARTEIN (OLAV) (1887–1952), Norwegian composer who spent his early years in Madagascar and then studied in Berlin coming (uniquely among Scandinavian composers of his generation) under the influence of Schoenberg and adopting the TWELVE-NOTE method, though not precisely as Schoenberg used it. Works include five symphonies, a violin concerto (a performance of which has been filmed), two string quartets.

VALENTINI, GIUSEPPE (1681–?), Italian composer, principally of chamber music; no relation of Pietro Valentini.

VALENTINI, PIETRO FRANCESCO (*c.* 1570–1654), Italian composer of operas, church music, madrigals, etc.

VALKYRIE, THE, see RING.

VALLS, JOSEP (b. 1904), Spanish (Catalan) composer, pupil of d'Indy in Paris. Works include a concerto for string quartet with string orchestra; symphony; songs.

VALSE (Fr.), equals WALTZ. So *La Valse*, 'choreographic poem' by Ravel for orchestra, 1920; *Valse Nobles et Sentimentales*, a set by Ravel for piano, 1911, afterwards orchestrated (Ravel intended homage to Schubert, who composed for piano some 'Valse Nobles' and some 'Valse Sentimentales'). So also *Valse triste* ('sad'), by Sibelius – originally for strings and occurring in the incidental music to the play *Death* by Arvid Järnefelt, afterwards scored for full orchestra and in this version first performed 1904.

VALVE, mechanism on brass instruments whereby, at the pressure of the player's finger, the current of air is diverted round an additional length of tubing. Thus the vibrating air-column becomes longer, giving a different HARMONIC SERIES from that of the unlengthened tube. By means of three valves, each giving a different additional length of tubing, and usable singly or in combination, the modern trumpet (and other instruments) can produce a complete chromatic scale; whereas the valveless trumpet of e.g. Bach's day, like a modern bugle, could produce only one harmonic series giving large gaps in the scale. All the brass instruments now normally used in the orchestra, military band, brass band, and dance band have valves – except the (normal) trombones, which have slides. For the exceptional *valve-trombone*, see TROMBONE.

VAMP, to improvise an instrumental accompaniment or introduction, e.g. to a song.

VAN, VAN DEN, VAN DER, prefixes to names – see next word of the name.

VANESSA, opera by Barber, produced in New York, 1958. Libretto by Gian-Carlo Menotti, about three women of the same family.

VAŇHAL, VANHALL, see WANHAL.

VARÈSE, EDGAR (1885–1965), French-born composer (pupil of d'Indy and Roussel) who settled in U.S.A., 1915, and cultivated music involving extremes of dissonance, unusual instrumentation, and (often) 'scientific' titles – e.g. 'Ionization' (percussion instruments only), 'Density 21.5' (flute solo), 'OCTANDRE'. Has also used ELECTRONIC instruments.

VARIABLE METRE, see BLACHER.

VARIATION, a passage of music intended as a varied version of some 'given' passage. So *Variations on* . . . a tune (whether or not the tune has been specially composed by the composer of the variations), the tune being called the 'theme' of the variations. Such variations may diverge only slightly from the theme, mainly by melodic ornamentation (as in Mozart), but the more recent tendency is to a looser type allowing a much freer form of composition, e.g. Elgar's 'ENIGMA VARIATIONS'. The terms CHACONNE and PASSACAGLIA also imply variations, of a specific type, and the term RHAPSODY may do so. See also following entries.

VARIATIONS AND FUGUE ON A THEME OF PURCELL (Britten), see YOUNG PERSON'S GUIDE.

VARIATIONS ON A THEME OF HAYDN, see 'ST ANTHONY' VARIATIONS.

VARNAY, (IBOLYKA) ASTRID (b. 1918), Swedish soprano, resident in U.S.A. since childhood; appeared at the Metropolitan Opera House, New York, from 1941, and later at Covent Garden.

VAUDEVILLE, French term of varying meanings, among them that of a song with verses sung by different characters in turn, each verse followed by the same refrain – as in the final number of Mozart's 'THE SERAGLIO'.

VAUGHAN WILLIAMS, RALPH (1872–1958), English composer, pupil of Stanford, Bruch (in Berlin), and Ravel (in Paris). Evolved distinctive musical idiom, much in association with Holst; greatly influenced by English folk-music, some of which he collected and arranged (see GREENSLEEVES, 'THE RUNNING SET'). Based his 'SINFONIA ANTARTICA' (Symphony no. 7) on his score for film *Scott of the Antarctic*, and brought out his last symphony (no. 9) at the age of 85. His first three symphonies are named 'SEA SYMPHONY', 'LONDON SYMPHONY', 'PASTORAL SYMPHONY'. Other works include operas 'HUGH THE DROVER', 'RIDERS TO THE SEA', 'PILGRIM'S PROGRESS' and others; ballet 'JOB'; many choral works ('MAGNIFICAT'; 'DONA NOBIS PACEM'; 'FIVE TUDOR PORTRAITS'; 'THIS DAY', etc.); 'SERENADE TO MUSIC', originally for sixteen solo voices and orchestra; orchestral works with solo instruments including 'FLOS CAMPI', 'THE LARK ASCENDING', 'Romance' (harmonica solo), tuba concerto; 'Fantasia on a Theme of Tallis' (see TALLIS) for strings; 'AN OXFORD ELEGY' (with speaker); Latin Mass; hymns, including 'For All the Saints'; two string quartets; songs including cycle 'ON WENLOCK EDGE'. Also conductor, especially choral, and hymn-book editor. O.M., 1935.

VAUTOR, THOMAS (?–?), English composer of 'Sweet Suffolk Owl' and other distinctive madrigals in a collection published 1619. (He was one of the last of the English madrigal school.)

VEALE, JOHN (b. 1922), English composer of two symphonies, clarinet concerto, etc.; pupil of Wellesz and, in U.S.A., of Roy Harris.

VECCHI, ORAZIO (1550–1605), Italian composer, also priest; holder of church and court musical posts. Works include madrigals, church music, and 'The Amphiparnassus' (It., *L'Amfiparnaso*), a work of dramatic form made up of madrigals – apparently not intended to be staged, but nevertheless a forerunner of opera.

VELOCE (It.), quickly – normally a direction to give an impression of uninterrupted swiftness, rather than to increase actual speed.

VENT (Fr.), wind; *instruments à vent*, wind instruments.

VENTADORN, BERNART DE (?–1195), French troubadour, some of whose surviving poems and melodies have been transcribed for modern use.

VENUS AND ADONIS, masque with music by Blow, produced in London about 1684; librettist unknown.

VERACINI, FRANCESCO MARIA (1690–*c.* 1750), Italian violinist, composer of twenty-four violin sonatas, etc. Twice visited London as performer, and his other works include opera 'Rosalinda' (after Shakespeare's *As You Like It*).

VERDELOT, PHILIPPE (?–*c.* 1567), Flemish composer who held church musical posts in Italy. Was one of the first madrigal-composers (see MADRIGAL, 1) and wrote also Masses, motets, etc.

VERDI, GIUSEPPE (FORTUNINO FRANCESCO) (1813–1901), Italian composer, born in Busseto of a poor family; became organist and composer in boyhood, but rejected by Milan Conservatory as over-age and insufficiently gifted. First opera, 'Oberto', 1839. Later operas – grafting an individual mastery (vocal, orchestral, and dramatic) on to traditional Italian models – include 'NABUCCO', 'MACBETH', 'RIGOLETTO', 'IL TROVATORE', 'LA TRAVIATA', 'SIMON BOCCANEGRA', 'A MASKED BALL', 'THE FORCE OF DESTINY', 'DON CARLOS', 'LUISA MILLER', 'AIDA', 'OTELLO' and 'FALSTAFF'. The last two are products of his 70s, and rely less on the appeal of successive 'set' numbers. Wrote also Requiem (sometimes called 'MANZONI REQUIEM') and a few other works to religious texts, though not himself a churchman; also string quartet – little else. In his earlier operas he became the symbol of resurgent Italian nationalism, and frequently clashed with censorships suspecting revolutionary implications; in 1860–5, himself sat as deputy in that part of Italy already unified. But later lived secludedly. Founded a home for aged musicians in Milan. After early death of his first wife, lived with and then married the singer Giuseppina Strepponi. Died in Milan.

VERESS, SÁNDOR (b. 1907), Hungarian composer, also pianist, now living in Switzerland; associated with Bartók in collecting and editing Hungarian folk-music. His works, having some NEO-MODAL tendencies, include violin concerto; 'Homage to Paul Klee' (one movement for each of seven pictures) for two pianos and strings; Sinfonia Minneapolitana (for the Minneapolis Symphony Orchestra).

VERETTI, ANTONIO (b. 1900), Italian composer, pupil of Alfano; has undergone various influences from jazz to TWELVE-NOTE technique. Composer of various orchestral works, a Divertimento for harpsichord and six instruments, ballet 'The Seven Sins', etc.

VERISMO (It.), realism – term applied particularly to Italian opera of about 1900 (e.g. Mascagni, Puccini) with reference to its 'contemporary' and often violent plots, sometimes amid sordid surroundings – e.g. Puccini's 'THE CLOAK', aboard a canal barge.

VERKLÄRTE NACHT, see TRANSFIGURED NIGHT.

VERMEULEN, MATTHIJS (b. 1888), Dutch composer formerly resident in France; works include five symphonies, and French songs. Is also critic.

VERSCHIEBUNG (Ger., a displacing), use of the soft pedal of the piano.

VERSE, term indicating, in English church music, the use of solo voice as contrasted with full choir; *verse anthem*, one using such a contrast.

VESTAL, THE (i.e. The Vestal Virgin; Fr., *La Vestale*), opera by Spontini, produced in Paris, 1807. Libretto by V. J. E. de Jouy. The heroine's religious vows conflict with human love.

VIA (It.), away with; *via sordini*, take off mutes.

VIA CRUCIS (Lat., The Way of the Cross), work by Liszt for solo singers, chorus, and organ, completed 1879; text, partly biblical, on the Stations of the Cross. Not performed until forty years after Liszt's death.

VIADANA, LODOVICO GROSSO DA (1564–1645), Italian composer who took the name Viadana from his birthplace (cp. PALESTRINA); was also monk. Held church musical posts, and wrote madrigals, etc., as well as church music – which includes 'One Hundred Church Concertos', giving an early example of CONTINUO-writing, though without figured bass.

VIBRAHARP (U.S.), equals VIBRAPHONE.

VIBRAPHONE, percussion instrument on which tuned metal bars (laid out on the pattern of a piano keyboard) are struck with small hammers; beneath the bars are resonators which, constantly opened and closed electrically, impart a vibrating sound to the tone. Compass from F below middle C, upwards for three octaves. Used by modern composers occasionally in symphonic and operatic music (e.g. by Berg in 'LULU') and also in modern dance music, etc.

VIBRATION, the side-to-side motion of a string, a struck surface, or air-column, by which musical sounds are produced. 'A vibration', as a measurement in acoustics, is defined as the total distance of movement from one side to the other and back. See FREQUENCY.

VIBRATO (It., vibrated), a rapid regular fluctuation in pitch – whether tasteful (e.g. as imparted by the oscillatory motion of a violinist's left hand) or exaggerated to a fault, as in a singer's 'wobble'. (Note the difference from *tremolo*, which is a fluctuation of intensity, i.e. loudness, not of pitch; but note also that some singing-teachers confusingly reverse the meaning of these two terms. See also TREMULANT.

VICTORIA, TOMÁS LUIS DE (*c.* 1548–1611), Spanish composer and poet who worked in Rome for nearly twenty years (hence Vittoria, the sometimes-encountered Italian form of his name). Then took up a church choirmaster's post in Madrid and died there. Composed only church music, including settings of all the hymns of the Roman Catholic liturgical year; other works include a notable Requiem Mass for the Spanish Dowager Empress, and other Masses and motets. His style, having points of contact with that of Palestrina (his colleague in Rome), is sometimes in a rich texture of up to twelve vocal PARTS.

VIELLE (Fr.), term normally meaning a HURDY-GURDY, but also used for a medieval stringed instrument played with the bow, a forerunner of the violin.

VIENNA BLOOD (Ger., *Wiener Blut*), operetta compiled from the music of J. Strauss the younger, with the composer's consent, by A. Müller; produced in Vienna, 1899. Libretto by V. Leon and L. Stein. Concerns romantic intrigue in Vienna, 1815, and is named from a Strauss waltz (1871) incorporated in it.

VIENNA PHILHARMONIC ORCHESTRA, an orchestra tracing its history to the Philharmonic Concerts begun in Vienna by Otto Nicolai in 1842. The orchestra also plays for the Vienna State Opera. It is self-governing.

VIER ERNSTE GESÄNGE, see FOUR BIBLICAL SONGS.

VIERNE, LOUIS (1870–1937), French organist and composer, pupil of Franck and Widor; blind from birth. Organist of Notre Dame, Paris; died while playing there. Noted travelling recitalist. Composer of six 'symphonies' and other organ solo pieces; also of Mass, string quartet, etc.

VIERTEL (Ger., quarter), crotchet (U.S. quarter-note).

VIEUXTEMPS, HENRI (1820–81), Belgian violinist (touring from age 7) and composer of six violin concertos and other works for his instrument. For a time taught in Russia. Died while visiting Algeria.

VIF (Fr.), lively.

VIHTOL, see WIHTOL.

VIHUELA, old Spanish musical instrument, shaped like guitar but strung and played like the lute; plucked either with the hand (*vihuela da mano*) or with plectrum. It became obsolete about 1700 and was superseded by the guitar.

VILLAGE ROMEO AND JULIET, A, opera by Delius, produced in Berlin, 1907. Libretto (after a story by G. Keller) by composer, in German (*Romeo und Julia aus dem Dorfe*), though no librettist's name is given in the printed score. The two lovers are the children of quarrelling landowners, and eventually commit suicide together.

VILLA-LOBOS, HEITOR (1887–1959), Brazilian composer, the first South American composer to become world-famous; was also pianist and teacher. Prolific output, including operas, ballets, eleven symphonies, two piano concertos, string quartets, songs, etc., in varied styles but frequently with pronounced 'national' flavour. Composed thirteen works called 'Choros' for various combinations (some including Brazilian native instruments), explaining the title as synthesizing 'the different modalities of Brazilian, South American Indian, and popular music, and having for principal elements rhythm and any typical melody of popular character'. His 'BACHIANAS BRASILEIRAS' are supposed evocations of Bach in a Brazilian spirit – the implied NEOCLASSICISM being also evident in certain works for guitar. He also composed some works based on notes written in a geometrical pattern derived from, e.g., a skyline.

VILLANELLA (It., country girl), type of Italian part-song to rustic words, flourishing in the 16th century. Not the same as VILLANELLE.

VILLANELLE (Fr., country girl), type of French poem of five three-line stanzas, or a musical setting of such. Not the same as VILLANELLA.

VINAY, RAMÓN (b. 1912), Chilean singer; began as baritone, won international fame as tenor – especially in 'heavier' roles, e.g. the title-rôle of Verdi's 'Otello'; in 1962, resumed baritone roles.

VINCI, LEONARDO (1690–1730), Italian composer and church musician; wrote operas, some in Neopolitan dialect. No relation of da Vinci the artist.

VIOL, type of bowed stringed instrument of various sizes, current up to about 1700 and thereafter superseded by instruments of the VIOLIN type; resuscitated in the 20th century, however, for old music. The viols differ from the violin family in shape, in having frets, and in the kind of bow and style of bowing used. The three principal sizes were the *treble viol*; *tenor viol* (or viola da braccio, i.e. arm-viol); and *bass-viol* (or viola da gamba, i.e. leg-viol, held between the legs), the last much used as a solo instrument. The *division viol* was a small bass viol suitable for such solos, of which the playing of DIVISIONS (i.e., variations) was a favourite type. The *violone*, corresponding to modern double-bass, was also used. Note that today the term *bass-viol* is also occasionally used (especially in U.S.A. and among non-musicians) not for the instrument here alluded to, but for the double-bass.

VIOLA, (1) bowed stringed instrument, a lower-pitched relative of the violin, invariably present in the orchestra and the string quartet (and used also as a solo instrument); its compass is from the C below middle C, upwards for more than three octaves; (2) Italian for VIOL; hence the following entries.

VIOLA D'AMORE (It., love-viol), bowed stringed instrument related primarily not to the modern viola but to the VIOL family – but, unlike them, having no frets. It has (usually) seven strings touched by the bow, and seven 'sympathetic' strings beneath them (hence the instrument's name) whose vibration is induced by the sounding of the upper set. The instrument is occasionally encountered in music of the late 18th and early 19th centuries (e.g. in Meyerbeer's 'THE HUGUENOTS').

VIOLA DA BRACCIO, DA GAMBA, see VIOL.

VIOLIN, bowed four-stringed instrument, the principal (and highest) member of the family of instruments (called 'the violin family') which superseded the VIOLS from about 1700. The other members are the viola and cello; the double-bass, less closely related, evolved from the corresponding member (*violone*) of the viol family. The violin is prominently used in the orchestra (where the players normally divide into first and second violinists, a division usually corresponding to higher- and lower-pitched parts) and in solo and chamber music. Its compass is from the G below middle C, upwards for three and a half octaves and more.

VIOLONCELLO, see CELLO.

VIOLONE, see VIOL.

VIOTTI, GIOVANNI BATTISTA (1755–1824), Italian violinist and composer (pupil of Pugnani) who came to London in 1792, and afterwards had varied career including the directorship of the Italian Opera in Paris. Died, impoverished, in London. Wrote twenty-nine violin concertos and other violin works; also ten piano concertos, songs, etc.

VIOZZI, GIULIO (b. 1912), Italian composer of opera 'Allamistakeo (title based on English words), 'Threnody' for two pianos, etc.

VIRELAI, type of medieval French song.

VIRGINAL(s), 16th- and 17th-century keyboard instrument of harpsichord type (i.e. the strings being plucked), but smaller and of different shape – oblong, and with its one keyboard along the longer side of the soundboard (not at the end). Revived for old music in the 20th century. Named probably from Lat. *virga*, rod or jack; just possibly from being played by maidens; but certainly not from the Virgin Queen, as it was known before her time. The Italian term *spinetto* is used both for this and for the wing-shaped but otherwise similar instrument; but the English practice is to confine the term SPINET to the latter type.

VIRTUOSO, a performer of exceptional skill, especially in the technical aspects of performance. Hence the term is sometimes used in a derogatory sense ('merely virtuoso music') to imply a contrast between technical accomplishment and an artist's inner sensitivity. The Virtuosi di Roma is a performing ensemble: see FASANO.

VITALI, GIOVANNI BATTISTA (*c.* 1644–92), Italian violinist and composer who held church and court posts; wrote dance music, sonatas for two and more instruments, psalm-settings, etc. Father of Tommaso Antonio Vitali.

VITALI, TOMMASO ANTONIO (*c.*1665–?), Italian violinist and composer of famous Chaconne for violin with keyboard accompaniment, also of other works for strings; edited a volume of music by his father (above).

VITO, GIOCONDA DE (b. 1907), Italian violinist, noted in concertos; married an Englishman and has been resident in London since 1949.

VITRY, PHILIPPE DE (1291–1361), French composer – also poet, priest, and French court official. Much esteemed in his day, but only a few of his motets survive. Exponent of ARS NOVA and author of a treatise on it; thought to have originated the ISORHYTHMIC motet.

VITTORIA, see VICTORIA.

VIVACE (It.), lively.

VIVALDI, ANTONIO (*c.* 1685–1741), Italian violinist and composer; also priest, nicknamed 'the red priest' (*il prete rosso*) from the colour of his hair. Pupil of Legrenzi. Long in charge of music at an orphanage-conservatory in Venice, but died in obscure circumstances in Vienna. Wrote more than 450 concertos (broadly conforming to the CONCERTO GROSSO type) with various solo instruments, many with illustrative titles, e.g. 'THE SEASONS'; also operas, church music, oratorios. Bach admired him and transcribed many of his works (e.g. Bach's concerto for four harpsichords and strings is a transcription of Vivaldi's concerto for four violins and strings); and there has been a notable revival of interest in his works in the 20th century.

VIVO (It.), lively.

VLAD, ROMAN (b. 1919), Rumanian-born Italian composer, also critic. Works include ballet 'The Lady of the Camellias' (after Dumas), Divertimento for eleven instruments, Variazioni Concertante for piano and orchestra.

VLADIGEROV, PANCHO (b. 1899), Bulgarian composer who studied in Berlin; works include opera 'Tsar Kaloyan', violin concerto, and piano concerto. Also pianist.

VLTAVA, see MY COUNTRY.

VOCAL CORDS (not 'chords'), see VOICE (1).

VOCAL SCORE, see SCORE.

VOCALISE (Fr., noun), a wordless composition for solo voice, whether for training purposes or for concert performance.

VOCE (It.), voice; *colla voce*, direction to play 'with the voice' (i.e. the accompaniment accommodating the singer on matters of tempo); *sotto voce*, under the voice, i.e. in a subdued tone; *voce di petto*, CHEST VOICE; *voce di testa*, HEAD VOICE.

VOGEL, VLADIMIR (RUDOLFOVICH) (b. 1896), Russo-German composer; born in Moscow, studied in Berlin under Busoni, and settled in Switzerland 1939. Has written memorial works to Busoni (for orchestra) and to Berg (for piano); chamber music; secular oratorios 'The Fall of Wagadu' and 'Thyl Claes' (the latter nearly four hours long, about the revolt of the Netherlands). Uses TWELVE-NOTE technique.

VOGLER, ABT, see next entry.

VOGLER, GEORG JOSEPH (1749–1814), German pianist, organist, and composer who travelled much and taught many, including Meyerbeer and Liszt; was also priest, and known as the Abbé Vogler ('Abt Vogler' in Browning's poem).

VOICE (1) the human (and animal) means of sound-producing using the two vibrating agents called the vocal cords (not 'chords'); hence (2) a separate 'strand' of music in harmony or counterpoint, whether intended to be sung or played. Thus a fugue is said to be in, say, four voices (or four PARTS), whether its four 'strands' are sung by individual voices, sung by several voices each, played by instruments, or all played on one instrument (e.g. piano). (3, verb), to adjust a wind-instrument or organ-pipe in the process of construction so that it exactly fits the required standards of pitch, tone-colour, etc.

VOICE-LEADING, see PART-WRITING.

VOIX (Fr.), equals VOICE (1st and 2nd senses); hence VOIX CÉLESTE.

VOIX CÉLESTE (Fr., heavenly voice), type of organ stop with two pipes to each note, tuned slightly apart and producing a wavering effect.

VOLANTE (It., flying), fast and light.

VOLKMANN, (FRIEDRICH) ALBERT (1815–83), German composer of symphonies, songs, etc., encouraged by Schumann; taught much in Vienna and in Budapest, where he died.

VOLKSLIED, see FOLK-SONG (the two terms not being quite identical).

VOLLES WERK (Ger., full apparatus), FULL ORGAN.

VOLTA (It.), time (in the sense of *prima*, *seconda volta*, 1st, 2nd time). See also LAVOLTA.

VOLTI (It.), turn (imperative); *volti subito* (abbr. V.S.), turn over the page immediately – direction used especially in old music to prevent a performer's ending or making a break in the music at the bottom of a page, or to warn, after 'rests' at the bottom of a page, that notes begin immediately overleaf.

VOLUNTARY, an organ piece of the kind used chiefly at the beginning and end of a church service. (For *trumpet voluntary* see under TRUMPET TUNE.)

VORSPIEL (Ger.), prelude. (Term used also e.g. by Wagner in the sense of overture, e.g. that to 'THE MASTERSINGERS').

VOX ANGELICA (Lat., angelic voice), delicate-toned organ stop – sometimes but not always having the wavering effect of the VOIX CÉLESTE.

VOX HUMANA (Lat.), organ stop imitating the human voice.

VRONSKY, VITYA, see BABIN.

VUATAZ, ROGER (b. 1898), Swiss composer of oratorios, Protestant church music, violin concerto, piano and organ works, etc.; also organist, Swiss radio conductor, and writer on music.

VUOTO, VUOTA (It.), empty – applied e.g. to a bar of music in which all performers' parts have a 'rest' (i.e. a 'GENERAL PAUSE'); *corda vuota*, open string.

VYŠEHRAD, see MY COUNTRY.

W

WAGENAAR, BERNARD (b. 1894), Dutch-born composer who settled in U.S.A., 1921, as orchestral violinist and then college teacher. Has composed opera 'Pieces of Eight'; triple concerto (flute, cello, harp); and various orchestral works, songs, etc. Son of Johan Wagenaar.

WAGENAAR, JOHAN (1862–1941), Dutch composer, broadly following 19th-century German models; also organist, and director of The Hague Conservatory. Father of Bernard Wagenaar. Works include operas, overtures to Shakespeare's *The Taming of the Shrew* and *Twelfth Night*, cantatas, songs.

WAGENSEIL, GEORG CHRISTOPH (1715–77), Austrian composer, pupil of Fux; also harpsichordist and organist. His symphonies are prophetic of those of the Viennese classical (Haydn-Mozart) era. Composed also operas, church music, keyboard works, etc.

WAGNER, (WILHELM) RICHARD (1813–83), German composer – also writer (of his own librettos, and of essays on musical and philosophical topics); also noted conductor, in which function he earned a living and visited London in 1855 and 1877. Born in Leipzig, travelled much, met much opposition. From 'RIENZI' (1842) went on to write successful operas 'THE FLYING DUTCHMAN', 'TANNHÄUSER', and 'LOHENGRIN'; then, exemplifying his new theories of the proper relation of music and drama, composed 'TRISTAN AND ISOLDE', 'THE RING' (cycle of four operas), and 'PARSIFAL'. These show a 'symphonic' conception of opera, proceeding by LEADING-MOTIVES (i.e. themes) not through the contrast of set 'numbers'. Wagner aimed at the *Gesamtkunstwerk*, the work of art uniting all the arts; the Festival Theatre at Bayreuth (opened 1876) was built to his own revolutionary design with this in mind. His only comic opera is 'THE MASTERSINGERS OF NUREMBERG'. Non-operatic compositions include 'A FAUST OVERTURE', 'SIEGFRIED IDYLL', and five song-settings with orchestra of poems by Mathilde Wesendonck, at that time his mistress. Afterwards he took as mistress Cosima, wife of Bülow and daughter of Liszt, and married her when his first wife died. He died in Venice. Influenced the course of music as much as any composer – as to operatic structure, harmony, and orchestration. Introduced the WAGNER TUBA.

WAGNER TUBA, type of instrument (more like a modified orchestral HORN than the usual tuba; see TUBA), made in two sizes (tenor and bass), designed to Wagner's specification and used by him (two of each) in 'THE RING'. The compass of the tenor is from the B♭ in the bass stave upwards for about two and a half octaves; the bass has a compass an octave lower. The instruments have been used also by Bruckner, R. Strauss, and a few others. (Note that the 'double-bass tuba', which Wagner uses with these instruments in 'The Ring' is not of this family: it is a 'real' TUBA.)

WAGNER-RÉGENY, RUDOLF (b. 1903), German composer, especially of operas, including 'The Favourite' and 'The Mine at Falun'.

WAIT, (1) a salaried musician acting as town watchman, or as a member of a court band, etc., in medieval England (the outdoor functions of the waits being alluded to in the modern application of the title to street-singers at Christmas-time); (2) obsolete reed instrument of the oboe type, much used by the medieval waits (above).

WALCHA, HELMUT (b. 1907), German organist, noted in recitals, almost exclusively of Bach: had defective sight since childhood, and later became blind.

WALD FLUTE, WALDFLÖTE (Ger., forest flute), organ stop of flute-like tone.

WALDHORN (Ger., forest horn), hunting-horn, i.e. a 'natural' horn having no valves. See HORN.

'WALDSTEIN' SONATA, nickname for Beethoven's piano sonata in C, op. 53 (1804), dedicated to Count Waldstein, a musical amateur who was one of Beethoven's patrons.

WALDTEUFEL, EMIL (1837–1915), French (Alsatian) pianist and composer of waltzes (including the well-known 'Skaters' Waltz') and other dance music. Was pianist to the Empress Eugénie of France.

WALKER, ERNEST (1870–1949), English composer, born in India; was also pianist, Oxford University lecturer, and writer of a history of English music. Composed choral works, chamber music, songs, piano solos, etc.

WALKÜRE, DIE, see RING.

WALLACE, WILLIAM (1860–1940), Scottish composer of 'The Passing of Beatrice' (1892), thought to be the first symphonic poem by a British composer; also of other symphonic poems, songs, etc. Was also writer on music, and ophthalmologist. No relation of William Vincent Wallace.

WALLACE, WILLIAM VINCENT (1812–65), Irish composer of once very popular opera 'MARITANA' (adapting Italian operatic model to English taste) and also of other operas, violin concerto, piano solos, etc. Originally violinist. Visited Australia and New Zealand as a young man, and N. and S. America later. Died in France.

WALMISLEY, THOMAS ATTWOOD (1814–56), English organist, professor of music at Cambridge, and composer chiefly of church and organ music.

WALTER, BRUNO (really Bruno Walter Schlesinger; 1876–1962), German-born conductor, also pianist; settled in Austria, then (as a Jew, on the Nazi rise to power) took French nationality; later settled in U.S.A., being naturalized there in 1946. Disciple of Mahler, and notable operatic and concert conductor; noted accompanist, acting as such e.g. for Kathleen Ferrier, whom he also coached.

WALTHEW, RICHARD HENRY (1872–1951), English pianist, and composer especially of chamber music; other works include piano concerto and operettas. Pupil of Parry.

WALTON, WILLIAM (TURNER) (b. 1902), English composer, largely self-taught; but former cathedral choirboy. Showed early influence of jazz and Stravinsky e.g. in 'FAÇADE' (reciter and instruments; later arranged for ballet) and overture 'PORTSMOUTH POINT'; has also stylistic contact with Elgar, e.g. in march 'CROWN IMPERIAL'. Other works, strongly rhythmical and predominantly diatonic, include two symphonies, concertos for viola (see HINDEMITH), violin, and cello; Sinfonia Concertante for piano and orchestra; overture 'SCAPINO'; cantata 'BELSHAZZAR'S FEAST' and smaller choral works; operas 'TROILUS AND CRESSIDA', 'The Bear'; arrangement of Bach for ballet 'THE WISE VIRGINS'; string quartet (1947) and violin sonata (1949), the latter having one of its themes constructed from all twelve notes of the octave successively (though the work is not in TWELVE-NOTE technique). Knighted 1951.

WALTZ, dance in triple time becoming universally known in the 19th century; characteristically harmonized with only one chord to each bar. (See also VALSE, and the following entry.)

WALTZ DREAM, A (Ger., *Ein Waltzertraum*), operetta by Oscar Straus, produced in Vienna, 1907. Libretto by F. Dörmann and L. Jacobson: a waltz is treated as the symbol of a nostalgic longing for Vienna.

WALTZER (Ger.), waltz(es).

'WANDERER' FANTASY, nickname given to Schubert's Fantasy for piano in C, 1822, because it makes use of material found also in his song 'The Wanderer' (1816). Best known as arranged by Liszt for piano and orchestra.

WANHAL(L), JOHANN BAPTIST (German form of Jan Křtitel Vanhal; 1739–1813), Bohemian composer; his name was sometimes (e.g. on English editions) spelt Vanhall, and he has thus been erroneously said to be of Dutch descent. Visited Italy but worked mainly in Vienna, where he died. Friend of Haydn and Mozart: composed about 100 symphonies, 100 string quartets, much church music, etc.

WAR REQUIEM, A, work by Britten for soprano, tenor, baritone, chorus and orchestra, first performed at Coventry, 1962; text, from Roman Catholic Requiem (in Latin) and Wilfred Owen's poems, carries an anti-war message.

WAR AND PEACE (Rus. *Voina i mir*), opera by Prokofiev; libretto, after Tolstoy's novel, by the composer and M. Mendelson-Prokofiev. First performance of first version (the work was later amplified), Moscow, 1944 (in concert form).

WARD, JOHN, English composer; dates unknown, but published a set of madrigals – the type of work for which he is noted – in 1619; wrote also music for viols, and church music.

WARD, ROBERT (b. 1917), American composer of operas 'He who gets slapped' and 'The Crucible' (after Arthur Miller); also of 3 symphonies, choral works, etc.

WARLOCK, PETER, pseudonym used as composer by *Philip Heseltine* (1894–1930), who wrote about music (e.g. a book on Delius) under his own name. Works include song-cycle 'THE CURLEW' and many other songs of distinct individuality (though showing influence both of Delius and of 16th–17th-century English song); also suite 'CAPRIOL', choral works, orchestral serenade for Delius's sixtieth birthday, etc. Also transcribed old English music. Committed suicide.

WARRIOR, THE, opera by B. Rogers, produced in New York, 1947. Libretto by N. Corwin, on the story of Samson and Delilah.

WAT TYLER, opera by A. Bush, produced in Leipzig, 1953. Libretto by Nancy Bush (the composer's wife) about the leader of the Peasants' Revolt in England, 1381.

WATER MUSIC, orchestral suite by Handel, originating in pieces written about 1715 for a royal procession on the Thames – the exact circumstances being uncertain. Published later as comprising twenty pieces, of which six were arranged by Harty in the (now standard) suite published in 1922. See also ROBERT RUSSELL BENNETT.

WATER ORGAN, see HYDRAULIS.

WEBBE, SAMUEL (1740–1816), English organist, composer of vocal music from Roman Catholic Masses and motets to glees and catches; father of Samuel Webbe (below).

WEBBE, SAMUEL (*c.* 1770–1843), English pianist, organist, composer of vocal music, etc.; also writer of textbooks. Son of the above.

WEBER, surname of two unrelated composers (separately below): the surname alone indicates reference to C. M. F. E. von Weber.

WEBER, BEN (b. 1916), American composer, largely self-taught; works include 'symphony' for baritone and chamber orchestra on poems by Blake, piano solos, ballet 'Pool of Darkness'.

WEBER, CARL MARIA FRIEDRICH ERNST VON (1786–1826), German composer, pupil of M. Haydn and Vogler; also conductor and pianist. Exponent of German ROMANTIC opera, particularly in 'DER FREISCHÜTZ', a lasting international success. Other operas include 'ABU HASSAN', 'EURYANTHE', and 'OBERON' – the last written in English for England, Weber dying in London after superintending the first production. (He had poor health, and was financially driven to overwork.) Also wrote incidental music to plays, including 'PRECIOSA' and 'TURANDOT'; two concertos and 'Concert Piece' for piano and orchestra; two concertos and one concertino for clarinet and orchestra; bassoon concerto; 'INVITATION TO THE DANCE' and other piano solos; church music, songs, etc. Also writer on music; wrote an unfinished novel *A Composer's Life*.

WEBER, LUDWIG (b. 1899), Austrian bass; at first a schoolmaster. Joined the Vienna State Opera in 1920, and has also worked much in Germany.

WEBERN, ANTON VON (1883–1945), Austrian composer, pupil of Schoenberg, whose TWELVE-NOTE technique he adapted to an individual style much concerned with establishing the relationship between a particular tone-quality and a particular note. His works, mainly vocal or in the nature of chamber music, are few and tend to extreme brevity: no. 4 of his 'Five Pieces for Orchestra' (1911), scored for nine instruments including mandolin, takes six and one-third bars and lasts nineteen seconds. Other works include two symphonies, variations for orchestra; cantatas; three works for string quartet; canons for voice, clarinet, and bass clarinet; songs. He was accidentally shot dead in the Allied occupation of Austria.

WECHSELDOMINANTE, see DOMINANT.

WECKERLIN, JEAN BAPTISTE THEODORE (1821–1910), French composer of operas, chamber music, etc., and editor of much old French music.

WEDDING, THE (Rus., *Svadebka*), ballet with music by Stravinsky (for chorus, four pianos, and percussion) produced in Paris, 1923. (The work having Russian words, there is no reason, outside French-speaking countries, for the name 'Les Noces'.)

'WEDGE' FUGUE, nickname given to the longer of Bach's two organ fugues in E minor, composed between 1727 and 1736; the opening subject proceeds in gradually widening intervals.

WEELKES, THOMAS (?–1623), English composer of many strongly individual madrigals – including 'As Vesta was from Latmos hill descending' in 'THE TRIUMPHS OF ORIANA'; also of BALLETTS and other secular vocal music, and of church music and pieces for viols including IN NOMINES. Also organist. Friend of Morley, in whose memory he wrote a three-part song. Birth-date unknown, but became Bachelor of Music at Oxford in 1602.

WEIGL, JOSEPH (1766–1846), Austrian composer of operas (chiefly comic) in German and Italian; also of church music, etc. Worked and died in Vienna, where he became musical director of the Opera. Godson of Haydn.

WEIHNACHTSORATORIUM (Ger.), equals CHRISTMAS ORATORIO.

WEIHNACHTSSYMPHONIE (Ger., Christmas Symphony), another nickname for Haydn's 'LAMENTATION' symphony.

WEILL, KURT (1900–50), German-born composer, pupil of Humperdinck and Busoni. Had early success with 'THE THREEPENNY OPERA' (Ger., *Die Dreigroschenoper*), modern adaptation of 'THE BEGGAR'S OPERA', exemplifying his leaning towards music consciously related to modern social problems, and with 'RISE AND FALL OF THE CITY OF MAHAGONNY'. But, condemned by the Nazis as a Jew and a composer of 'decadent' music, settled in U.S.A. 1935; thereafter his music took on a less 'modernistic' and more 'folky' character, e.g. in the opera 'DOWN IN THE VALLEY' (originally for students) and various Broadway musical plays including 'Lost in the Stars'. Other works include cantata 'Lindbergh's Flight' (1929), symphony, concerto for violin with wind instruments.

WEINBERGER, JAROMIR (1896–1967), Czech composer who studied with Reger in Berlin, lived in U.S.A. 1922–26, and settled in U.S.A. 1939. Works include opera 'ŠVANDA THE BAGPIPER' – internationally the most popular Czech opera, apart from Smetana's 'THE

BARTERED BRIDE', but almost the only work by which its composer is well known. Other works include various operas, orchestral Variations and Fugue on 'Under the Spreading Chestnut Tree', and various works of an American connexion, e.g. 'The Legend of Sleepy Hollow' for orchestra (after Washington Irving).

WEINER, LEÓ (b. 1885), Hungarian composer of three Divertimenti and other orchestral works, piano pieces, etc.; is not a prolific composer, and follows 'classical' (19th-century German) techniques rather than cultivating Hungarian musical nationalism like Bartók and Kodály.

WEINGARTNER, (PAUL) FELIX (1863–1942), Austrian conductor, succeeding Mahler at the Vienna Court Opera and afterwards touring much – in Britain, U.S.A., and elsewhere. Also composer (opera, six symphonies, etc.) and writer of a noted textbook on conducting.

WEINZWEIG, JOHN JACOB (b. 1913), Canadian composer who uses TWELVE-NOTE technique; is also conductor and teacher. Works include orchestral suite 'The Land' (originally from a documentary radio feature) referring to Canada.

WEISGALL, HUGO (b. 1912), American composer (born in Czechoslovakia); works include operas 'The Stronger' (after Strindberg), 'The Tenor', and other operas.

WEISS, FLEMMING (b. 1898), Danish composer showing some French influence; works include two symphonies, wind quintet, cantata 'The Promised Land'; songs in Danish, German, and Swedish.

WEISS, SYLVIUS LEOPOLD (1686–1750), German lutenist and composer for his instrument, working at various courts.

WELDON, GEORGE (1908–63), English conductor of the City of Birmingham Symphony Orchestra, then (from 1952) assistant conductor of the Hallé Orchestra (Manchester).

WELDON, JOHN (1676–1736), English organist and composer of church and stage music; pupil of Purcell.

WELITSCH, LJUBA (really Welitschkova; b. 1913), Bulgarian soprano who settled in Austria but toured widely (London from 1947), especially in 'heavy' operatic parts – e.g. the title-role of Strauss's 'ELEKTRA'.

WELLESZ, EGON (b. 1885), Austrian-born composer who settled in England, 1939, as Oxford University lecturer. Pupil of Schoenberg, and wrote operas (including 'ALKESTIS') in a Schoenberg-influenced technique; but his opera 'Incognita' (Oxford, 1951) is in a back-to-Mozart vein similar to R. Strauss's. Other works include cantata 'The Leaden Echo and the Golden Echo' (Gerard Manley Hopkins) for soprano and four instruments; Roman Catholic church music; violin concerto, songs.

WELLINGTON'S VICTORY, *or The Battle of Victoria* (Ger. *Wellingtons Sieg, oder Die Schlacht bei Victoria*), orchestral work by Beethoven, 1813. (He wrote 'Vittoria' by mistake.) Also known as the

'Battle Symphony', it is illustrative of an English victory over Napoleonic forces at Victoria, Spain, and quotes various national airs.

WELL-TEMPERED CLAVIER, THE (Ger., *Das wohltemperierte Clavier*), title given by Bach to his twenty-four preludes and fugues, 1722, in all the major and minor keys, and applied also to a further similar twenty-four (1744); the title is thus now applied to the two sets together, which are also known as 'the Forty-eight'. The use of all the major and minor keys demonstrated the facilities offered by the (then new) system of 'equal TEMPERAMENT'. The word *clavier*, meaning any keyboard instrument, is correct here – not clavichord, Bach not intending the work exclusively for that instrument.

WERLE, LARS JOHAN (b. 1926), Swedish composer of 'Dreaming about Thérèse', opera designed with special instrumentation to be performed 'in the round' (orchestra encircling audience encircling singers); also of 'Sinfonia da Camera', ballet 'Zodiac', etc.

WERT, GIACHES DE (or Jaches de; 1535–96), Flemish composer who went to Italy as a boy chorister and settled there, dying in Mantua. Wrote madrigals, motets, etc., and held court and church musical posts.

WERTHER, opera by Massenet, produced (in German) in Vienna, 1892; libretto, in French, by E. Blau, P. Milliet, and G. Hartmann – after Goethe's *The Sorrows of Werther*, the hero being driven by sentimental love to suicide.

WESLEY, CHARLES (1757–1834), English organist, harpsichordist, and composer (concertos, anthems, etc.); a youthful prodigy who did not fulfil his early promise. Pupil of Boyce. Nephew of John Wesley, the founder of Methodism, and brother of Samuel Wesley.

WESLEY, SAMUEL (1766–1837), English organist and composer; despite his family background (see preceding entry) became Roman Catholic, and wrote mainly Roman Catholic (but some Anglican) church music; also symphonies, organ concertos, etc. A head injury in youth caused his later mental instability. Was among the first British enthusiasts for Bach; hence, doubtless, the middle name of his son (below).

WESLEY, SAMUEL SEBASTIAN (1810–76), English composer, illegitimate son of the preceding; also organist, finally at Gloucester Cathedral, and a fighter against the slackness in Anglican cathedral music at that time. Wrote much church music; also choral 'Ode to Labour' and some piano pieces.

WHETTAM, GRAHAM (b. 1927), English composer, mainly self-taught; works include four symphonies, viola concerto, 'Concerto scherzoso' for harmonica and orchestra.

WHIP, percussion instrument imitative of the crack of a whip and consisting of two pieces of wood joined in V-shape: the player snaps the arms loudly together.

WHISTLE, (1, verb) to produce a vocal sound through a small aperture in the lips, the pitch being governed by the shaping of the mouth as a resonating chamber. A few professional whistlers have occasionally penetrated to the concert-platform. (2, noun) general name for various wind instruments, usually of primitive construction (and sometimes played with the nose) giving a sound similar to human whistling – a Western mouth-blown example being the TIN-WHISTLE.

WHITE, MAUDE VALÉRIE (1855–1937), English composer, born in France; wrote mainly songs, in French, English, and German; also a few piano pieces, etc.

WHITE, ROBERT (or Whyte; *c.* 1530–1574), English composer who died of the plague; wrote church music (chiefly but not entirely to Latin texts), and also music for viols, for organ, etc. Married Ellen Tye, probably a daughter of the composer Tye.

WHITE PEACOCK, THE, work for piano by Griffes (1915), later orchestrated; after a poem by William Sharp, and originally forming one of four 'Roman Sketches'.

WHITHORNE, EMERSON (originally Wittern; b. 1884), American composer – also pianist, pupil of Leschetizky in Vienna; lived for a time in England and in China. Works include 'New York Days and Nights' and other piano pieces; symphonic poems, chamber music, etc.

WHITHORNE, THOMAS, see WHYTHORNE.

WHITLOCK, PERCY WILLIAM (1903–46), English organist, and composer chiefly of organ and church music.

WHITTAKER, WILLIAM GILLIES (1876–1944), English writer on music, educationist, folk-song arranger, composer of part-songs, etc.

WHOLE-NOTE (U.S.), equals SEMIBREVE.

WHOLE-TONE, two semitones, e.g. the interval from C up to the adjacent D – divisible into the two semitones C–C♯ and C♯–D. So *whole-tone scale*, a scale progressing entirely in whole-tones, instead of partly in whole-tones and partly in semitones like the major and minor scales and the old MODES. Only two such whole-tone scales are possible – one 'beginning' on C, one on C♯, though in fact each scale can equally well begin on any of its notes, since (owing to the equal intervals) there is no note which presents itself as a point of rest equivalent to a keynote. Debussy and other composers have used the whole-tone scale pronouncedly for chords and short passages, but not for an entire piece consistently.

WHYTE, IAN (1901–60), Scottish conductor and composer, pupil of Stanford and Vaughan Williams. Conductor of BBC Scottish Orchestra from its foundation in 1935. Works include ballet 'Donald of the Burthens' (using a bagpipe with orchestra), and other works with Scottish associations; also two symphonies, etc.

WHYTE, ROBERT, see ROBERT WHITE.

WHYTHORNE, THOMAS (b. 1528, d. after 1590), English composer who travelled in Italy and elsewhere, and wrote songs anticipating the AYRES of Dowland and his time; wrote also vocal duets to religious and secular words.

WIDOR, CHARLES MARIE (JEAN ALBERT) (1844–1937), French organist, composer, writer on music, and teacher of the organ and of composition. Wrote many organ solos including ten 'symphonies'; also symphony for organ and orchestra, two other symphonies, three operas, etc. The last surviving pupil of Rossini.

WIECHOWICZ, STANISLAW (1893-1963), Polish composer, chiefly of various choral works (unaccompanied, with orchestra, with organ, with two pianos); also orchestral works and many songs. Is also conductor, music critic, and writer of text-books.

WIEGENLIED (Ger.), cradle-song; the one sometimes attributed to Mozart ('Schlafe, mein Prinzchen' – 'Sleep, my little prince') is really by J. Bernhard Flies, an amateur composer born about 1770.

WIENER BLUT, see VIENNA BLOOD.

WIENIAWSKI, HENRYK (1835–80), Polish violinist, composer of two concertos (no. 2, Lisztian in construction, is the well-known one) and other music for his instrument. Toured much (in U.S.A. with Anton Rubenstein), taught many years at the Brussels Conservatory, and died in Moscow.

WIHTOL, JOSEPH (1863–1948), Latvian composer, pupil of Rimsky-Korsakov in Russia; director of the Latvian National Opera, and wrote various works with Latvian associations – including folk-song arrangements, a Fantasy on Latvian Folk-songs for cello and orchestra, etc. Died in Germany.

WILBYE, JOHN (1574–1638), English composer, particularly of madrigals (including 'Flora gave me fairest flowers') – of which form he is reckoned among the greatest exponents. His other works, which are very few, include a little church music (in Latin and English), and some pieces for viols. Contributor to 'THE TRIUMPHS OF ORIANA'. In service to noble English families.

WILHELMJ, AUGUST (EMIL DANIEL FERDINAND) (1845–1908), German violinist who in 1893 settled in London as teacher, and died there. Wrote cadenzas for celebrated violin concertos, arrangements of works for violin, etc. – e.g. the so-called 'Air on the G string' (see AIR).

WILLAERT, ADRIAAN (*c.* 1490–1562), Flemish composer who worked chiefly in Venice as church musician, achieving high influence and dying there. Was one of the first to compose madrigals, to write independent instrumental pieces (of the type of the *fantasy*, etc.), and to employ double choirs antiphonally – later a characteristic of Venetian music. Composed Masses, motets, a Magnificat, and various vocal pieces to secular words.

WILLAN, HEALEY (1880–1968), English-born organist and composer who settled in Canada (Toronto University post, 1914). Composed symphony, cantatas, church and organ music, etc.

WILLIAM TELL (Fr., *Guillaume Tell*), Rossini's last opera, produced in Paris, 1829. Libretto by V. J. E. de Jouy and H. L. F. Bis – after Schiller's drama about the Swiss national hero.

WILLIAMS, ALBERTO (1862–1952), Argentinian pianist, conductor, and composer of nine symphonies (all but no. 1 having illustrative titles), piano solos, choral works, etc. Pupil of Franck in Paris, but influenced by Argentinian folk-music and considered a national figure in his country. He was of British and Basque descent.

WILLIAMS, GRACE (b. 1906), Welsh composer, pupil of Vaughan Williams (no relation) in London and of Wellesz in Vienna. Works include 'PENILLION' for orchestra, Symphonic Variations 'Owen Glendower', and other works with Welsh associations; also opera 'The Parlour', Sinfonia Concertante for piano and orchestra, trumpet concerto, songs, Welsh folk-song arrangements.

WILLIAMS, RALPH VAUGHAN, see VAUGHAN WILLIAMS.

WILLIAMSON, MALCOLM (b. 1931), Australian composer resident in England since 1953; also organist and pianist. Works include 'OUR MAN IN HAVANA', 'Julius Caesar Jones' and other operas; also symphony, string quartet, and piano and organ pieces, and Roman Catholic Church music in modern popular-song style.

WILSON, HENRY LANE (1870–1915), English composer of songs, editor of old English songs, and pianist – especially song-accompanist.

WILSON, JOHN (1595–1674), English lutenist, singer, viol-player, and composer of songs (some to words by Shakespeare), catches, church music, etc. Is thought to be identical with the 'Jack Wilson' who acted in Shakespeare's company in *Much Ado About Nothing*. Later, court musician to Charles I and Charles II.

WIMBERGER, GERHARDT (b. 1923), Austrian composer of 'Lady Goblin' (after Calderon's 'La dama duende') and other operas; 'Figures and Fantasies' for orchestra; cantatas, etc.

WIND INSTRUMENT, generic name for musical instruments in which the sound is produced through the vibrations of a column of air which is set in motion by the player's breath – such instruments being commonly divided into WOODWIND and BRASS (convenient labels to classify differing types of mechanism, though the implication that all the former are made of wood and the latter of brass is misleading). Instruments in which the effect of the breath is mechanically simulated, e.g. organ and accordion, are not normally understood by the term *wind instruments*.

WIND-BAND, term used to describe a band of mixed wind-instruments; MILITARY BAND is, however, the more usual British term (a BRASS BAND being of brass alone, not mixed with woodwind). Haydn's so-called *Wind-Band Mass*, however (in B♭, 1802; Ger., *Harmoniemesse*) got its nickname only because wind instruments are used in it prominently, not exclusively.

WINDGASSEN, WOLFGANG (b. 1914). German tenor (though born in Switzerland); noted in Wagner at Bayreuth, Covent Garden, etc.

WIND-MACHINE, theatrical 'effects' machine simulating wind (usually by means of the rotation of a fabric-covered barrel) used in a few musical works – e.g. R. Strauss, 'DON QUIXOTE'.

WINTER JOURNEY, THE, (1) song-cycle by Schubert, 1827 (Ger., *Die Winterreise*), on twenty-four poems by W. Müller about an unrequited love; (2) cantata by A. Bush, 1946, with words by R. Swingler on the story of the Nativity.

'WINTER WIND' STUDY, nickname for Chopin's Study in A Minor, op. 25 no. 11, 1834.

WINTERREISE, DIE, see THE WINTER JOURNEY.

WIRE BRUSH, type of drumstick with a head of several stiff wires, used to give a 'brushing' sound to a side-drum – an effect chiefly used in dance-bands.

WIRÉN, DAG IVAR (b. 1905), Swedish composer who studied in Paris and became influenced by Honegger; has also been a music critic. Works include Serenade (for strings), four symphonies, violin concerto, piano concerto, cello concerto, stage and film music, string quartets. He has discarded some early works.

WISE VIRGINS, THE, ballet with music arranged by Walton from Bach; produced in London, 1940.

WISHART, PETER (CHARLES ARTHUR) (b. 1921), English composer of violin concerto, operas 'The Captive' and 'Two in a Bush', organ and piano music, etc.; pupil of N. Boulanger. Also college teacher.

WITCHES' MINUET, see 'FIFTHS' QUARTET.

WITT, JEREMIAS FRIEDRICH (1771–1837), Austrian composer of Masses, orchestral works, etc.; see JENA.

WITTGENSTEIN, PAUL (1887–1961), Austrian pianist who lost his right arm in the First World War and for whom R. Strauss, Ravel, Britten, and others wrote piano works for left hand alone (with orchestra). Resident in U.S.A. from 1939.

WOHLTEMPERIERTE CLAVIER, DAS, see THE WELL-TEMPERED CLAVIER.

WOLF, (1) a jarring sound sometimes occurring through unintentional vibrations on stringed instruments; (2) an out-of-tune effect occurring in certain keys on old organs tuned in 'mean-tone temperament' – not in 'equal temperament' by which all keys are equally 'in tune'. (See TEMPERAMENT).

WOLF, HUGO (1860–1903), Austrian composer chiefly of songs, usually grouped by their literary sources – e.g., 'ITALIAN SONG-BOOK' and 'SPANISH SONG-BOOK' (German translations of Italian, Spanish poems), MÖRIKE SONGS, songs by Goethe (Wolf wrote fifty-one). These are reckoned as a peak within the general German Romantic type of song; as in Schumann's, the piano parts are very important. A few of the songs also have orchestral (as well as piano) versions of the accompaniments. Wolf wrote also opera 'The Corregidor'; 'ITALIAN SERENADE'; and a few other works. Lived largely in poverty; proved himself unfitted to conducting;

was an aggressive music critic (extolling Wagner, decrying Brahms); became insane in 1897 and was confined from 1898 till death.

WOLF-FERRARI, ERMANNO (1876–1948), Italian-born composer, son of a German father and Italian mother; pupil of Rheinberger. Works, in a straightforwardly lyrical idiom, are principally operas (in Italian, though some were first given in German). They include 'SCHOOL FOR FATHERS' (*I quatro rusteghi*), 'SUSANNA'S SECRET', 'THE JEWELS OF THE MADONNA', and 'CINDERELLA'. Wrote also cantatas, chamber music, etc.

WOLFF, ALBERT LOUIS (b. 1884), French operatic and concert conductor; also composer of opera 'The Blue Bird' (after Maeterlinck), etc.

WOLSTENHOLME, WILLIAM (1865–1931), English organist and composer, blind from birth; composed chiefly for the organ. Also violinist (taught by Elgar) and pianist.

WOMAN'S LOVE AND LIFE (Ger., *Frauenliebe und -leben*), song-cycle by Schumann, 1840, to eight poems by Chamisso – male poet proclaiming woman's adoring submission.

WOOD BLOCK (or CHINESE BLOCK), a rectangular block of wood, hollowed out for resonance and used as a percussion instrument in certain 20th-century works, e.g. Lambert's THE RIO GRANDE. A related type is the TEMPLE BLOCK.

WOOD, CHARLES (1866–1926), Irish organist, composer, professor of music at Cambridge. Composed cantatas, church music, songs (including 'Ethiopia Saluting the Colours'), etc.

WOOD, HAYDN (1882–1959), English composer chiefly famous for 'Roses of Picardy' and similar popular sentimental songs, and of orchestral pieces in similar vein; but also wrote piano concerto, 'Philharmonic Variations' for cello and orchestra, a Fantasy-Quartet for strings, etc.

WOOD, HENRY (JOSEPH) (1869–1944), English conductor, in boyhood a church organist; began a famous series of Promenade Concerts in London in 1895, continuing till death, and notably introducing new works both British and foreign. Also arranger e.g. of the so-called 'Trumpet Voluntary' (misattributed to Purcell, see CLARKE) for organ, brass, and kettledrums; and, under the name 'Paul Klenovsky', of Bach's organ Toccata and Fugue in D minor as orchestral work. Knighted 1911.

WOOD, HUGH (b. 1932), English composer, pupil of Hamilton and Seiber; Works include two string quartets and 'Scenes from "Comus"' (Milton) for soprano, tenor and orchestra.

WOOD, RALPH WALTER (b. 1902), English composer of piano concerto, three string quartets, etc.; also writer on music.

WOOD, THOMAS (1892–1950), English composer (pupil of Stanford), and author. Travelled to Australia and popularized the song 'Waltzing Matilda' outside Australia. Works, in straightforward traditional English idiom, include unaccompanied cantata 'Chanticleer'; 'The

Rainbow' (male voices and brass band) on the Dunkirk episode in the Second World War.

WOODWIND, collective name for those types of wind-instrument historically and generally made of wood – either blown directly (e.g. flute, recorder), or blown by means of a reed (e.g. clarinet, oboe,) and in either case consisting basically of a tube with holes which, closed or opened by the player's fingers, shorten or lengthen the vibrating air-column and thus vary the pitch of the note emitted. The term *woodwind* is also used for cover instruments conforming to this but made of metal (e.g. saxophones, and some models of flute and clarinet). The distinction between *woodwind* and BRASS, apart from material, is that in the latter the player blows not by the methods described above but by pressing his lips against a cup-shaped or funnel-shaped mouthpiece. In the symphony orchestra, *double woodwind* indicates two players of each 'standard type' (flute, oboe, clarinet, bassoon), as usually specified e.g. by Beethoven; *triple woodwind* indicates three of each, one player normally also taking an 'extra' related to the four 'standard' instruments above – respectively, piccolo, English horn, bass clarinet, double-bassoon.

WORDSWORTH, WILLIAM (BROCKLESBY) (b. 1908), English composer; a descendant of Christopher Wordsworth, brother of the poet. Works include five symphonies, four string quartets, songs.

WORKING-OUT, synonym for DEVELOPMENT, e.g. in sonata-form.

WORLD OF THE MOON, THE, (*It.* 'Il Mondo della luna'), comic opera by Haydn, produced in Eszterhaza, 1777. Libretto by Goldoni, about an astronomer so absorbed in his study of the moon that he allows his daughters to accept 'unsuitable' suitors.

WOYTOWICZ, BOLESLAW (b. 1899), Polish composer of symphonies, 'Cantata in Praise of Work', piano studies, etc.; also pianist.

WOZZECK, opera by A. Berg, completed 1921, produced in Berlin, 1925. Libretto by composer; Wozzeck is a simple, persecuted, feeble-minded private soldier. The play on which the opera is based is by Georg Büchner, 1836; another opera on it, by M. Gurlitt, appeared in 1926.

WURLITZER ORGAN, trade name of a type of UNIT ORGAN used in cinemas and incorporating 'freak' effects (bells, motor-horns, etc.).

WYK, ARNOLD VAN (really Arnoldus Christiaan Vlok van; b. 1916), S. African composer and pianist who studied in England, returning to S. Africa in 1946 and later holding a university post there. Works include two symphonies, 'Christmas Cantata', chamber music, song-cycle 'Of Love and Forsakenness' (in Afrikaans, as 'Van Liefde en Verlatenheid').

WYSS, SOPHIE (b. 1897), Swiss-born soprano who settled in England, 1925. Works in French have been written for her by Britten, Berkeley, and other British composers.

X

XENNAKIS, IANNIS (b. 1922), Rumanian-born composer of Greek parentage; uses complex mathematical formulas – and sometimes a computer, as in part of 'Eonta' (Gk, 'Beings') for piano and five brass. His 'Metastaseis' ('After-standstill') is for sixty-one individual instrumentalists.

XERXES (It., *Serse*), opera by Handel, produced in London, 1738. Libretto by N. Minato about a Persian king. Contains the famous aria 'Ombra mai fù' (in praise of a tree's shade) known as 'Handel's Largo' – arbitrarily, since Handel actually headed it 'Larghetto'.

XYLOPHONE, percussion instrument consisting of tuned wooden bars (hence the name, from Greek for 'wood' and 'sound'), arranged in order as on a piano keyboard and struck with small hard-headed sticks. Compass from middle C upwards for three octaves. Introduced from Eastern Europe; used in the orchestra in Saint-Saëns' 'DANSE MACABRE' 1874, and afterwards gaining general currency for special effects. (The toy instruments usually called xylophones, but having metal bars, are really toy glockenspiels.)

Y

YEOMEN OF THE GUARD, THE, *or The Merryman and his Maid*, operetta by Sullivan, produced in London, 1888. Libretto by W. S. Gilbert, the title referring to the Warders of the Tower of London, and the action set in the 16th century.

YODEL (Ger., *Jodel*), type of singing for men alternating between natural voice and falsetto, practised particularly in the Tyrol (in Austria). It is used for simple dance-like tunes.

YON, PIETRO ALESSANDRO (1886–1943), Italian-born organist and composer who settled in U.S.A., 1907. Wrote a 'Concerto Gregoriano' for organ and orchestra (with themes from plainsong), Masses, organ solos, songs, etc.

YONGE, NICOLAS (?–1169), English singer; see MUSICA TRANSALPINA.

YOUNG, WILLIAM (?–1671), English flutist, violinist, and composer who worked abroad and published at Innsbruck (1653) the earliest English sonatas for two or more violins with bass viol and continuo – i.e. the type of TRIO-SONATA later used by Purcell. Afterwards returned to England and became a member of the court band.

YOUNG FRANCE (Fr., *La Jeune France*), group formed in 1936 by four French composers – Baudrier, Jolivet, Lesur, and Messiaen – championing the traditional idea of a 'personal message' in musical composition, at that time rather out of fashion.

YOUNG LORD, THE (Ger., *Der junge Lord*), opera by Henze, produced in Berlin, 1965; in Ingeborg Bachmann's libretto, the 'English nobleman' is really a dressed-up ape.

YOUNG PERSON'S GUIDE TO THE ORCHESTRA, THE, variations and fugue by Britten (1945) on a theme of Purcell (from the play 'Abdelazer', 1695).

YRADIER, SEBASTIÁN (1809–65), Spanish composer of 'La Paloma' (Sp., The Dove) and other popular songs. The Habanera in Bizet's 'CARMEN' is an adaptation of one of Yradier's songs.

YSAŸE, EUGÈNE (1858–1931), Belgian violinist, pupil of Wieniawski and Vieuxtemps; toured much, played many new works (including Franck's violin sonata); was also conductor and composer – mainly of six concertos and other works for violin, but also of an opera in Walloon (a Belgian dialect of French).

Z

ZACHAU, FRIEDRICH WILHELM (1663–1712), German composer, chiefly of church and organ music; teacher of Handel.

ZADOK THE PRIEST, no. 1 of four anthems by Handel for the coronation of George II, 1727; performed at every English coronation since.

ZAFRED, MARIO (b. 1922), Italian composer of five symphonies (no. 4 in honour of the wartime Resistance), flute concerto, harp concerto, three piano sonatas, songs, cantata 'Duino Elegy' (poem by Rilke), etc.; pupil of Pizetti. Also critic.

ZAMPA, *or The Marble Betrothed* (Fr., . . . *ou la Fiancée de marbre*), opera by Hérold, produced in Paris, 1831. Libretto by A. H. J. Mélesville; Zampa, a 16th-century pirate, is dragged down to death by a marble statue. (The statue is female, but cp. DON GIOVANNI.)

ZANDONAI, RICCARDO (1883–1944), Italian composer of operas in the conventional Italian style of his period – including 'Giulietta e Romeo' (on Shakespeare's *Romeo and Juliet*) and 'Francesca da Rimini' (after D'Annunzio's play). Also composed orchestral works, songs, etc.

ZAPATEADO (Sp.), vigorous Spanish dance for a single performer, in which the heels tap out rhythmic patterns.

ZAR UND ZIMMERMANN, see TSAR AND CARPENTER.

ZARZUELA (Sp.), type of traditional Spanish musical stage entertainment, with spoken dialogue, often satirical.

ZAUBERFLÖTE, DIE, see THE MAGIC FLUTE.

ZECCHI, ADONE (b. 1904), Italian composer – also violinist, conductor, critic. Has written orchestral works; Divertimento for flute, harp, and strings; piano trio; Requiem for male choir and orchestra. Pupil of Alfano.

ZELTER, CARL FRIEDRICH (1785–1832), German composer, chiefly of vocal music, including song-settings of Goethe which won Goethe's approval; teacher of Mendelssohn.

ZIEHHARMONIKA (Ger.), equals ACCORDION.

ZIGEUNER (Ger.), gipsy; so *Zigeunerbaron* – see GIPSY BARON; *Zigeunerweisen* (Gipsy Airs), work in gipsy style for violin and piano (or orchestra) by Sarasate, published 1878.

ZIMBALIST, EFREM (b. 1889), American violinist composer of an 'American Rhapsody' and other works, and director of the Curtis Institute of Music, Philadelphia.

ZIMMERMANN, BERND ALOIS (b. 1918), German composer, pupil of Jarnach, Fortner, and Leibowitz; works include four symphonies, violin sonatas (unaccompanied and with piano), violin concerto, cantata 'In Praise of Stupidity' (on texts by Goethe), 'The Soldiers' and other operas, etc.

ZINGARELLI, NICCOLÒ ANTONIO (1752–1837), Italian composer of many operas (one on *Romeo and Juliet*), also of church music, etc.; holder of church music posts. Teacher of Bellini.

ZITHER, stringed instrument laid on the knees or table, and plucked; usually, some strings can be 'stopped' (as on a violin), and others are fixed in pitch and used for accompaniment. It is a 'folk' instrument native to Central Europe but widely adopted elsewhere.

ZOPPA (It.), a limp; *alla zoppa*, term used of music having a prominent SCOTCH SNAP or a pronounced regular syncopation.

ZWÖLF (Ger.), twelve; *Zwölftonmusik*, TWELVE-NOTE music.

MORE ABOUT PENGUINS

Penguin Book News, which appears every month, contains details of all the new books issued by Penguins as they are published. From time to time it is supplemented by *Penguins in Print*, which is a complete list of all books published by Penguins which are in print. (There are nearly three thousand of these.)

A specimen copy of *Penguin Book News* will be sent to you free on request, and you can become a subscriber for the price of the postage – 3s. for a year's issues (including the complete lists). Just write to Dept EP, Penguin Books Ltd, Harmondsworth, Middlesex, enclosing a cheque or postal order, and your name will be added to the mailing list.

Some other books published by Penguins are described on the following pages.

Note: *Penguin Book News* and *Penguins in Print* are not available in the U.S.A. or Canada

THE SYMPHONY

VOLUME I: HAYDN TO DVORÁK
VOLUME 2: ELGAR TO THE PRESENT DAY

Robert Simpson

This completely new work in two volumes provides a comprehensive introduction to the whole symphonic scene from Haydn to the present day.

Robert Simpson – himself a well-known symphonist – has done more than compile programme notes of the great symphonies: he has, in his two introductions, analysed the essence of symphonic form. By identifying the elements of rhythm, melody, harmony, and – vitally important – tonality as *all* being present in full measure in any successful symphony, he has provided a frame of reference which binds together symphonists from Haydn to Holmboe, from Mozart to Martinu.

His team of distinguished contributors, which includes Deryck Cooke, Hans Keller, and Hugh Ottaway, has thus been able to provide a connected, unified study of all major composers who have 'attempted to achieve in an orchestral work the highest state of organization of which music is capable'.

INTRODUCING MUSIC

Ottó Károlyi

Some acquaintance with the grammar and vocabulary of music – enough to understand the language without speaking it – greatly broadens the pleasure of listening.

Introducing Music makes the attempt to convey the elements of the art to music-lovers with no technical knowledge. Setting out from the relatively open ground of tones, pitches, timbres, sharps, flats, bars and keys, Ottó Károlyi is able to conduct the reader out into the more exciting territory of dominant sevenths and symphonic structure. His text is clearly signposted by musical examples and illustrations of instruments described, and no intelligent reader should have any difficulty in following the path. On arrival at the end, in place of being confused by the technicalities of a programme note, he should be within reach of following the music in a score.

CHAMBER MUSIC

Edited by Alec Robertson

Chamber music has frequently and rightly been described as the music of friends, in allusion to the intimate teamwork the playing of it involves and its special character. The term itself covers a huge field of beautiful, and still far too little known, music, the exact limits of which no one has been able to define precisely. For the purpose of this book it is taken to range from duet works to octets, and to cover the time from the early eighteenth century to the present day. The book, among whose contributors are not only established names but also many younger writers, will be of use and interest to record collectors as well as to concert-goers, since chamber music is ideally suited to the gramophone and a very large repertoire of it is available on records.

THE PELICAN HISTORY OF MUSIC

Edited by Alec Robertson and Denis Stevens

The concert-goer and music-lover, anxious to discover some of the hidden wealth of musical history, will find in this series of three volumes an account of many kinds of music: primitive and non-Western, liturgical, medieval, renaissance, baroque, classical, romantic, and modern. Although there is some technical analysis, the authors and editors have concentrated on fitting music into its proper frame, whether ecclesiastical, courtly, or popular.

Each musical epoch is discussed by an expert who considers the music at its face value, instead of thinking of it merely as a link in a chain of development ending in the music of Beethoven or Boulez. The reader can therefore come to understand musical trends and styles both within and outside the normal orbit of concerts and opera, and be able to enjoy unfamiliar music as well as the accepted classics.

Volume 1
Ancient Forms to Polyphony

Volume 2
Renaissance and Baroque

Volume 3
Classical and Romantic